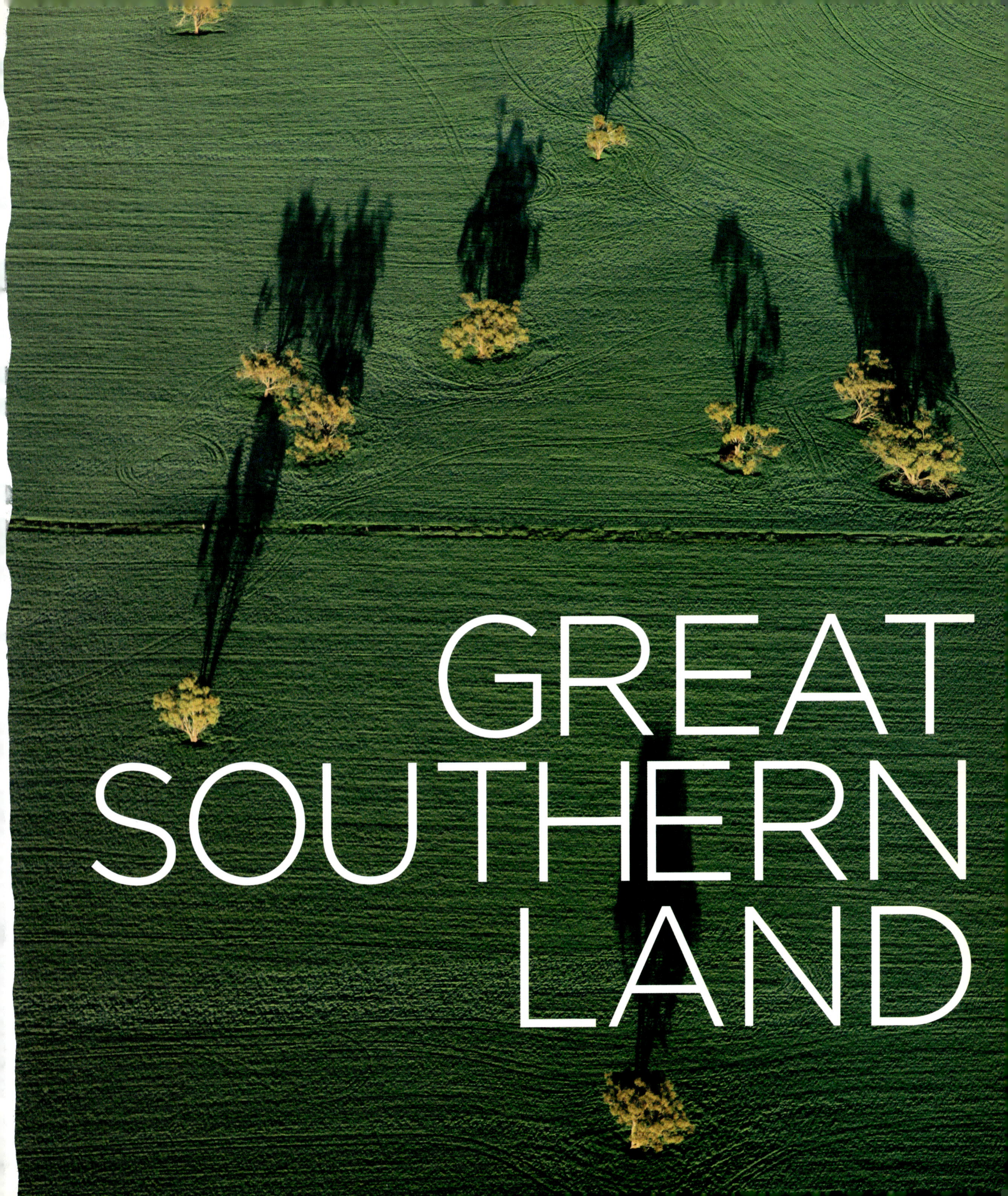
GREAT
SOUTHERN
LAND

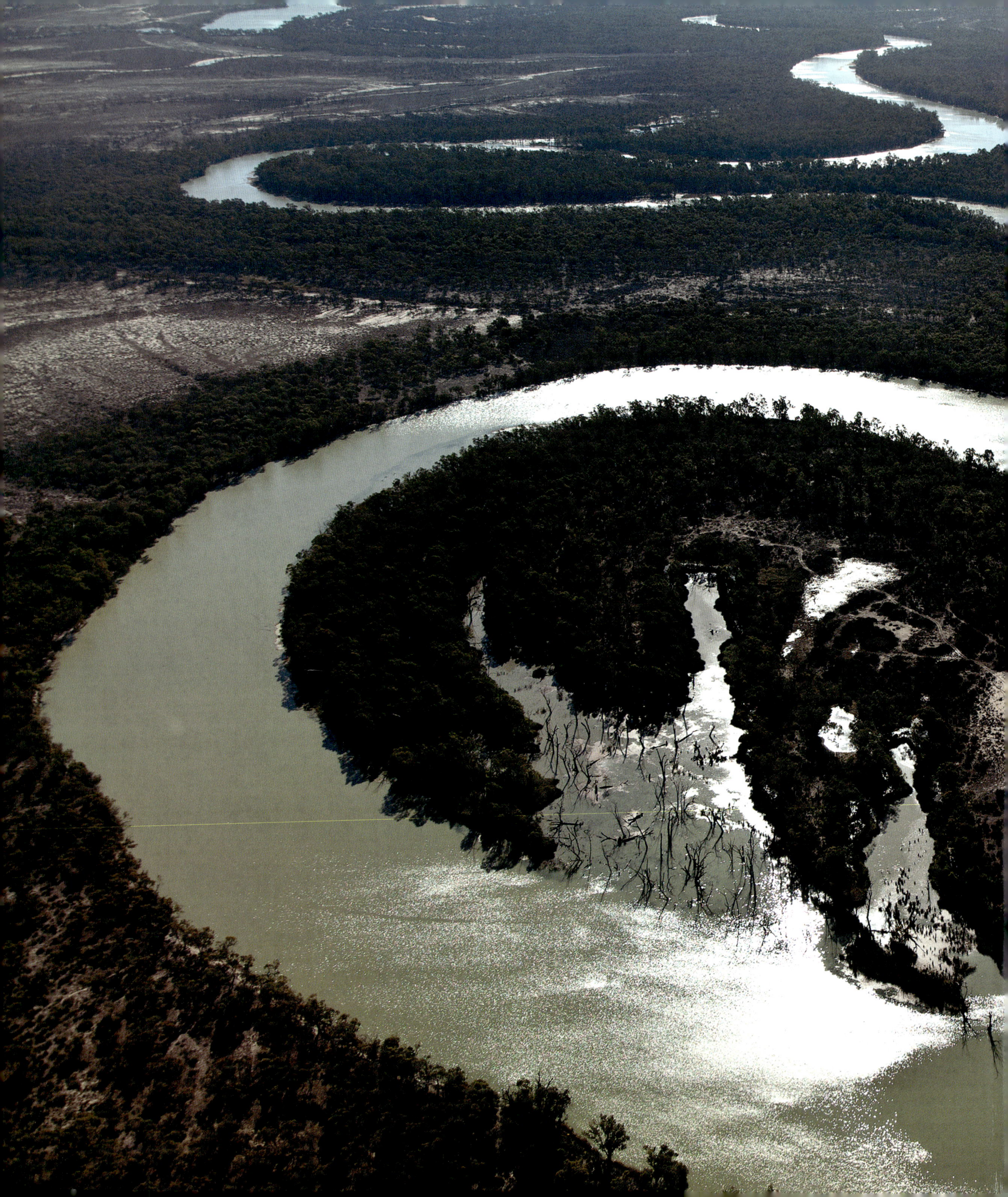

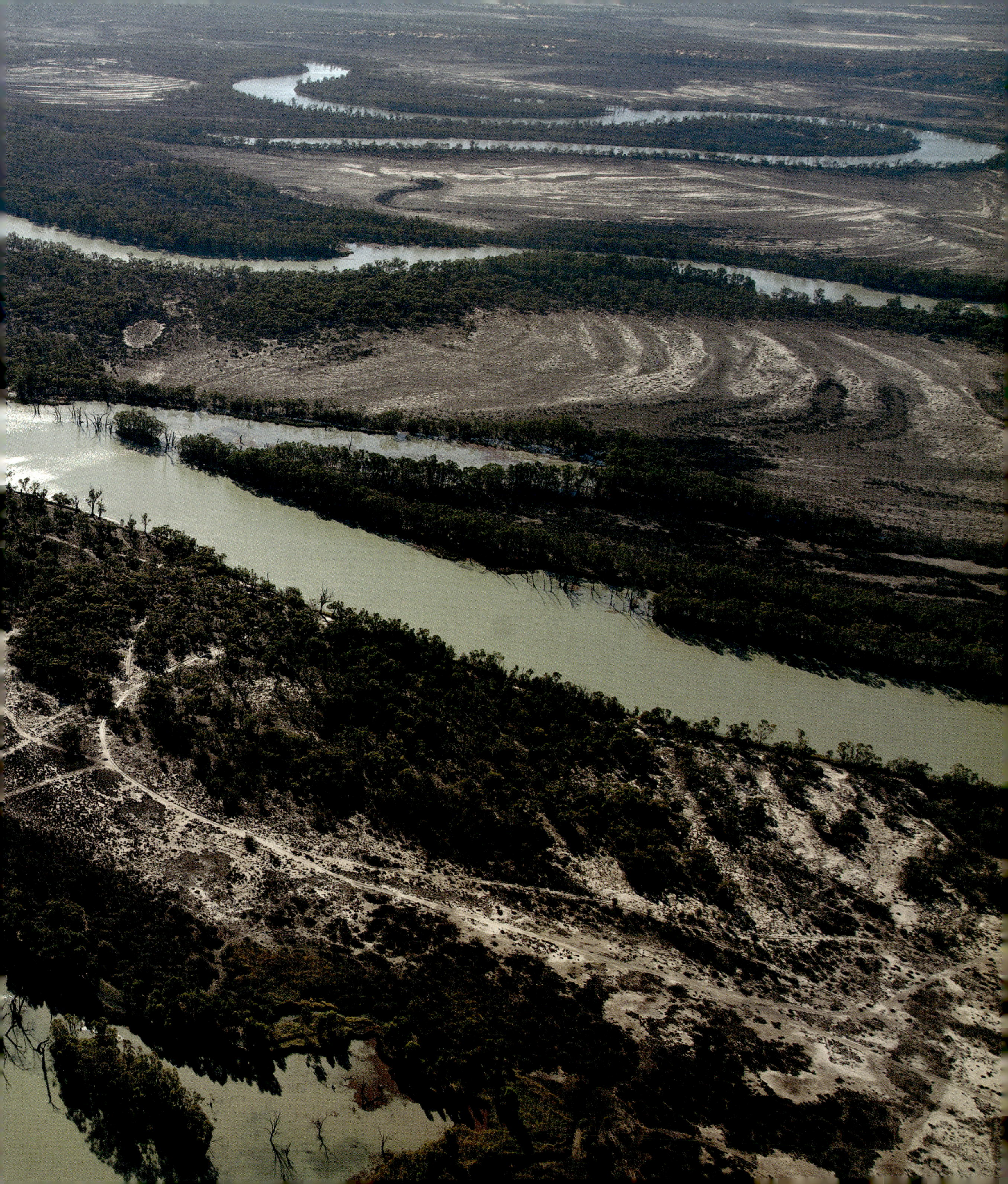

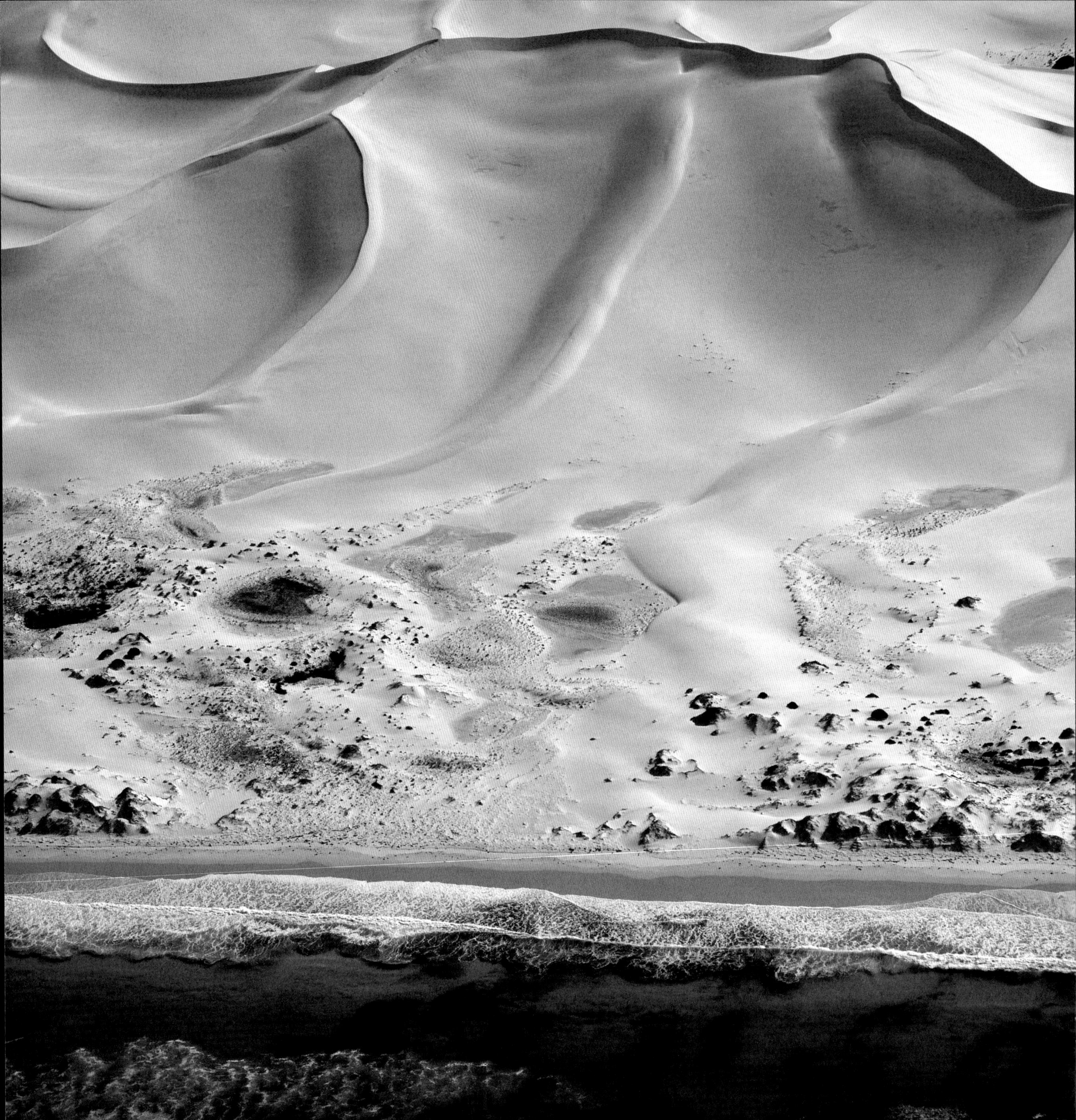

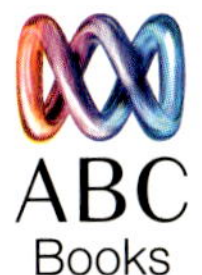

GREAT SOUTHERN LAND

IVAN O'MAHONEY & STEVE BIBB

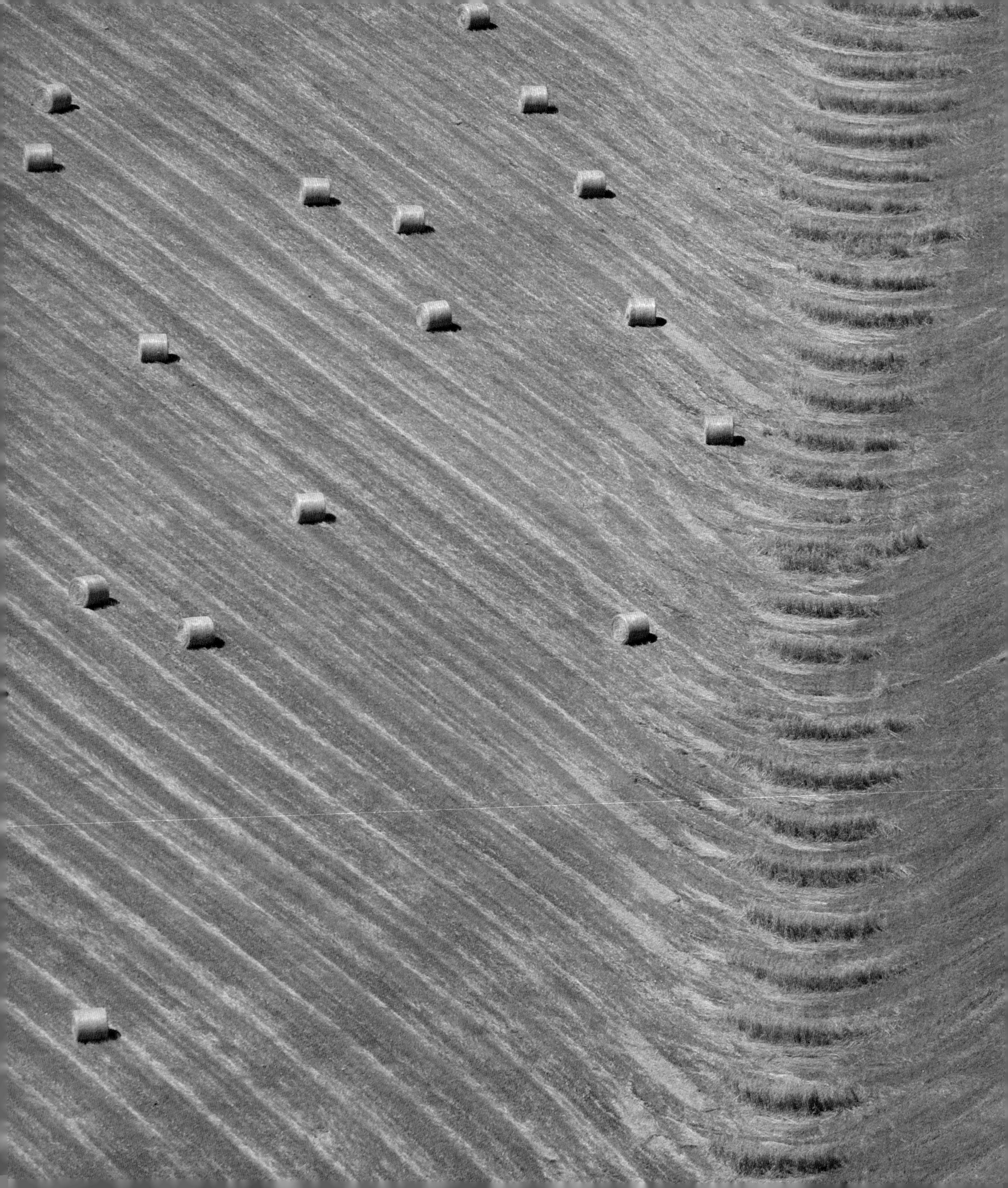

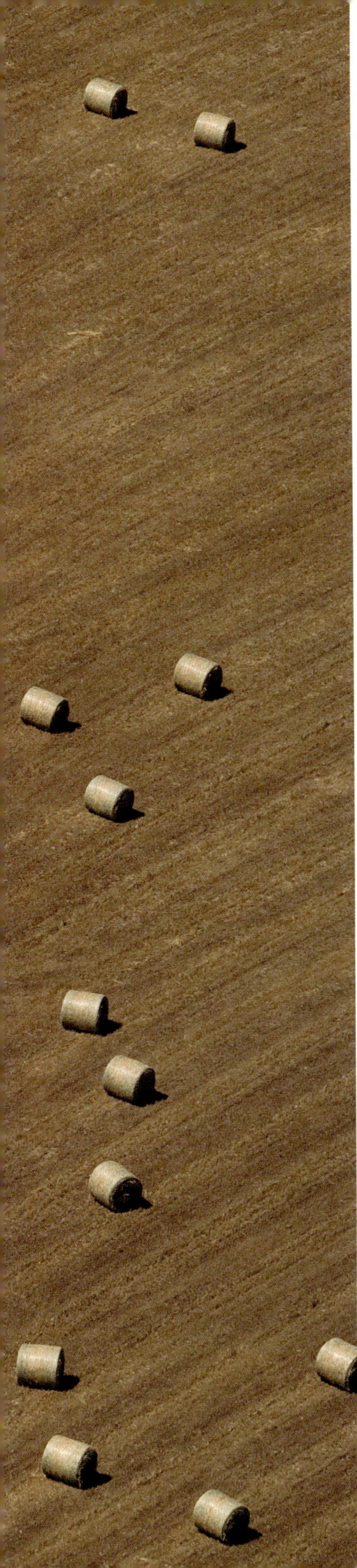

CONTENTS

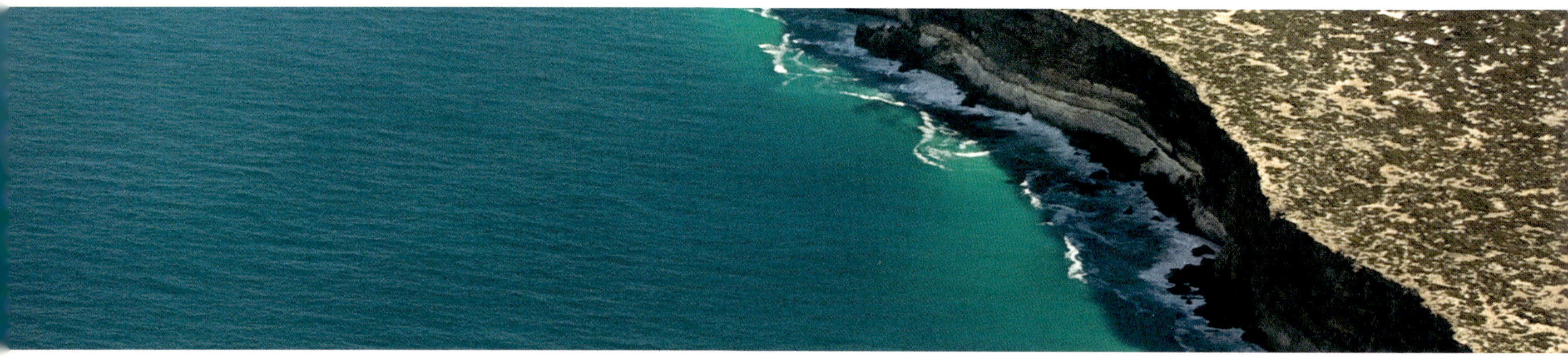

FOREWORD

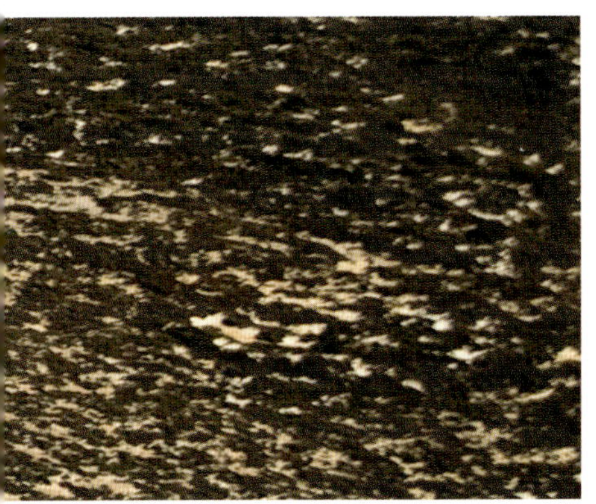

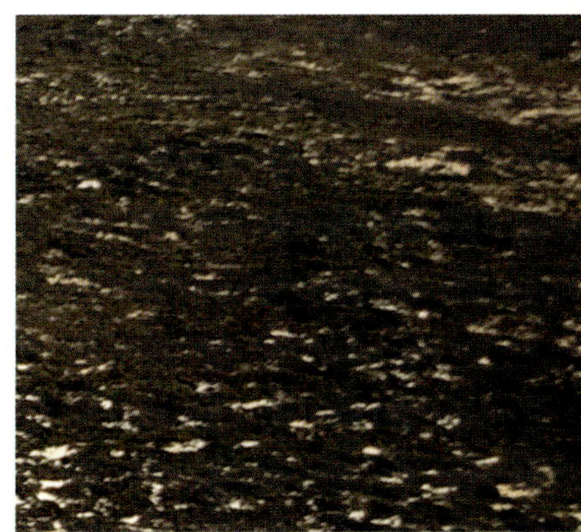

This book is a pictorial record of a remarkable story; the story of how modern Australia works, and of the ordinary people doing extraordinary things who make sure that it does work – most of the time. I had the privilege of hosting the accompanying television series – an experience I will treasure, because of the people I met, the opportunity I had to get to know my own country better, and for the chance to spend more time in the air than I had ever imagined, or, to be frank, wanted. For, you see, I don't much like heights.

In the television series we set out to document the state of affairs in modern Australia – to provide an account of how 23 million of us manage to cling to the edges of this huge, dry continent and make our way in the world as a thriving advanced economy. The challenge for us as a nation is to balance meeting our needs and lifestyle aspirations, without compromising the health of our environment, or of ourselves. We addressed some of the major issues, contradictions and compromises involved in achieving that balance, and provided a rich assortment of supporting facts and figures. Our aim was to explain the issues and ask the big questions, not to proselytise or harangue. The facts are there – it's up to us and our political leaders to decide what sort of country we want for our children and grandchildren.

While high on a tower above the grain port terminal at Port Kembla, south of Sydney, I realised what I most love about living in Australia. I was standing in the midst of one the greatest concentrations of heavy industry in the country, yet in 10 minutes I could have been sitting on the pristine white sands of a surf beach or sipping a coffee in one of Wollongong's cafes or bushwalking in the Royal National Park with nobody else in sight and only the parrots and lyrebirds for company. How good is that? After a recent rescue of a bushwalker in the Blue Mountains, west of Sydney, a friend pointed out that there are few places in the world where you can travel an hour from the centre of a major city, get lost and die.

This personal realisation, triggered by the view from a tower at Port Kembla, is but one small example of how taking an aerial view provides a clarity hard to achieve when you're in the midst of things. As a scientist, I'm used to trying to understand complex systems – whether they be how locust swarms affect the livelihoods of one in ten people on the planet, or how our risks of developing obesity, diabetes and cardiovascular disease are affected by the complex interactions between our biology, psychology, social pressures, the built environment, the food production system, economics, politics, and more. The only way to come to grips with such complexity is to start by describing the entire system, then to focus in on the component parts.

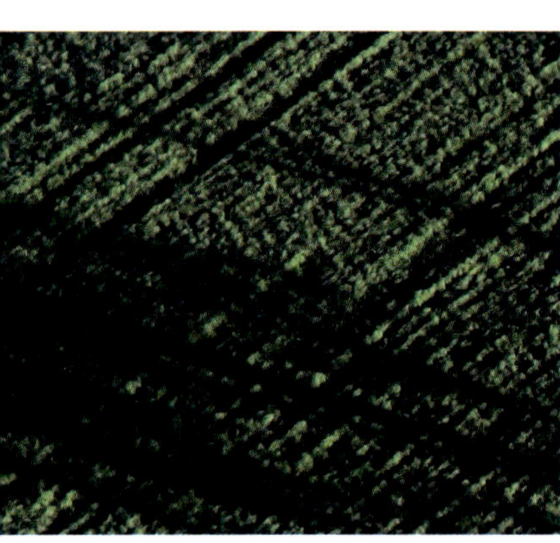

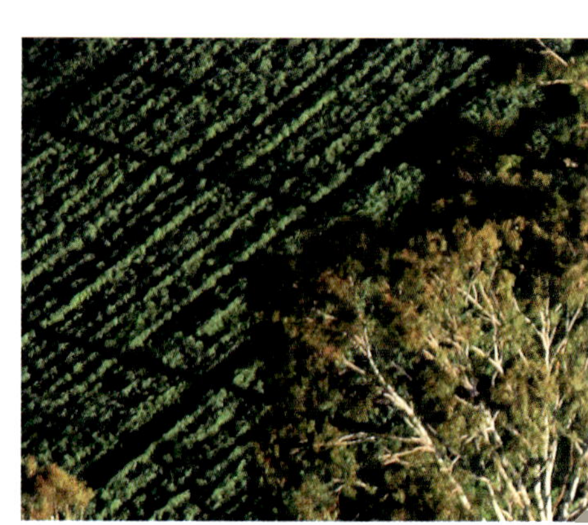

In *Great Southern Land*, when it came to trying to describe and understand how we feed and power ourselves, the extent and implications of urbanisation, or the logistics of communication and transportation, there was only one place to start – from above. This would be true for any country, but Australia uniquely lends itself to an aerial perspective. That's because ours is the flattest continent on Earth, which means that even the slightest relief on the landscape gives a vantage point. Many of the paintings depicting Aboriginal stories of Dreaming exemplify this point – it seems that Australians have always conceived their landscape from above. Our highest mountains may be paltry by world standards – mere worn down stubs sitting on a barely rippled landscape – but the view from the top of Mount Townsend in Kosciuszko National Park is as majestic as any I've seen in Europe, Asia or the Americas.

Taking an aerial view was especially useful for appreciating our interactions with the natural world. While flying over the floods near Griffith in the Riverina, I experienced firsthand the juxtaposition between the havoc and heartache created for the local community, and the river red gum forests prospering from the much-needed water and thronging with birdlife. Herein lies one of the fundamental truths of life in Australia: our ecology is adapted to extremes – indeed, it requires them. Intermittent floods, fires and even locust plagues are essential to the health of our environment, providing pulses of nutriment to ancient, impoverished soils, and synchronising patterns of reproduction and growth among native plants and animals. But the downside, of course, is that such events make Australia a punishing place for us to live, especially for those living on the land, upon whom we all rely for our food.

Having gained the big picture from above, the next step in understanding any complex system is to focus in on the parts that make it all work, and that means the people who dedicate their working lives to keeping the country functioning. It was these personal stories that for me were the highlight of *Great Southern Land*.

Among the many wonderful people we met, I was especially impressed by the farmers; by their ingenuity and willingness to adapt in the face of a changing world, while remaining true to their rural roots and retaining their deep connection to the land – a connection born of reliance. Watching a shy, young Afghani refugee, the sole survivor of his family, proudly working in a high-tech tomato farm near Adelaide; sharing a day with a family of wheat farmers near Deniliquin, New South Wales; seeing how a feedlot near Roma in Queensland appears to be squaring the circle of intensifying beef production without compromising animal health and welfare – these and other similar experiences were heartening. We will come to rely ever more heavily on our farmers' ingenuity to ensure the sustainable use of our precious arable land, as our population grows larger and our climate changes.

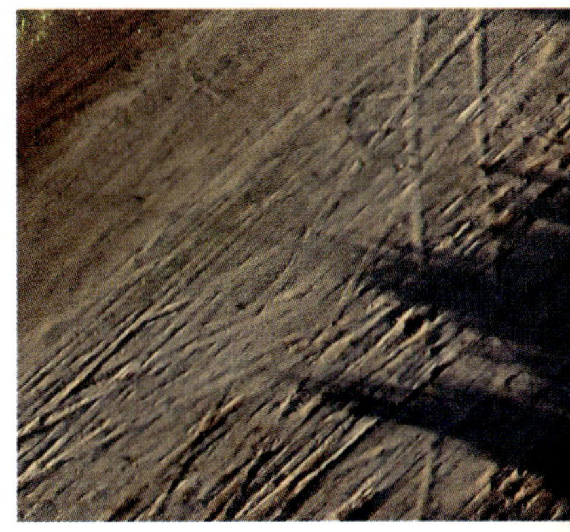

More disquieting, however, was an appreciation of how many of us are at risk of losing our connection with the land. A pervading theme in *Great Southern Land* is the extent of urbanisation in Australia. We like to think of ourselves as an outdoor society. For many of us, the bush and the beach are dear to our identity, but the reality is that most of us live in the suburbs and, apart from an occasional visit to a beach, we all too rarely get out into the natural landscape.

It is precisely because Australia is such a vast and unforgiving place that we cluster together in towns and cities, mostly within a short distance of the coast. But urbanisation competes with arable land, places strain on communication and transport systems, and demands more of our environment to sustain us. Up to a point, these are manageable challenges, which are being tackled all the time by dedicated people, usually without the rest of us even realising it.

In some notable cases, urbanisation can even benefit the environment, as I observed from a rickety aerochute, soaring above the Werribee marshlands with their abundance of migratory birds making the most of the thousands of tonnes of treated effluent flowing each day from Melbourne. Nevertheless, the systems and networks that keep us fed, moving and communicating are fragile and Australia's natural resources are finite.

And that is where I think *Great Southern Land* has much to offer as a documentary series. It helps us to understand the implications of living in Australia: where our food comes from, what food production and distribution entails, and what it means when we make decisions about population growth, town planning, mining, forestry, fishing and conservation. These are tough decisions, which can only be made with a proper understanding of the issues – and of what is at stake.

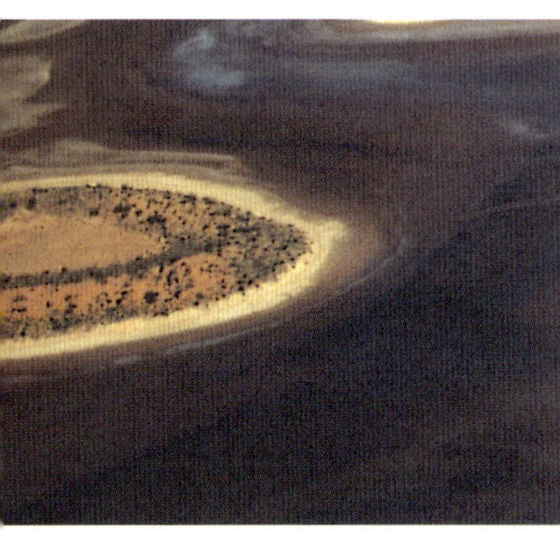

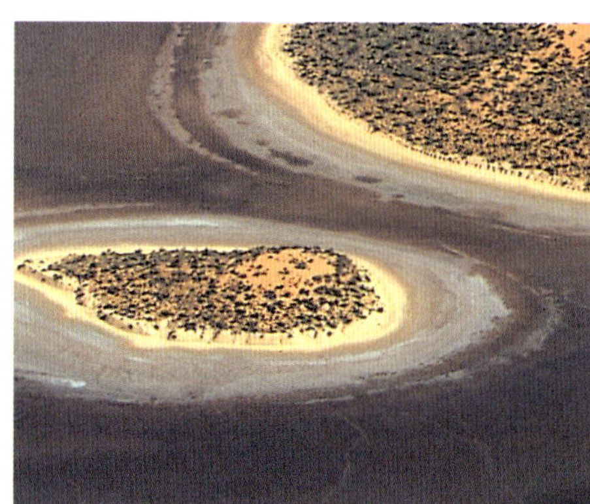

It also takes courage and vision to make the right decisions. Here, the hope is that we can emulate some of the successes of previous generations. Thanks to the foresight of our forebears, many of us are fortunate in having easy access to large tracts of bushland in our national parks. In Sydney we are especially lucky – a perspective especially evident while suspended from a hang-glider over the cliffs of the Royal National Park. My other favourite example of past visionary thinking came from flying at dawn in a hot-air balloon over the Goldfields Pipeline, which runs nearly 600 kilometres from Perth to Kalgoorlie, and is internationally recognised as one of Australia's three great engineering achievements, along with the Snowy Mountains Hydro-electric Scheme and the Sydney Harbour Bridge. The design and building of the pipeline, completed in 1903, was overseen by C.Y. O'Connor, Engineer-in-Chief of the newly founded state of Western Australia. But weeks before it opened, and secure in the knowledge that it would work, O'Connor succumbed to years of intense criticism from the press and his political enemies about the extravagance and wastefulness of the project. They also questioned his probity, and claimed that it was being built for the benefit of 'Easterners', not true Western Australians. O'Connor rode his horse into the surf one morning and shot himself. His suicide note made a final suggestion for inserting baffles into the header dam to improve flow. These are still in place and water has flowed continuously for the past 110 years, nourishing farmlands and communities over a huge area.

Offsetting the spectacular views provided from above, I became acutely aware on numerous occasions that those who fly, let alone leap out of, small aircraft risk their lives each time they take off. In this regard, I would like to offer a tribute to Maurice Little, the gentlemanly and highly skilled glider pilot who flew me across the wind farm at Ararat in Victoria. Tragically, he and a young passenger were killed a few months after we filmed the segment.

The structure of this book loosely follows the path laid out by the documentary series. Part One, entitled 'Great Australian Bite', reveals what it takes to satisfy two of our great hungers in Australia: the seemingly unquenchable desire for power and food. Part Two, entitled, 'Tug of War', exquisitely captures our complicated and challenging relationship with the natural world in Australia. Part Three, 'On the Move', takes us to the cities – with a diversion or two into the bush. It shows the pressure we place on the networks and systems that transport us en masse. Finally, Part Four, entitled 'Living on the Edge', looks at what it takes to sustain our mostly coastal dwelling existence. This final chapter also provides fine examples of antidotes to the stress of our urban sprawl existence.

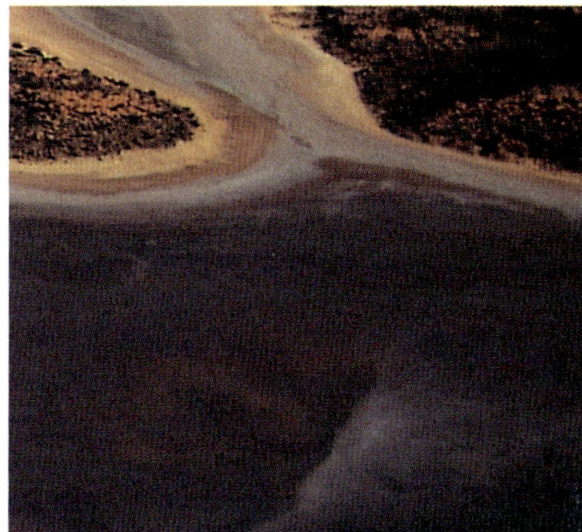

The images in this book are a stunning pictorial record of modern Australia. Inspired by the television series, they are a celebration of the life we have built, here in our Great Southern Land.

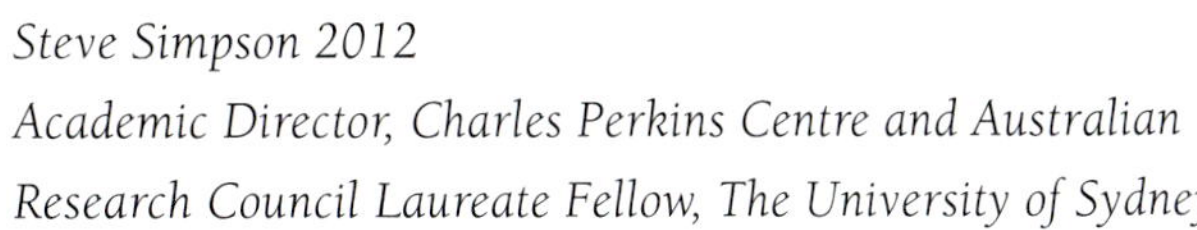

Steve Simpson 2012
Academic Director, Charles Perkins Centre and Australian Research Council Laureate Fellow, The University of Sydney

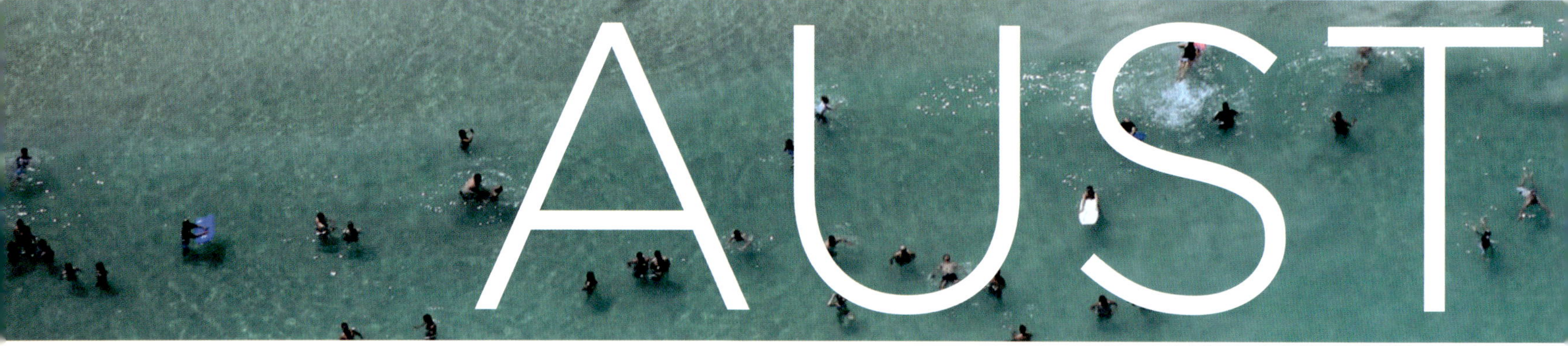
AUST

GREAT

RALIAN

BITE

In Australia we have a voracious appetite, a ceaseless craving, for two of life's vital ingredients: food and power. And we have come to expect those appetites to be satisfied almost instantly. Happily, through hard work and ingenuity, we have managed to turn our vast natural resources into powerhouses and our parched countryside into a colossal food bowl – a triumph not just against the odds but sometimes logic, too.

We can pretty much eat what we want when we want. We have built the systems and networks to keep the lights on, air conditioners humming and our television and computer screens flickering – 24 hours a day. Our ever-increasing needs and demands, though, put an awful lot of strain on our farms, transport systems and grids, and on those expected to keep it all running, mostly hidden from view.

Behind the scenes, how we survive and thrive in this hostile corner of the world is often a tale of considerable drama. It is the story of the men and women who, with perseverance, tenacity and sometimes at great risk to their own health, keep Australia fed and powered. Like Lori Folino. As a 'bare hander' employed in Victoria to maintain high-voltage transmission lines, Folino scales dangerous heights and takes extraordinary risks, just so others can go about their daily lives as normal and have a cup of tea, for instance.

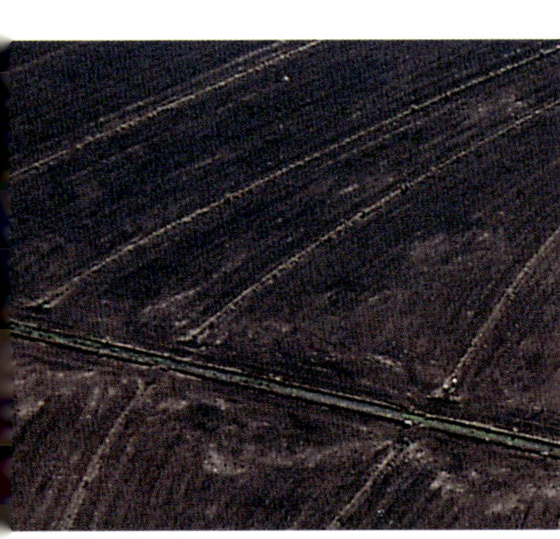

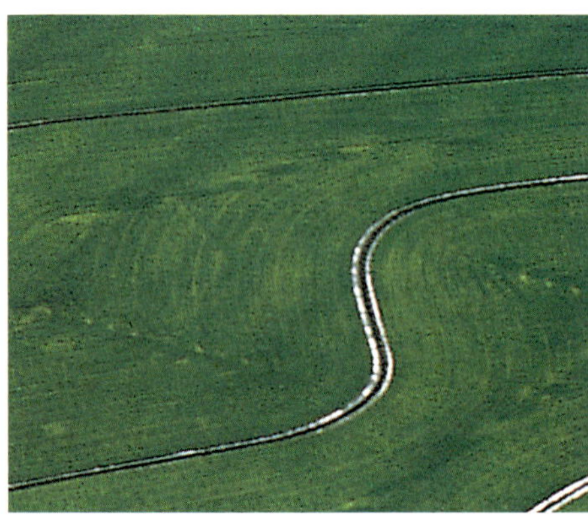

'We have 1.2 million customers we need to supply,' says Folino. 'It's very important that we keep the power on and keep it running.' For Folino that means going up 35 metres in a cherry picker, then hooking himself to a 500,000 volt power line and, finally, crawling on it. 'There is a feeling of excitement as you're about to bond on,' says Folino. 'You hear that loud electricity and you can see it. People say that you can't see electricity, but guess what … we can.'

Folino is one of 70 such bare handers – wirewalkers who clean and repair the infrastructure that delivers power to a nation. The only reason Folino and his colleagues don't get electrocuted is the gear they wear. Bare handers call it a Faraday suit, named after the English physicist who discovered that a metallic cage conducts electricity without affecting what's inside. The suit is made of 25 per cent stainless steel, and protects Folino in the same way the fuselage of a plane protects passengers when hit by lightning. A clever solution if ever there was one.

Folino's many missions typically include repairing faulty spacers, the devices that hold lines apart, and making sure they don't touch and short out. If that were to happen, thousands of homes would be without power. From the point where he bonds on, it can be a 25-metre crawl. 'The feeling of freedom going along a power line – it's an exciting part of my day,' says Folino. 'Sometimes I do have to stop to think about the job we are doing. Normal people don't get on power lines with half a million volts running through them.'

Our ability to scale heights and take to the air is crucial in keeping the lights on. To maintain power 24 hours a day, energy supply companies in Western Australia now also deploy low-flying helicopters carrying high-pressure water hoses to blast dirt and bird droppings from insulators, which could otherwise malfunction. This, too, is very risky business. The choppers fly just metres from the lines and if the water isn't pure enough, contaminants can act as an electrical conductor, turning the helicopter into a huge fireball.

In Queensland, energy suppliers have built semi-automated flying machines – curious-looking hybrids between fixed-wing aircraft and helicopters – to monitor the network. These aircraft are designed to fly at low speeds, for hours on end, using cameras and light pulses to calculate the distance to, and properties of, an object. That way they are able to create a 3D representation of the power network and everything near it – most importantly, vegetation. If trees or plants threaten infrastructure, engineers can quickly be dispatched to chop them down or cut back their branches.

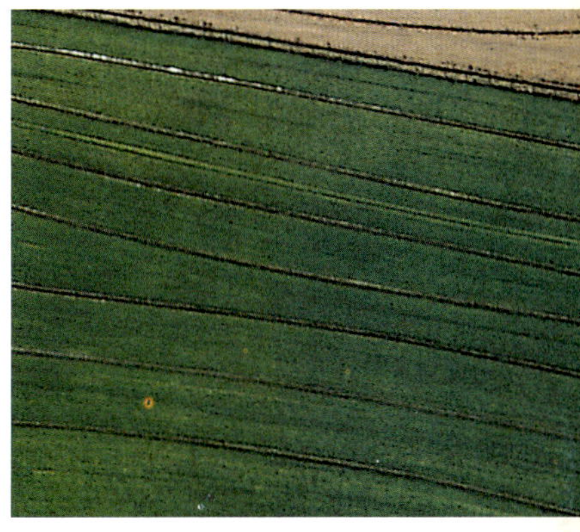

In a country with 900,000 kilometres of power lines, and an environment as harsh as ours, maintenance is always needed. Our demand for electricity is so overwhelming we simply cannot afford to shut down power lines. During the past 20 years, peak demand for electricity has soared 70 per cent. Energy suppliers blame the increase on our growing desire for cool air, and they have the numbers to back it up. In our sweltering suburbs, we're willing to put up with fewer and fewer of life's discomforts.

The Australian Bureau of Statistics surveys our domestic energy habits every couple of years. The results sometimes seem whimsical. For instance, there are more dishwashers in ACT households than in any other part of Australia; laptops are becoming more popular than desktop computers; we buy fewer stereo systems and more DVD players. Sure. But the big news is the rise of the air conditioner. Two decades ago only one in three homes had an air conditioner. Now, almost three-quarters of us bathe in cool air whenever the going gets hot. And it's that increase in peak demand that is pushing our infrastructure to the brink, putting pressure on suppliers and producers.

In Australia, most of us are hooked onto the national grid. It's a curious name, as it covers neither the Northern Territory nor Western Australia, each running its own mainly gas-fired systems. But the national grid is still enormous. In fact, with more than 200 power stations pumping out 25 billion watts every day, it is the largest integrated power grid in the world, stretching 5,000 kilometres from Port Douglas in northern Queensland to Port Lincoln in South Australia. Transported through the grid at the speed of light, most of our nation's electricity still comes from coal, which is mainly dug up from open cut mines in the Hunter Valley, the Bowen Basin and the Latrobe Valley.

But we do go underground for coal as well. And, in the future, as our more convenient resources on the surface dwindle, we might be forced to go deeper still. At the Mandalong mine, near Lake Macquarie in New South Wales, mine deputy Paul Morris already spends a third of his life in the dark, often getting up at four in the morning and not getting home till seven at night. 'Some times of the year I just don't see the sun for three days straight,' says Morris, although dealing with sun deprivation is the easy bit. At a depth of 300 metres, Morris and his six-man team operate a huge machine called a shearer. It shaves enormous lumps of coal from the seam, but in doing so it also unlocks methane, a highly explosive gas.

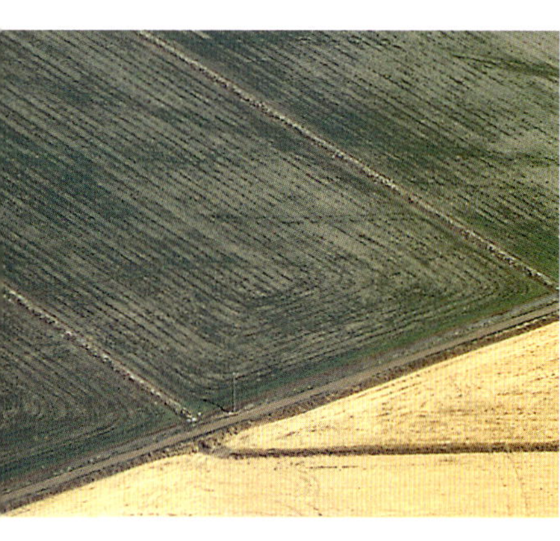

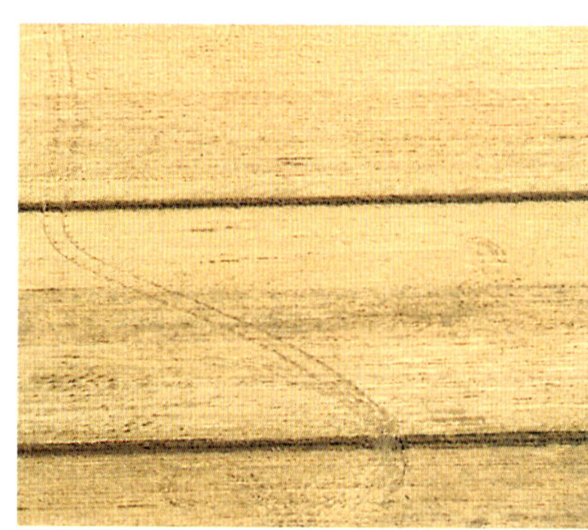

'That's the biggest fear of an underground miner,' says Morris. 'If you get an ignition source and the right combination of gas levels, you can get an explosion.'

Morris knew colleagues who died in mining accidents, but it doesn't deter him from digging deep every day. 'I'm not a brain surgeon, I'm not curing cancer, but I am playing my role in society,' he says. 'People just take electricity for granted – walk over and flick the switch. But you don't think about the process involved.'

Like the bare handers, Morris and his team risk their lives so we can keep the lights on. The black coal they help dig up is responsible for more than half of Australia's electricity production. Add its brown cousin to the mix and that goes up to 75 per cent. In fact, add natural gas and we depend on fossil fuels for 90 per cent of all our electricity.

Maybe our love affair with carbon was meant to be. After all, Captain Cook's HMS *Endeavour* was a converted coal carrier, and two other great maritime explorers, Bass and Flinders, were the first to discover coal in Australia, initially in the area of Wollongong and later further north – a find so important it led to the establishment of the convict settlement of

In Australia, most of us are hooked onto the national grid. It's a curious name, as it covers neither the Northern Territory nor Western Australia, each running its own mainly gas-fired systems.

Newcastle on the Hunter River, now the world's largest coal port.

It's hard not to marvel at the scale of the coal industry, but it's not without its problems. It's dirty, it's a major source of CO_2 build-up in our atmosphere and our known reserves will run out in a few decades. Thankfully, in the lucky country, there are other ways to power our lives – if we choose to embrace them. According to the Australian Academy of Science, the sun's energy falling on Australia in one day is equal to half the total annual energy required by the whole world. That's truly an extraordinary thought.

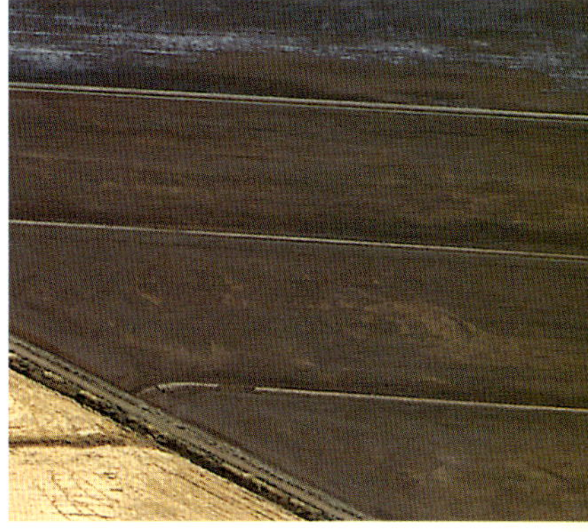

The Liddell coal power station in New South Wales is the first of its kind to harness some of that solar potential. Five hundred mirrors are used to reflect sunlight onto overhead tubes containing water to produce steam. Liddell eats through 5.5 million tonnes of coal each year, and its solar component only brings that down by 2,000 tonnes. That's a drop in the carbon ocean. Nationwide, solar contributes less than half a per cent to our electricity production.

There is no denying that costs and technology are obstacles but, in this sun-drenched land, it does seem the biggest power deficit is political willpower. We do fare a little better, but only just, in capturing that other great infinite clean resource: wind. Harnessing wind is hardly a novel idea, of course. Ask any Australian farmer using windmills to pump water from bores and wells to irrigate fields. There are thousands of them. We have some of the best wind resources in the world, but wringing electricity from the breeze has yet to be embraced with similar determination and enthusiasm.

Wind exists because the sun unevenly heats the surface of the Earth. As hot air rises, cooler air fills the void. So as long as the sun shines, the wind will blow. And as long as the wind blows, we can harness it to power our lives. The Commonwealth has legislated that by the year 2020, 20 per cent of all our energy must come from renewable resources. In South Australia, wind already contributes that much to the energy mix, but around the country it's a little more than two per cent.

There is, however, a revolution of sorts, in the air. There are more than 50 wind farms around Australia and in the windswept plains of Macarthur, in country Victoria, construction of the largest yet is under way. When this billion-dollar project is finished, 140 turbines, spread over 5,500 hectares, will harvest a whirlwind of energy, powering more than 220,000 homes. That's roughly the size of the Gold Coast – or Wollongong, Newcastle and Parramatta in Sydney combined – all powered from wind.

Macarthur is ideally placed, right in the path of the Roaring Forties. But constructing its enormous turbines is a funny business. It requires Mother Nature to play nice. Each blade is 54 metres long, weighs six tonnes, and needs to be craned 90 metres into the air. It's a difficult and potentially hazardous operation. If wind speed gets beyond 36 kilometres an hour, work has to stop. But ironically, if it were too easy to build the turbines, they would be in the wrong place.

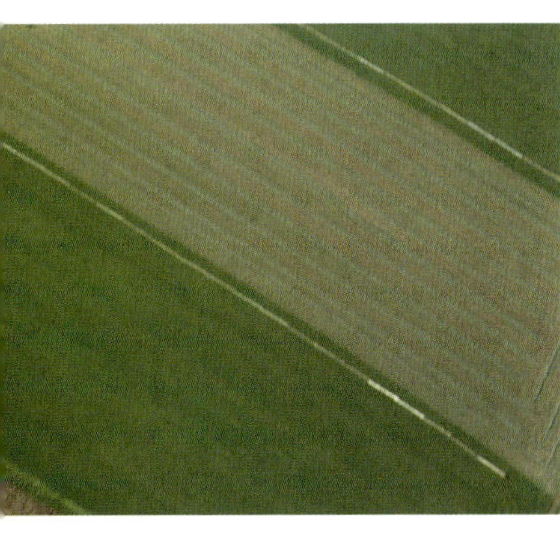

As Macarthur joins the fray, Victoria is definitely playing catch-up in the clean energy race. But in the world of renewable power, Tasmania outstrips all others. Courtesy of its high rainfall in the west of the island, the state's hydroelectric scheme produces 75 per cent of its electricity. Tasmania represents only one per cent of the Australian landmass, but holds 12 per cent of its freshwater resources. It's a very wet place. Water discharged at the end of the Derwent River chain of generators equals twice the total water usage in South Australia.

The march of renewables finds itself at an interesting crossroads. In our desire to unlock more energy from the natural world, we are also turning food crops and their by-products into fuel and electricity. Much has been made about the use of corn to produce bioethanol, but in the Burdekin region of northern Queensland the effort has a distinct Australian flavour. This is sugarcane country, which is best known for its iconic harvest burns.

The farmers there are no longer just sweetening our lives: at local refineries, they are turning cane molasses into biofuel and burning another by-product – bagasse – to create electricity. That electricity, in turn, runs the mill, but if it produces more than it needs, the overflow is fed into the grid. Australia's 4,000 sugarcane farms hug 2,100 kilometres of coastline from northern New South Wales to the north of Queensland – indeed, a treasure trove of energy.

But even our individual best efforts may come to very little without more of the kind of thinking that launched Australia's first foray

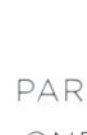

into renewable energy, and created not only one of our largest energy generators, but allowed for large scale irrigation at the same time: the Snowy Hydro Scheme. At more than 2,000 metres, you can't get any higher on our ancient eroded stub of a continent. But where some saw gnarled gum trees and white powder good only for skiing, others saw the awesome power lying dormant in those fabled high altitude snowfields.

Sixty years ago, work started on the scheme that would become one of the world's most impressive hydroelectric systems, diverting water from the Snowy and Eucumbene rivers, among others, to help irrigate drought-prone farms to the west of the Great Dividing Range. Along the way, the liberated spring water also helps drive huge turbines that generate 42 per cent of renewable energy in mainland Australia's national electricity market. In the Snowy Mountains, our two great appetites for food and power found one audacious and hard-won solution. More than 120 workers died during construction and it's no wonder the scheme is often credited with forging our multicultural nation, much like 'mateship' is linked to the trenches of Gallipoli – both defining points in our history.

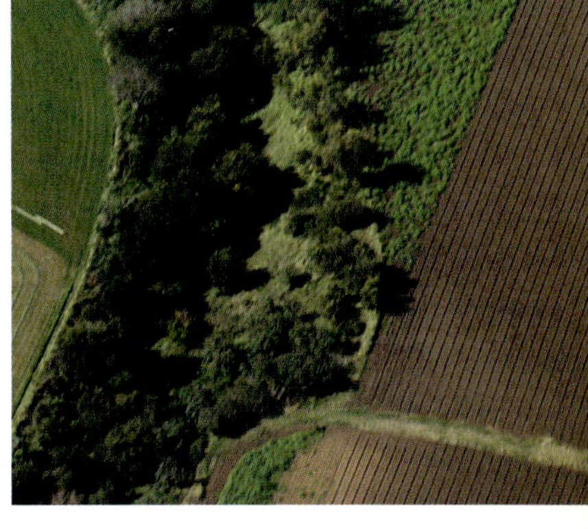

More than 100,000 people came to work on the scheme, many from war-ravaged Europe, some from countries that had just been adversaries. But in the harsh and unforgiving mountains there was neither time, nor patience, for lingering animosities. 'You aren't any longer Czechs or Germans,' chief engineer Sir William Hudson told them. 'You are men of the Snowy.'

The Snowy Hydro's brave workforce built 16 dams, seven power stations and 225 kilometres of pipelines, aqueducts and tunnels. Ideally suited to cover peak load demands as it can instantly create extra electricity when needed, the hydro scheme also sends more than 2,000 billion litres of water a year to the Murray and Murrumbidgee rivers, to irrigate the farms that feed us.

The scheme helps to explain how our 120,000 farms produce 93 per cent of the fresh food we eat each day – but also how we export enough food to feed another 60 million people overseas. Producing that much food in a country with only six per cent of arable land takes hard work, technology, sunshine, soil and, of course, water. And indeed, we have become very adept at squeezing the last drop out of our most limited of resources.

We irrigate almost two million hectares of farmland with water drawn from dams, rivers, canals, aquifers and even from treated effluent.

North of Adelaide, carrot farmer John Bergamin relies on recycled water from the Bolivar sewerage plant. In most years, his corner of the country receives just 500 millimetres of rain. That's less than half the rain that falls in Brisbane or Sydney. But thanks to the treatment plant, Bergamin's able to pump 300 million litres of cleaned-up water onto his 44 hectares. 'Beforehand we had underground water and it used to be artesian,' he says, 'but they pumped the water almost out of existence.' Bolivar water came just in time. 'We're paying for it, naturally, but it is an excellent source.' says Bergamin.

Our great water rush began 125 years ago when Mildura, a dusty sheep station in Victoria, became the first purpose-built irrigation town. From there, irrigation fever spread along the Murray, into the Murrumbidgee and along the Darling. The Murray–Darling Basin today sprawls from South Australia all the way into Queensland, bolstered by the diverted waters from the Snowy Hydro Scheme, which irrigate one million square kilometres, a territory twice the size of Spain. The basin is responsible for producing one-third of everything we put on our plates.

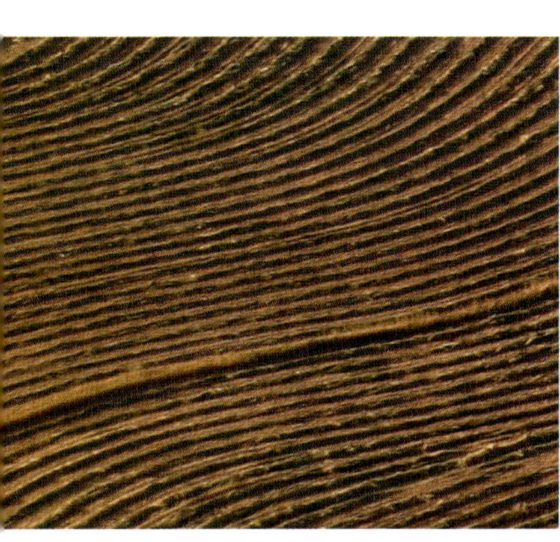

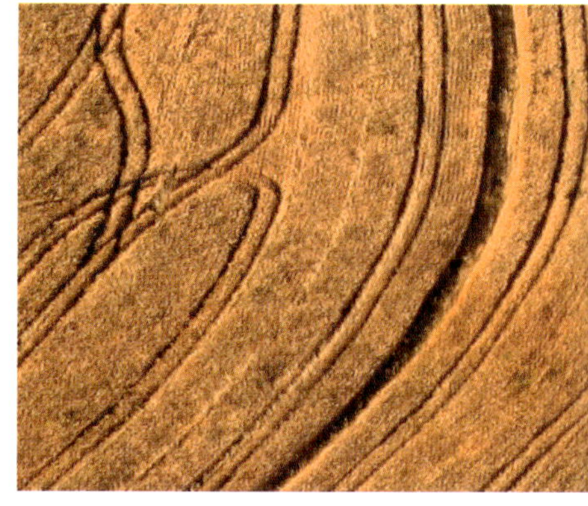

In New South Wales and Victoria, irrigation has spurred the growing of some rather exotic – and often perhaps questionable – crops. On the driest inhabited continent in the world, we flood our river valleys with millions of litres of water to grow rice. You can forget images of barefoot farmers wading patiently through tropical paddies. In Australia, growing rice is a hi-tech affair in which farmers use special temperate varieties suited to our climate. 'We need to feed people and we need to do that as efficiently and effectively as we possibly can,' says Les Gordon, a third-generation rice farmer in Deniliquin, southern New South Wales. 'It's what we know. It's what we do.'

And the way we do it, once again, involves jumping in a plane. Specially trained pilots fly 'air tractors', planes engineered to sow from the air. They release germinated rice seeds, using GPS for pinpoint accuracy. On Gordon's farms, seventy hectares of flooded paddocks are covered in just a few hours. Down on the ground, that same job would take several labourers two days. In such a dry land it's a sometimes contentious business, but this is ideal rice country, with dense clay just beneath the plains holding water tightly. 'You watch it and marvel at how far things have changed', says Gordon. 'I wonder what my grandkids will be looking at and what technology will bring over the next twenty, thirty, forty or fifty years.'

The march of renewables finds itself at an interesting crossroads. In our desire to unlock more energy from the natural world, we are now also turning food crops and their by-products into fuel and electricity.

Australian paddies can produce a million tonnes of rice a year. After milling, 80 per cent goes overseas, mostly to Asia, including our major markets of Indonesia, South Korea and Japan. Rice, though, is just a small part of the equation. Not only do we have the potential to feed our entire population, we export a staggering 60 per cent of everything we grow, sending our produce all over the globe, effectively feeding a country the size of France.

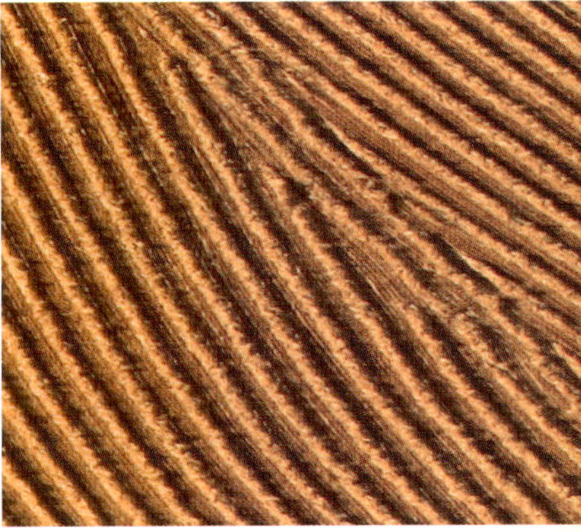

Our biggest food export is wheat. In its raw form we export more than 20 million tonnes each year, which makes Australia the world's second largest exporter after America. Western Australia is the largest grower of wheat – the state producing 40 per cent of Australia's annual crop. A total of 90 per cent is exported from the west, mostly through the Kwinana terminal, south of Perth. At the 19 grain ports around the country, bulk carriers take on as much as 55,000 tonnes a time. It's big business. Half of all our cropped land, 14 million hectares, is devoted to wheat.

In such a dry and barren land it's no overstatement to say it's a miracle that we are able to produce as much food as we do. In total, we dedicate more than 400 million hectares, about half our land surface, to agriculture. And we only need to take a closer look at our 'simple' everyday comfort foods to realise just how complex our system of food production and distribution really is. The Aussie hamburger is a prime example.

The burger bun may have started life in the vast wheatbelts of Western Australia or the Murray–Darling Basin, but the other ingredients will also be well travelled when they come together at your local takeaway. For instance, beetroot comes from Queensland's Lockyer Valley. There, a mere nine farmers grow 90 per cent of all the beetroot we eat. And eat we do. We consume more bulbous red tubers per capita than any other country. Pineapple will have grown at the foot of the Glasshouse Mountains in Queensland. Iceberg lettuce may well have journeyed from the Mornington Peninsula in Victoria, while in Dampier and Adelaide, huge ponds of seawater are evaporating to make salt.

Just up the road from South Australia's capital, in Two Wells, is the grand home of the tomato – a juicy, healthy bit of our hamburger – grown in a crystal palace that rises from the desert. 'These are truss tomatoes,' says manager Jon Jones. 'The vines are 25 centimetres when they come in and then 51 weeks later they are 18 metres long.' Only from above can you really appreciate the scale of the enterprise. Under 120,000 panes of glass, 600,000 hydroponic plants grow not in soil but in nutrient rich water, largely drawn from a nearby treatment plant and collected from the vast rooftop. These plants produce 10,000 tonnes of vine-ripened tomatoes a year.

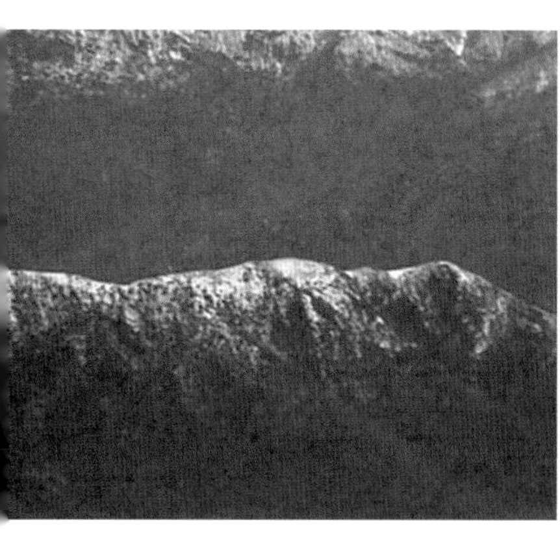

It's a factory for all seasons, but sealed off from the elements so the plants need a helping hand. Workers whiz by on automated trolleys to shake the stems – taking the place of bees in pollination. The glasshouse makes sure the tomatoes are grown in an optimal environment. 'Tomatoes love to be in a particular temperature range and also humidity,' says Jones. 'The glasshouse keeps it in that range – 23 degrees and 70 per cent, all year round.' It's an efficient solution. One hectare of glasshouse grows ten times the amount of a same-sized open field.

With growing populations worldwide, it seems we have no choice but to find more intensive ways of farming. It not only affects tomatoes. It also has implications for the production of red meat, the last ingredient of our hamburger. Our appetite for steaks, hamburgers and sausages far outstrips the carrying capacity of our land. And so a new industry has sprung up to keep the barbies sizzling and the burgers filled.

The Brindley Park Feedlot, near the town of Roma in Queensland, is home – a temporary one really – to 20,000 prime beef cattle. Like the glasshouse in South Australia, a feedlot eliminates seasonal uncertainties. Cattle are fattened in a manner that is both more intensive and efficient than any traditional farm could offer, especially those on the impoverished lands of the Australian Outback. 'They stay for about 60 days and that gets them up to around 500 kilo live weight,' says Mick Lee, whose grandfather started this feedlot in the early 1980s.

To get the cattle from 380 kilos, their arrival weight, to the magic 500, they are fed a wheat-based grain mix – carb and protein loaded, designed for rapid weight gain. Next stop, the slaughterhouse. At Brindley Park, 120,000 cattle pass through its pens every year. Together, Australia's 600 feedlots produce 70 per cent of all supermarket beef.

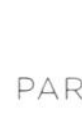

'We need to be producing that amount of beef to meet consumer needs,' says Lee. 'I think that if we were trying to get that type of number of animals through, off just grass or just the properties, it would be a real challenge and require a lot more land.' Feedlots are an example of consumer demand dictating food production.

The burger reveals what it takes – and the distances travelled – to put a meal on our plates. As we rear ourselves ever more intensively in our crowded cities, it follows that we'll have to intensify our food production systems. The question is, how do we do that? While the impact of food miles is a serious issue, how do we maintain a sustainable, affordable, nutritious supply of food without compromising the environment, animal health and welfare, or divorcing food production from its original rural roots?

Sustainability questions arise too when it comes to satisfying our appetite for electricity. We are addicted to fossil fuels, but they pollute the planet and they'll run out. Our only hope is that renewables will soon increase their presence in the energy mix. Future generations will judge us on our ability to harvest and harness the natural world without emptying or exhausting it. It's a delicate and difficult balance, but one we must strike.

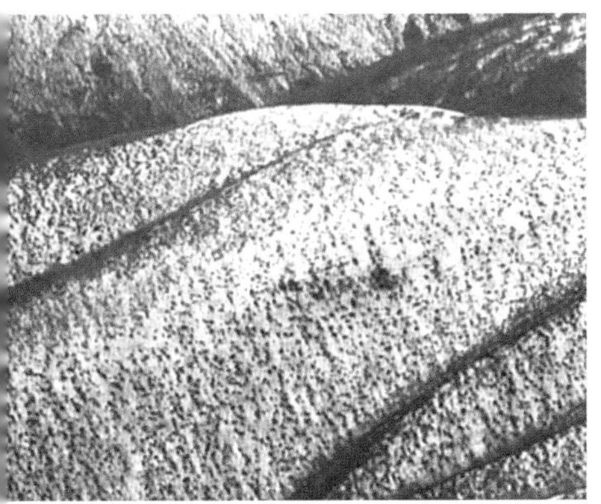

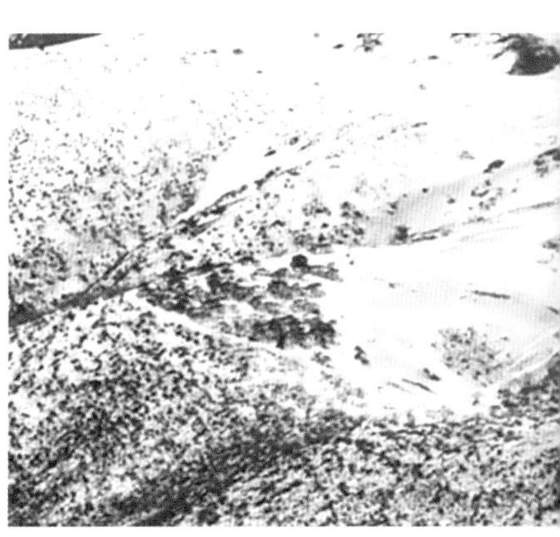

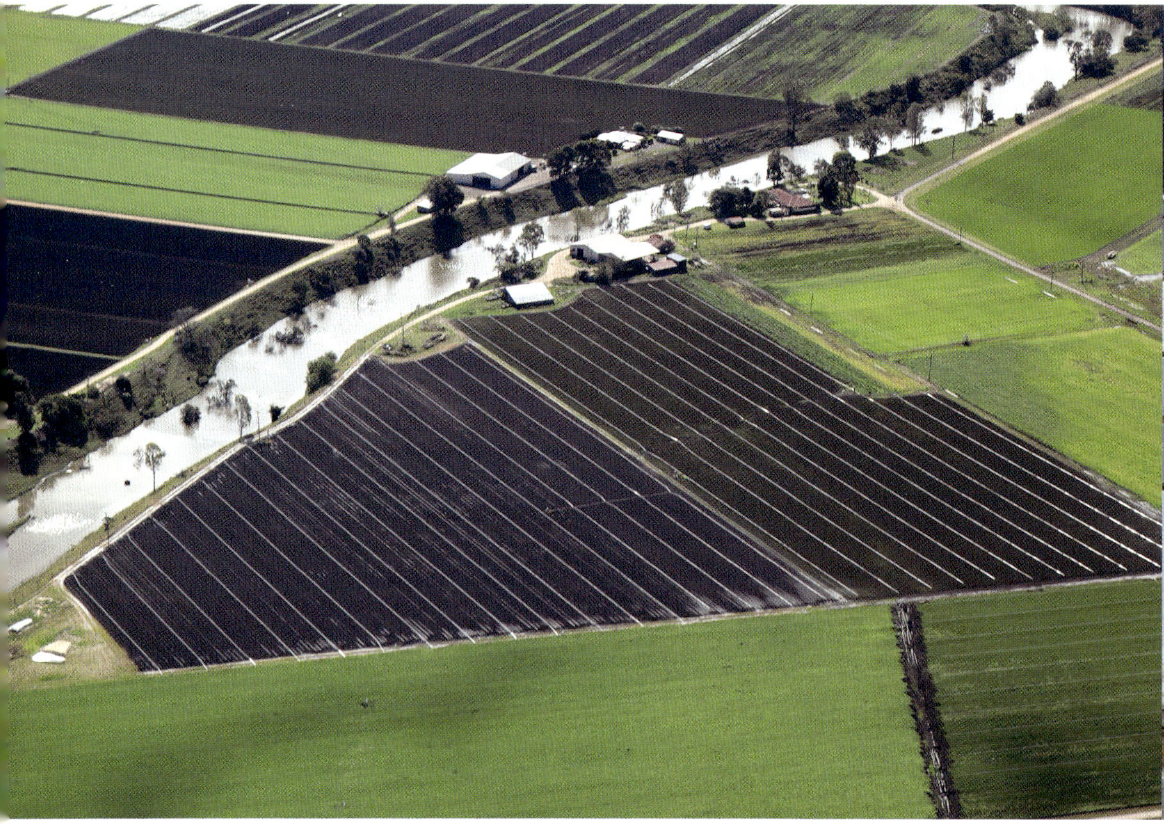

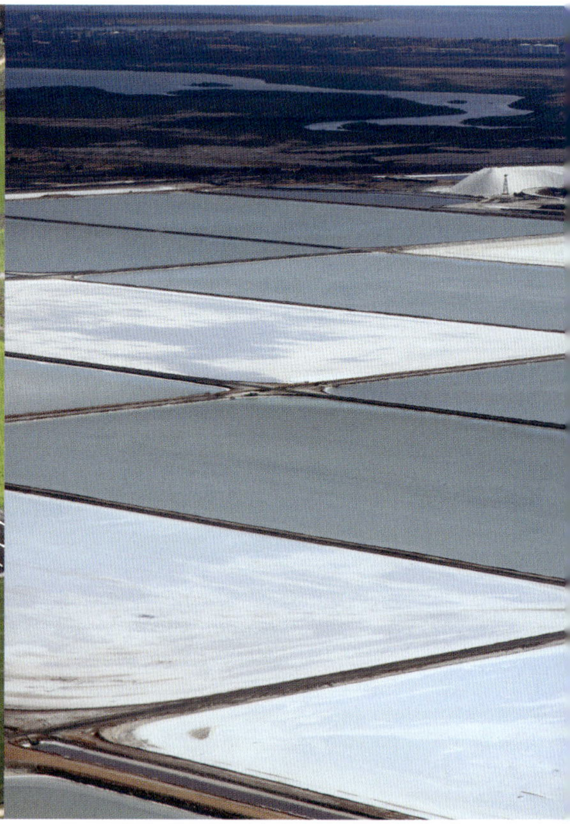

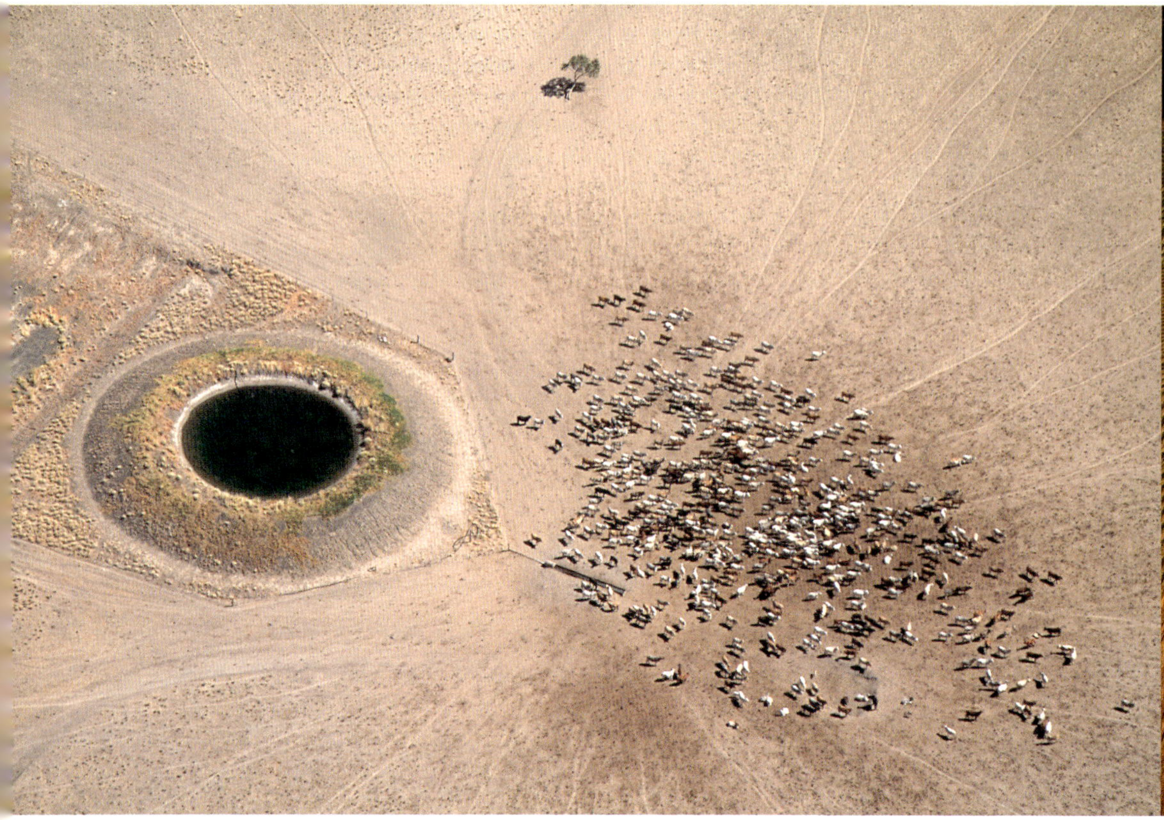

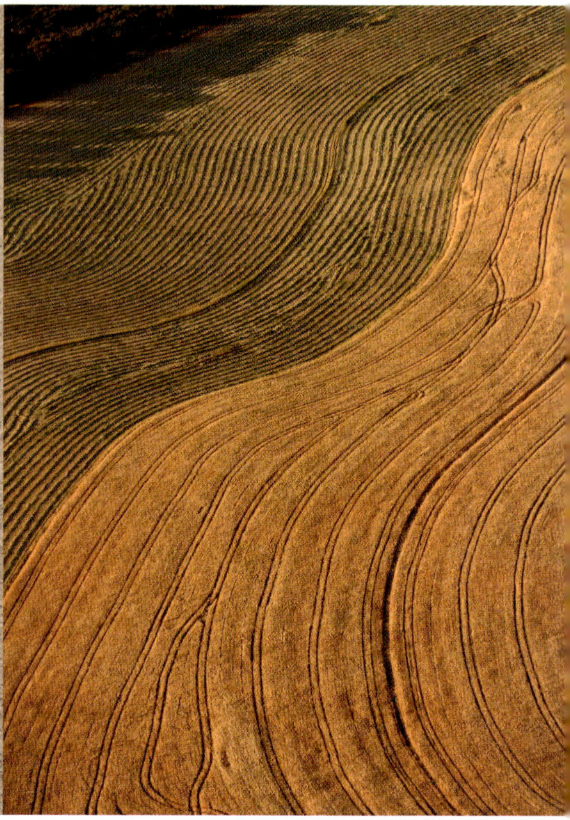

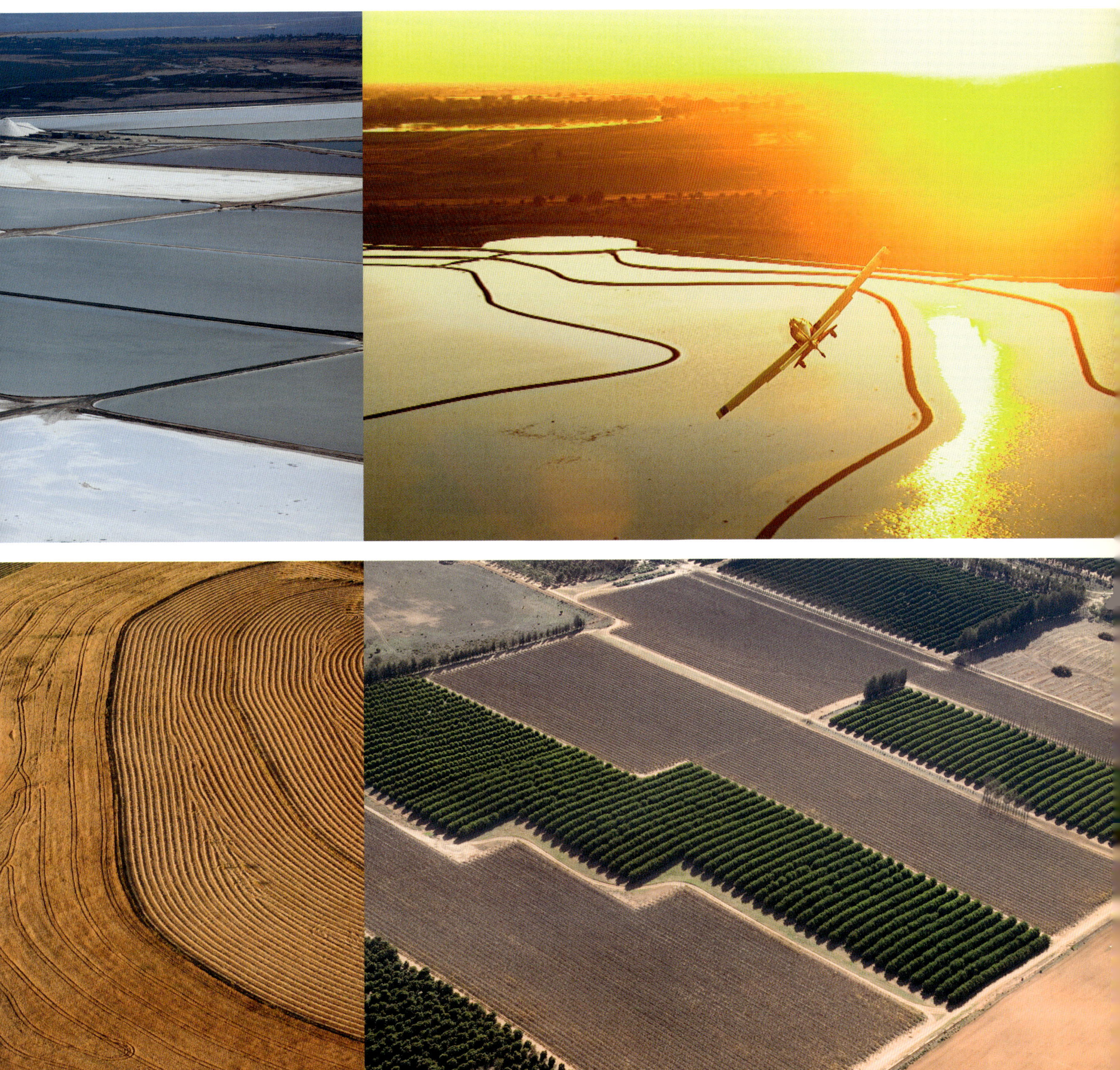

BELOW: Netted vineyards north of Hobart, Tasmania. Throughout the country, 2,000 wine companies have 154,000 hectares under vine. Australia produces more than a billion litres of wine a year, three quarters of which is shipped overseas, mainly to the US, the UK and Canada. Australia is the world's fourth largest exporter.

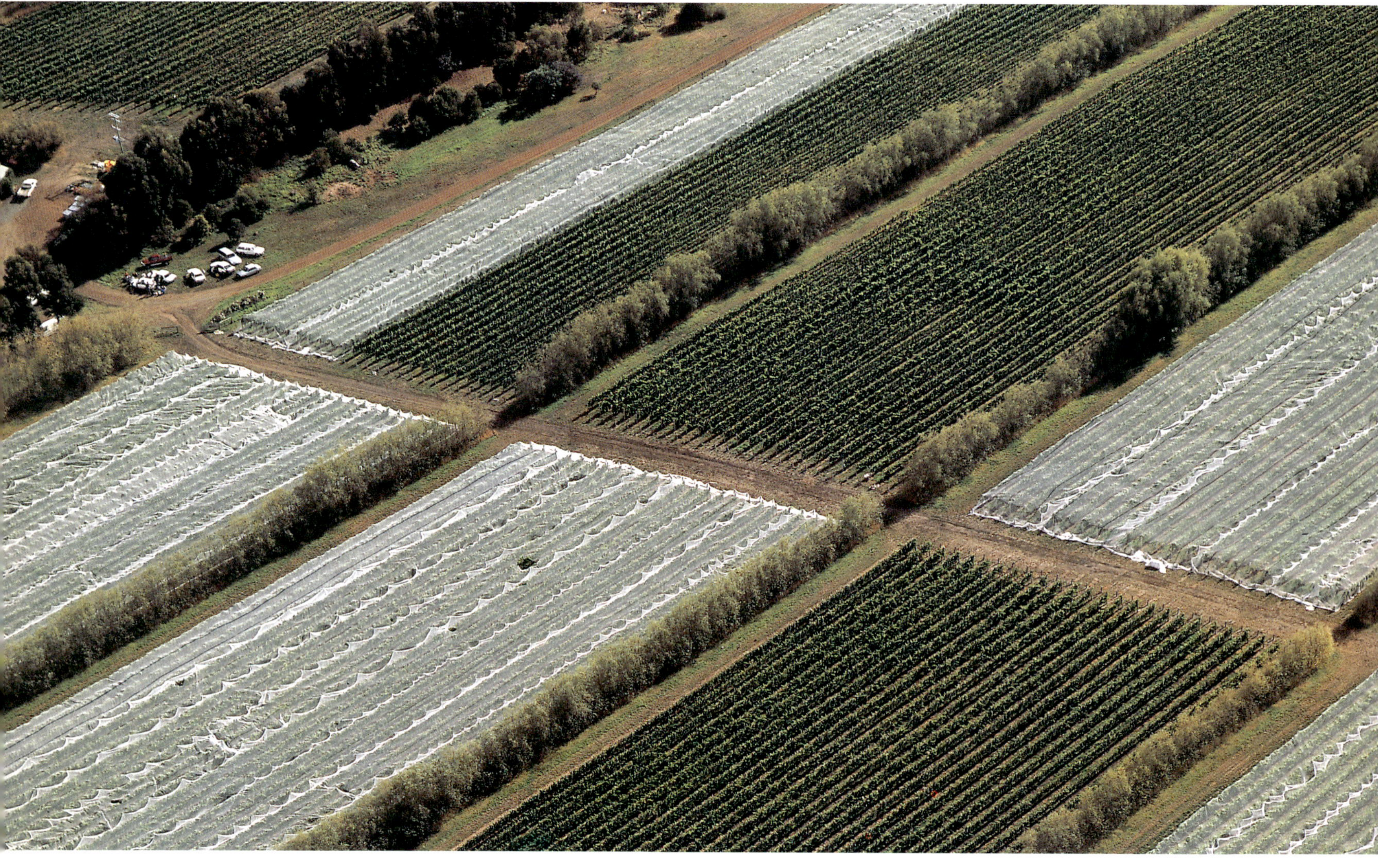

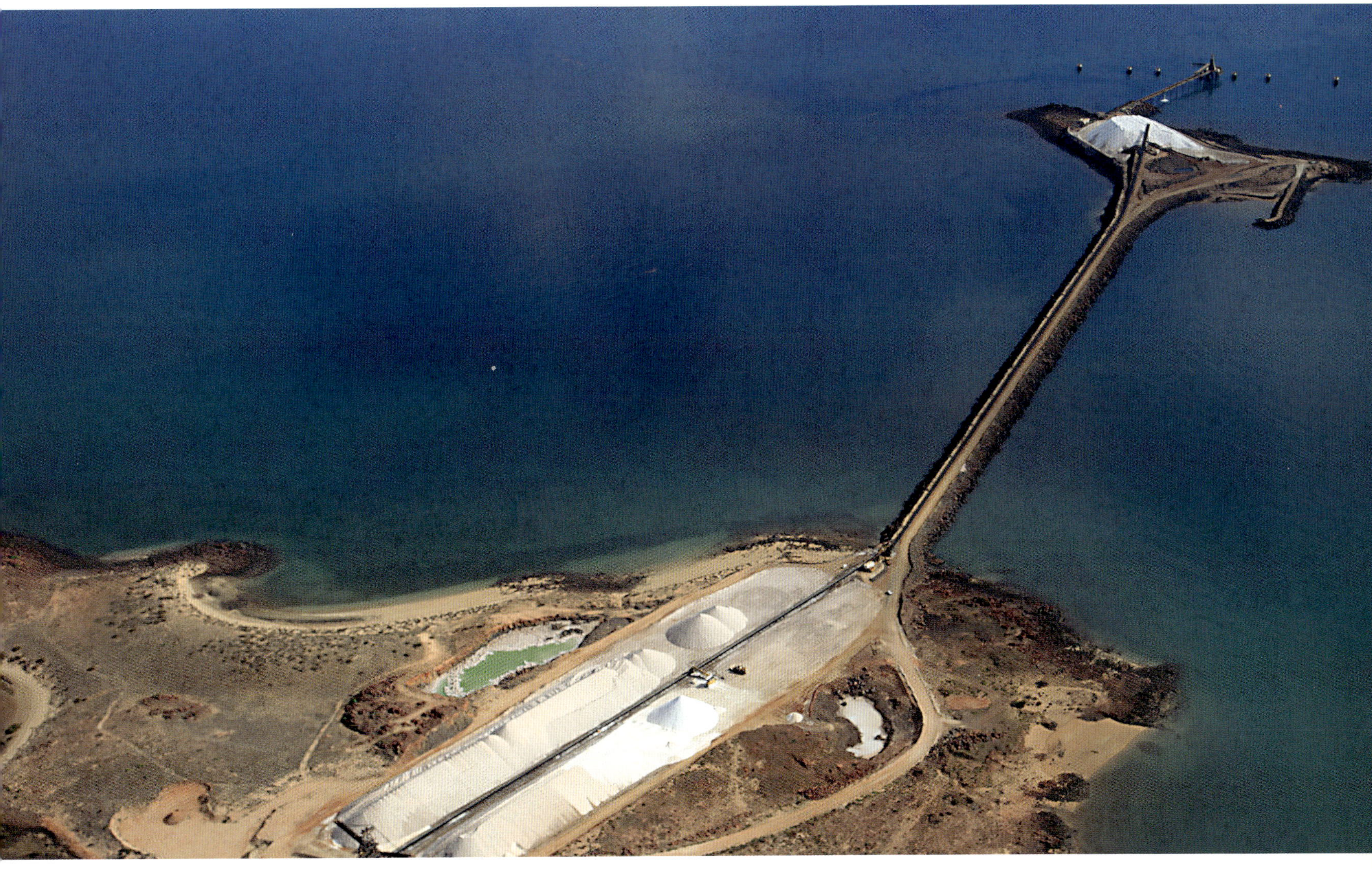

ABOVE: Salt shipping terminal, Dampier, Western Australia. Extracted from inland waters, salt domes and sedimentary deposits, salt's most abundant source is the ocean. It takes a year and a half to move the sea water through a series of evaporation ponds and to prepare the salt for harvesting. Dampier is the world's largest exporter of solar salt. **FOLLOWING PAGES:** The Tumut Pond Dam. This concrete arch was built as part of the Snowy Hydro scheme between 1955 and 1959. At a height of 86 metres and width of 217 metres, it collects the inflows of the Tumut river and the waters diverted through the Tooma and Eucumbene tunnels.

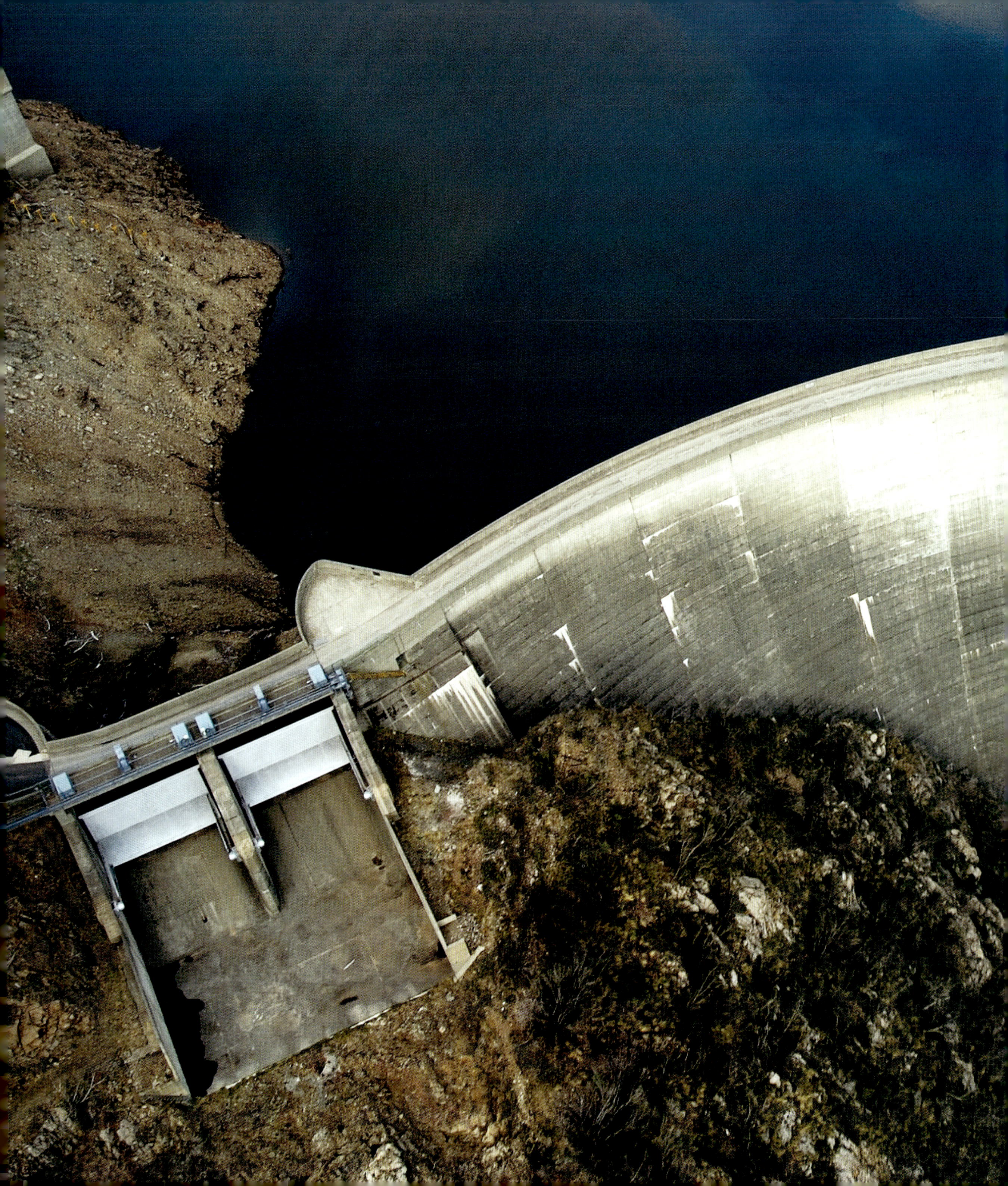

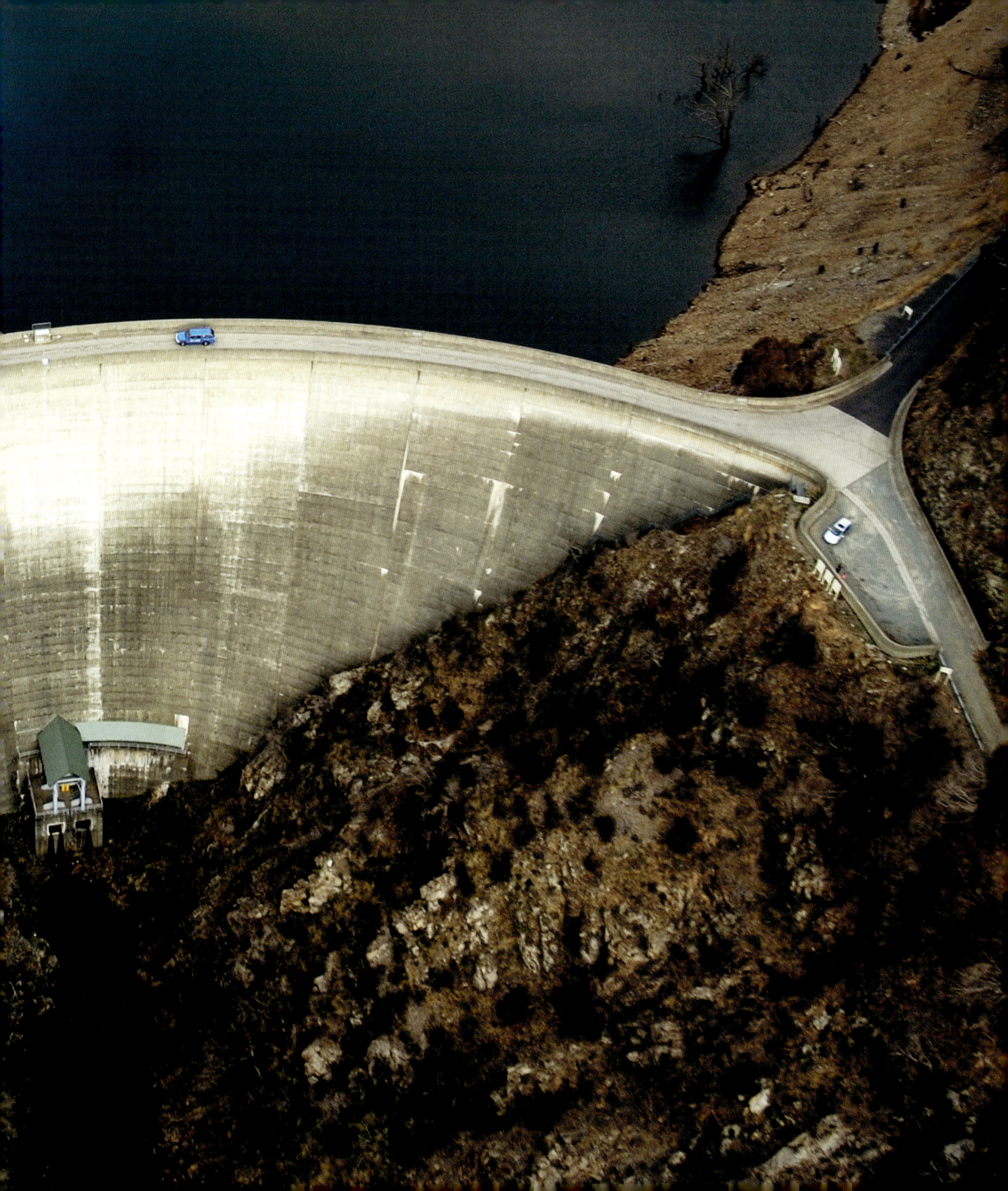

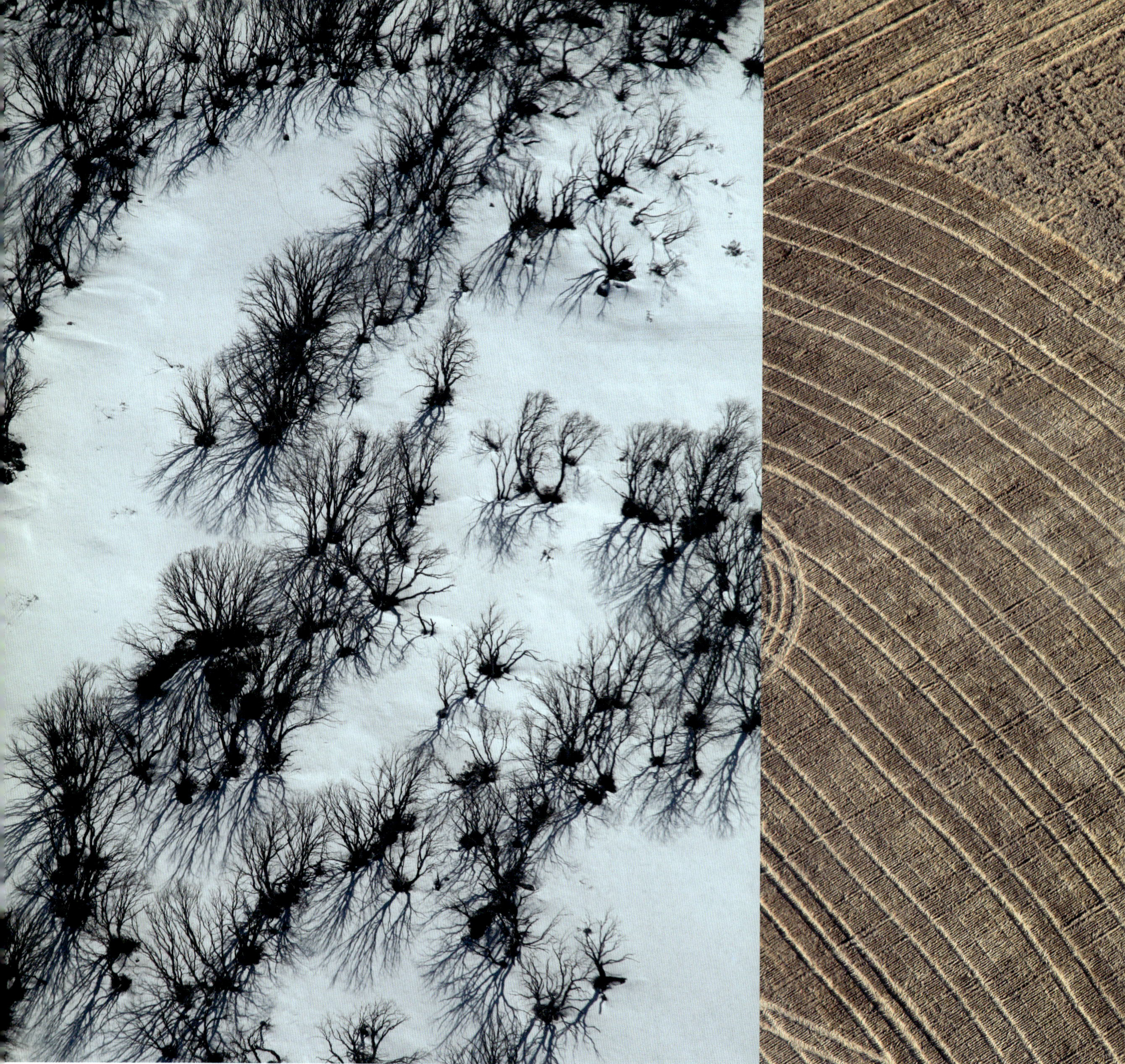

LEFT: Snow in Mt Hotham, Victoria. Once thawed, the water will feed Victoria's Kiewa hydroelectric scheme and help irrigate farms. **MIDDLE:** A combine harvester at work in York, Western Australia. The world's first commercial combine harvester was invented by Australian Hugh Victor McKay, patented in 1885. Driven by climatic extremes and vastness of properties, such Australian innovations have kept the country at the vanguard of international agriculture.

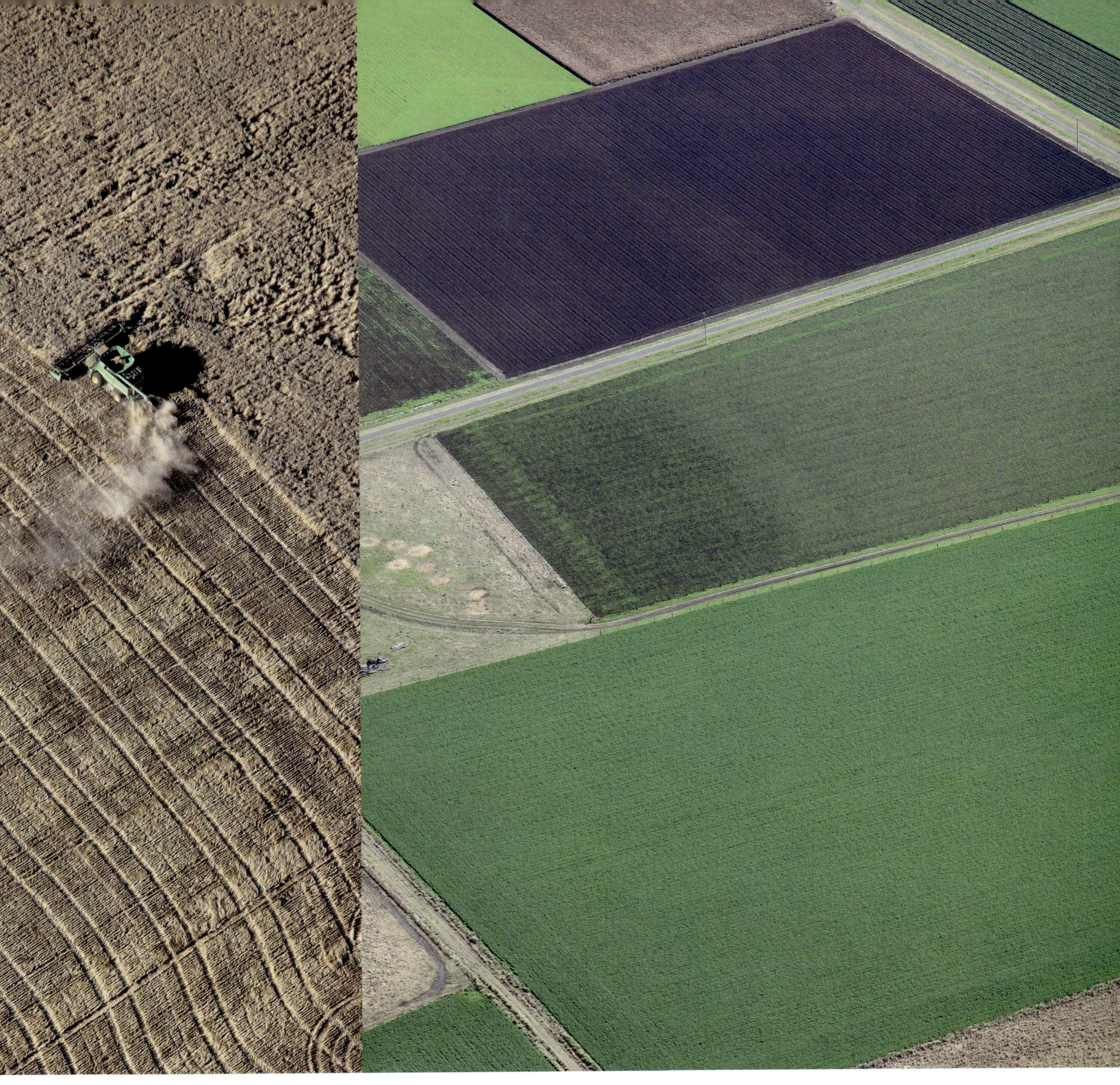

RIGHT: Mixed crops in Laidley, Queensland. These irrigated farms in the Lockyer Valley draw water from the northeastern tip of the Murray–Darling Basin. The basin, a territory twice the size of Spain, is responsible for a third of everything Australians eat.

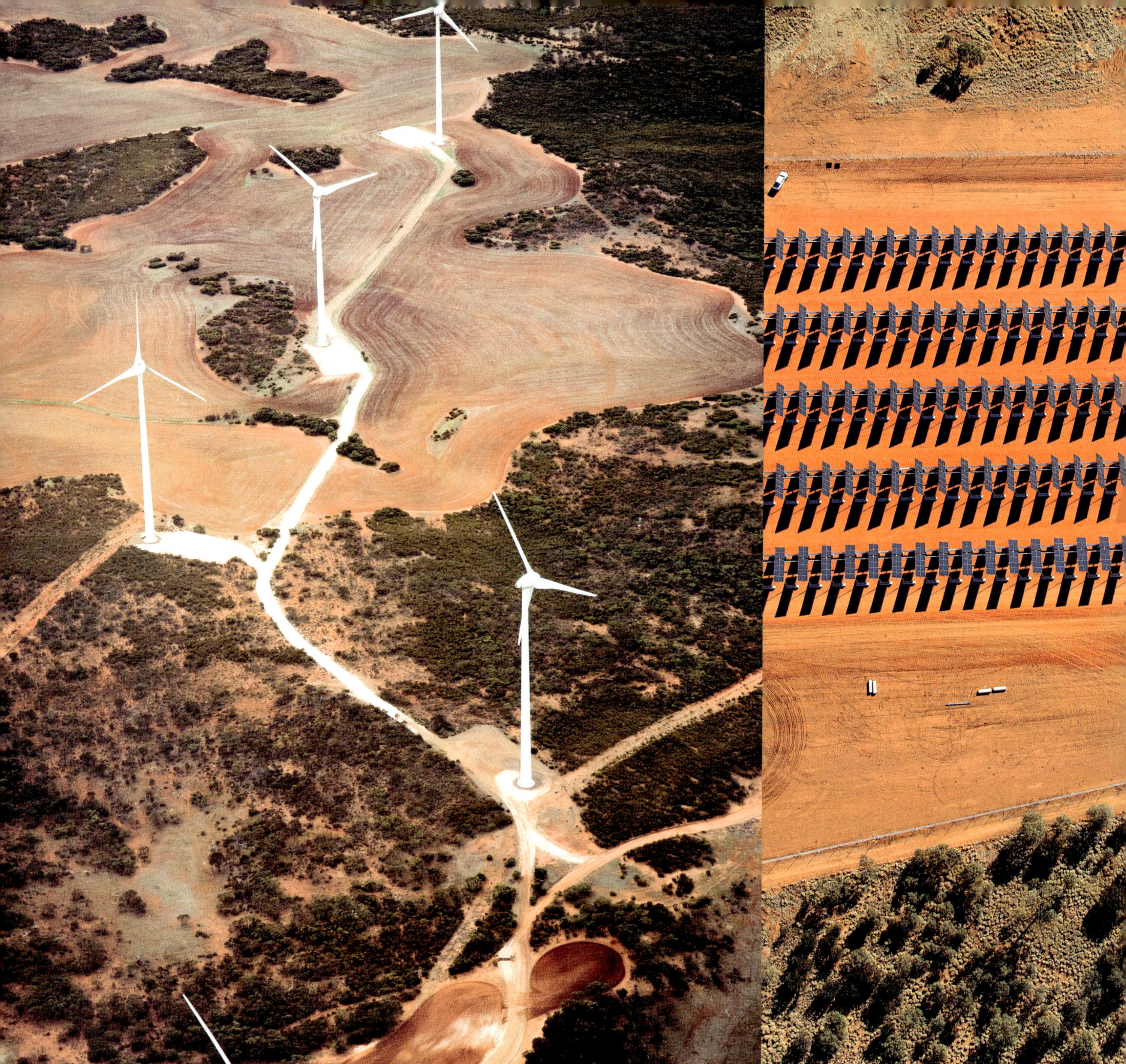

LEFT: The Mumbida Wind Farm near Geraldton, Western Australia. Under the federal government's Renewable Energy Target, 20 per cent of energy must come from renewable resources by 2020. There are currently 59 operating wind farms in Australia, with a total of 1,345 turbines. **MIDDLE:** The Uterne Solar Power Station in Alice Springs, Northern Territory, powers 270 homes. Its name means 'bright sunny day,' in the local Arrernte language. Across the nation, despite

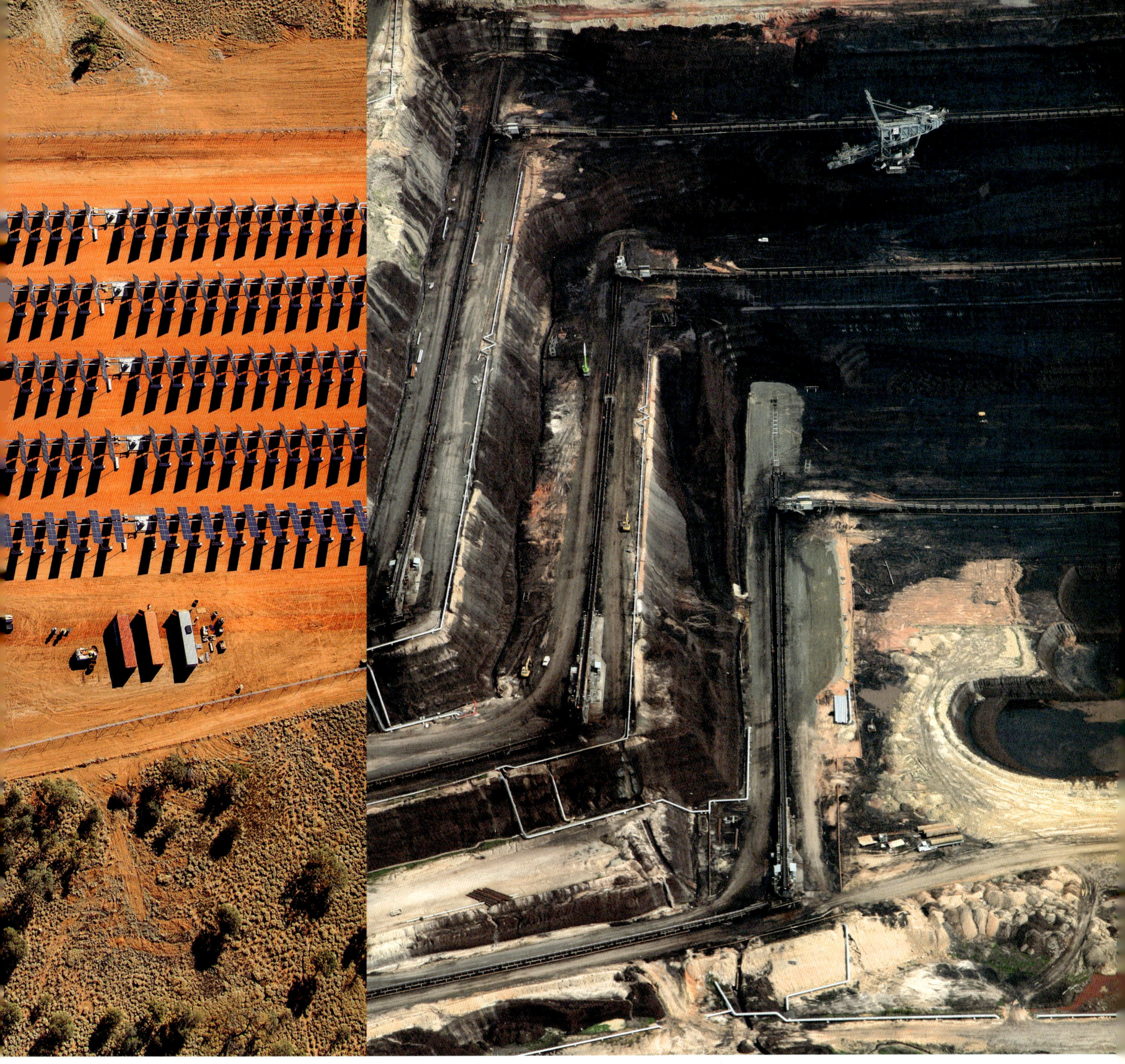

an abundance of bright sunny days, solar energy makes up less than half a per cent of electricity production. **RIGHT:** Brown coal in the Latrobe Valley, Victoria. Australia holds a quarter of the world's brown coal reserves but it is mined solely for domestic energy production. 75 per cent of Victoria's electricity relies on it.

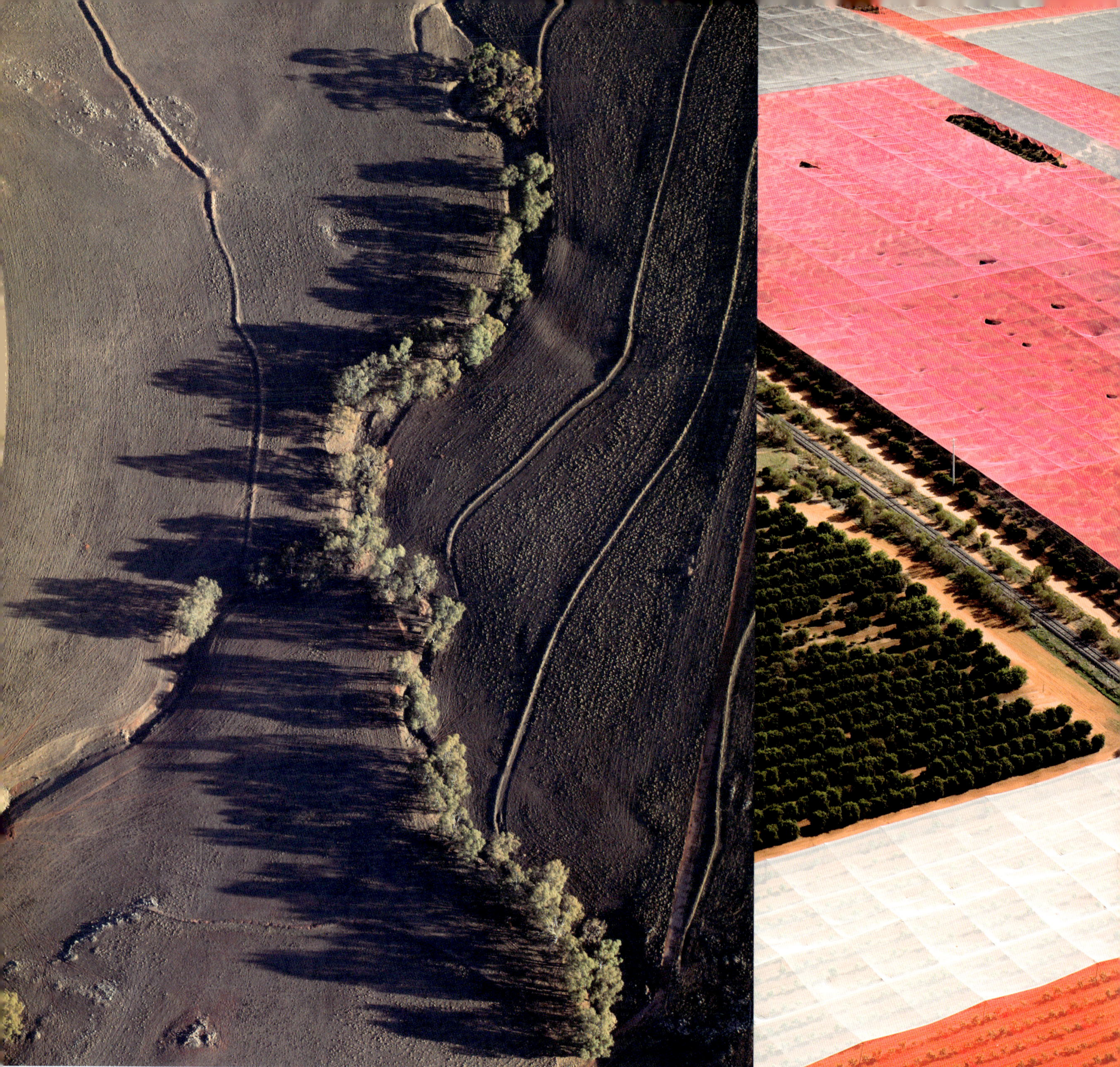

LEFT: Contour farming in Western Australia's Wheatbelt. The nation's 120,000 farms produce 93 per cent of the fresh food eaten each day. On top of that, Australia exports enough food to feed another 60 million people overseas.
MIDDLE: Shade cloths protect farmed trees in Mildura, Victoria. Located on the banks of the Murray River, Mildura went from being a dusty sheep station 125 years ago to Australia's first purpose built irrigation town.

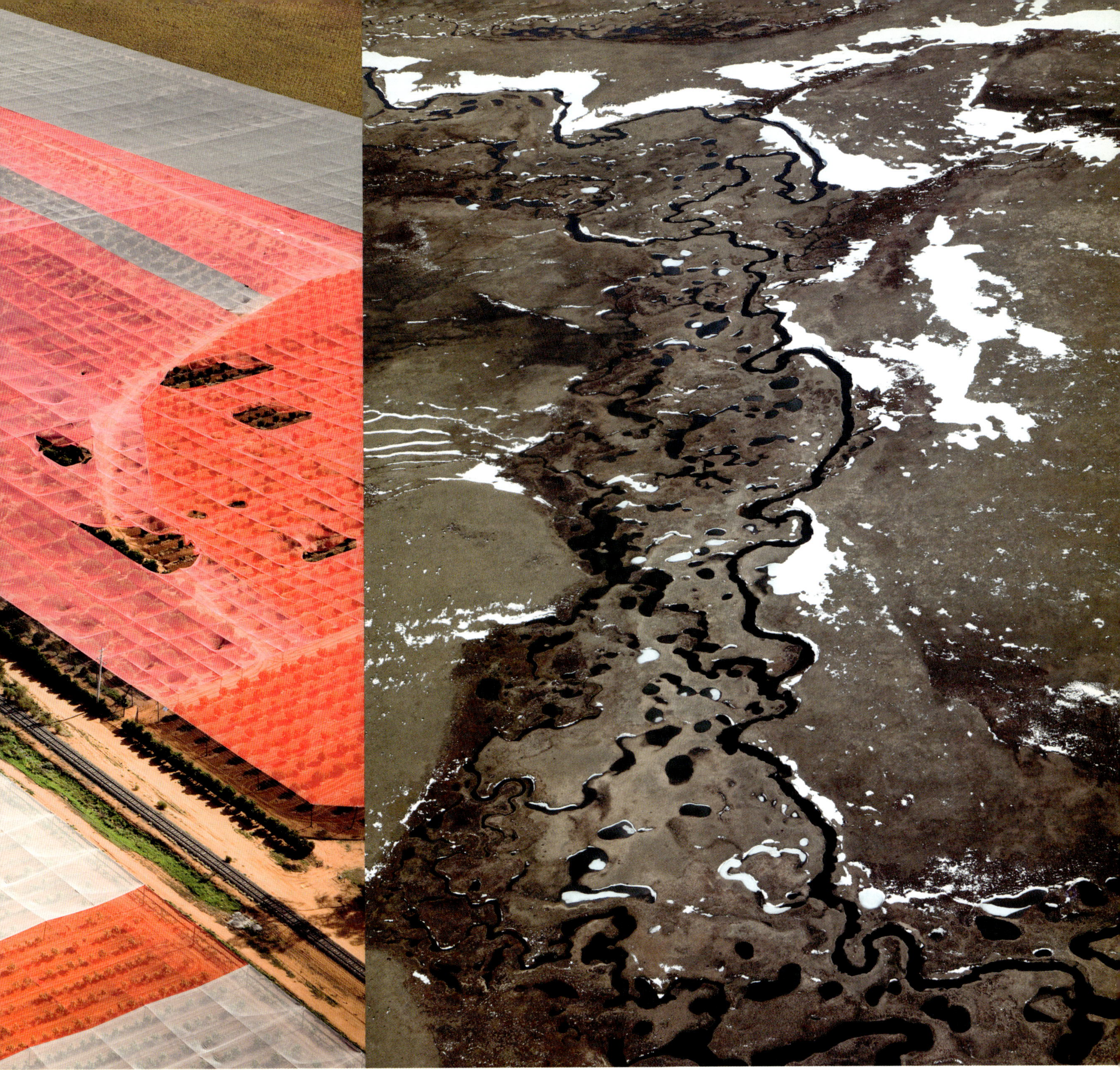

RIGHT: Melting snow and waterways between Hotham and Falls Creek in the Victorian Alps. Many of the state's major rivers, including the Murray, Goulburn and Kiewa, have their sources in these alpine and sub-alpine areas.

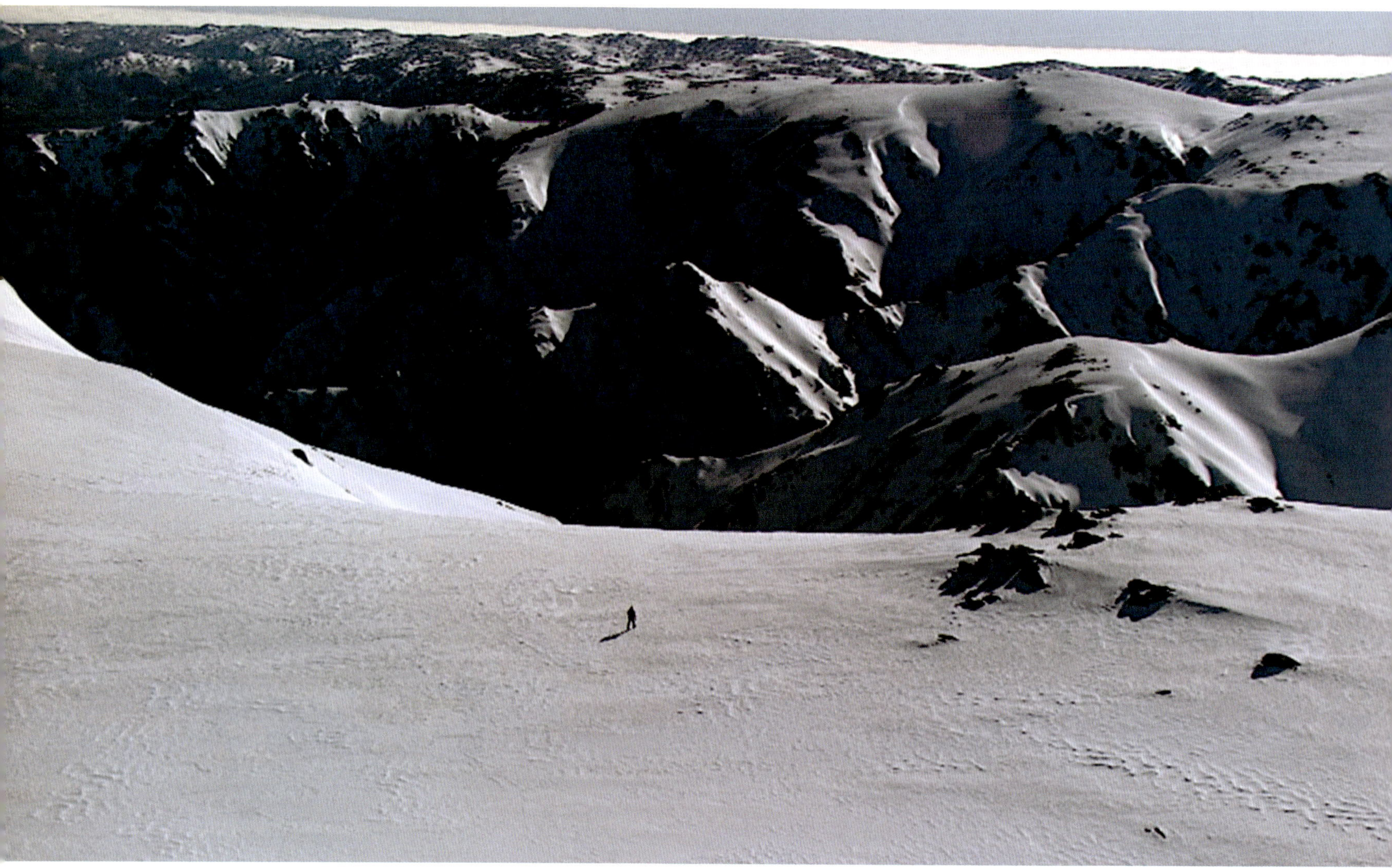

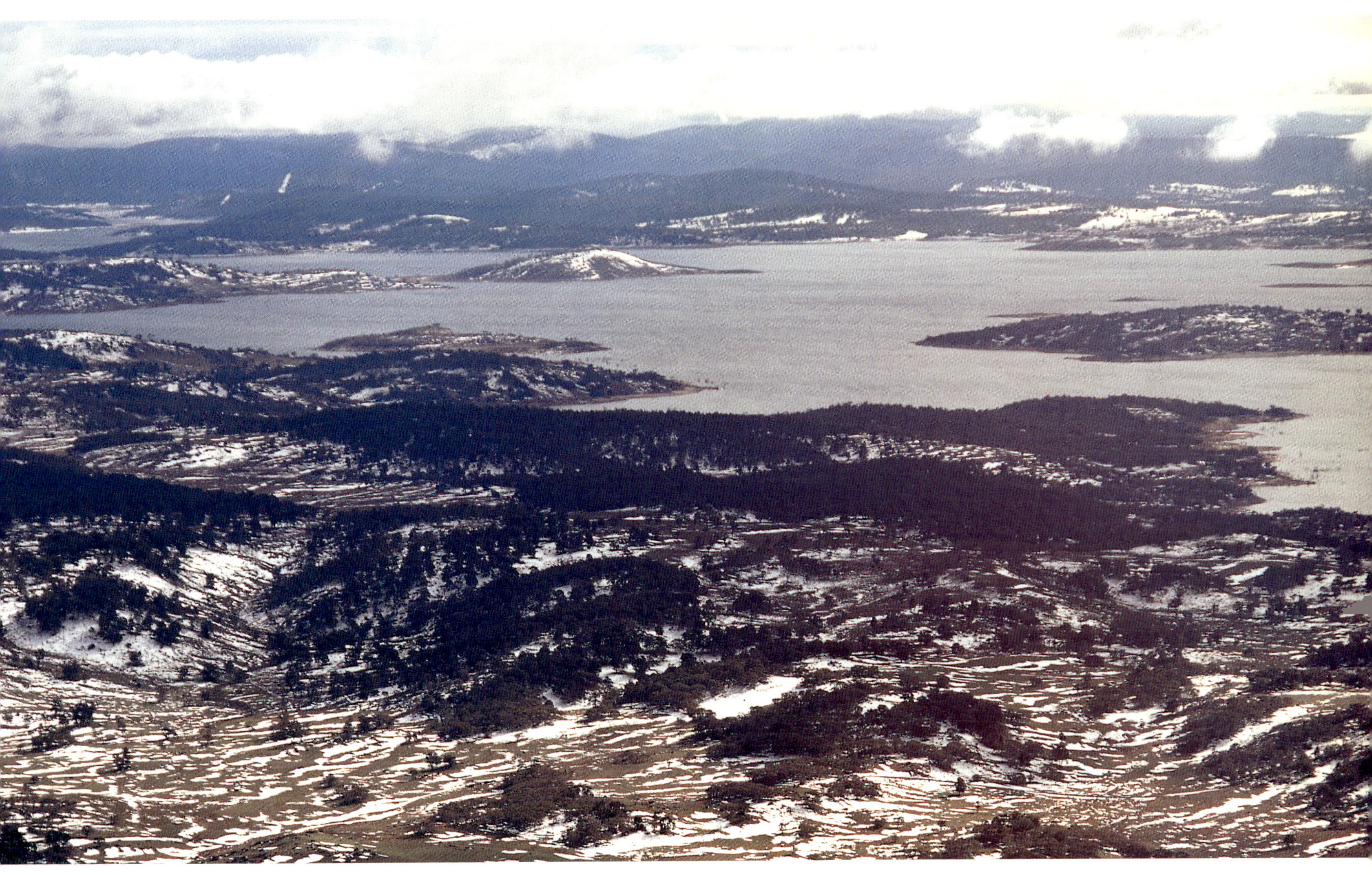

LEFT: Australia's rooftop: Mt Townsend in the Snowy Mountains, New South Wales. The 'snowies' are the highest part of the Great Dividing Range, a collection of mountains and plateaux which run 3,000 kilometres from northern Queensland to central Victoria. **RIGHT:** Lake Eucumbene in the Snowy Mountains. This man-made lake was created as part of the Snowy Hydro scheme. The dam that created the largest reservoir of the scheme was completed in 1958. At the bottom of the lake lies the flooded town of Old Adaminaby, sacrificed on the altar of progress.

LEFT: According to the Australian Academy of Science, enough solar energy falls on Australia in two days to power the world for a year. The Academy reports that to power all of Australia's energy needs would require only 0.3 per cent of the land surface to be devoted to solar power generation. **RIGHT:** A coal carrier is loaded for export at Hay Point near Mackay, Queensland. It's one of nine such terminals in Australia, the world's leading black coal exporter. Despite growing concerns about climate change, coal still generates 42 per cent of the world's electricity.

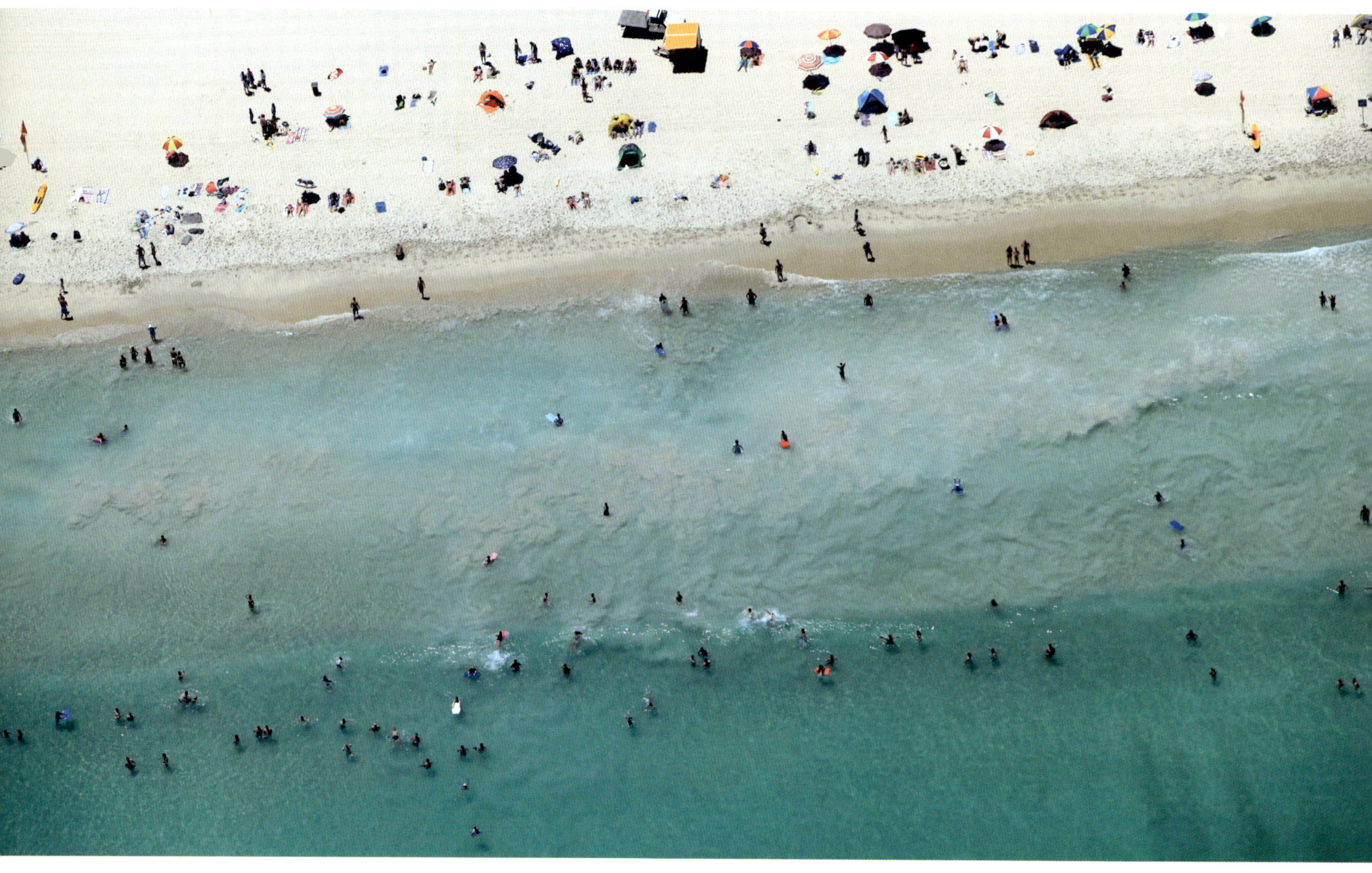

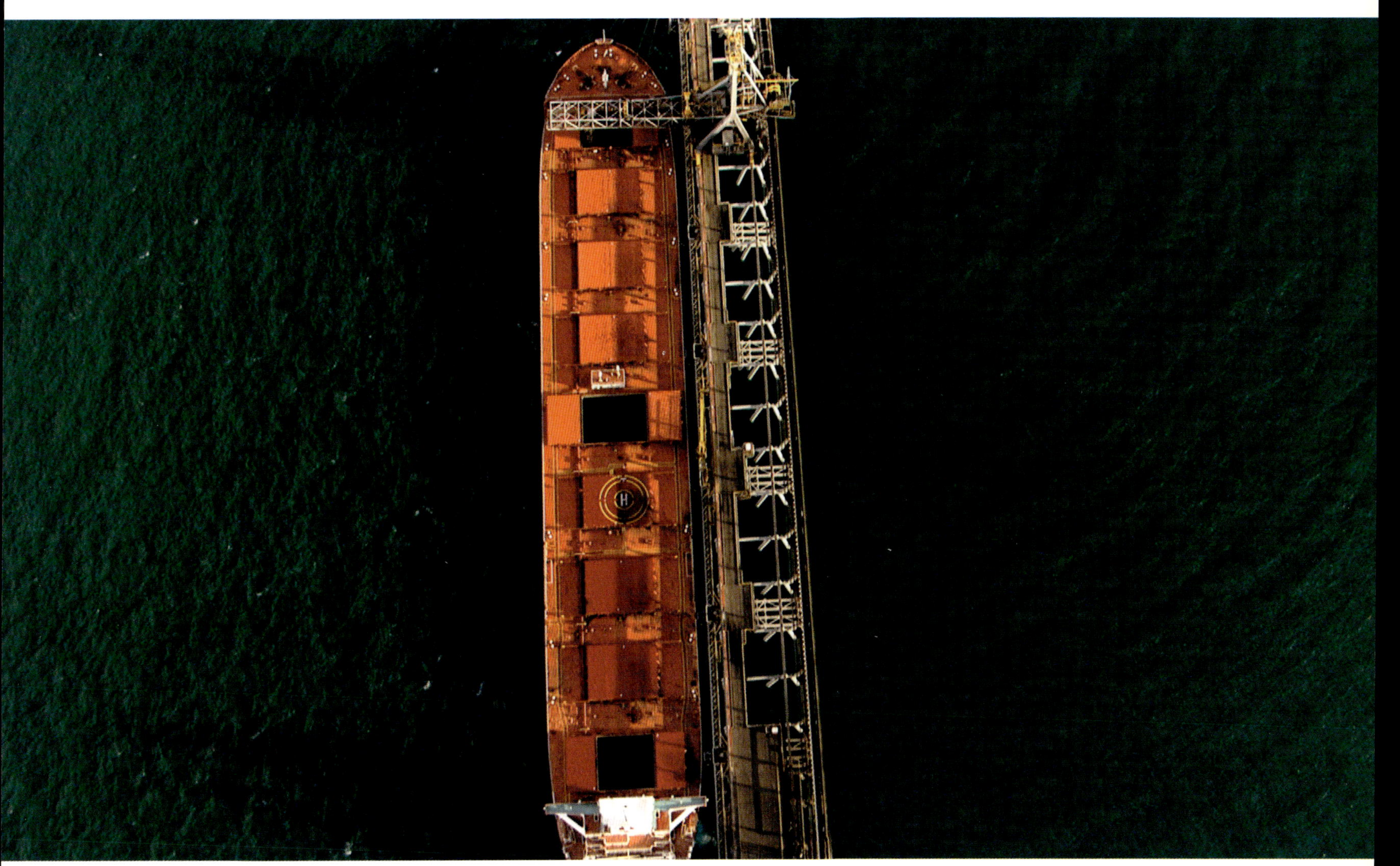

LEFT: Solar salt evaporation ponds at Lake MacLeod, Western Australia. It takes 60 million tonnes of sea water to produce one million tonnes of salt. Staggeringly, there is enough salt in the oceans to cover the world's continents to a height of 35 metres. **RIGHT:** Australian rice fields can produce up to one million tonnes of rice a year. In a typical production year, Australian rice helps feed up to 40 million people every day. A sometimes controversial industry in a dry country, Australian rice growers are efficient, using up to 50 per cent less water to grow a kilo of rice than the world average.

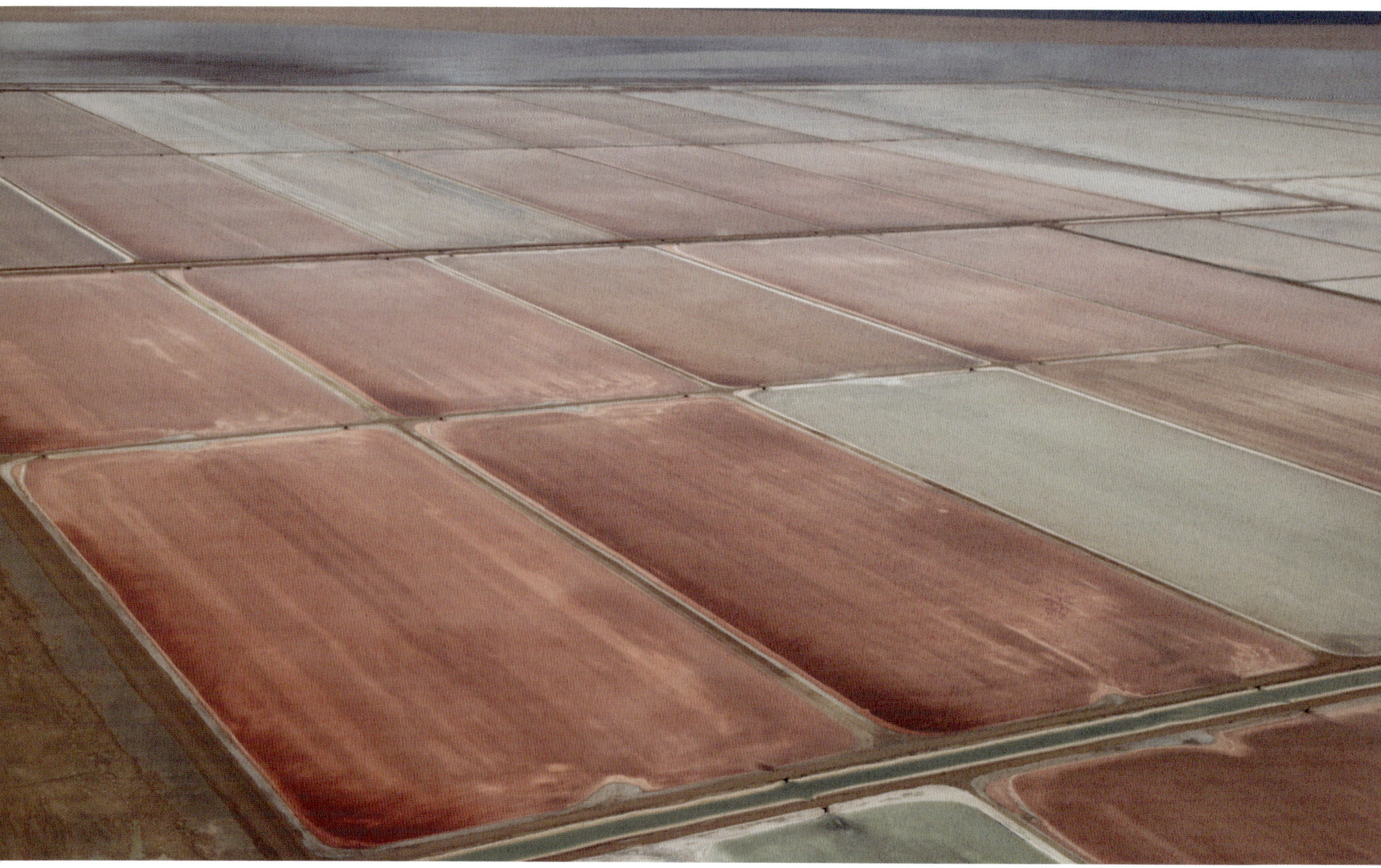

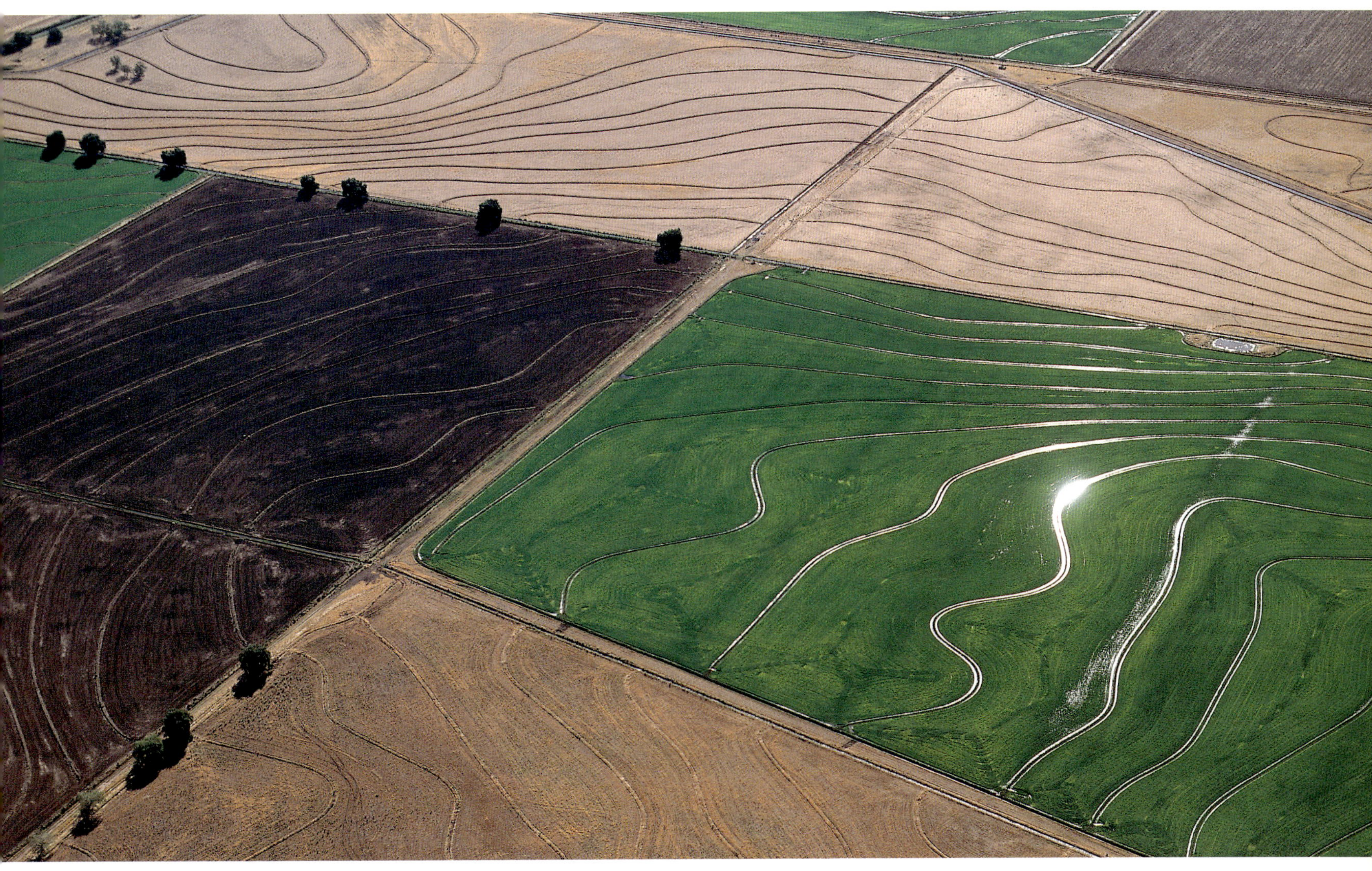

FOLLOWING PAGES: The dense clay soil in Deniliquin, New South Wales, is perfect for holding water for thirsty rice crops. The flowing lines follow surface contours while the straight lines have been cut using laser-precision technology.

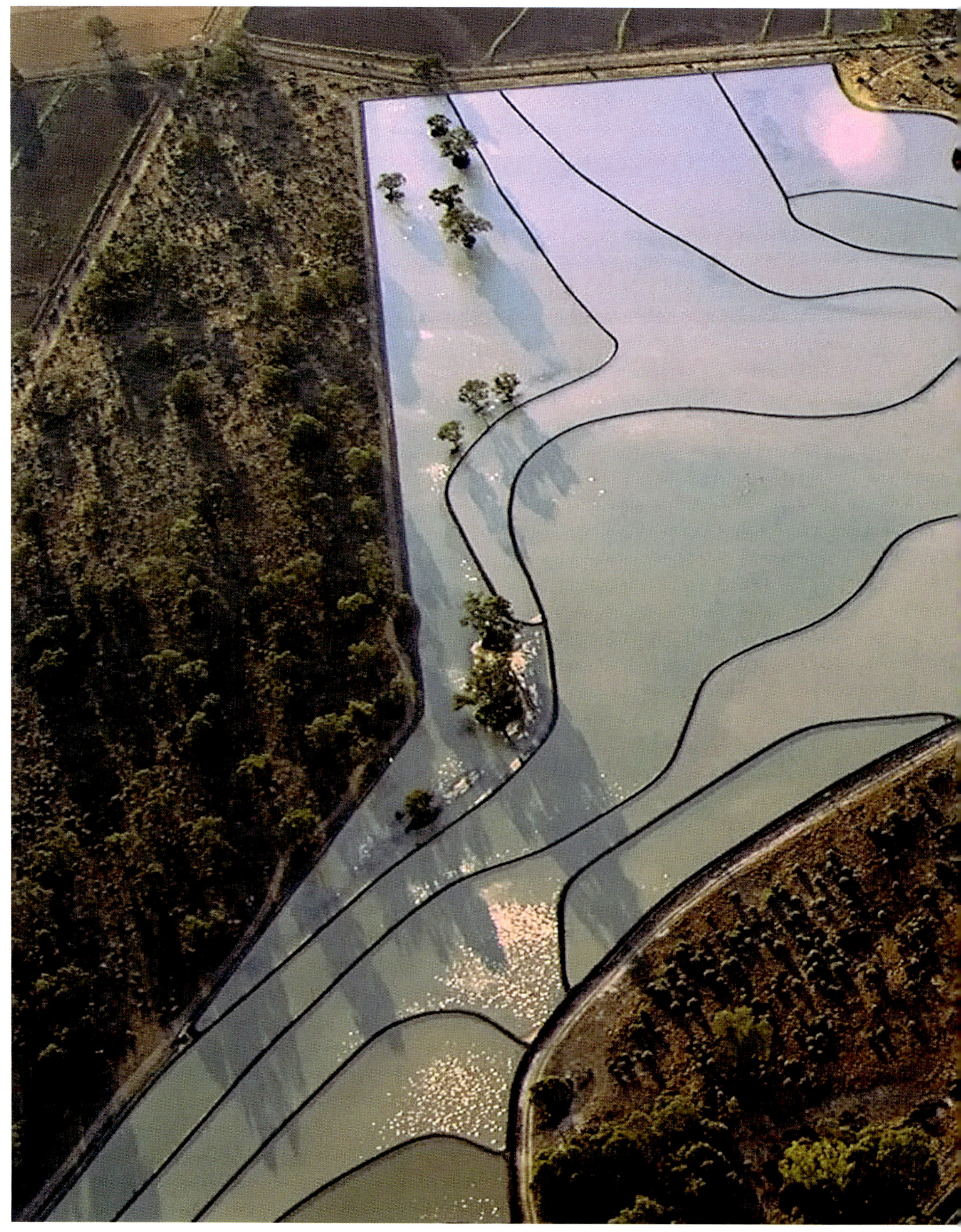

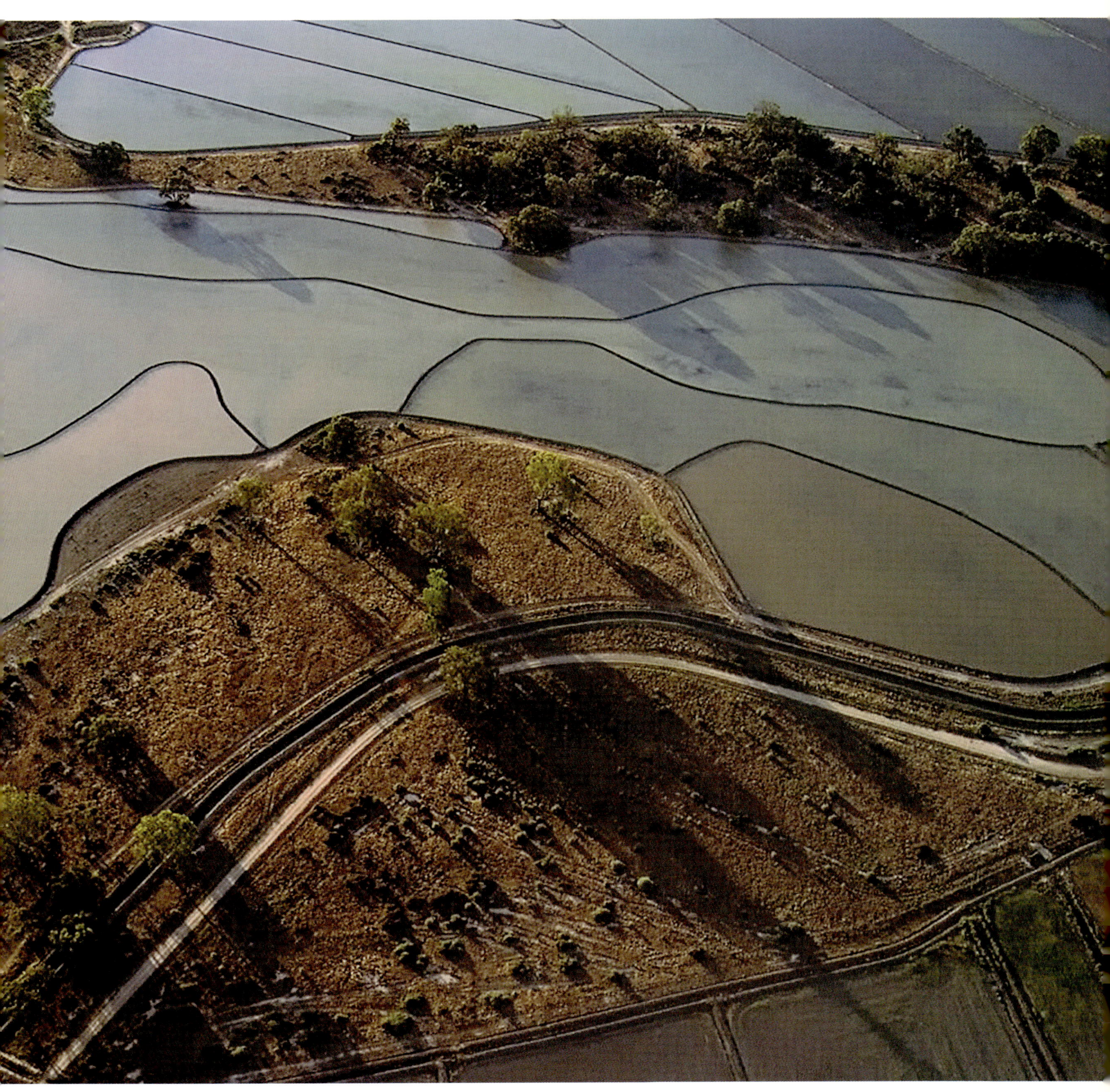

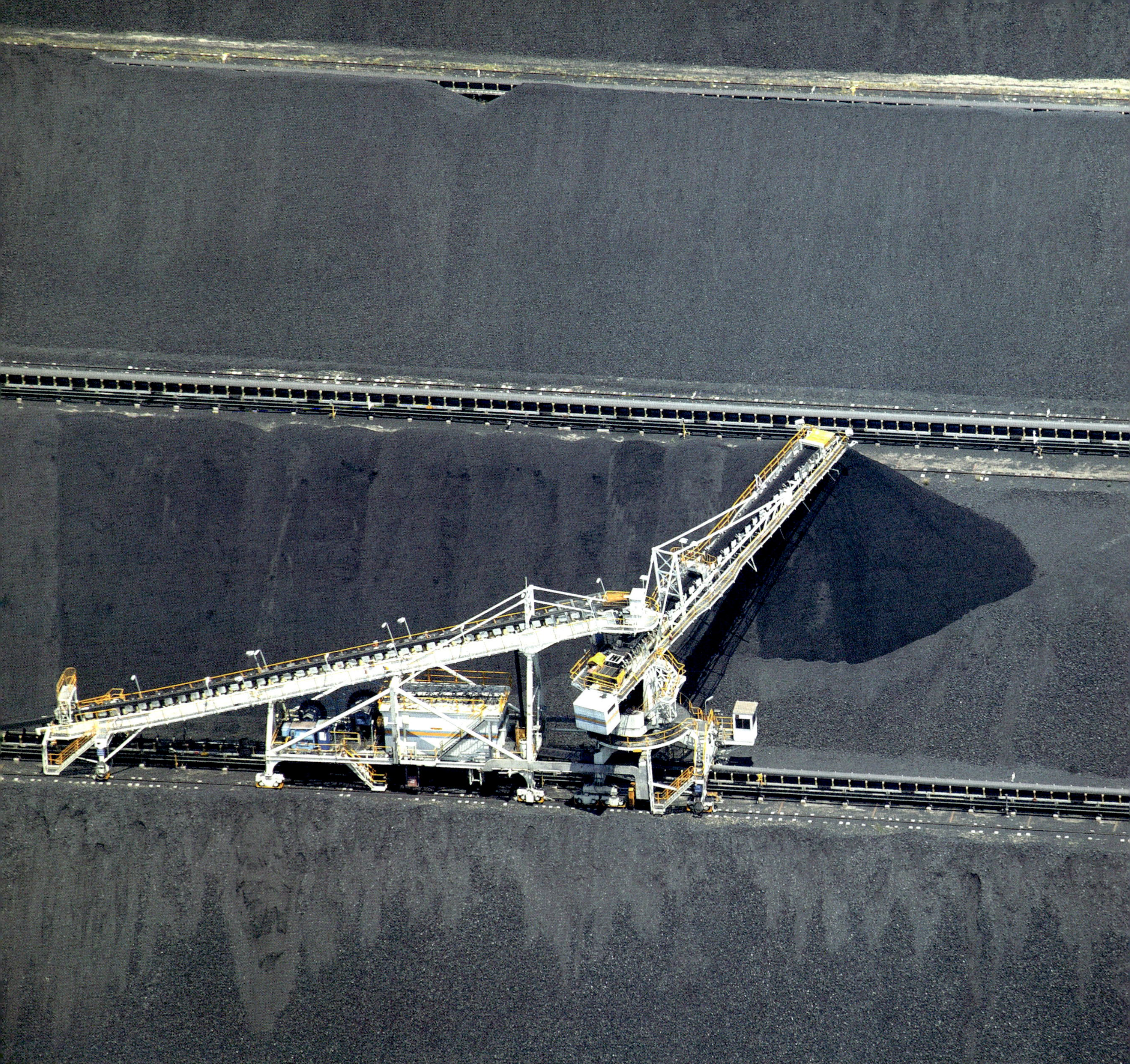

LEFT: Black coal mining at Mt Thorley in the Hunter Valley, New South Wales. From here, coal is transported 90 kilometres to the Port Waratah terminal in Newcastle for export. Domestically, black coal generates 55 per cent of electricity. If brown coal and gas are added, fossil fuels make up 92 per cent of the energy mix. **RIGHT:** Black coal waiting for export at Wollongong, New South Wales, the site of Bass and Flinders' first major coal find in Australia.

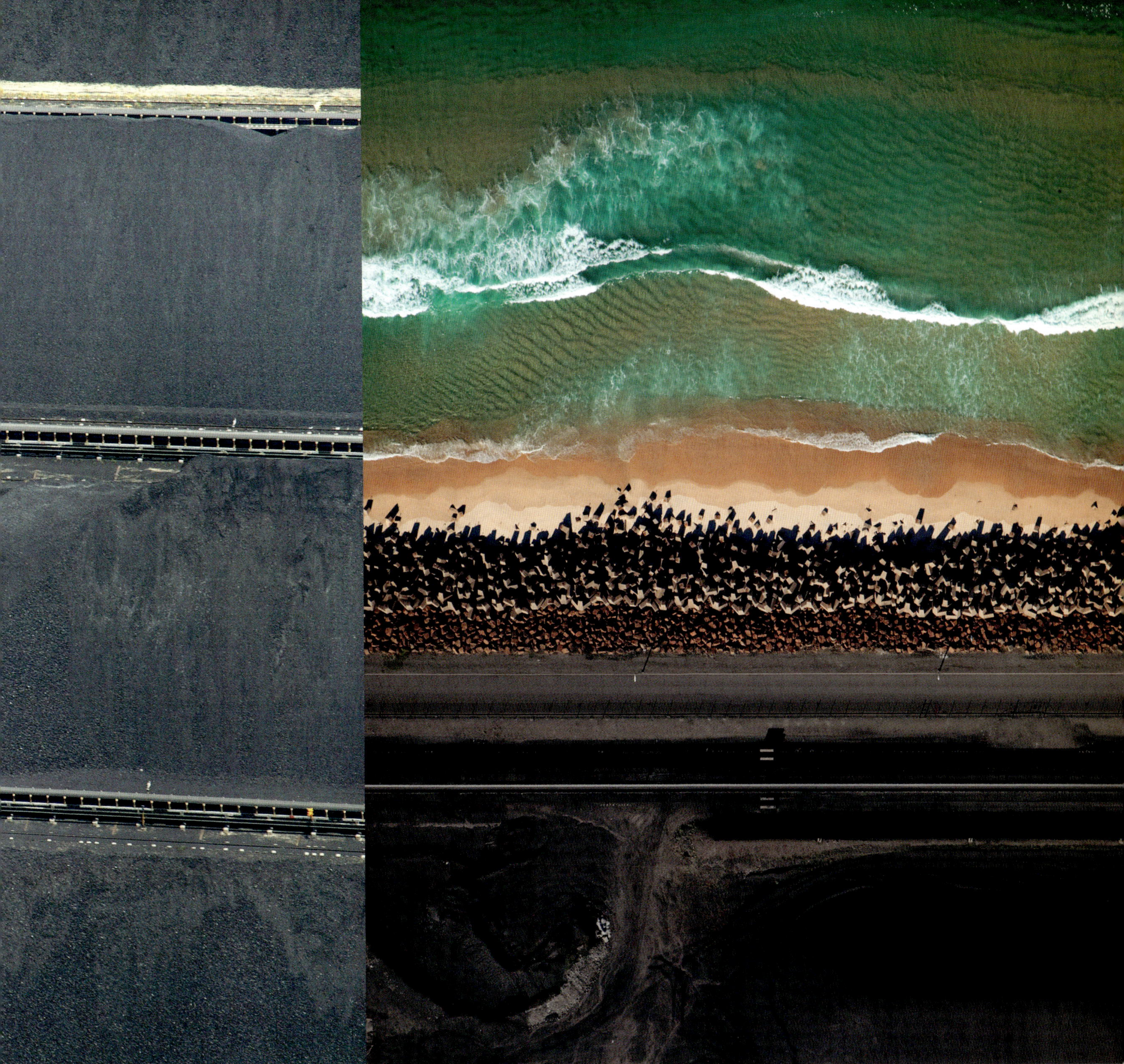

LEFT: The Australian Alps deliver 9,600 gigalitres of water to the Murray–Darling Basin, roughly a third of the basin's total average annual flow and the equivalent of almost four million Olympic swimming pools. **RIGHT:** Completed in 1974, the Snowy Hydro scheme consists of 16 major dams, seven power stations, one pumping station, and 225 kilometres of tunnels and aqueducts. Only ten per cent of the scheme is above ground.

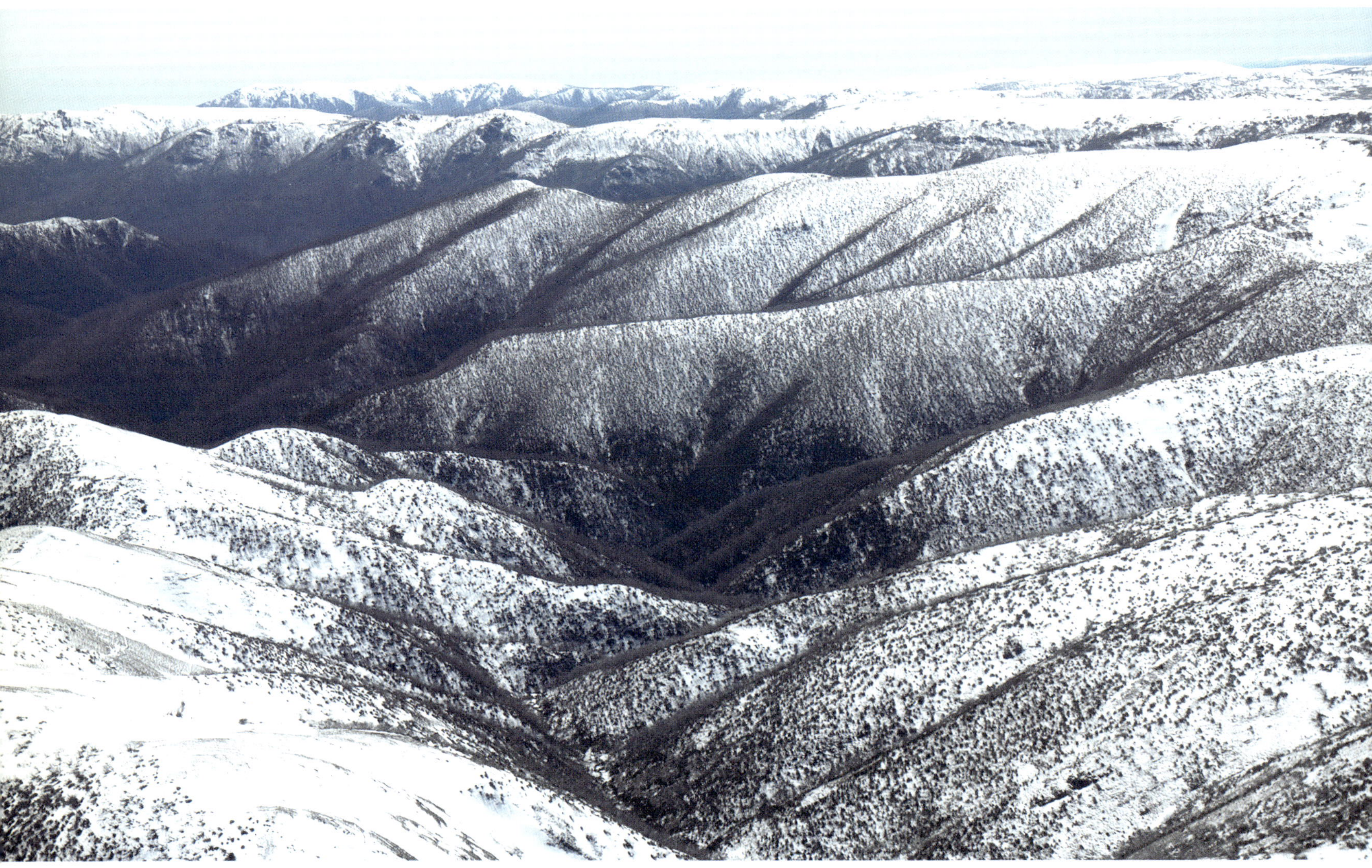

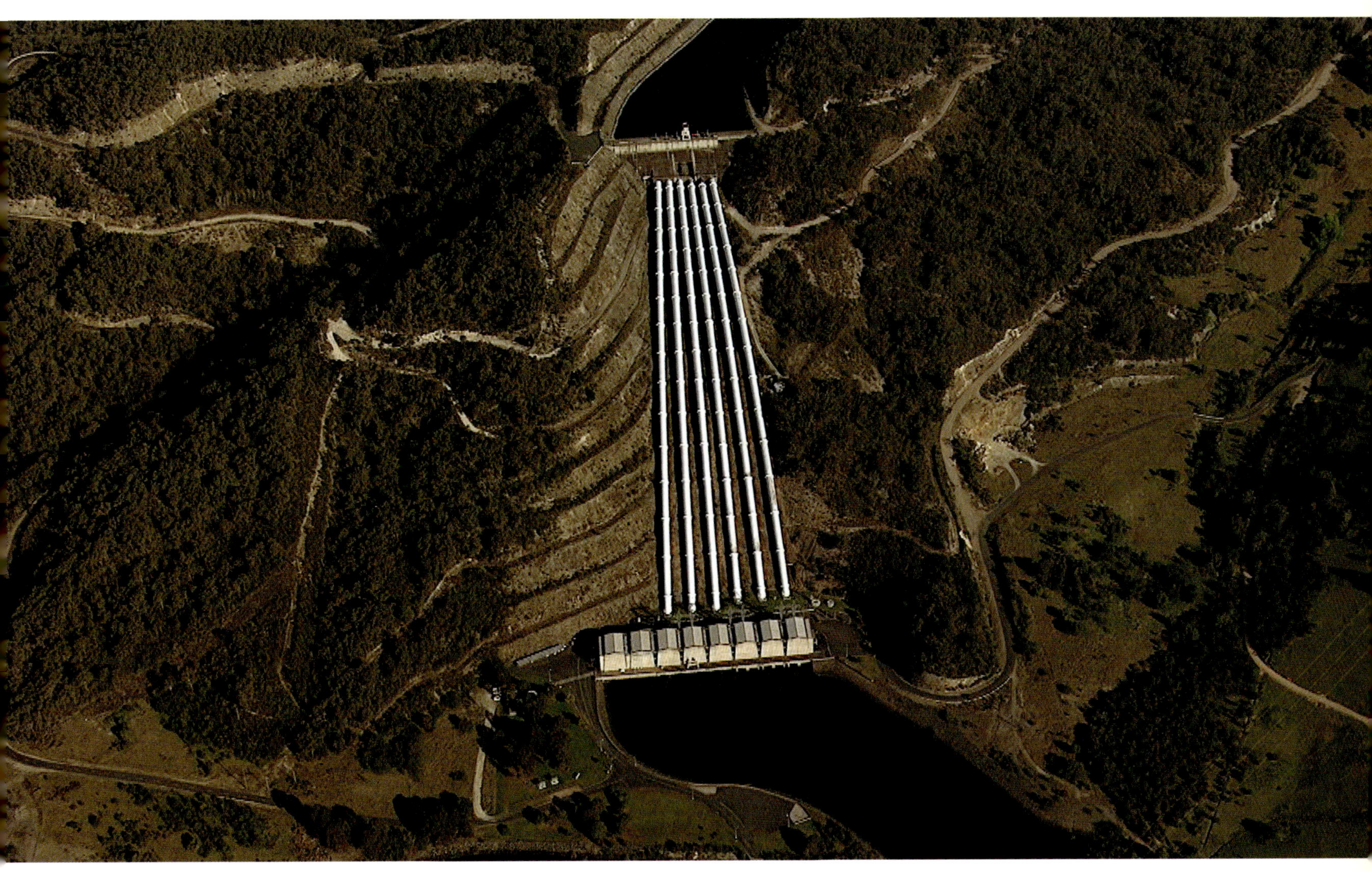

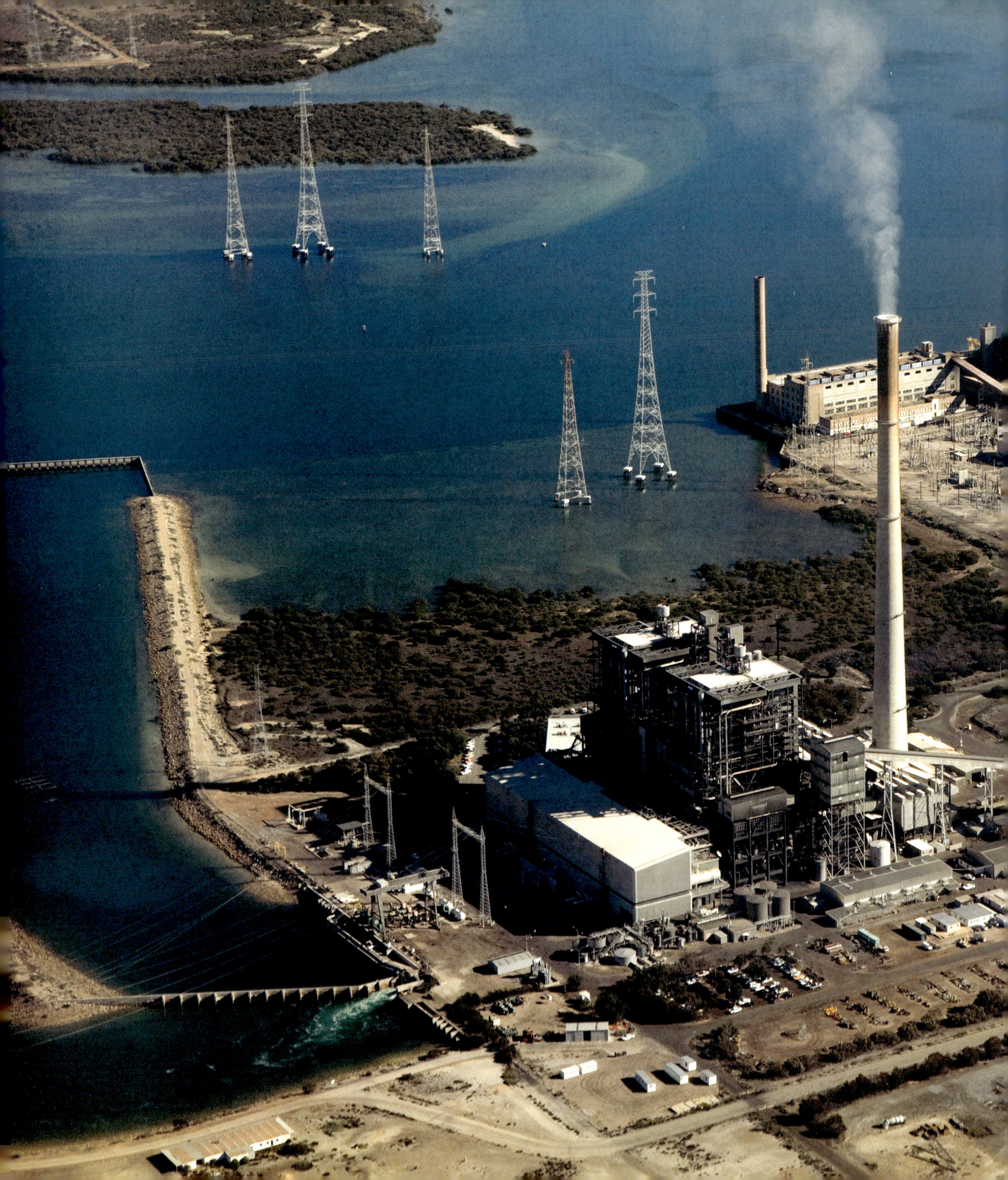

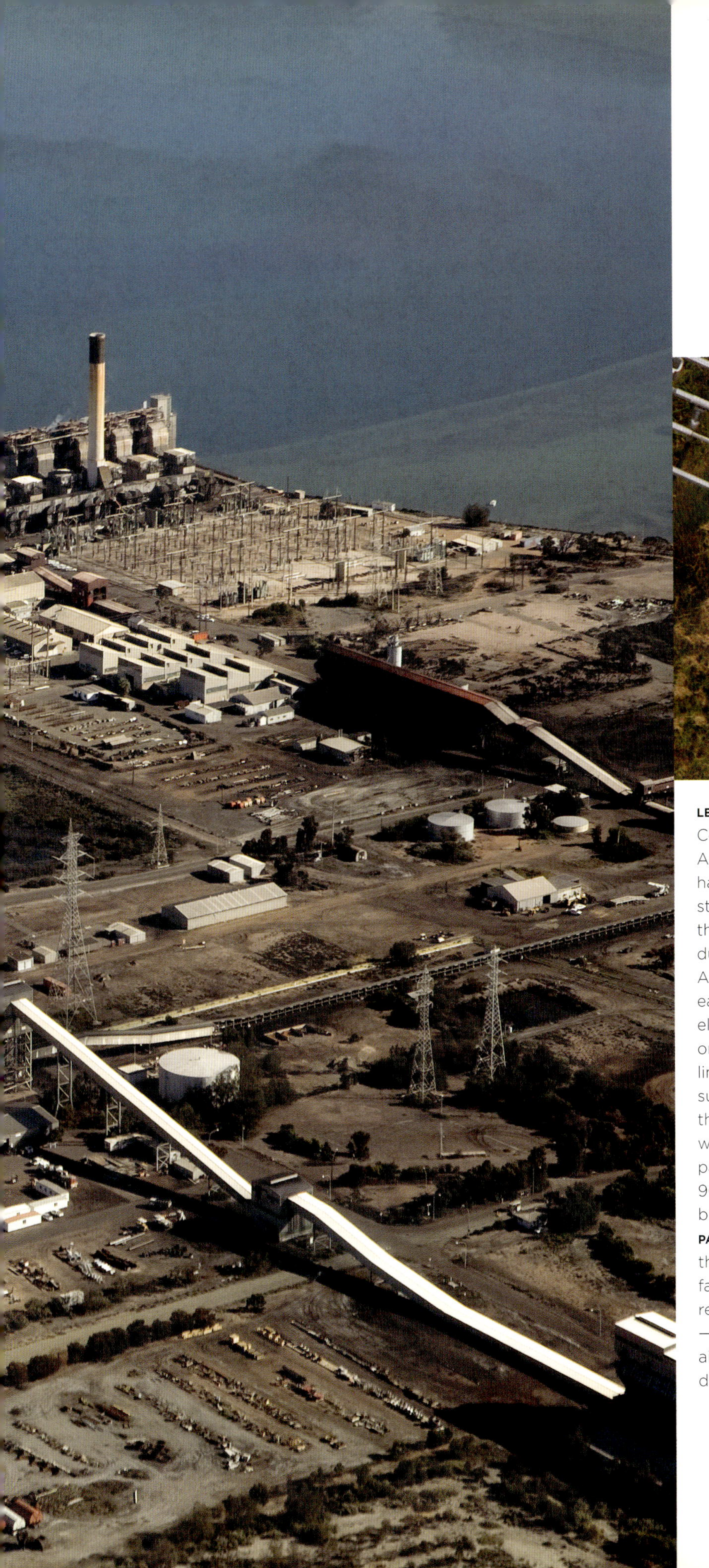

LEFT: A sign of things to come? Coal-fired power stations in Port Augusta, South Australia. Operators have effectively shut the Playford station on the right, while operating the Northern station on the left only during summer months. In South Australia, wind energy and coal now each provide a quarter of that state's electricity. **RIGHT:** A bare hander sits on a live 500,000 volt transmission line, protected only by his Faraday suit. It's a conductive contraption that keeps him safe in the same way the fuselage of a plane shields passengers if hit by lightning. There are 900,000 kilometres of such lines to be maintained in Australia. **FOLLOWING PAGES:** A wind glider is pulled into the sky over the Chalicum Hills wind farm in southwest Victoria. Once released, the glider navigates thermals — columns of hot rising air. The cold air, which fills the void, causes wind, driving the turbines on the ground.

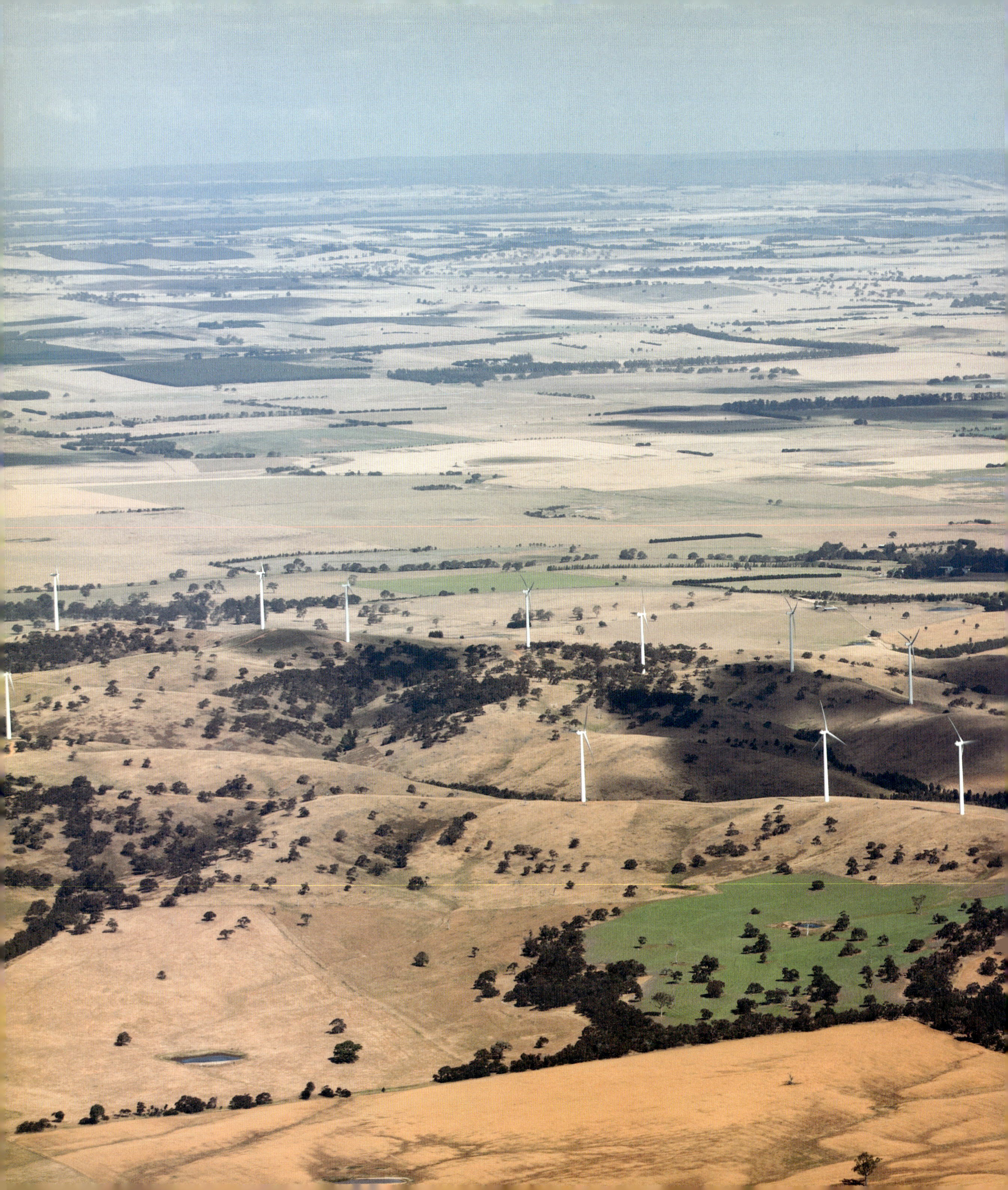

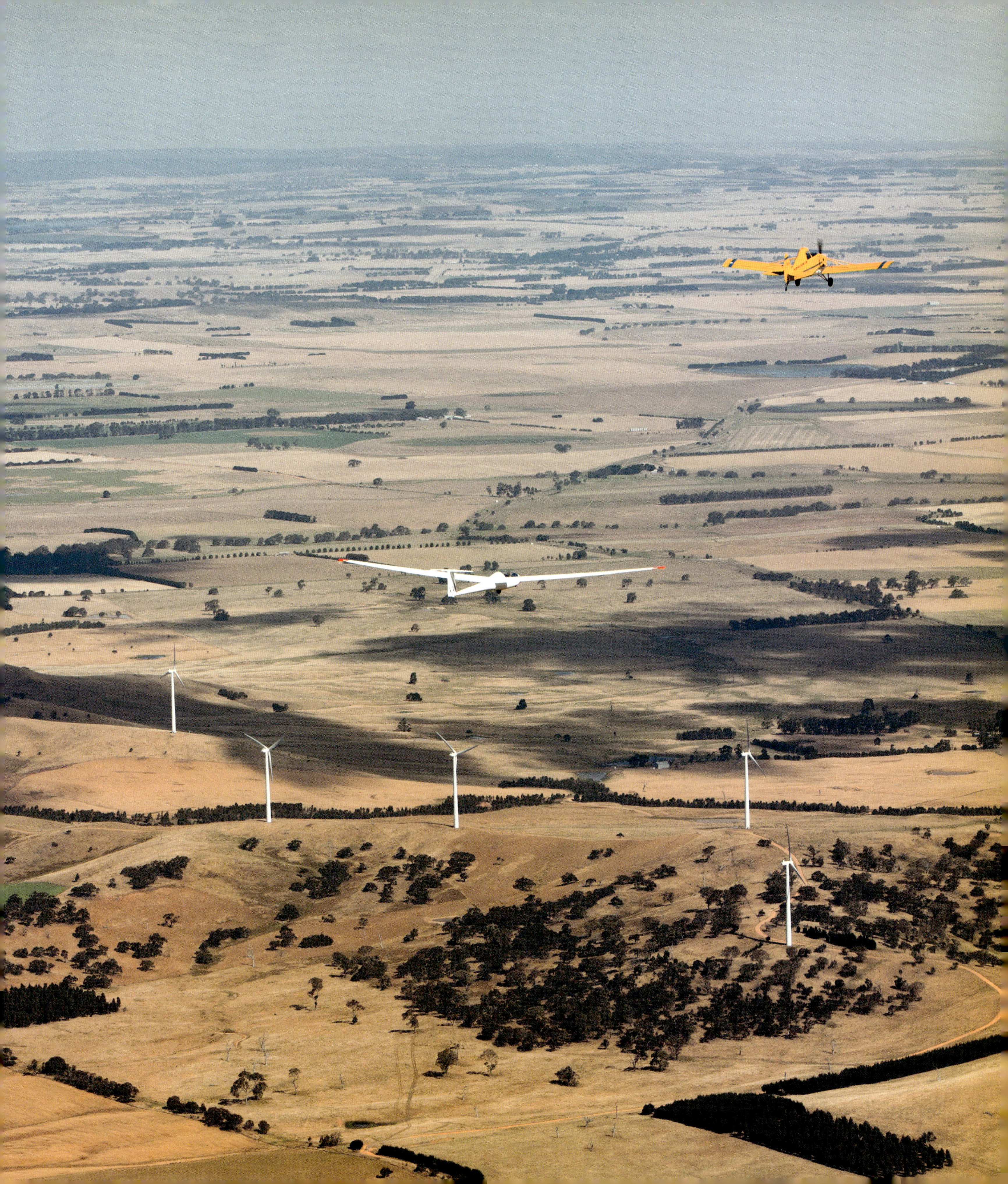

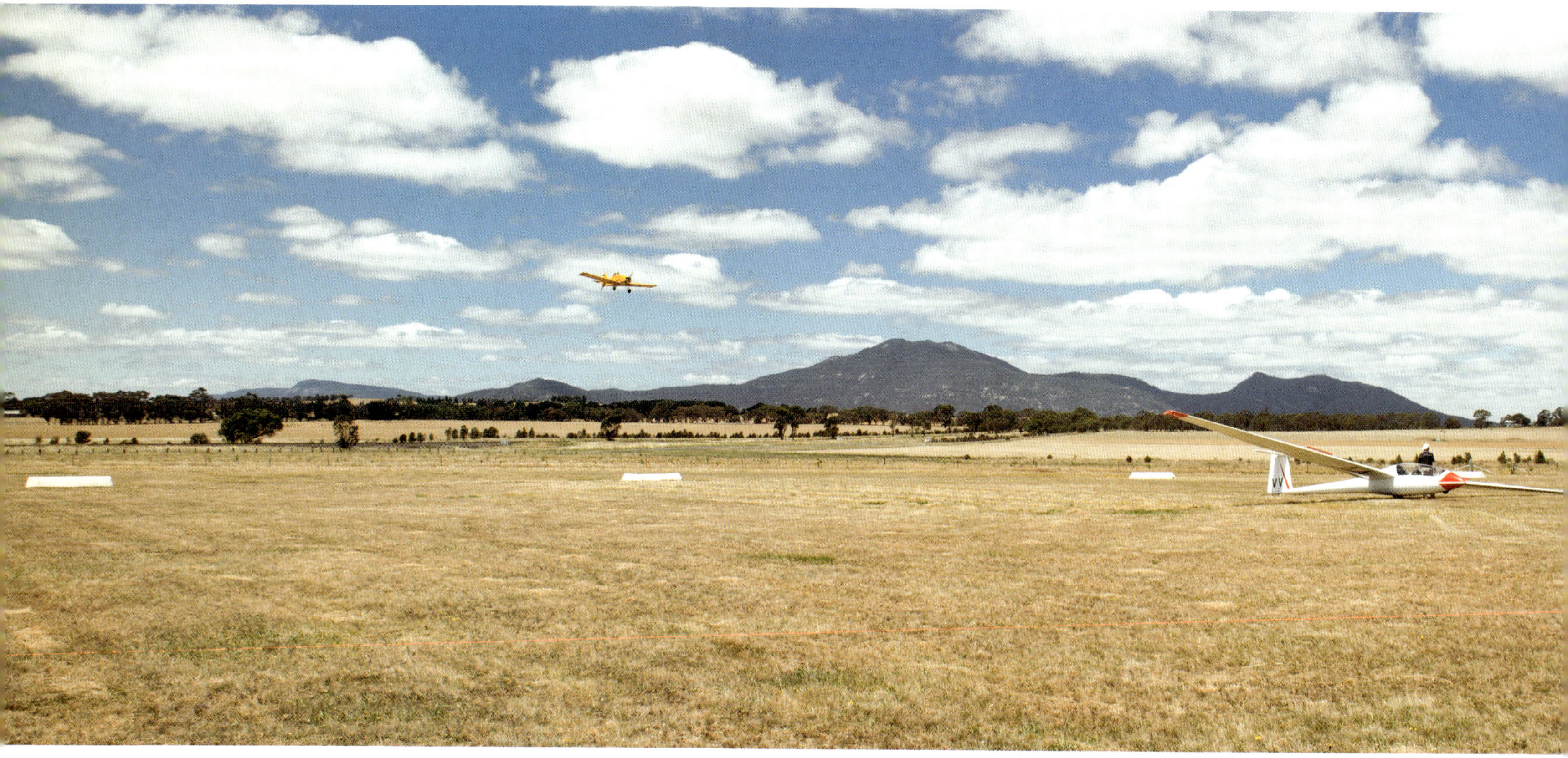

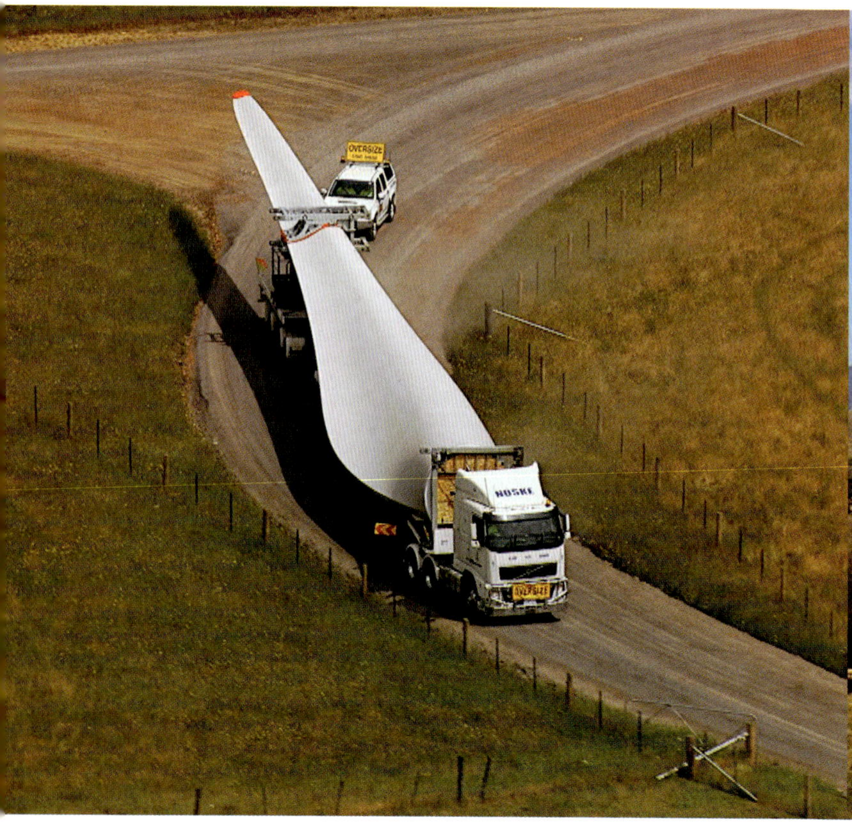

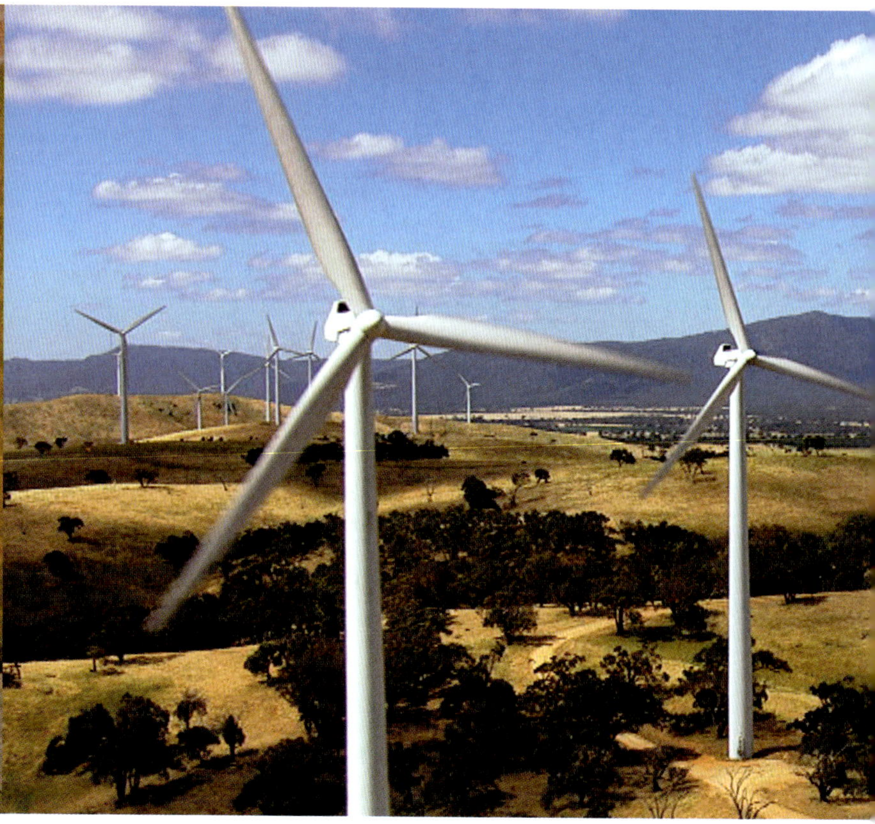

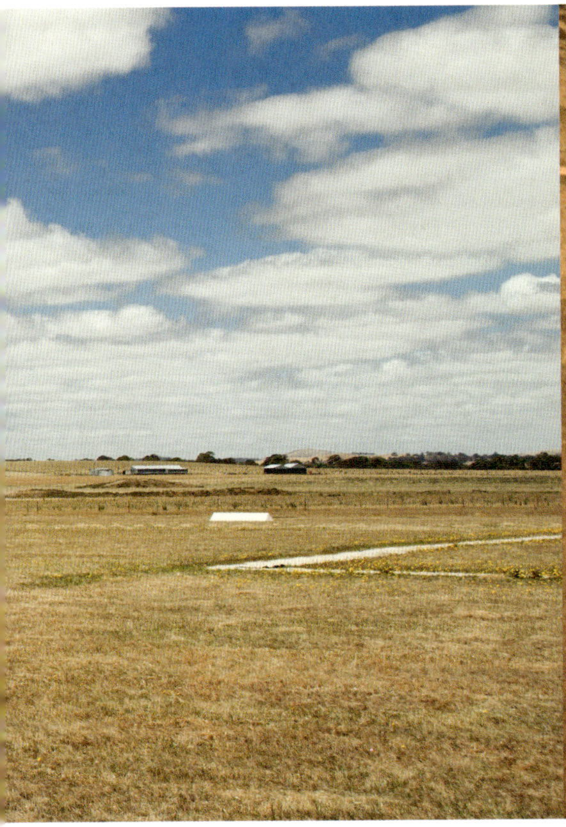

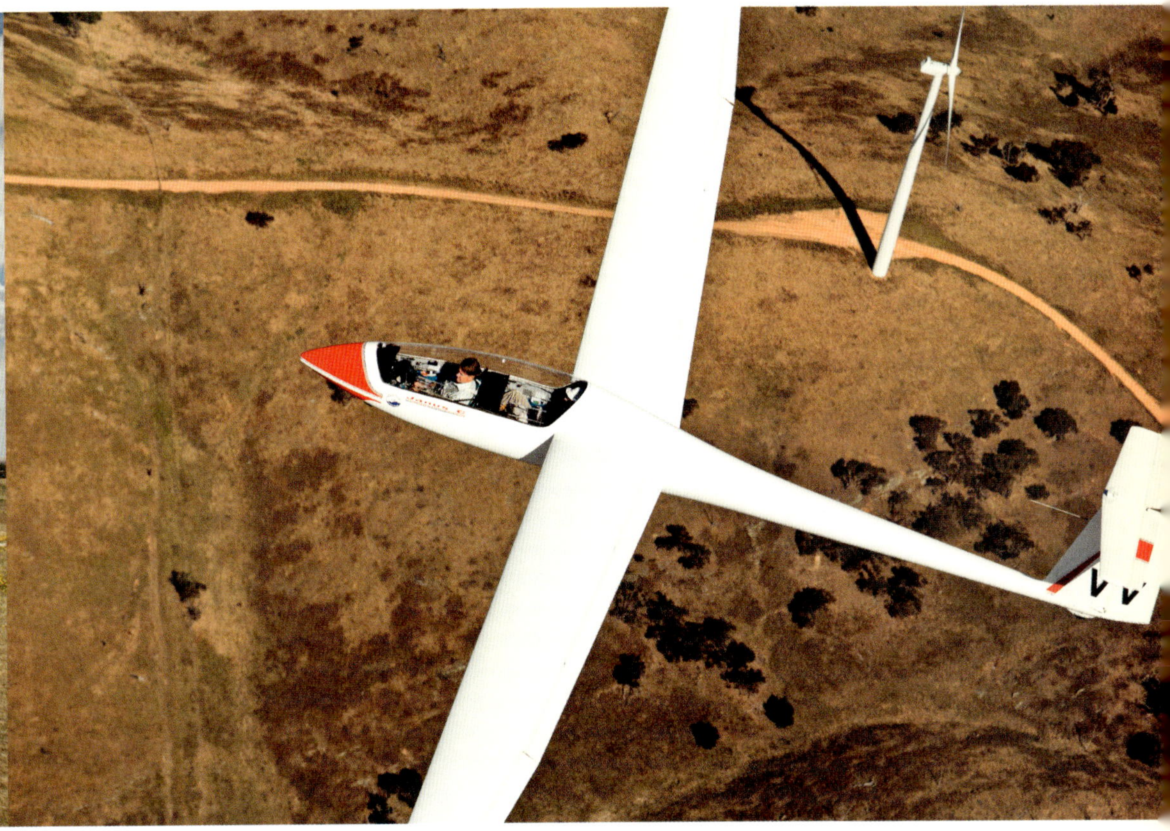

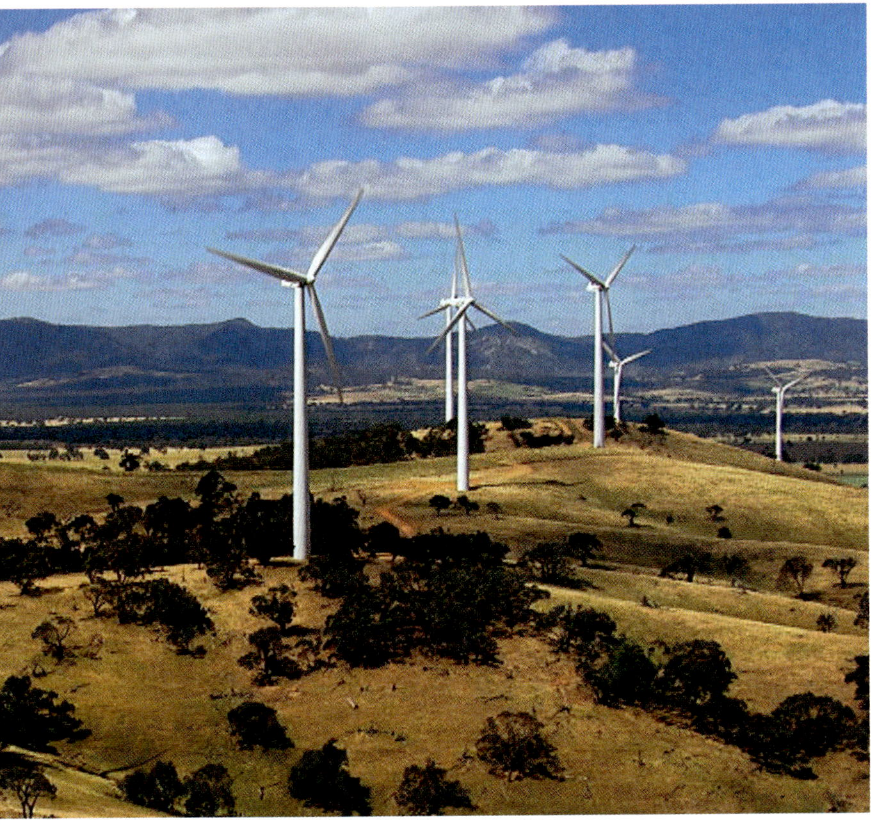

TOP LEFT: Ararat in southwest Victoria lies in the path of the Roaring Forties, strong westerly currents between latitudes of 40 to 50 degrees. It's a prime location for wind gliding and building wind farms. **TOP RIGHT:** Glider over one of Chalicum Hills' 35 wind turbines. **BOTTOM LEFT:** A 55-metre blade is transported to Macarthur, Victoria, where it will be hoisted 90 metres into the air as part of a new turbine. The future home to 140 such turbines, Macarthur wind farm is set to be the largest in the Southern Hemisphere. **BOTTOM RIGHT:** The Chalicum Hills wind farm generates enough electricity to power 26,000 households a year. Nationwide, wind energy contributes just 2 per cent to the energy mix, even though Australia has some of the best wind resources in the world.

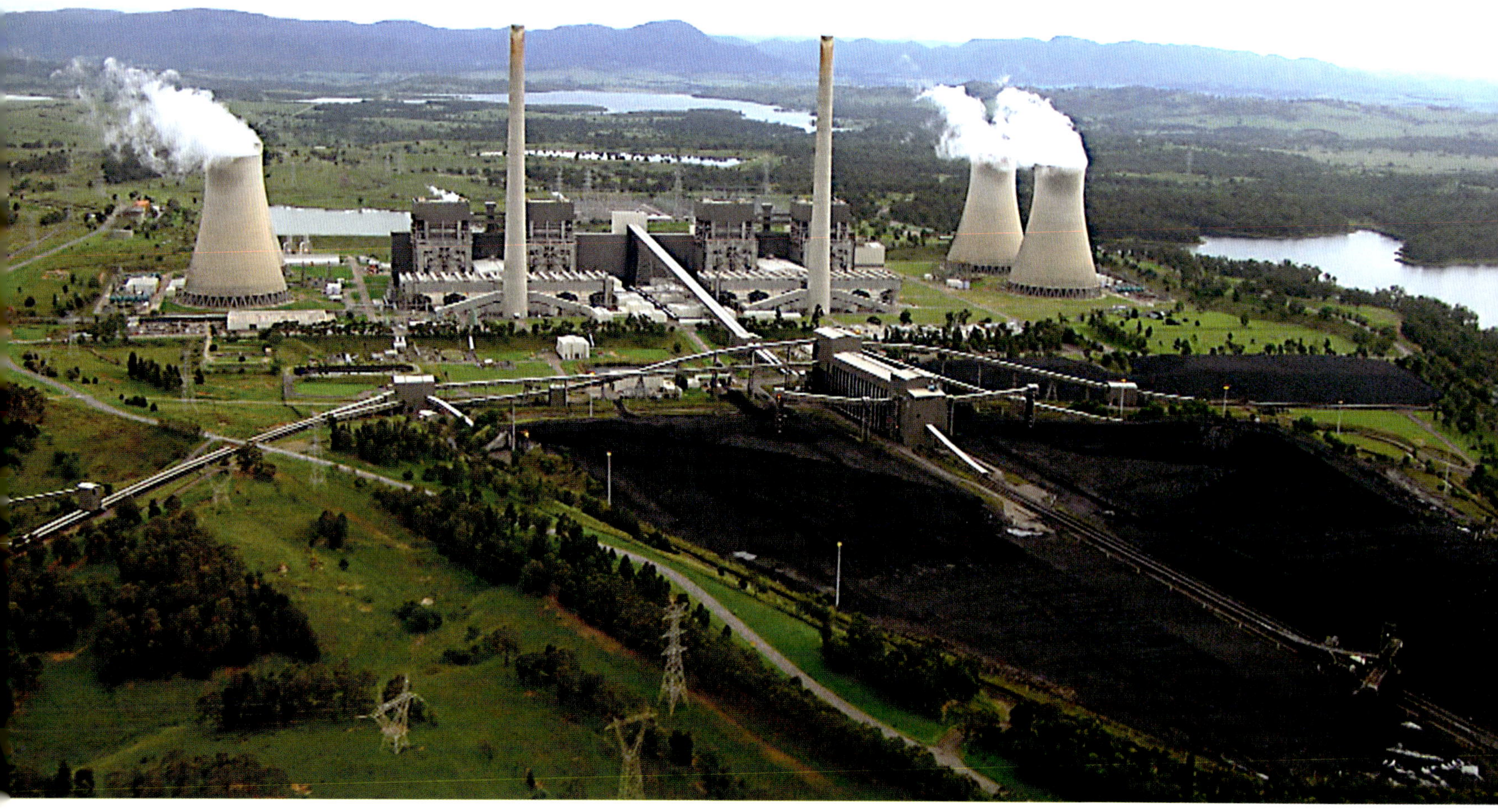

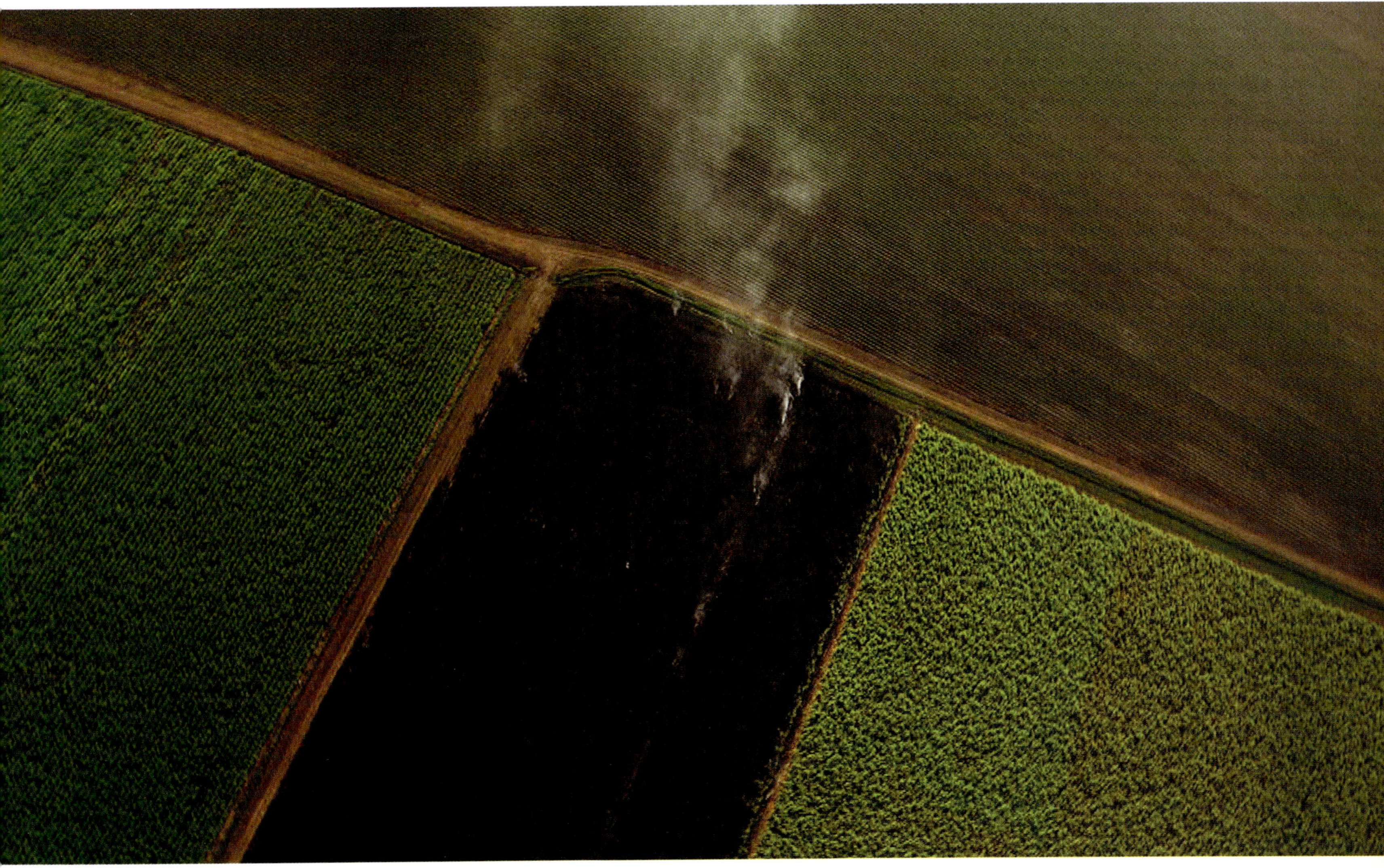

LEFT: The Liddell Power Station in the Hunter Valley, New South Wales, is one of 200 major electricity generators feeding the national grid. The largest integrated power grid in the world, it stretches 5,000 kilometres from Port Douglas in northern Queensland to Port Lincoln in South Australia. **RIGHT:** A smouldering cane field in far north Queensland. With new harvesting techniques allowing for 'green' harvesting, eliminating the need to first burn the leaves of the stalks, these iconic cane burns may soon be a thing of the past.

LEFT: Australian cane fields are no longer producing just raw sugar. Increasingly, the by-products — molasses and bagasse — are used to make bioethanol and electricity. Other such bioenergy sources are food processing waste, sewage gas, landfill gas and forestry wastes. **RIGHT:** Circular irrigation in New South Wales. The 400-metre irrigation arm moves around a central pivot, while sprinklers water the crops. Only five per cent of tilled agricultural lands are irrigated, but that portion produces a third of all agricultural crop output.

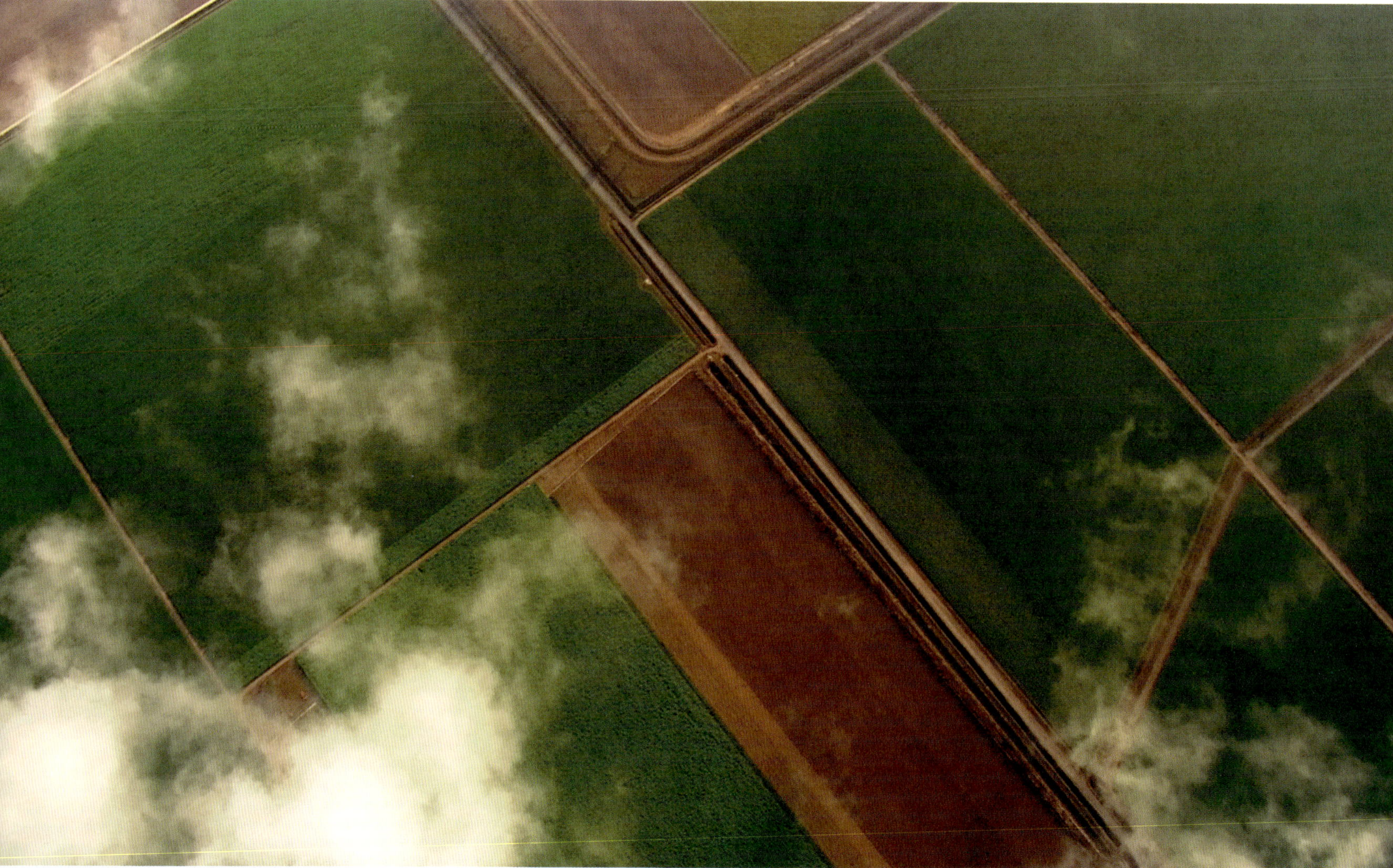

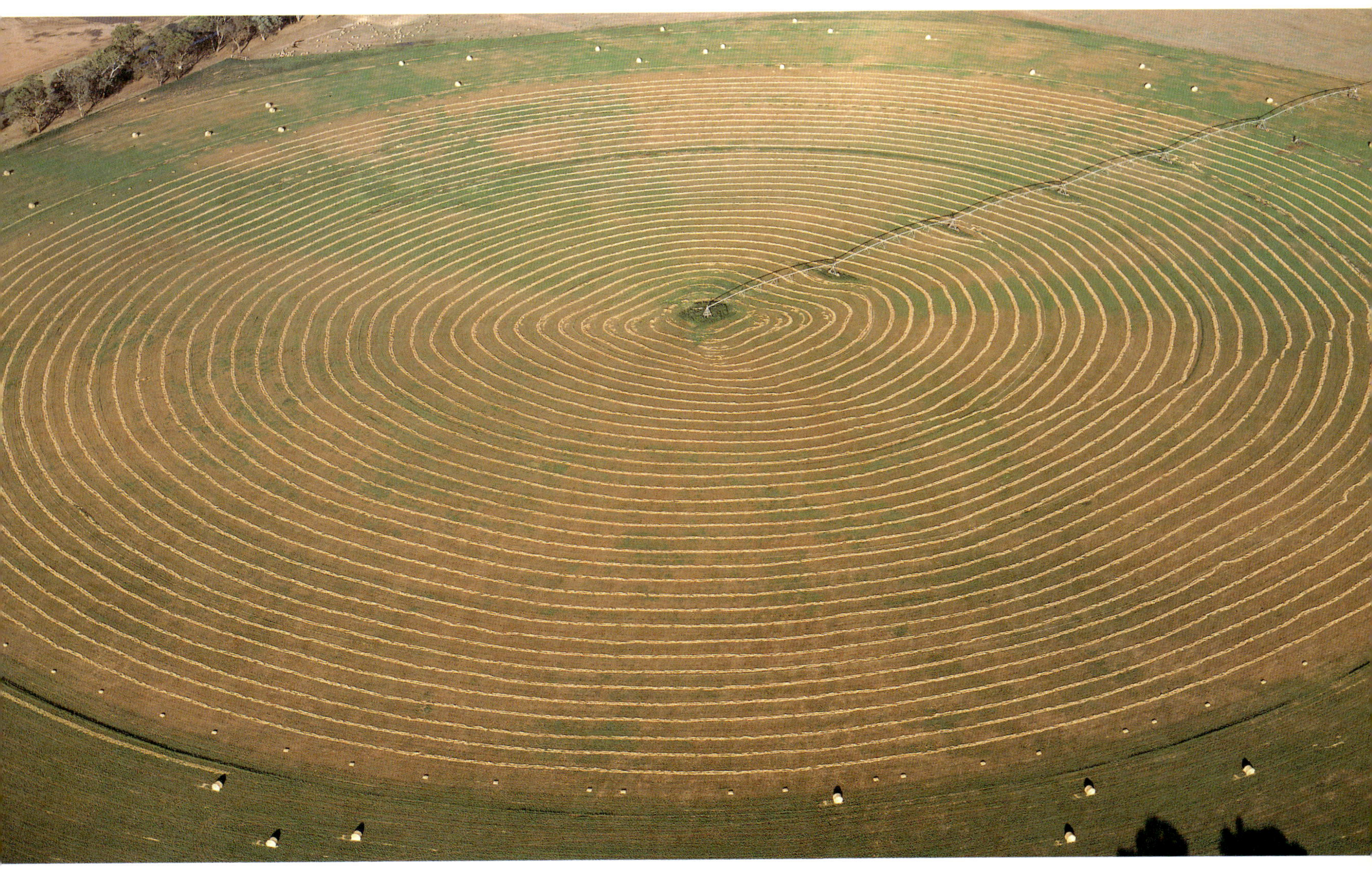

LEFT: Irrigated farmland in Mildura, Victoria. There are 40,000 irrigators in Australia whose total production is valued at $10 billion a year. In Australia, irrigation accounts for a whopping 60 to 70 per cent of water withdrawn for human consumption.

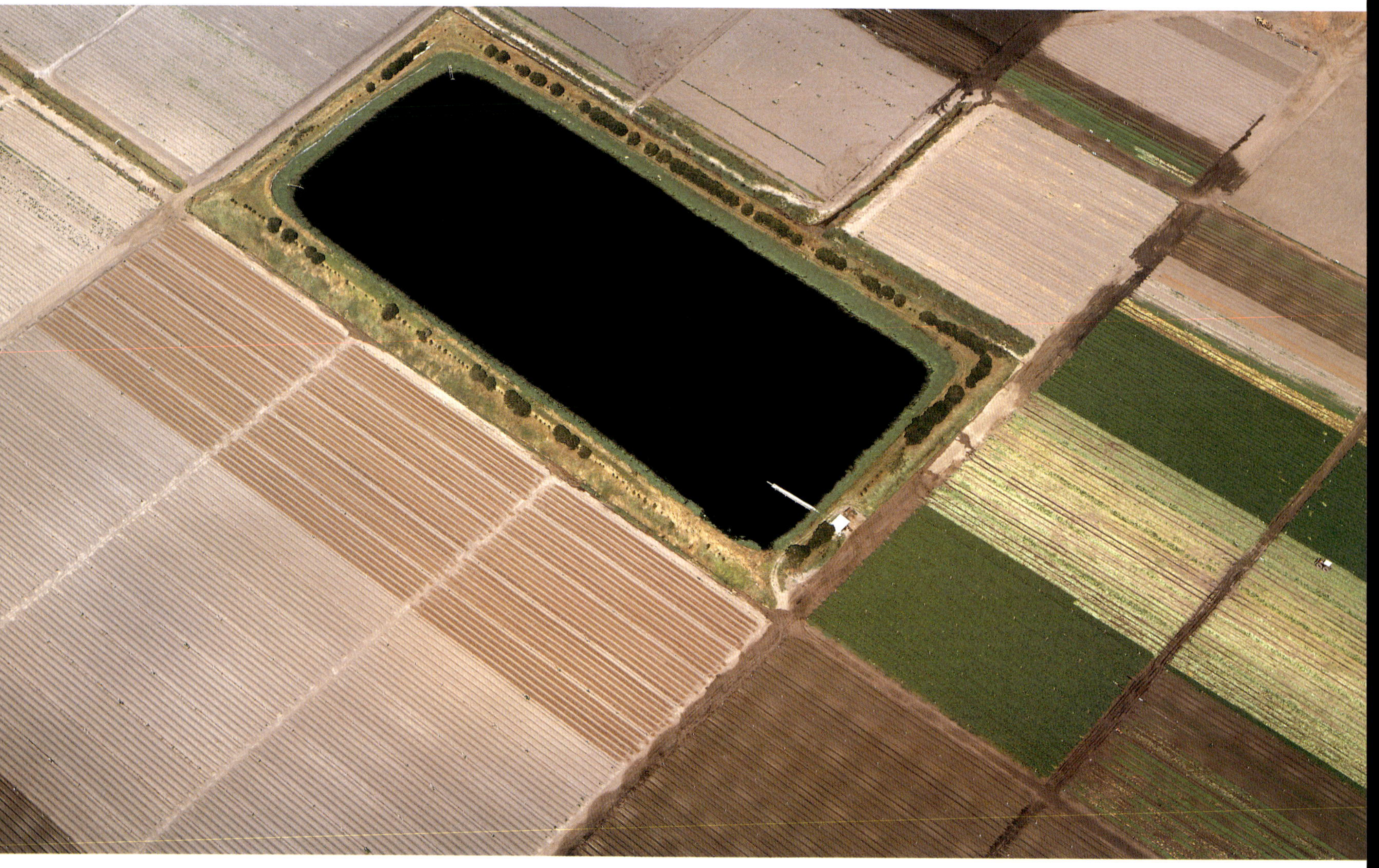

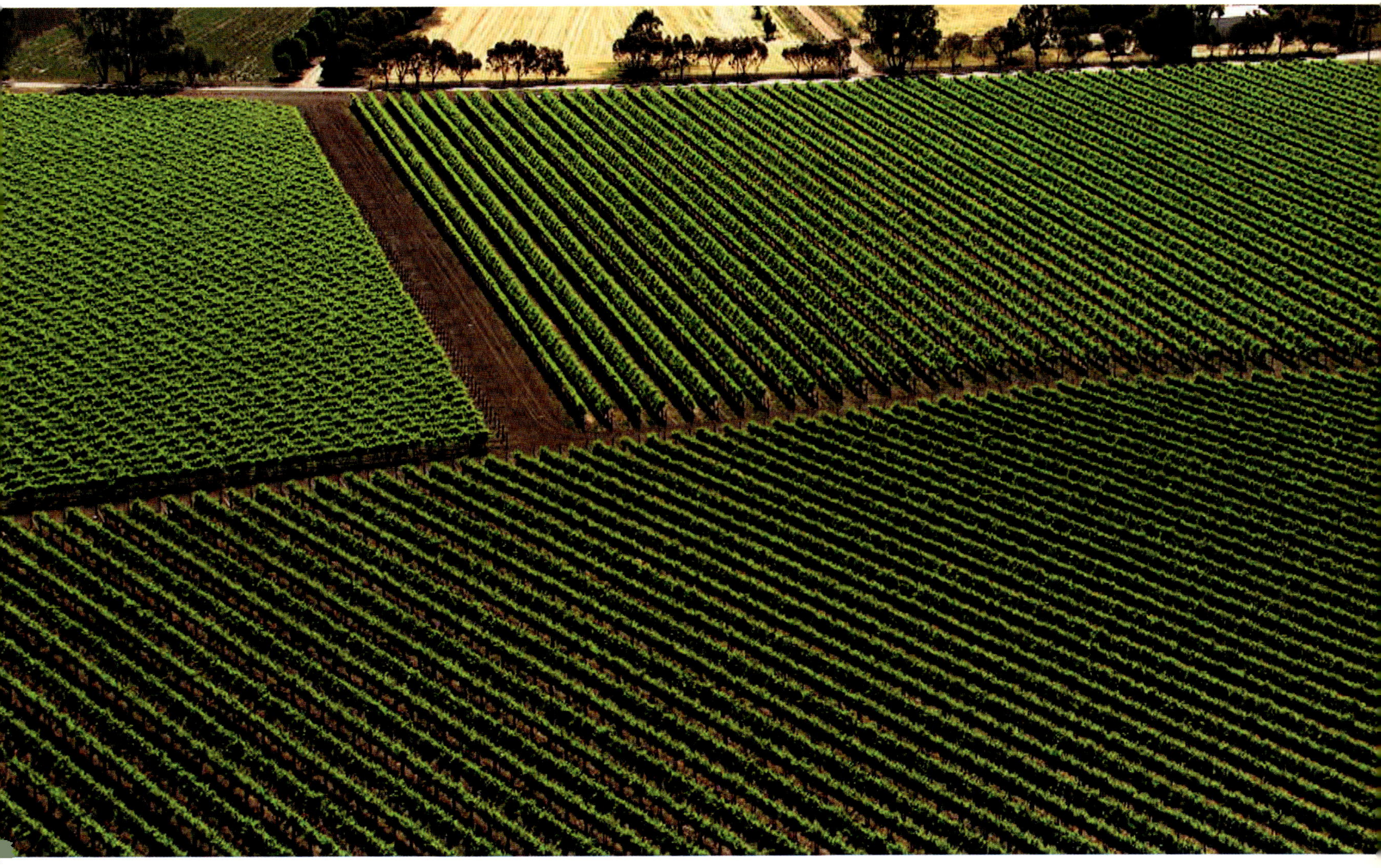

RIGHT: Wakool, New South Wales. Water drawn from the nearby Murray and Murrumbidgee rivers allows for an extraordinary variety of crops, from grapes to oranges and stone fruits, including peaches, apricots, nectarines, prunes and cherries. **FOLLOWING PAGES:** Sheep near Toodyay, Western Australia. The national flock is 73 million head and is kept at over 40,000 properties. Australians eat nine kilos of lamb per person a year. Almost 50 per cent of lamb meat is exported. A quarter of it goes to the Middle East, the biggest export market.

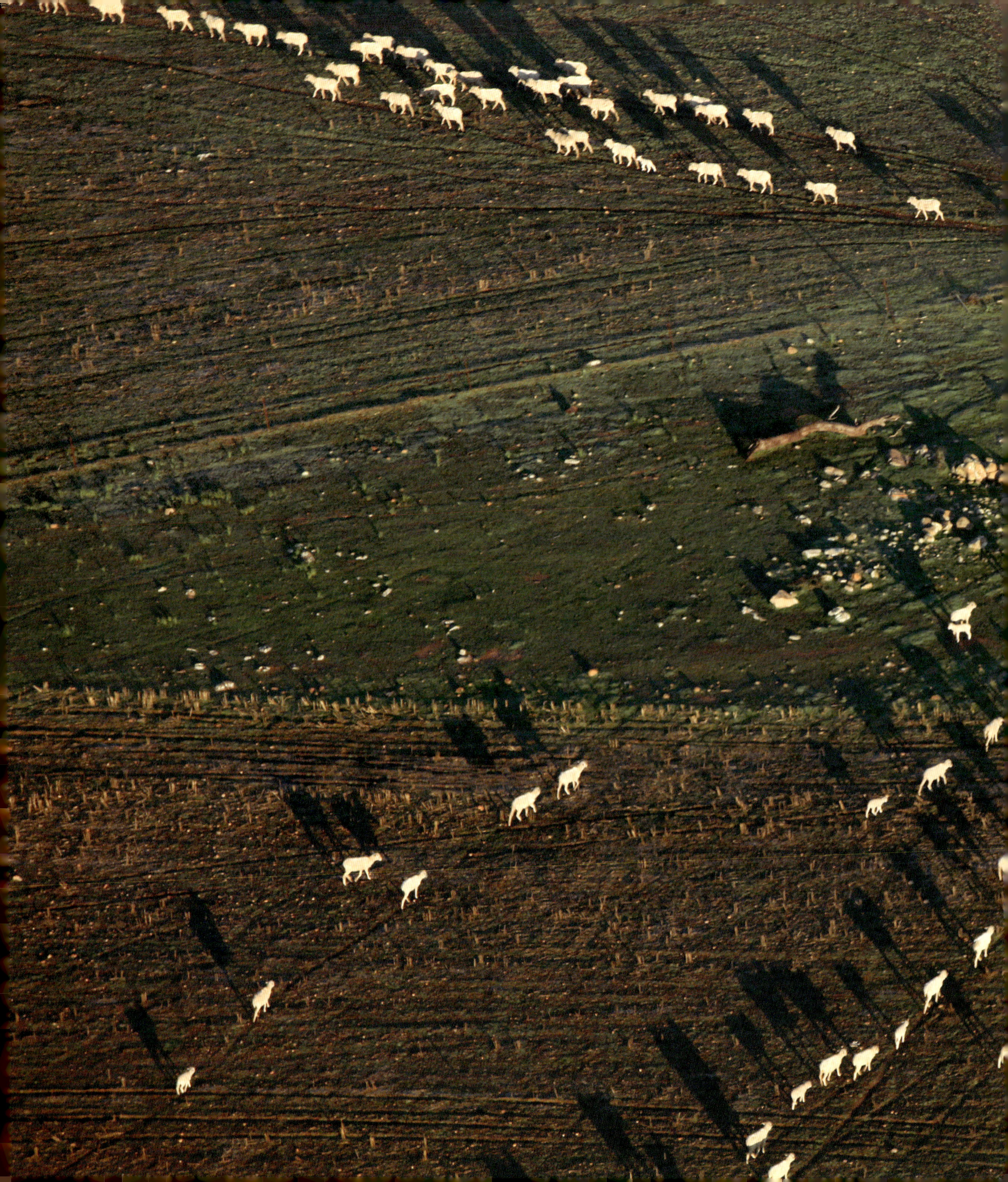

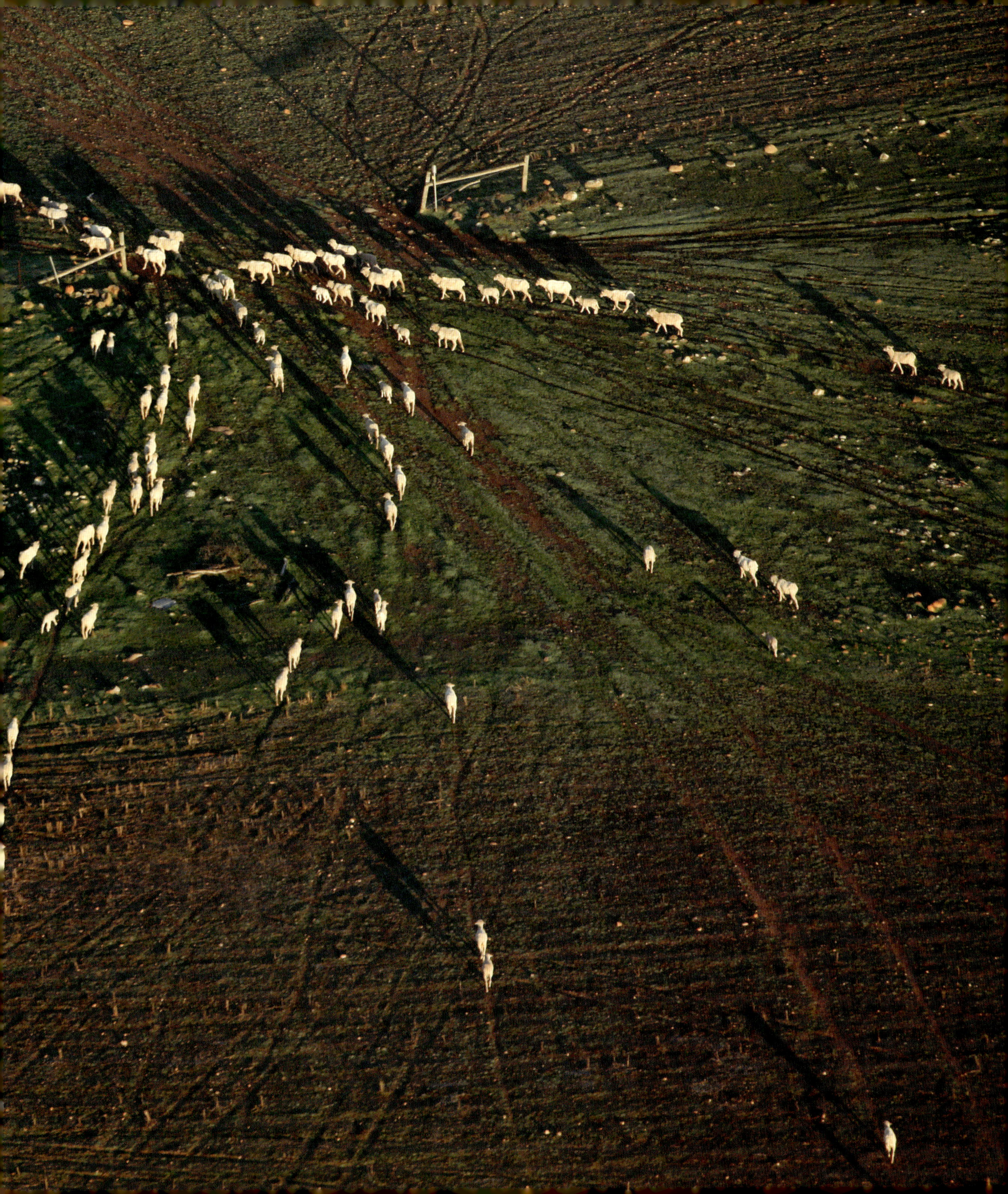

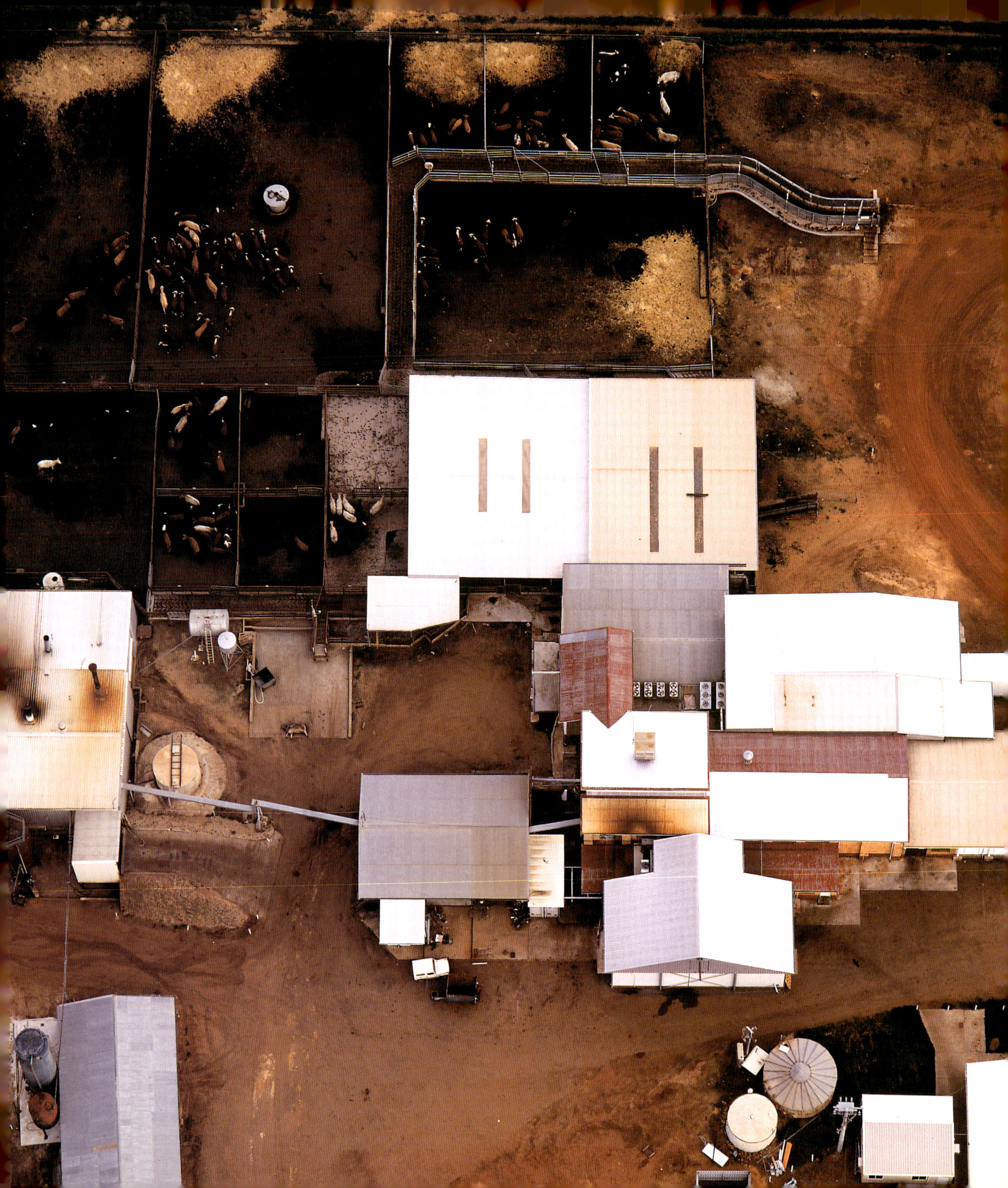

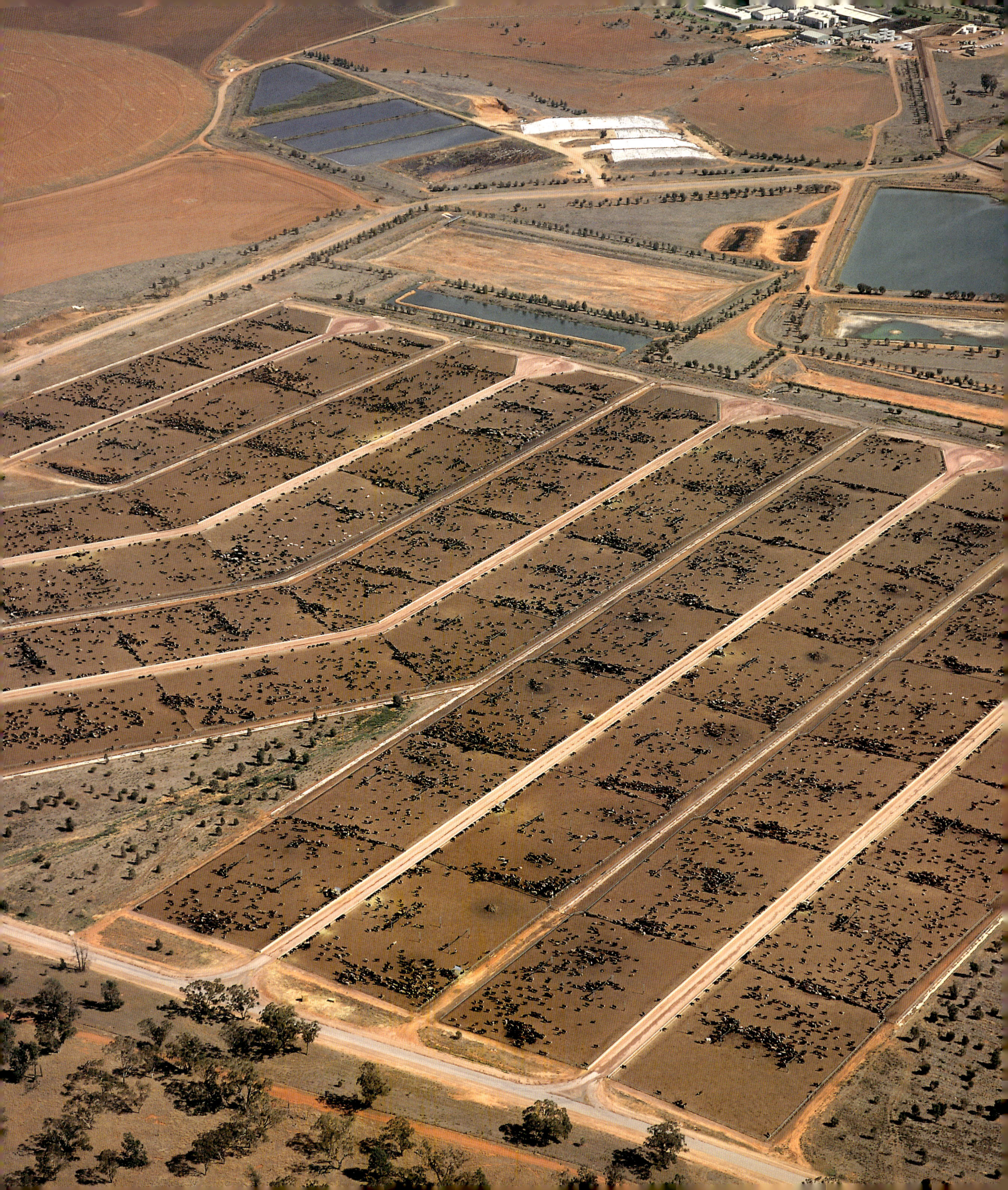

PREVIOUS PAGE LEFT: An abattoir near Perth. Around Australia, there are about 600 abattoirs or 'meat processors'. Cattle slaughtering can reach over 600,000 per month. Add to that 45,000 calves, 500,000 sheep, 1.7 million lambs and 380,000 pigs — enough to keep barbecues sizzling, here and abroad. **PREVIOUS PAGE RIGHT:** Thousands of cattle at a feedlot near Griffith, New South Wales. In just 60 days, cattle can be fattened from their arrival weight of 380 kilos to the slaughter weight of 500 by feeding them a protein- and carb-loaded wheat-based grain mix. Australia's 600 feedlots produce 70 per cent of supermarket meat.

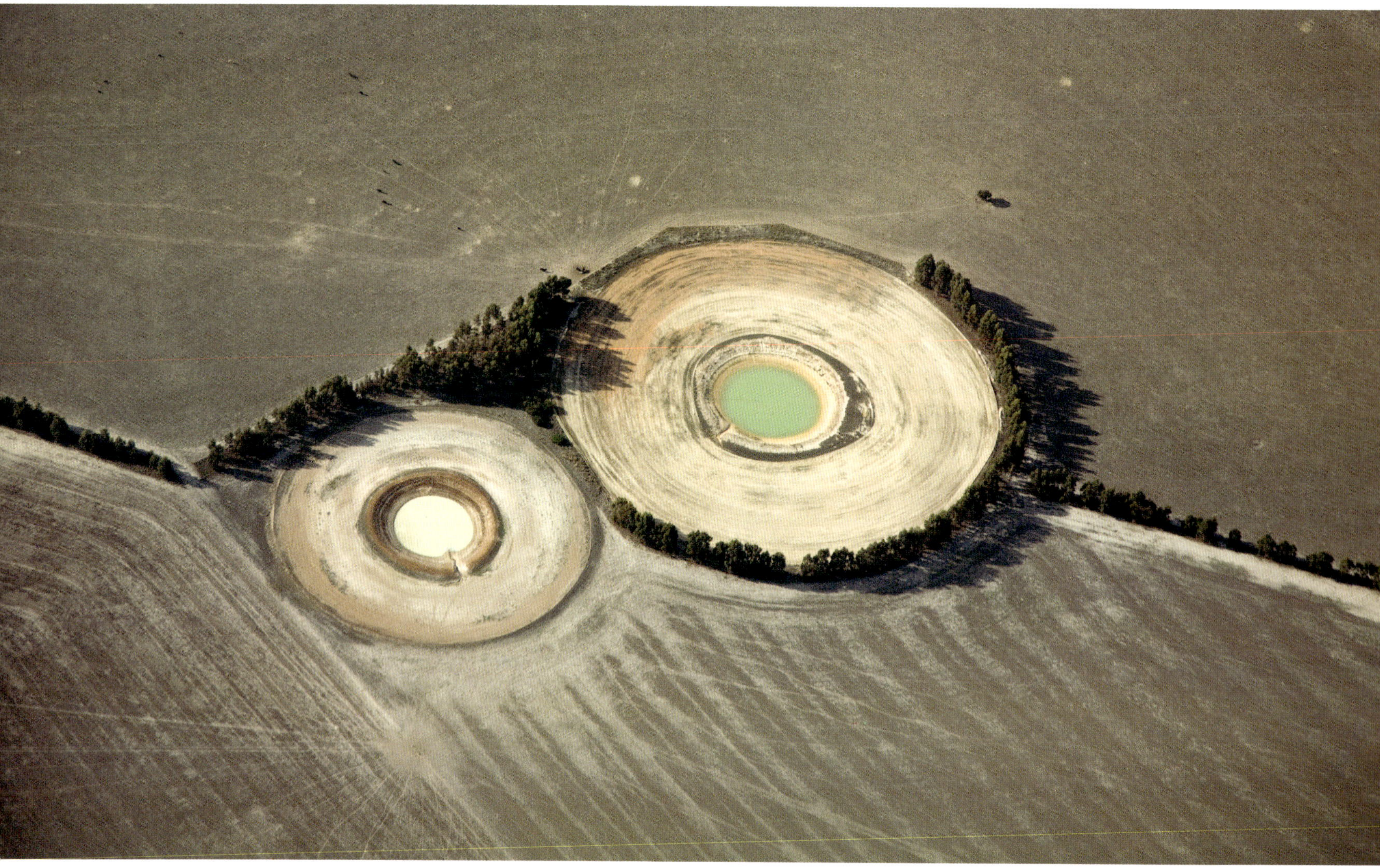

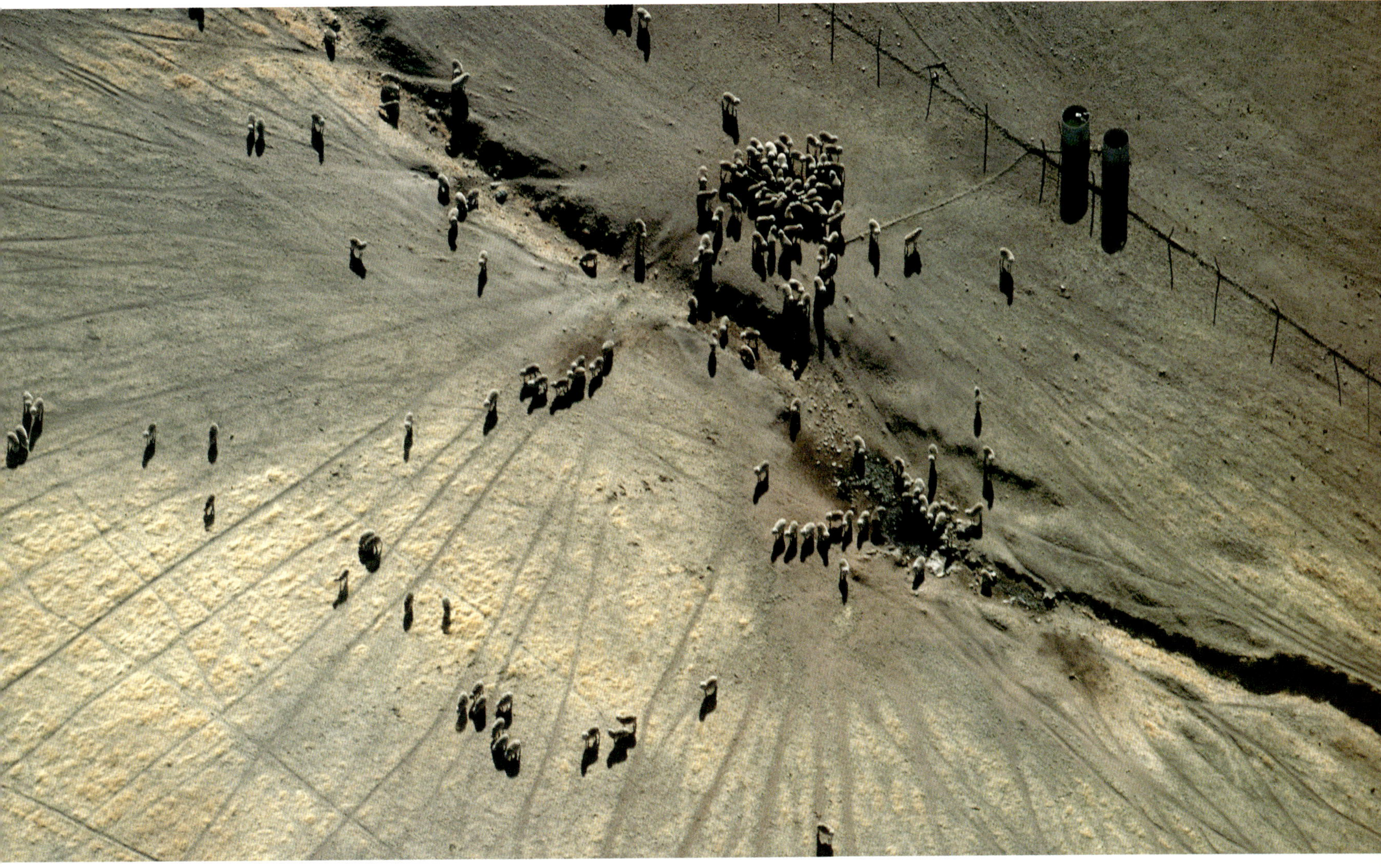

LEFT: A stock dam in the southwest of Western Australia, with a ring of trees planted around it to minimise evaporation otherwise increased by wind. The ring also prevents dam damage through wave action and reduces erosion and sedimentation. Windbreaks can protect areas of up to 12 times the height of the trees. **RIGHT:** Wool is produced in varying climates, from the highlands of New South Wales and Tasmania, to the pastoral zones of Queensland, South Australia and Western Australia. Australia may no longer be riding the sheep's back but with 350 million kilos of wool shorn per year, Australia is still the world's largest producer.

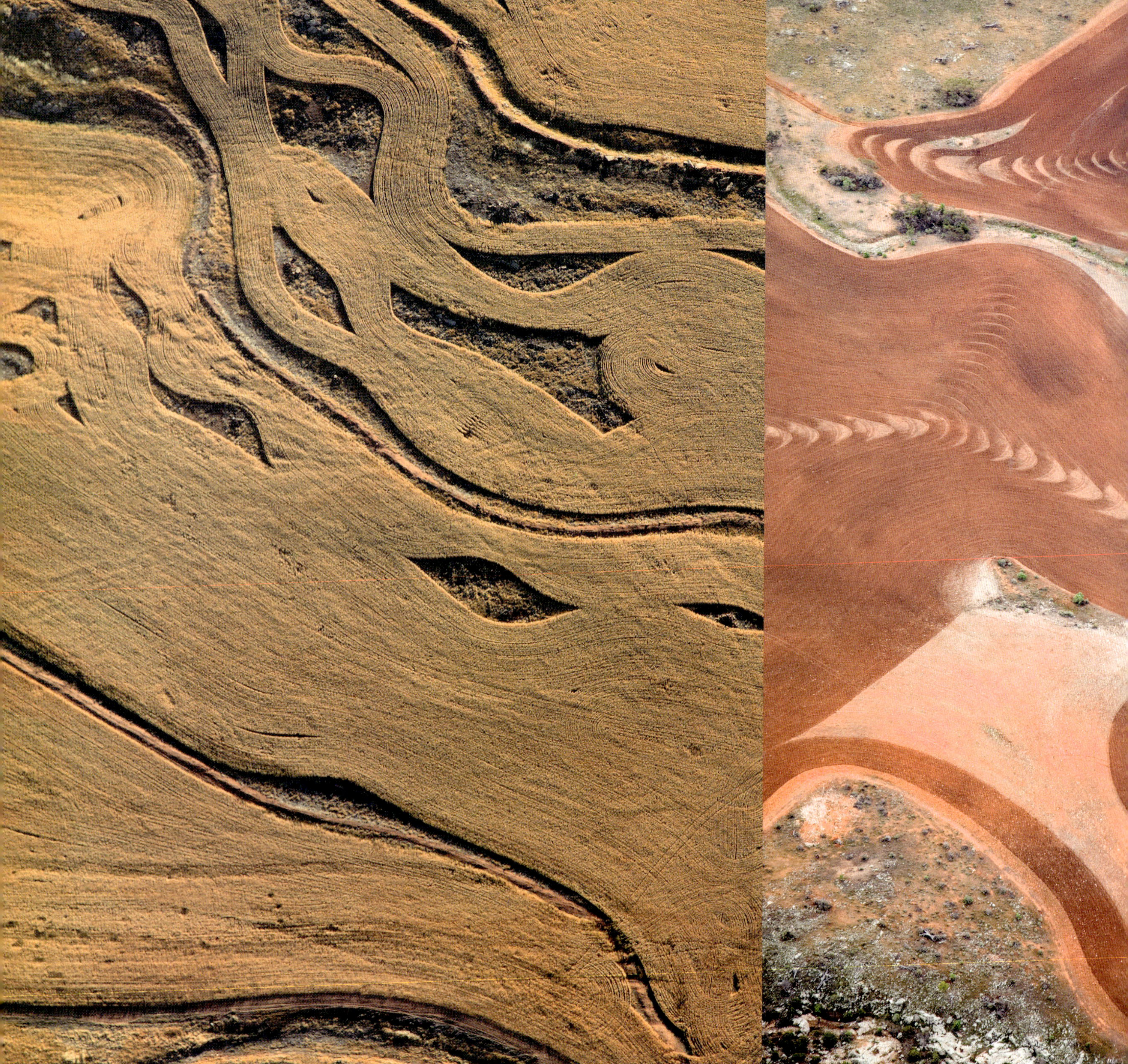

LEFT: Wheat fields near York, Western Australia. In this rugged landscape, farmers make use of every centimetre of farmable soil. Half of all cropped land, 14 million hectares, is devoted to wheat. **MIDDLE:** Extraordinary contours emerge from this Eyre Peninsula wheat farm in South Australia. In its raw form, Australia exports more than 20 million tonnes of wheat each year, which makes Australia the world's second largest exporter after America.

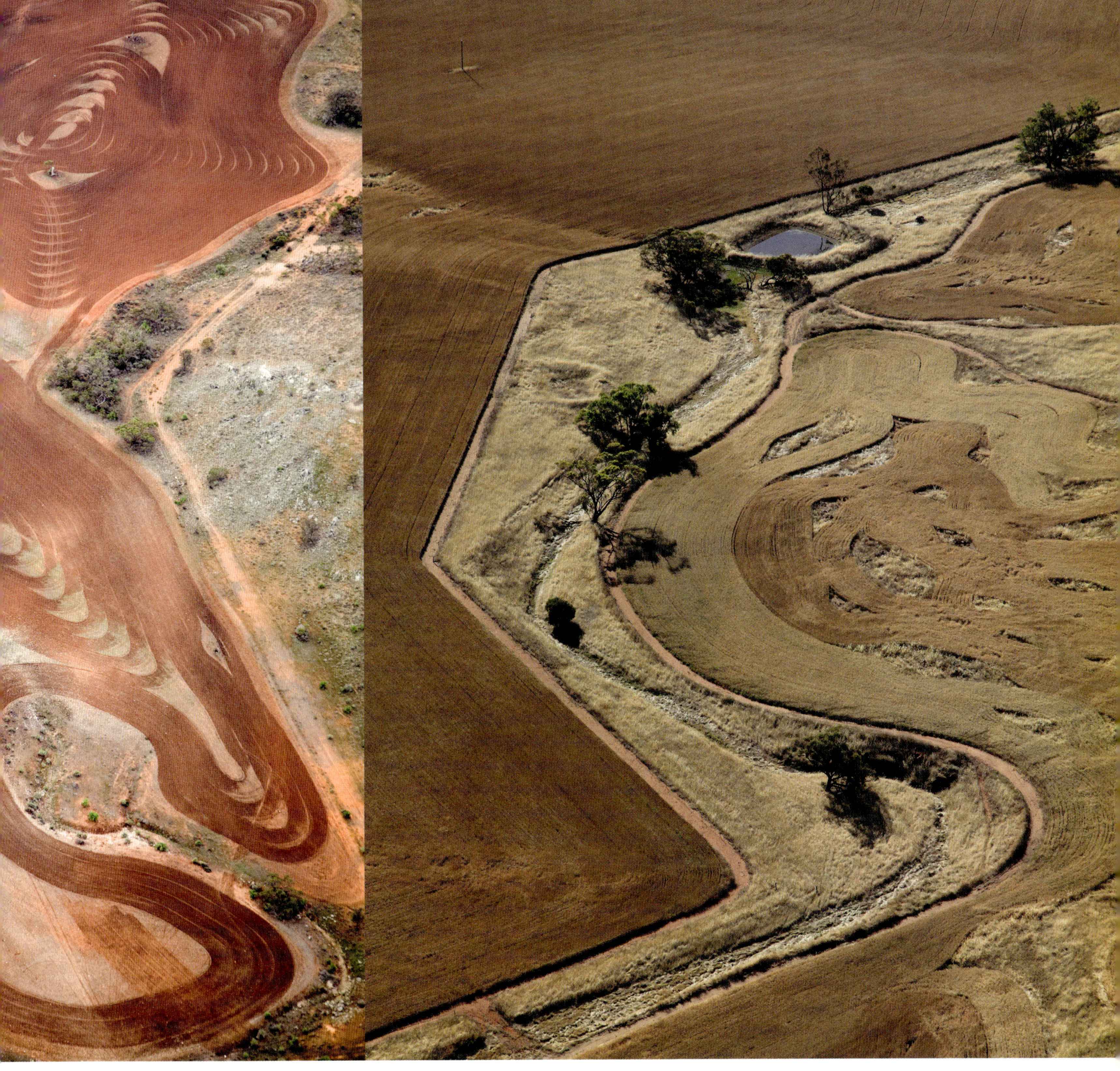

RIGHT: Western Australia is the largest grower of wheat, producing 40 per cent of Australia's annual crop. A total of 90 per cent is exported from the west mostly through the Kwinana terminal, south of Perth. **FOLLOWING PAGES:** Hay bales northeast of Northam, Western Australia. Mostly used as animal fodder for cattle, horses and sheep, hay's availability helps farmers deal with seasonal uncertainties when grazing pastures produce too little food or food that is too rich.

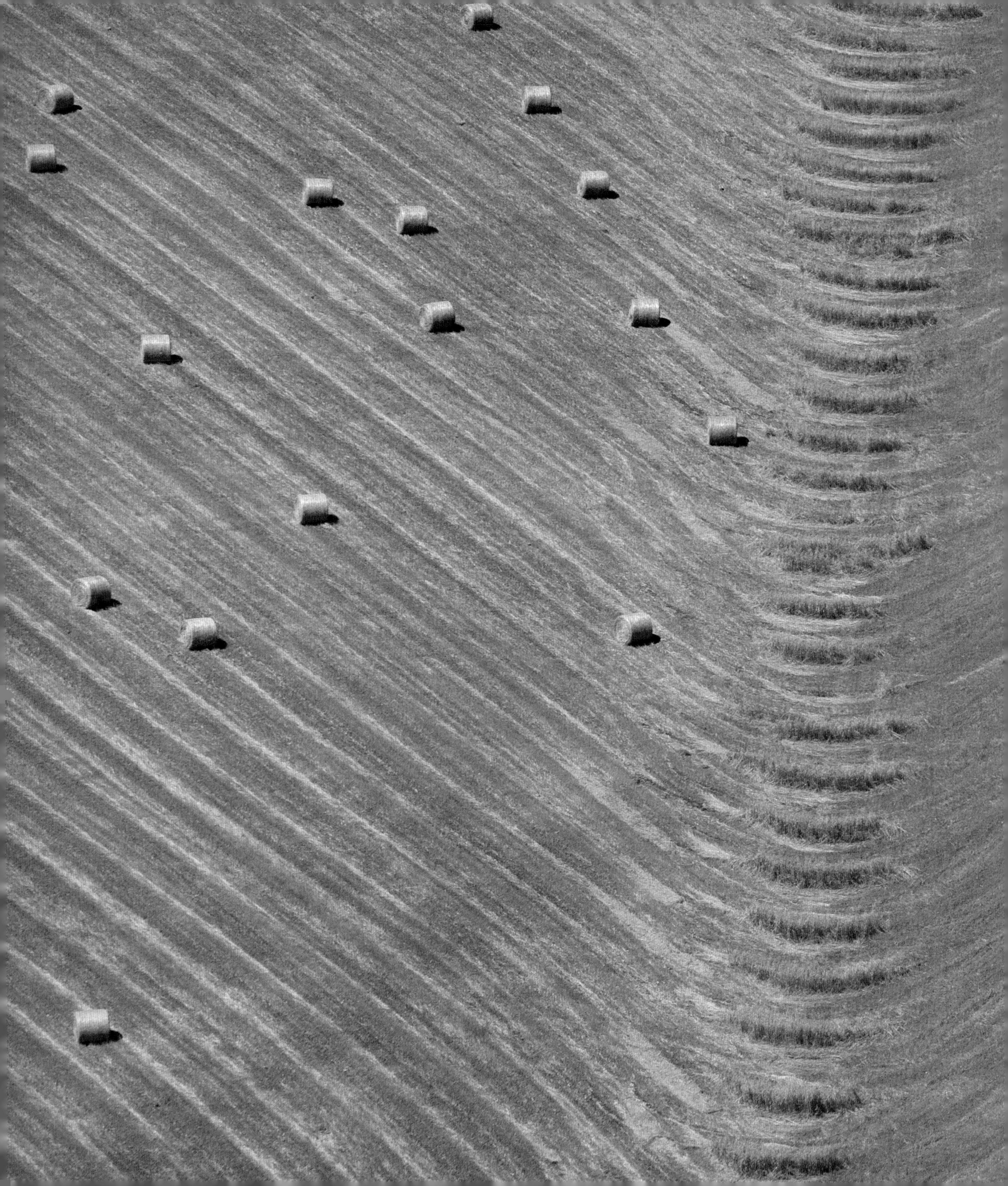

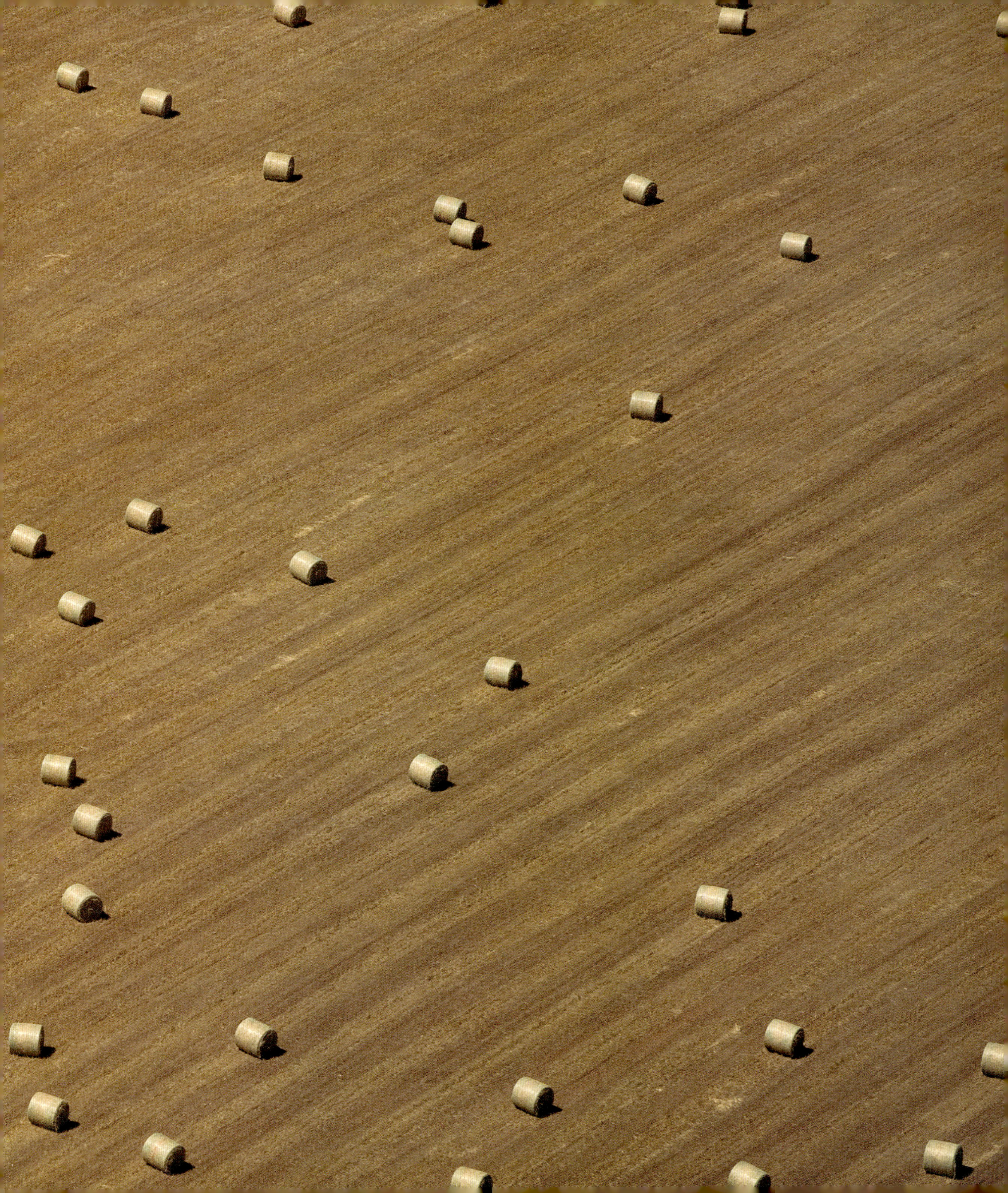

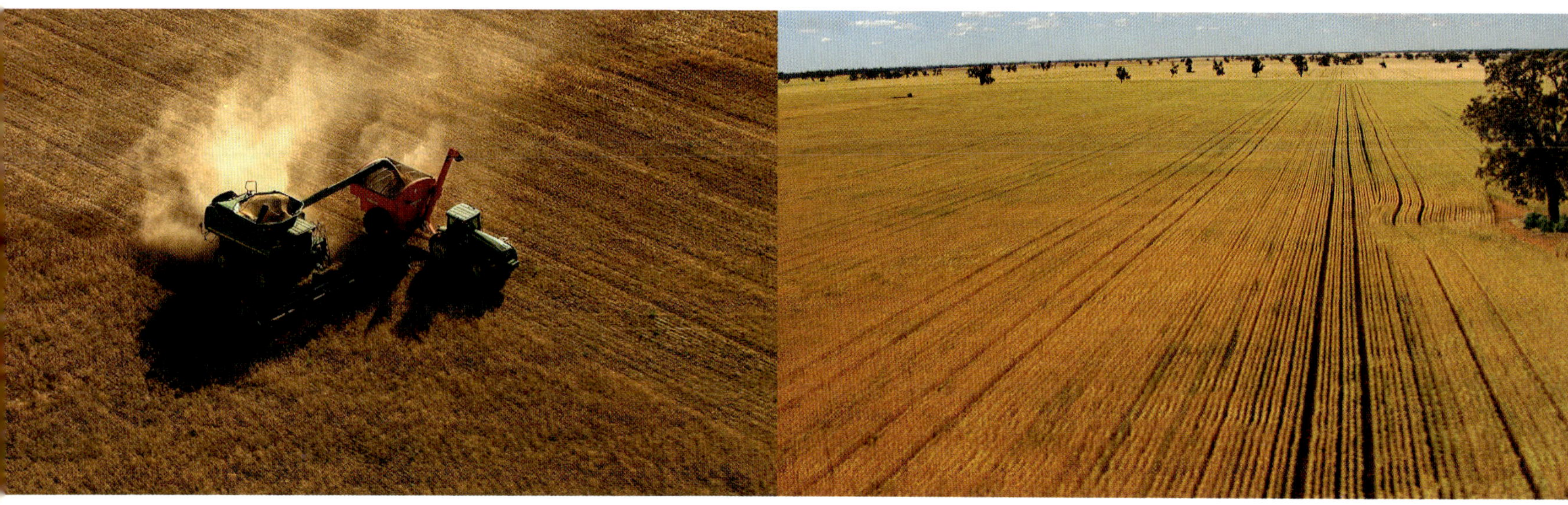

LEFT: Dry wheat being harvested in Burraboi, New South Wales. Varieties like this 'dwarf' wheat are crossbred to stay short and quickly mature, thus eliminating the need for irrigation. **MIDDLE:** Crisp straight wheat field lines. Thanks to GPS technology, sowing and harvesting can now take place with pinpoint accuracy, maximising yield. Agricultural satellite navigation systems vary in price from $2,000 to $20,000. **RIGHT:** A harvester at work in Wakool, New South Wales. Harvesters like this can cost up to $500,000. If equipped with GPS technology, they can steer themselves while producing yield maps that show where the crops are performing well and where they need fertilising.

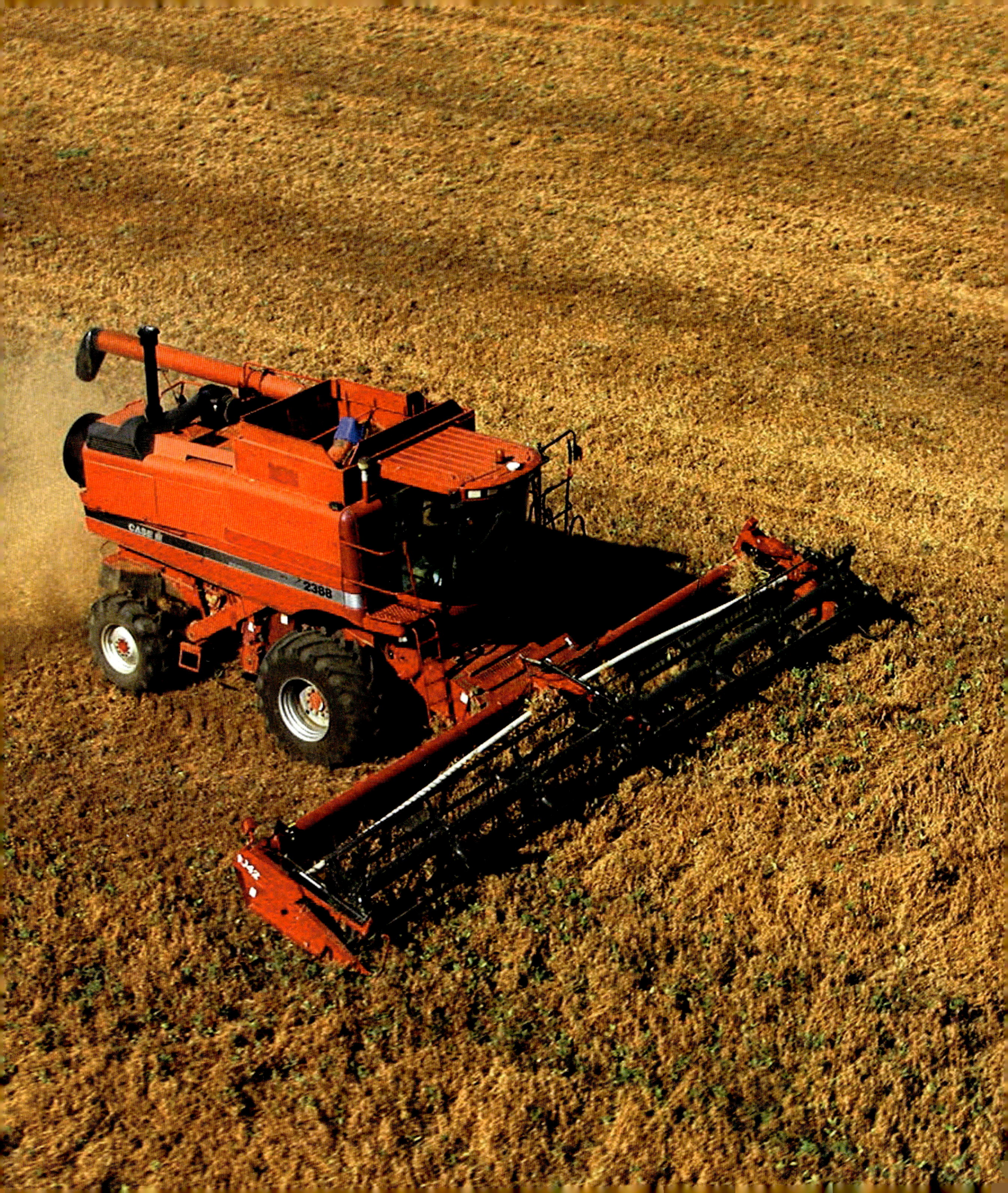
2388

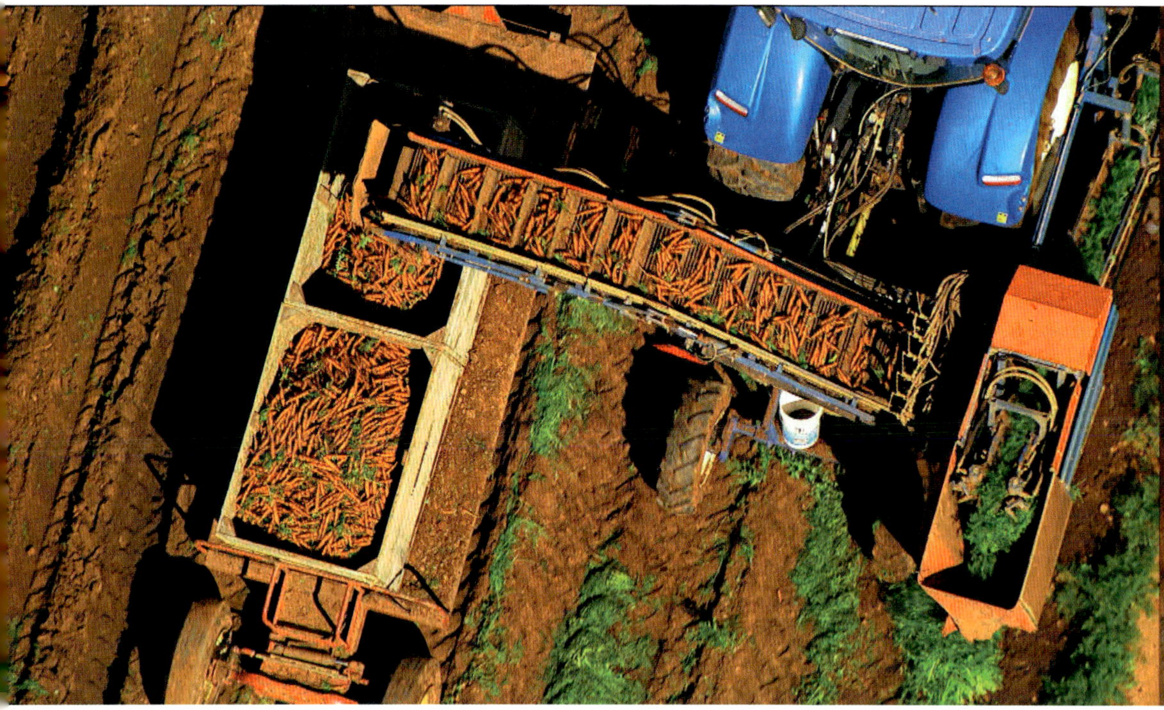

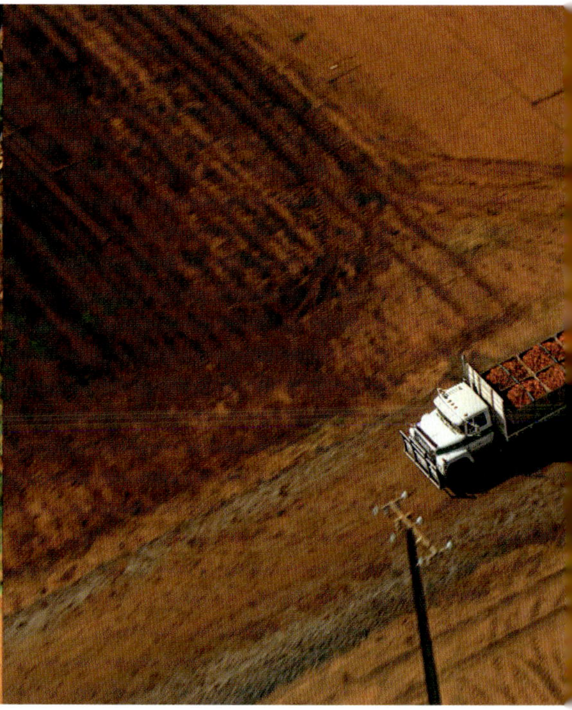

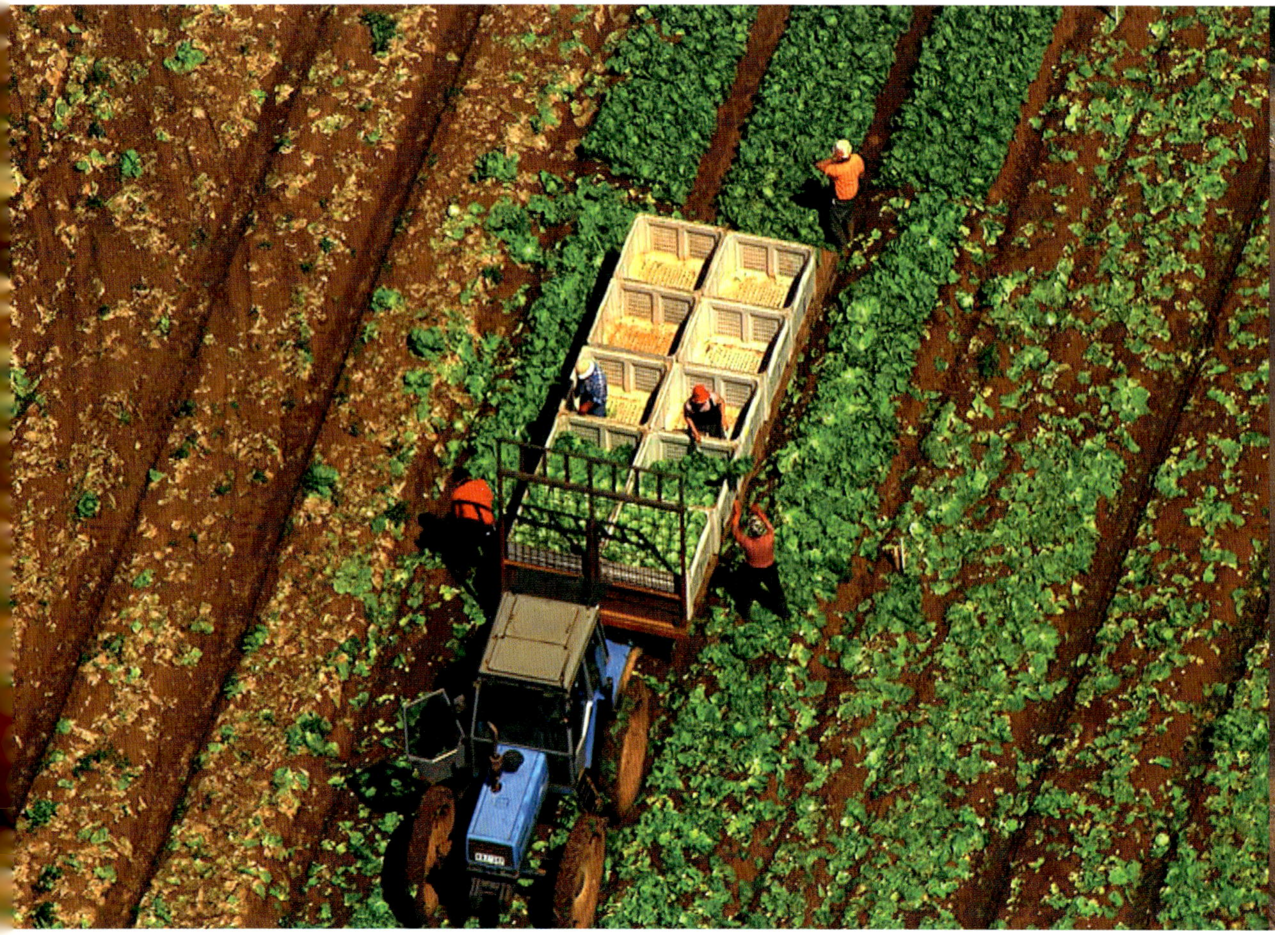

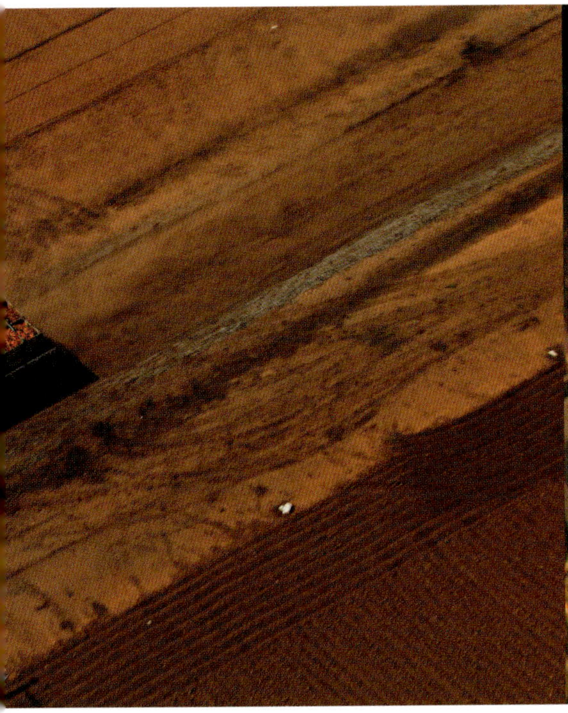

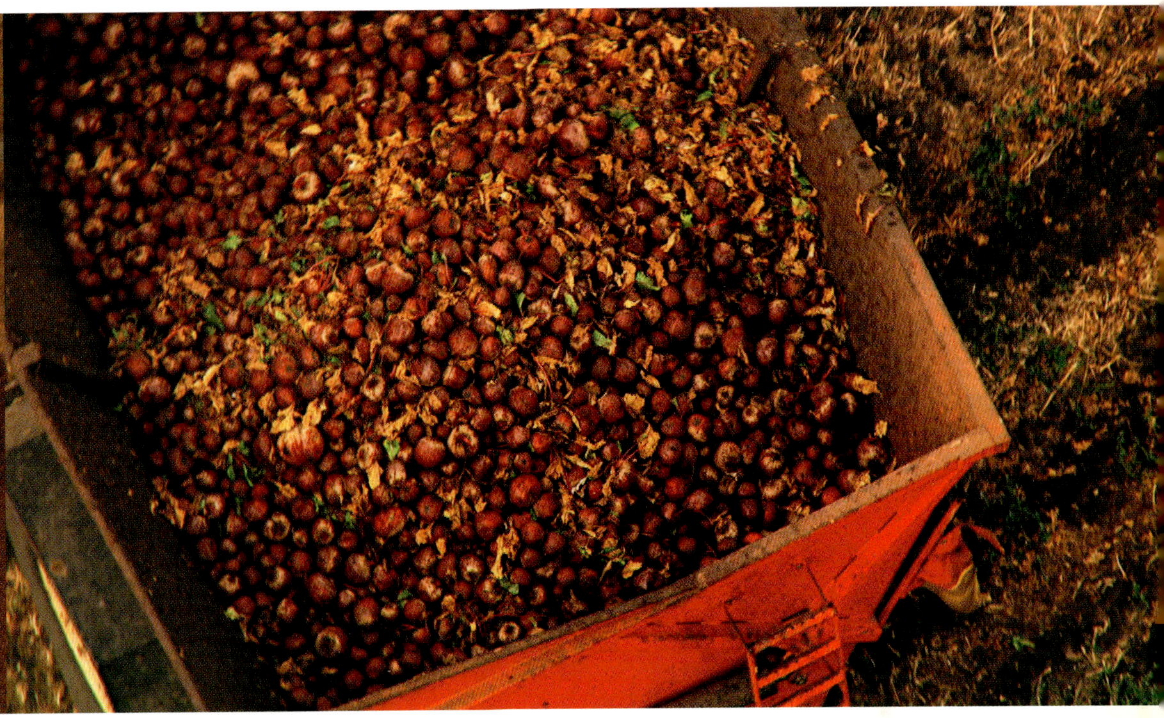

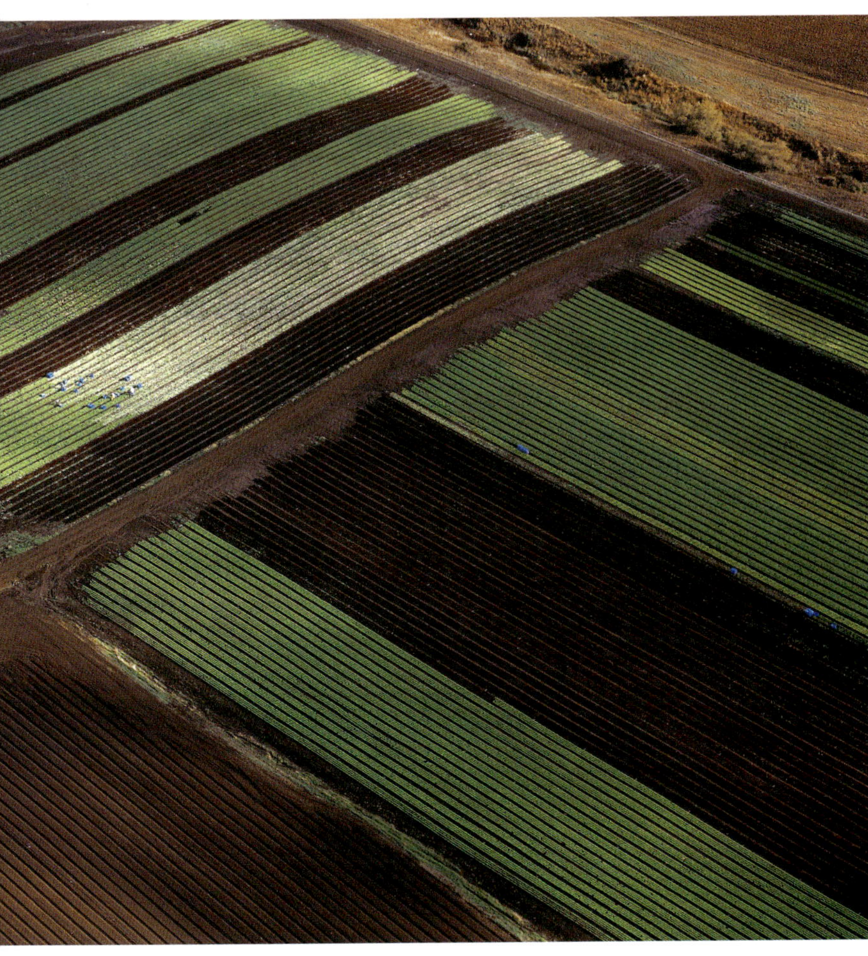

TOP LEFT: Carrots being harvested in Virginia, South Australia. A nearby sewerage plant provides the treated water needed for growing these crops in an otherwise dry environment. **TOP MIDDLE:** A truck laden with carrots departs dry and dusty Virginia. In most years, this corner of the country receives just 500 millimetres of rain. That's less than half the rain that falls in Brisbane or Sydney. **TOP RIGHT:** Australians eat more beetroot than anyone else in the world. In the Lockyer Valley, Queensland, just nine farmers grow 90 per cent of all beetroot. **BOTTOM LEFT:** On the Mornington Peninsula, Victoria, iceberg lettuce is handpicked to meet the summer's spike in demand. **BOTTOM RIGHT:** Lettuce is harvested in Tasmania.

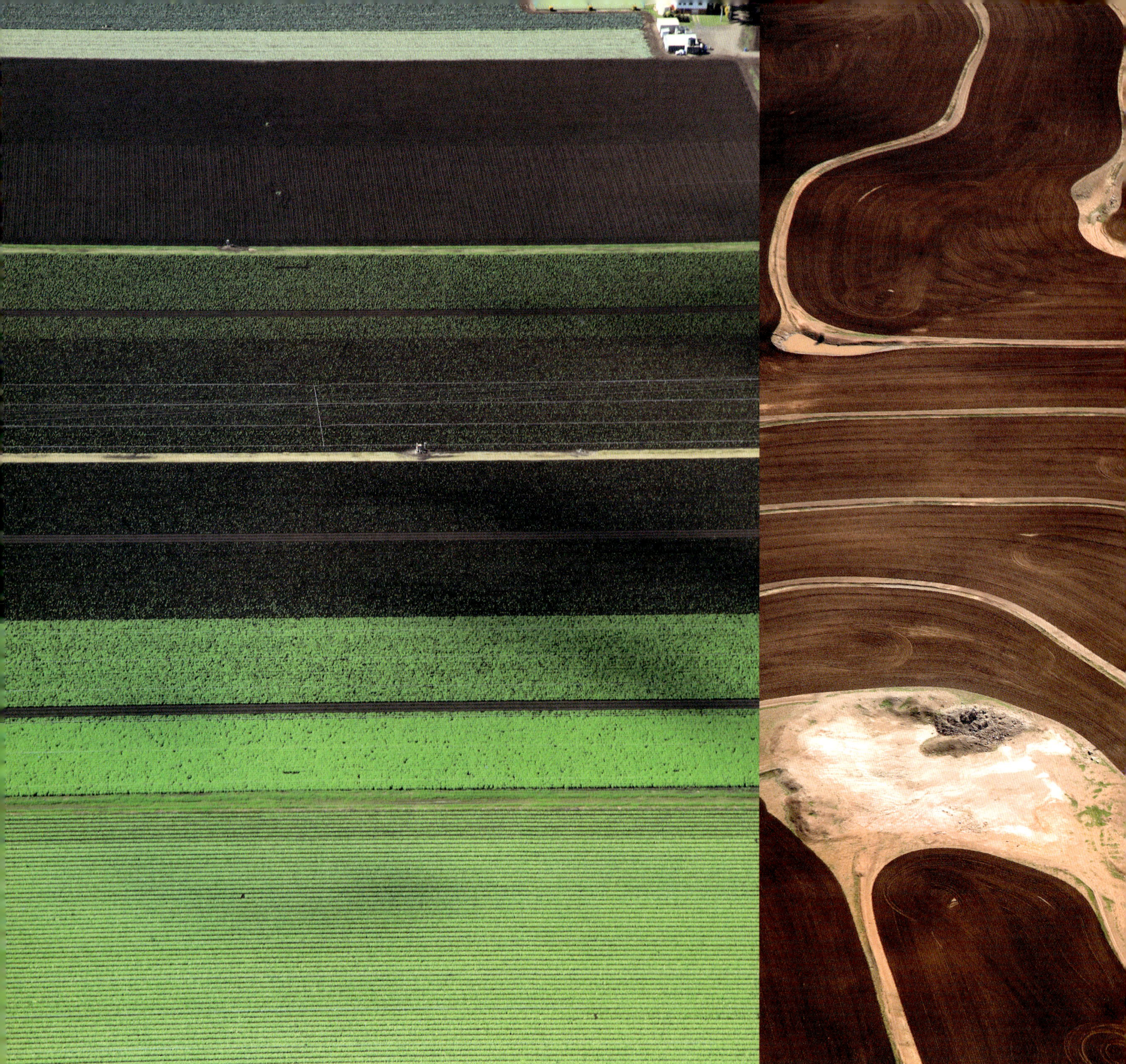

LEFT: Mixed crops grow near Toowoomba, Queensland. Dubbed Queensland's Garden City, Toowoomba is positioned on the northeastern tip of the Murray–Darling Basin. **MIDDLE:** Contour farming on the southwestern end of the Murray–Darling Basin, near Adelaide. By following the natural elevation of slopes, the rows ensure slow water run-off after rainfall, maximising water uptake and minimising erosion. **RIGHT:** Farm fields near Griffth, New South Wales.

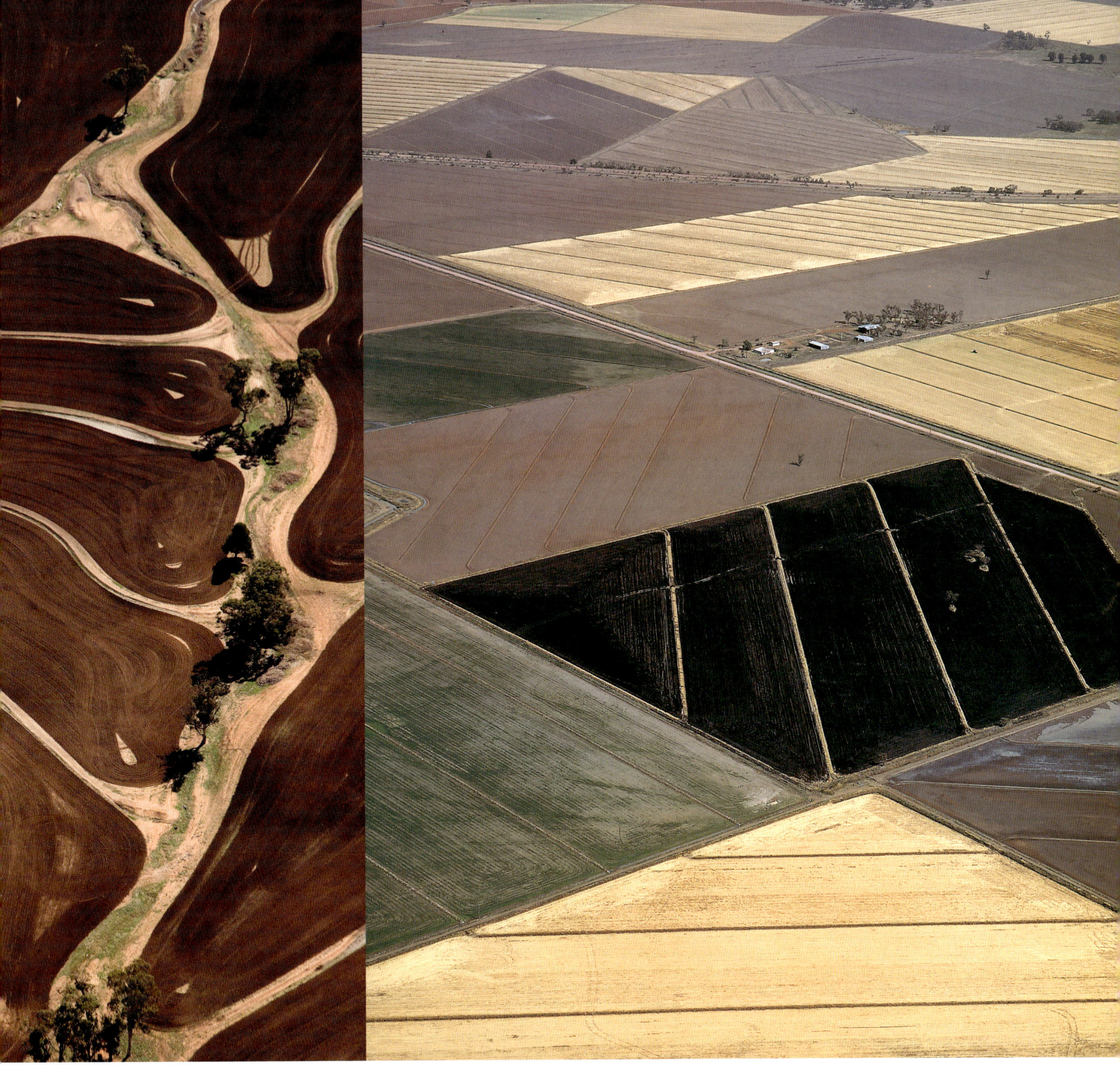

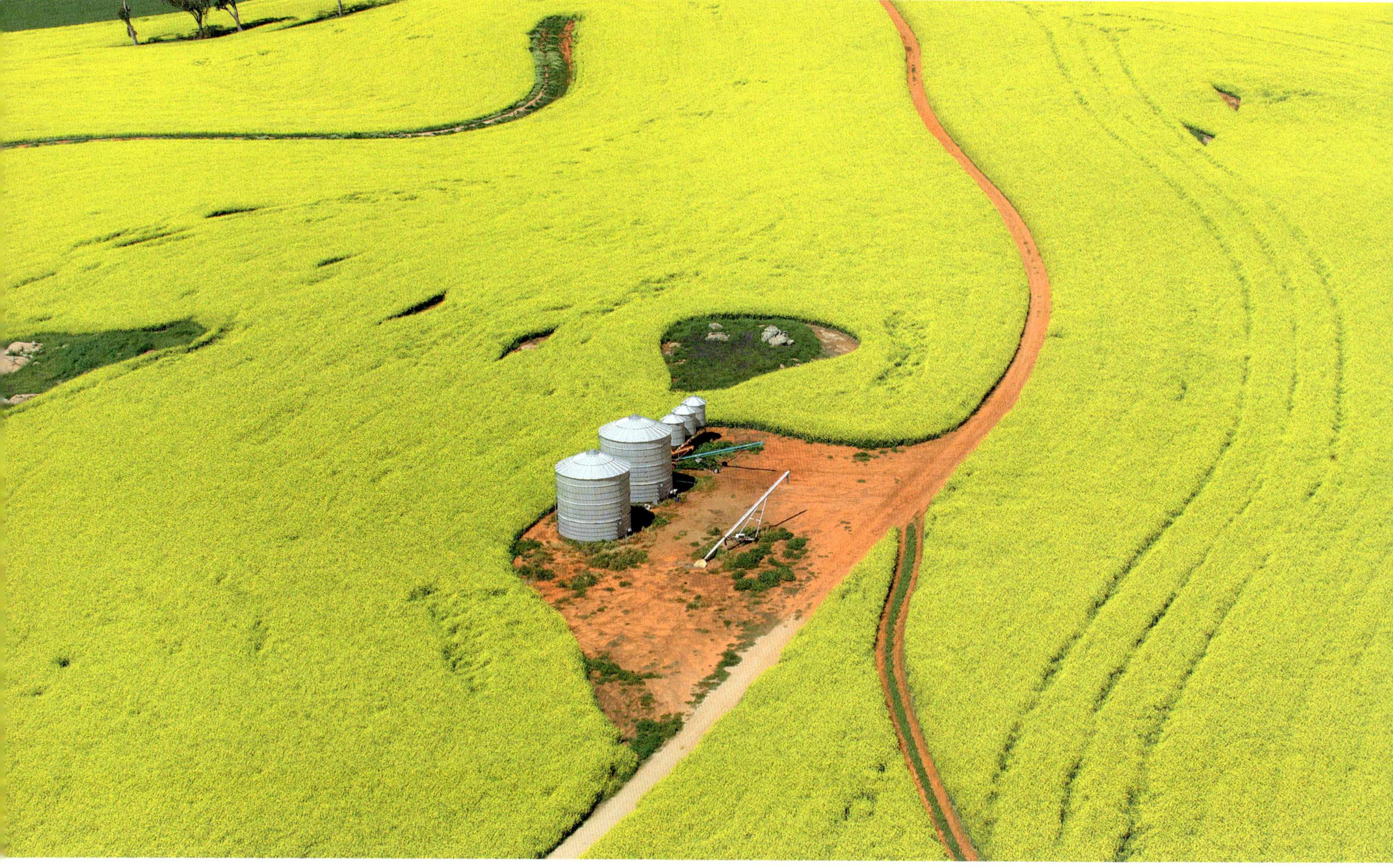

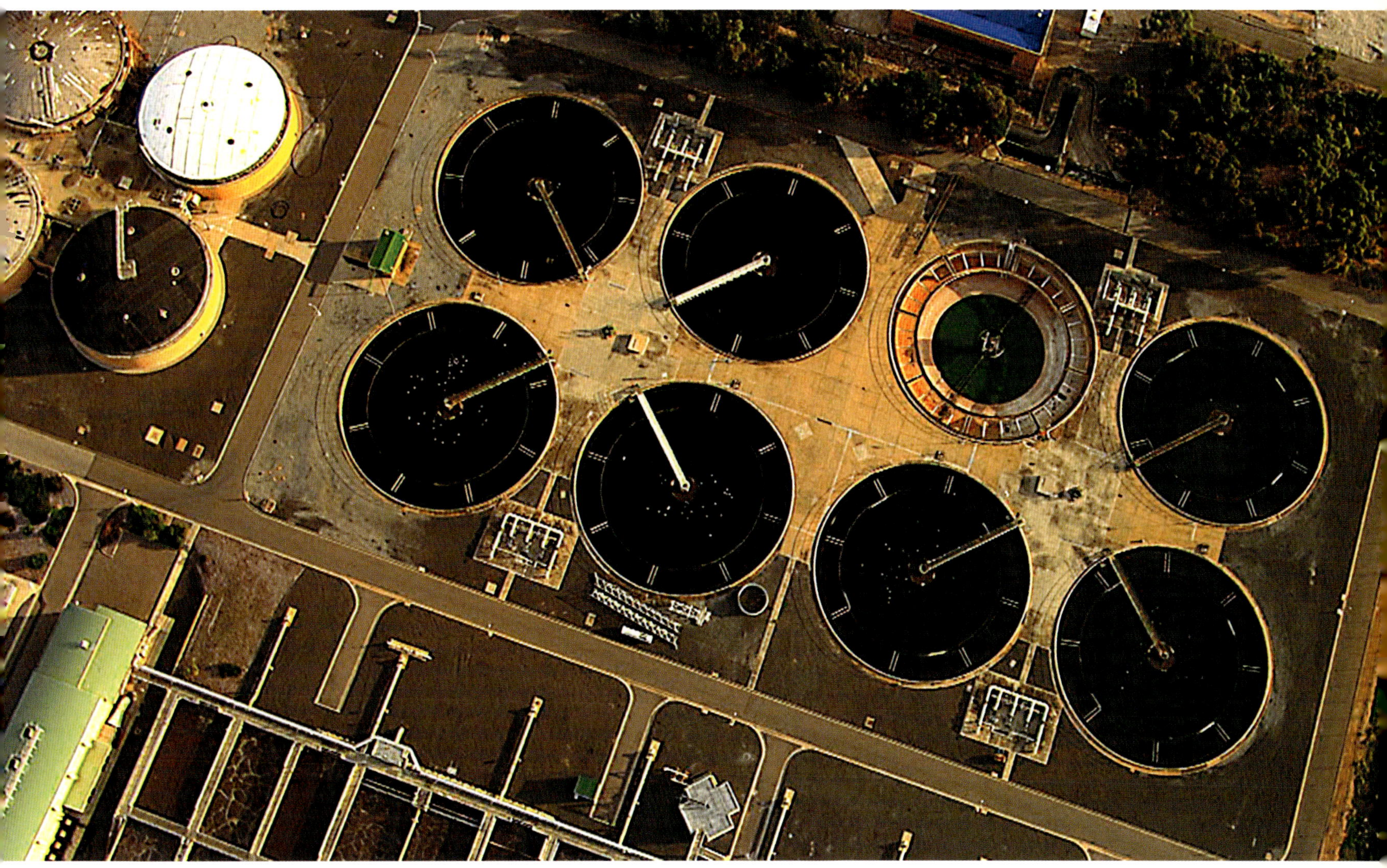

LEFT: Canola fields in western New South Wales. Introduced to Australia in the late 1960s, canola is used to produce oil for cooking and spreads, while its by-products end up in stock feed. **RIGHT:** Treated wastewater from the Bolivar sewerage plant near Adelaide helps irrigate nearby farms and hydroponic crops such as tomatoes grown in greenhouses. Organic material, collected during wastewater treatment, is repurposed as fertiliser.

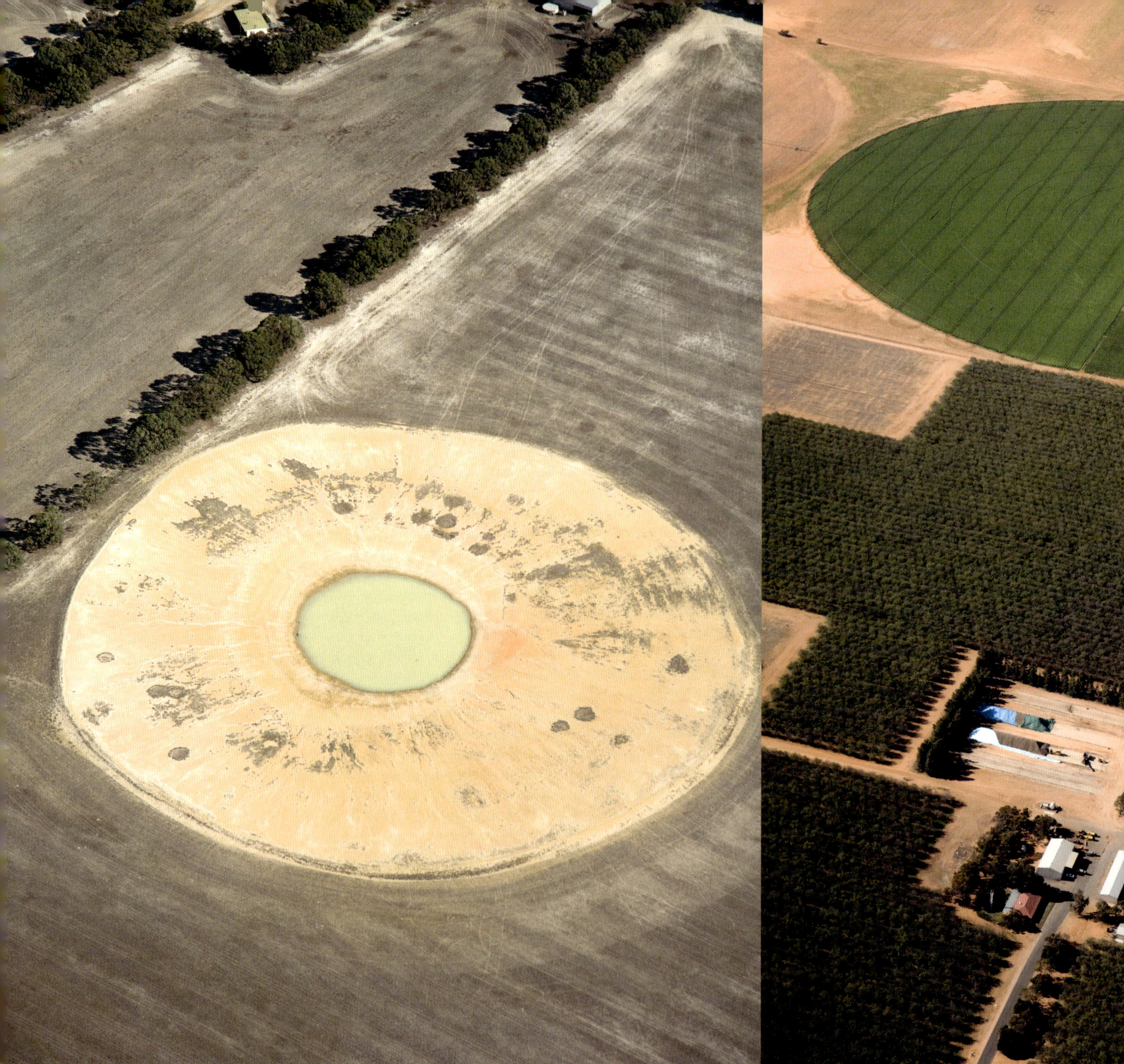

LEFT: A stock dam near Adelaide. Such dams are mostly constructed in regions deprived of suitable quality groundwater, or where water is too deep and costly to extract. **MIDDLE:** Circular and linear irrigation in action, side by side, to grow produce in Renmark, South Australia, drawing water from the Murray–Darling Basin.

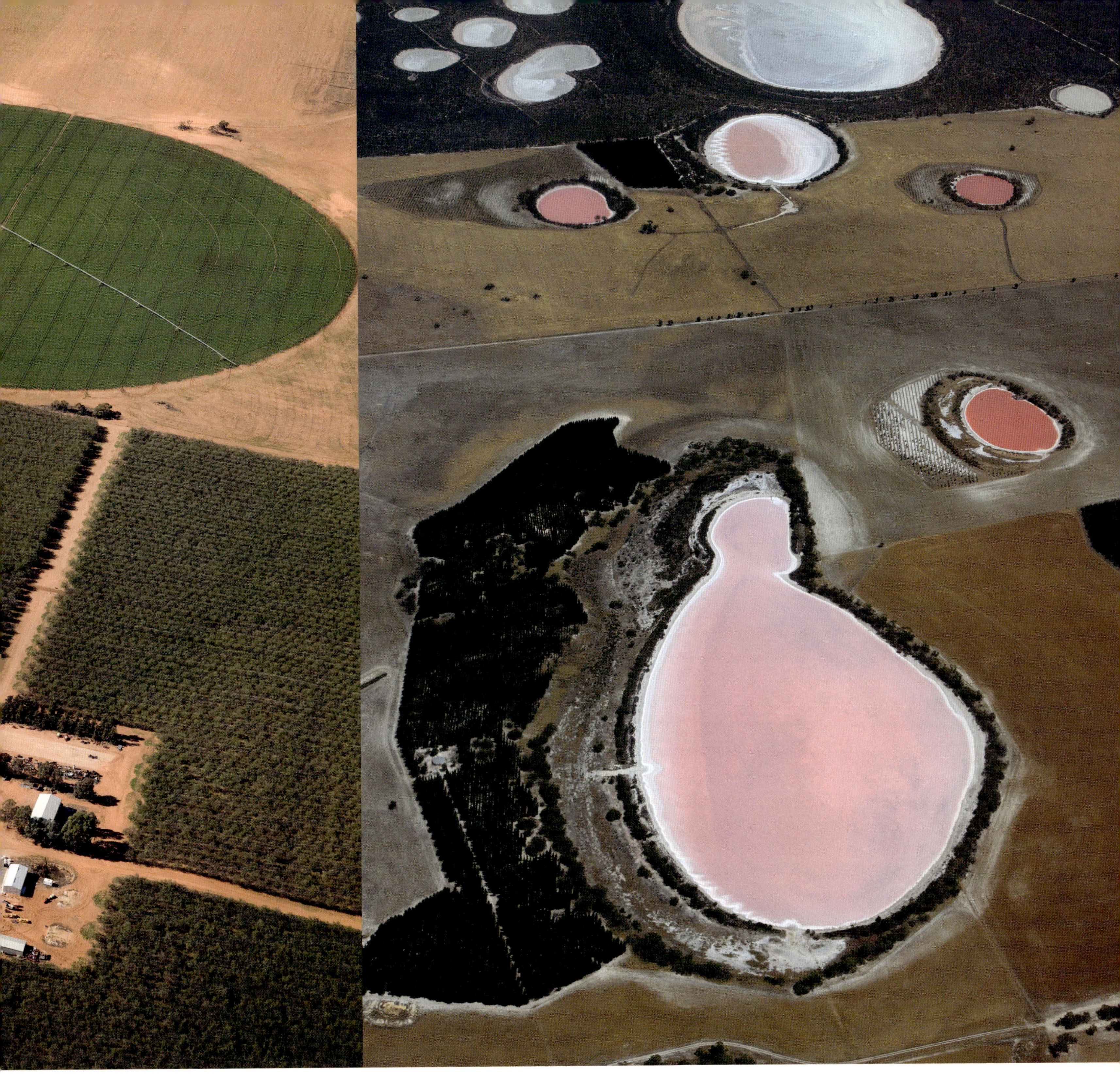

RIGHT: Naturally occurring salt ponds north of the Stirling Ranges, Western Australia. The pink colour comes from a pigment called betacarotene, naturally produced by algae. When a lake dries out, the top turns white as the algae die from lack of water.

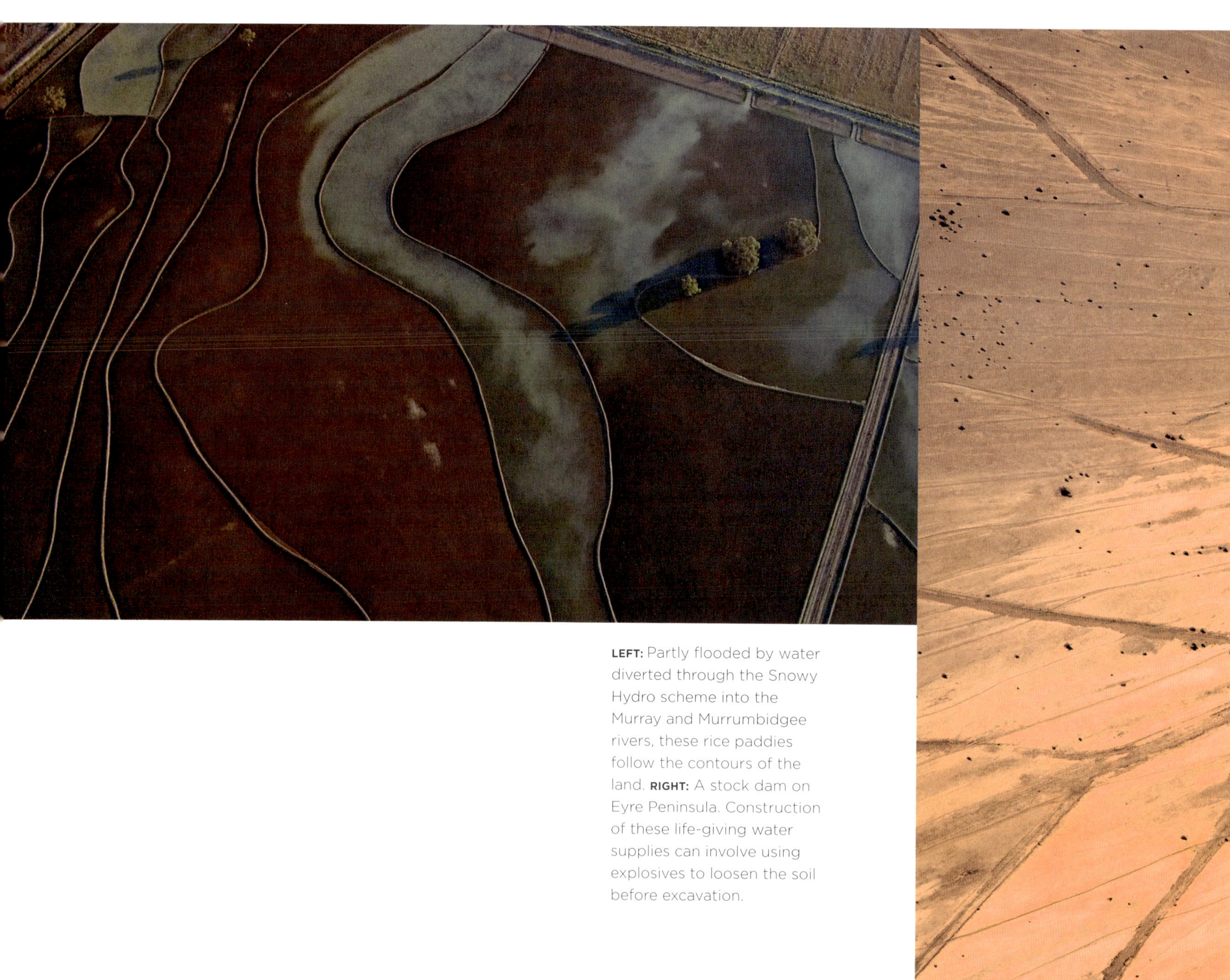

LEFT: Partly flooded by water diverted through the Snowy Hydro scheme into the Murray and Murrumbidgee rivers, these rice paddies follow the contours of the land. **RIGHT:** A stock dam on Eyre Peninsula. Construction of these life-giving water supplies can involve using explosives to loosen the soil before excavation.

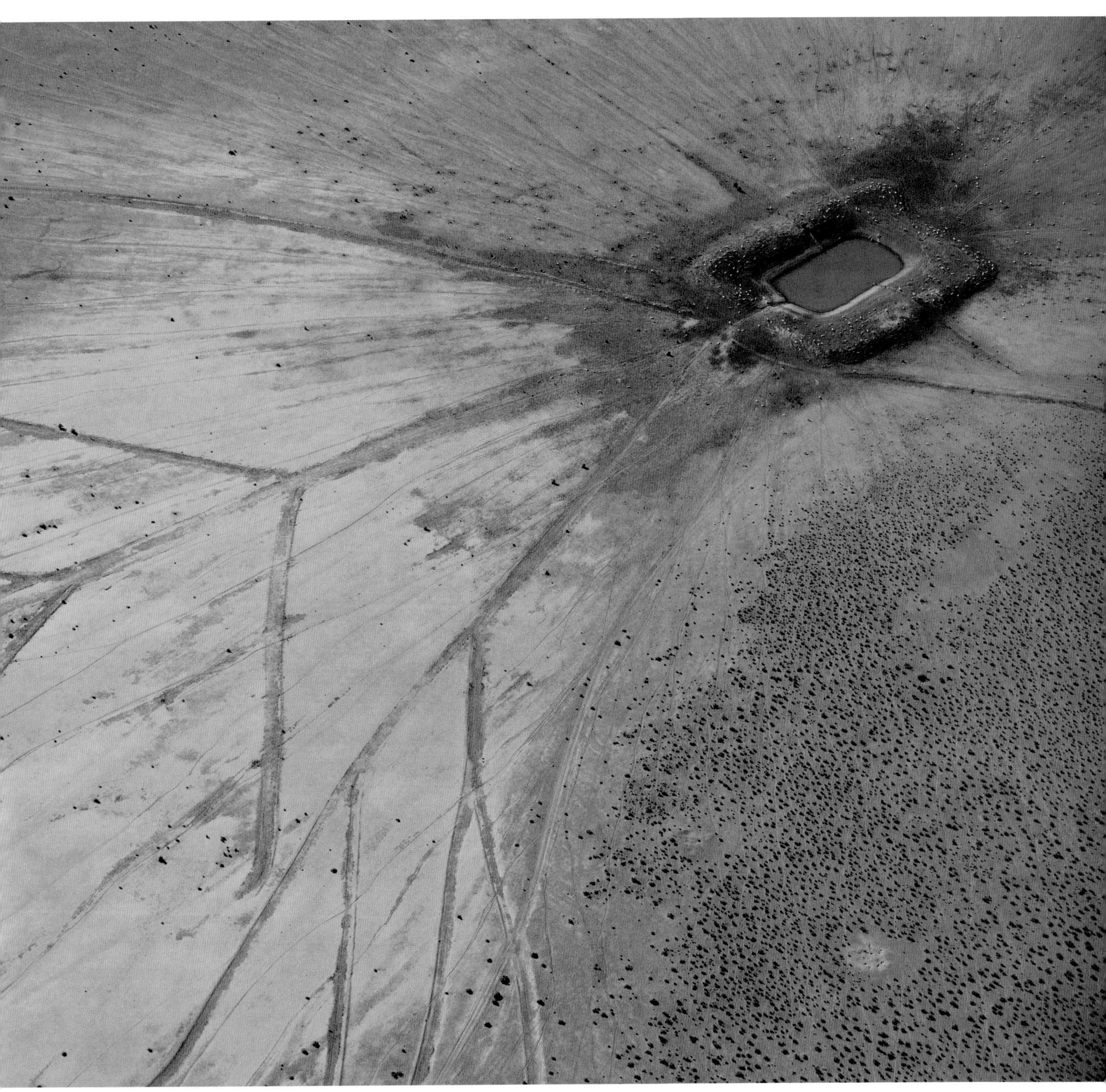

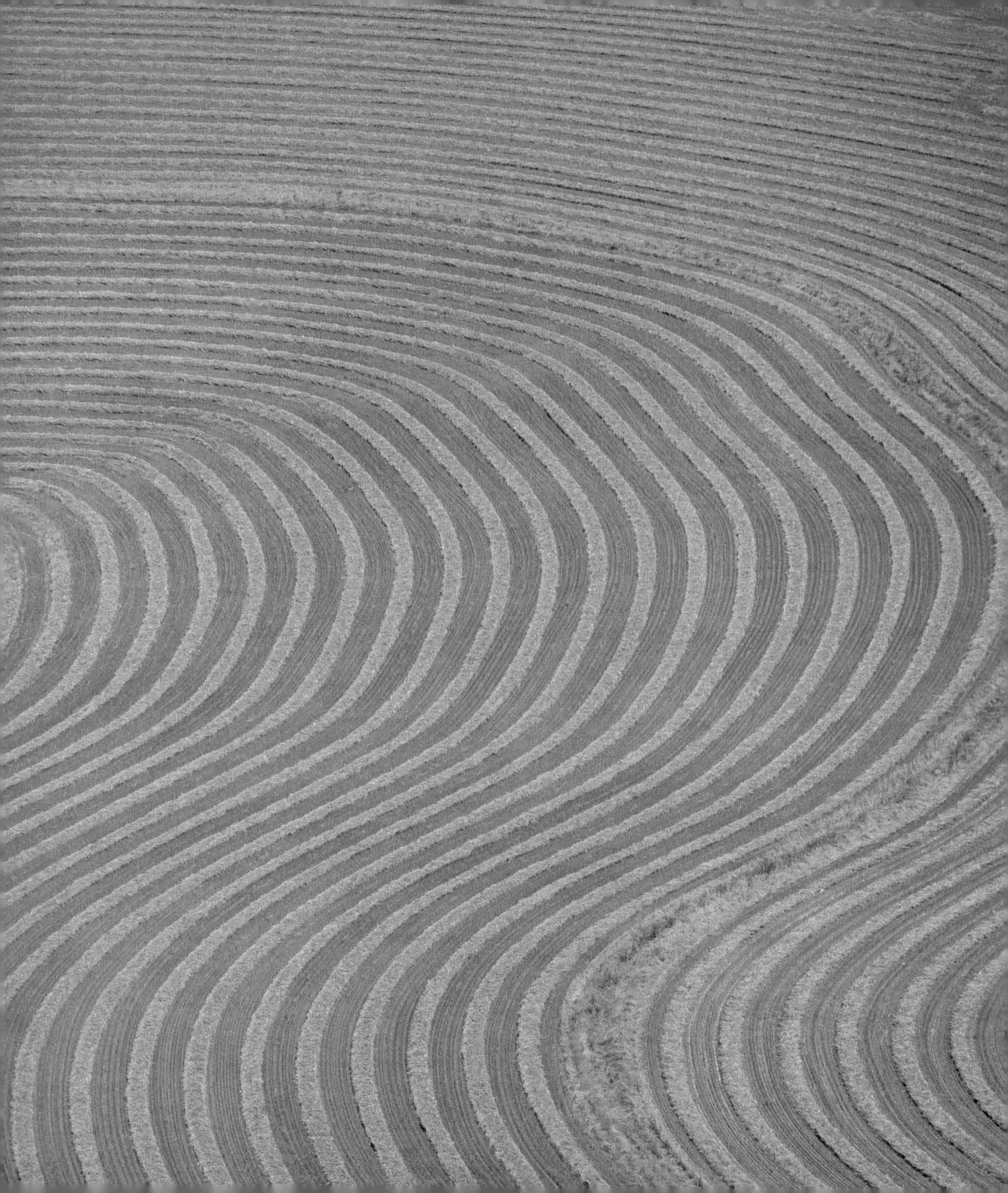

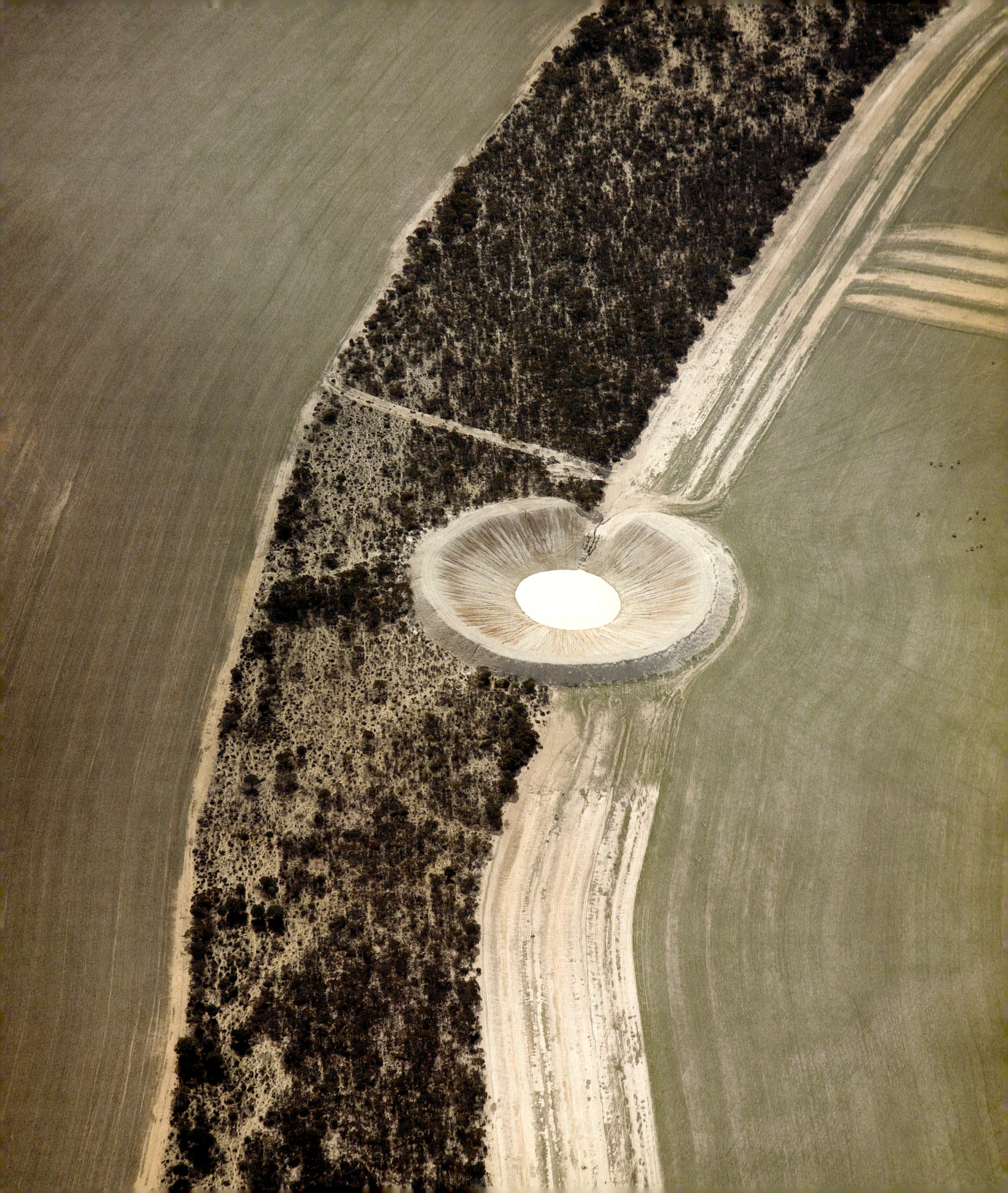

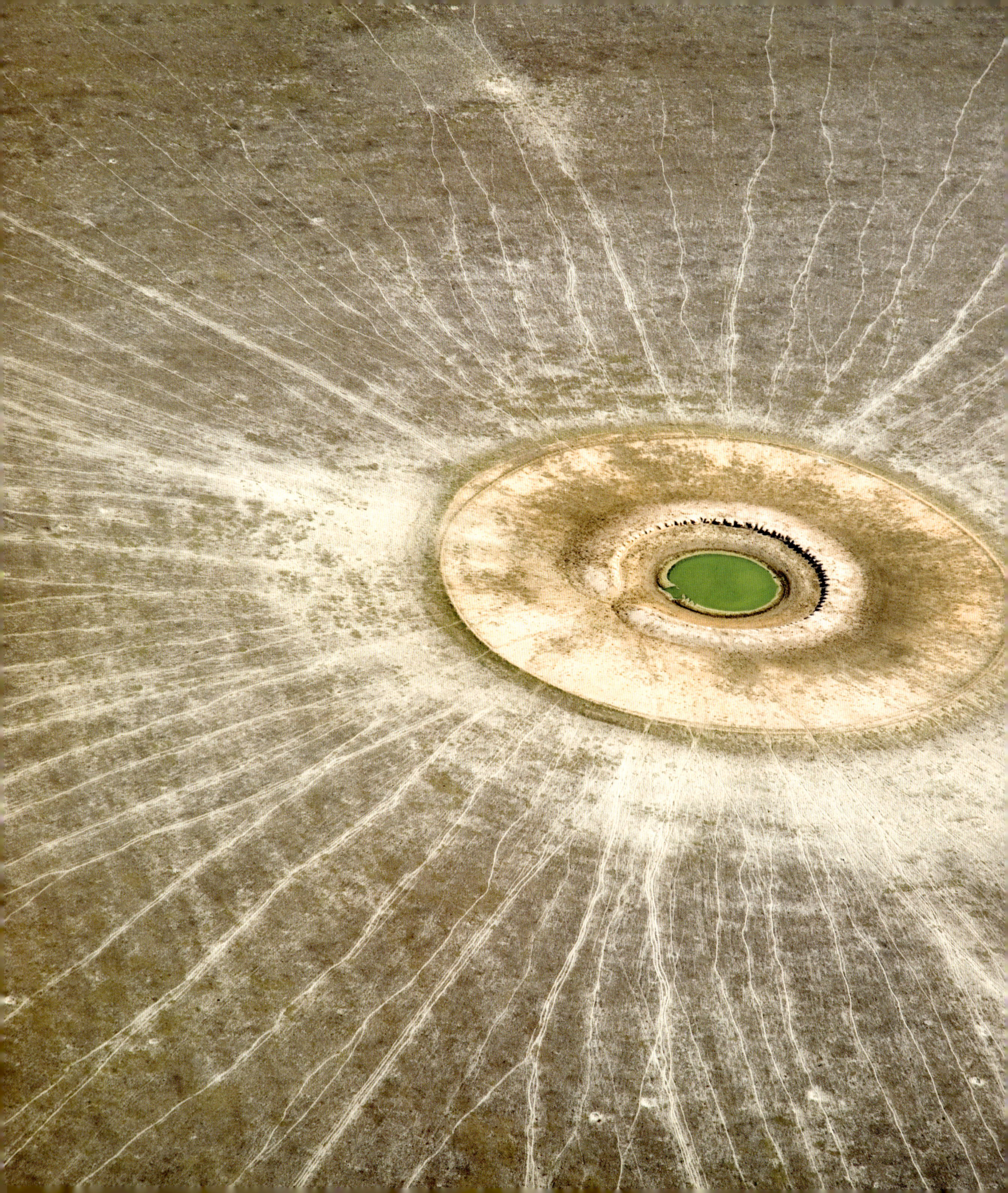

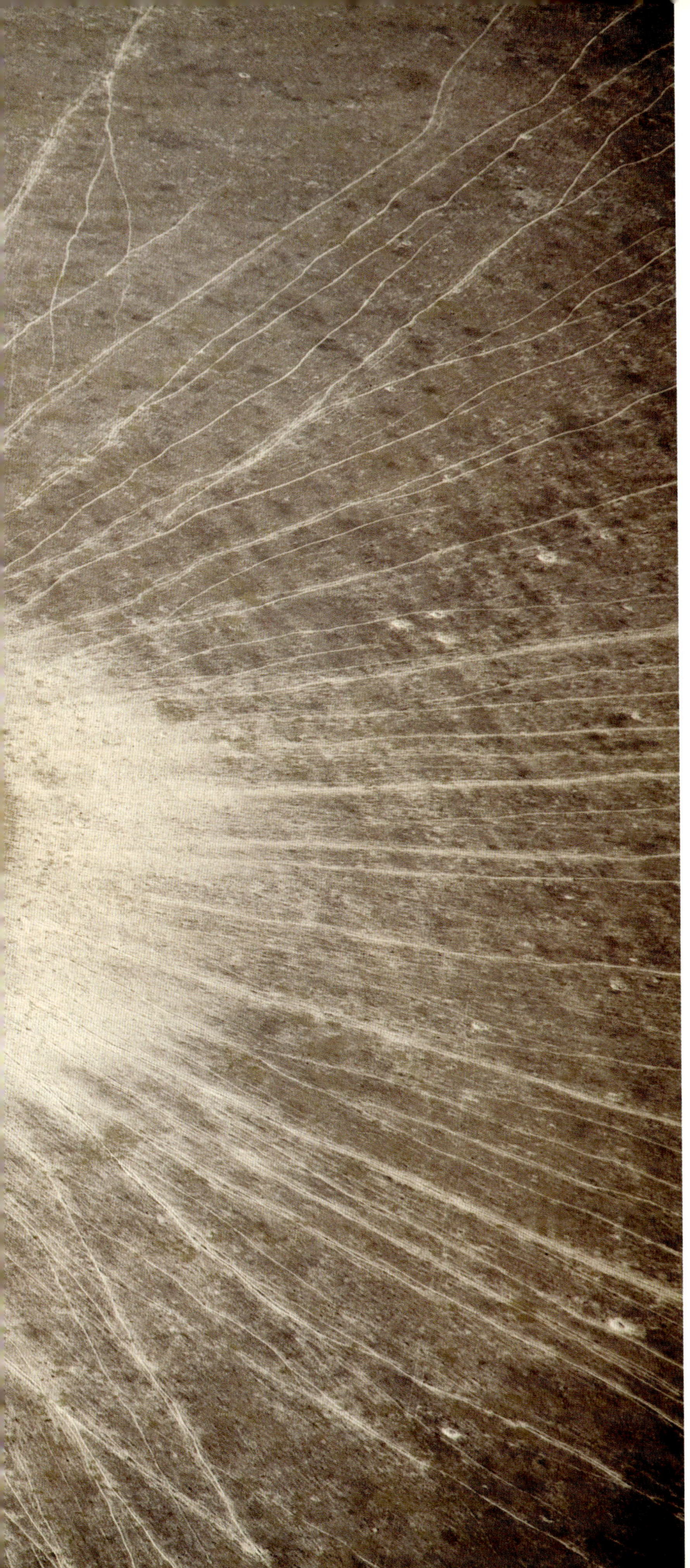

PREVIOUS PAGE LEFT: Cut hay in Western Australia's Wheatbelt is drying, waiting to be baled.
PREVIOUS PAGE RIGHT: A stock dam and shelterbelt separate paddocks east of Newdegate, Western Australia. Shelterbelts help protect cropping land from the harsh winds common in the area, provide protection for livestock from temperature extremes and can reduce stock deaths during lambing. They are also useful residual habitats for local flora and fauna.
THIS PAGE: Stock dam in Western Australia's Wheatbelt. Experts say that circular dams are the most cost effective for stock watering purposes. Comparatively, they provide less stored water than a conventional square dam but the effective storage life in a drought is similar because it is deeper and has less evaporative losses.

LEFT: An 'air tractor' approaches a flooded rice paddy, ready to release germinated rice seeds. What used to take several people a couple of days on the ground is done by one pilot in a couple of hours. Such technology makes Australia a highly efficient and competitive rice producer. **RIGHT:** Cane country. Queensland's Burdekin region lies at the northern tip of a cane-growing region that hugs 2,100 kilometres of coastline and stretches south to New South Wales. Four thousand farmers produce up to five million tonnes of raw sugar, which makes Australia one of the world's leading suppliers of sweetness.

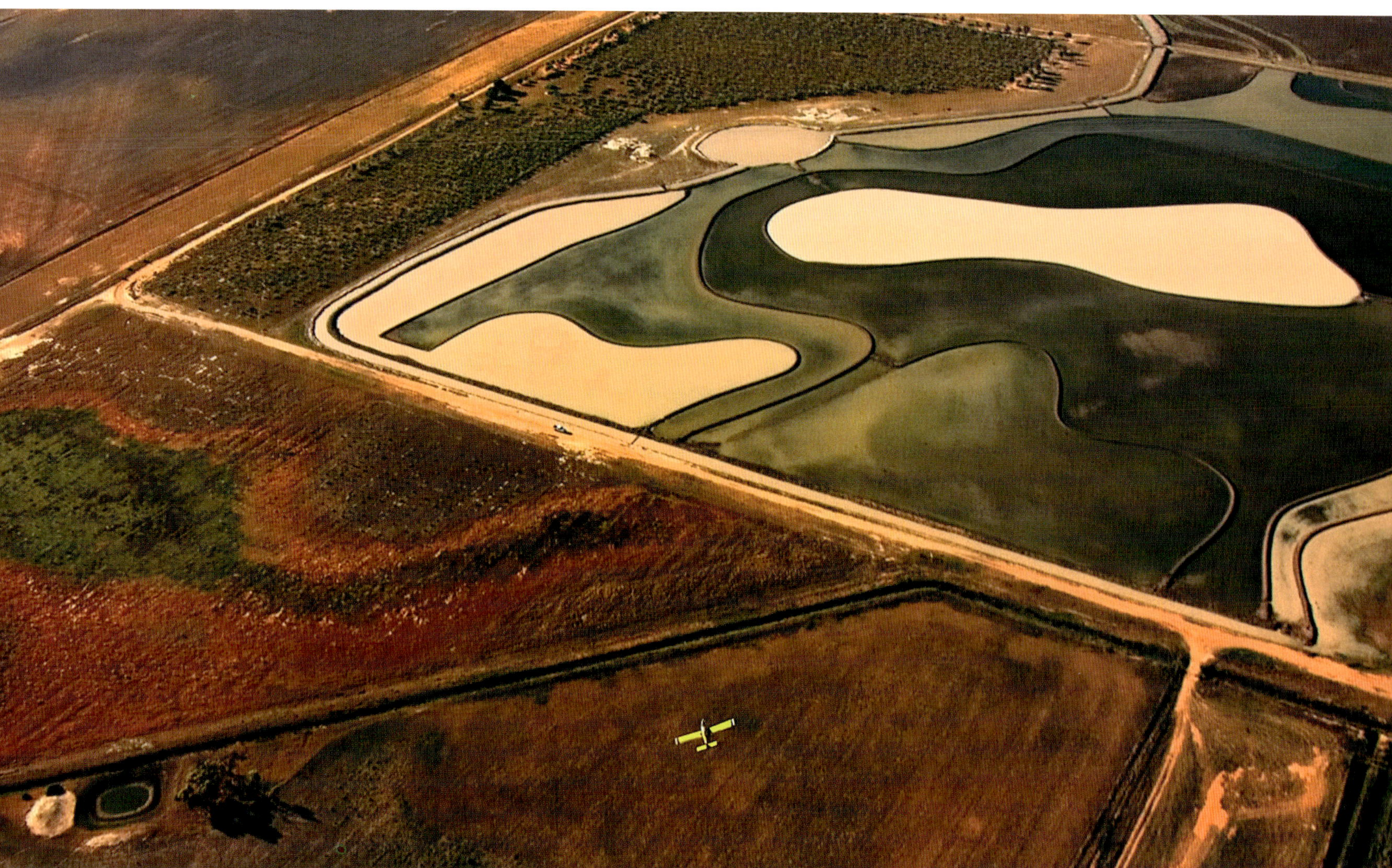

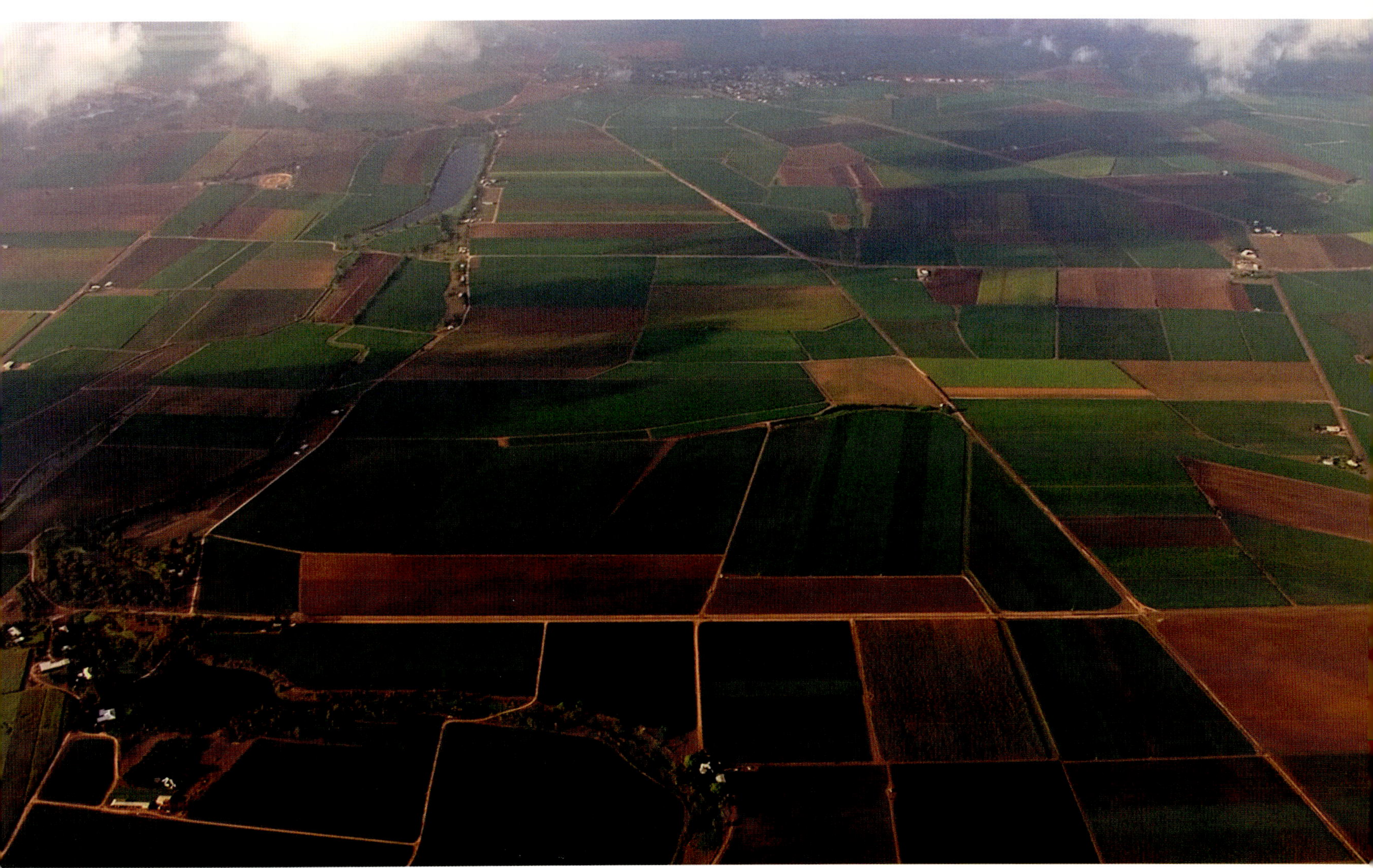

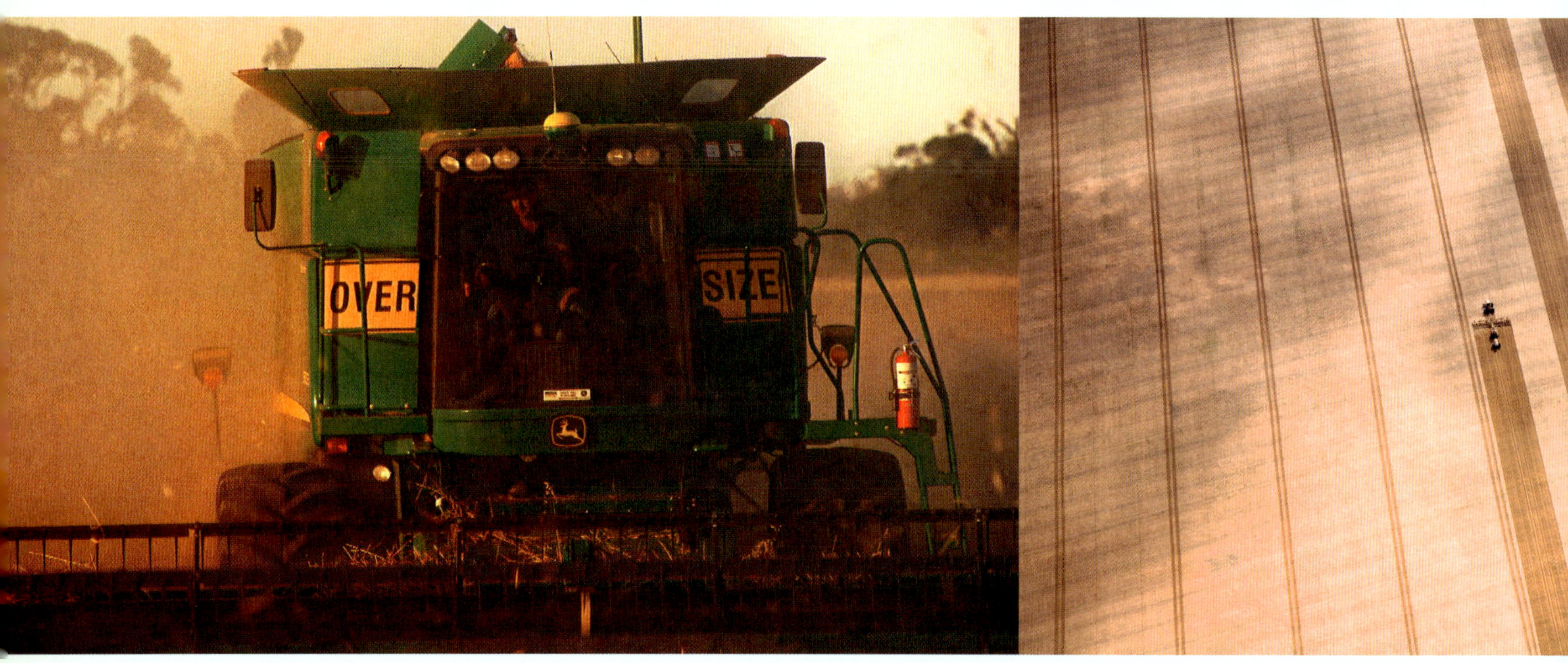
OVER
SIZE

HARVEST FROM THE HEAVENS

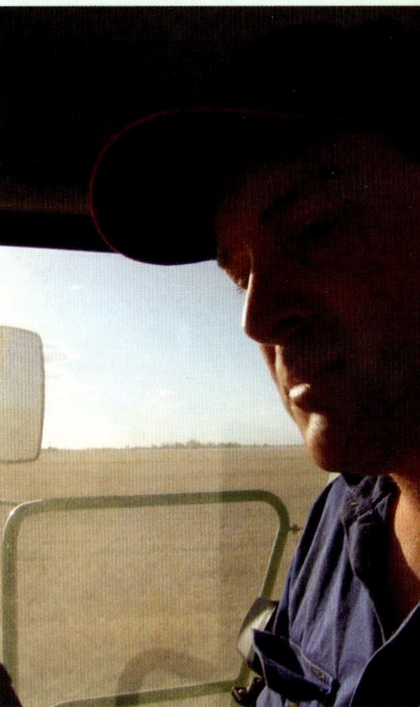

IN BURRABOI, SOUTHERN New South Wales, Neville Hollins is busy reaping what he sowed, showing off the technology that gives Australian wheat farmers a leg-up. 'This is a dry land variety,' he says as his harvester makes its way through a golden field. 'It goes along not too bad at all — providing it rains.' Hollins calls this type a 'dwarf wheat'. It is especially crossbred to keep it small and to mature quickly, thus needing less water and so not dependent on irrigation.

With half a million dollars invested in his harvester, you would expect Hollins to keep his eyes on the growth and his hands on the wheel. Instead, Hollins is able to make business calls and enjoy a cup of tea because modern harvesting machines are driven by something else — satellites. 'We are collecting a signal from the sky and it's going to a beacon on the tractor,' says Hollins, a fourth-generation farmer. 'It's pretty good. Take your shoes off, put your feet up on the glass. It's all a bit easier. You wonder how you went without it, actually.'

GPS allows Hollins to harvest his 3,000-hectare property with extraordinary precision. 'You're not overlapping the crop like you might be if you are steering it,' he says. 'Our line is dead straight. At the end of the day we are going to get a lot more done.'

But his $20,000 satellite system does more than that. 'The main thing,' he says, 'is that we can take home yield maps of what the crop has done.' As the header cuts through the paddock, the onboard computer tracks the results, marking them in different colours. 'The green bits are exceptional,' says Hollins. 'Four tonnes a hectare. Purple is below half a tonne. At the moment we are getting between one and three tonnes to the hectare.'

Further analysis of the maps will tell Hollins exactly where his crops are roaring and where they need some extra fertiliser. And that adds up to giving this farmer a much-needed edge in a competitive world market.

POWER TO THE RAINMAKERS

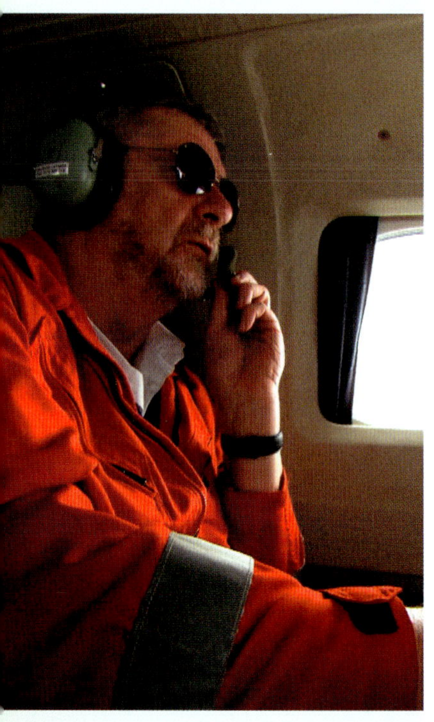

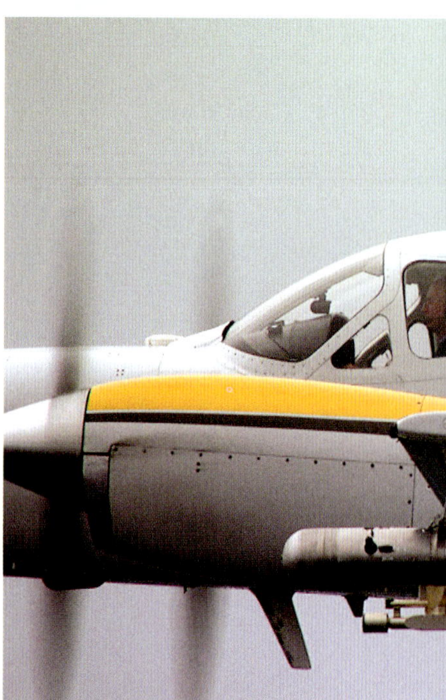

DESPITE THEIR VAST fresh water resources, Tasmanians are still not convinced nature works hard enough. Rain, they say, is inconsistent, regional and seasonal. To make sure the state's hydroelectric reservoirs are always at capacity, they call on people such as Vaughan Latimer, a man who takes to the skies so we can charge our phones and computers, heat our water or vacuum the house. Latimer's job is to 'seed' clouds to make them rain harder and more focused. To do that, Latimer navigates Tasmania's humid air in a plane modified to disperse silver iodine particles in the atmosphere, looking for a storm.

'In pilot training,' says Latimer, 'you're trained not to fly into icing conditions. We're flying into icing conditions. Other pilots think you're a bit of a silly bugger. They think you're a little stupid.' Latimer's work, however, is anything but stupid. The particles he releases from the plane, like the naturally occurring ice nuclei they supplement, allow ice crystals to form and grow and ultimately become raindrops.

Cloud seeding is a technique pioneered by General Electric in the United States shortly after the Second World War. The first man-made rain in Australia, brought about by the CSIRO, fell in Bathurst, New South Wales, in 1947. In Tasmania, they have been cloud seeding since 1964.

A successful mission requires perfect conditions. The outside temperature, for instance, needs to be between minus six and minus 13 degrees Celsius. And that can happen at challenging times of the day. 'If an event happens at midnight, then you make sure you get a sleep in the afternoon, and then we take off at midnight or take off about an hour before midnight to do the cloud seeding,' says Latimer.

It's not a job for the faint-hearted. 'You're surrounded by cloud. You've got a very rough motion from the turbulence, you can't see out so you can't see a horizon, so there is nothing to focus on,' says Latimer. In Tasmania, cloud seeding increases rainfall between five to 13 per cent. On average, there are 25 flights a year at a total cost of $1 million. That sounds like a lot of money but it's a worthwhile investment, says Latimer. 'The return from cloud seeding is somewhere between seven to ten times the amount of money we put into it.'

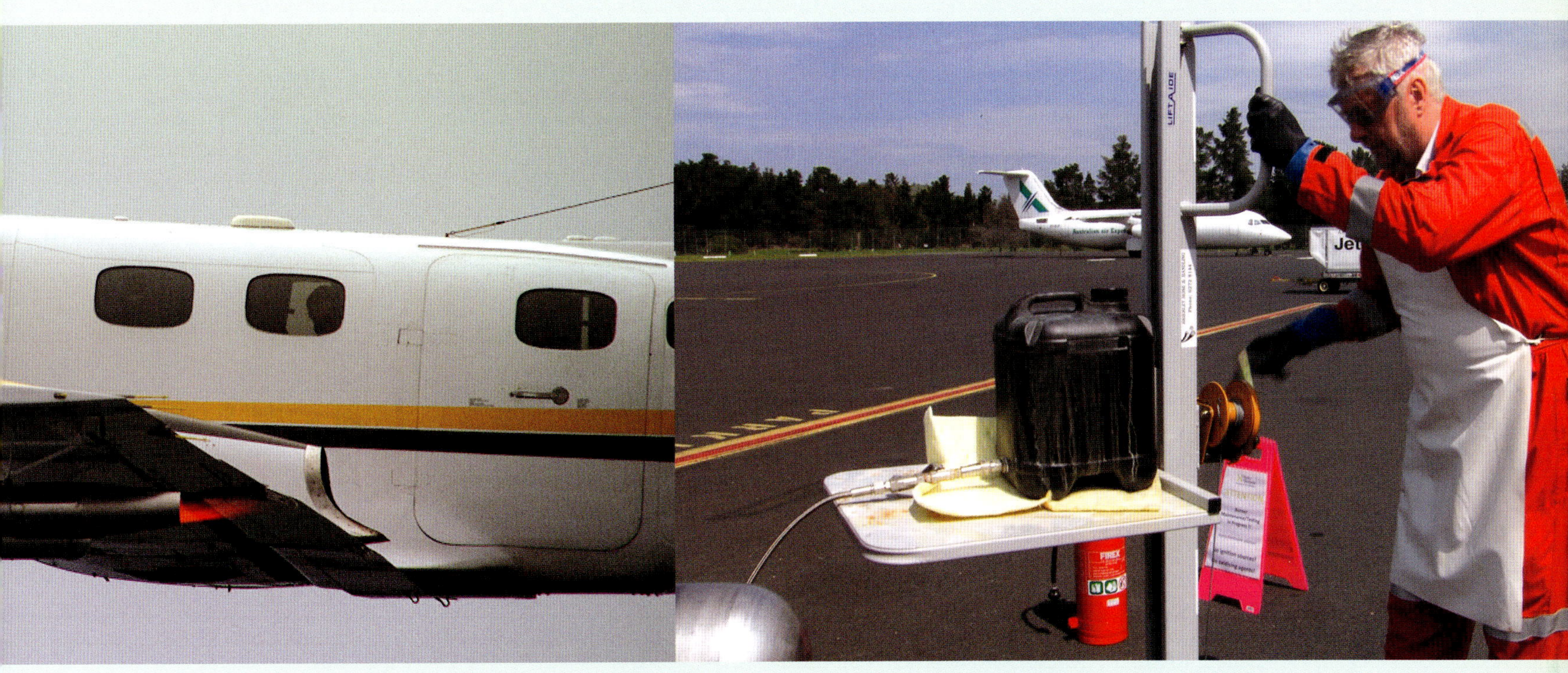

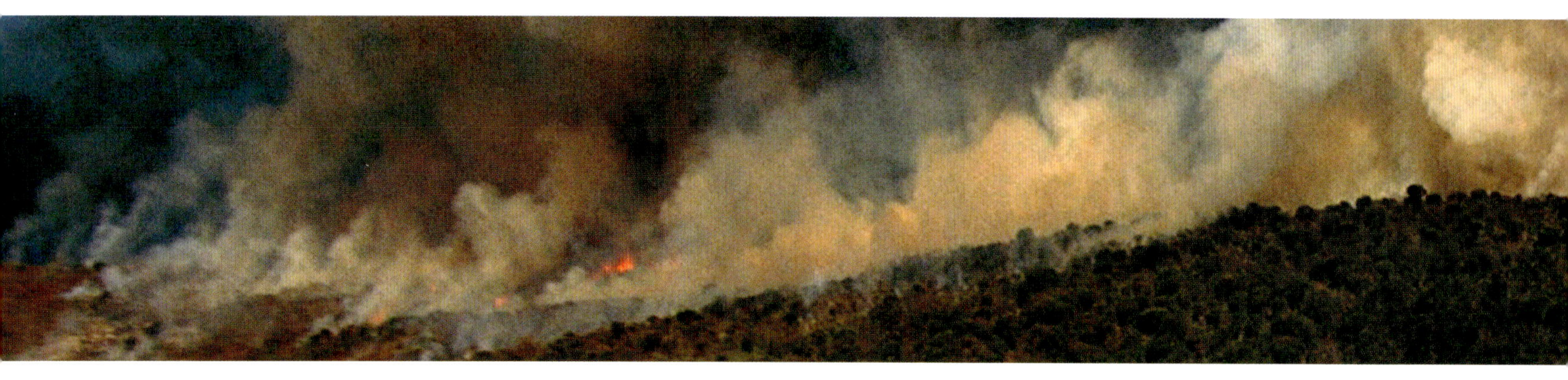

TUG OF WAR

Eternal vigilance, it is said, is the price of freedom. But in Australia – with its cycles of floods, fires and droughts – it is the price of simply getting by. On this magnificent but complicated continent we have a delicate and often uneasy relationship with the natural world. It's true we are inordinately blessed with wondrous treasures. Everywhere around us there are places of quiet refuge – mountains, bush and beaches. Places to which we retreat from the hectic pace of our modern lives and soak up the simplest of pleasures – sheer natural beauty.

But Mother Nature is a cruel mistress. With her looks comes a temperament to match. No corner of our continent is left untouched by the fury she so regularly unleashes. Life in Australia is a constant tug of war. In this country of extreme weather, predatory animals and feral pests wreaking havoc, we find ourselves forever locked in battle. But it's also a battle in which *we* can be the aggressors. We harvest nature for what she is worth; often marching onwards with scant regard for the environment that ultimately sustains our lives.

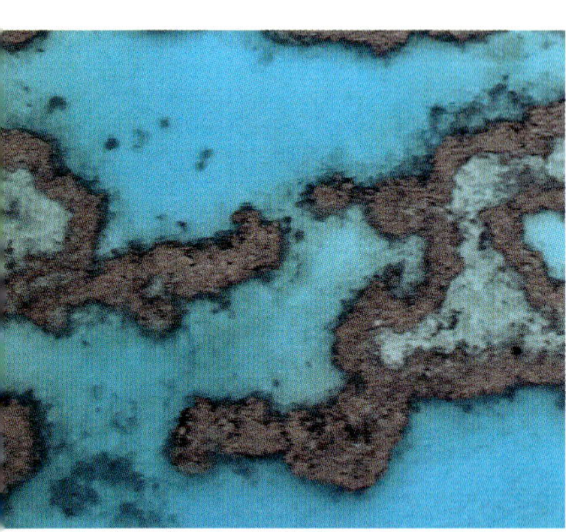

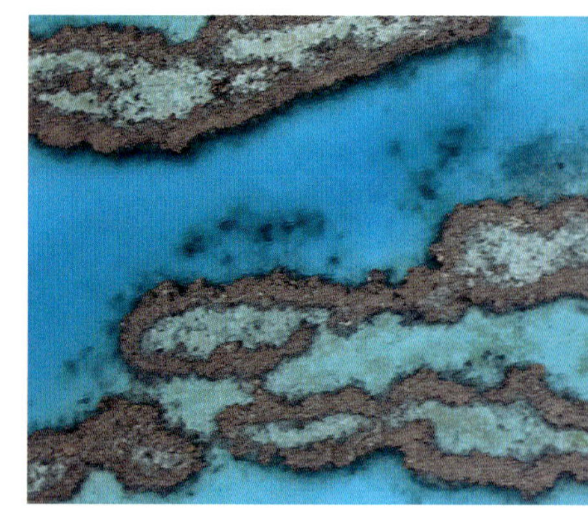

In a country this big, it's only from the air that we can truly see what's at stake. Flying above the land, we start to understand that while we *are* in a tug of war, it's a war that can't, nor should be, won. If we try, it will be at our peril. To survive, we need a sustainable truce, an equilibrium in which we play the cards we are dealt the best we can, while making sure we don't make an already tough situation worse simply for the pursuit of short-term material gain. Getting it right will always be a balancing act.

No one is more aware of that than the men and women on our front lines, those who keep us, and the environment, safe from harm. People such as Rob Laver. As an aerial incendiary supervisor for the South Australian government, Laver spends his days up high in a helicopter, igniting controlled bushfires by setting alight the landscape below him. Being able to take to the skies, he says, relieves pressure on ground crews and is an invaluable tool in the battle with nature.

'One of the greatest challenges in this part of the world is the topography,' says Laver, 'and our only safe access to light a burn like this is using aircraft. It's just not safe to have crews in there while we're doing a burn of this type. We also can provide situation reports back to the operations officer on the ground of what's happening in real time, so they get first-hand intelligence on what the fire is doing.'

Laver's job is to identify areas of high vegetation growth and burn them before nature does it for us with far greater devastation. In Australia, there are more than 50,000 bushfires a year. A small fire now, he says, can prevent a much bigger one in the future. Deep Creek Conservation Park 100 kilometres south of Adelaide, where Laver and his team plan to burn 80 hectares, is a case in point. The park hasn't seen substantial flames since 1983, the same year in which the Ash Wednesday fires blackened 300,000 hectares and killed 75 people. 'Extreme conditions can decimate the whole park,' says Laver, 'and then once it gets out of the park it can threaten assets and life as well, so we want to reduce that.'

Typically, controlled burns like the one at Deep Creek involve Laver dropping burning jellified petrol, or napalm, from a drip torch slung below his helicopter. Ridges are strategically set on fire, causing burns that will ultimately die out without the need to intervene from the ground. 'The fire will be controlled with natural control lines, topography, creek lines and the weather,' says Laver, who also uses computer models to forecast expected fire behaviour. 'There is a lot of science behind it. Relative humidity, fuel moistures – it's all taken into account.'

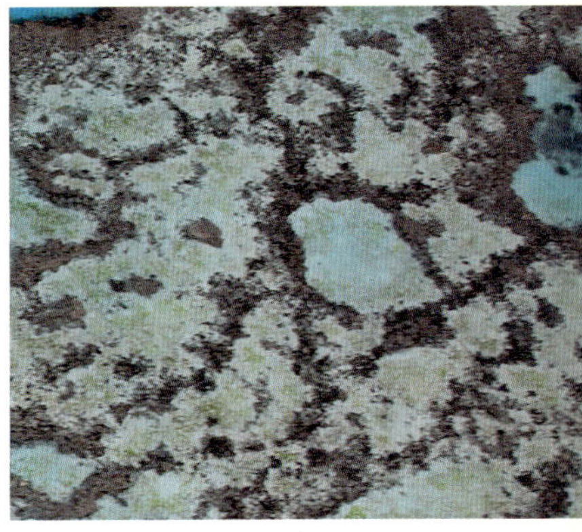

Yet, caution remains. Water bombers are on standby and fire crews are deployed at the edge of any predicted burn should the fire 'escape'.

Laver also stresses it's crucial to have an experienced pilot. 'The pilots are immensely skilful. It's important the pilot knows fire behaviour, and knows how to navigate his way through smoke.' As Laver and his pilot coordinate their efforts there is little margin for error. As soon as Laver pushes the button, the burning jelly falls from the sky and attaches itself to the vegetation, burning it down in a matter of seconds. The irony is despite the dangers bushfires pose, the Australian landscape requires fires to regenerate. Many native species actually need heat and smoke cues to germinate. Or, as Laver puts it, 'A lot of our vegetation encourages fires. It's got a lot of flammability'. Few people will disagree with that.

Following particularly bad fires that swept through New South Wales and the Australian Capital Territory in the early 2000s, the federal government decided a national system was needed to spot and monitor fires early. And to do that, taking to the skies wasn't enough. We needed to take to the heavens. Our major scientific organisations – the CSIRO, Geoscience Australia and the Defence Imagery and

Geospatial Organisation – banded together to devise a system known as Sentinel Hotspots. It's a web-based mapping tool using information drawn from NASA's Earth Observation satellites as they orbit over Australia.

Accessed at any one time, Sentinel Hotspots is likely to show hundreds of active fires raging somewhere on our vast continent. Most are bushfires ignited by lightning strikes. Some fires will have been lit by humans, maliciously by arsonists or for benign reasons by farmers. Seen from space, it's a hot country indeed. To the untrained eye these fires may look random, but mapped out over time, a clear pattern emerges, creating a year in the life of fire.

For instance, shortly after winter we would see small stubble burns lighting up the Murray–Darling Basin. Then, in the tropical north — Cape York, Arnhem Land and the Kimberley — hundreds of small fires herald the start of the dry season. In August, large areas are ablaze in the Red Centre; some are huge infernos half the size of Tasmania. It's only from above that we can appreciate the size of these fires. Unusually wet winters lead to vegetation growth in an otherwise barren outback. From October to December, satellites reveal the fire activity shifts north to the Gulf of Carpentaria region and the Pilbara.

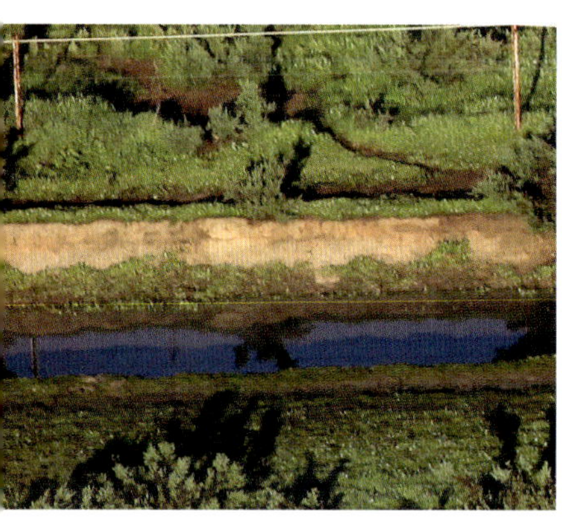

In the Burdekin, pre-harvest cane burns join bushfires in regional Queensland. Heavy rains make for a quiet autumn but in April, stubble burns light up Western Australia's Wheatbelt before the cycle shifts back to the Murray–Darling Basin.

The satellite information is a crucial asset in controlling and predicting the direction of bushfires. But NASA's eyes in the sky orbit Australia just once a day, and that isn't always enough. Some of our cities' crucial infrastructure is surrounded by bush and needs constant monitoring. And to do that, we rely on a group of highly specialised and fearless folk best described as 'smoke jumpers'.

One such team is based near the Nepean Dam on the fringe of Sydney. The smoke jumpers job is to put out spot fires as soon as they've been ignited by summer lightning strikes. The team is there to protect the city's drinking water. Sydney's water storage and supply areas, or catchments, are enveloped by 370,000 hectares of native bushland. The land protects water quality by filtering out pollutants, but it's highly fire prone. If the bush is lost in a blaze, its demise can lead to erosion, exacerbated by the rains that often follow. Run-off then transports ash into the streams and rivers that feed into the dam

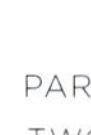

Accessed at any one time, Sentinel Hotspots is likely to show hundreds of active fires raging somewhere on our vast continent. Most are bushfires ignited by lightning strikes. Some fires will have been lit by humans, maliciously by arsonists or for benign reasons by farmers. Seen from space, it's a hot country indeed.

storages, causing algal blooms and cloudiness. And that's bad news for our health.

At a cost of $1 million a year, the Catchment Remote Area Fire Teams, or CRAFT, are on alert. Winched in from helicopters, their firefighters aim to be on the scene within 30 minutes and contain fires to less than 10 hectares. If a seriously bad storm is on the horizon, they may even fly right behind it, jumping out as soon as thunderbolts ignite the ground. During dry summer months, hundreds of fires are kept under control and extinguished in this way.

We live in a boom-or-bust landscape where the might of fire is matched only by the force of floods. When a mighty river such as the Murrumbidgee bursts its banks, the consequences can be intimidating – inundating hundreds of square kilometres of farm and parkland. In the Riverina, the task of park ranger Dave Parker is to help assess flood damage to humans, crops, livestock and native flora and fauna. From his chopper Parker takes in the devastation. It's been ten years since the area has been this wet. Below him, everyone's working hard at keeping the water at bay: houses surrounded by walls of sandbags, stranded cattle, and farmers moving not in tractors but canoes.

'They're certainly close-knit communities,' says Parker. 'From filling up a sandbag to getting to an actual location, everyone gets involved and it's a coordinated effort, everyone draws together.' The floods in southern New South Wales in 2012 saw 2,000 properties cut off and 9,000 people evacuated. Then there's the perished livestock, submerged buildings and lost crops. On average, lost income and repair work caused by floods cost the nation $400 million a year.

But just like the bush needs fire, the plains Parker traverses need flooding. 'These flood events are part of the natural environment,' he says. The countryside thrives on them. The gum trees can barely keep their canopies above water but Parker says they have adapted to their environment. 'These species are Black Box,' he says. 'They don't mind being wet.' The upside for nature is manifold. 'We are seeing southern bell frogs, a threatened species that hasn't been seen for many years. During drought times they get stressed, but as soon as the flood comes they revitalise so quickly.'

And while farmers will see their harvests diminished, there *are* long-term gains for them too. A year and half ago there were major locust outbreaks in this region. Now, the egg beds they left will drown, minimising the chance of yet more swarms destroy crops this season. 'The agricultural systems short term are damaged, but in the long term they may well benefit,' says Parker.

If the floods and fires aren't enough to deal with, our farmers face challenges from elsewhere too. On the edge of Kosciuszko National Park, dog trapper Mick Filtness steers his four-wheel drive slowly over a fire trail. 'The next-door neighbour heard some dogs howling here about two weeks ago,' he says. 'I caught one but another one is still out there.'

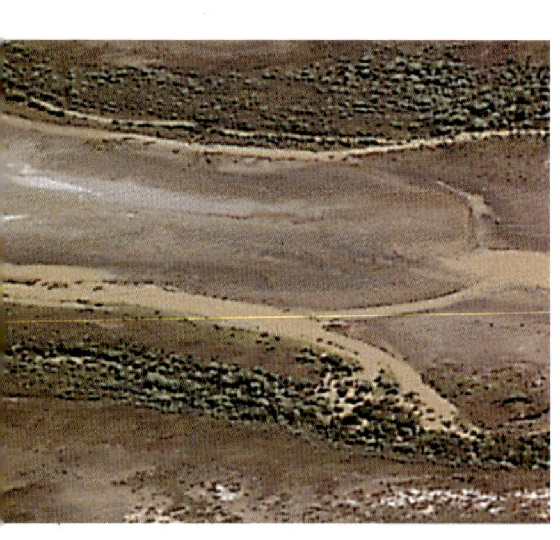

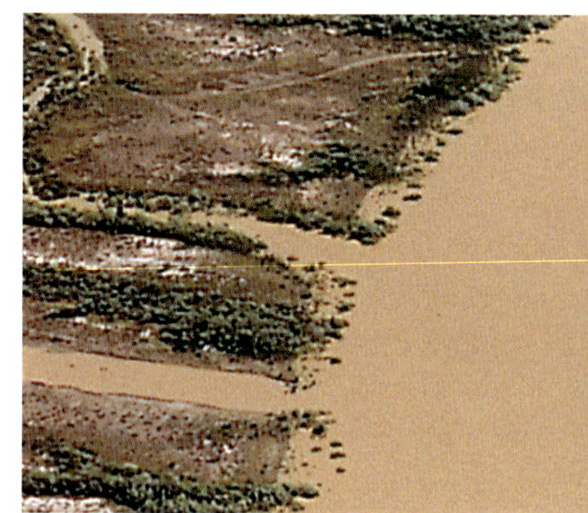

Filtness sets traps to catch troublesome wild dogs – predators known to kill and maim sheep. Some are native dingoes, but most are hybrids – dingoes interbred with domestic dogs. It is estimated the loss of income and replacing sheep killed by wild dogs costs farmers $60 million every year. Catching the perpetrators is a tough proposition. By trapping wild dogs, fitting them with GPS collars and then tracking them via satellites, scientists have established that in the high country, these animals roam from as little as a couple of hundred to more than 10,000 hectares.

It all depends on the availability of prey – wallabies, kangaroos *and* sheep. 'The hybrid can cause a lot of problems,' says Filtness. 'I don't want the landowners to have any stock losses.' To find wild dogs, the trapper runs his *own* dogs – trained to spot signs of their feral compatriots – in front of his car. If one stops and starts scraping the soil, it's time for Filtness to pull over. 'It's a good sign that a wild dog has been around that area within the last week or so,' he says. Then Filtness pulls a trap from the boot and gets to work. 'I push the dirt in and around the trap, so if the dog puts his foot at the edge of the trap it's nice and firm.' Filtness's hope is that the wild dog will be drawn to the smell of the urine around the trap and set it off. While he points out the traps have padded jaws so the animal doesn't suffer unnecessarily, in the end the dog's fate isn't any happier. 'As soon as

I see him,' Filtness says solemnly, 'I just have to put the animal down with a rifle.'

But we aren't always at war with the natural world. Sometimes humans and animals team up to fight common feral foes. Case in point: our major cities are plagued by an invasion of pigeons, turning towers into toilets. It's hard to keep these flying vermin at bay, but bird handler Paul Mander says he's found an environmentally friendly and casualty free solution – a solution that requires the services of another bird, his native wedge-tailed eagle, Soren.

'He was born twelve years ago and he has been raised with my family,' says Mander. 'He's like a third child. Our relationship is very close. He looks menacing but he is a big softie.' On the roof of a fancy Gold Coast hotel, at the heart of what locals call 'the glitter strip', Mander demonstrates Soren's capabilities. His mission is to intimidate and harass the pigeons that have taken up residency. When Mander releases Soren from his arm, the raptor takes to the skies with an imposing wingspan of 2.5 metres. 'Pigeons have a built-in, innate response towards birds of prey. They won't stick around and get to know them.'

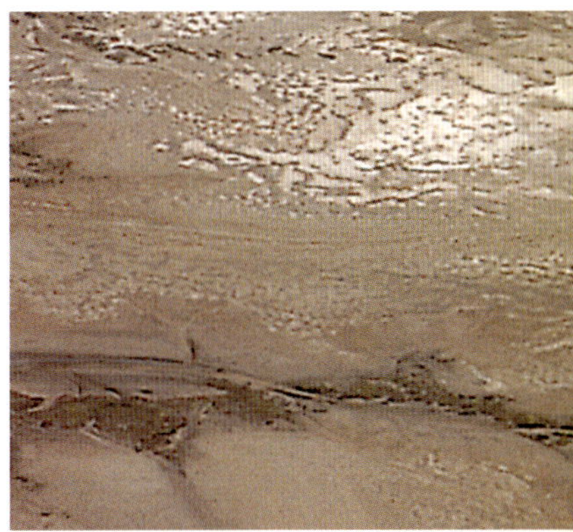

It's a matter of shock and awe. Soren soars through the air at up to 100 kilometres an hour. The pigeons disperse with little desire to further test this native jetfighter's capacities. Normally, it takes Paul and Soren about two days to evict flying ferals from a building. The problem is that, while the pigeons are successfully chased away, they will come back eventually or cause trouble elsewhere. Despite our best intentions and myriad approaches, no major feral species has been wiped out in Australia. Camels, cane toads, pigs, horses, rabbits, foxes, cats, water buffalo, deer – the list is long – are all here for the time being.

As these destructive pests live on, so does the debate on how to manage *them* and other, more fearsome, creatures. For it isn't always a love affair with our native species either, especially when our paths cross in water. Humans might be at the top of the food chain on land, but in the ocean we meet our match. It's a battle for supremacy that we sometimes lose. Shark attacks make regular headlines and terrify us. The fear, statistically at least, is also somewhat irrational. In the past half century there's been an average of one fatality a year. But each one *is* a tragedy and, indeed, enough to send us to the skies for protection.

Around the country there are half a dozen shark patrols – men and women flying in small, slow aeroplanes, spotting sharks from the air. Pilot Nick Skewes is a spotter for the South Australian government. From his superb high-vantage point, Nick's job is to alert the swimmers of Adelaide's beaches if a shark is in the vicinity. The plane is equipped with a very noisy alarm system – a good thing in this case. Skewes spots about a hundred sharks a year in Gulf St Vincent, much to the relief of the otherwise unsuspecting holiday-makers in the waters below him.

Swimmers jumping off jetties are of particular concern to Skewes, but it's not they who are increasing the sharks' curiosity. 'A lot of people fish off the jetty,' Skewes says. 'We have seen sharks sitting at the end; it's a prime place.' Spotter planes are a tried and true warning system, but their effectiveness depends on resources and the availability of aircraft and staff. Scientists, though, are now working on ways for sharks *themselves* to tell us when they are near.

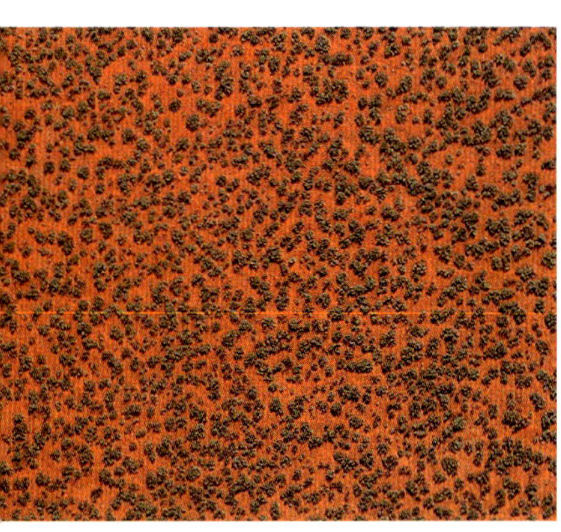

And that, too, involves a bit of fishing. It's not unusual for ecologist Charlie Huveneers to find himself on a boat in Gulf St Vincent at 2am, pulling sharks from the ocean. Every successful catch is followed by Huveneers surgically inserting an acoustic tag, while keeping the shark alive by running water through its gills with a hose.

'We really want to try to get a better estimate of the proportion of the sharks tagged here that go to the metropolitan region, up and down Adelaide,' says Huveneers, 'and how much time they spend in this area.' And so Huveneers tags as many sharks as possible, more than 100 so far. 'The tag transmits a little pulse every two to three minutes,' he explains, 'with the pulse having within its coding the actual ID of individual tags.' Listening stations, or receivers, are dotted around the Gulf. They pick up a shark's signal if it comes within 500 metres – data that Huveneers uses to examine the shark's migratory movements.

The clever twist, though, is the beacons can also be equipped to send an email alerting nearby lifeguards. Hundreds of such beacons are already deployed around the coastline, waiting to be enlisted. Tracking every shark is clearly impossible, but understanding the behavioural patterns of the ones that *are* tagged may help save lives.

Technology is always changing our dealings with the natural world. It helps us to prepare for the extremities of our weather and informs our interaction with pests and predators. Now, it also helps us unlock Earth's hidden treasures.

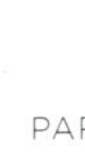

Despite our best intentions and myriad approaches, no major feral species has been wiped out in Australia. Camels, cane toads, pigs, horses, rabbits, foxes, cats, water buffalo, deer — the list is long — are all here for the time being.

In the Outback, a skirmish between humans and nature is about to play out in a hot and hostile landscape. The spoils in this veritable game of hide-and-seek for big boys are untold riches. The mining industry contributes $120 billion to the Australian economy annually. We're the world's largest producer of iron ore and the third largest producer of gold, uranium, zinc and coal. Prospecting these resources is no easy task. Mother Nature has hidden them well, often in faraway, inhospitable locations. But technology and wings are turning the odds in our favour.

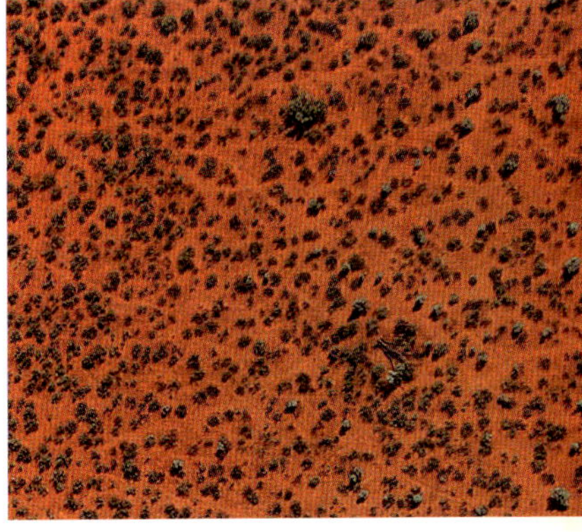

Near Uluru, Carel Lubbe is rising to the challenge – taking to the skies in a converted Second World War transporter plane. Lubbe calls it *Pinocchio*, and it does look rather peculiar: a long nose, extended tail, and cables wired all around its extremities. The real name of this flying Hills Hoist is an airborne electromagnetic surveying system. And despite its advanced age, the aircraft is anything but old-fashioned, jam-packed with hi-tech gadgets that effectively turn it into an enormous flying metal detector.

Its mission is to scour the land for minerals; precious metals such as gold, silver or nickel. 'One of the areas that really hasn't been prospected is the outback of Australia,' says Lubbe, who is the system's operator. 'Most of the mining companies have found quite a good potential of base metals out there.' These companies pay the plane's owners handsome money to act fast and efficiently. A typical prospecting flight will set you back $75,000, but it does in weeks what would have taken years on the ground.

In the back of the plane are the controls for two 'birds' – million dollar receivers that drag behind the aircraft. To do the job properly, the aircraft must drop to an altitude of just 100 metres and fly a grid pattern. The DC-3 sends electromagnetic signals half a kilometre below the earth's surface. If there is anything metallic, it will be detected by the birds. In the cabin, pilot Lee Szick is locked in battle with the elements, trying hard to stay on course.

'If you think about it,' says Szick, 'you are trying to keep 13 tonnes within six metres. You have the wind against you and the sun in your eyes. Most guys only get to an hour and then they start to tire.' As Szick struggles on, printouts rattle out of Lubbe's computer. The data needs to be analysed by geophysicists back at base, but the flight may well have been worth the effort. 'There is definitely something reacting underneath the ground and that is exactly what our clients want. So this is a good area to go prospecting on,' says Lubbe. If he is right, it won't be long before the next mining pit opens up.

Of all the feats allowing us to carve not just pits but a life in the harsh lands, one outshines all – the Goldfields Pipeline. Built more than a century ago and completed in 1903, it is the longest freshwater pipe in the world, stretching 560 kilometres from Perth to the arid goldfields of Kalgoorlie. A structure this big can only be properly appreciated from the air. 'The pipeline is a central part of people's lives,' says Anne Brake from the National Trust. 'It follows the railway and road. When it disappears and comes back again, it's like an old friend coming back and travelling with them down the highway.'

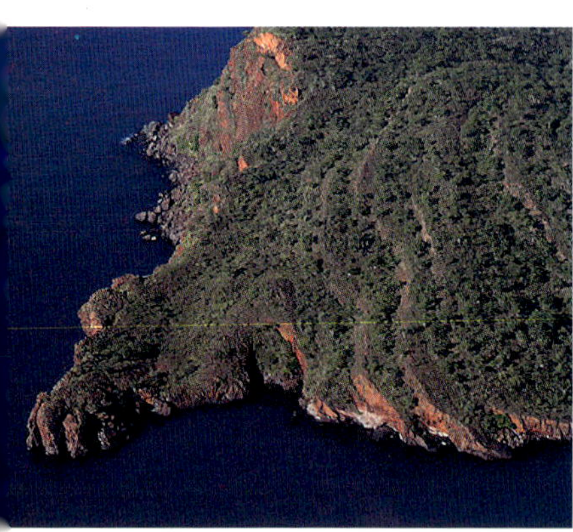

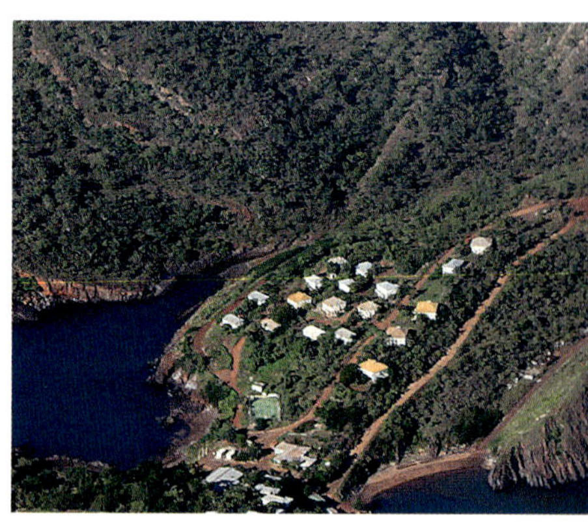

Engineer Rod Higgins has an even more intimate relationship with the pipeline. Rod and his team don't travel *alongside* it but *inside* the pipeline. It's up to Higgins' crew to rejuvenate the aging centenarian by relining its inner wall. 'People are a little bit astounded to hear that we actually go inside the pipe to do the repairs,' Higgins says. 'We are totally replacing the existing with a new, complete inside concrete lining that is sprayed on by the lining vehicles.'

The term 'lining vehicles' make the wheelie contraptions sound a lot bigger then they are. The workers lie down on a tiny self-propelled trolley, which carries wet cement and a sprayer. This is not a job for the faint-hearted or claustrophobic. After a temporary bypass is built to ensure water flow, the men enter the pipe with only a few centimetres' clearance. And with 15 kilometres to cover in 15 months, Rod's team will spend an awful lot of time in the dark. But they are proud of their work and have a strong incentive. 'We just haven't got any other water options up at this end,' says Higgins. 'This pipeline is absolutely critical. This is the lifeline to the goldfields. A lot of people might not realise it, but without the pipeline they just wouldn't be here.'

Bringing water to the desert is a benign victory over nature; if the pipe spills, it leaks water – in the desert there will be few complaints.

But elsewhere in Australia, to keep our economy satisfied, we often take very big environmental risks. Striking the balance in *that* tug of war – economy versus environment – can sometimes fall on the shoulders of just one person.

In a chopper high above the Great Barrier Reef, John Foley is on his way to work – and about to prevent a potential disaster. Foley is a reef pilot. His job is stopping large coal carriers from destroying the precious and fragile world beneath him. 'Someone once said that war is 90 per cent boredom and 10 per cent sheer terror,' says Foley as his chopper lands on *Mega Ocean*, the ship he is about to guide. 'We have to be spot-on with every aspect of our pilotage to make sure the ship stays in safe waters.'

Mega Ocean, a bulk ore carrier, is heading for Hay Point in Queensland, one of the world's largest coal ports. John's task is to shepherd the vessel through a short cut in the reef called Hydrographers Passage. It saves shipping companies almost 500 kilometres and therefore millions of dollars in fuel and wages. But the 220-kilometre passage, charted by the navy in 1981, is narrow – at times just one kilometre wide. That may sound a long way but steering a giant steel ship in strong currents and bad weather tests the nerves. The *Mega Ocean*, for example, can carry 80,000 tonnes of coal, steam at 35 kilometres an hour and is 300 metres long; it takes five kilometres for the behemoth to come to a halt.

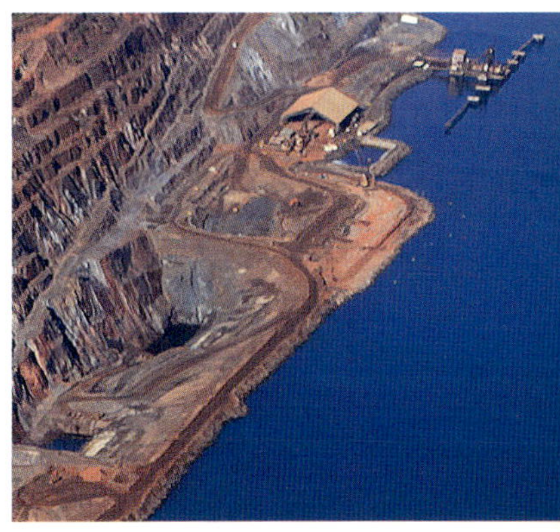

On jobs like this, Foley will draw on everything he's learned in his 27 years as a reef pilot. A single error can lead to ruptured tanks and an oil spill, threatening the world's largest living organism and the thousands of species it harbours – as well as Australia's environmental reputation. 'It can still happen,' says Foley. 'Something goes wrong. Somebody is not paying attention or there is equipment failure, and ships go aground. As far as my role is concerned, I think the best way to describe it is as a guardian of the reef. We are here to guard the reef.'

On North Stradbroke Island, just off Brisbane, another group of marine guards reports for duty. But their mission is conducted in secret and under cover of night. Australia's fishing zone stretches 370 kilometres out to sea. The zone is bigger than our landmass and the seafood it produces is worth $2 billion a year – making it a drawcard for illegal fishermen: foreigners and Australians alike. The men at North Stradbroke Island have access to cutting-edge technology to help combat the illicit harvesting of our waters – gadgets developed for military battlefields but now making their way into civilian law enforcement.

Most people would call these new weapons drones, but in military circles they are referred to as unmanned aerial vehicles. This one is just over a metre long with a wingspan three times that length. In Australia, drones don't carry bombs but a sophisticated set of infrared cameras. Pilot Nigel Meadows oversees the trial at the request of Queensland Boating and Fisheries Patrol. It's a unique collaboration – for the first time, a remotely operated plane will fly into controlled civilian airspace. Big Brother has landed a business-class seat.

'We don't need a runway, we don't need airfields to operate and launch from,' says Meadows. 'We have a caravan-like device that we operate the aircraft from, and that can travel anywhere in Australia.' Compressed air is used to launch the unmanned aeroplane, which beams back images to the mobile control centre on the beach almost as soon as it has taken off. From 1,500 metres up, it's a pretty good view.

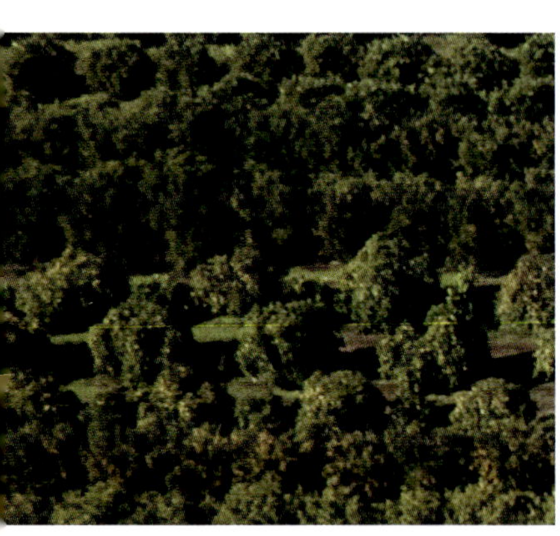

'We can see from a fairly reasonable distance somebody who's smoking a cigarette,' says Meadows. 'And we can see them throw that cigarette on the ground or into the water.' The screens show a trawler north of the command centre, heading east at two or three knots, trawling as it pushes along. As the spy in the sky focuses its image, the trawler's nets are just being put back in the water.

With nothing untoward taking place, the drone continues to drift through the night – the tug of war for the oceans' riches covertly controlled from the skies. Defending the world's third largest fishing zone is serious business. Fishermen caught in regional waters controlled by the states are subject to fines. But foreign trawlers caught further afield face the full wrath: their owners deported and the boats burned. These measures seem extreme, but the authorities say they need to send a signal that there are lines that cannot be crossed.

It's a difficult balance to strike – the natural world needs to be protected from our excesses. It's hard to argue that unfettered plundering and abuse of our most precious resources will not lead to catastrophic consequences. At the same time, we have an economy to run. Twenty-three million Australians depend on its health. The challenge is to find solutions that aren't mutually exclusive.

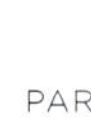

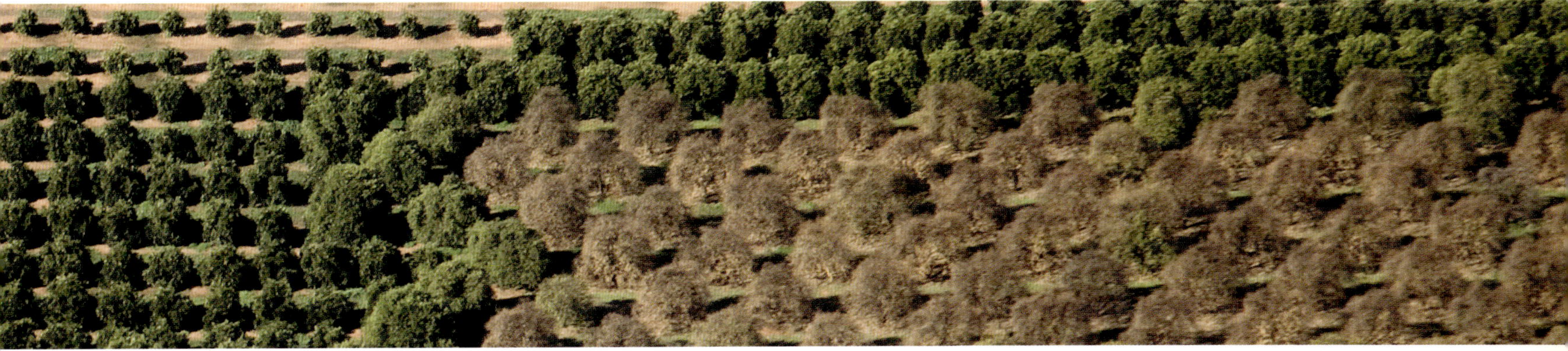

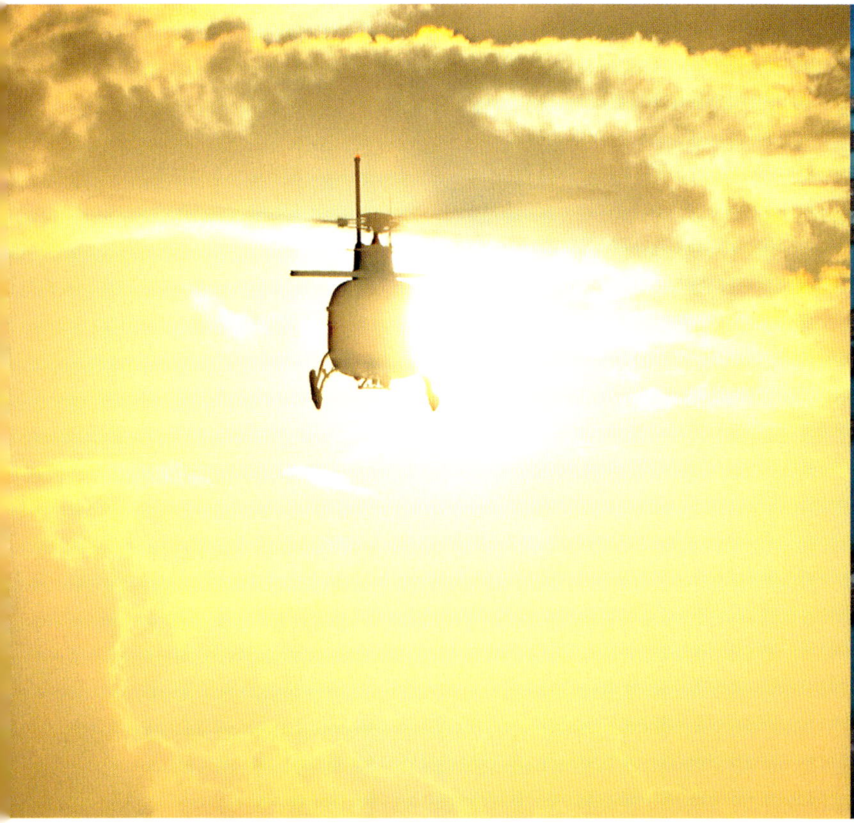

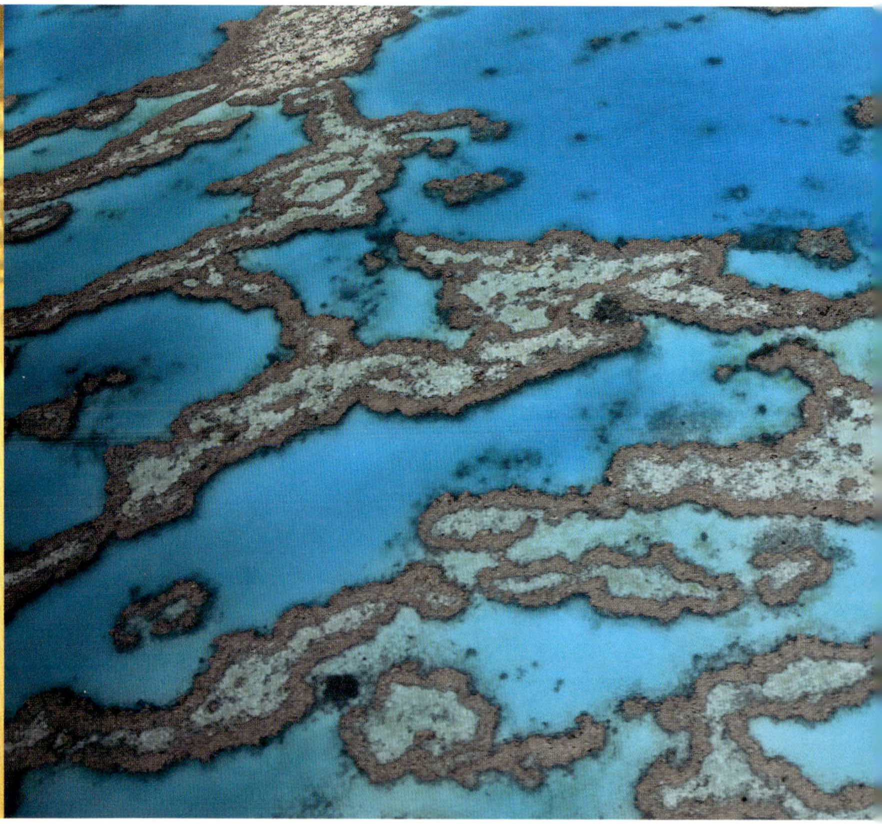

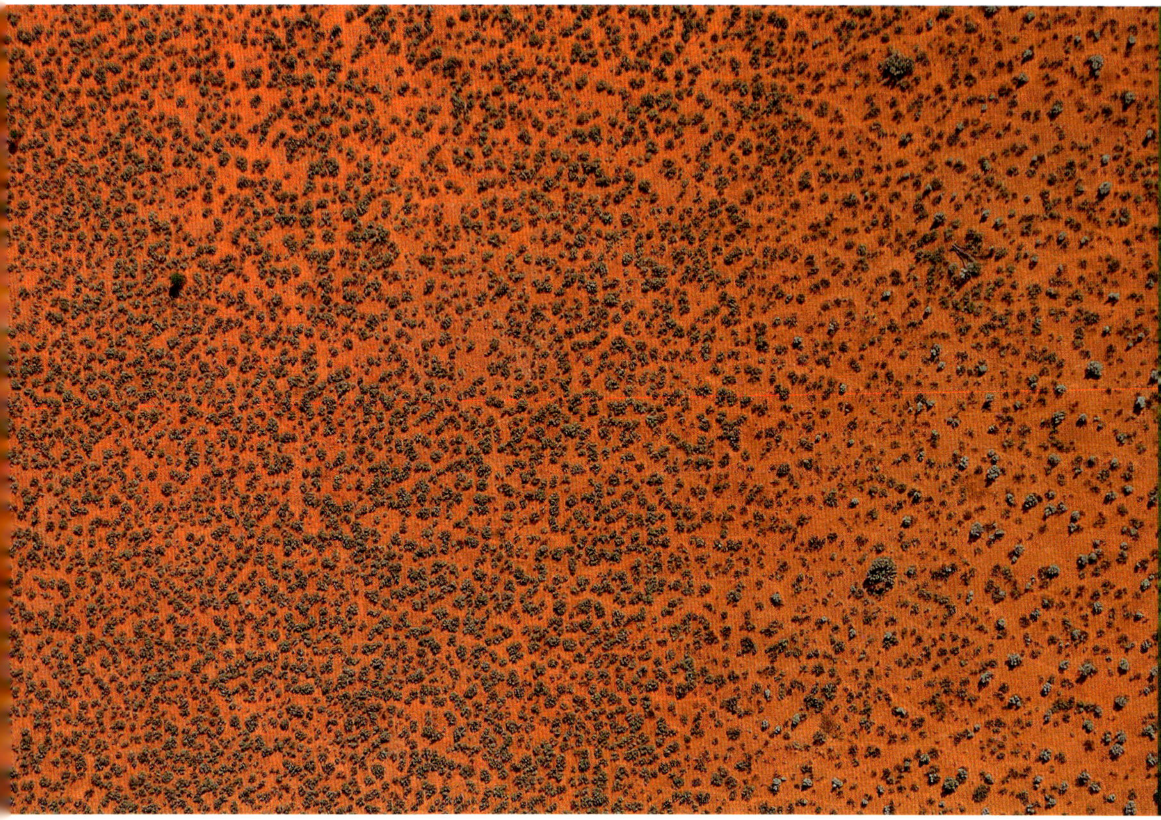

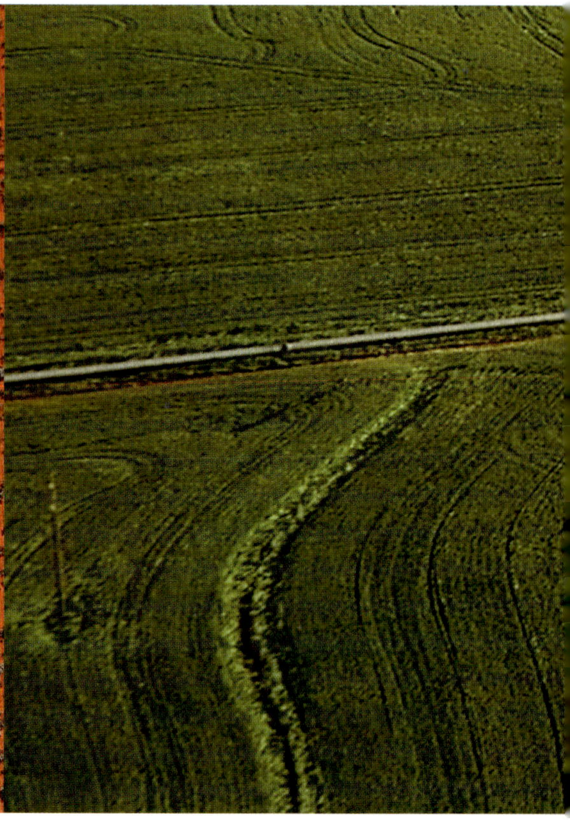

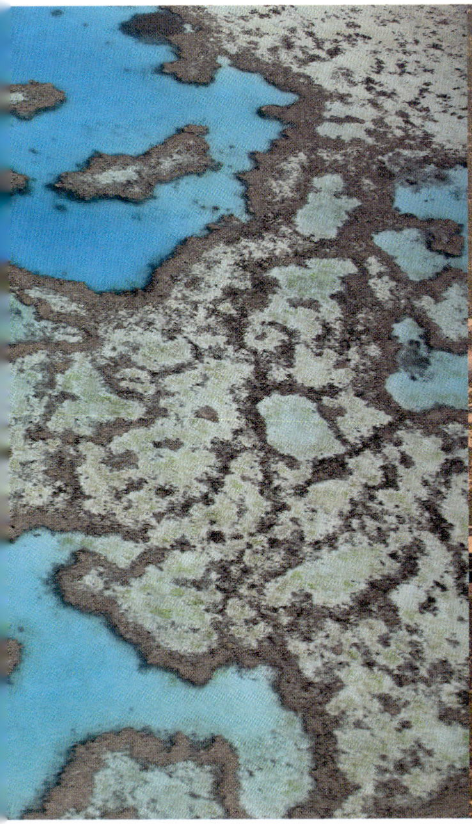

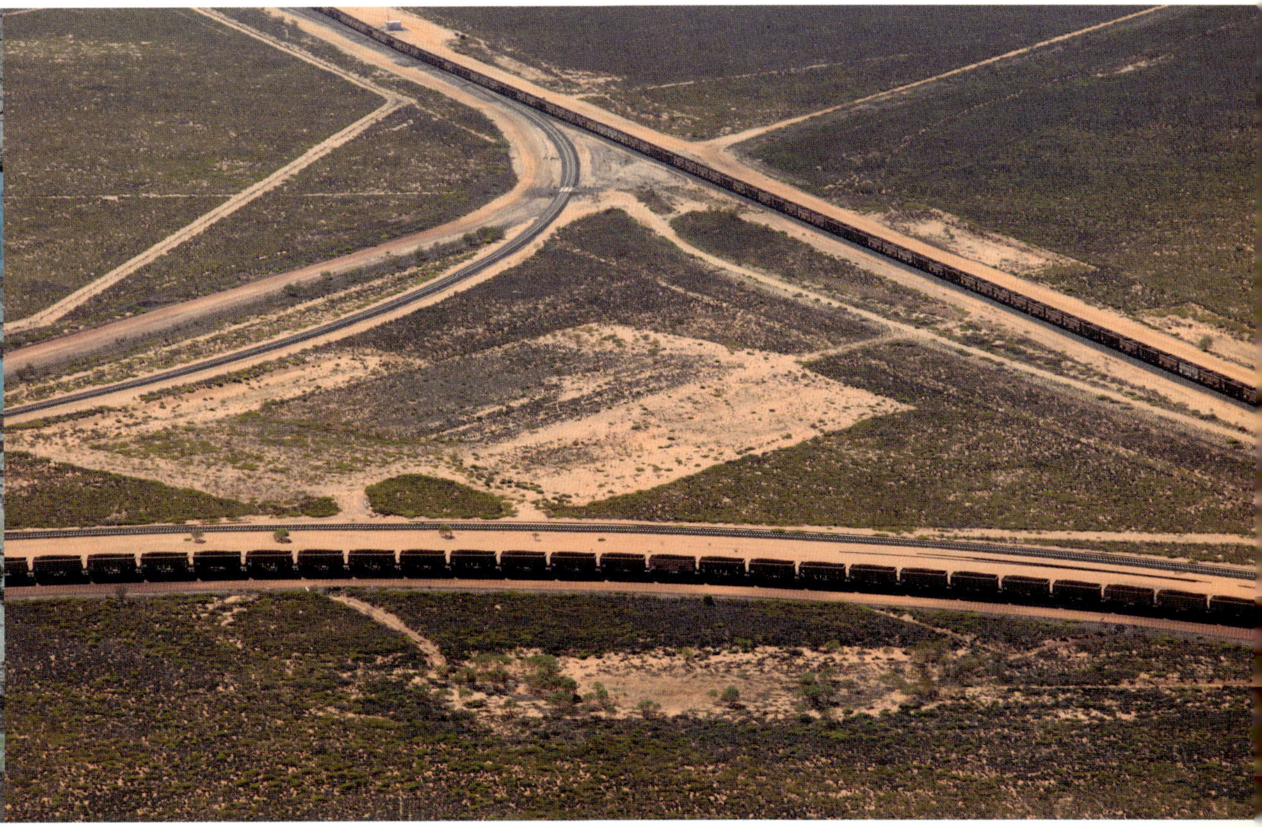

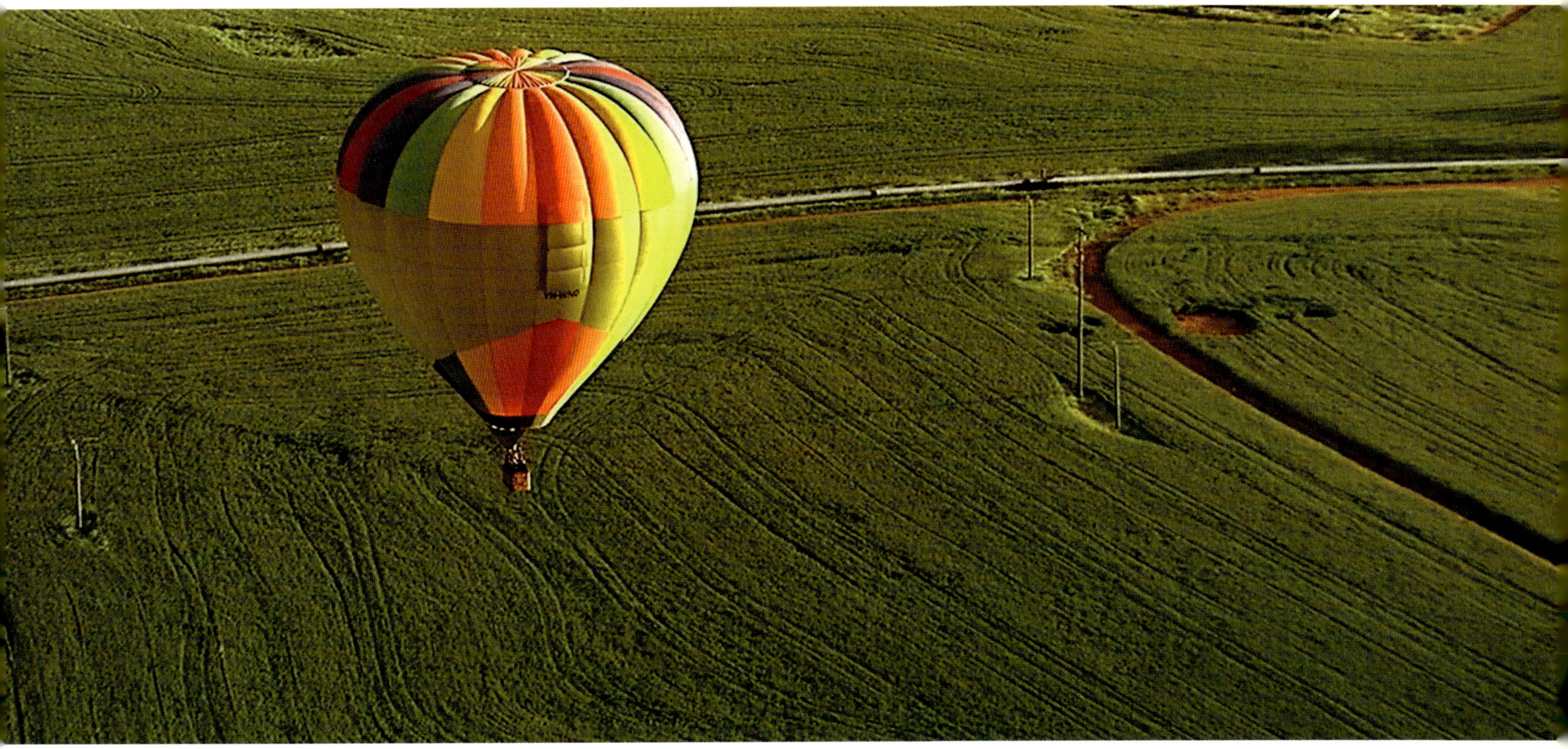

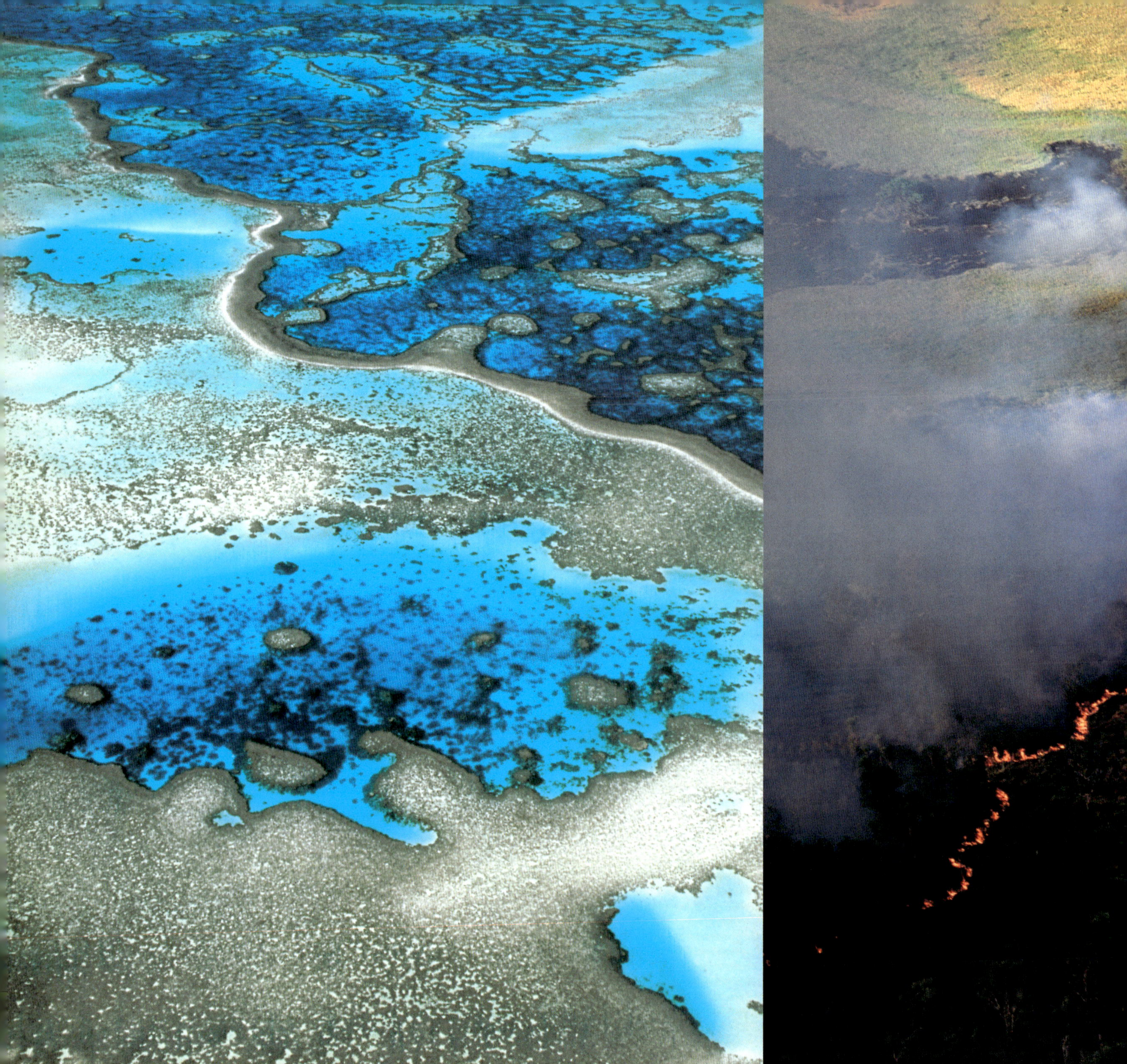

LEFT: The Great Barrier Reef near Gladstone, Queensland. Comprised of over 2,500 individual reefs, this UNESCO World Heritage site is home to 400 coral species, 1,500 fish species and 4,000 types of invertebrates. It covers an area of 348,000 square kilometres. **MIDDLE:** A controlled burn of bushland in Jabiru, Northern Territory. Such grass burns take place early in the dry season to prevent later fires consuming huge areas, making sure local communities and infrastructure are

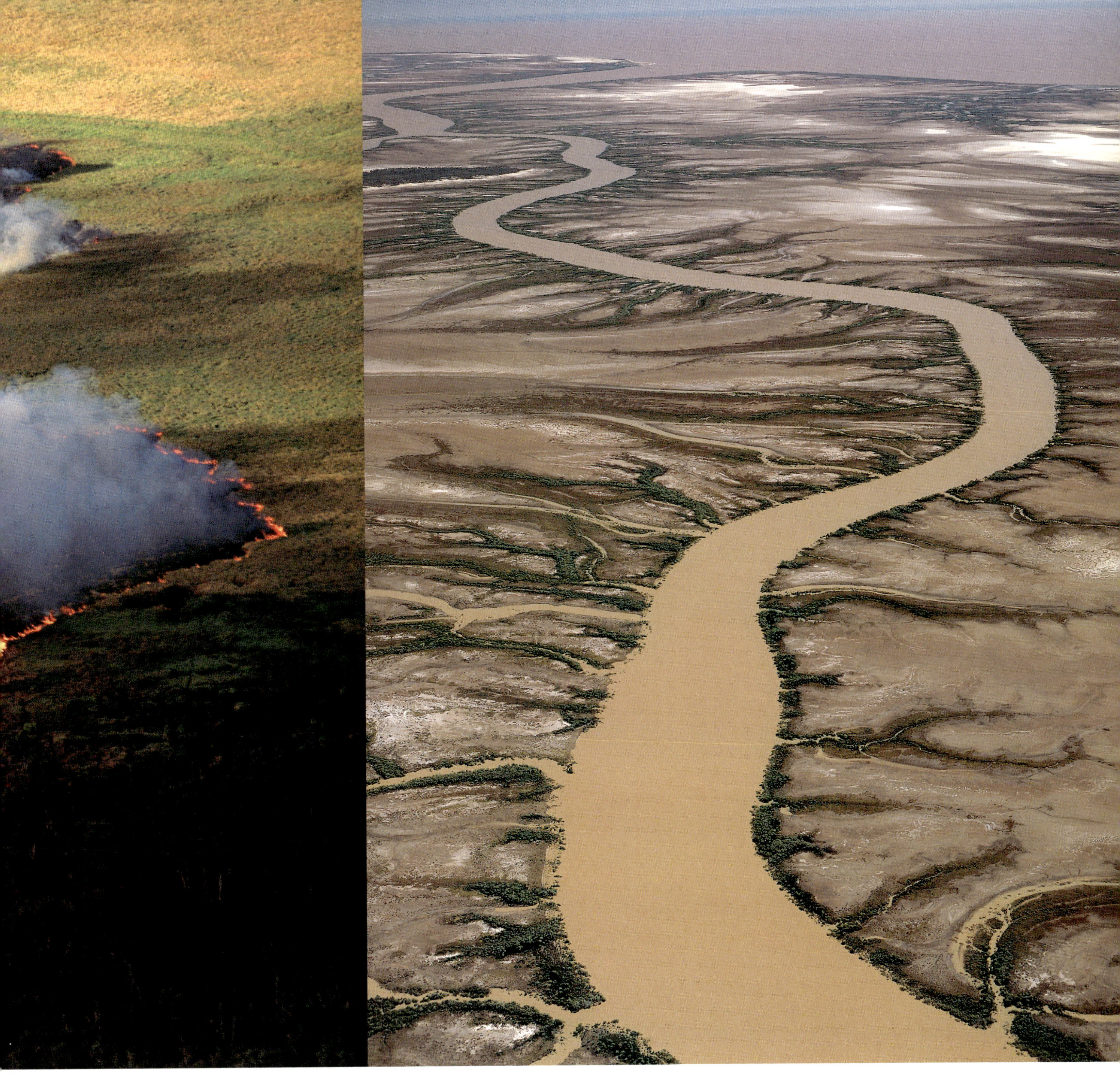

protected. Local Indigenous groups are involved with fire management and maintain some of their traditional fire uses such as burn-assisted hunting. **RIGHT:** The flood plains of the Victoria River, Northern Territory. Seasonally swollen by the 'big wet', the river starts on Riveren Station and winds over 700 kilometres through grasslands, savannahs and spinifex country. Its mouth, at the Joseph Bonaparte Gulf, is 10 kilometres wide and characterised by mangroves and mud plains.

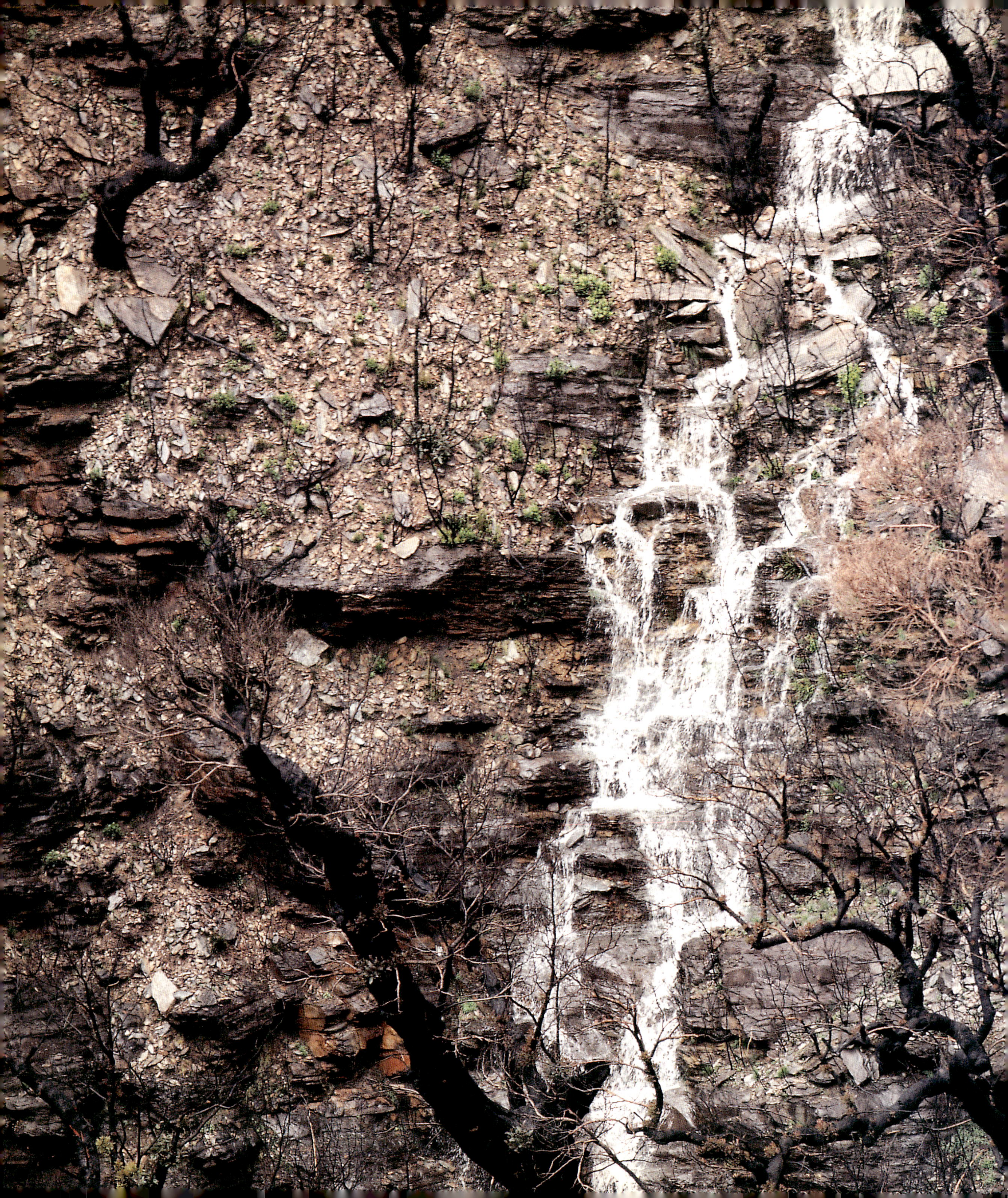

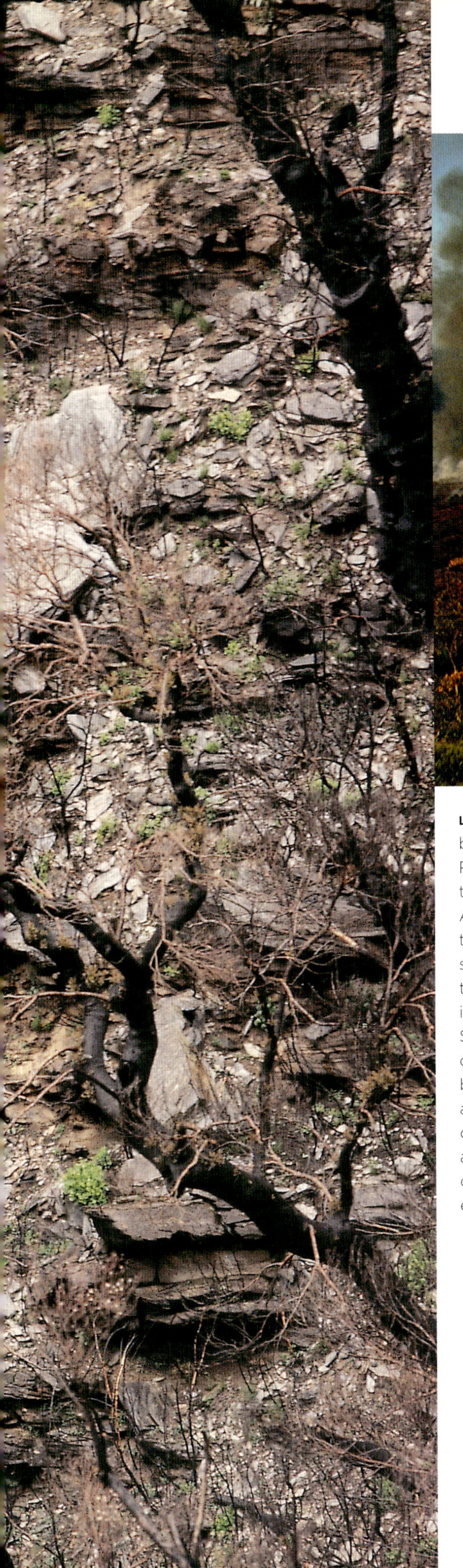

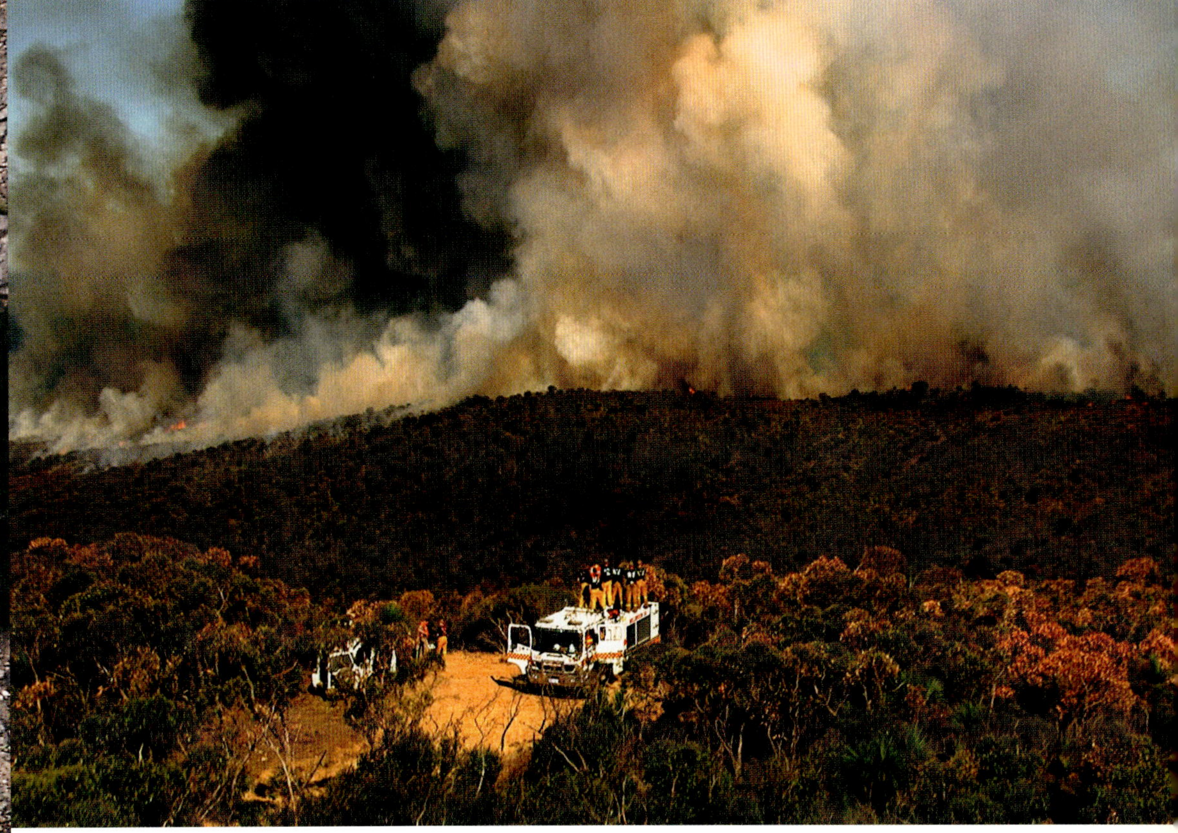

LEFT: A waterfall runs through burned bush in the Stirling Ranges, Western Australia. Despite the danger bushfires pose, the Australian landscape needs fire to regenerate — some native species even use fire and smoke to germinate. **RIGHT:** Firefighters in Deep Creek Conservation Park, South Australia, stand guard as a controlled burn takes place. The burn is to minimise the fuel load and prevent a much bigger fire later on. The fire has been lit from the air, using a helicopter. The ground crew has to ensure the fire doesn't escape its planned boundaries.

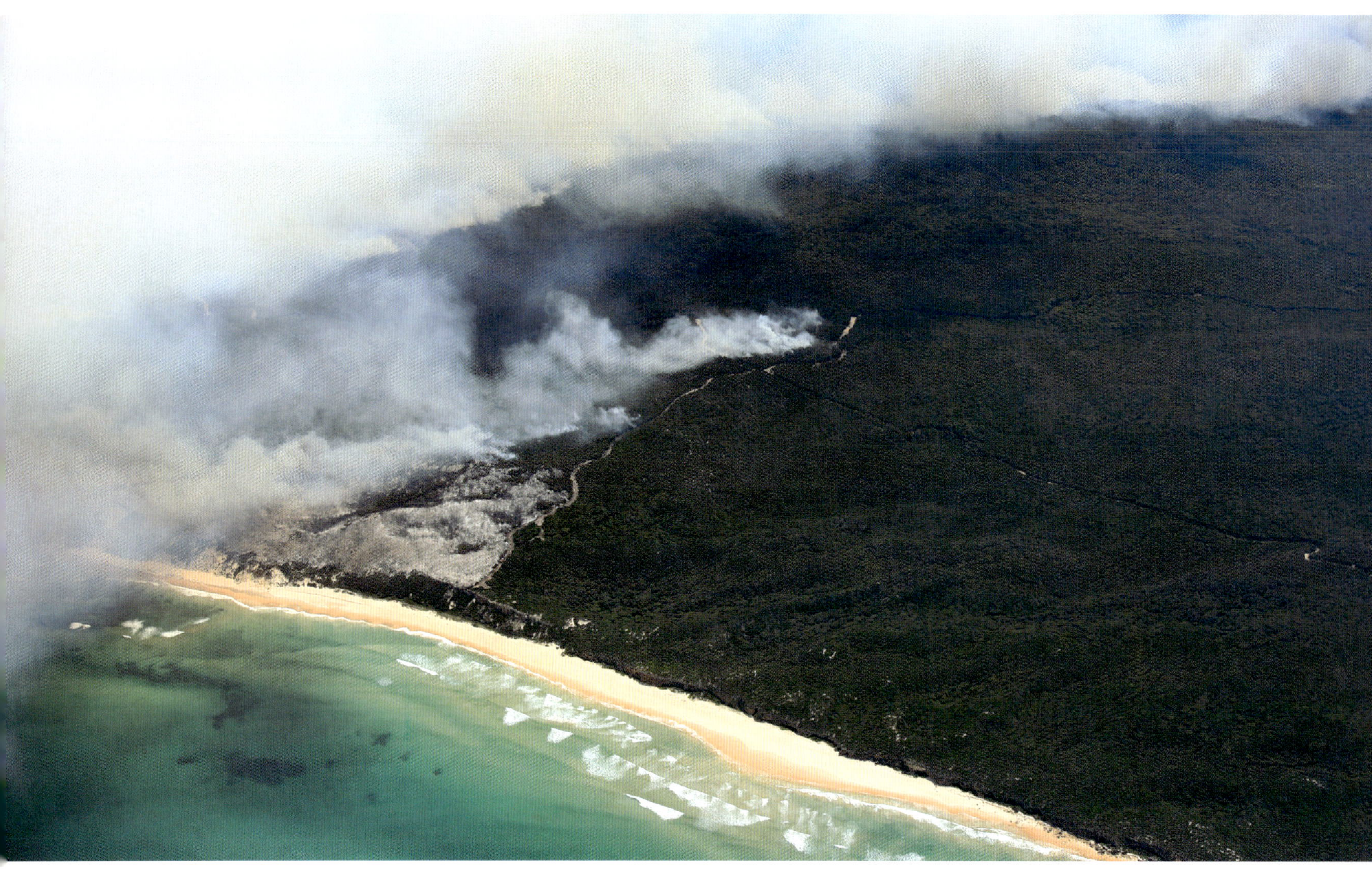

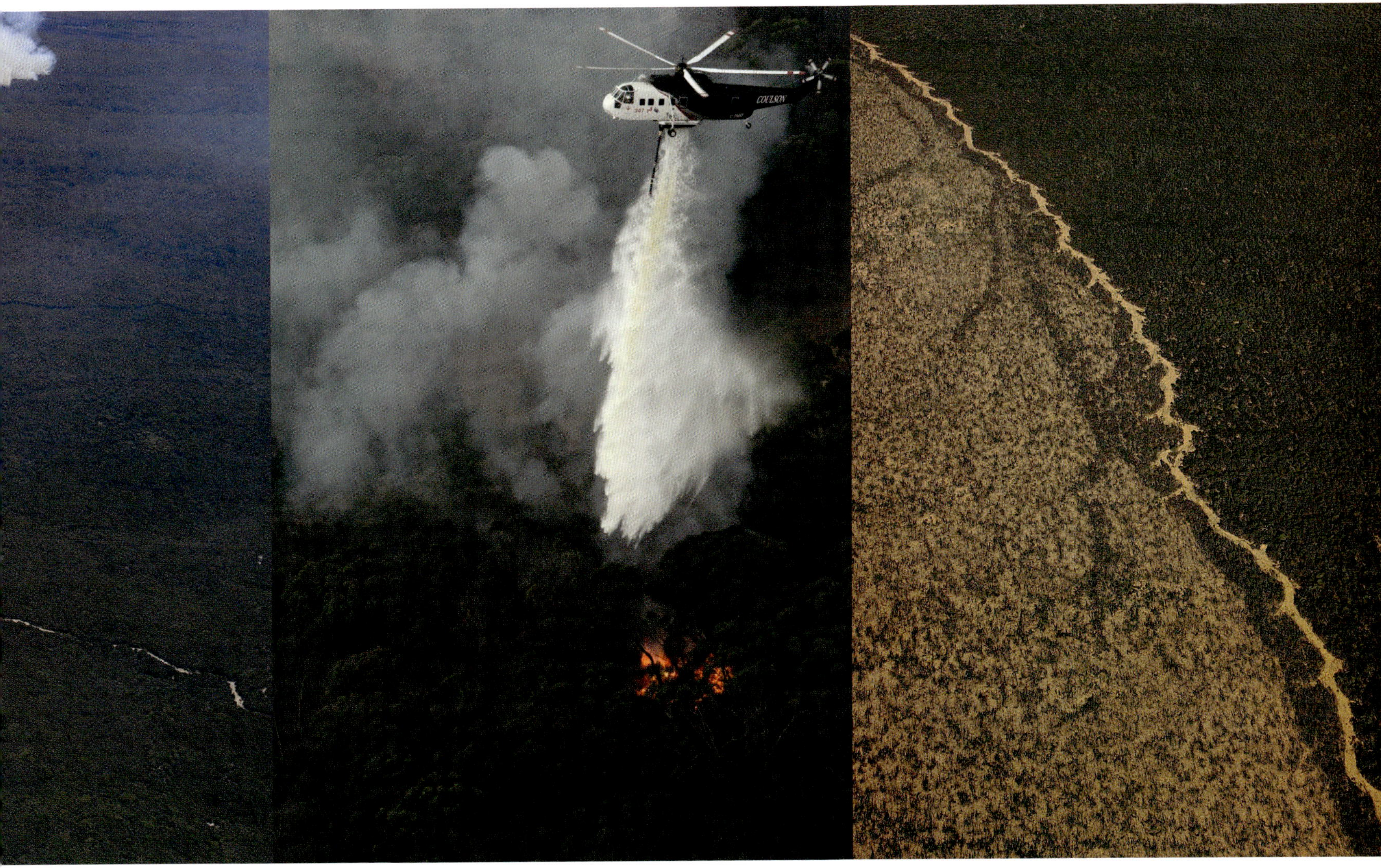

LEFT: A bushfire eats its way through the landscape near Walpole, Western Australia, on the edge of the Great Australian Bight. Annually, there are more than 50,000 bushfires in Australia. **MIDDLE:** A Sikorsky S-61N water-bombing helicopter is deployed to douse flames in the aftermath of Victoria's Black Saturday fires in the area between Kilmore and Flowerdale. The fires killed 173 people and destroyed more than 2,000 houses. **RIGHT:** A line of scrub has been cleared by bulldozers to create a firebreak north of the highway between Kalgoorlie and Coolgardie, Western Australia. A fire raged on the left side of the control line but, deprived of fuel, was unable to spread to the right.

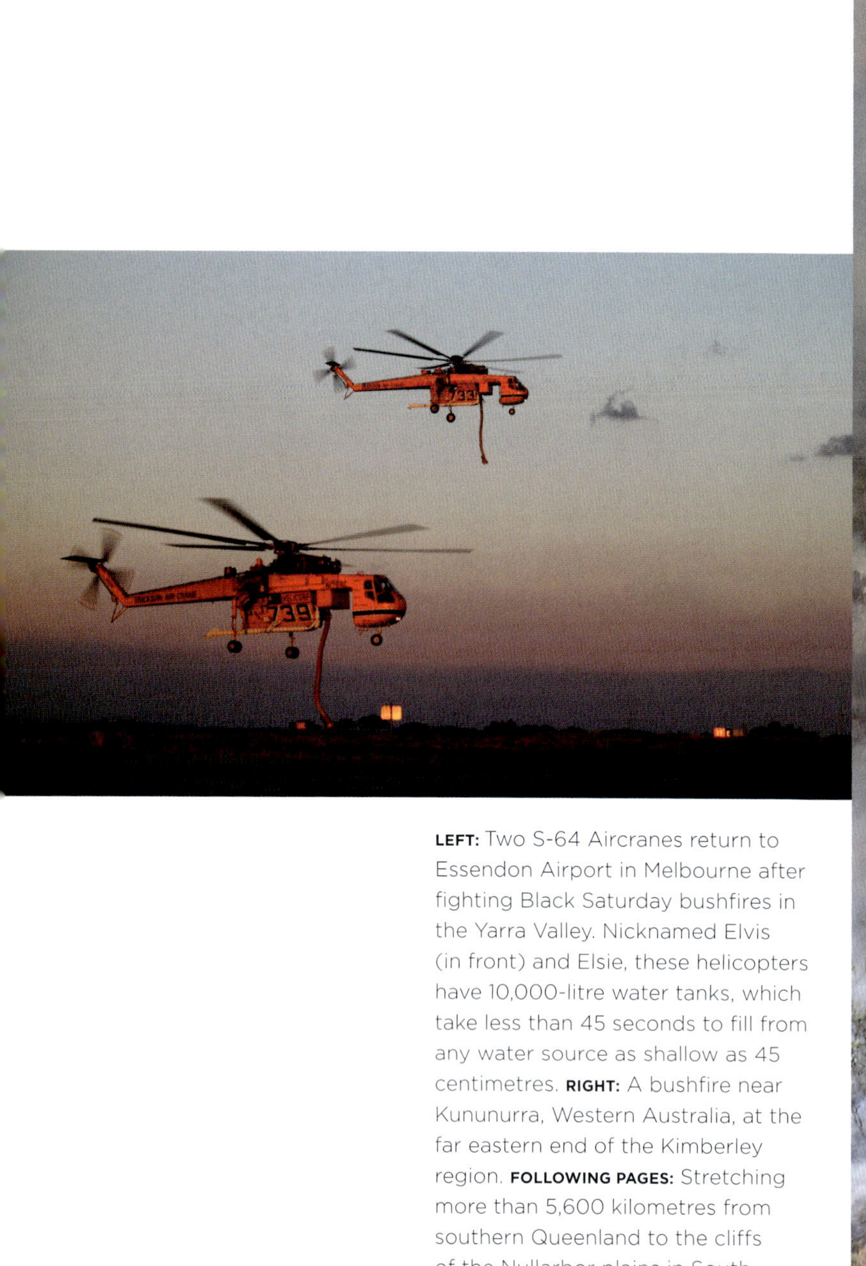

LEFT: Two S-64 Aircranes return to Essendon Airport in Melbourne after fighting Black Saturday bushfires in the Yarra Valley. Nicknamed Elvis (in front) and Elsie, these helicopters have 10,000-litre water tanks, which take less than 45 seconds to fill from any water source as shallow as 45 centimetres. **RIGHT:** A bushfire near Kununurra, Western Australia, at the far eastern end of the Kimberley region. **FOLLOWING PAGES:** Stretching more than 5,600 kilometres from southern Queensland to the cliffs of the Nullarbor plains in South Australia, the dingo fence is the world's longest man-made structure. Built in the 1880s to keep dingos from killing sheep and cattle, the fence protects properties the size of small European countries. Several parts have been electrified to keep feral camels at bay.

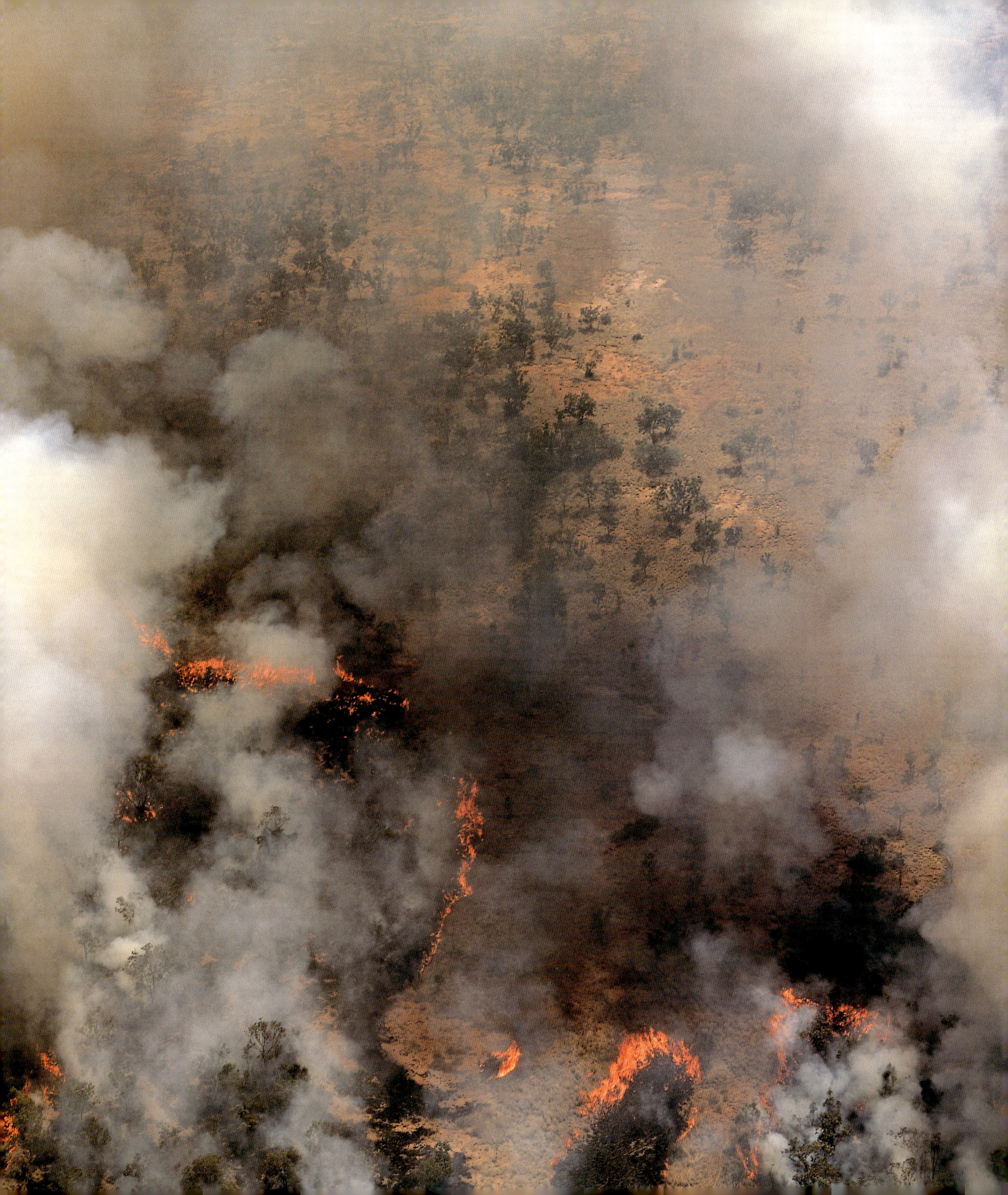

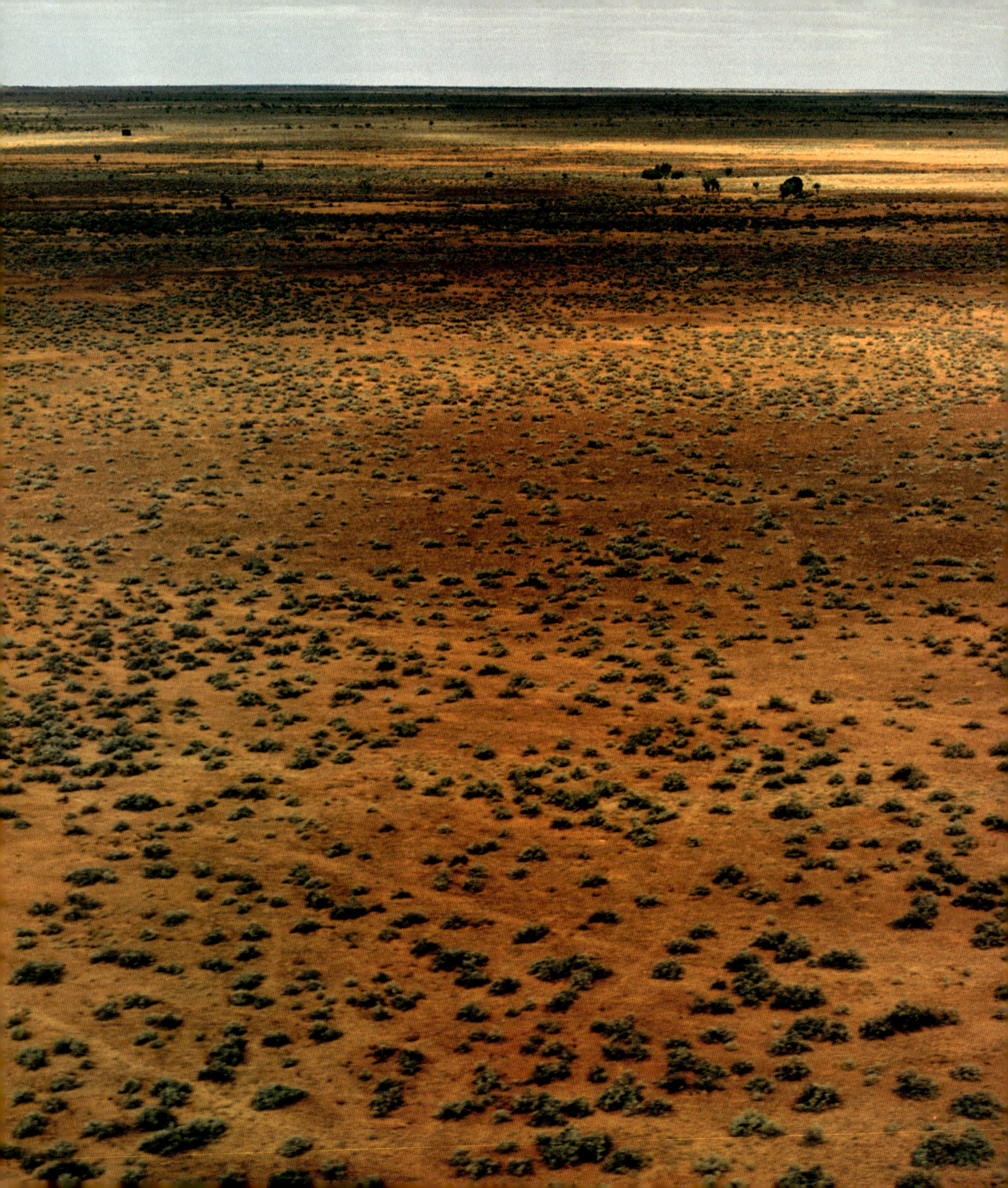

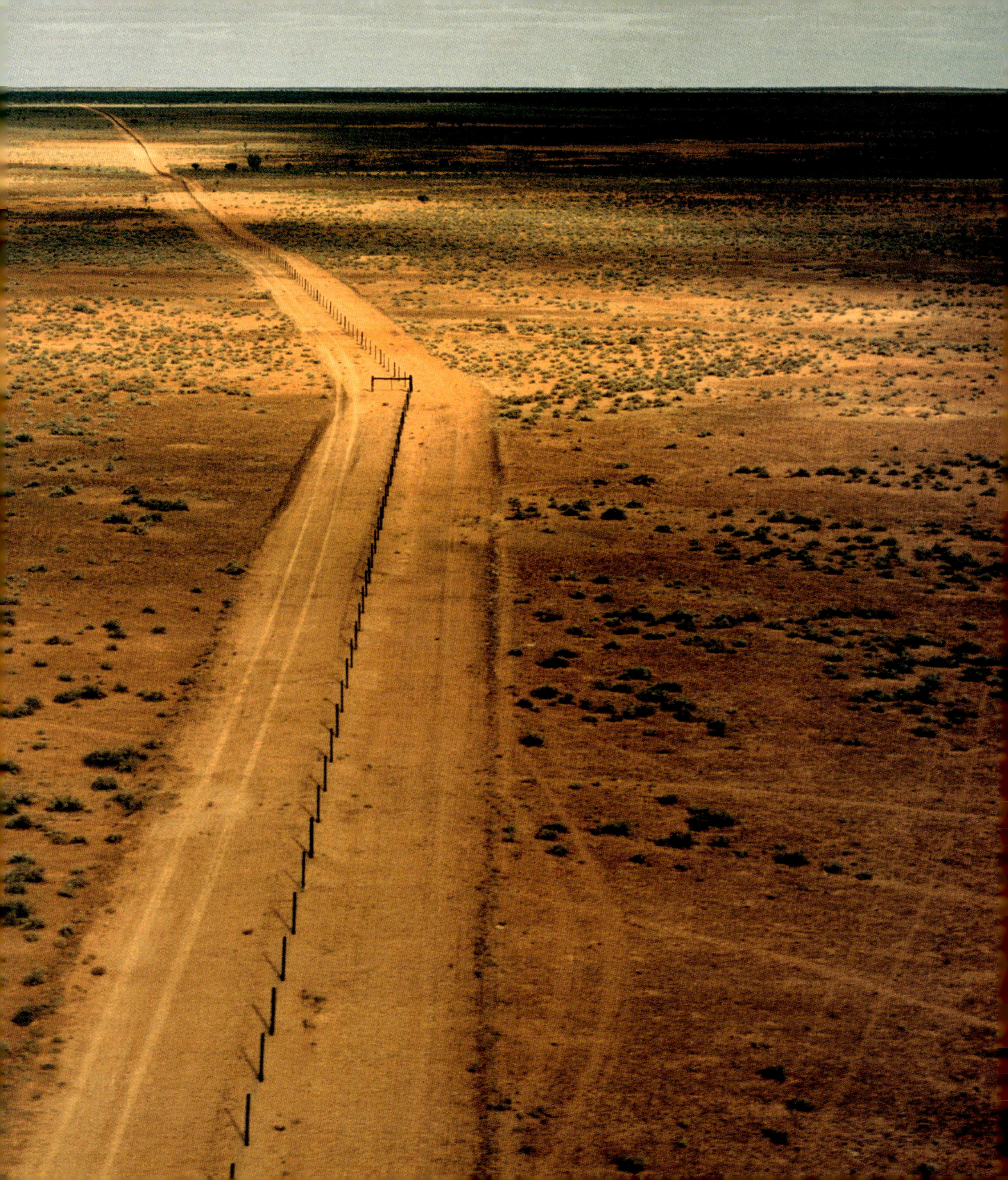

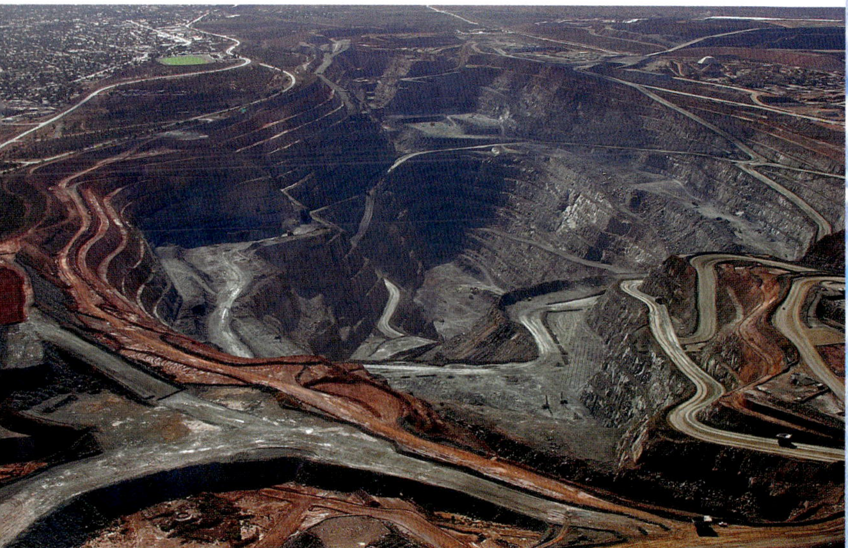

LEFT: The Super Pit lies on the edge of Kalgoorlie, Western Australia. At four kilometres long, 1.5 kilometres wide and 600 metres deep, it is the biggest open pit gold mine in the country. It runs around the clock and keeps 1,000 people in work, harvesting 800,000 ounces of gold every year. **RIGHT:** An electromagnetic prospecting aeroplane takes off from Conellan airport near Uluru, on its way to survey an area 500 kilometres to the northwest. In essence a flying metal detector, the aircraft and crew will scour the earth for nickel, gold or other minerals. In such a vast country, prospecting from the air is an expensive but efficient way of exploration.

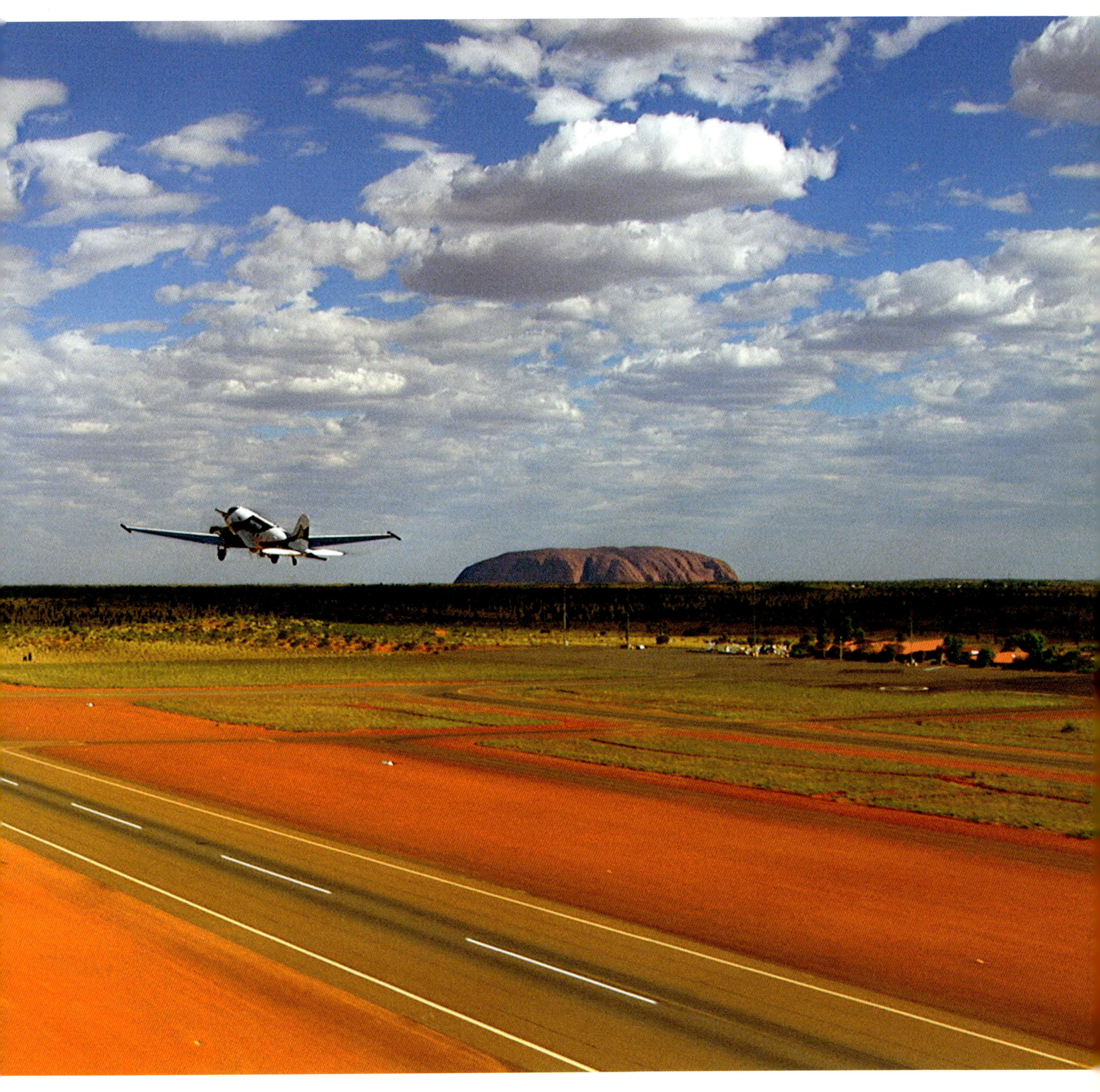

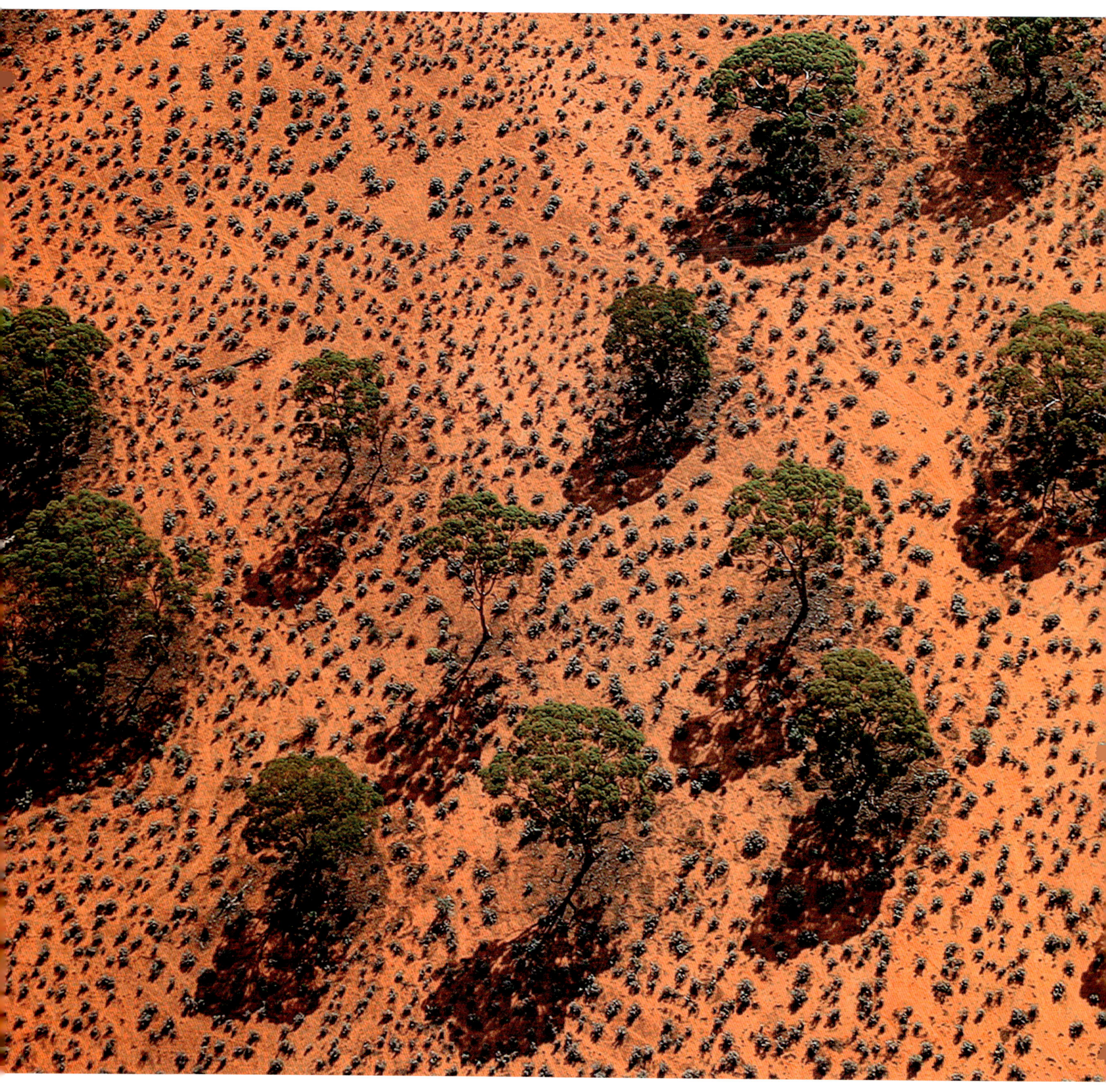

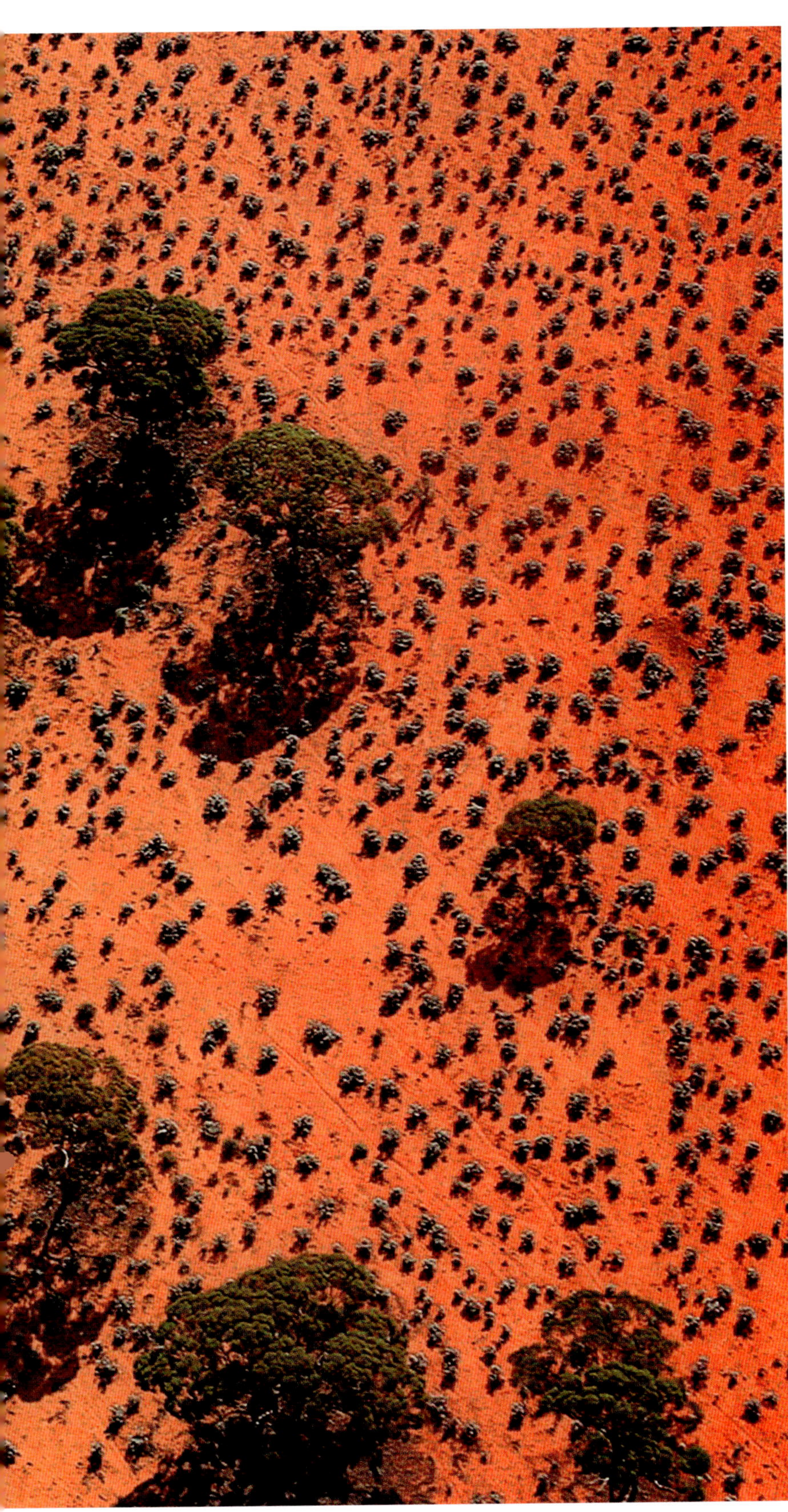

LEFT: Iron oxide gives the soil of the arid Outback of Australia its distinctive red colour.

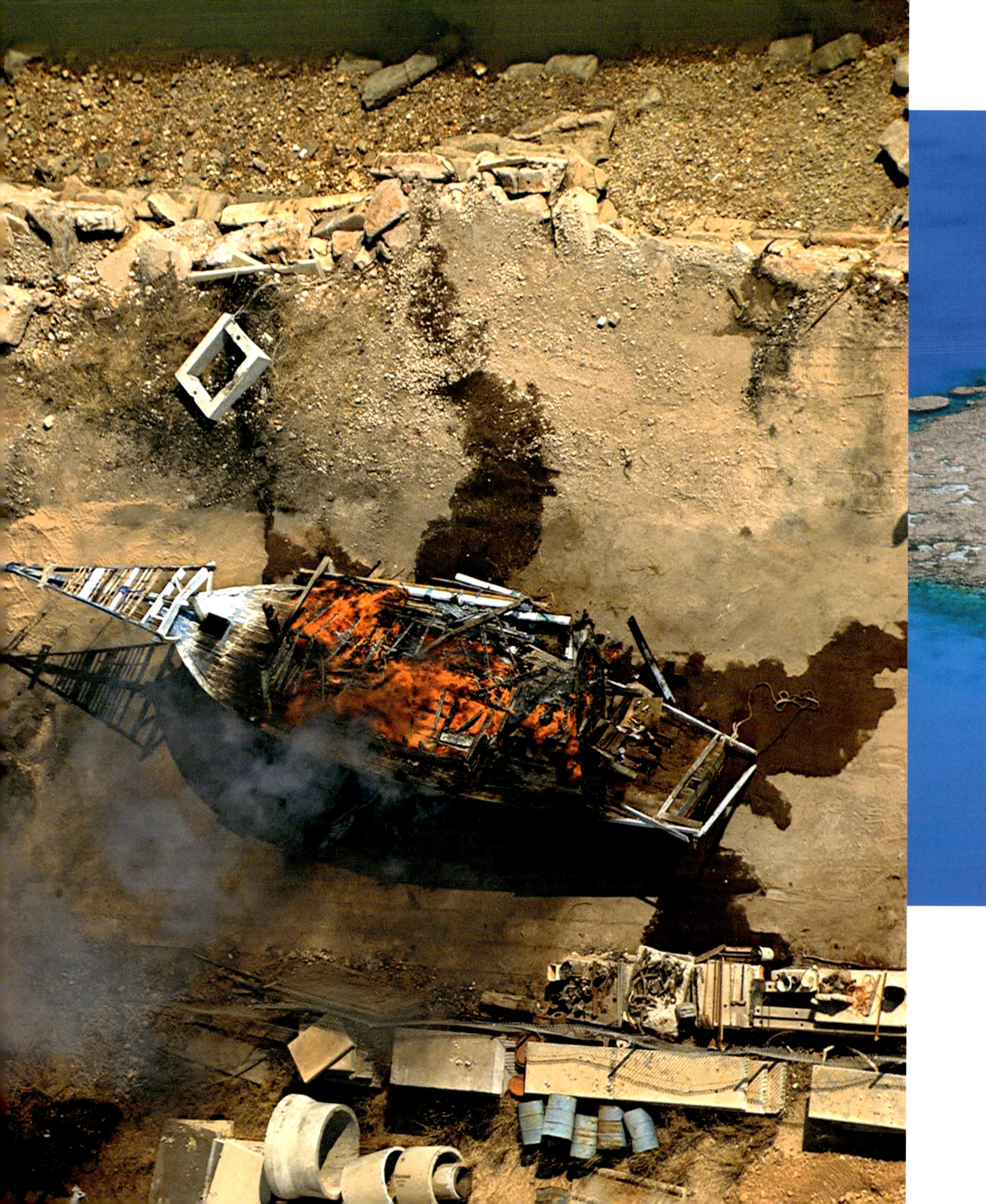

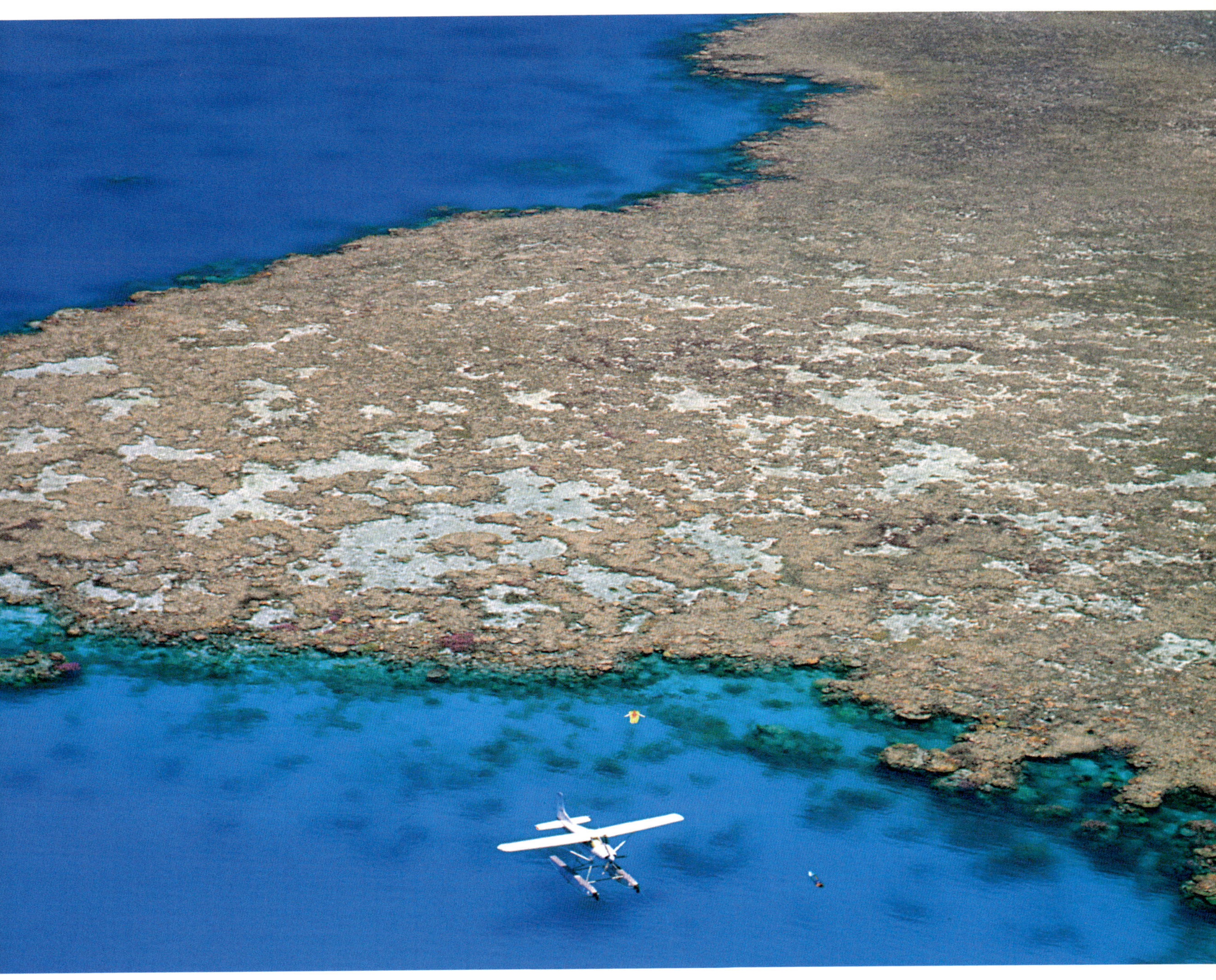

LEFT: An Indonesian vessel, caught fishing illegally in Australian waters, goes up in flames on an industrial site in Darwin. Its destruction was ordered by the Australian Fisheries Management Authority, which oversees the world's third largest fishing zone, extending 370 kilometres out to sea. **RIGHT:** A seaplane takes off from Hardy Reef, 60 kilometres east of Airlie Beach, Queensland. Part of the Great Barrier Reef system, it harbours hundreds of fish species including trevally, cuttlefish, angelfish and gropers as well as starfish and giant clams.

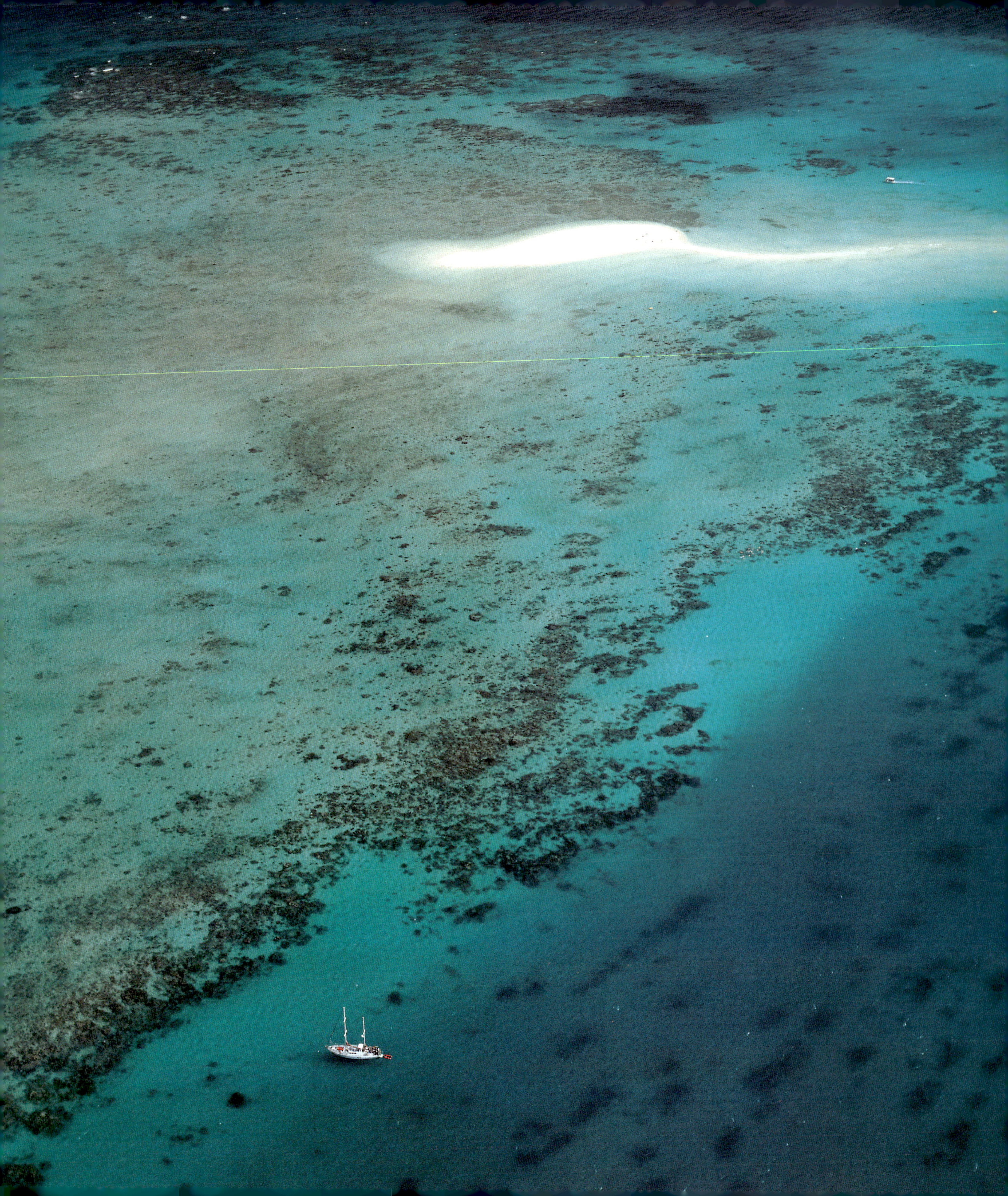

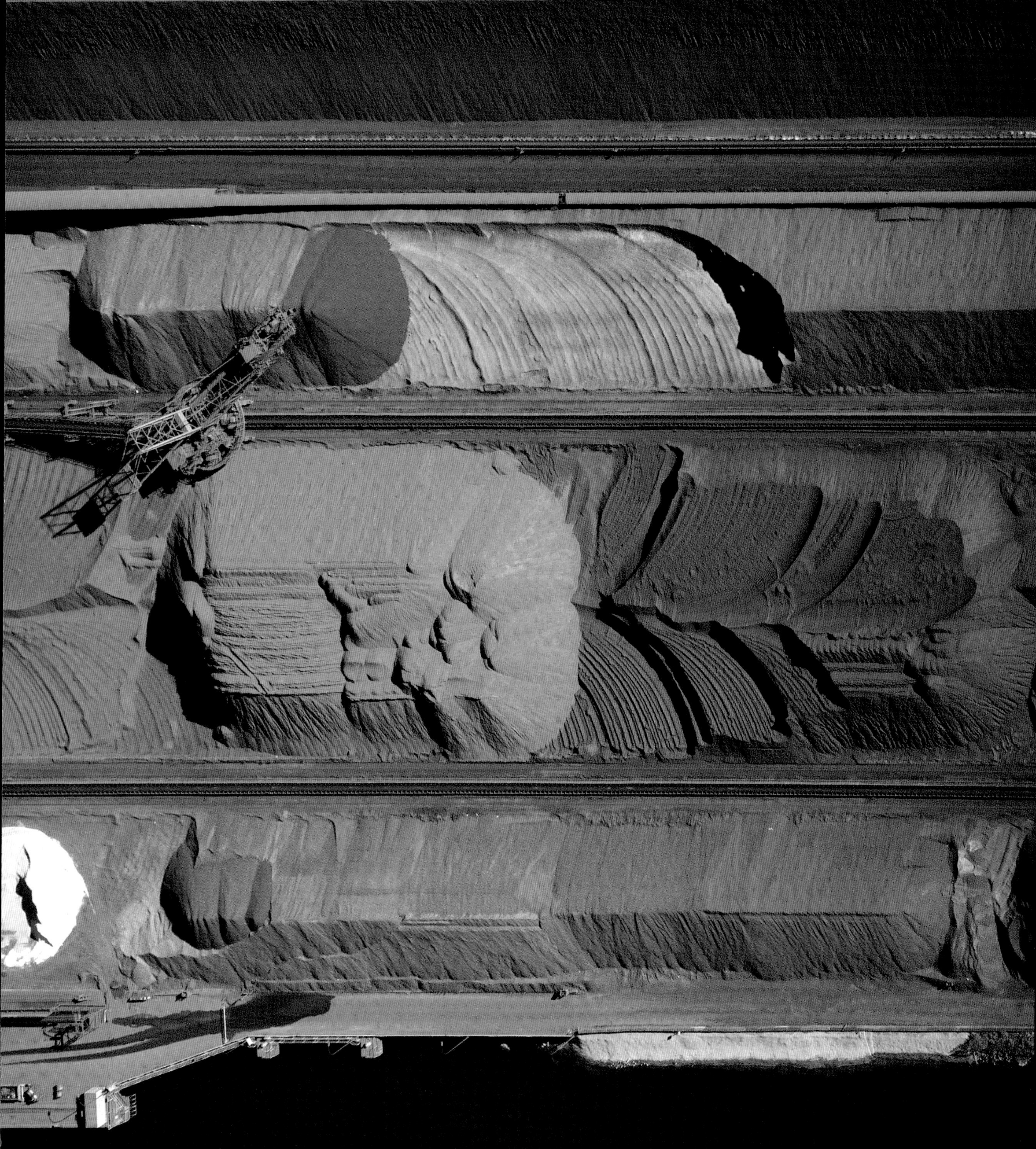

PREVIOUS PAGE LEFT: The Great Barrier Reef near Cairns, Queensland. **PREVIOUS PAGE RIGHT:** Piles of iron ore unloaded at Port Kembla, New South Wales. Different types of iron ore are blended before being used in the nearby blast furnaces. While the Port Kembla steelworks produce 2.6 million tonnes of crude steel annually, most of Australia's iron ore, in its raw form, is exported to Asia.

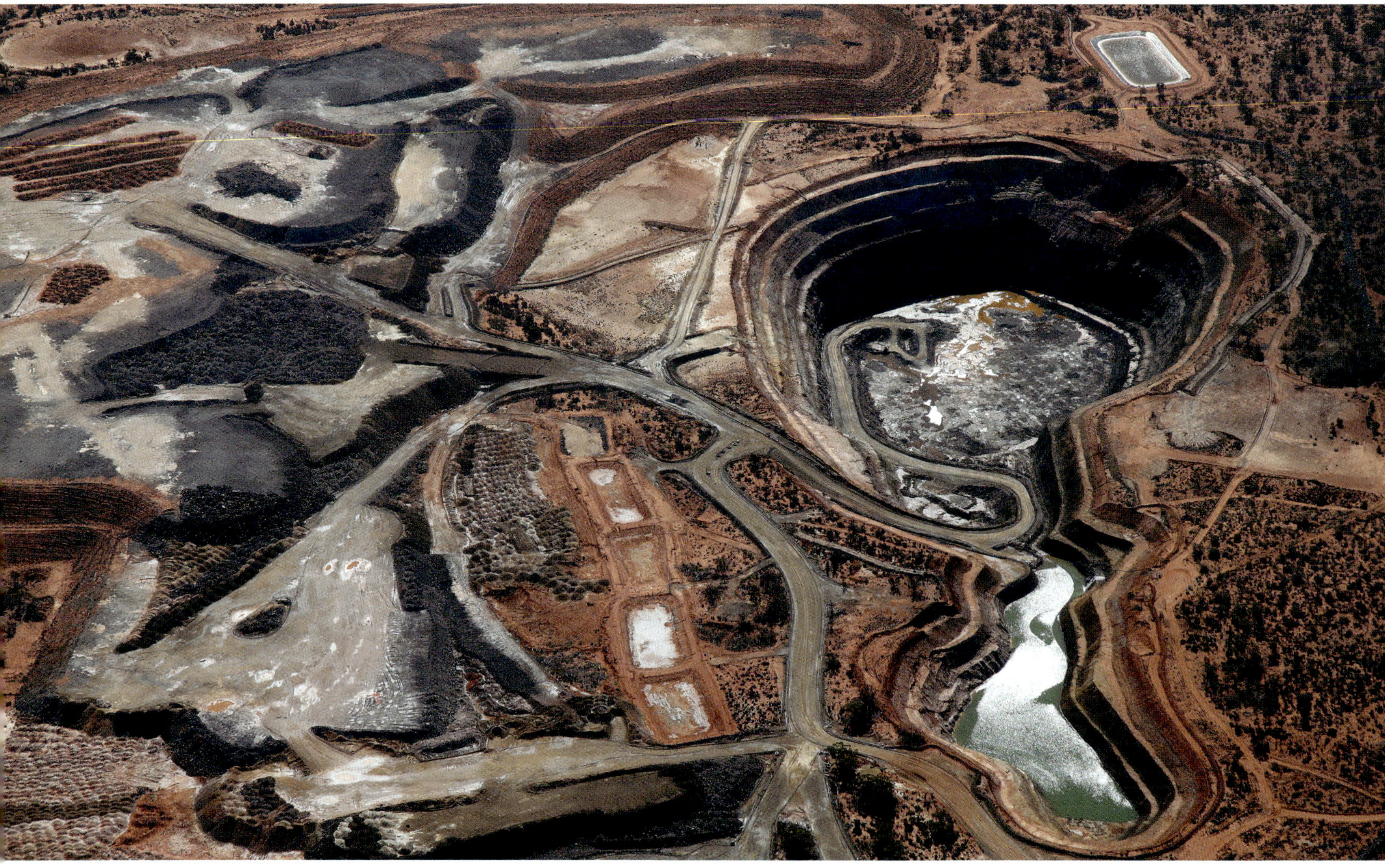

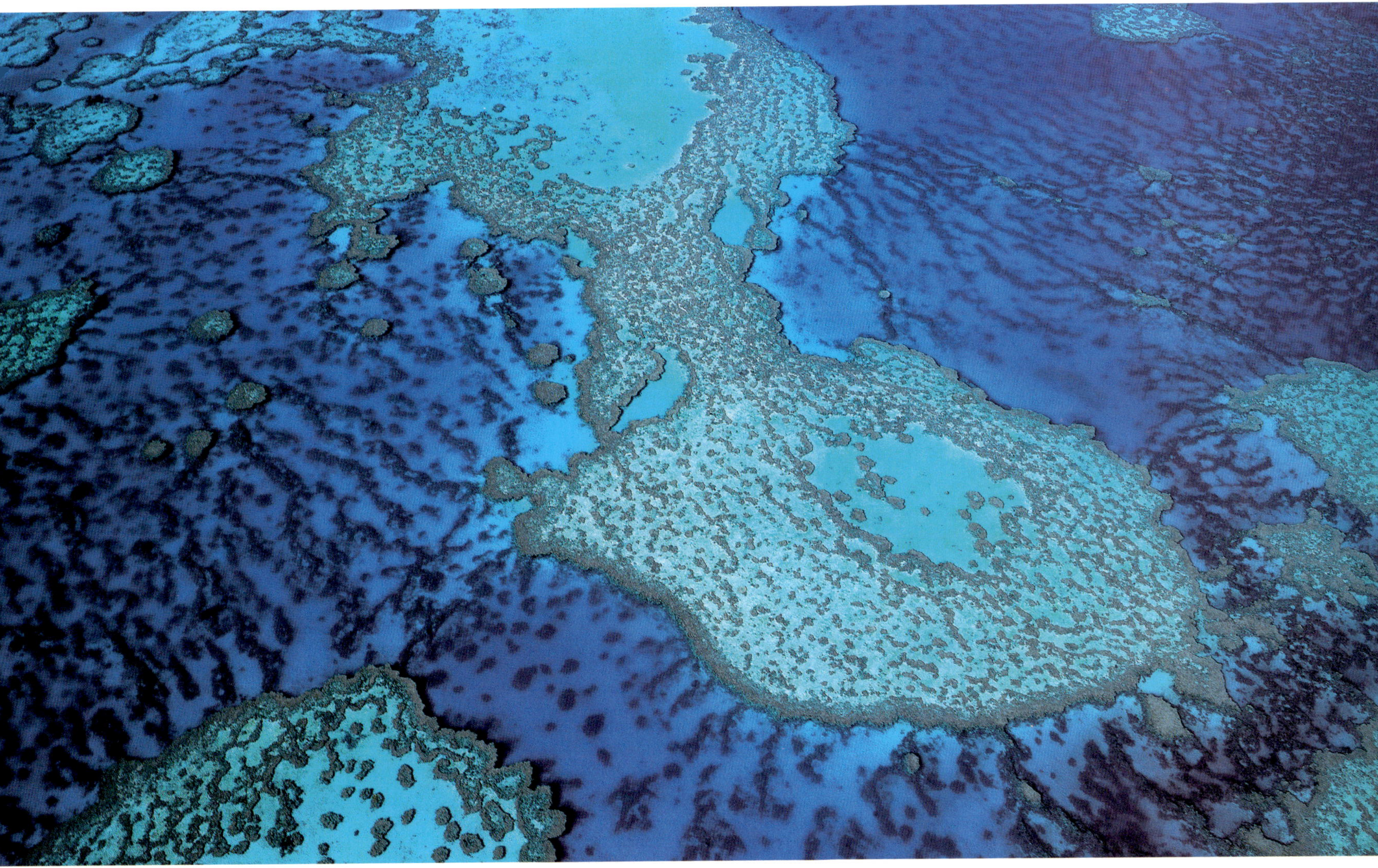

LEFT: The White Foil gold mine, 23 kilometres southwest of Kalgoorlie. Australia is the world's third largest producer of gold after South Africa and the US. The open pits are generally huge as gold often has a concentration of less than five grams in every tonne of rock that is mined. **RIGHT:** Mining, oil drilling and exploration were banned when the Great Barrier Reef Marine Park was created in 1975.

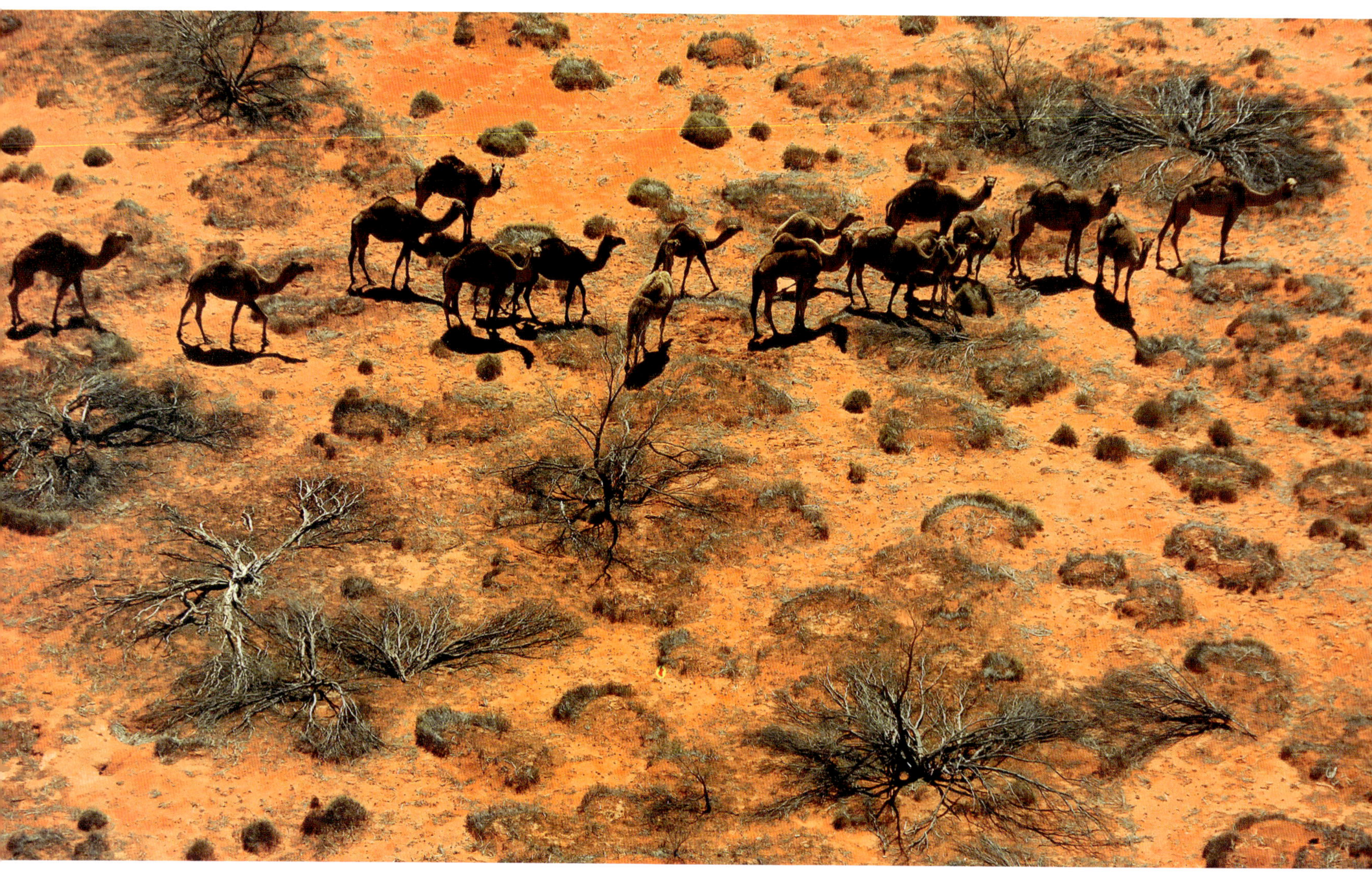

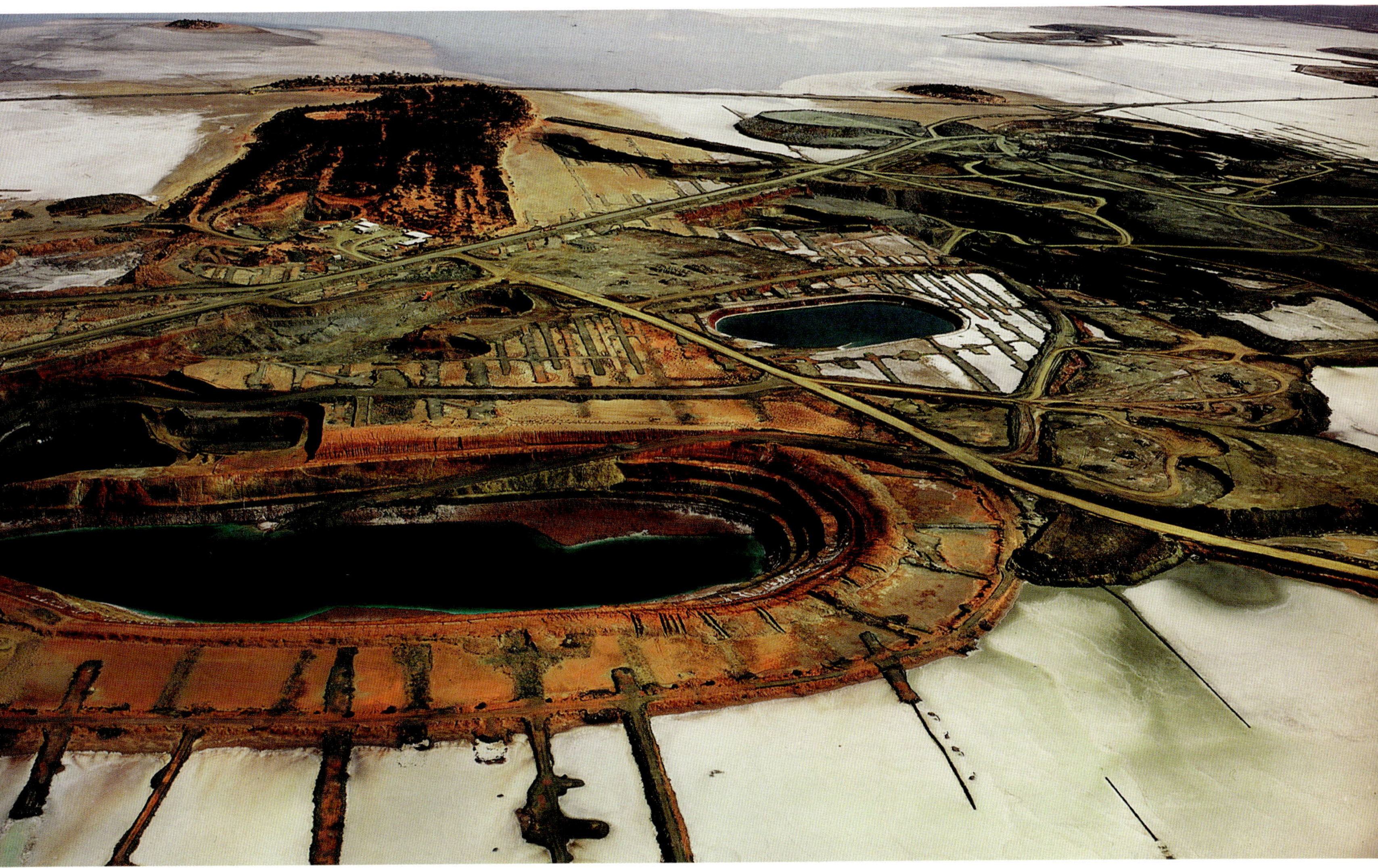

LEFT: More than a million feral camels roam the Australian Outback. Brought in originally in small numbers to help unlock the hinterland and build the Overland Telegraph Line, their feral descendants are now a major concern, roaming an area of more than 3 million square kilometres. They cause damage to infrastructure and sites of biological and cultural significance. **RIGHT:** Gold and nickel mines dot the landscape near Kambalda, Western Australia, and are surrounded by the vast white expanse of Lake Lefroy, a 500-square-kilometre inland salt lake. This is the Revenge open-cut gold mine, which has now been closed, as evidenced by the water that has flooded the pit.

LEFT: A dolphin pod at Esperance, Western Australia. There are 45 species of whales, dolphins and porpoises in Australian waters. Some reside permanently while others only pass through when migrating from their summer feeding grounds in the Antarctic to the warmer waters in the north. **RIGHT:** A bushfire in the Darling Ranges, Western Australia. Most bushfires are caused by lightning strikes.

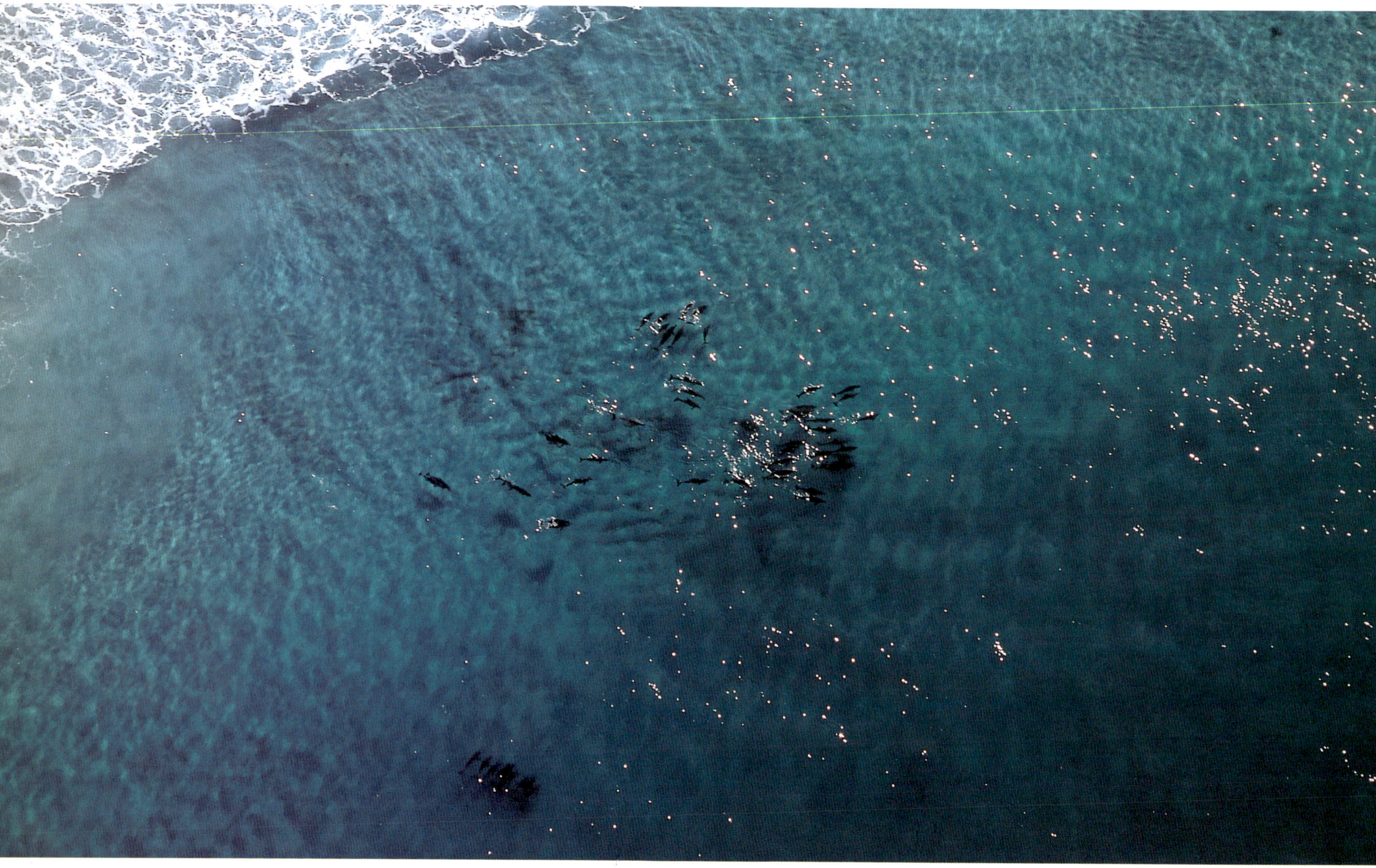

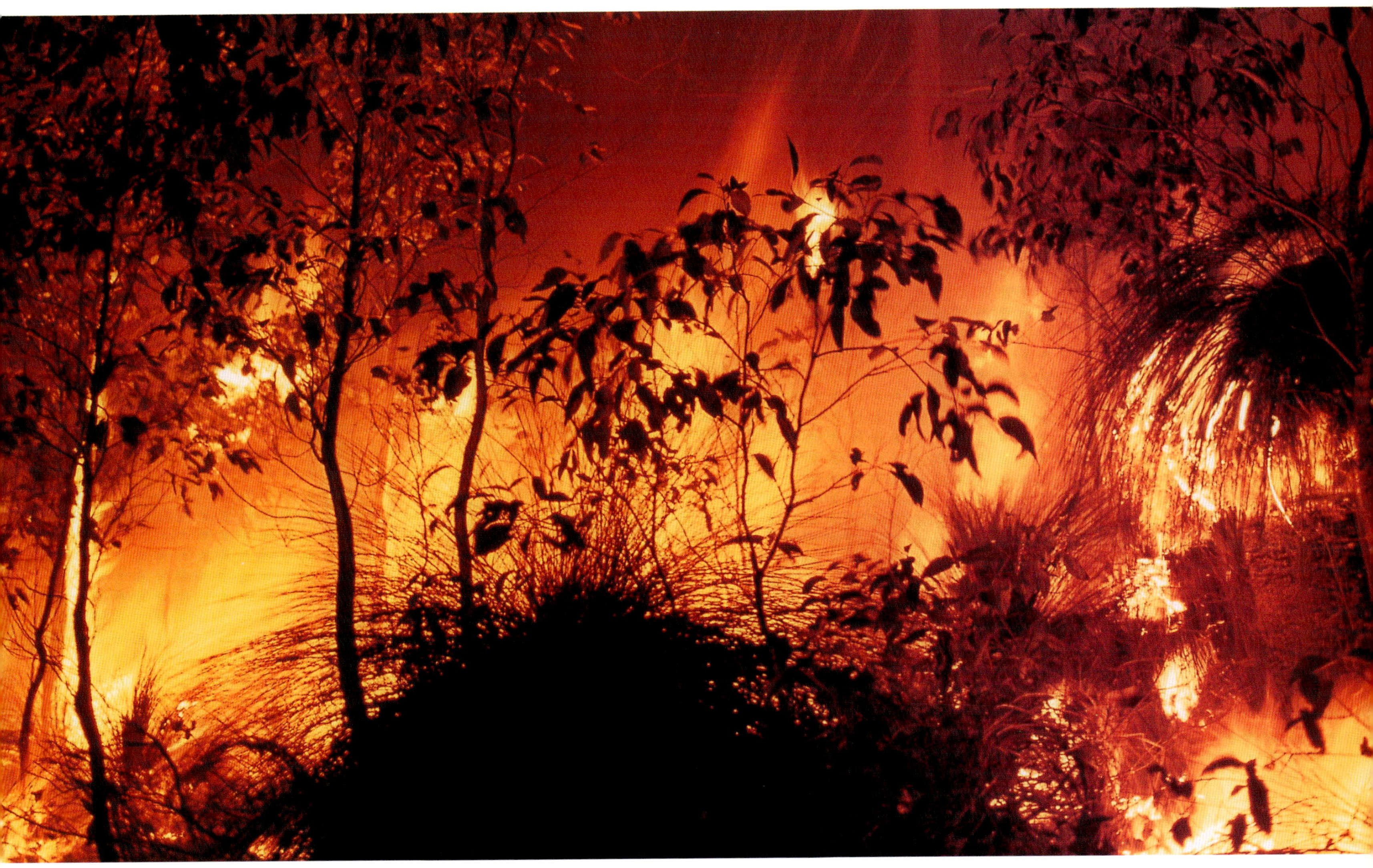

LEFT: A flock of magpie geese flies over the bush in the Northern Territory. Habitat destruction and drought have all but eliminated the geese from the country's south, but in the Northern Territory, this iconic water bird continues to thrive. **RIGHT:** A part of the Port Kembla steelworks known as the recycling area. By-product material from steel smelting, such as blast furnace slag, is processed into products for the construction industry. The plant also processes reclaimed metal for use in the steelmaking process.

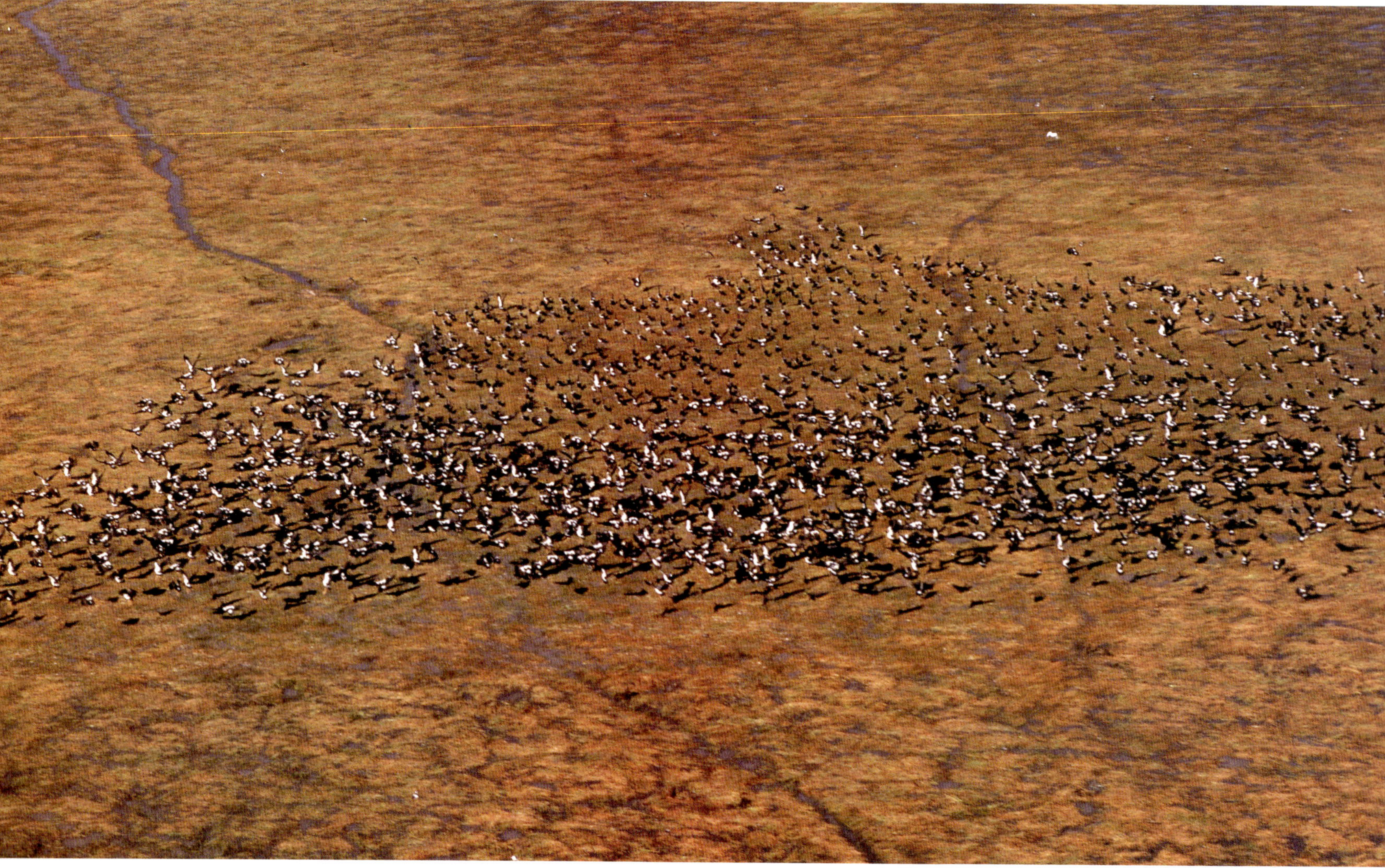

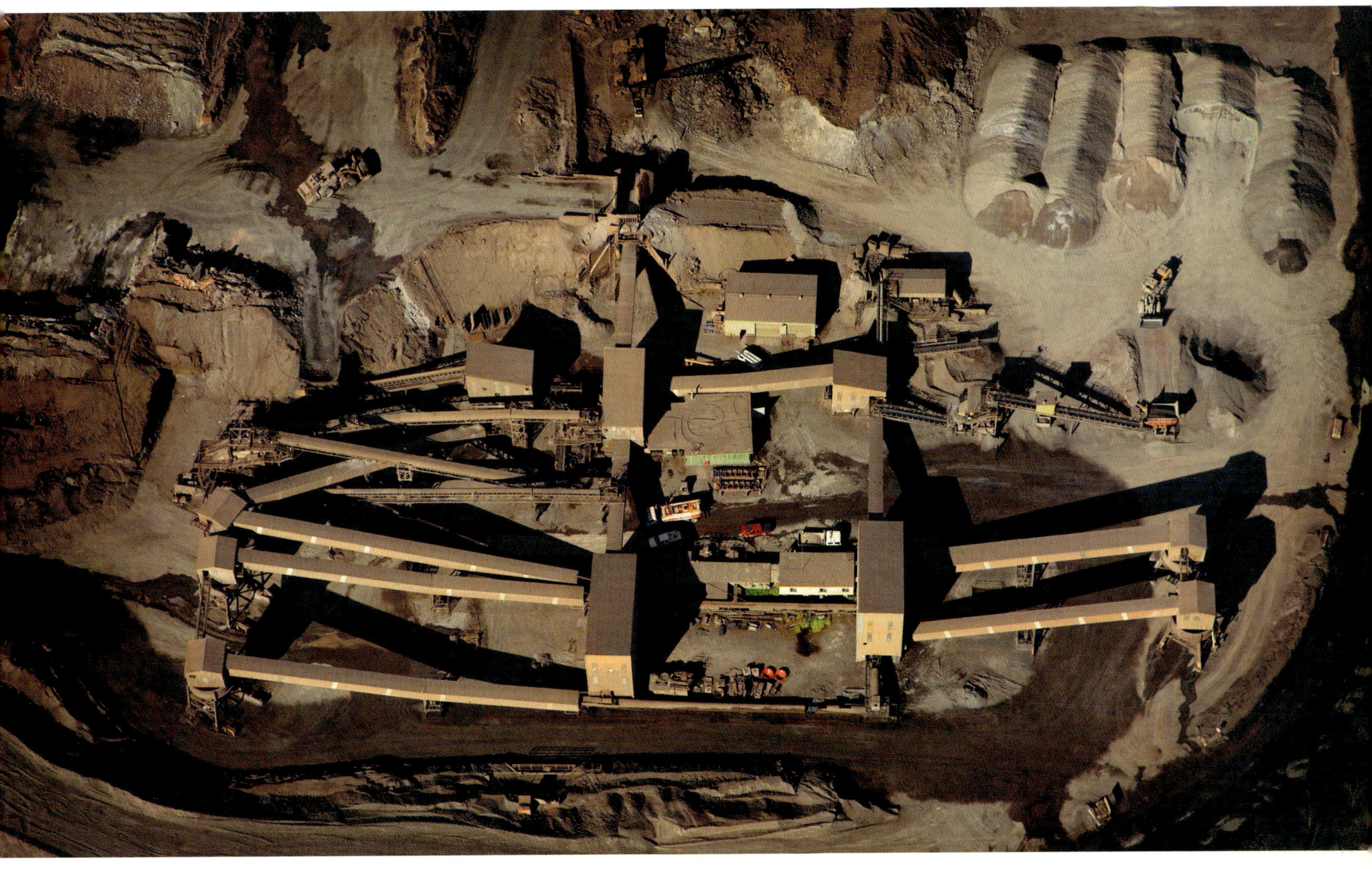

FOLLOWING PAGES: The Goldfields Pipeline. Completed in 1903, it is the longest freshwater pipe in the world, stretching 560 kilometres from Perth to the arid goldfields of Kalgoorlie. It can take a drop of water up to 11 days to travel from one end of the pipe to the other. It holds a staggering 300 million litres of water with 100,000 people depending on the pipe for their livelihood.

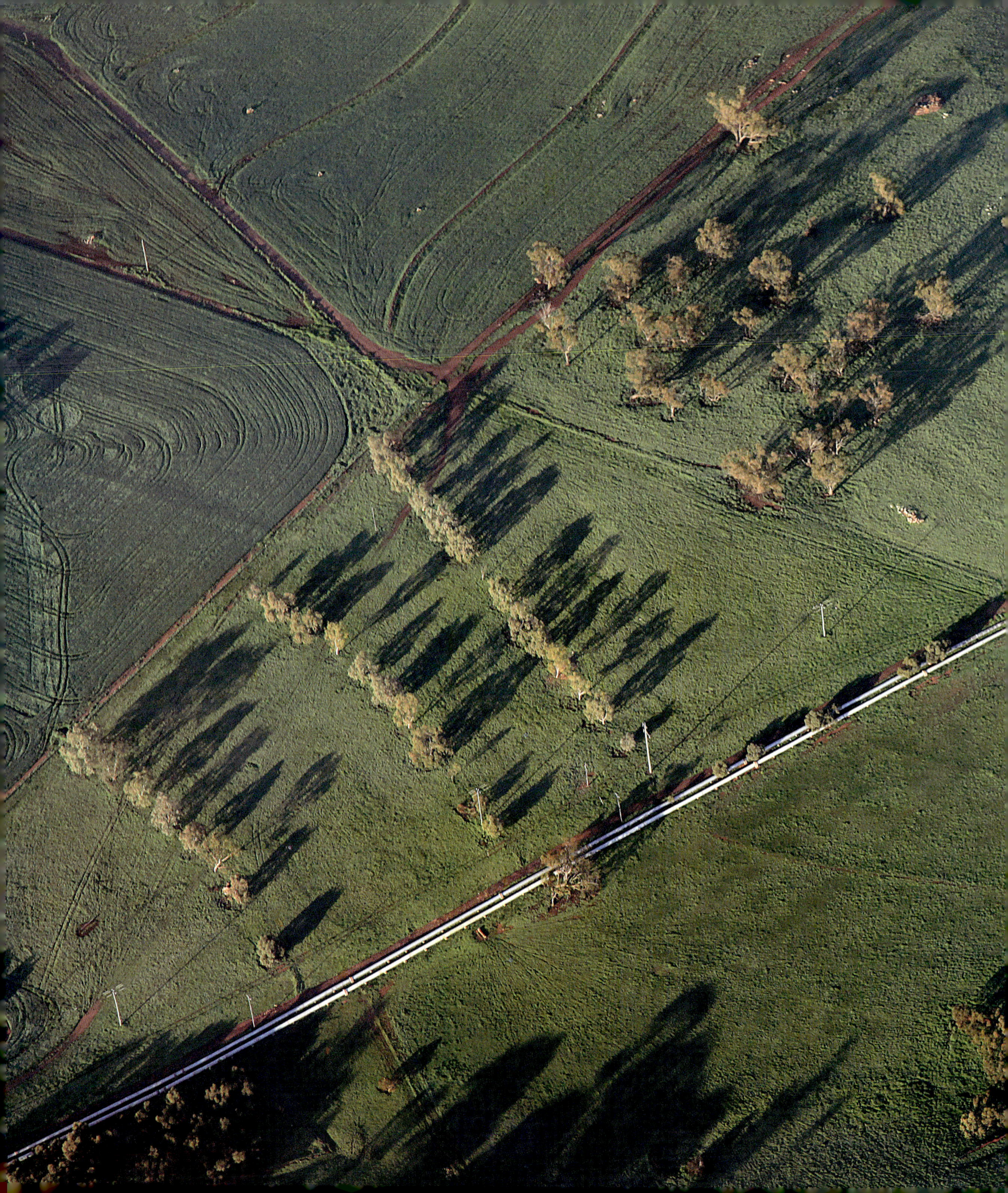

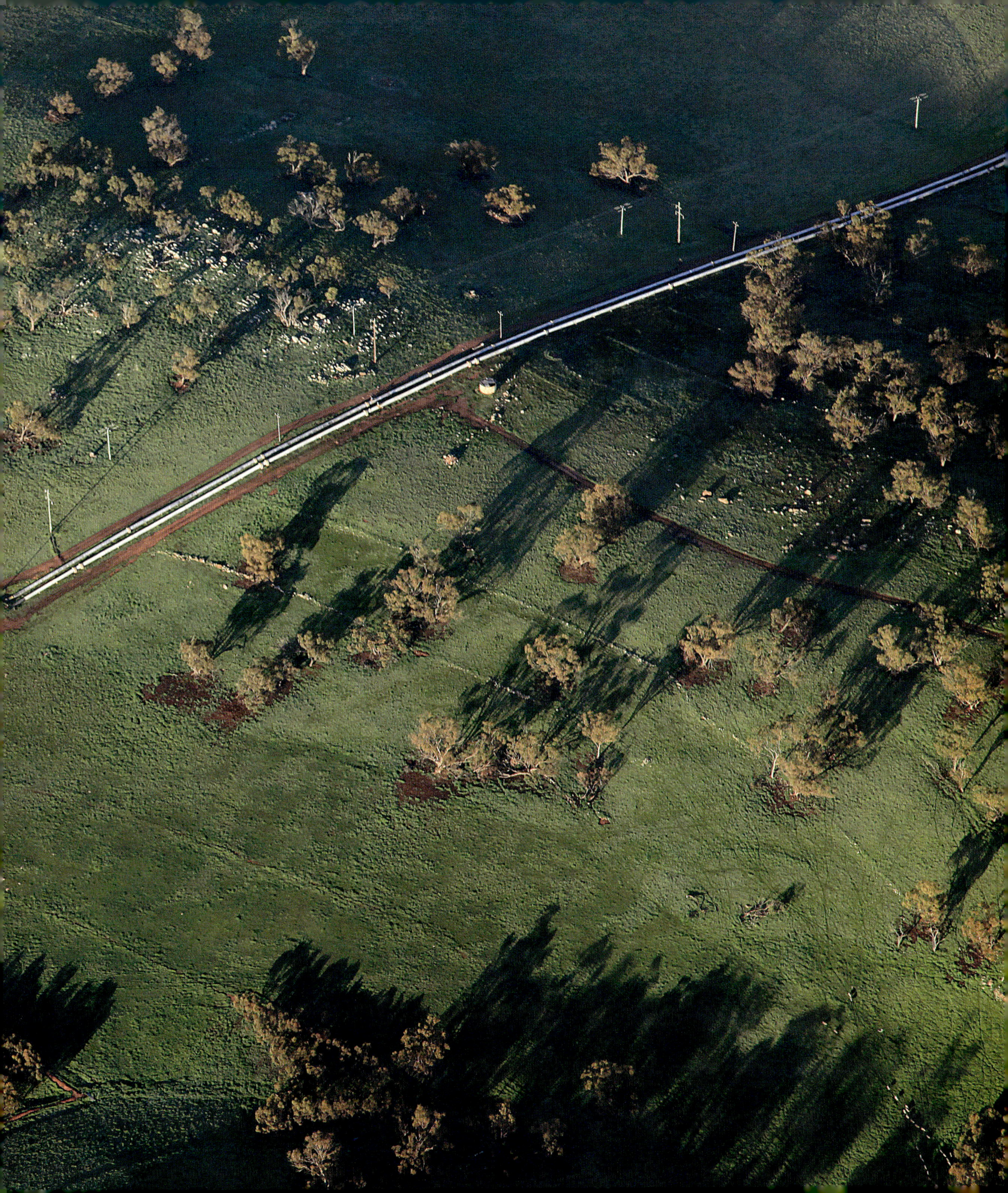

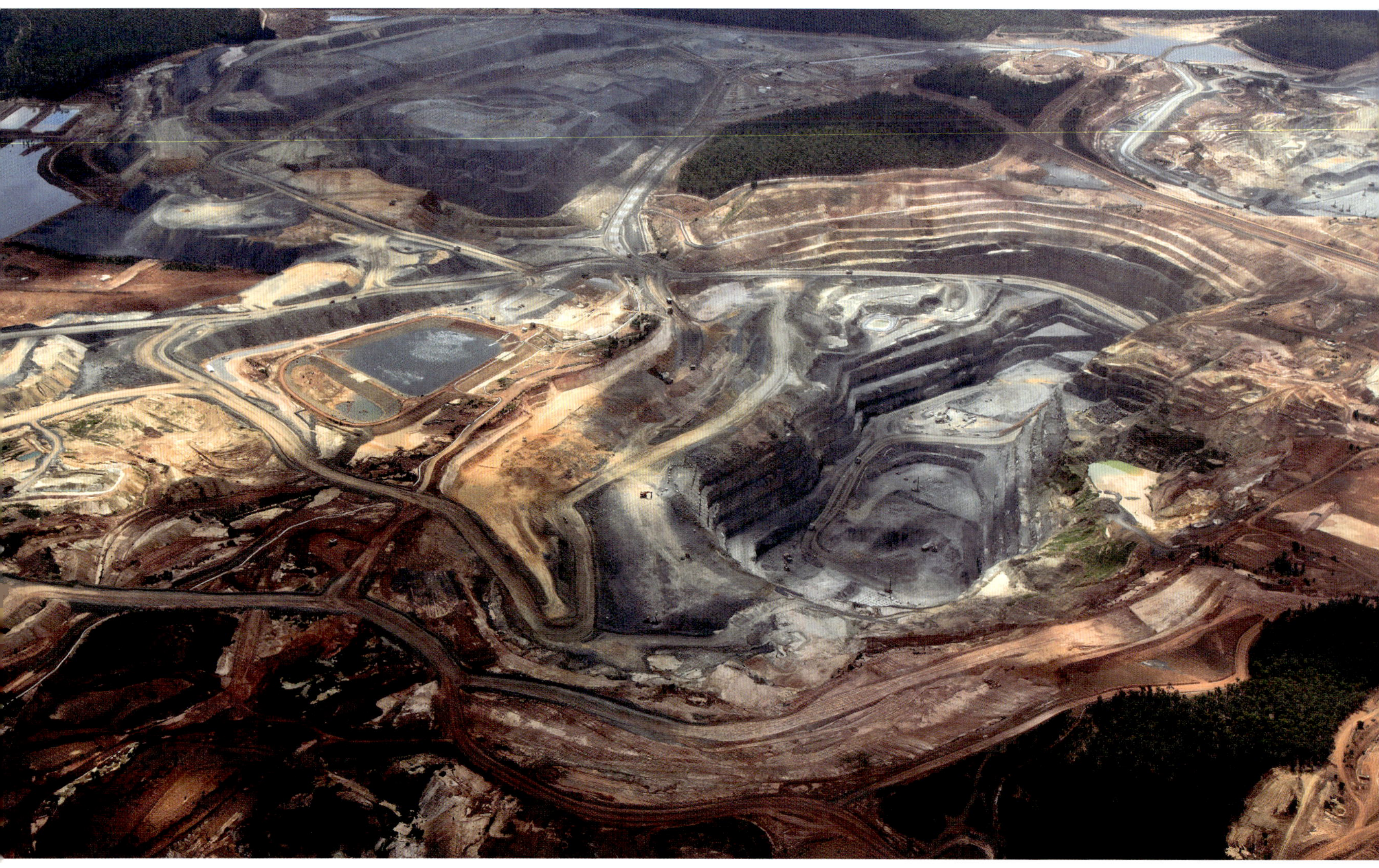

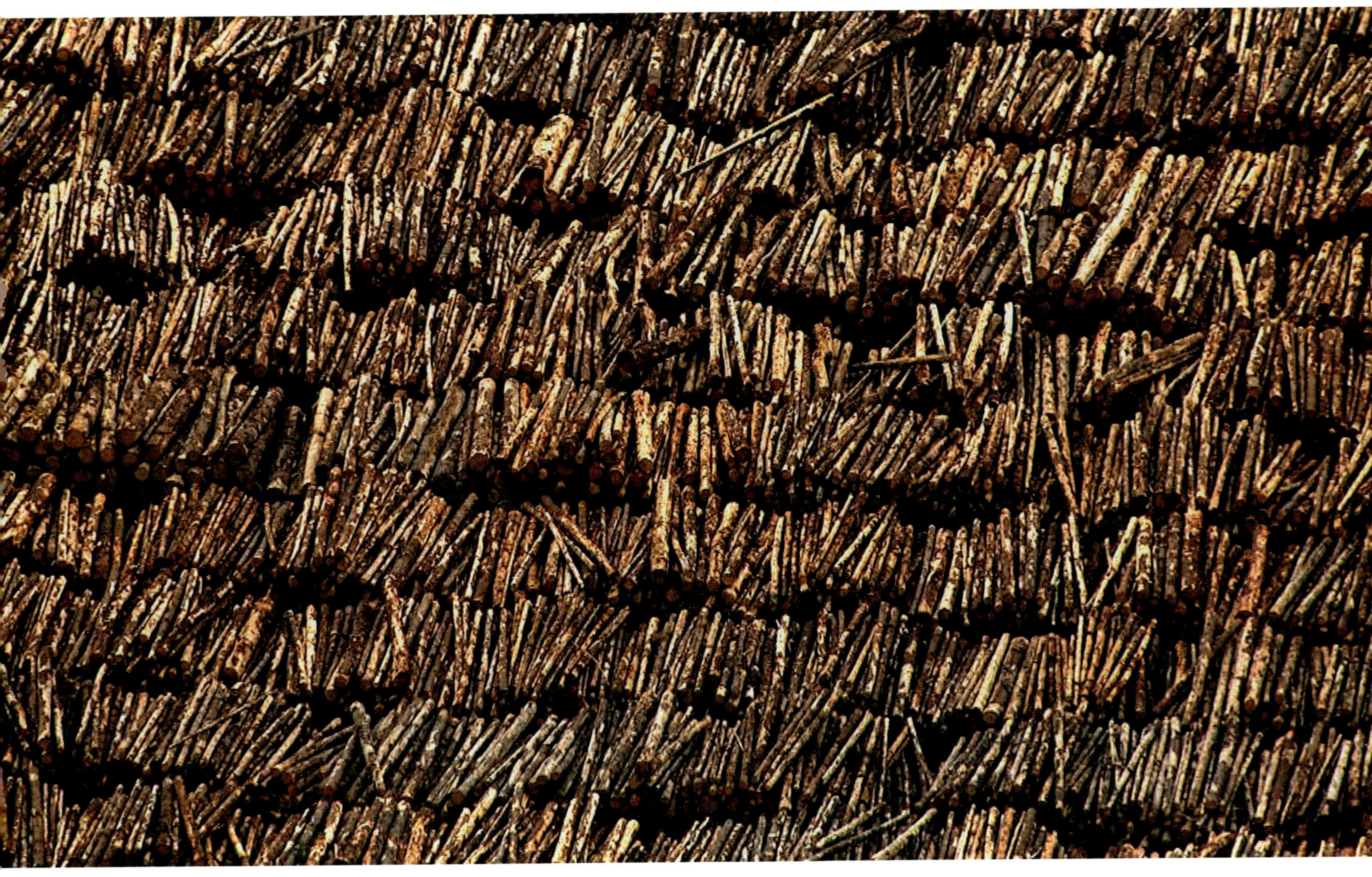

LEFT: The Boddington Gold Mine, Western Australia, was opened in 2009. Australia's economic gold resource is estimated at 5,200 tonnes. While sixty per cent of all deposits are located in Western Australia, all states and the Northern Territory have gold. Most of Australia's gold production comes from open-cut mines. **RIGHT:** Logs in Tasmania. Forestry is a sometimes-controversial industry. In Tasmania, 10,000 people depend on it for their jobs. In a typical year, more than 25 million cubic metres of logs are harvested from the country's production forests — around two-thirds from plantations, with the remainder from native forests.

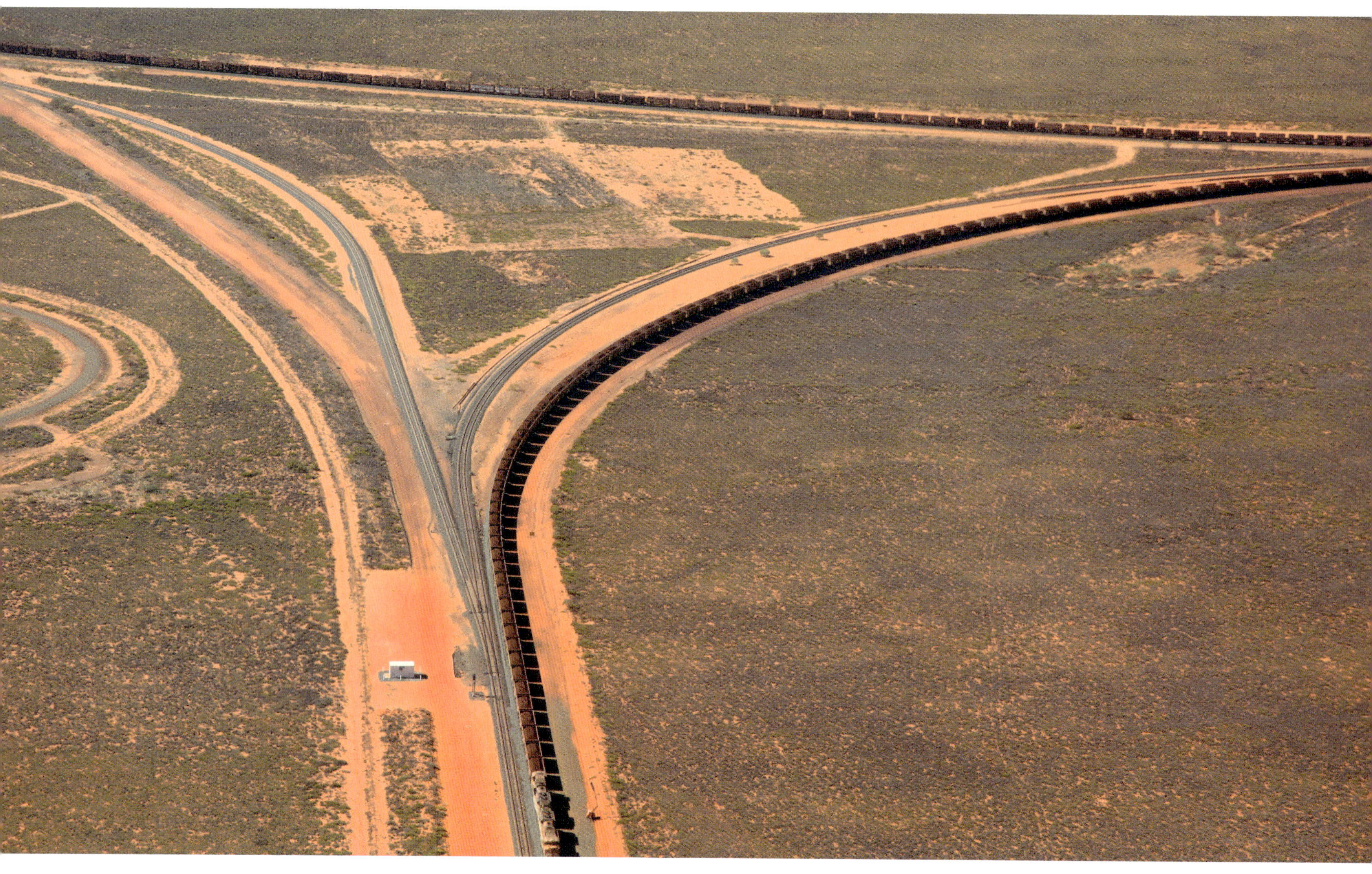

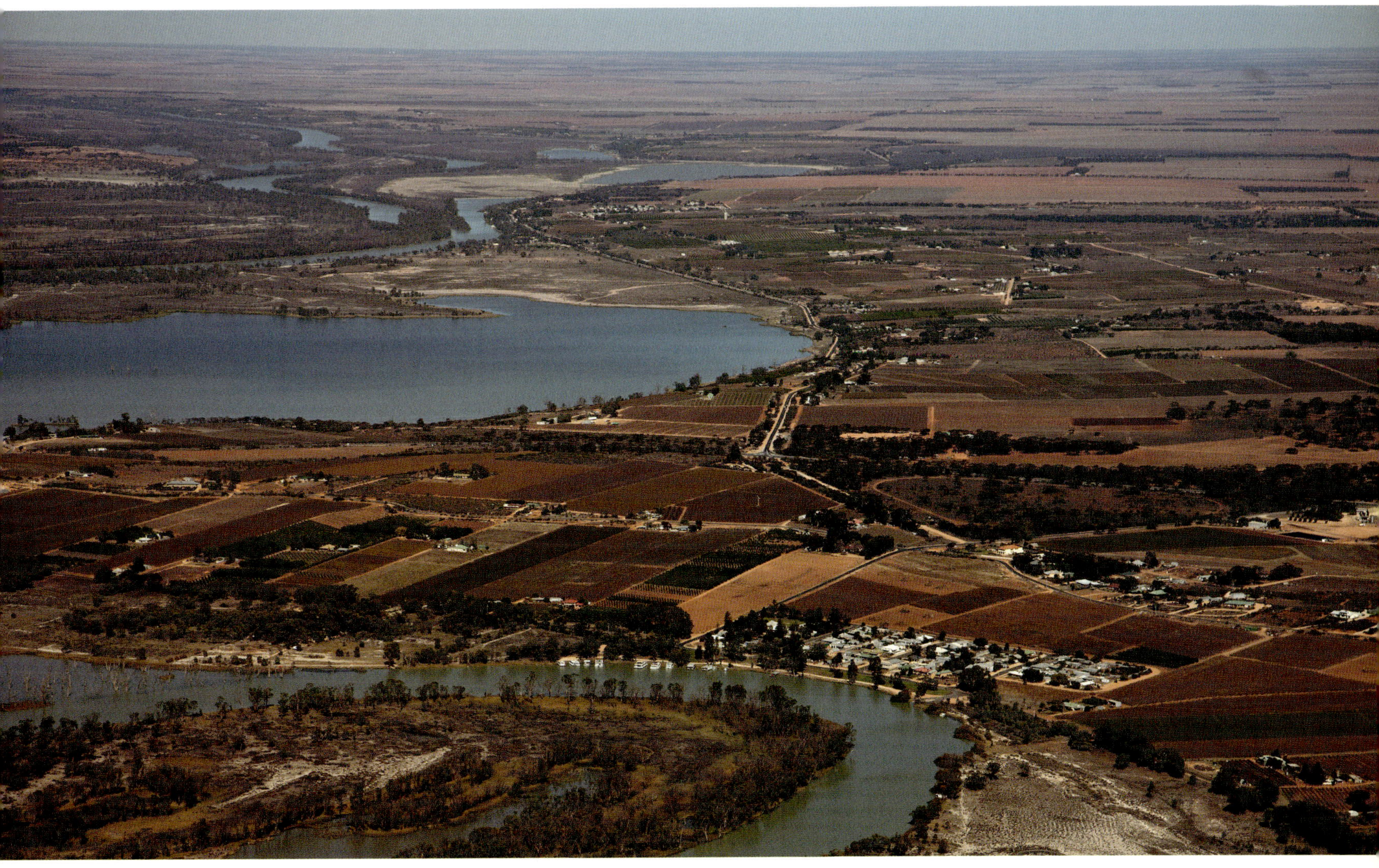

LEFT: An iron ore train makes its way from the Pilbara hinterlands to the coastal ports of Dampier or Port Hedland, Western Australia. Australia's known resources are 28 billion tonnes with 98 per cent in Western Australia. Iron ore trains are more than two kilometres long and consist of more than 200 cars, each loaded with more than 100 tonnes of ore. **RIGHT:** Farms along the Murray river near Renmark, South Australia, benefit from irrigation the river provides. Like Mildura in Victoria, Renmark was set up in the late 1800s by the Canadian Chaffey brothers, who had successfully developed irrigation schemes in California, USA.

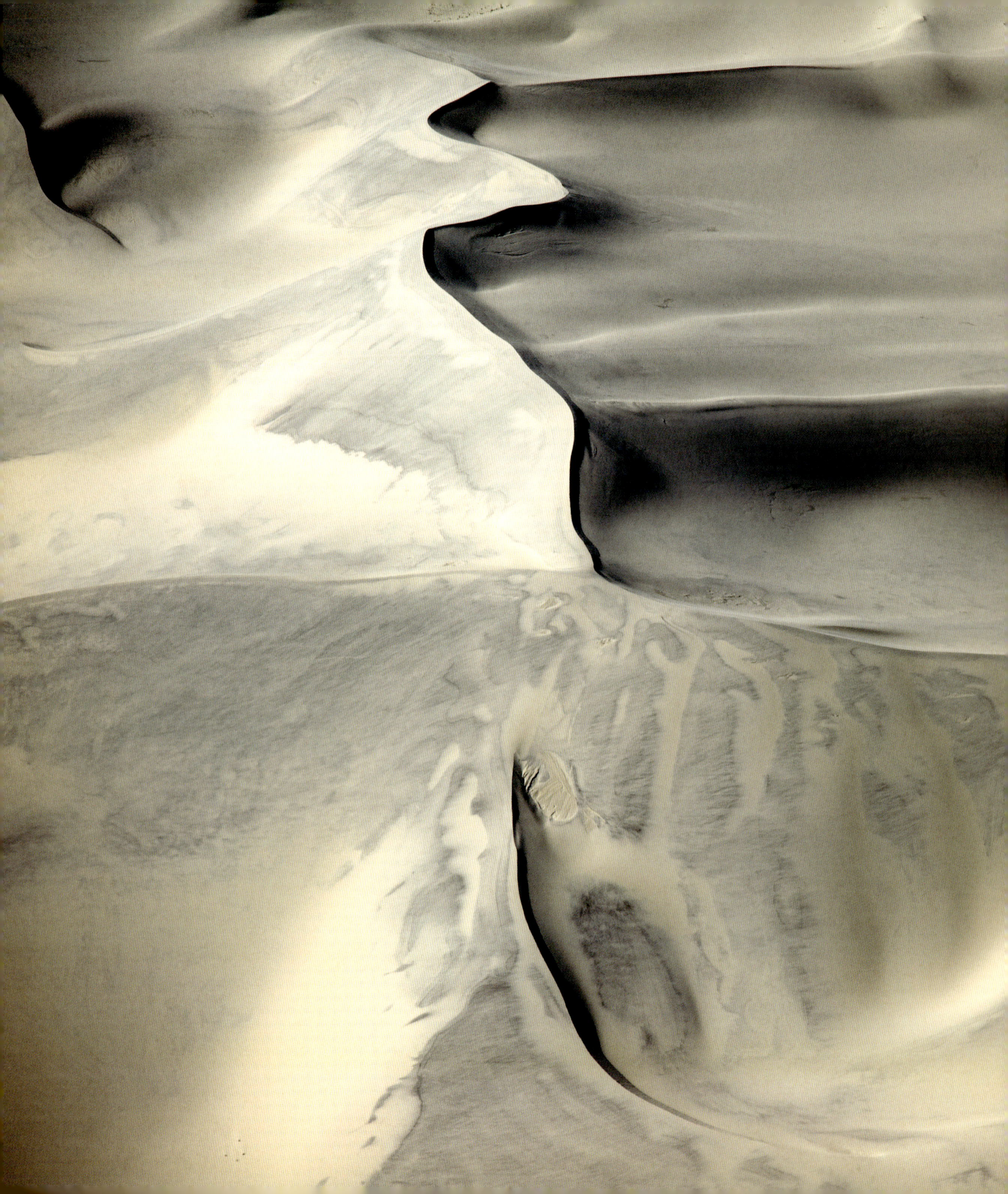

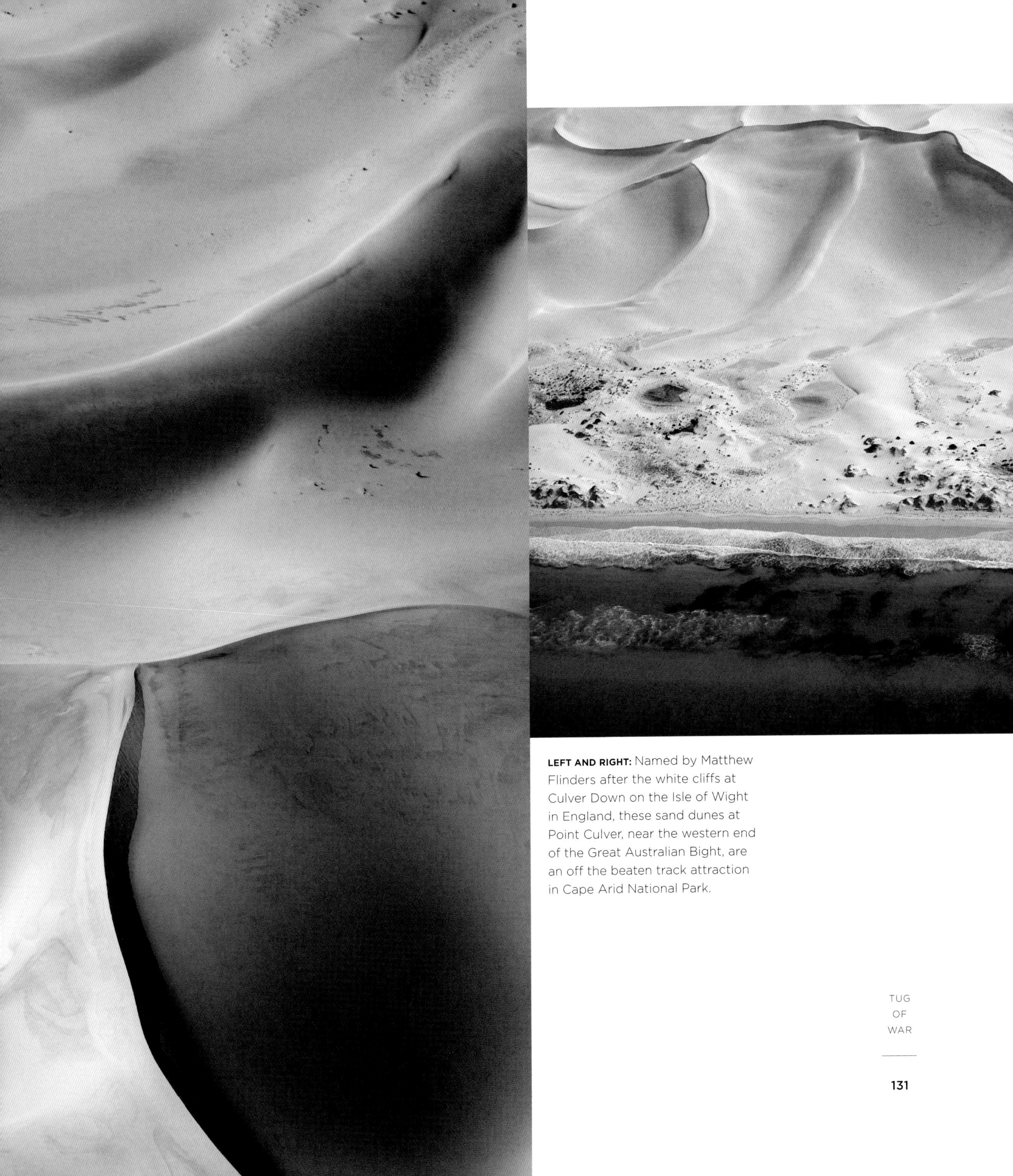

LEFT AND RIGHT: Named by Matthew Flinders after the white cliffs at Culver Down on the Isle of Wight in England, these sand dunes at Point Culver, near the western end of the Great Australian Bight, are an off the beaten track attraction in Cape Arid National Park.

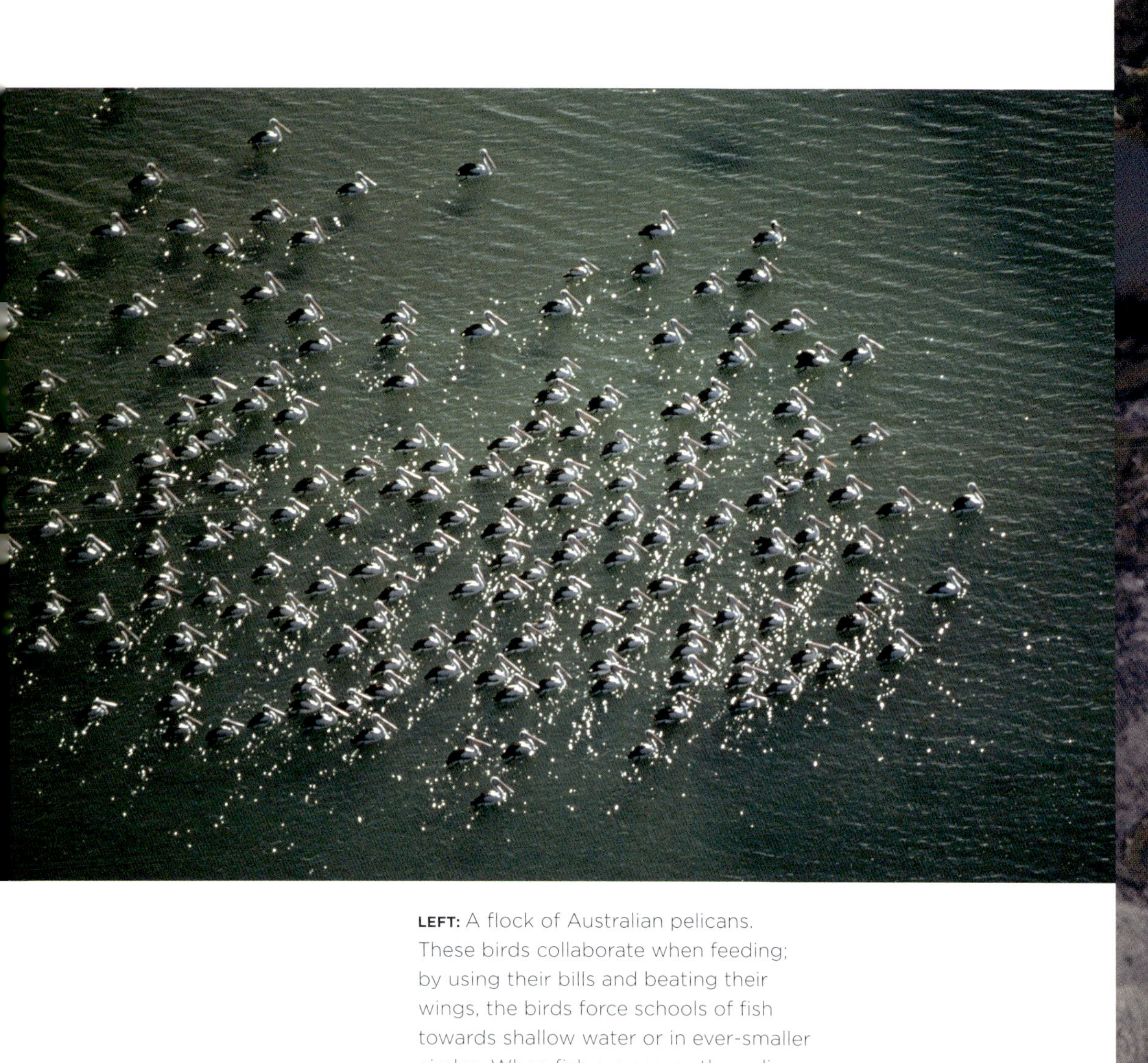

LEFT: A flock of Australian pelicans. These birds collaborate when feeding; by using their bills and beating their wings, the birds force schools of fish towards shallow water or in ever-smaller circles. When fish are scarce the pelicans feed on seagulls, crustaceans and turtles. **RIGHT:** Bushfire scars in Margaret River, Western Australia. These are the result of a prescribed burn in nearby Leeuwin-Naturaliste National Park, 13 kilometres northwest of the township. The fire broke its boundaries and became a wildfire, destroying 32 homes and burning out 3,400 hectares.

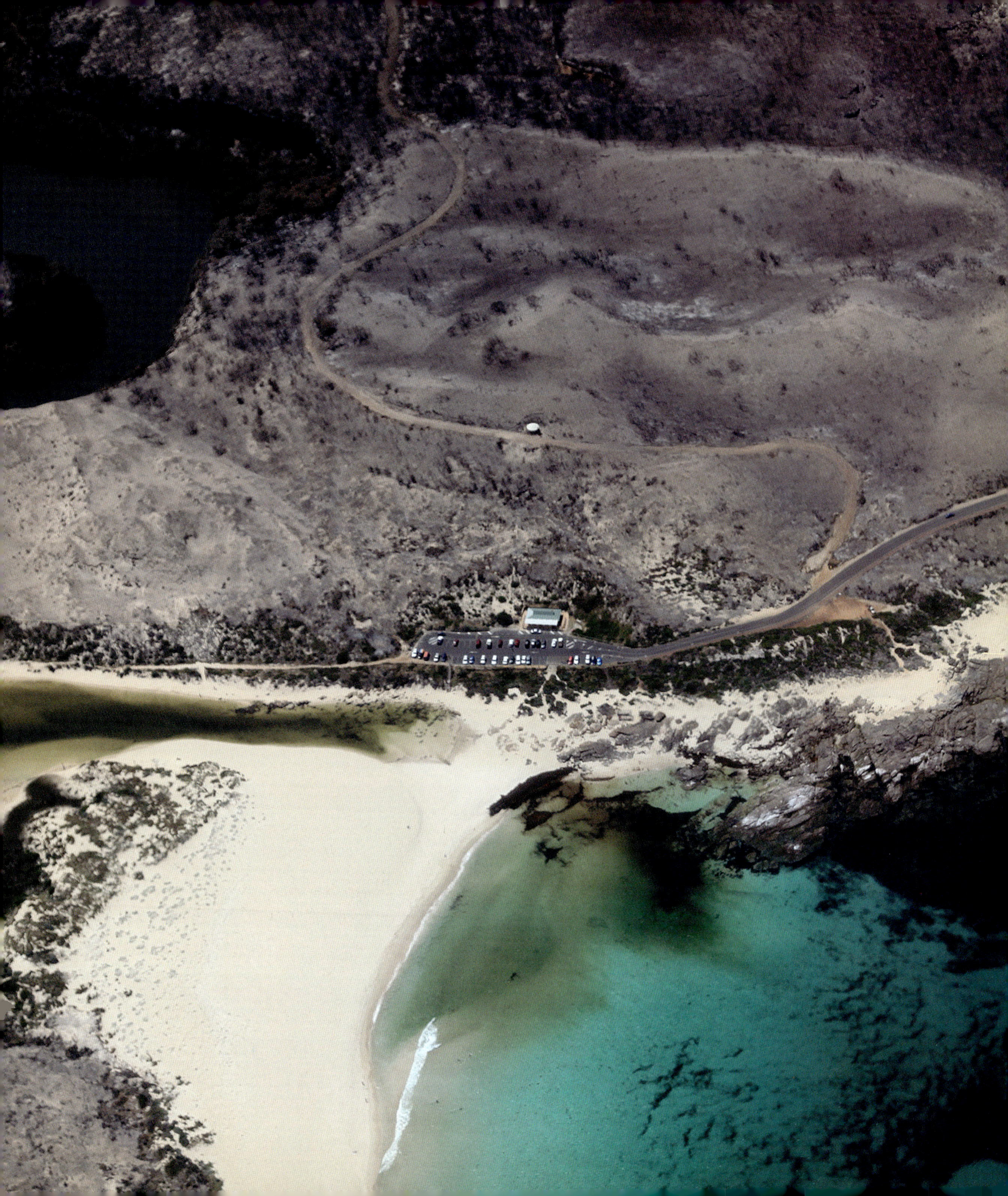

LEFT: The Talbingo Dam, on the Tumut River in southern New South Wales is the largest in the Snowy Mountains Scheme and was completed in 1970.
RIGHT: Cockatoo Island in the Buccaneer Archipelago near Broome, Western Australia. Mining for its high-grade iron ore began in the 1950s. Gradually the western side of the island was shaved off. When deposits were discovered below sea level, a seawall was built to prevent tidal waves from flooding the pit.

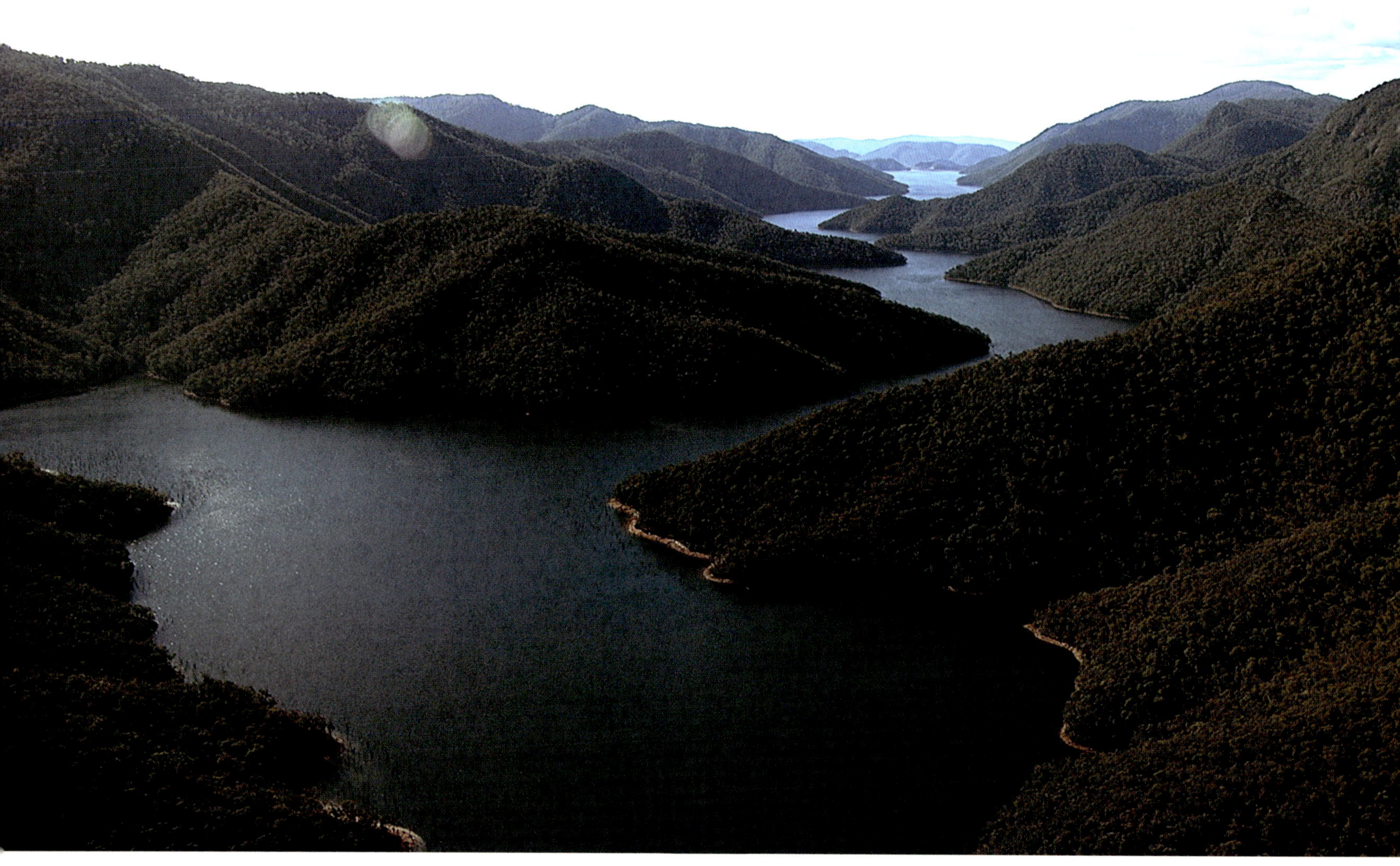

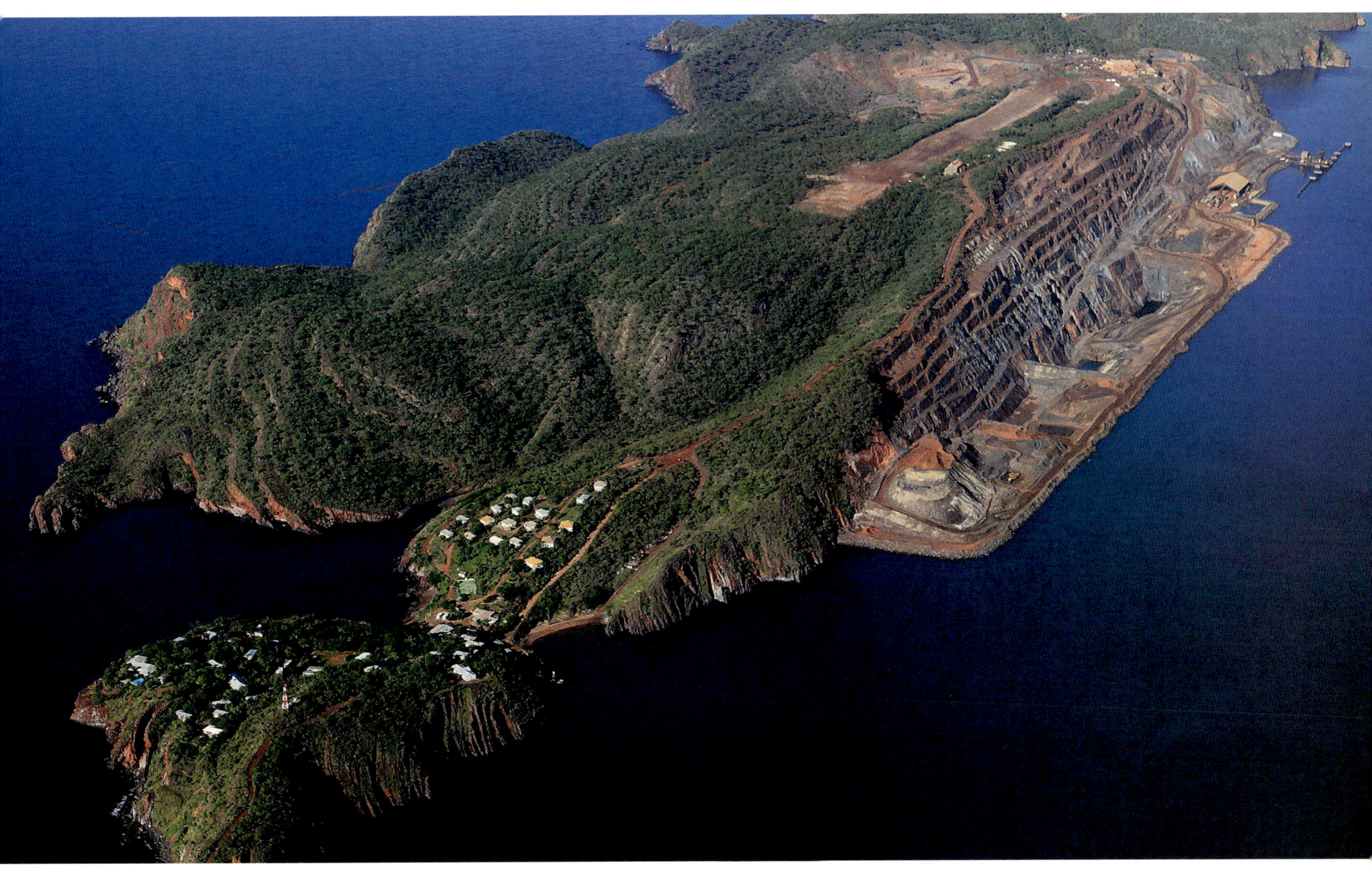

FOLLOWING PAGES: A helicopter from the New South Wales National Parks and Wildlife Service surveys the damage after the Murrumbidgee River broke its banks and flooded farms in the Riverina. On average, lost income from perished livestock, replacing destroyed crops and repair work caused by floods cost the nation $400 million a year.

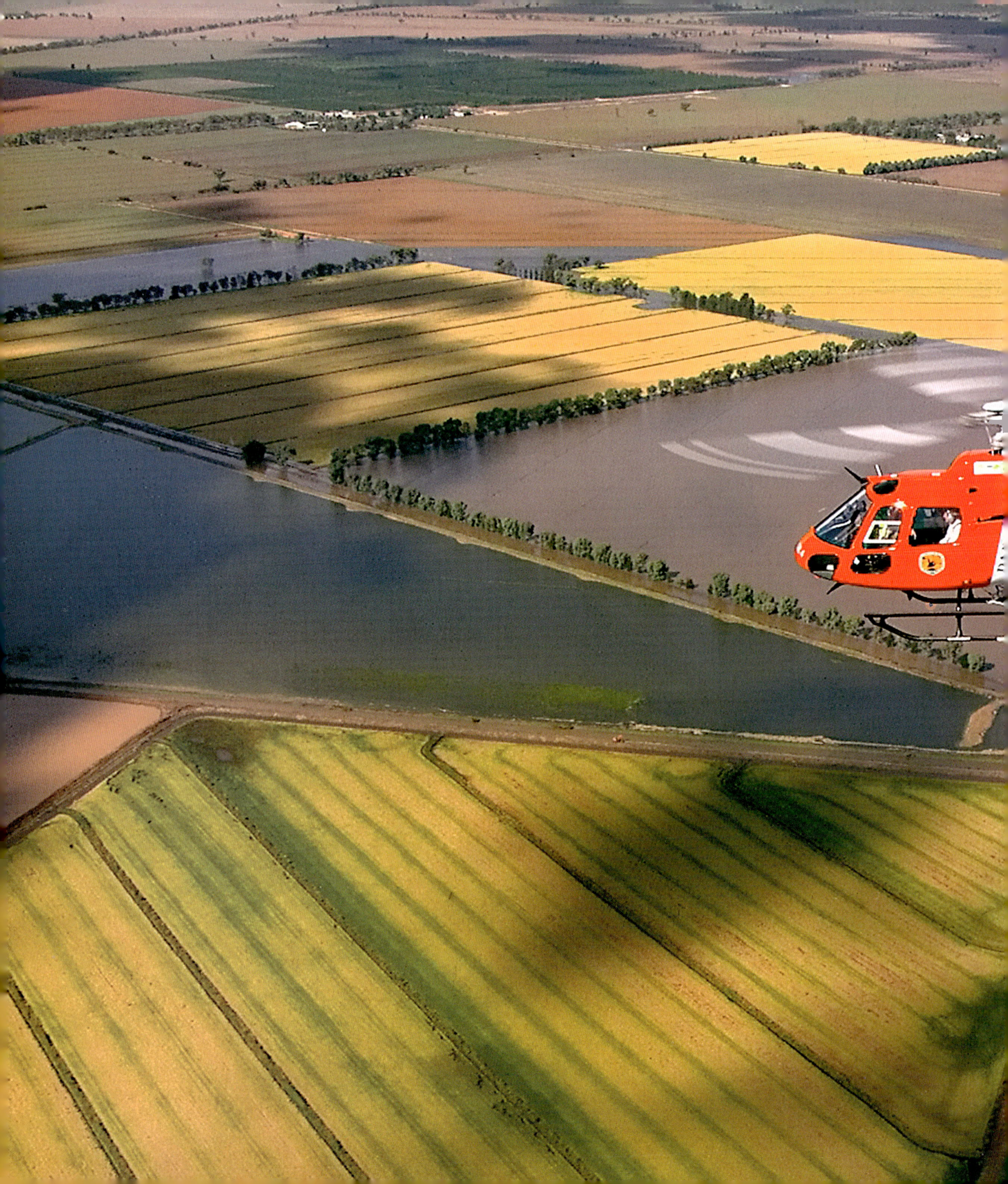

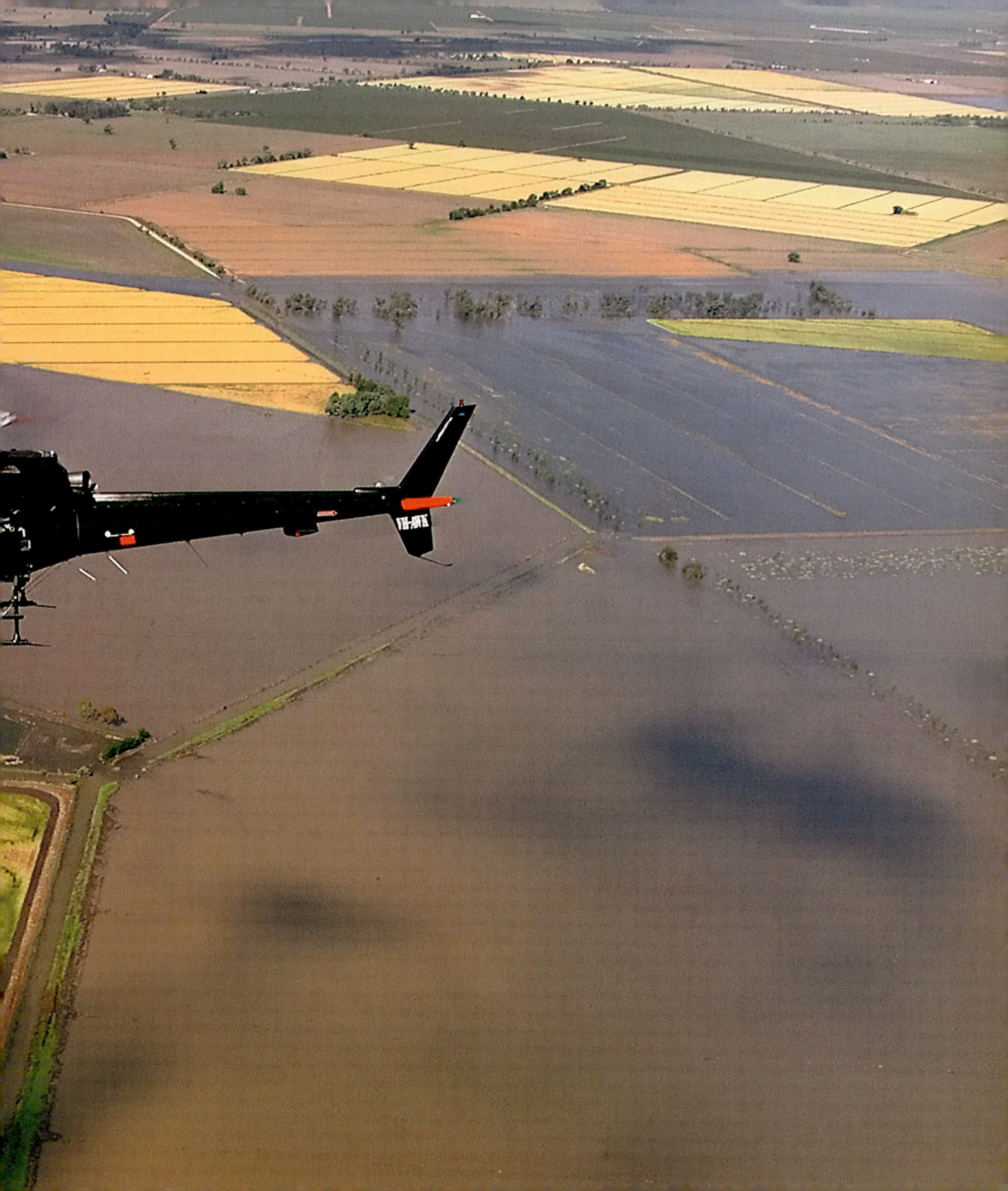

LEFT: A boat has pulled up alongside a farm near Griffith, New South Wales. With trucks and cars no longer able to move, it is the most convenient mode of transport. The 2012 floods saw 2,000 properties in New South Wales cut off and 9,000 people evacuated. **RIGHT:** The Great Barrier Reef.

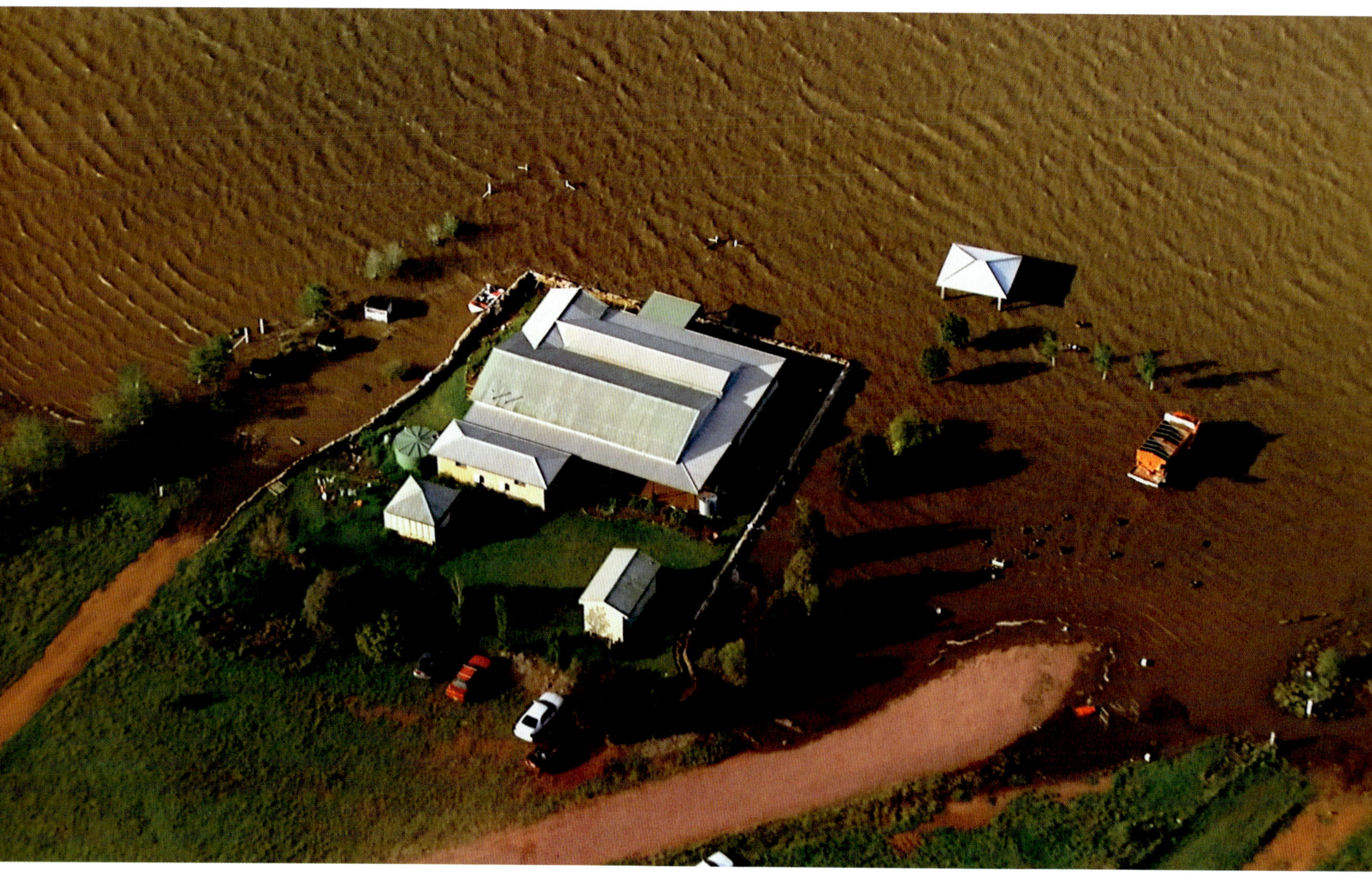

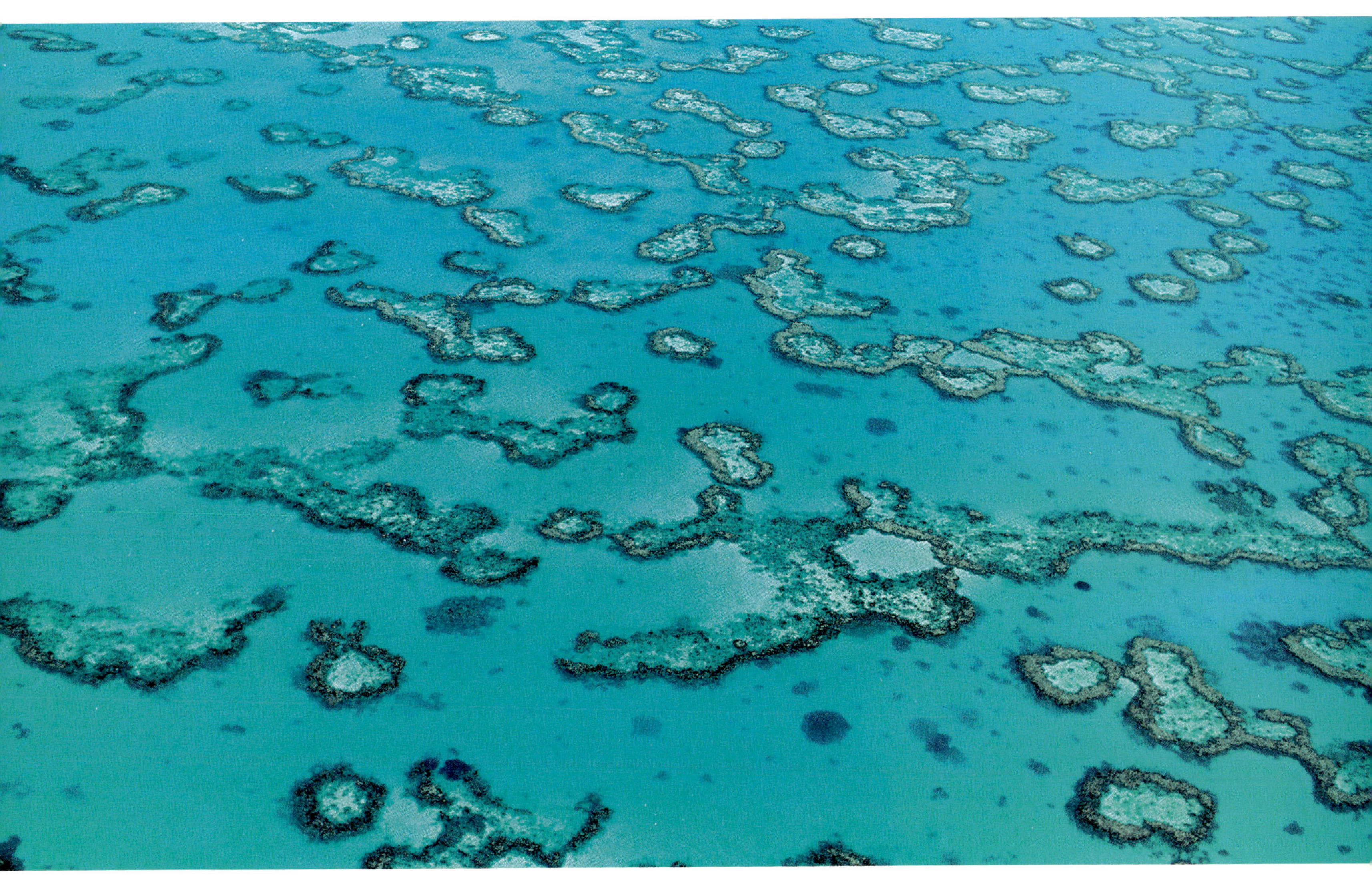

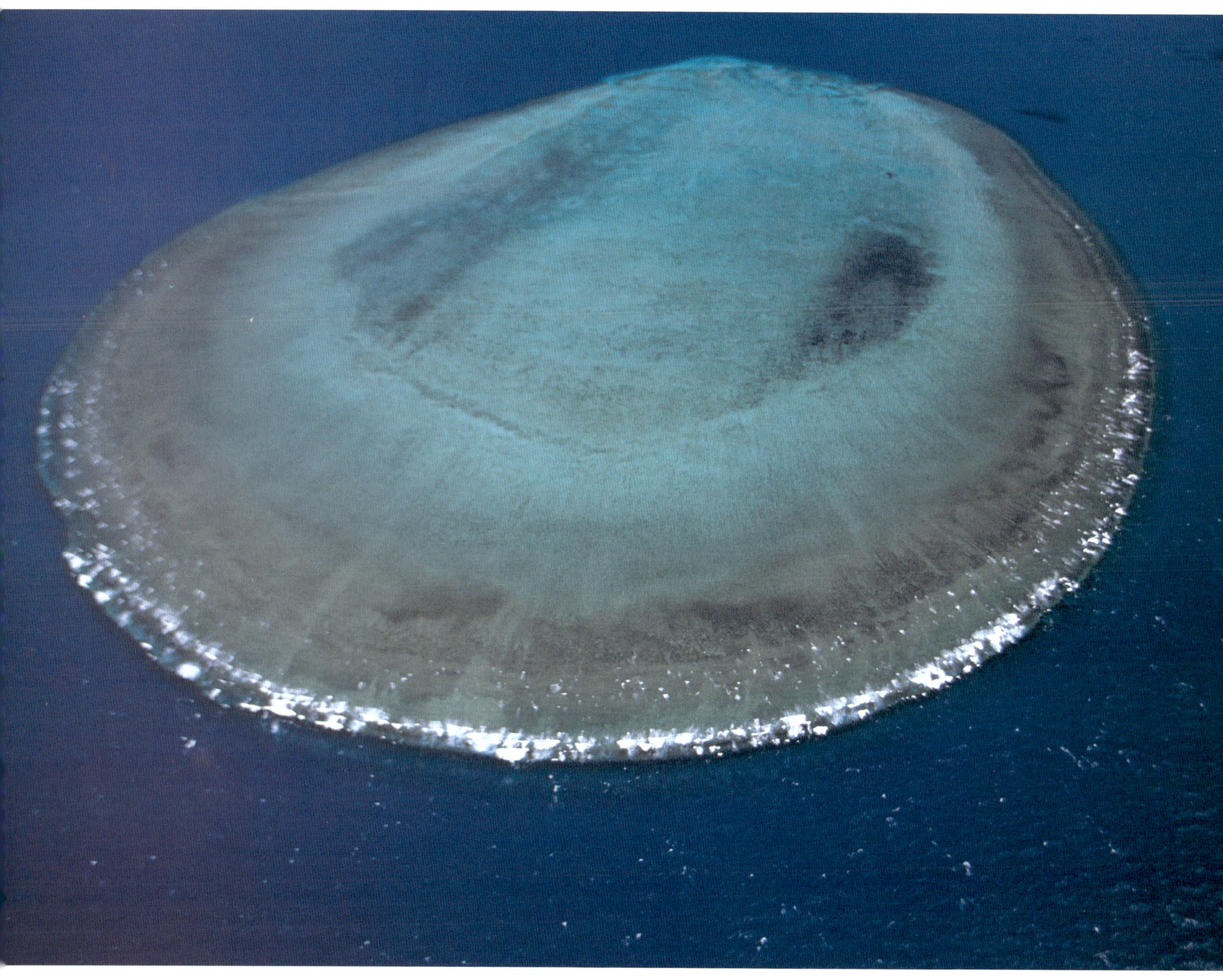

LEFT: An island in the Great Barrier Reef, north of Cooktown, Queensland. There are 900 islands in the Great Barrier Reef system, from small and sandy to much bigger and vegetated cays, as well as large continental islands which can rise to 1,100 metres above sea level. **RIGHT:** Marine farming in Tasmania. Each circular net holds up to 50,000 Atlantic salmon. The industry is worth $350 million a year. By 2025, according to the United Nations Food and Agriculture Organization, more than half of all seafood consumed globally will be farm-produced.

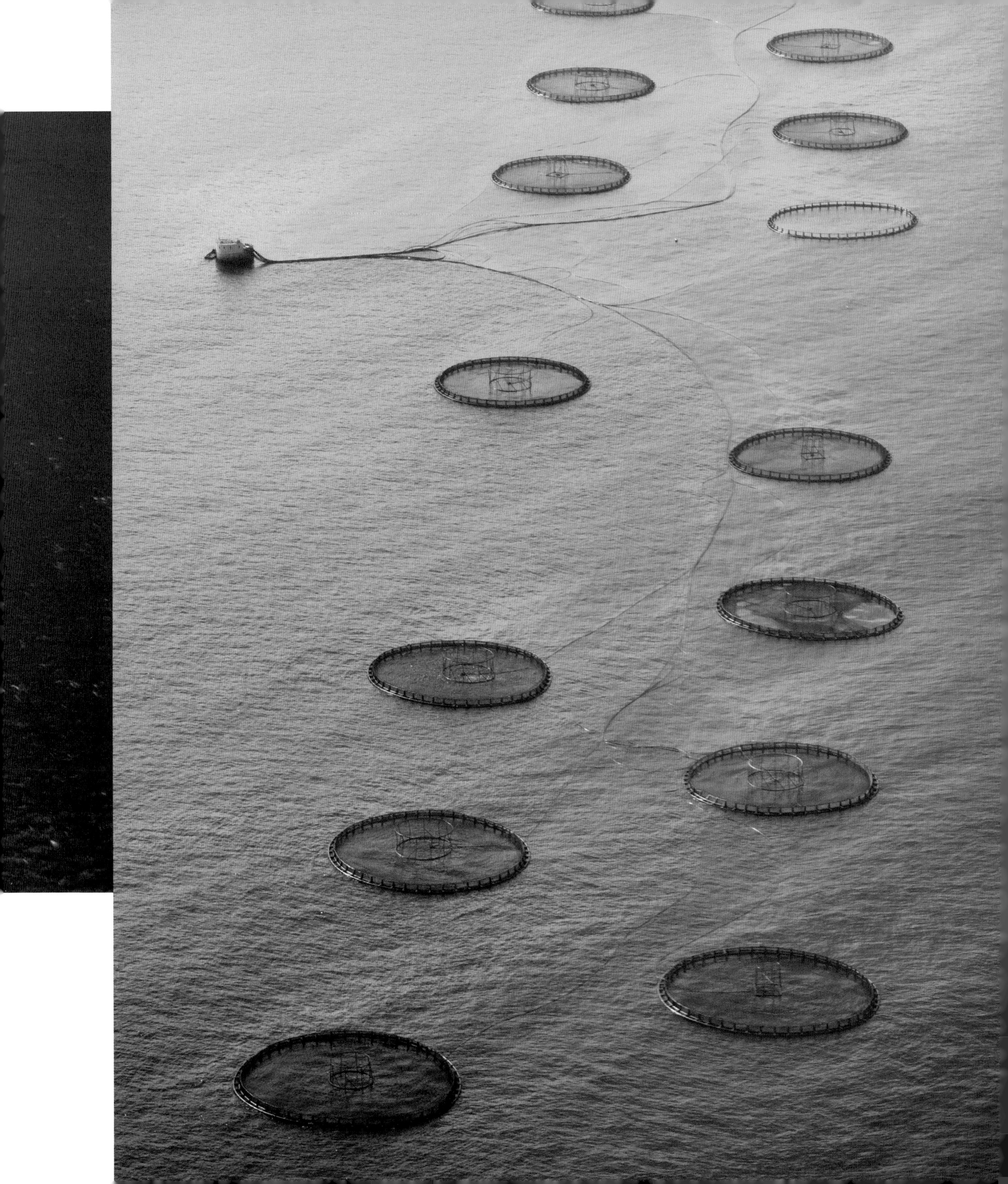

LEFT: A helicopter carrying a reef pilot lands on a Chinese coal carrier in the Great Barrier Reef. The pilot will take control of the vessel to shepherd it safely through a narrow passage to reach Hay Point, one of the world's largest coal ports. **RIGHT:** A coal carrier makes its way through Hydrographers Passage in the Great Barrier Reef. First charted by the navy in 1981, this shortcut to Hay Point saves shipping companies 500 kilometres in travel distance.

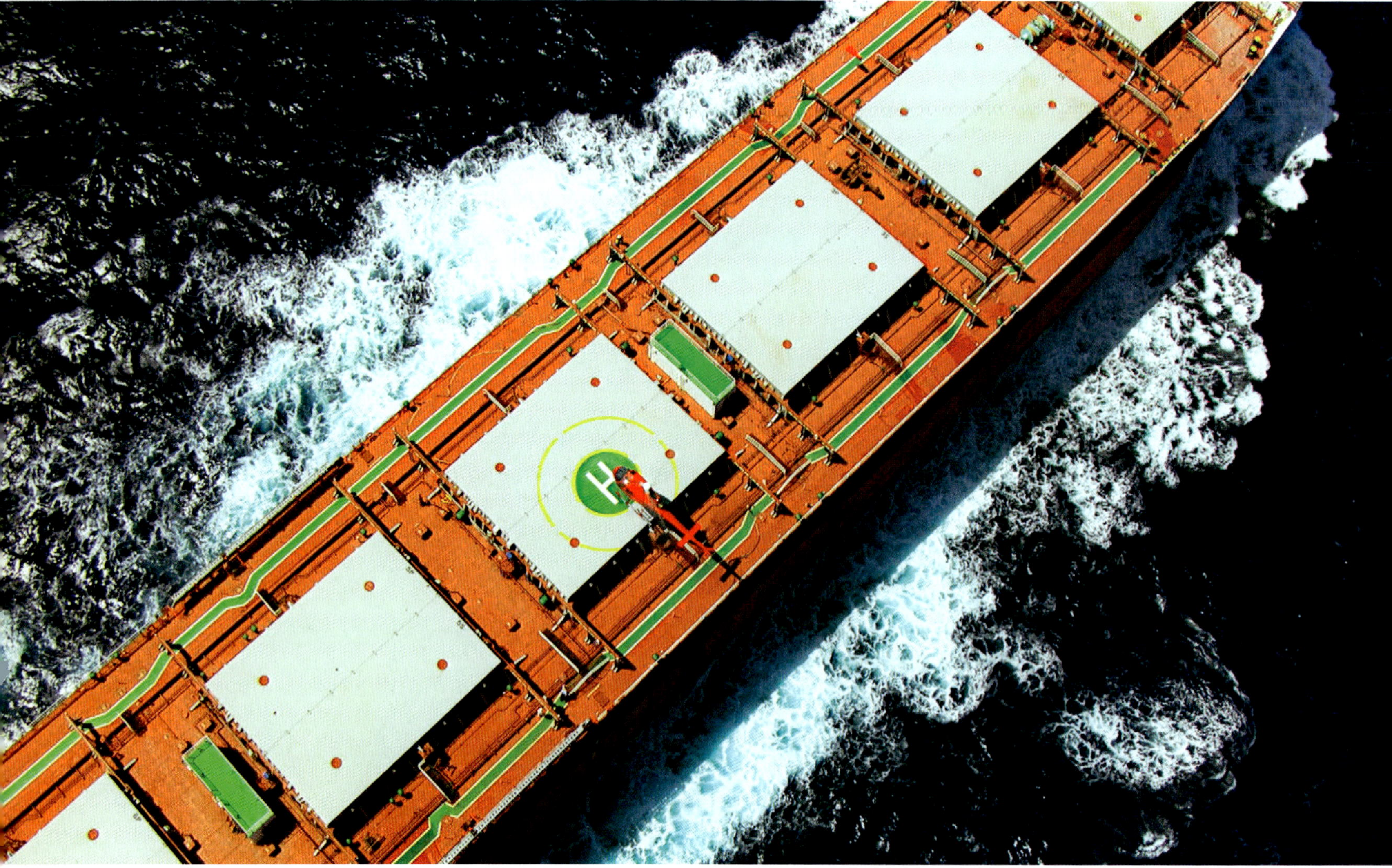

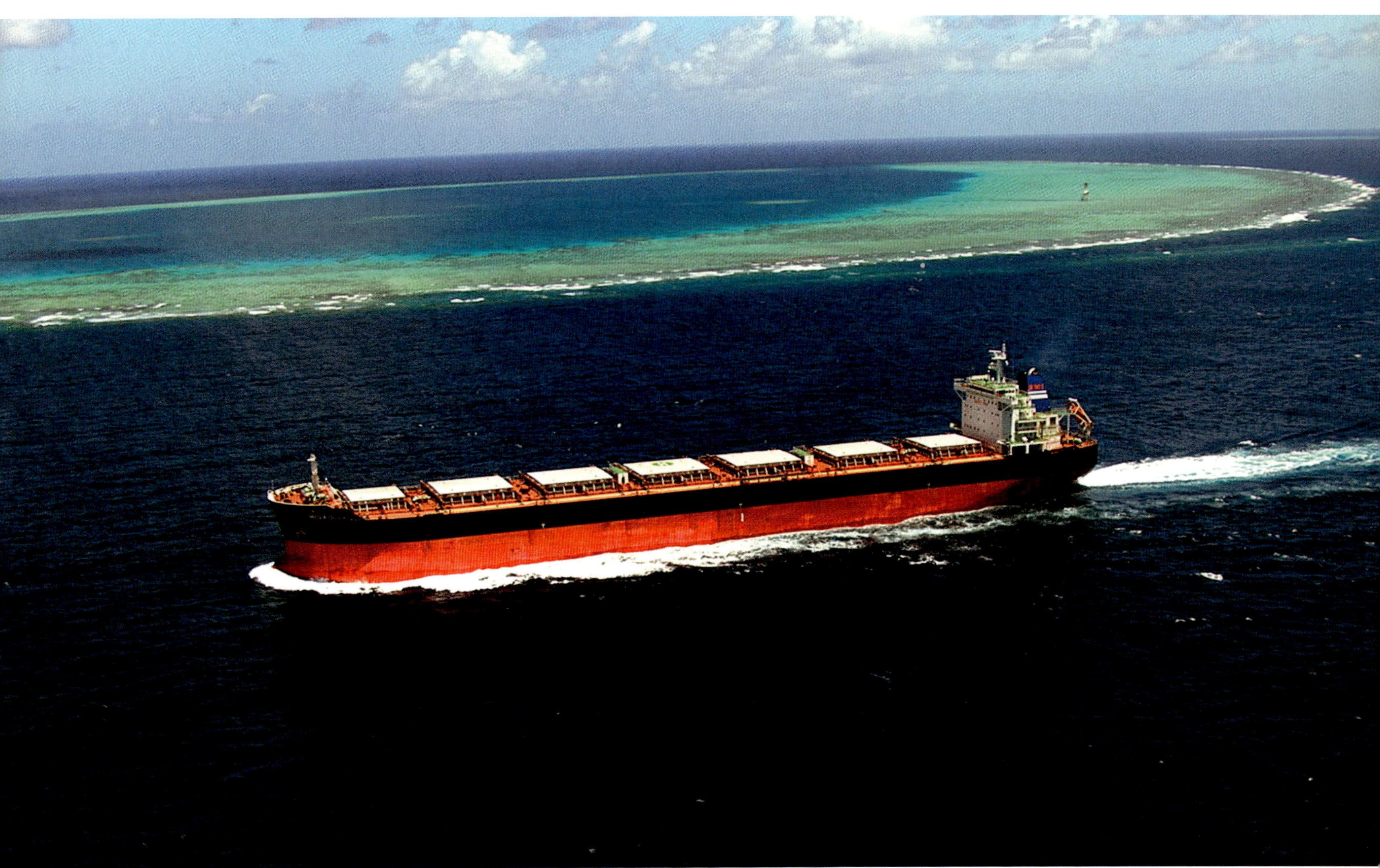

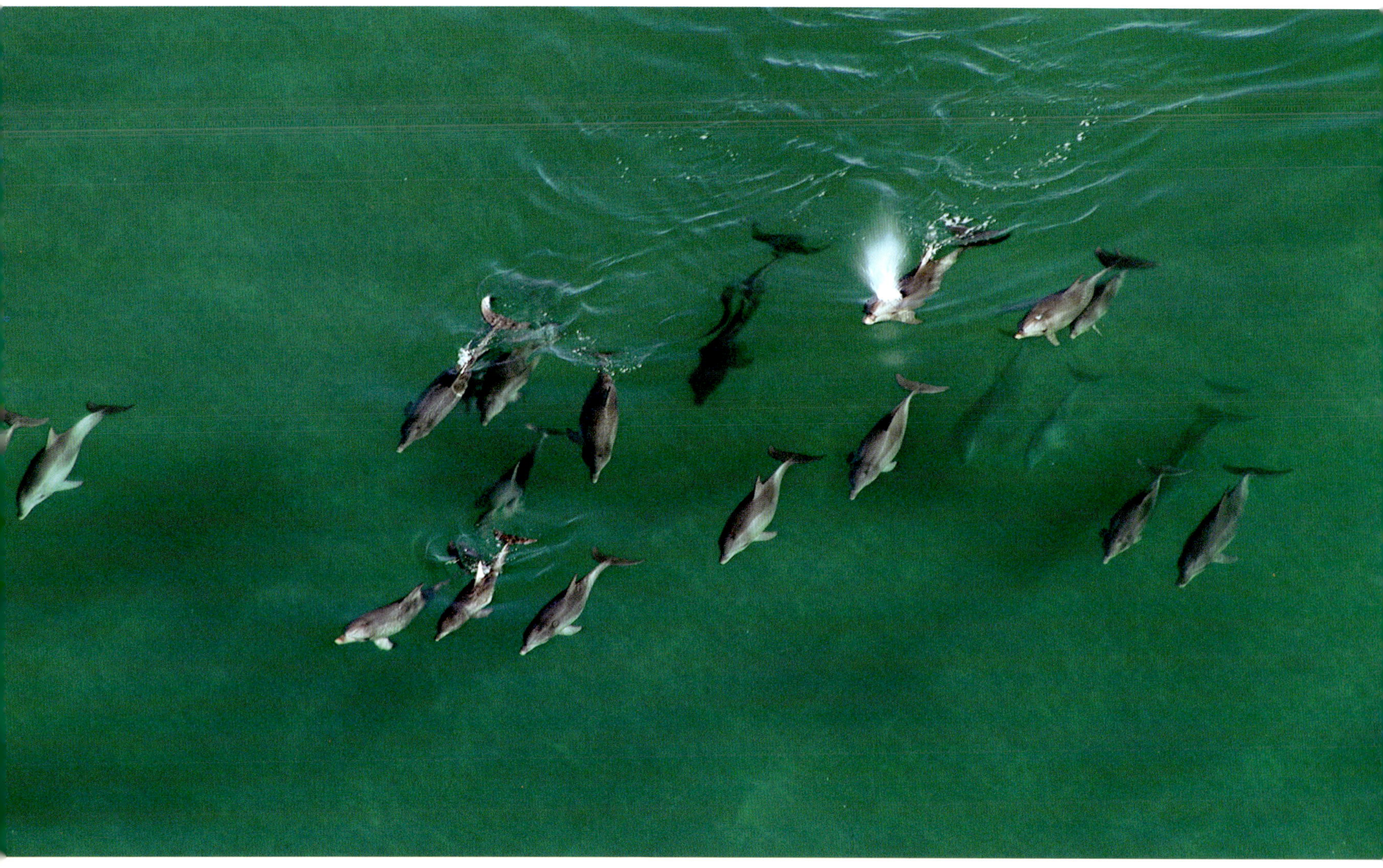

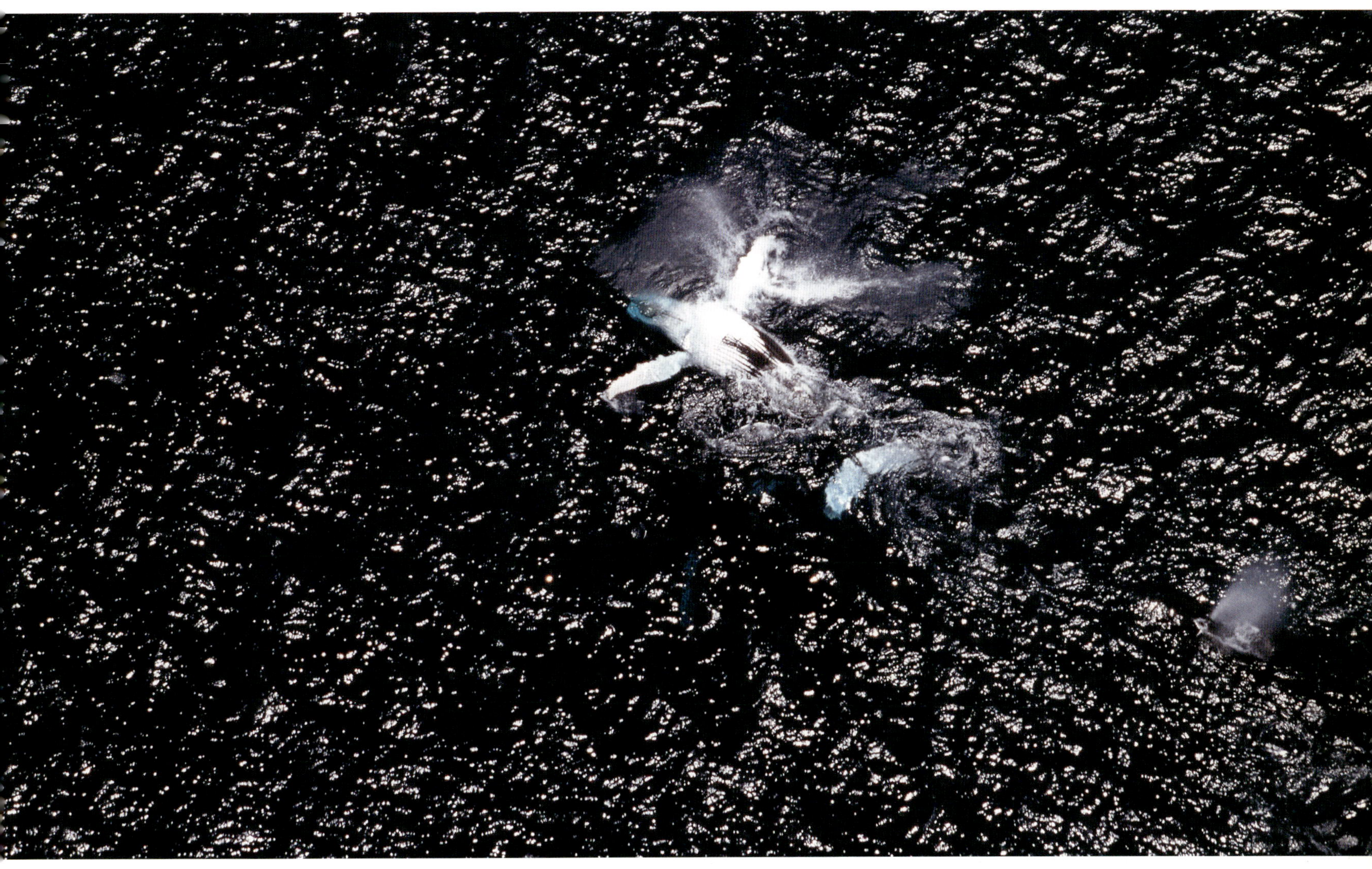

LEFT: About 30 Indo-Pacific bottlenose dolphins have made a permanent home in the Port River and Barker Inlet in Adelaide, South Australia. The sea grasses, marshes, tidal flats, estuaries and mangroves provide habitat and food. In 2005, the area was proclaimed a dolphin sanctuary. **RIGHT:** A humpback whale off Eden on the south coast of New South Wales. From April to November, these gentle giants migrate north to subtropical waters to mate and give birth after feeding on krill in the Antarctic during the summer months.

LEFT: Logging trails in the Darling Ranges look like a river system from above. Located in the southwest of Western Australia, it is the only region in the world where the *Eucalyptus marginata* grows. Known better by its Aboriginal name, jarrah, it is a much sought after hardwood for flooring, musical instruments and cabinet making. **RIGHT:** Many regions in the Murray–Darling basin suffer from extensive soil erosion caused by grazing, land clearing and rabbit plagues going back 150 years.

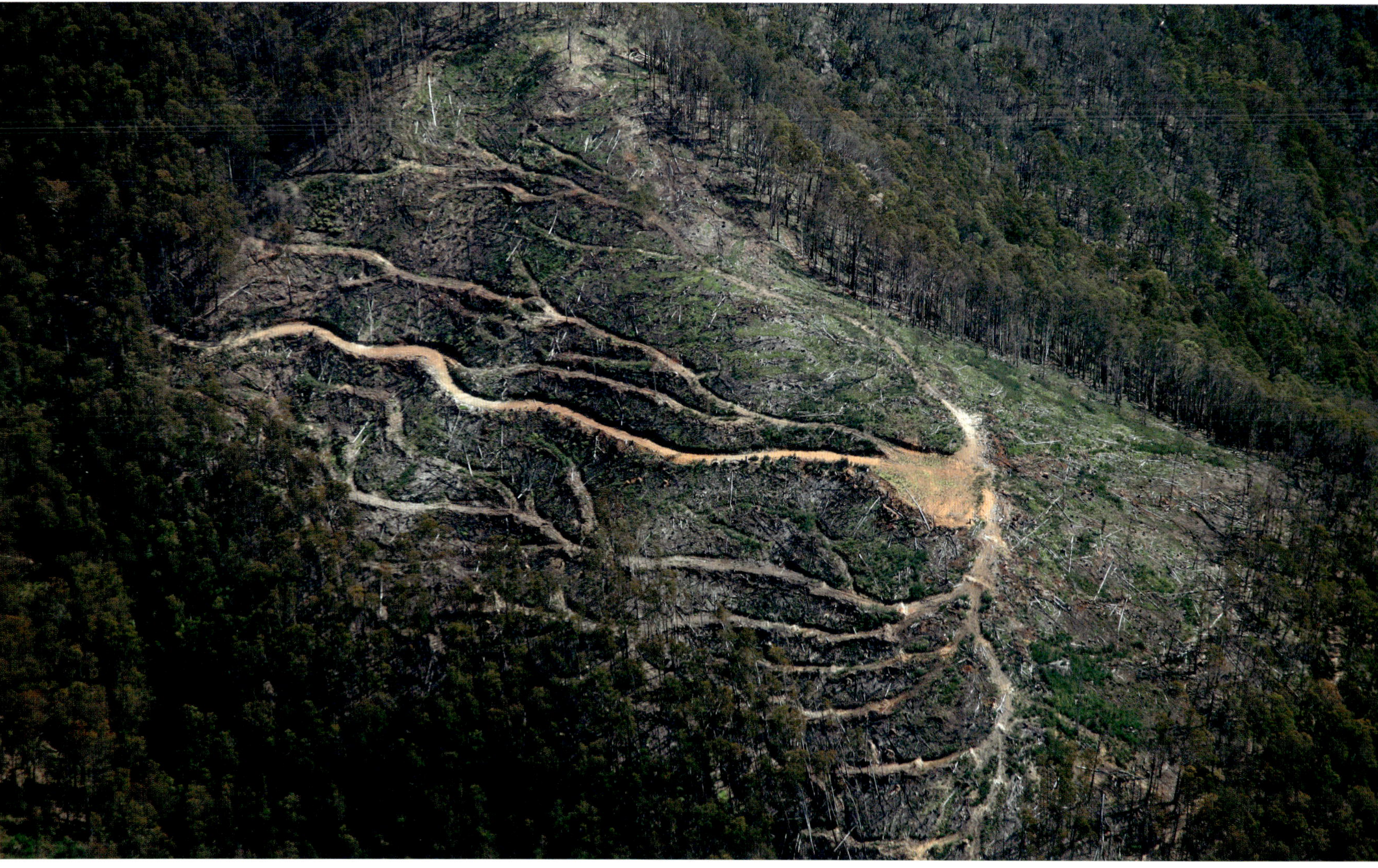

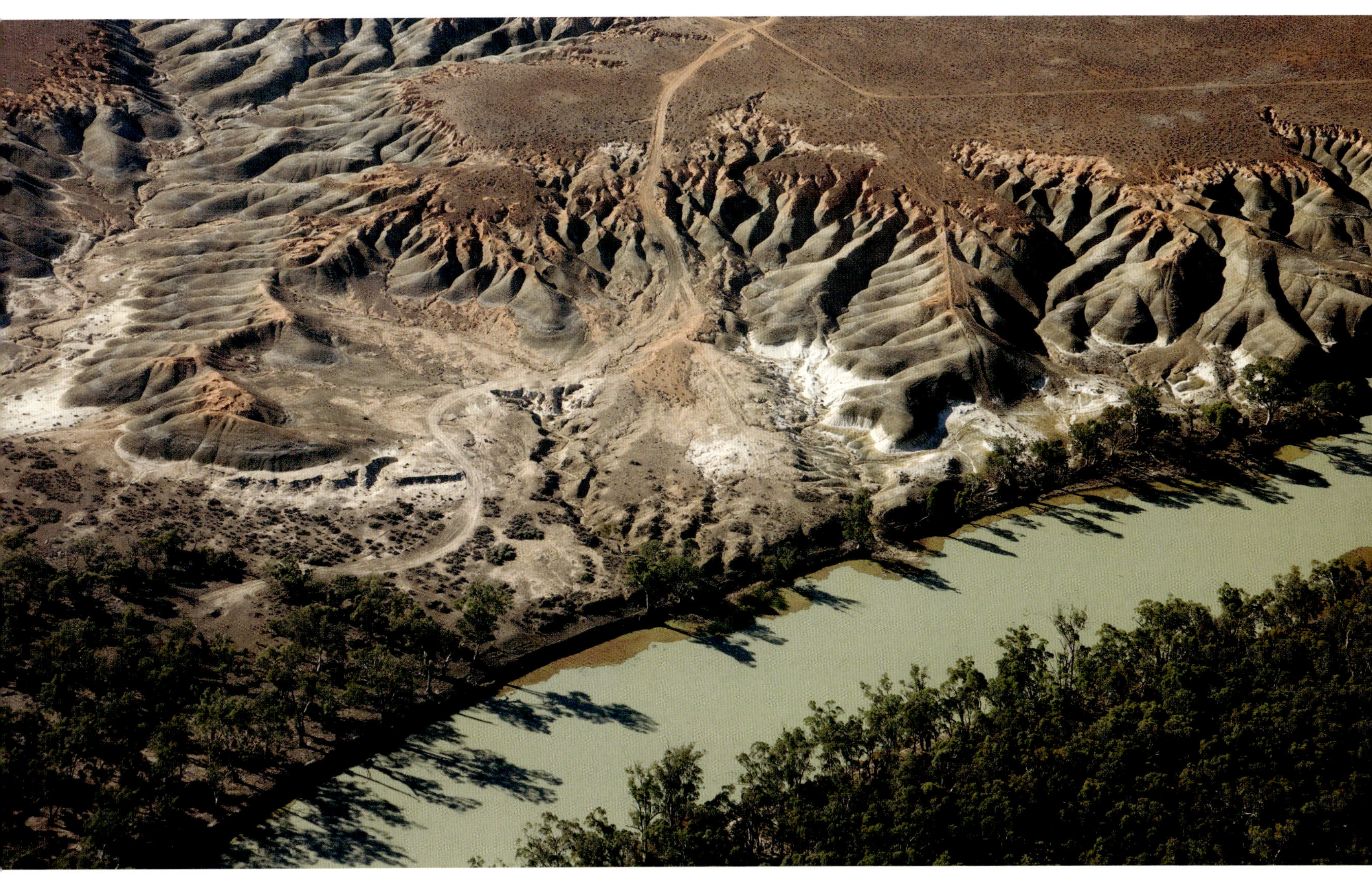

FOLLOWING PAGES: A noose around the neck of the forest? Logging karri trees in Western Australia's southwest botanical province. These eucalypts are among the tallest hardwood trees in the world.

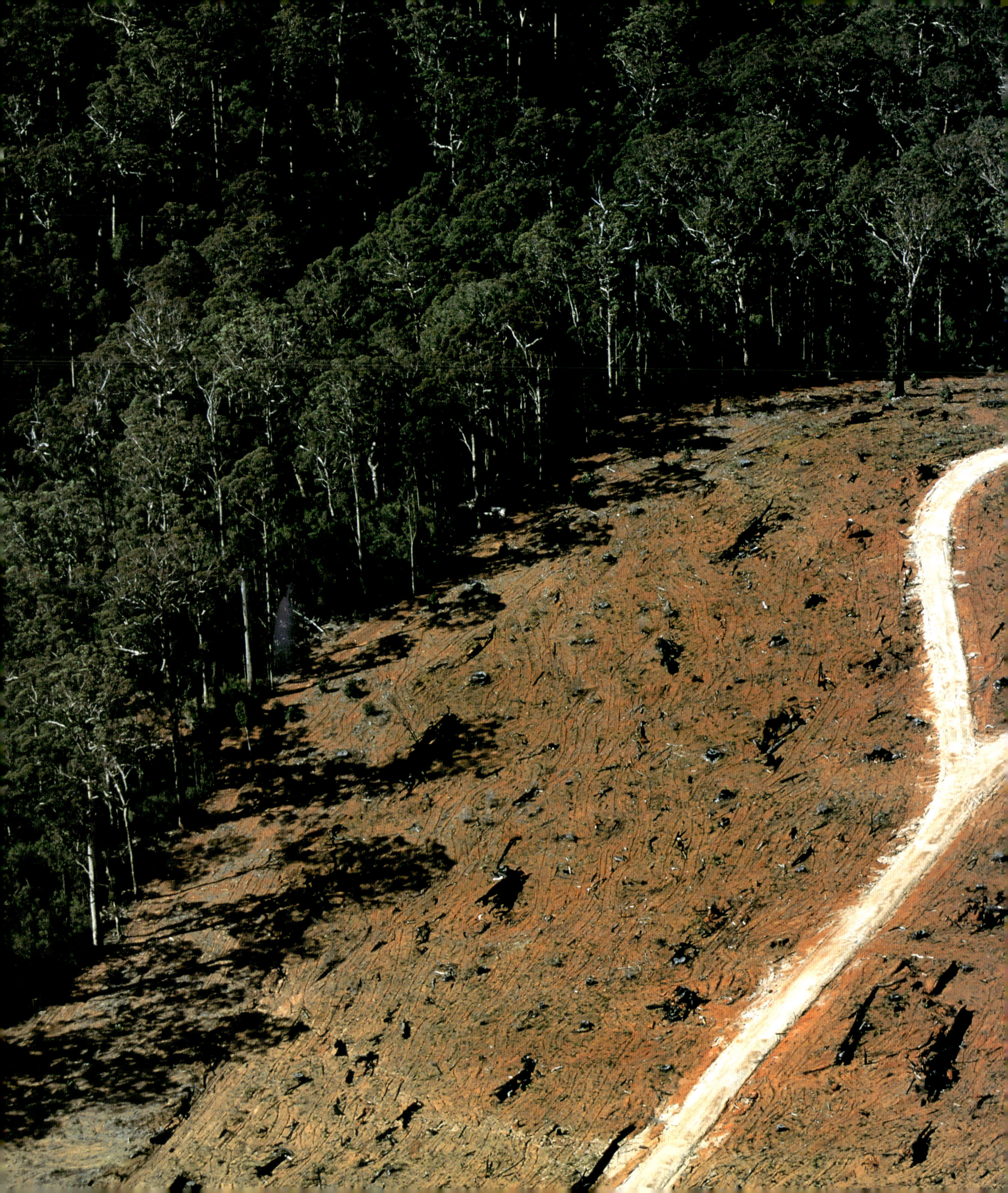

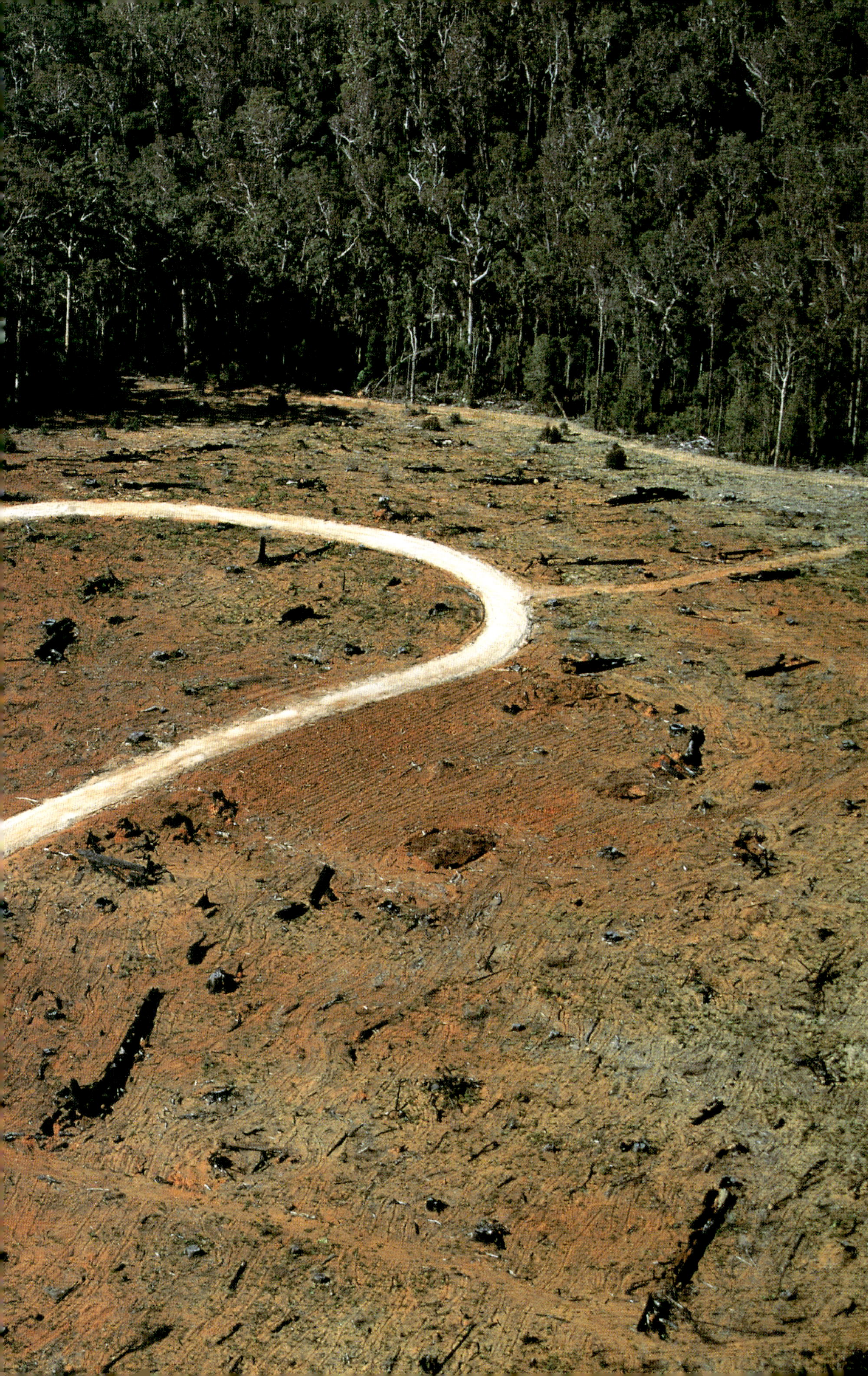

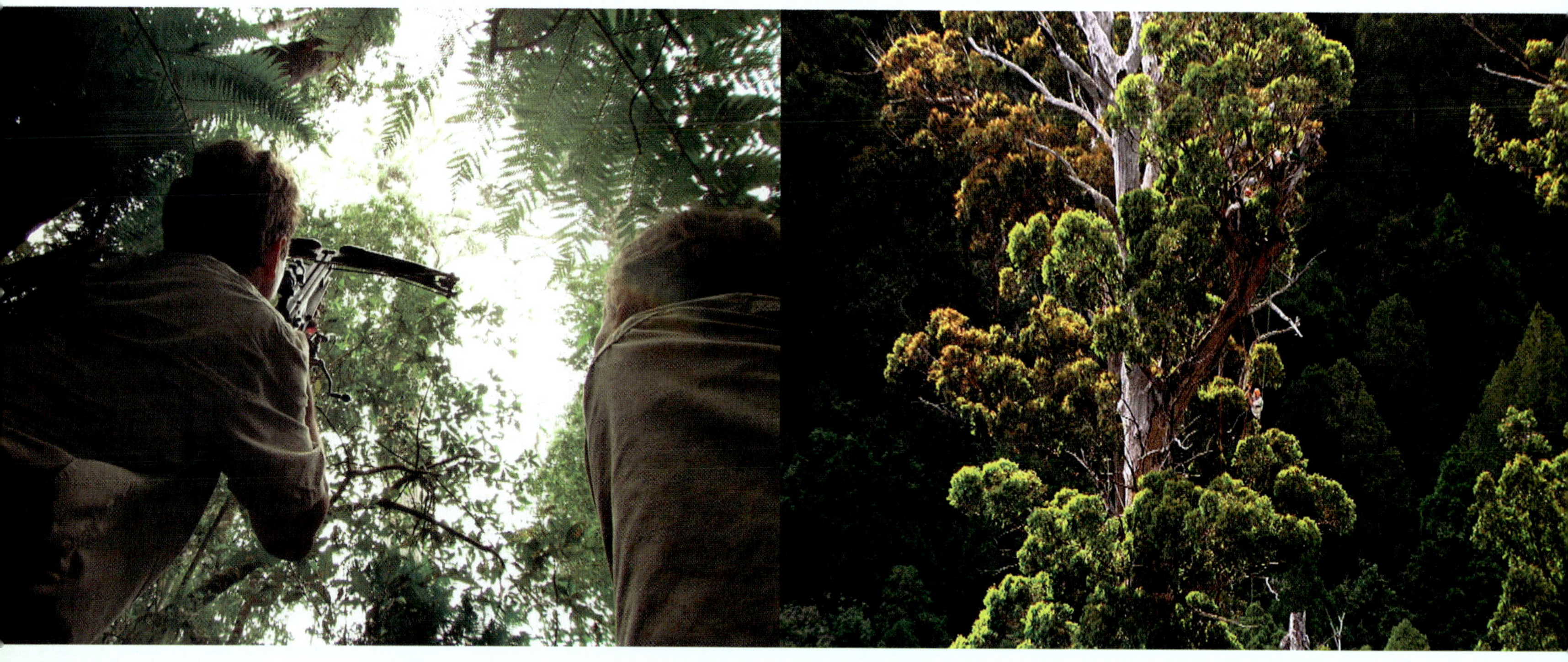

STANDING TALL FOR EUCALYPT GIANTS

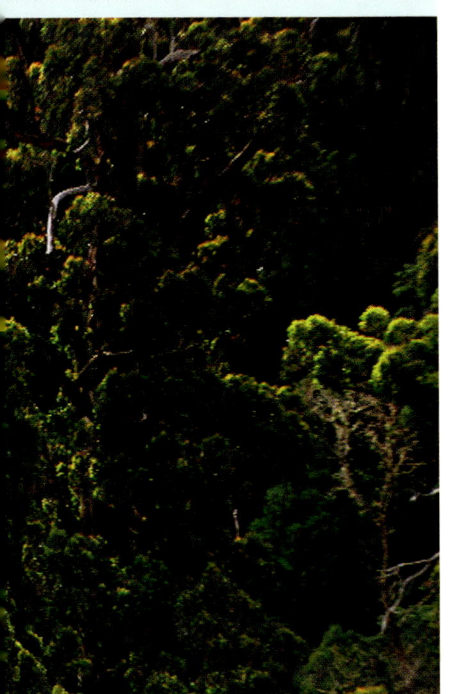

AUSTRALIA HAS ALMOST 150 million hectares of forests, mostly native and some plantations. These forests cover about a fifth of the continent. They are also at the centre of our tug of war with the natural world. In Tasmania, especially, that battle is carved in its rugged landscape. The logging industry is vital to the state's economy, employing 10,000 people. Since European settlement, though, 70 per cent of native forests have been lost, either to harvesting for logs or clearing for agriculture.

In a dense forest southwest of Hobart, friends Tom Greenwood, Brett Mifsud and Grant Harris are making their way to a tree named Toby Bennett. It isn't just any tree — it's a giant eucalypt, *Eucalyptus regnans*. But Greenwood and his mates are not ordinary bushwalkers either. The three specialise in climbing tall trees. Greenwood, a professional arborist, is a three-time national tree climbing champion. The native eucalypts they seek out are the world's tallest hardwood trees.

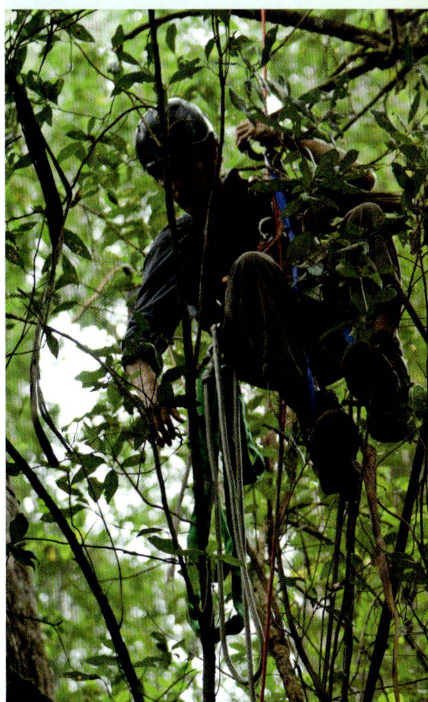

The team climbs and then measures the trees to provide scientific data to researchers and to help save the giants from being cut down. Local forestry regulations classify a tree of 85 metres in height, or a volume of 285 cubic metres, as a giant. And while that protects that particular tree from logging, Greenwood says more should be done. 'They are protected, but if you only protect a small area around the giants, you still hasten their decline. Our big thing is protecting these trees with space.'

Before the climb to measure Toby Bennett begins, Greenwood shoots a crossbow arrow with a setting line attached to it over a branch at the top of the tree. It's all very Robin Hood and quite difficult.

'On a good day you can get it first go, if it really goes well,' says Greenwood. 'The longest I have ever spent setting a line is seven hours.' Once the line is secured, the climb begins. The adventurers strap themselves in a harness and make their way up. The tree is like a highway for creepy-crawlies. Arboreal ants run up and down, emphasising that these giants are effectively high-rise developments for other life forms. They are also carbon dioxide sinks, trapping greenhouse gas for centuries.

The eucalypts are extraordinarily fast-growing. They reach 50 metres in 50 years after which they live half a millennium. Toby Bennett measures 79 metres in height — the equivalent of a 25-storey building — and 315 cubic metres in volume. This tree will be safe from logging but other old growth forests remain vulnerable. In years to come we will have to ask the question of whether these trees are worth more to us dead or alive.

FOOD BOWL OF THE SEA

AARON JONES IS first mate on the New Fish II, one of 52 trawlers that fish for prawn in the mighty Gulf of Carpentaria, a sprawling expanse that's five times the size of Tasmania. The fleet targets nine species of prawn including Brown Tiger, White Banana and Blue Endeavour. 'It is sort of a primitive thing,' says Jones. 'You are out there hunting, gathering food. I like to feed people. I think that is what draws me to it.'

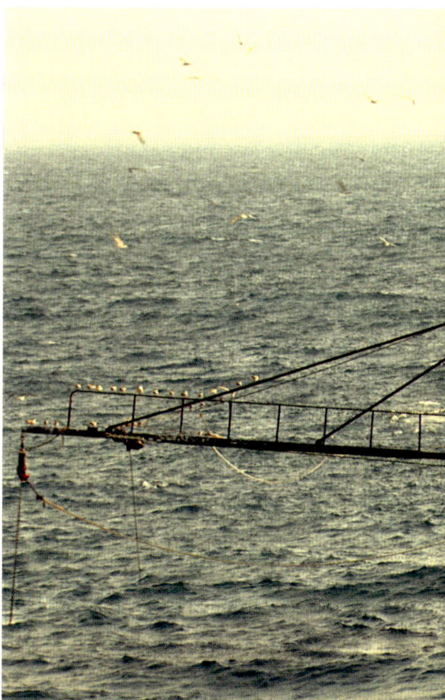

On a typical night, Aaron and his crew hope to catch 500 to 600 kilograms of prawns. To do that they trawl in the dark when the prawns emerge en masse from the muddy depths to feed. It's an effort, Jones suspects, which few folks on land really appreciate. 'A lot of people I speak to,' he says, 'don't know where prawns come from. They come from the supermarket as far as they are concerned.'

Prawn fishing is hard work. Once caught, each individual prawn is picked up by hand and sorted by size. There are no machines involved. 'It's quite physical, you do a lot of hours,' says Jones. But it is a worthwhile pursuit — the little crustaceans fetch $90 million a year.

As the sun sets, Jones and his crew release the nets for the first haul. There will be several attempts throughout the night, using nets that have been designed to allow big fish and turtles to escape while keeping the prawns in. 'I like the sustainability of it,' says Jones. 'Hammerhead sharks, groupers, anything massive all go through. They don't get dragged around in the net all night and end up dying.'

At 5am, Aaron and his now weary crew bring in the last of the night's catch. Another backbreaking 12 hours in the Gulf prove to have been productive. New Fish II harvested half a tonne of prawns worth $14,000. Before the crew can rest, though, they need to offload their snap-frozen booty to a mother ship that services the wider fleet. That vessel will take the prawns to Cairns where they are distributed throughout Australia and abroad.

For fisherman Jones there is a delicious irony. 'All your larger prawns that we get the best money for, they'll go to Tokyo,' he says. 'That is not such a bad thing that they don't end up in Australia because larger prawns are horrible really. They are just big and tough and I don't understand why people like them. I think it is just the presentation of it.'

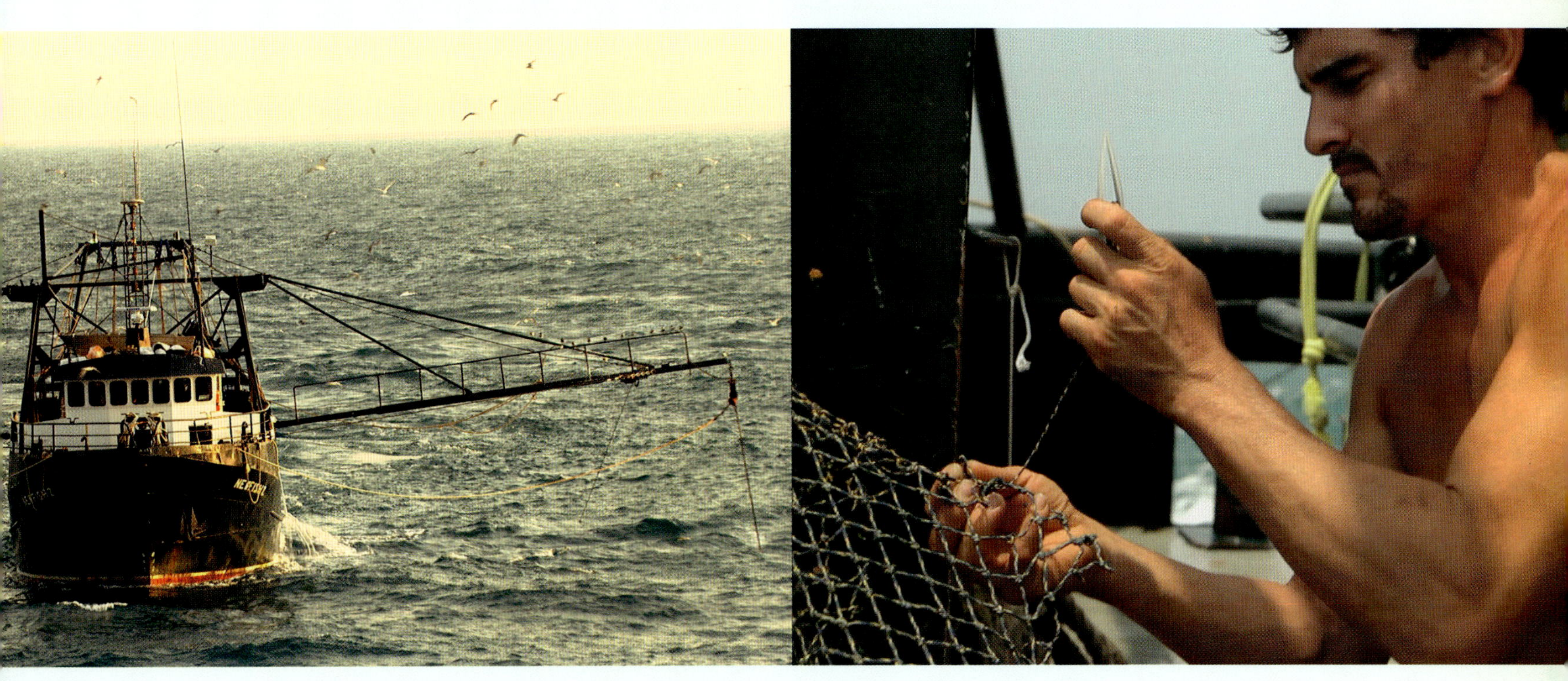

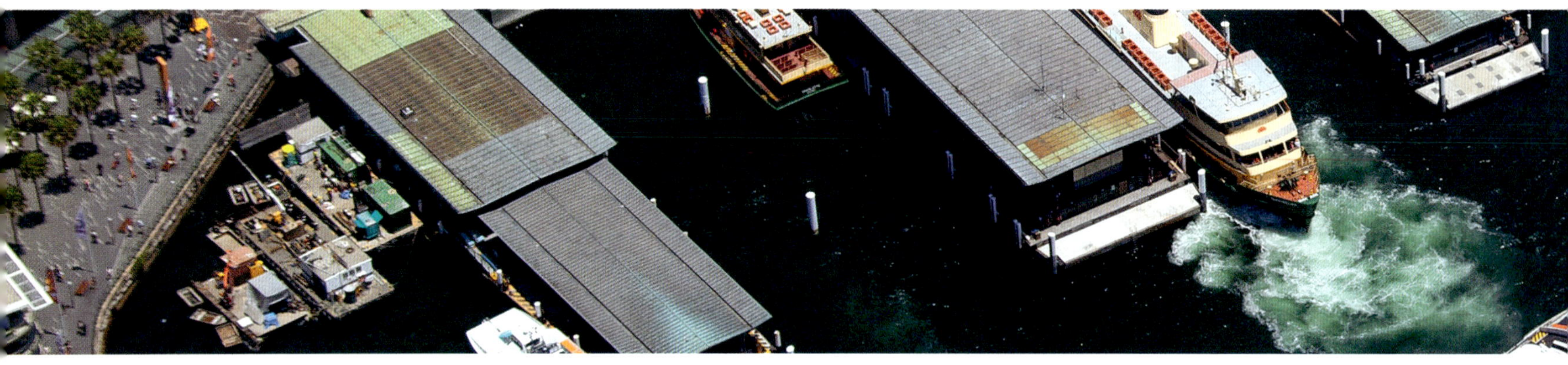

ON THE MOVE

We are a country of daily mass migrations – by road, rail, air and even cyberspace. As a sparsely populated but highly urbanised nation, we rely on an intricate web of transport networks to keep us connected and on the move.

These systems are remarkably fragile yet strangely robust. They teeter forever on the edge of chaos but are somehow in firm control. Our nation of 23 million people is constantly on the move and there's a lot more going on to support that than meets the eye.

As dawn breaks from east to west, we wake to rituals that have a distinct Australian feel – swimmers take a dip in rock pools, rowers stroke our rivers and lakes, golfers squeeze in a quick nine holes. All gentle moves but harbingers of the early morning movement madness that is about to unfold.

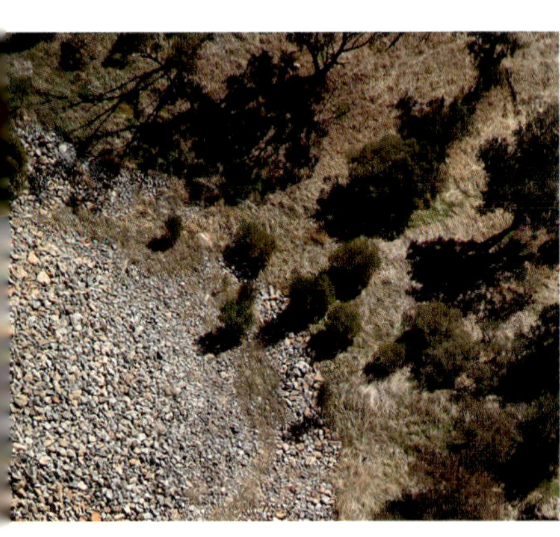

Soon, in Melbourne, carriages will roll onto the world's largest tram network; almost 500 trams on 500 kilometres of track. 'It's just another working day,' says tram driver Desmond Barboza. He's been on the job for 11 years during which, he estimates, he transported between three to four million people. 'Today, I expect to pick up 2,000 passengers.'

In the heart of Brisbane, early morning trains shuttle in and out of South Bank and Roma Street stations, while in Adelaide, commuters pour out of the main station in a rush to the city centre. On Sydney Harbour, ferries deliver the first of 90,000 passengers. Many more commuters will arrive at Central Station by train. Fewer than 100,000 people call Sydney's CBD home, but every day its population mushrooms to a million.

Our skies are about to be filled with flight, as well. A staggering 55 million passengers fly from place to place within Australia in one year, covering 63 billion kilometres in the air, the equivalent of 164,000 trips to the moon.

Sydney Airport sits at the centre of a patchwork of 185 airports, aerodromes and regional landing strips. Subject to a strict curfew, the first planes move no earlier than 6am, but preparations to help take us to the sky begin well before that. Captain Elyse Fordham is getting ready for the departure of QF401, the first flight to Melbourne. Early morning is her favourite time of the day to fly. 'It's lovely and calm,' she says, 'and just very peaceful.' Before take off she inspects the exterior of the plane, checking the wings, tyres and everything else to ensure a safe flight. Meanwhile, luggage is loaded and snacks brought on board.

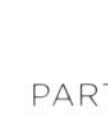

On a typical day, 150 domestic flights connect Sydney and Melbourne. It is the world's second busiest corridor, only beaten by planes between Rio de Janeiro and Sao Paulo in Brazil. 'It can feel like a traffic jam,' says Fordham, 'because there is so much traffic going into Sydney and Melbourne and there is only a certain amount of tarmac that the aircraft can land on.'

The congestion leads to the holding patterns so many of us are familiar with. 'It involves a racetrack type of pattern to go round and round in circles because we simply can't pull over and park the plane,' says Fordham.

On an average day she flies between the two great cities four times, clocking up 4,000 kilometres in the air. And as she does so, a crucial network to watch over her is in full flight down below, on the ground. In Melbourne, Jeff Whitely and his team of air controllers look after half the nation's airspace. They take charge as soon as flights leave local control. By 7am, QF401 is just one in a long line of aircraft waiting to land.

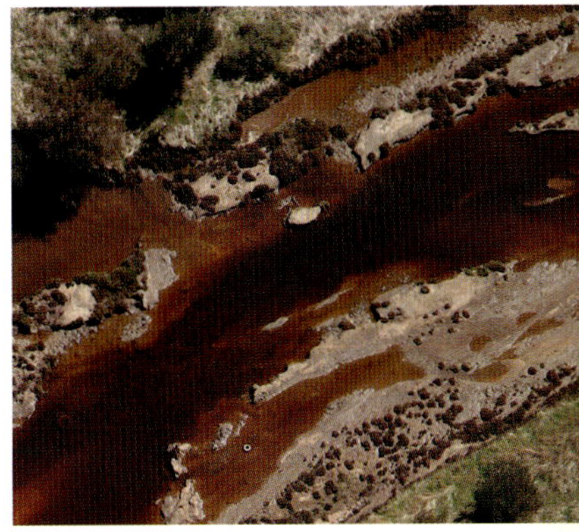

Whitely's crew deals with domestic and international carriers. Last year, 27 million people flew in and out of the country on international flights. 'It's endless really,' says Whitely. 'Each one is neatly spaced with about three minutes between each and every one, and that will just continue for the next few hours.'

In the past five years, flights between Sydney and Melbourne have soared 20 per cent to more than 50,000 a year. This route, and indeed all such highways in the sky, will expand even further as our economy and population grows.

Already, 12 million people – more than half the population – commute by air, land and sea every day across Australia. It leads to one transport system piling on top of another, piling on top of yet another. Across the country, two million people catch trains. Two-thirds of all school children are dropped off by car, and then 80 per cent of us take that car to work. It's an extraordinary figure and, surprisingly, pretty much the same across all our cities.

With that in mind, it's hard to deny we are a nation of car lovers – only outdone by the Americans – and that love affair shapes our cities, our lifestyles and even our health. Three-quarters of us complain about stress while in traffic. When you are stuck in it, looking at your watch, pondering whether to just suck it up or whether it's worth an attempt at jumping lanes, it is easy to think that nobody cares. Quite the opposite is true.

Around Australia, small groups of experts sit glued to screens taking live video feeds from thousands of cameras watching traffic from above. Phones ring and workers bark orders trying to keep traffic on the move. In Sydney, a dedicated band of brothers in the NSW Transport Management Centre watches morning traffic across the state with a birds-eye view. From the outside, their building looks like any other suburban, bland, office block. But inside it is a 350-square-metre, hi-tech, glitzy and buzzing operation. A 15-metre screen displays a mosaic of images provided by 1,500 traffic cameras around the state. On either side of the video wall, 15 more monitors show what drivers on the state's 180,000-kilometre road network are up to. The video installation looms over the centre's 18 traffic managers, who guide 120 million vehicles a year. 'I think the centre is the best-kept secret in Sydney,' says Alan Cohen. 'I really don't think most commuters understand the degree of the monitoring and the efforts put in to try to make the network run on a daily basis.'

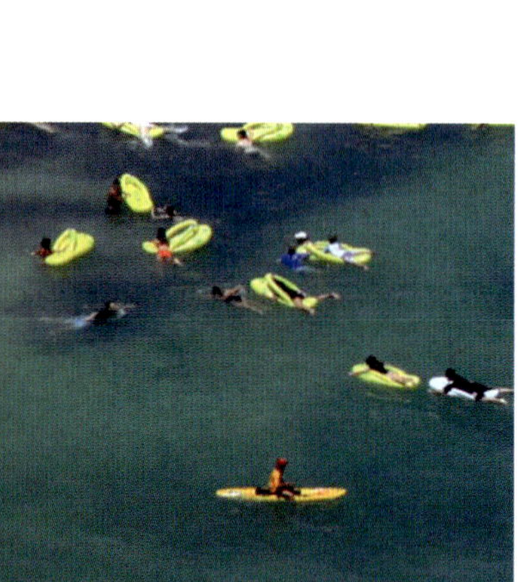

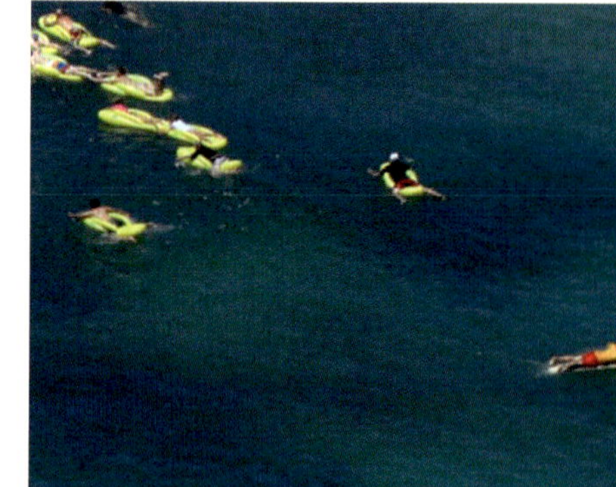

Cohen is in charge of the country's busiest road – the one crossing the Sydney Harbour Bridge. 'It's like being a police officer or an ambulance officer or a fireman. You never know what's coming next,' he says. Typically, Cohen can deal with anything from tipped-over trucks to rescue helicopters landing on the bridge, to broken-down trains needing a traffic lane for passengers to disembark.

About 300 vehicles break down on the bridge every year. The surveillance operation makes it easier to catch collisions and other problems more quickly, but it still takes time to tow cars off the bridge or attend to accidents. And with 160,000 vehicles a weekday crossing the 'Coat Hanger,' just one breakdown can stop all drivers in their tracks. Frustratingly for Cohen, every solution to a problem potentially causes another set of issues that need to be resolved. 'What we've got to decide,' he says as he looks at the big screen, 'is whether we can afford to take a lane away from the people coming *out* of the city and give it back to the people going *into* the city.' These are big decisions, made far away from the public's gaze.

Whether competing for space in Sydney, jostling on the Pacific Motorway next to the Brisbane River or sitting trapped at Adelaide's reviled Britannia roundabout, it is the same story around the country. Demand outstrips supply. For Sydney taxi driver Stephen Hemsley, that deficit is annoyingly clear, every day. Like his colleagues in other cities, Hemsley struggles to navigate a road system that was mostly

A staggering 55 million passengers fly from place to place within Australia in one year, covering 63 billion kilometres in the air, the equivalent of 164,000 trips to the moon.

laid out before the birth of the modern car. 'There's just basically not enough roads to handle the cars,' he sighs as he sets off for his night shift. 'The only reason I survive it really is knowing the rat runs and that I can use the bus lanes during peak hours so I can skirt around traffic jams.'

During his 27 years on the road, Hemsley has seen journey times become longer and more unpredictable. But he has also witnessed a surprising change in passenger attitudes, a simple acceptance that they'll be late for work. 'In the commercial world a lot of people are working extra hours for nothing,' Hemsley says. 'The company's already sucking more out of them than is on the contract anyway, so you know … it's not as if the boss can chip them too much.'

Australia's 66,000 taxi drivers pick up and deliver 372 million fares every year. If that sounds like a lot, Hemsley believes using even *more*, not fewer taxis is part of the solution. 'If people realised how much of their life is a habit, they may realise that it is actually better not to have a car at all,' he says. 'Not even look at it as a save the planet thing, just look at their own life and see how many journeys they make where a car is essential. Most of the journeys aren't.'

Traffic is one of those subjects everyone has an opinion on. Yet, few will be as informed as Vic Lorusso. As an airborne traffic reporter, Lorusso spends 400 hours a year hovering over our anger and anxiety.

'Peak hour, in my eyes, can stretch from 4.30 in the morning right up to midday,' he says. 'If you talk to the professional drivers – the couriers, the truck drivers out there – during the day, their peak hour extends well into the early hours of the afternoon. If you are not on the road before 5am from the western suburbs, it's going to be very tough to get into Sydney on time.'

From his helicopter, Lorusso is witness to Sydney drivers crawling to work at an average of just 26 kilometres an hour. That's worse than Greater London. Australia's lucky city is Perth, where drivers race along at a brisk 38 kilometres an hour. Traffic jams cost $13 billion a year in lost productivity, which is estimated to soar to $20 billion if changes aren't made soon. And it may come as a surprise that some of these traffic jams aren't even real – they aren't, in fact, caused by anything. 'They are phantom traffic jams,' explains Lorusso. Below him cars are pulling up, only to hit the brakes just metres further along. 'No accident, no breakdown, just massive congestion. You get a group of motorists accelerating when they get a little bit of stretch of clear traffic and then they're breaking all of a sudden. And that's what causes the backlog.'

Academic researchers using mathematical models are trying to work out how we would need to change driving behaviour to avoid these phantom jams, but so far the answer eludes us all. Fewer cars on the road would be a good start but how realistic is that? At the moment only one in five commuters takes public transport to work. And if roads seem prone to moving in slow motion, our rail networks can be fragile too.

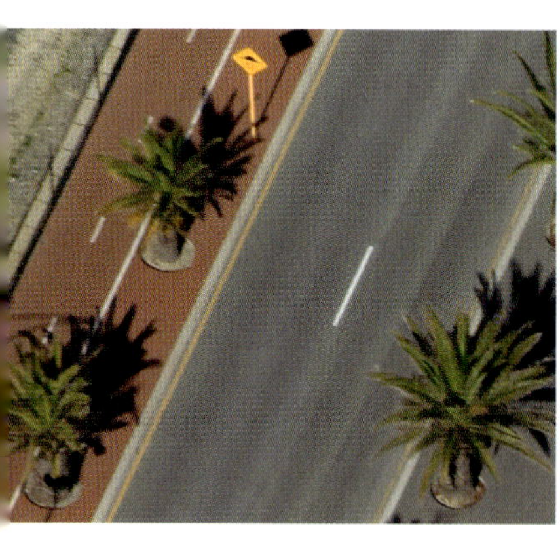

Ask Steve Chay. He is the shift manager at Sydney's Rail Management Centre, which runs Australia's largest urban rail network. Like his road colleagues, Chay and his colleagues track traffic on his 1,600-kilometre network via a gigantic screen, each of his 340 trains represented by a blinking light. At its peak, Central Station – the network's main hub – will see the arrival of a train every three minutes. That's if everything runs smoothly. But seemingly small incidents such as a gas pipe rupturing can easily throw a spanner in the works.

Gas leaks can mean vital signals – the stop and go lights - aren't working and, in this case, trains cannot move across 20 kilometres of the network, virtually crippling the entire system. 'If this was to continue right through until the afternoon peak, it would affect everyone,' says Chay. 'We carry somewhere between five hundred and six hundred thousand people between 2pm and 7pm.'

Engineers will fix the leak, but meanwhile the nerve centre is in overdrive to resolve the knock-on effects. 'Incident response personnel,' specially trained staff to deal with emergencies, are dispatched to several key locations where passengers need to be evacuated from trains and moved onto buses. Sounds easy enough, but buses are actually hard to come by. It's morning and most buses normally available as emergency backups are busy doing school runs. In some cases, Chay must resort to organising taxis. Chay and his team may also change the direction of other trains to operate on

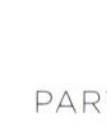

different lines outside the stretch of track that is paralysed. 'This in itself causes other delays,' explains Chay, 'as the trains are now operating on longer journeys.'

In the end, it takes 45 minutes to repair the broken gas pipe but it will be hours before everything is 'back to normal'. It seems congestion, in one shape or another, is an unfortunate price we must always pay for living in the city. Moving ourselves, though, is just one part of life's big puzzle in Australia; moving data is the other.

We live in the modern information age. And keeping in touch across our huge harsh continent is no mean feat. Our telephone network consists of more than 11,000 exchanges, connecting 11 million landlines. But in these wireless times, we are hanging up on landlines. There are now 23 million mobiles in Australia, one for every man, woman and child. That's a 400 per cent rise in a decade. But with mobile phones, digital technology and internet all the rage, it's sometimes easy to forget that the backbone to our data transfer system is actually 200 years old. Moreover, it's still going strong ... and on foot.

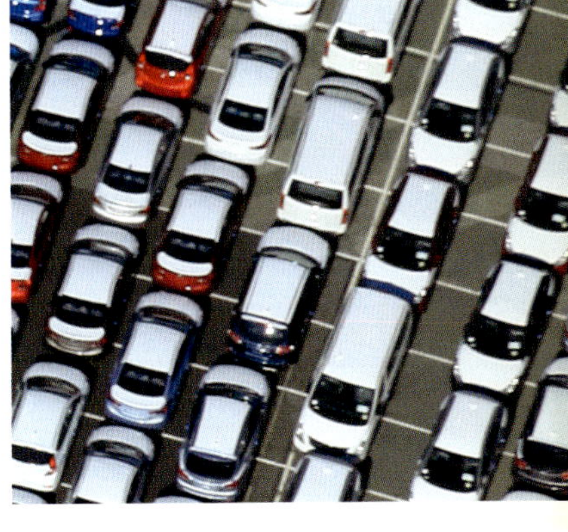

Dave South is a suburban postie, a human fibreoptic cable delivering data to your door. 'Every day,' he says, 'I reckon I deliver about 1,200 letters and maybe another 300 large letters on top of that.' Across the country posties deliver 100 million items a week. Arguably, it is the nation's largest information network, even if much of that information now consists of bills rather than love letters. 'I think the personal letters are on the decrease,' says South, 'because the biggest thing is email. It is just quicker to email or text someone these days.'

A generation ago we'd wait in eager anticipation for the rattle of the letterbox but today it's rare for anyone but the dog to get excited. 'Years ago there used to be lots of people home when you delivered the mail,' South laments. 'These days you hardly see anyone come out and collect the mail. People don't stop and talk as much as they used to. Everyone's in a hurry.' Ironically, if the web heralded the end of the personal letter, it may also be the postman's saviour. 'The internet has impacted on my job by really changing the type of mail we get,' says South. 'But the increase in online shopping makes us deliver quite a few more parcels, and that's taken up a bit of the slack.'

Whether it's letters in the mail or billions of megabytes carried over the internet, Australians rely on information in almost every aspect of their lives. Take the weather. In Melbourne, on the edge of the Docklands precinct, a $30 million machine processes more than 100 billion pieces of data a second. Why? Well, on one level, to see whether it will rain in Dubbo on Tuesday.

This digital giant is a so-called super computer, owned by the Bureau of Meteorology. There are only three such computers at work in weather centres around the world. The other two are stationed in Washington D.C. and Moscow. Chris Ryan, of the bureau's National Climate Centre, quips that the correct weather forecasts are easy to forget, and that it is only the wrong ones people remember. But, he says, the super computer plays a huge role in their lives.

'A lot of people do appreciate that there are satellites, balloons, radars and so on,' he says, 'but there are a lot of things that are hidden. The millions of pieces of data that flow in every day, they're all invisible and people tend to take it for granted.' Ryan stresses people make decisions often without even thinking about the fact that they are getting that input. 'From the trivial,' he says, 'like not taking an umbrella to work … to the really significant decisions by farmers about whether to plant, or sailors about whether to go out or stay at home.'

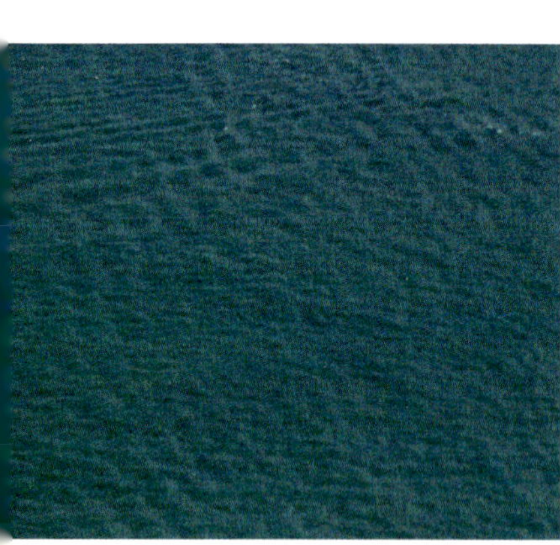

Of course, some events go ahead come rain, hail or shine. And when they do, they cause a perfect storm of data and human movement to collide. In Melbourne, on AFL Grand Final day, thousands of fans flock to the Melbourne Cricket Ground. Inside the stadium, two teams will battle it out for the premiership, as 100,000 fans put their hearts and lungs to the test, let alone the purveyors of pies, the sellers of beer, the toilets and sewerage system. But there is an even greater, unseen, challenge about to arise. And that's because virtually every fan is carrying, and using, a mobile phone – many are so-called smart phones. Luckily, 15 kilometres from the stadium, another team is at work trying to avoid mass mobile meltdown.

Steve Callinan works inside Telstra's Global Operations Centre. Think of any movie showing NASA's Houston control centre and multiply what you think of by five. That's roughly how big the Melbourne nerve centre is. On an average day, Steve and his colleagues handle five million mobile calls and three and a half million text messages. But this is no ordinary day. 'Last Saturday would have been fairly similar to the Saturday before that and so on,' Callinan says. 'This Saturday, though, is very different.'

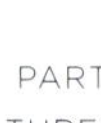

There are now 23 million mobiles in Australia, one for every man, woman and child. That's a 400 per cent rise in a decade.

The company has deployed a string of base stations in the MCG capable of upping the bandwidth. The infrastructure should cope with a surge in demand but if it doesn't, frustrated fans find themselves unable to make calls, send text messages and pictures or surf the internet. 'With the Grand Final on, there is a definitive flow of core traffic at the start of the game. People are calling their friends going "Yeah I got my gear on, I've got my face painted, I'm fired up, I'm here with the kids",' says Callinan.

Throughout the afternoon, the mobile network is pushed and pulled. 'When that first bounce goes,' he says, 'you can see the network traffic around that area basically just stops. It falls off the planet because the game is on.' But the main break sees an explosion of data traffic. In the MCG, 60,000 phone calls are made at the same time. Add to that half a million text messages.

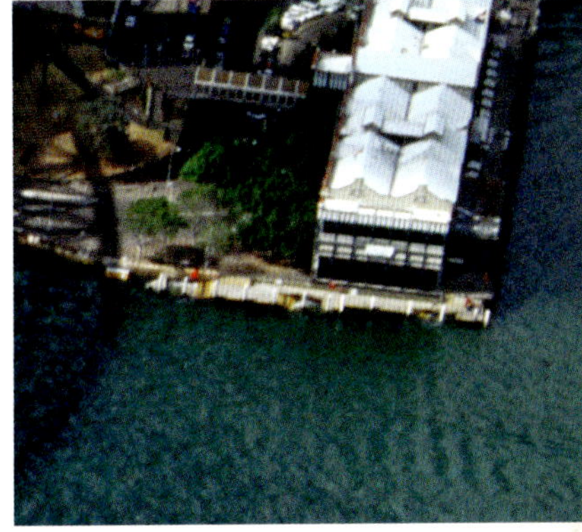

Steve and his colleagues carefully monitor the network, keeping the fans connected. 'If it all goes well, they don't care about us because it just gets done,' says Callinan. 'I think we're okay with that. We'd rather not be mentioned and just have it all happen and everyone's happy.'

Like their peers at control centres around the country, Steve's team works tirelessly behind the scenes to keep us mobile. Modern Australia is alive with daily mass movement. If we're to propel a successful nation, we can't stand still. We need to get right the networks and systems that connect and transport us. When they break down, or let us down, it's easy to get annoyed and frustrated. But bear in mind the folk doing their utmost to make sure that doesn't happen.

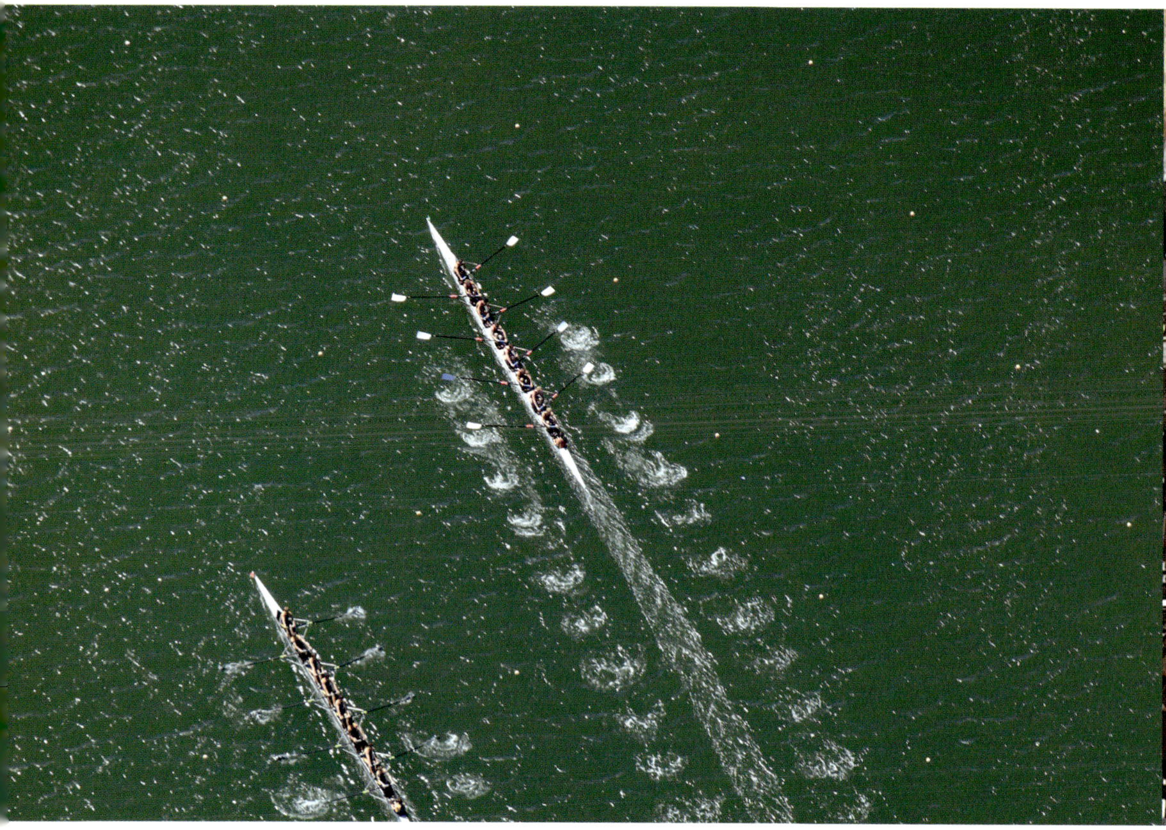

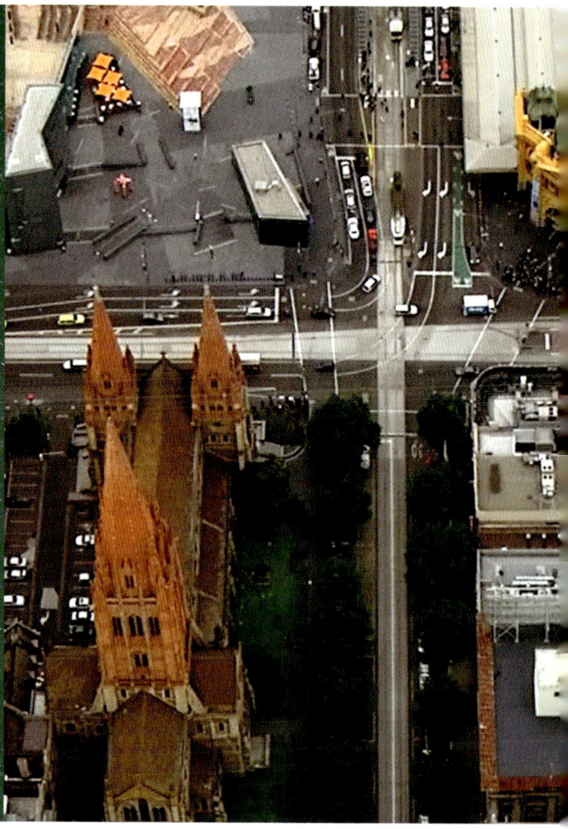

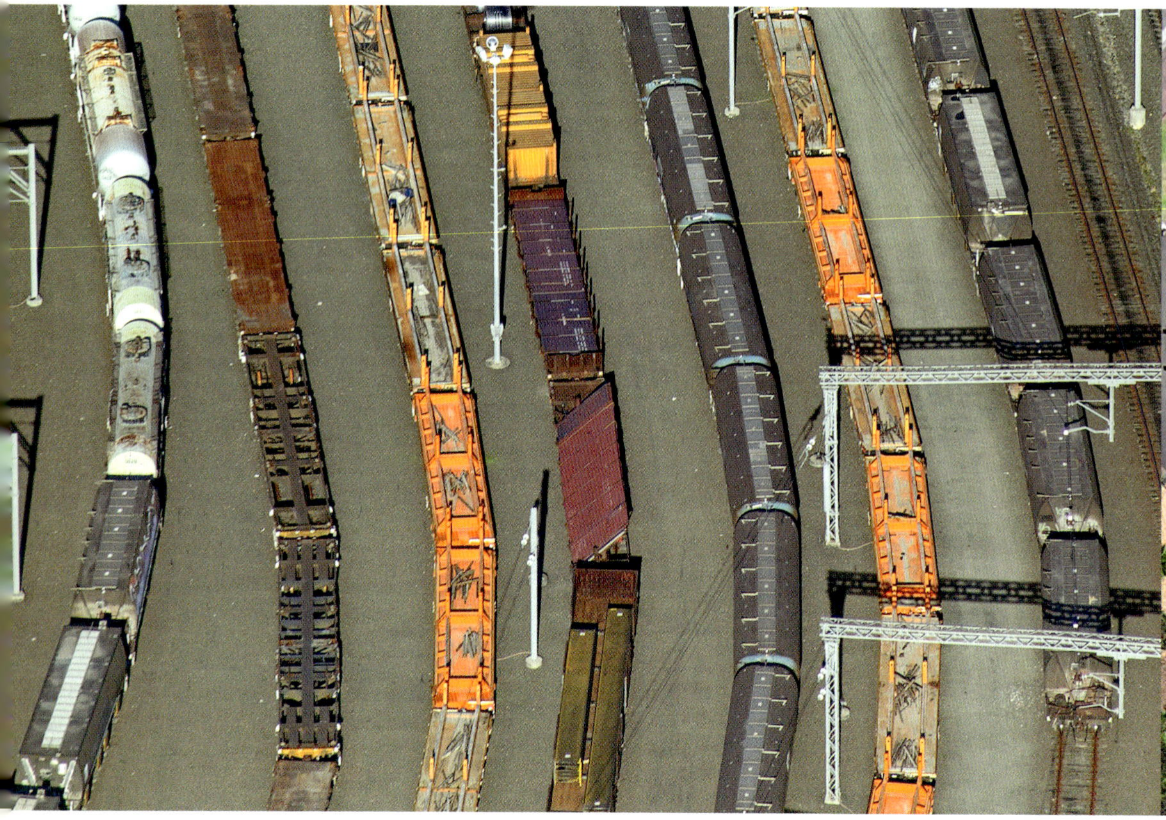

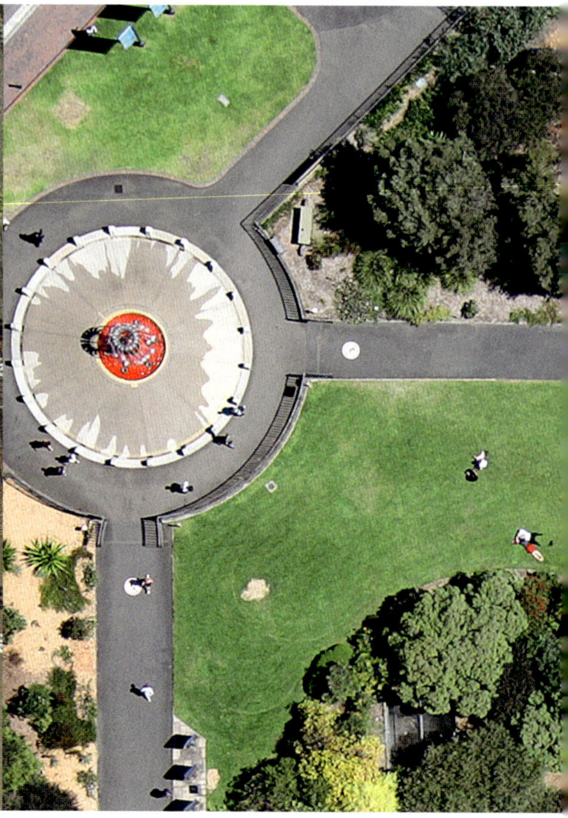

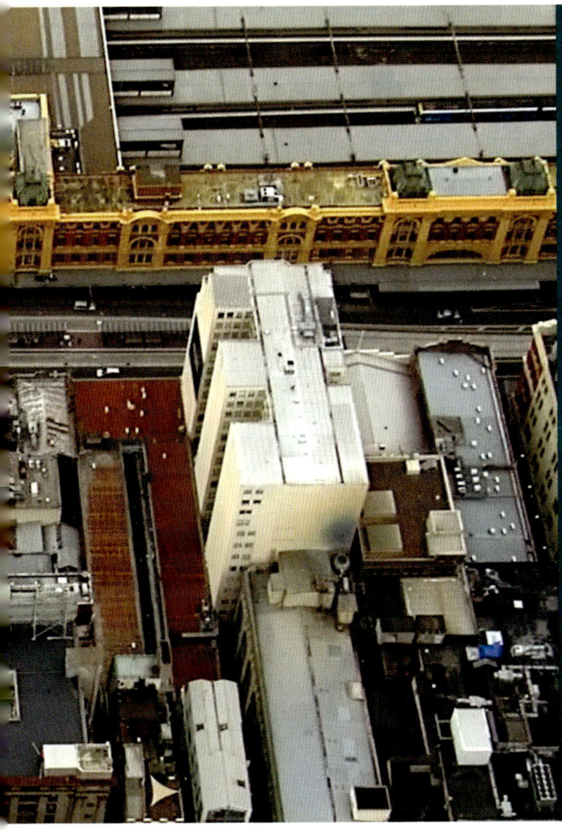

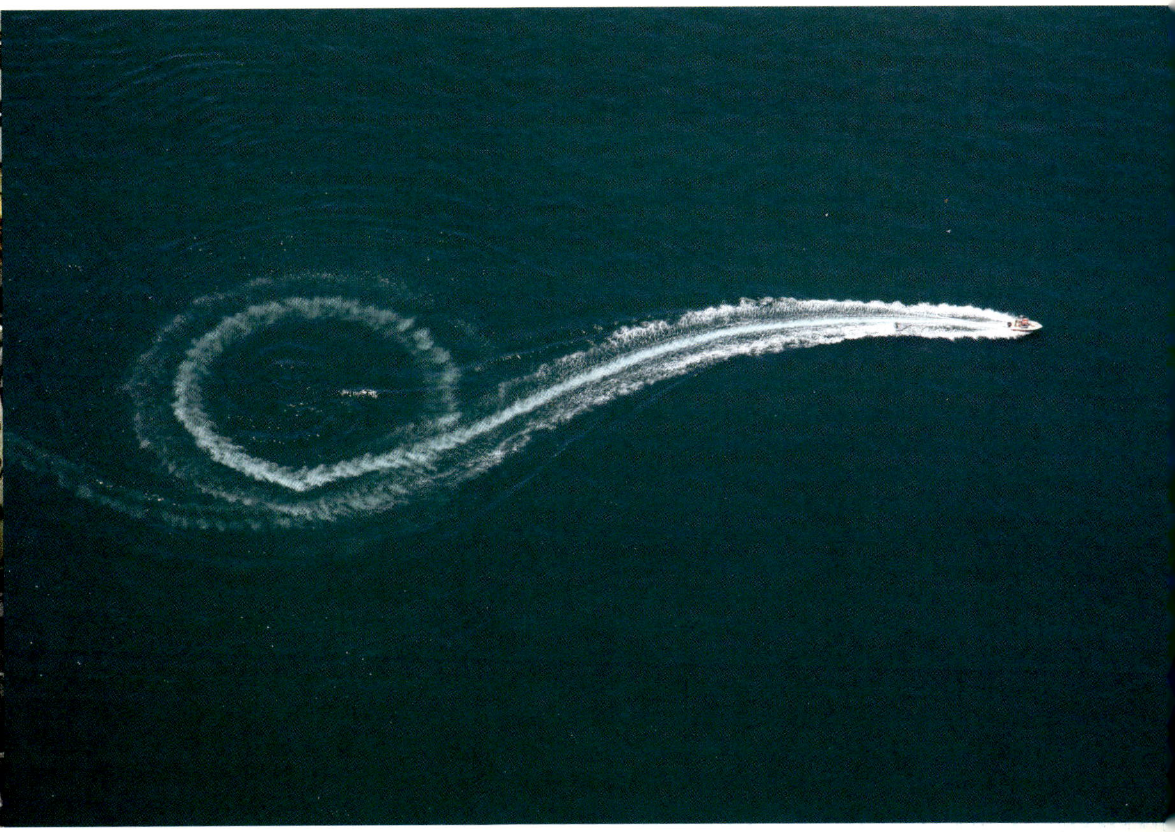

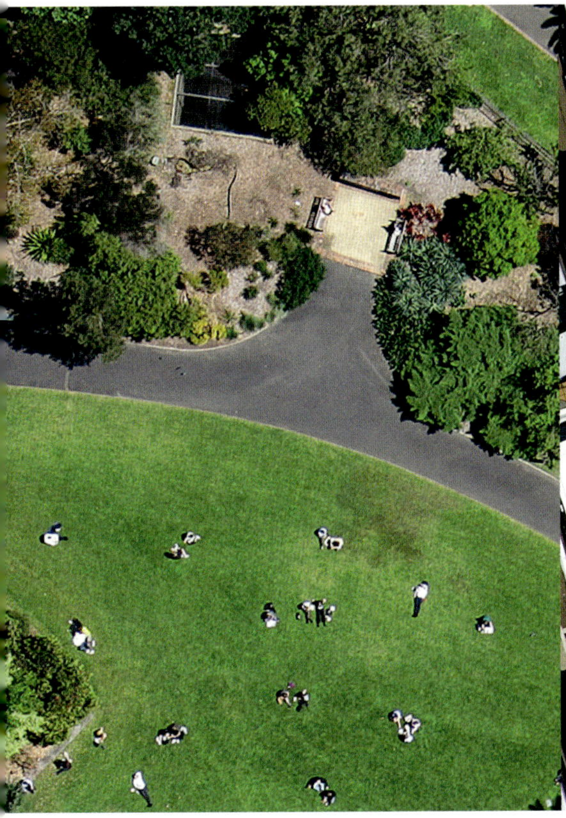

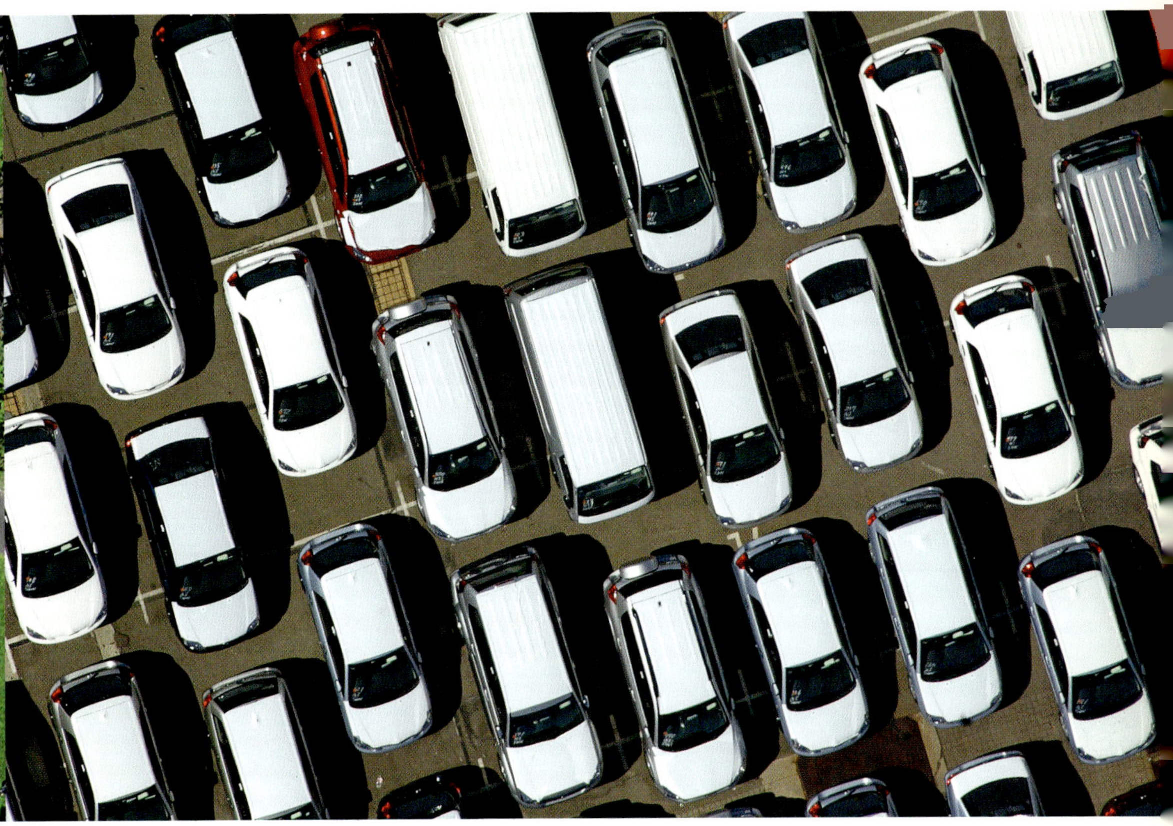

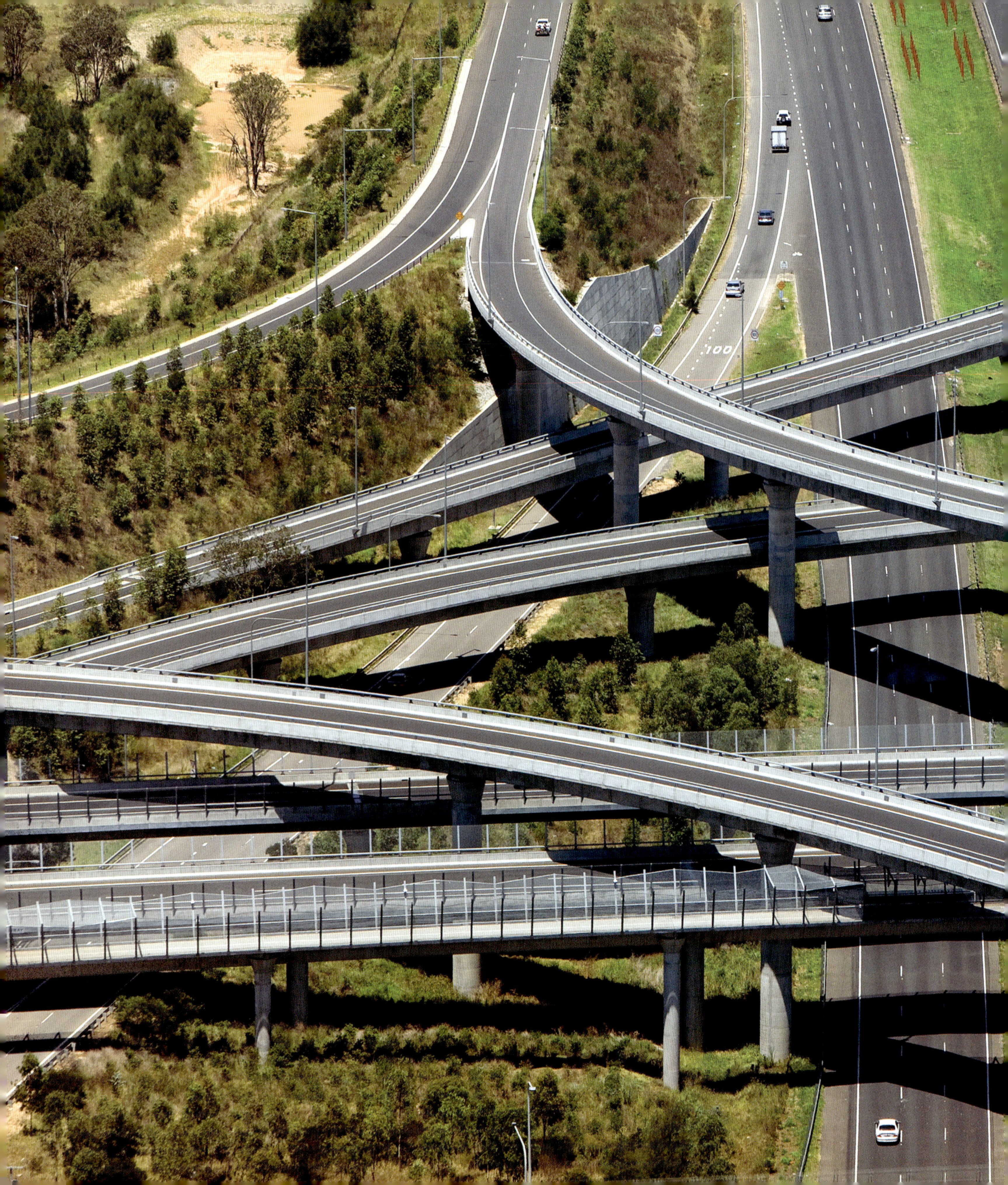
100

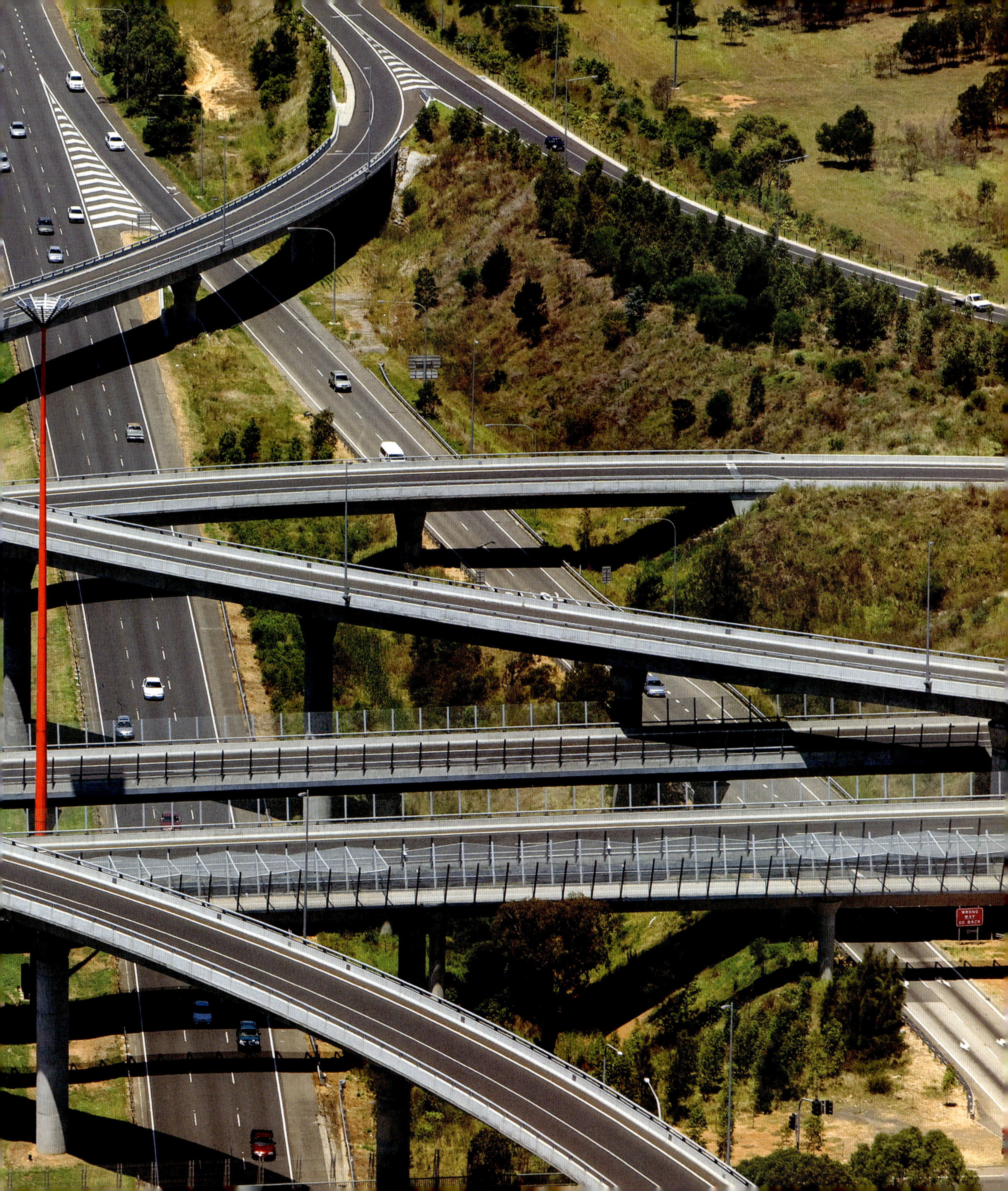
WRONG
WAY
GO BACK

PREVIOUS PAGES: A red mast in the heart of the Light Horse Interchange in western Sydney is both a tribute to the Light Horse Brigades and Australia's love of cars, roads and commuting. The interchange connects the M4 and the M7. Sydney drivers can average just 26 kilometres an hour in the rush to work.

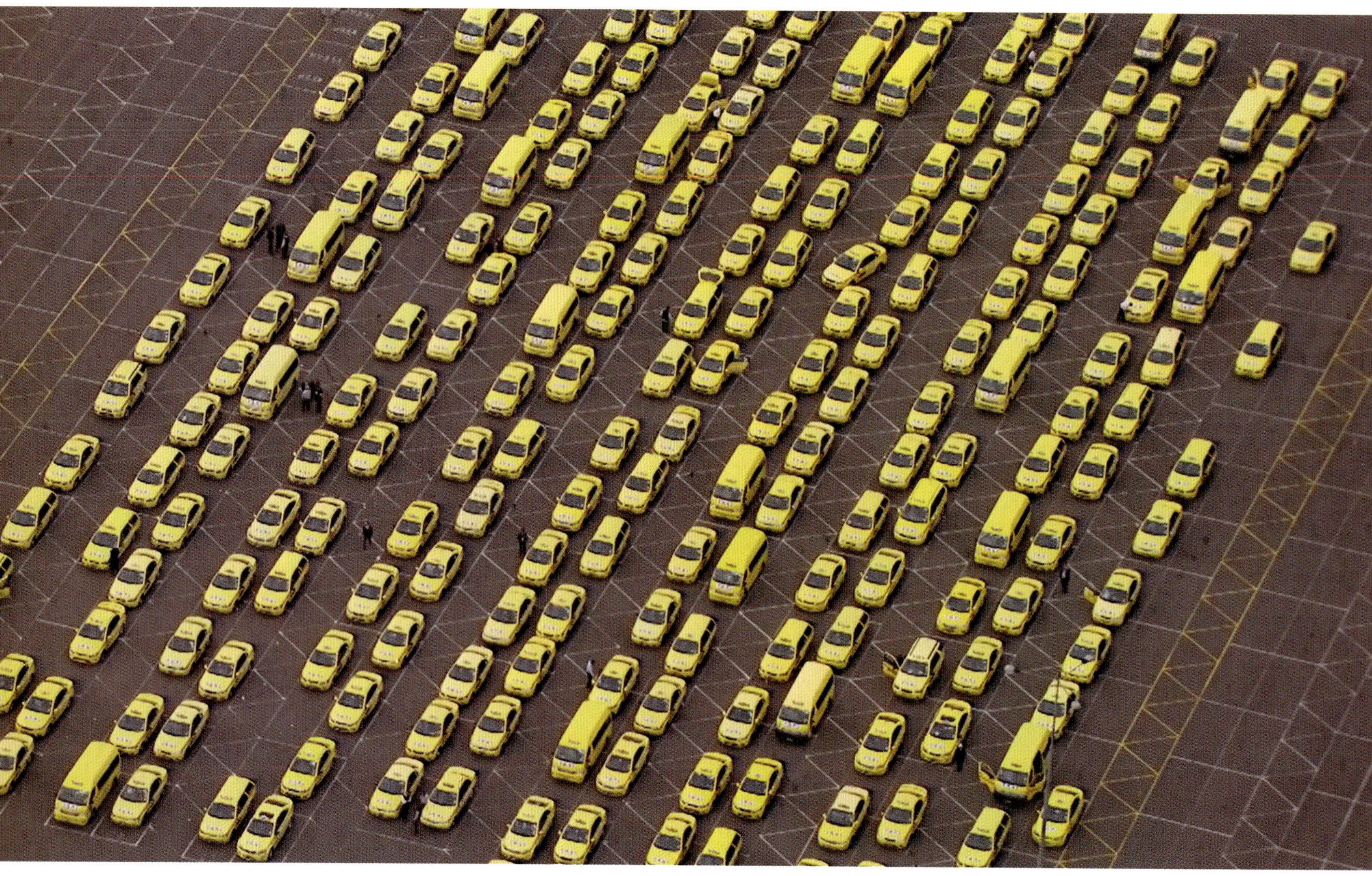

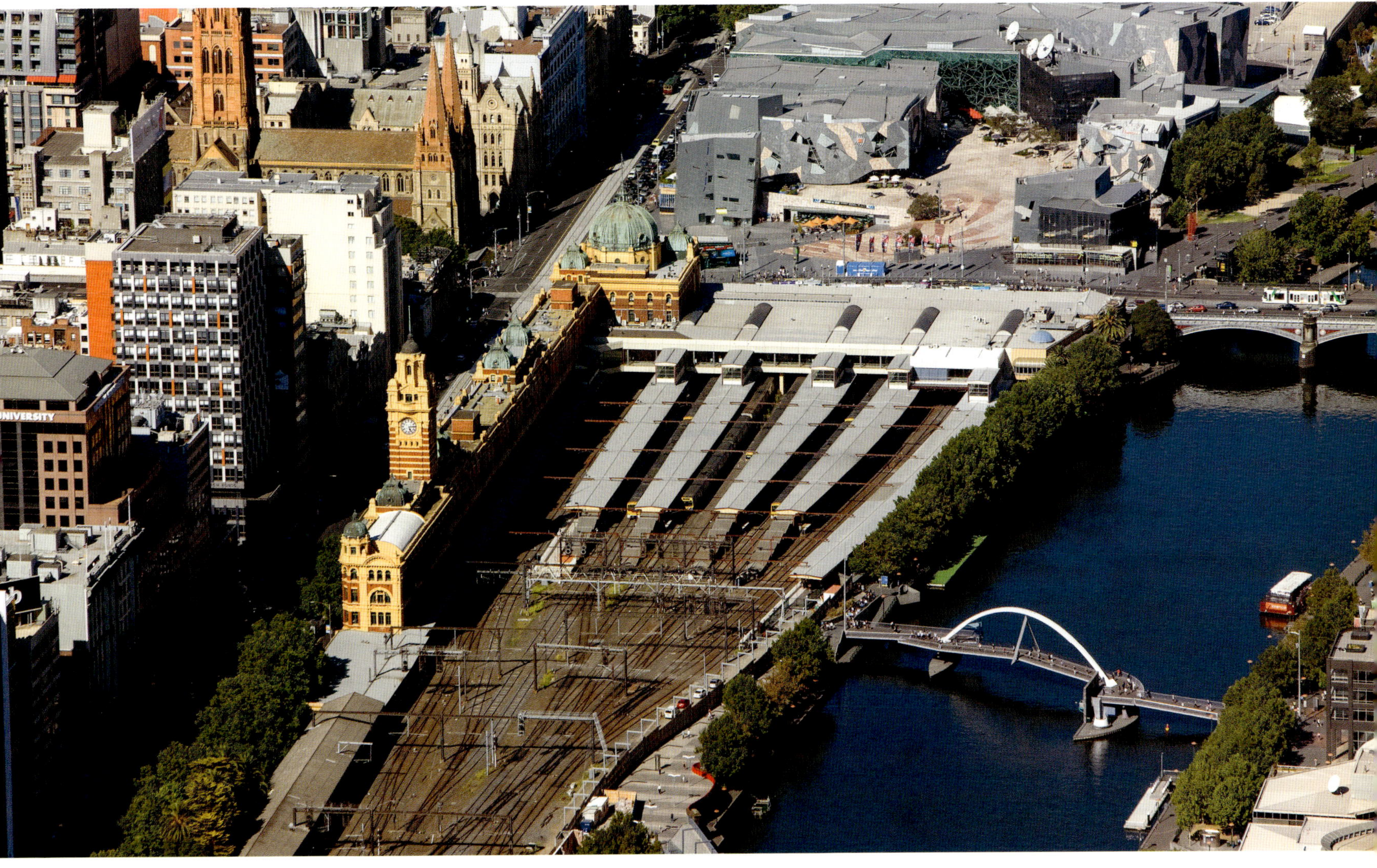

LEFT: Yellow taxis wait patiently to join a queue for passengers at Melbourne airport. **RIGHT:** Flinders Street Railway Station in the centre of Melbourne, where more than 100,000 commuters pass through every day.

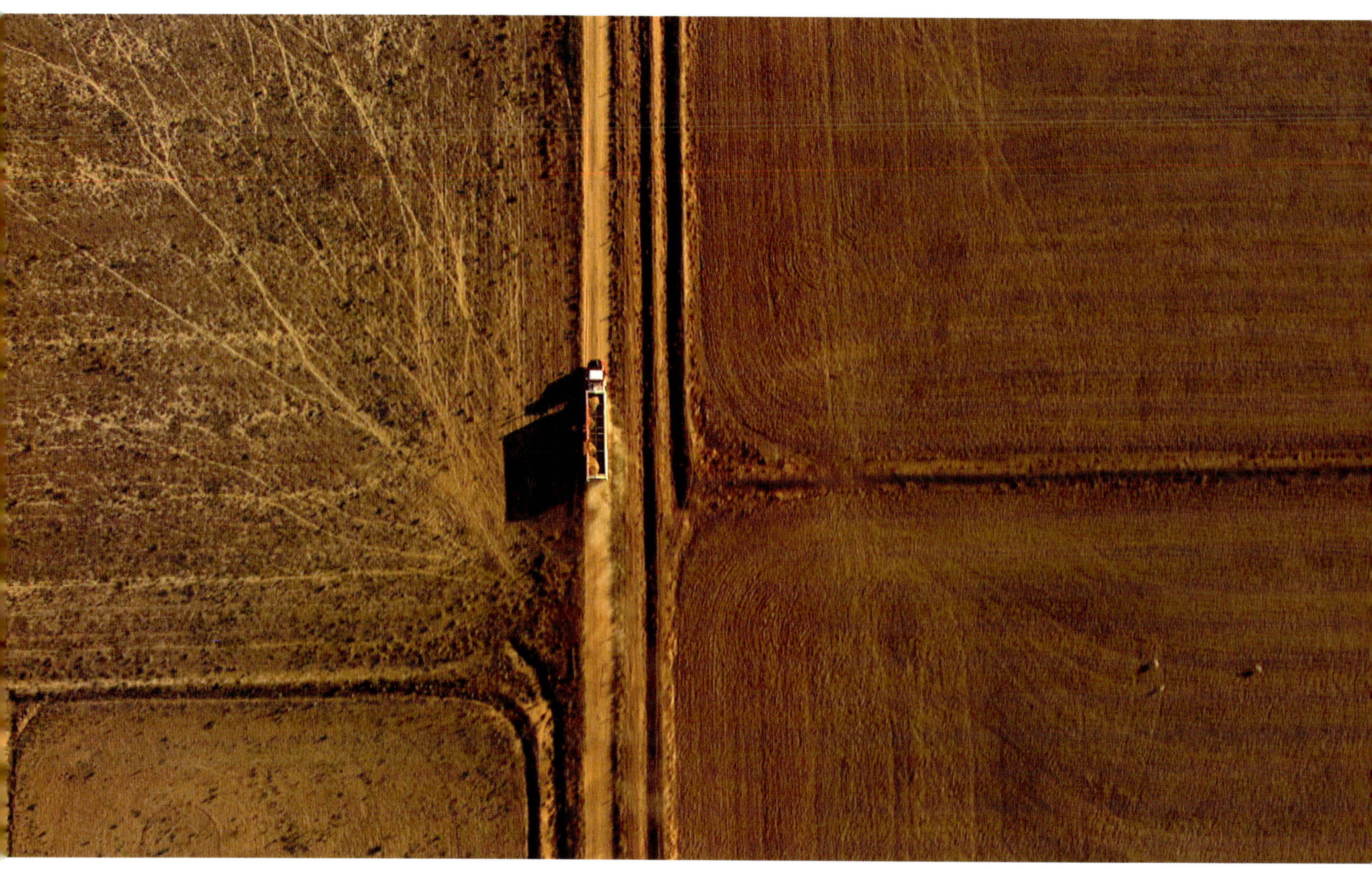

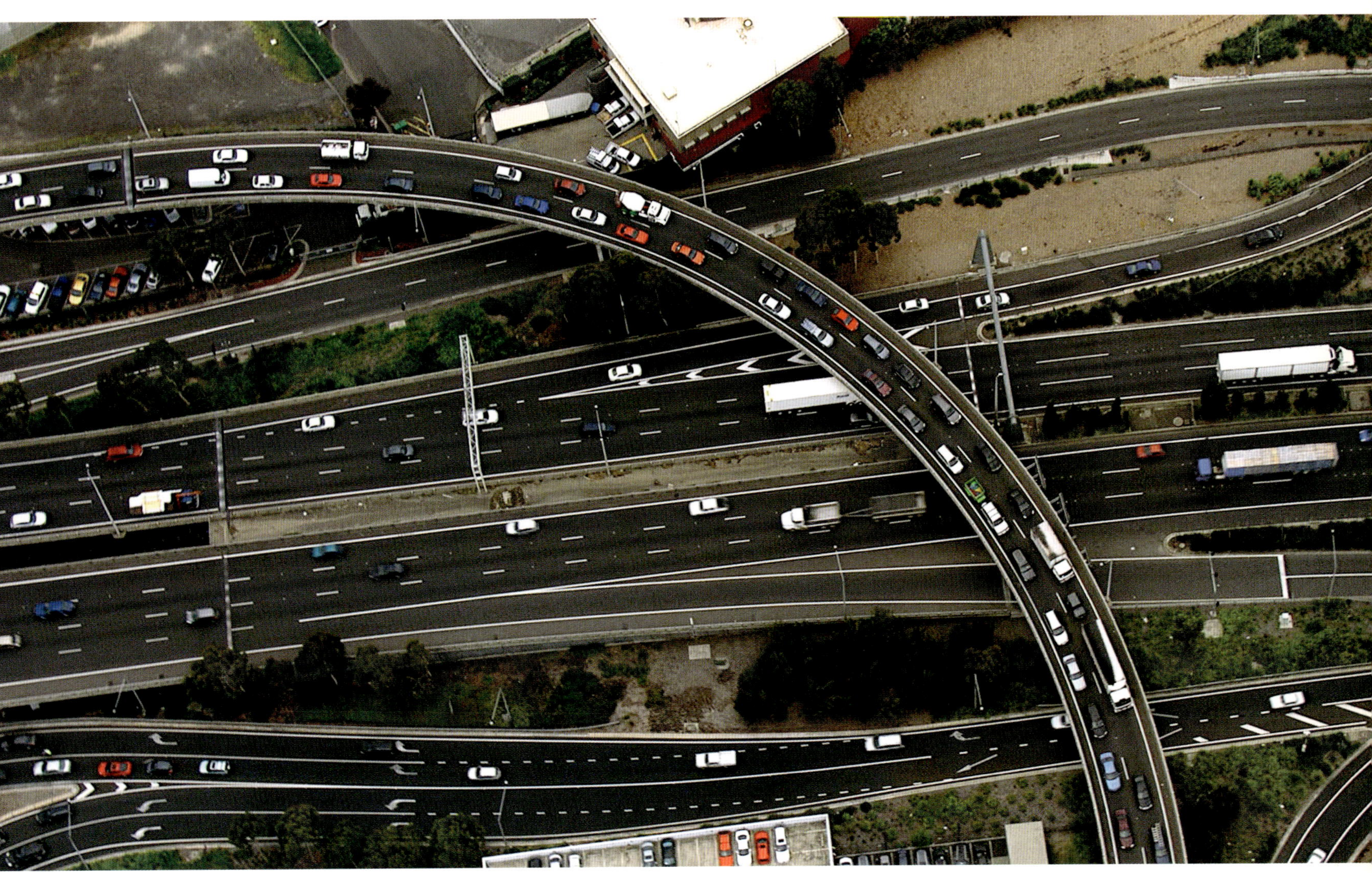

LEFT AND RIGHT: From lonely brown dirt in the Outback to the busy bitumen in the cities, Australia is a nation connected by, and dependant on, roads. There are more than 820,000 kilometres of sealed and unsealed roads in Australia.

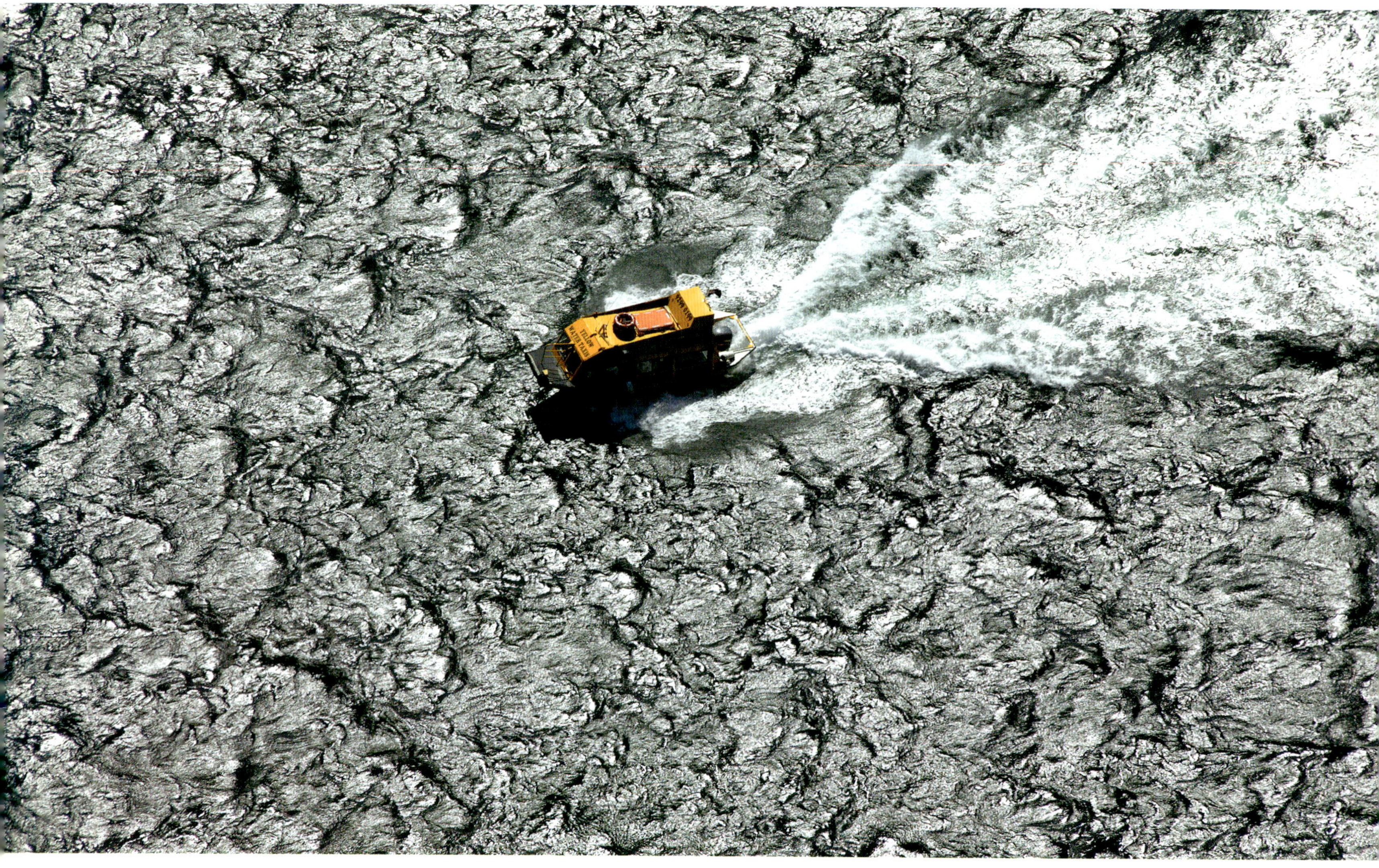

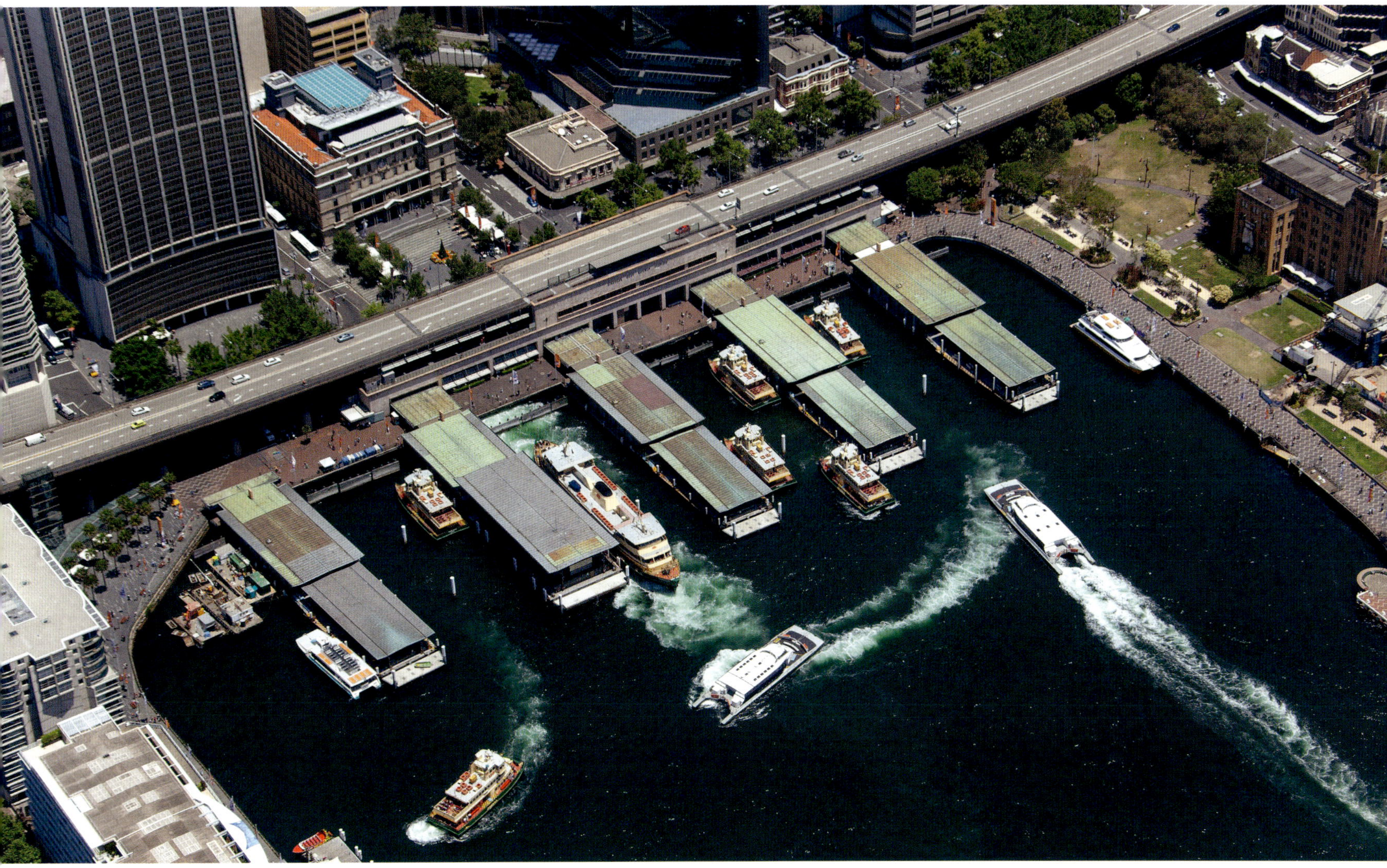

LEFT: A water taxi races a passenger across Sydney Harbour. **RIGHT:** Ferries and River Cats move commuters to and from Circular Quay. Sydney Ferries carry 14.7 million passengers a year. **FOLLOWING PAGES:** Austinmer ocean baths on the Illawarra coast, south of Sydney, were built in 1917 to provide an antidote to the pressures of modern life.

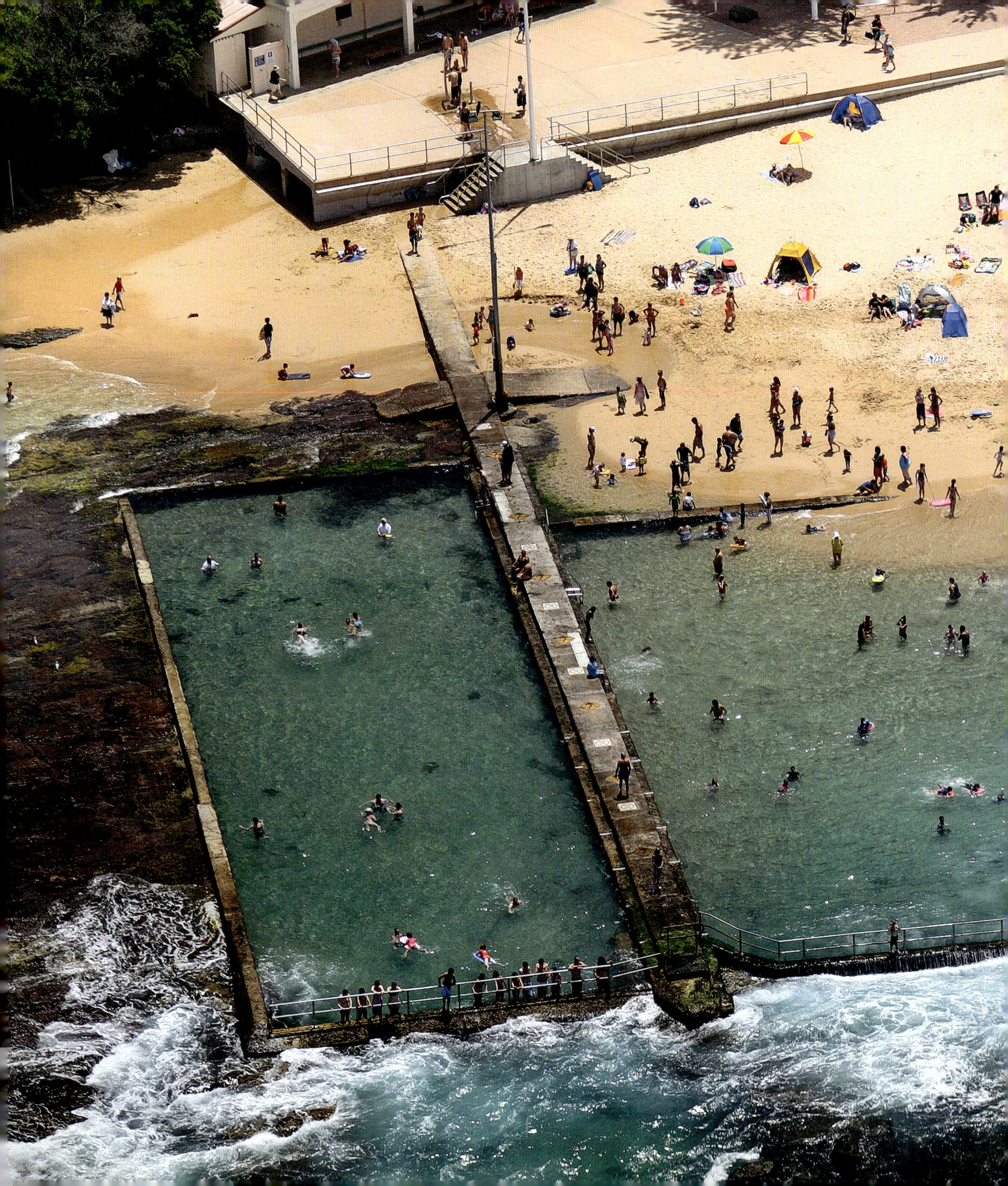

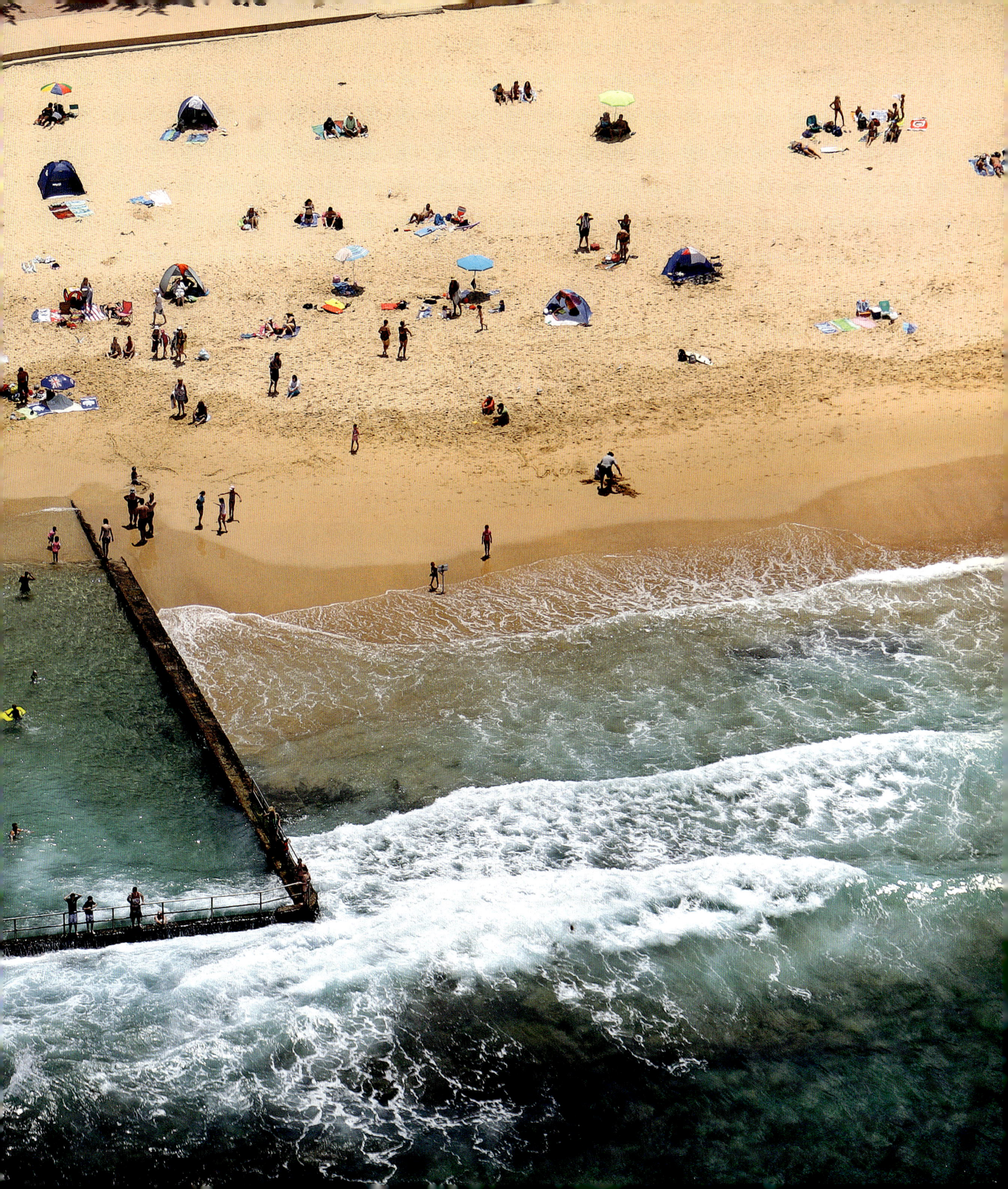

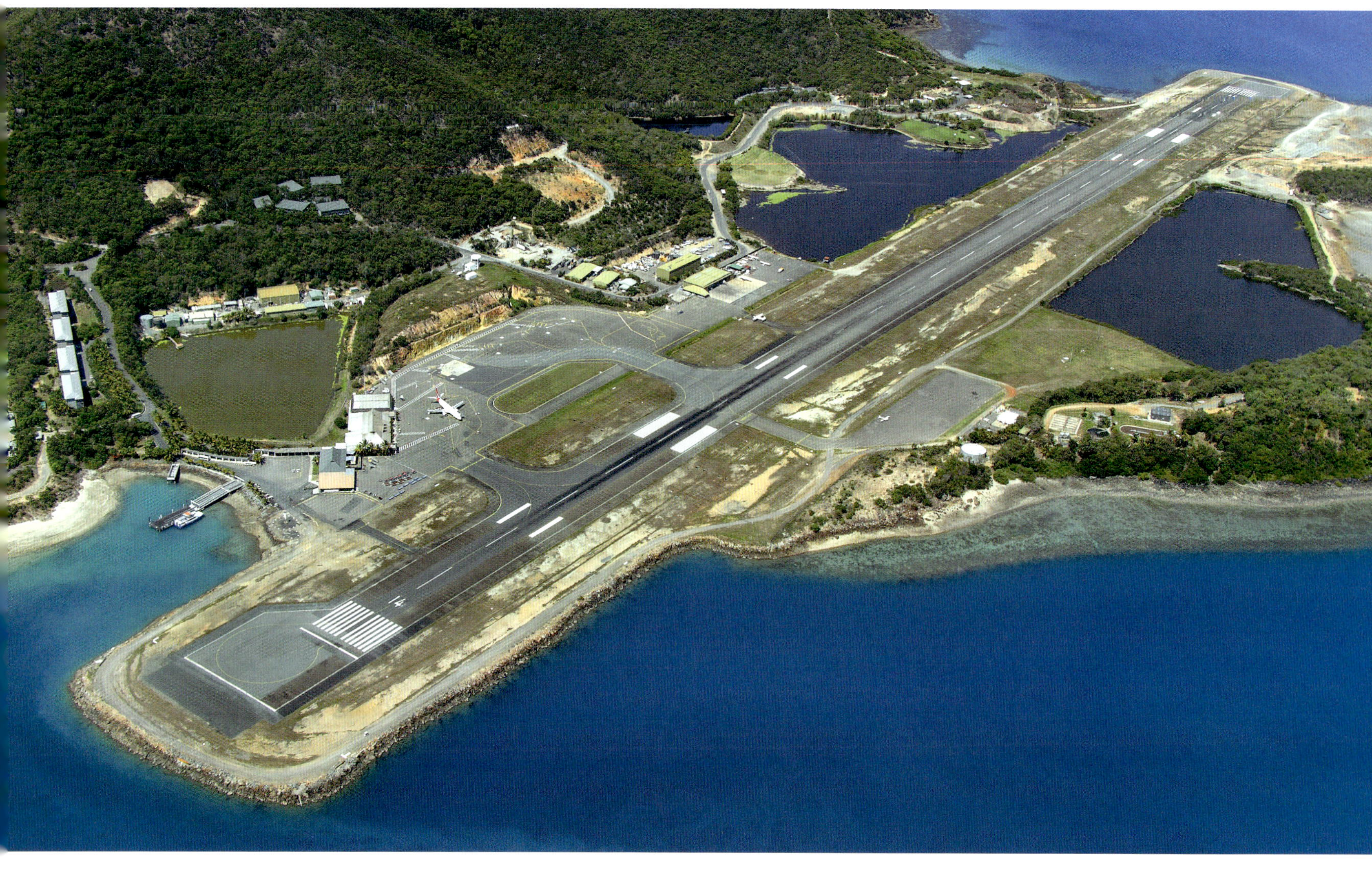

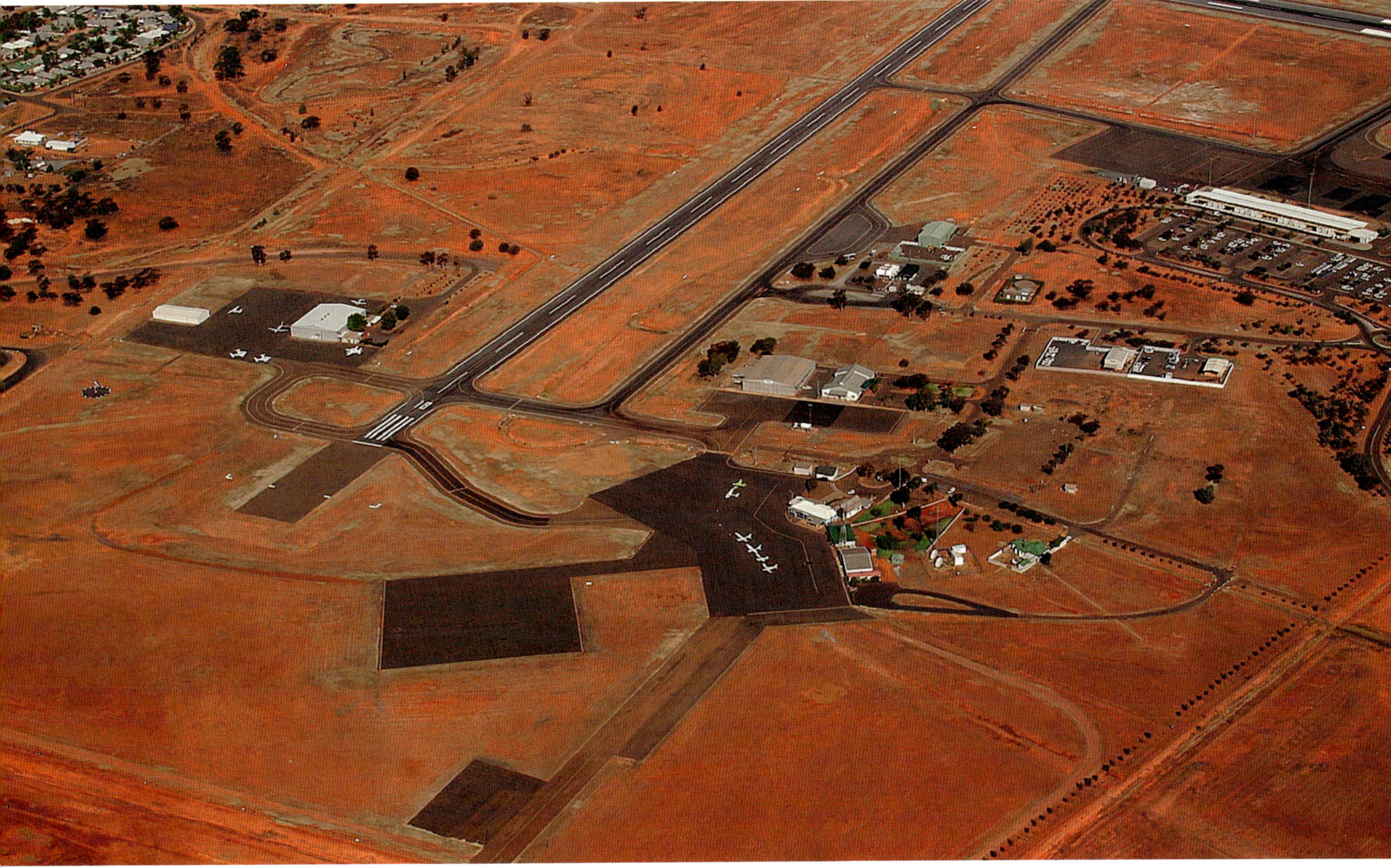

LEFT: The single airstrip on Hamilton Island, Queensland, is 1,764 metres long and built mostly on reclaimed land. **RIGHT:** The airport in Kalgoorlie, Western Australia, is a major fly-in, fly-out hub because of the local gold mines. There are 333 airports with sealed runways in Australia. **FOLLOWING PAGES:** Eucla airport on the border of South Australia and Western Australia. The dirt strips sit between the Eyre Highway and the Great Australian Bight and are used by small aircraft, including the Royal Flying Doctor Service.

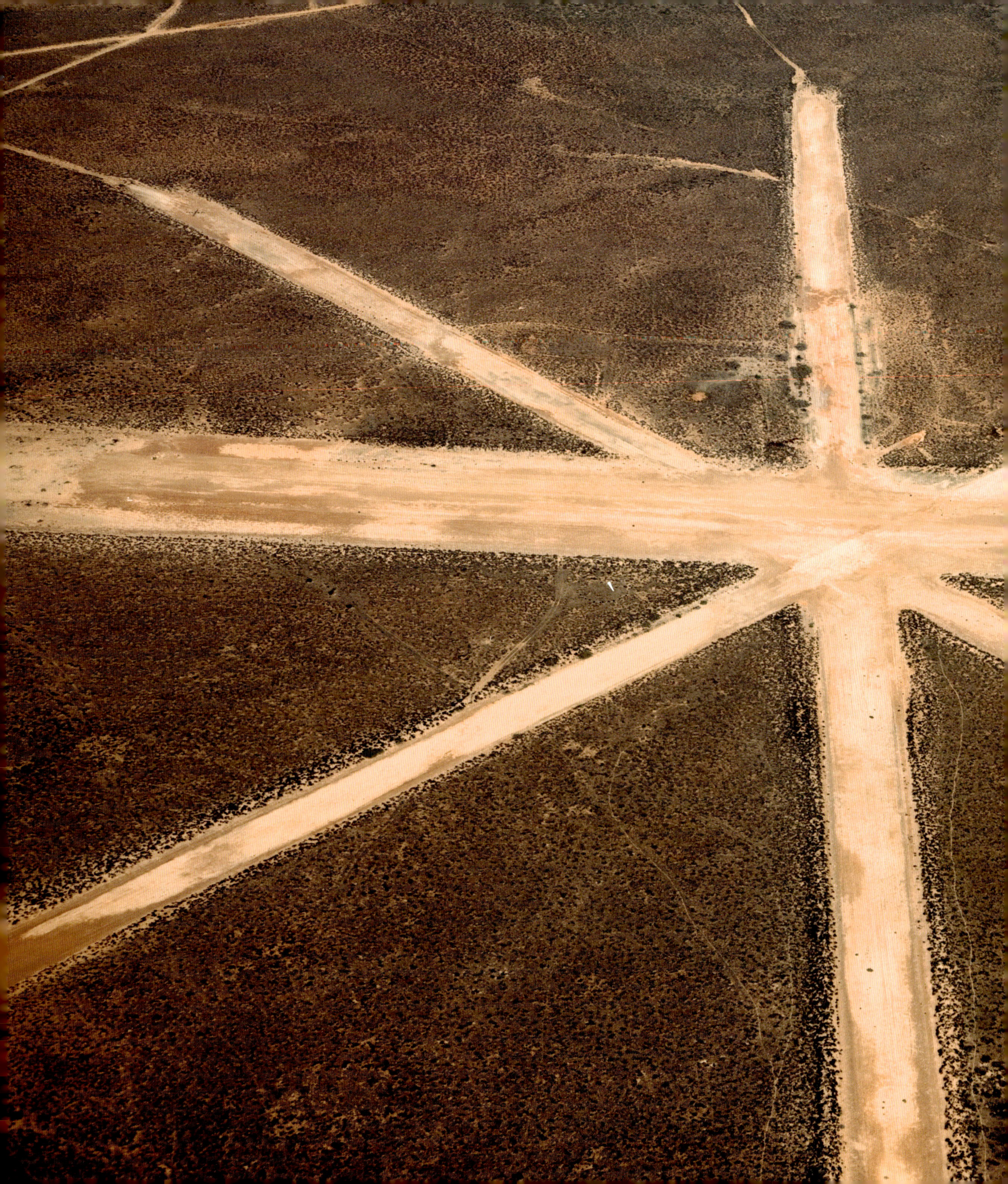

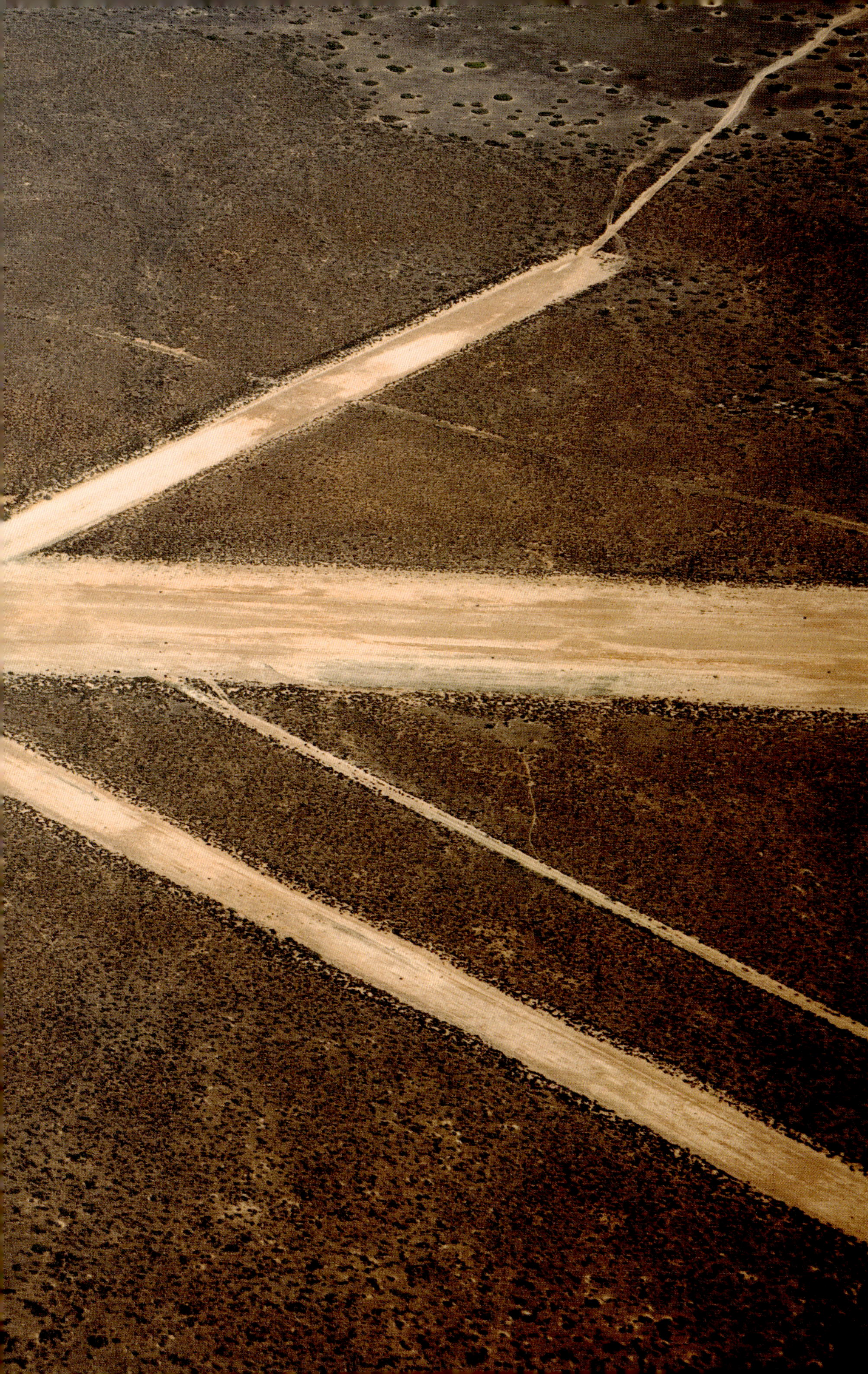

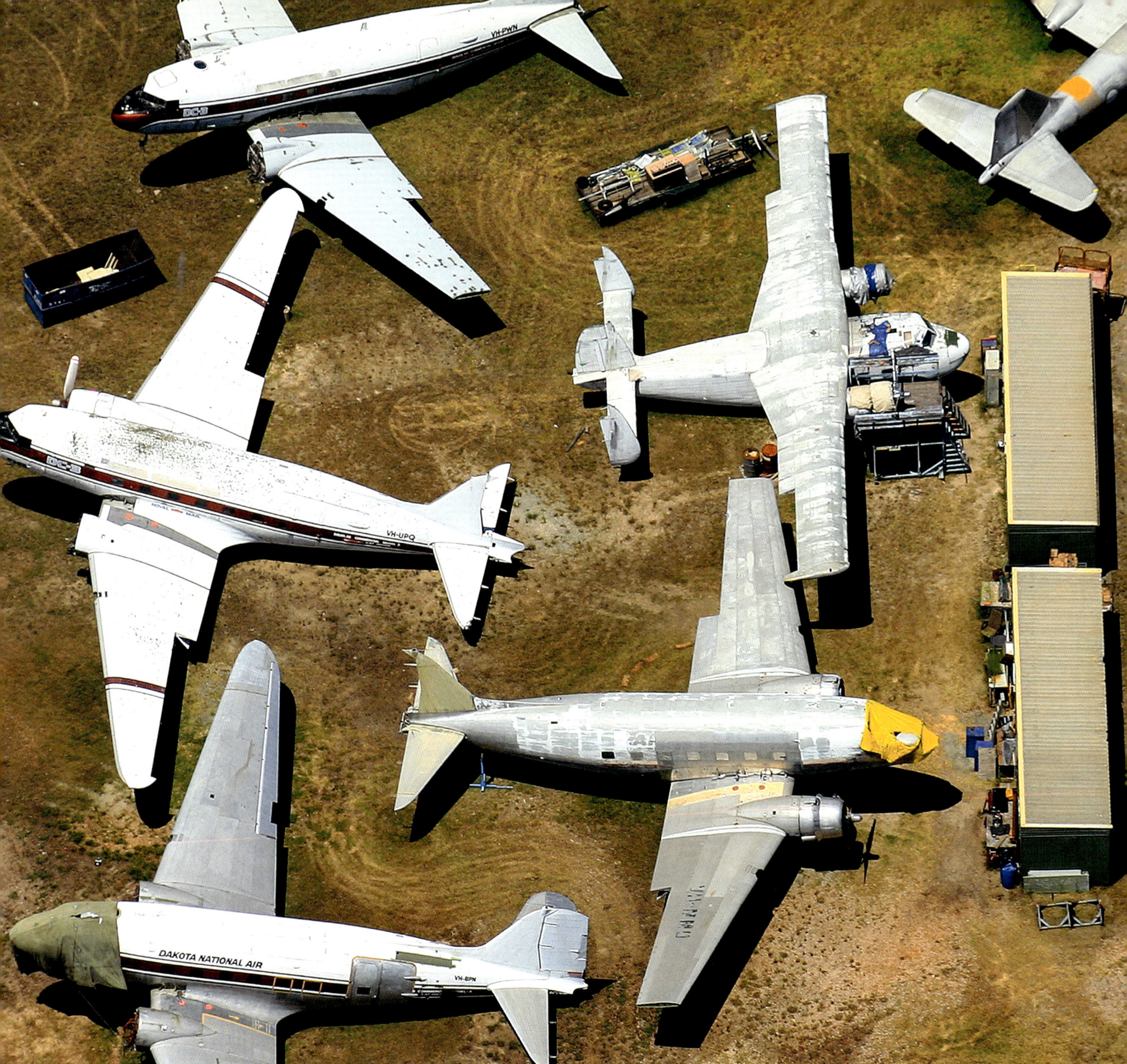

LEFT: The Australian Aviation Museum at Bankstown Airport in Sydney is a tribute to commuting from a bygone era. **RIGHT:** A seaplane takes off from Rose Bay on Sydney Harbour for a scenic flight.

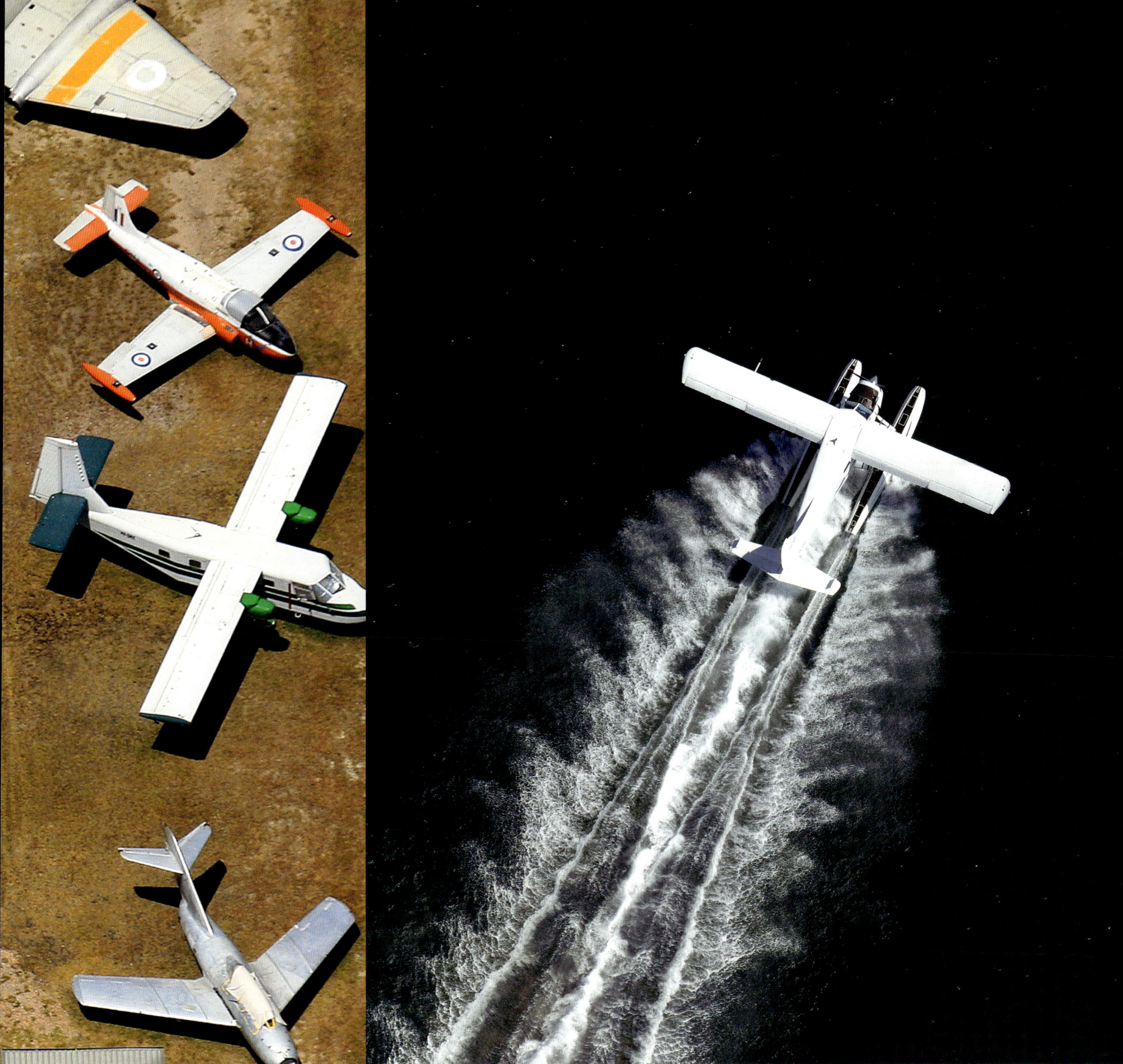

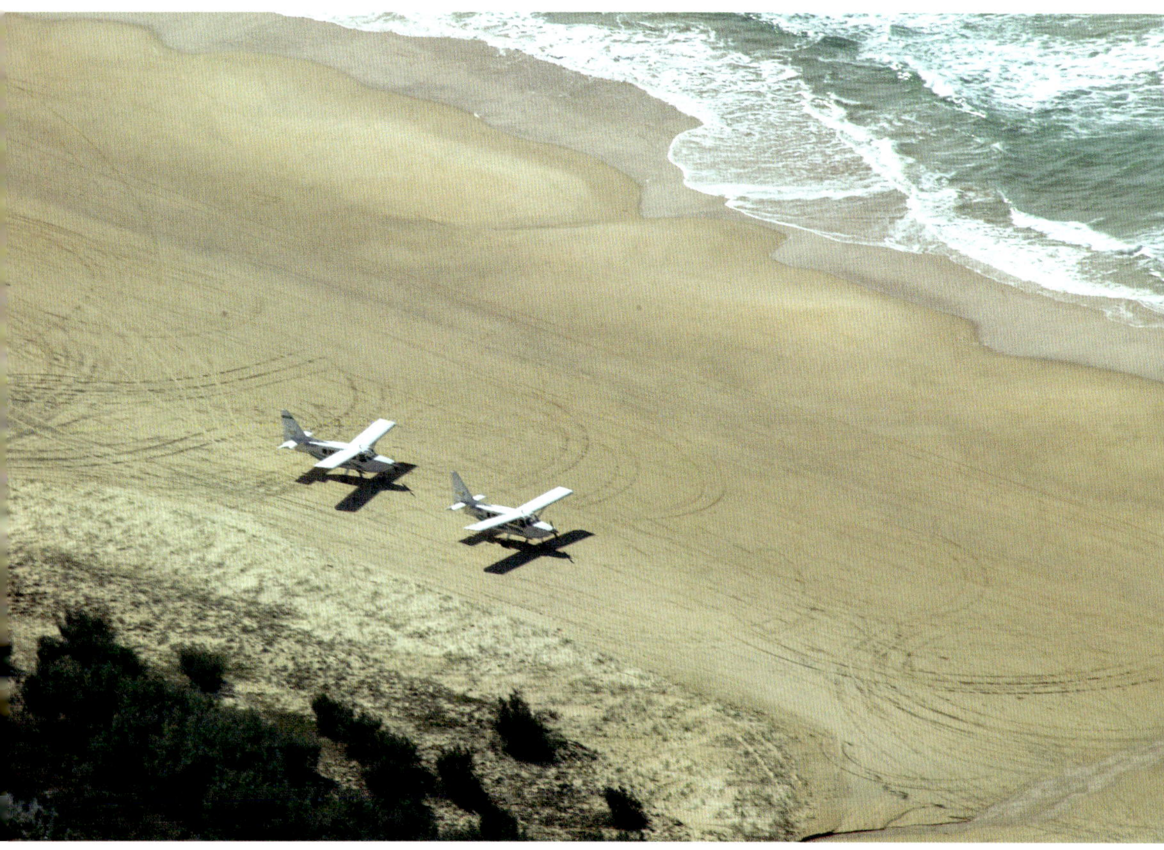

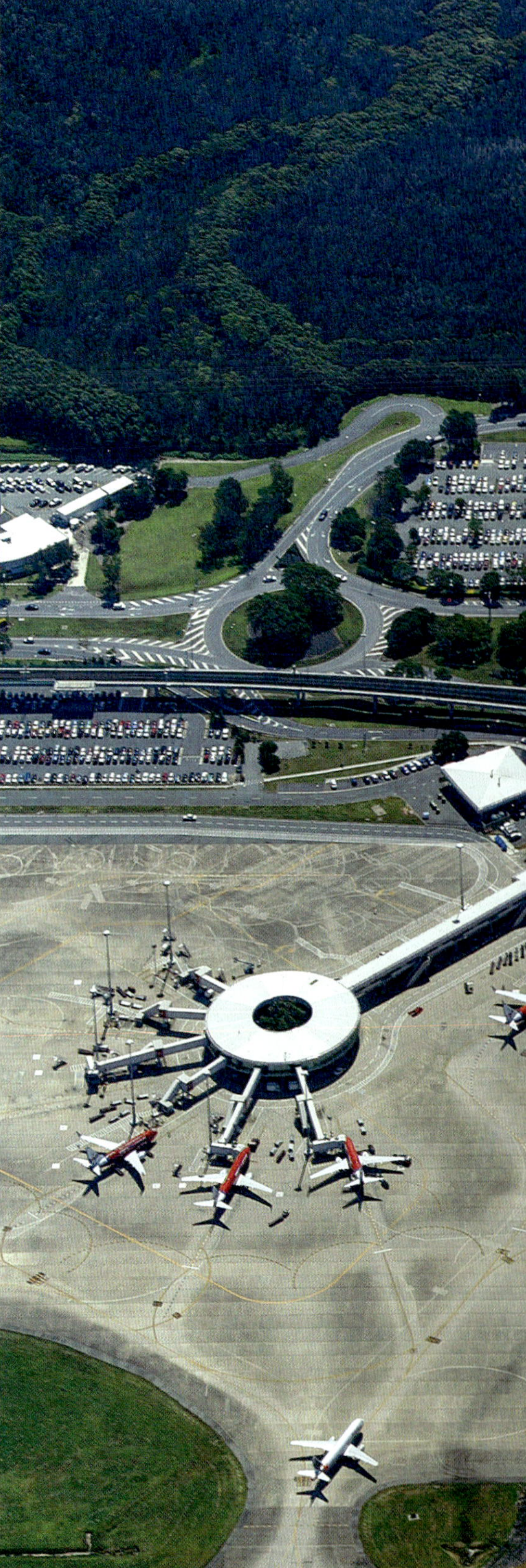

LEFT: Fraser Island's famous beaches act as a landing strip for sightseers. **RIGHT:** Passenger planes, cars and taxis make for a busy afternoon at Brisbane's domestic airport. Almost 20 million passengers pass through Brisbane's domestic and international terminals a year.

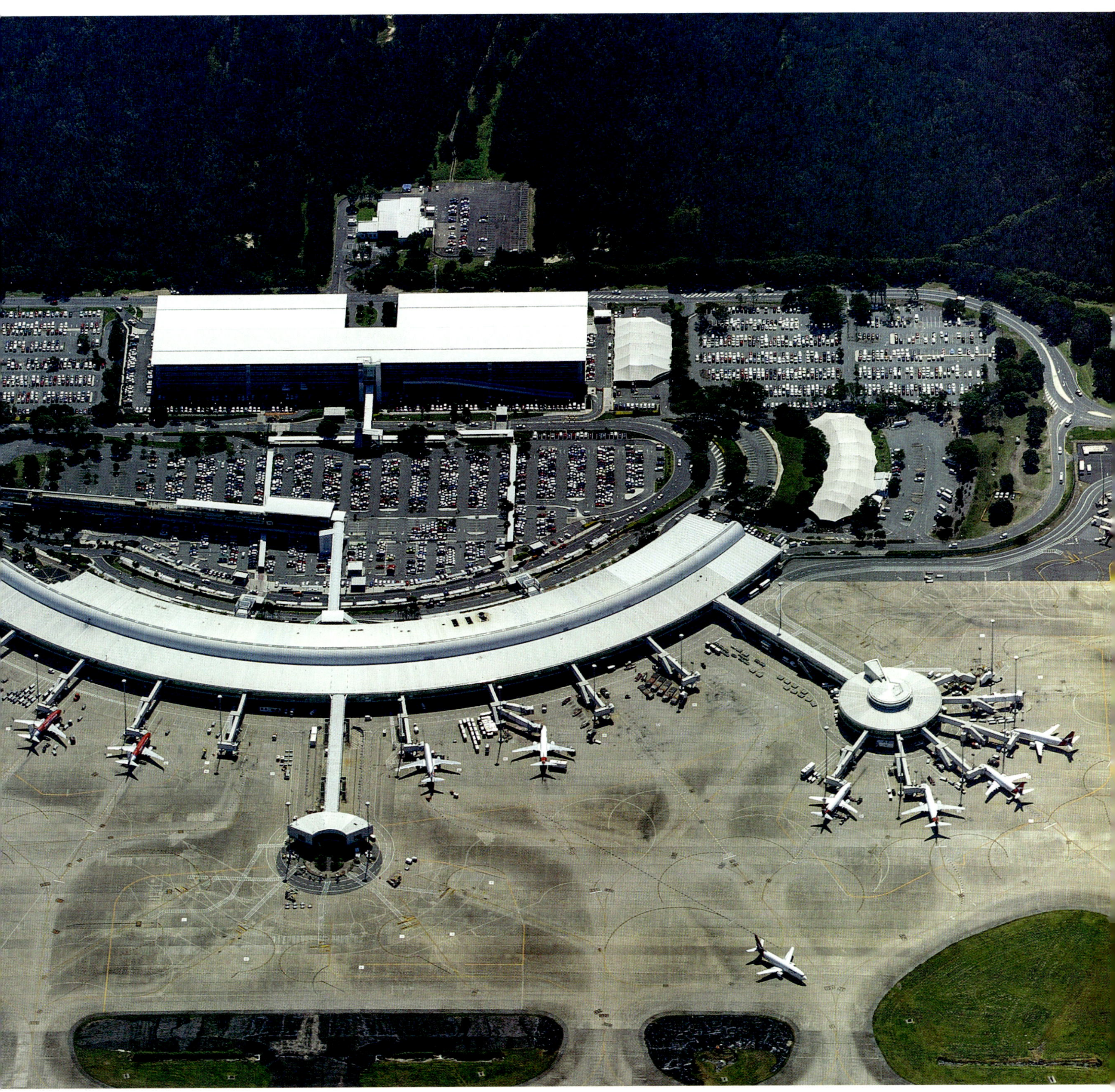

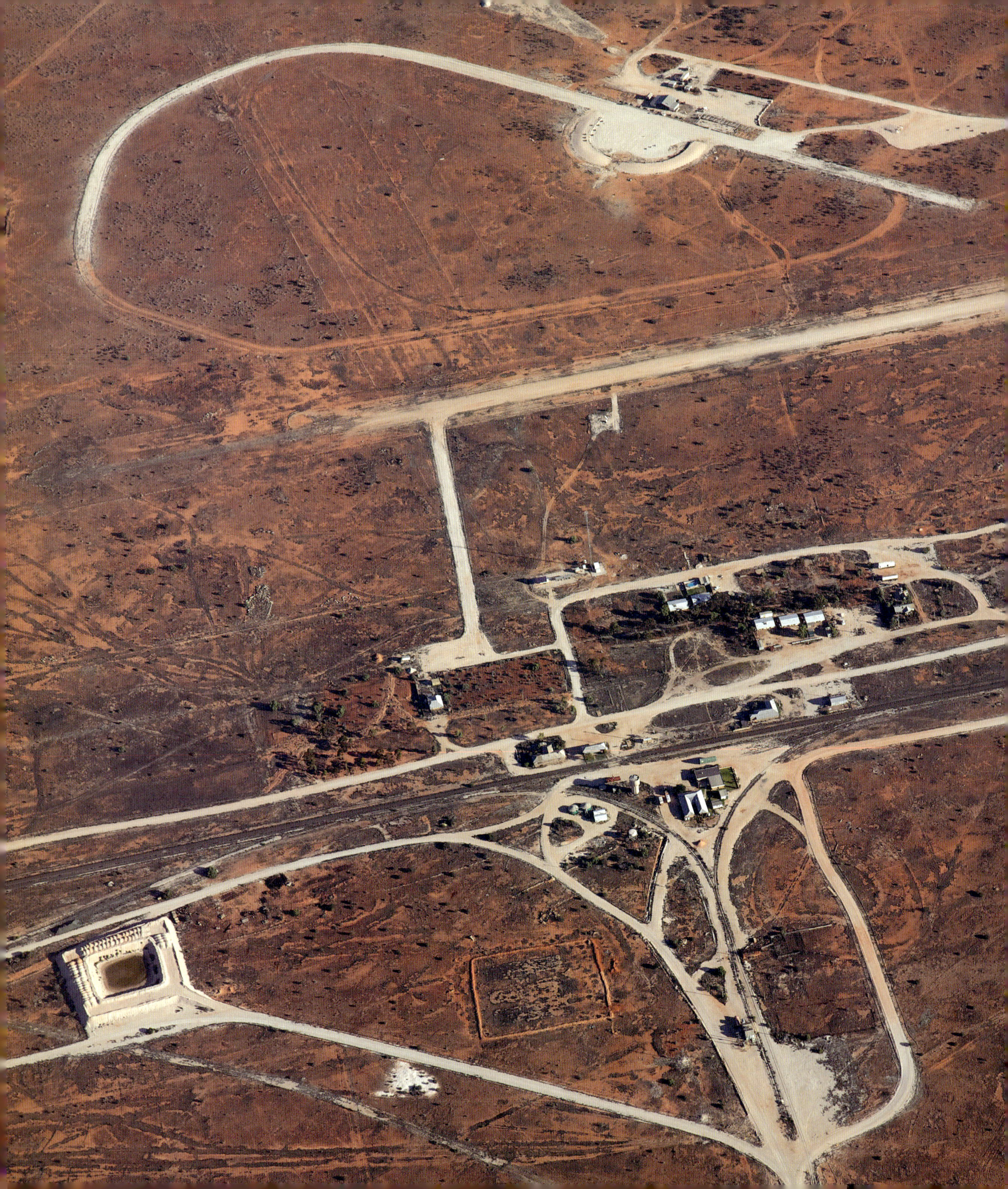

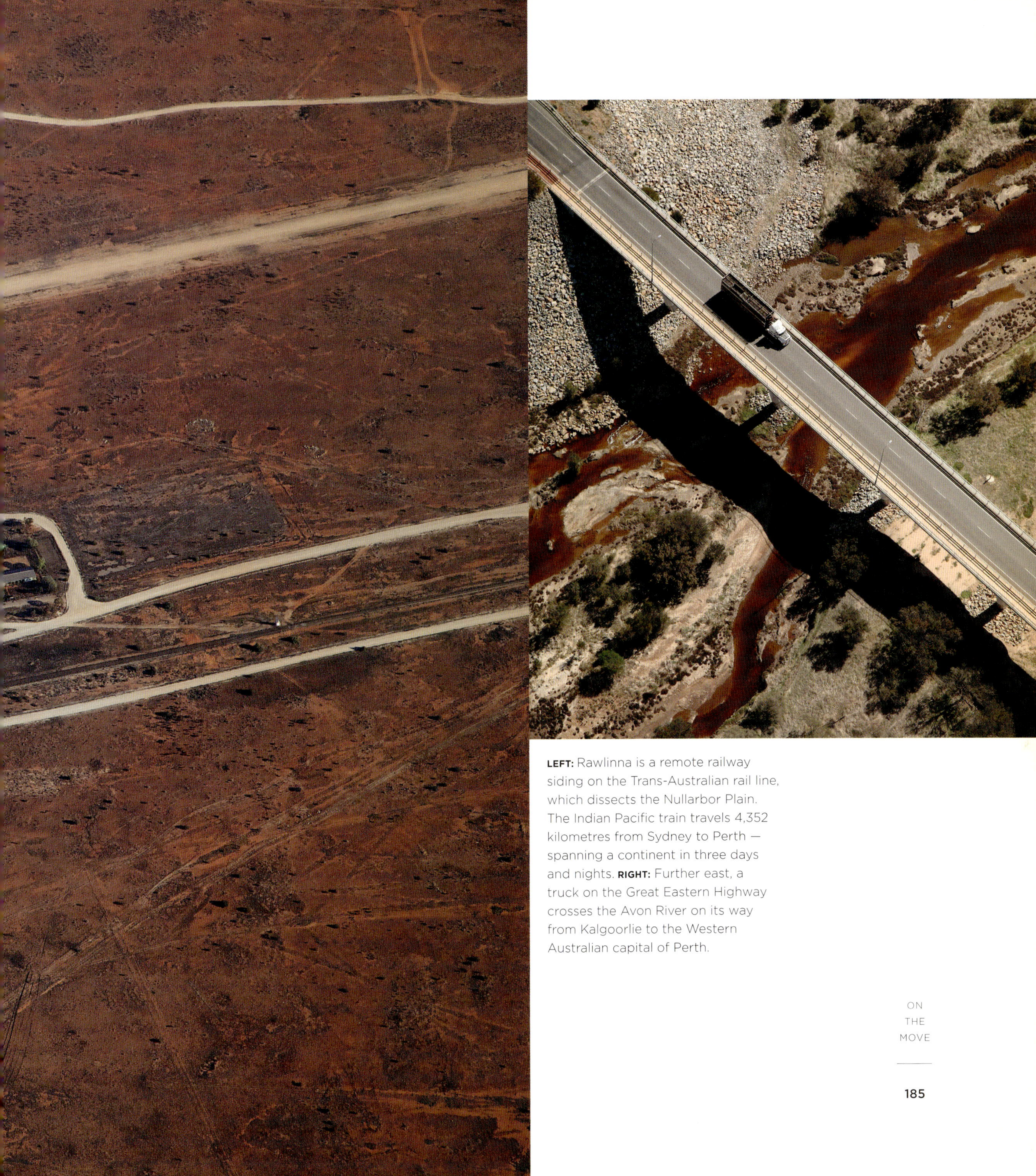

LEFT: Rawlinna is a remote railway siding on the Trans-Australian rail line, which dissects the Nullarbor Plain. The Indian Pacific train travels 4,352 kilometres from Sydney to Perth — spanning a continent in three days and nights. **RIGHT:** Further east, a truck on the Great Eastern Highway crosses the Avon River on its way from Kalgoorlie to the Western Australian capital of Perth.

LEFT: Thousands of city dwellers gather on Australia Day at Cottesloe Beach in Perth to attempt to break the world record for the longest line of inflatable thongs. **RIGHT:** The bush unites at the start of the ute muster in Deniliquin, southern New South Wales. The event holds the Guinness World Record for the largest gathering of people wearing blue singlets — 3,500 in 2010.

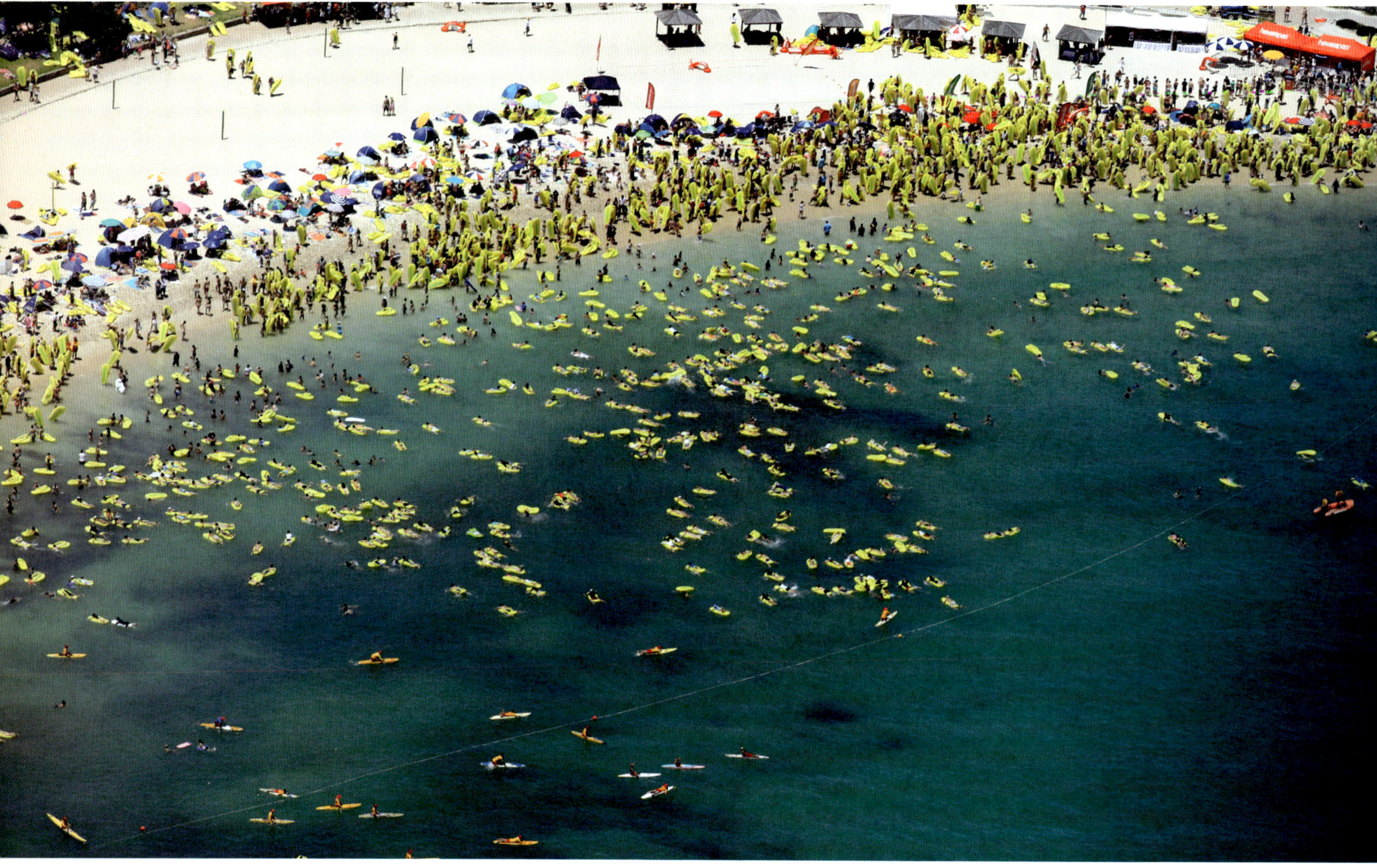

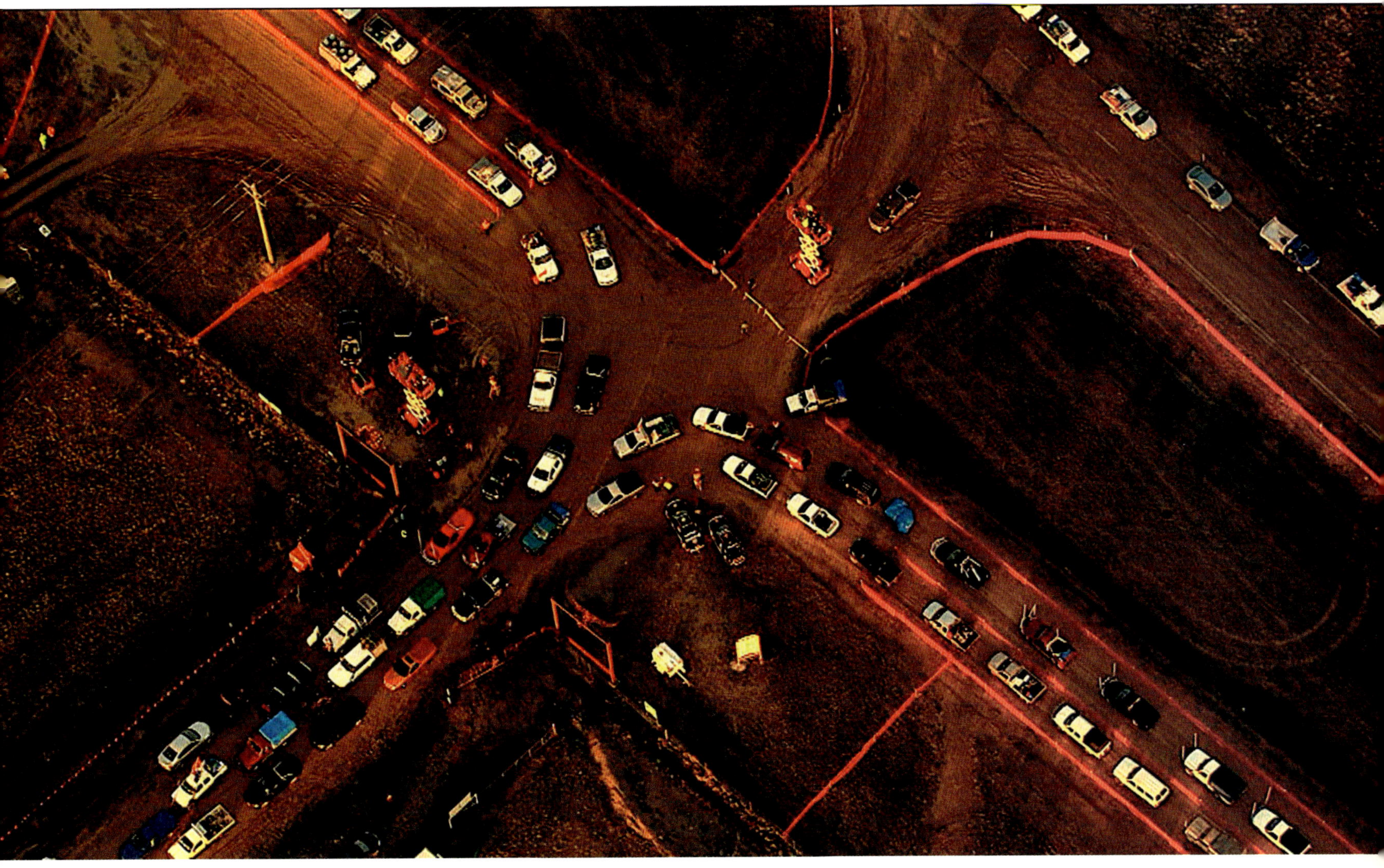

Two events that attract people from around the world. **LEFT:** The neat and orderly world of the Byron Bay Blues Fest on the east coast of Australia. The site caters for 17,500 festival-goers per day, and 6,500 campers over the length of the festival. **RIGHT:** Racing yachts moments before the start of the Sydney to Hobart Bluewater Classic. This yacht race is widely regarded as one of the most dangerous and challenging in the world.

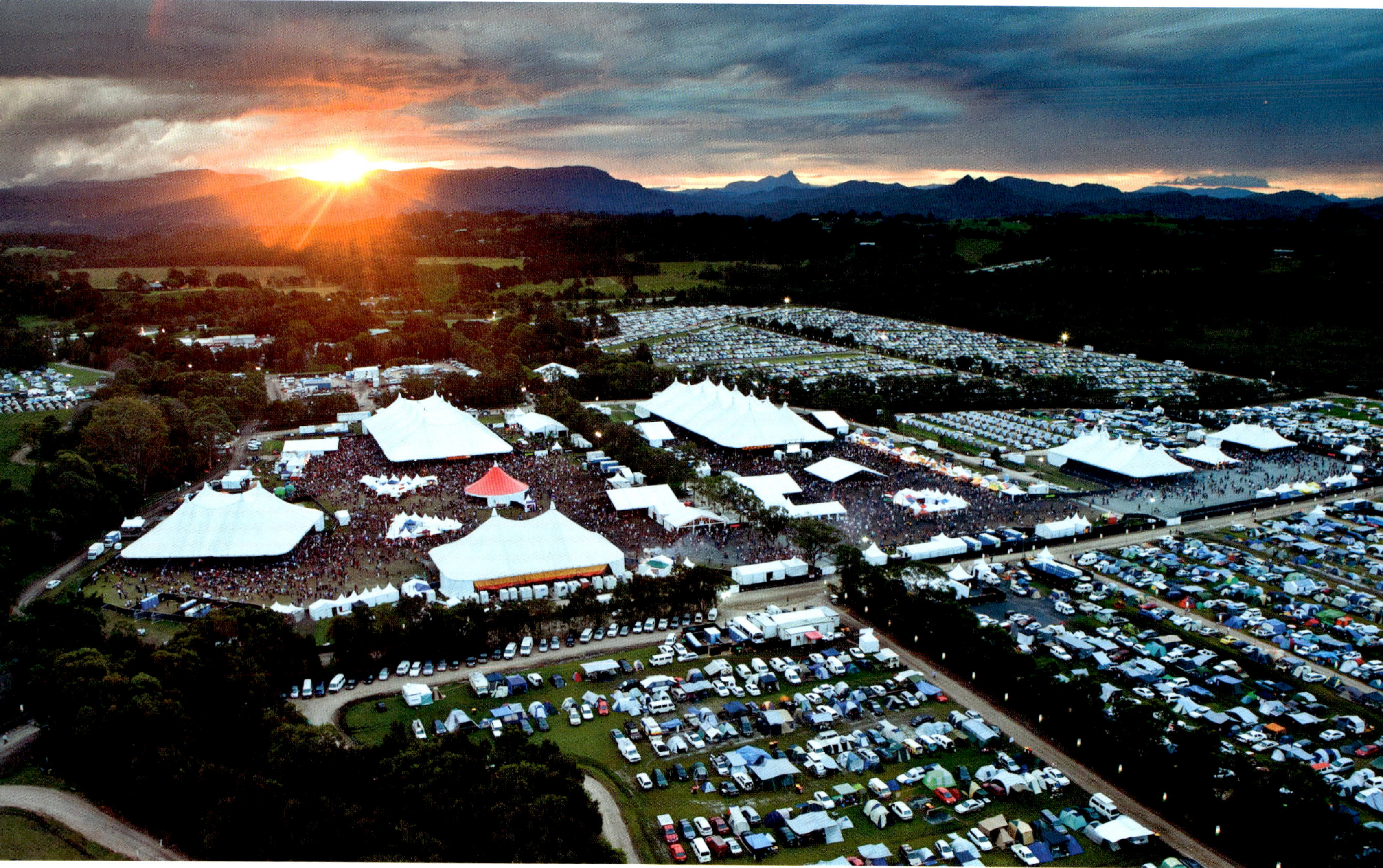

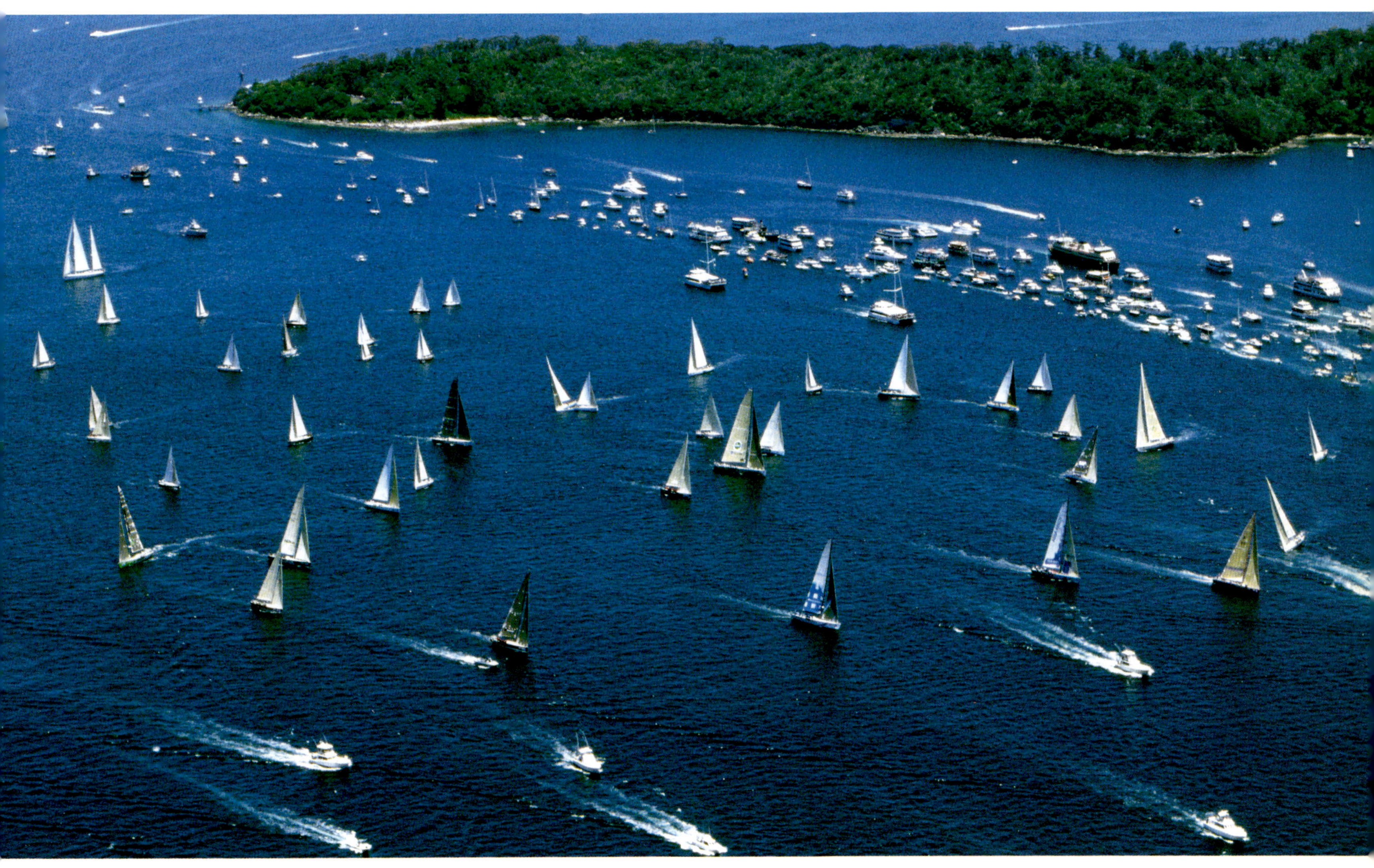

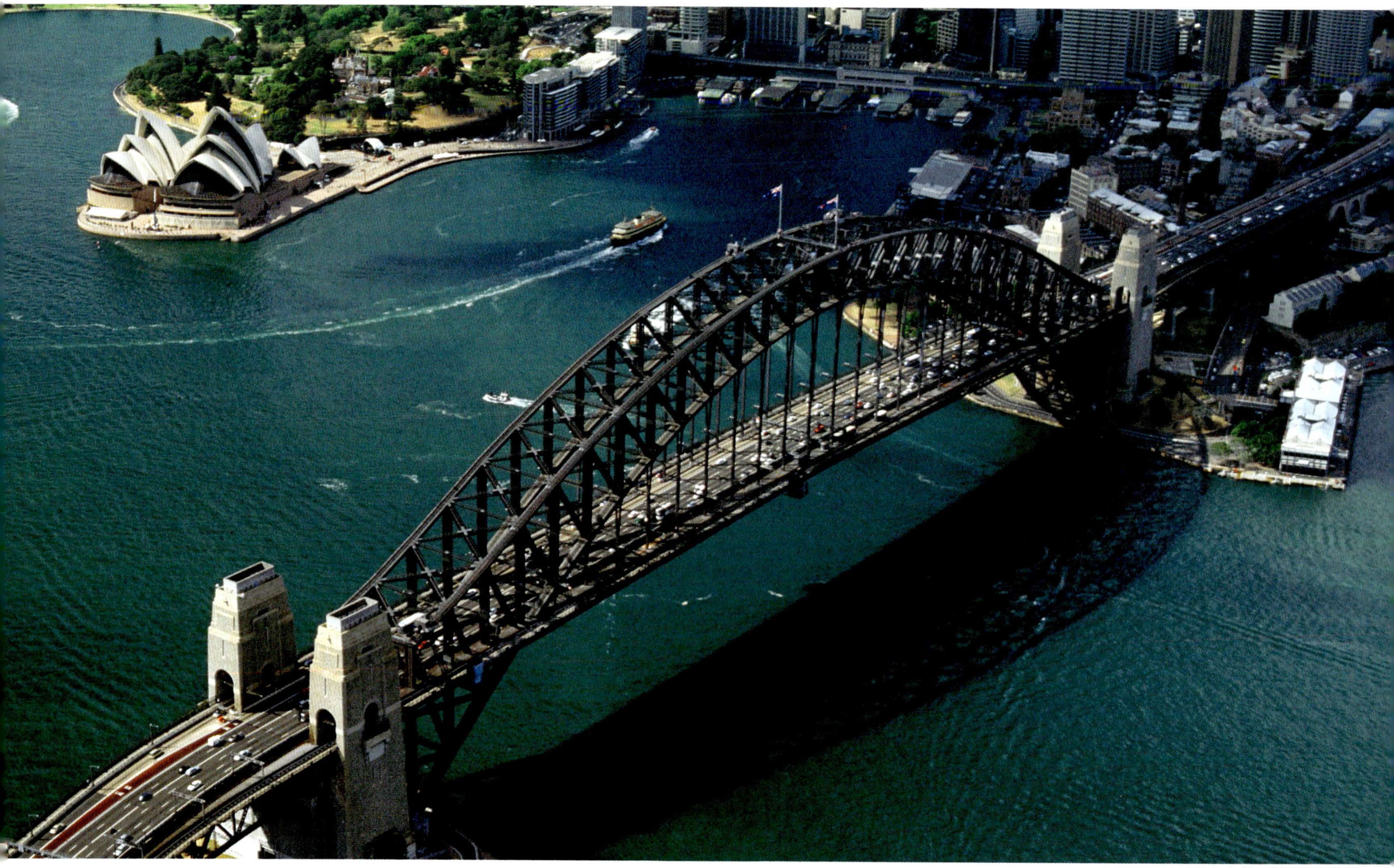

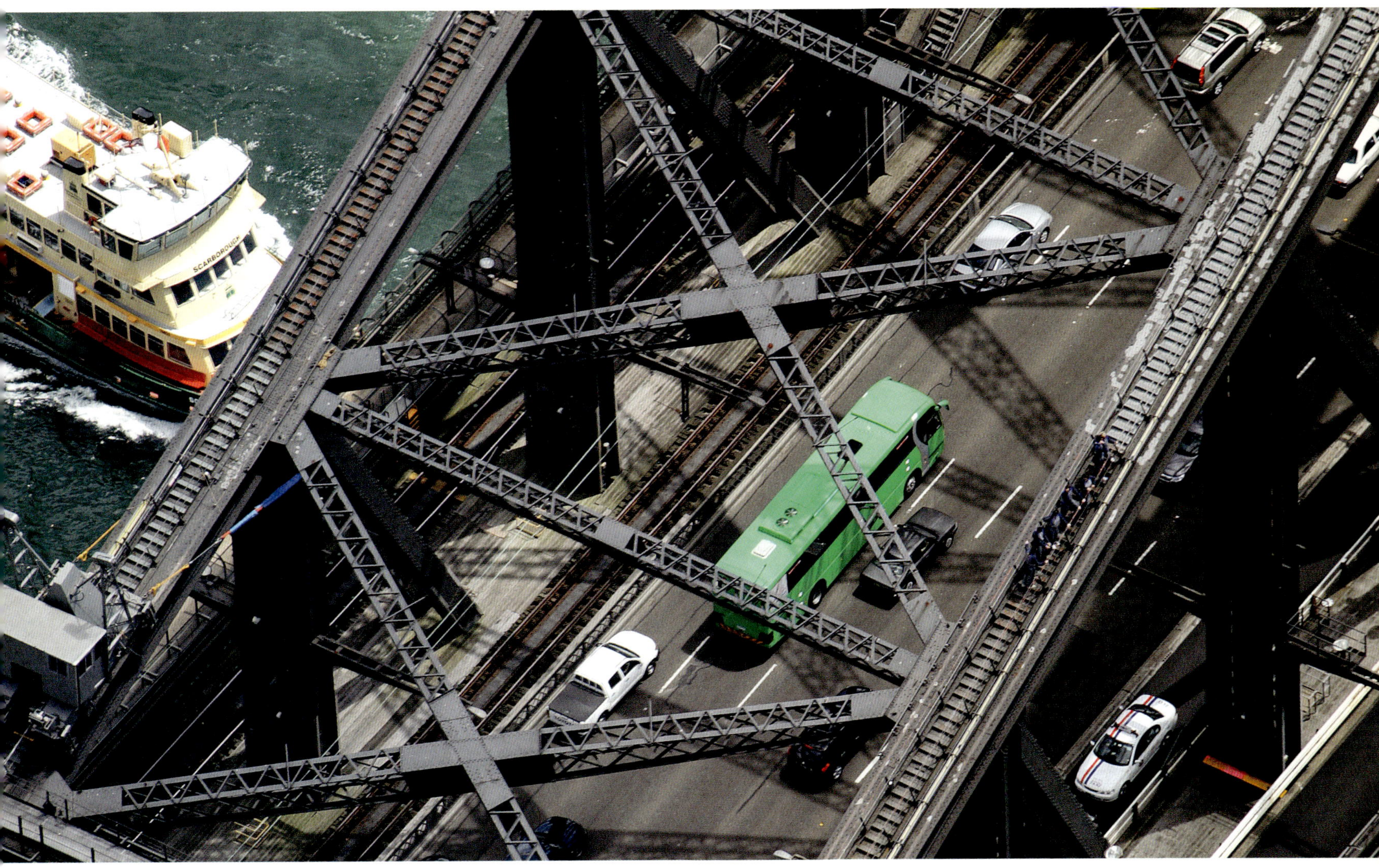

LEFT AND RIGHT: The Sydney Harbour Bridge — Australia's busiest road — carries more than 160,000 vehicles every working day. Another 100,000 vehicles use the Sydney Harbour Tunnel.

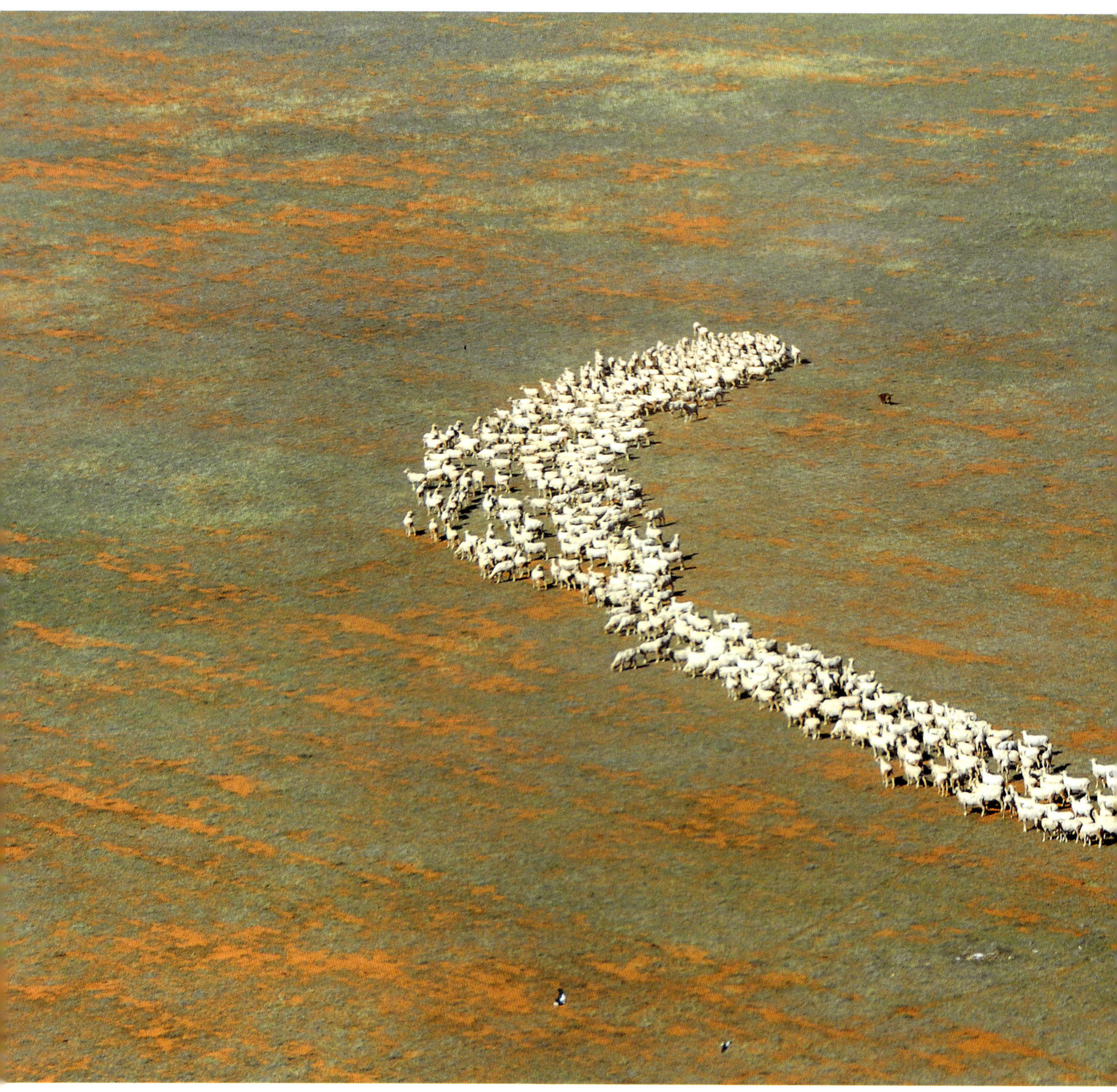

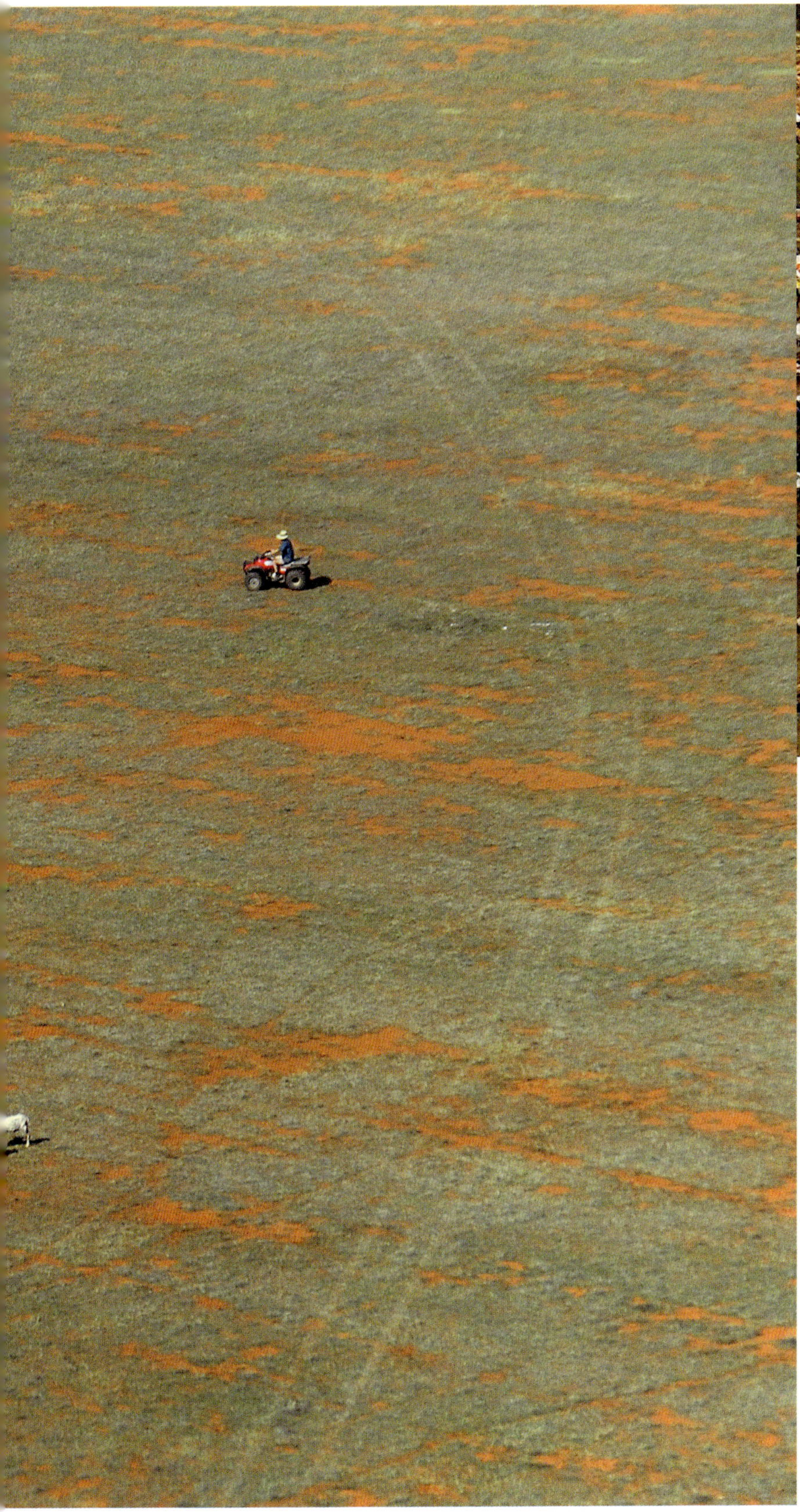

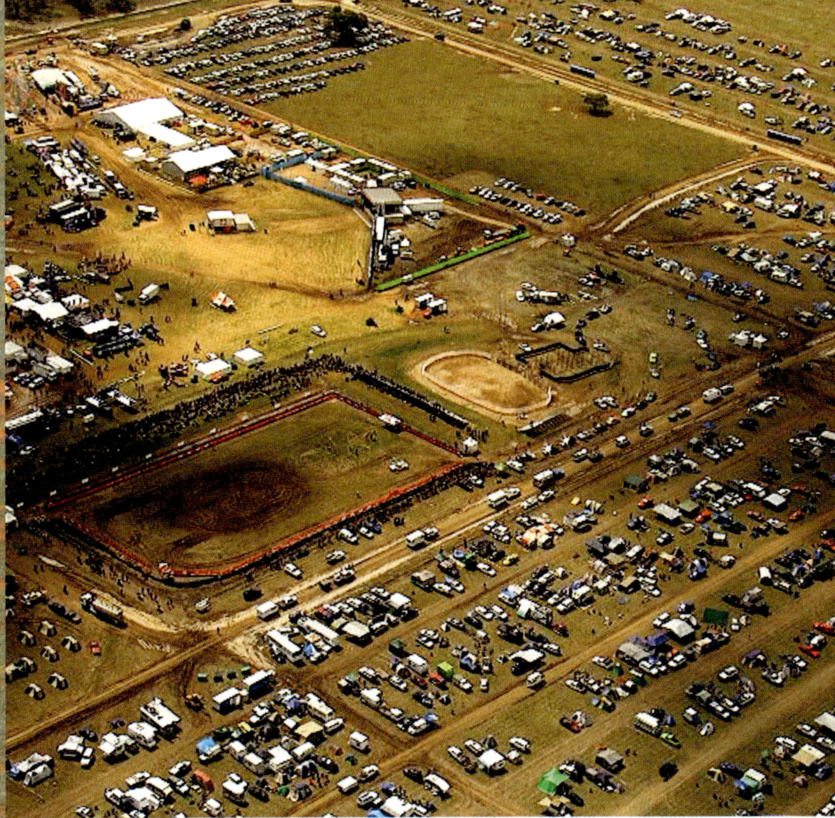

A tale of two musters. **LEFT:** A farmer and his dogs round up sheep near the small country town of Caragabal in the central west region of New South Wales. **RIGHT:** Ute lovers gather in Deniliquin, New South Wales. In 1999, the ute muster set the world record for the highest number of legally paraded utes at 2,839. **FOLLOWING PAGES:** Ore wagons in Newcastle, New South Wales. Australia is the world's largest exporter of iron ore with most destined for the mills of China, Japan and South Korea.

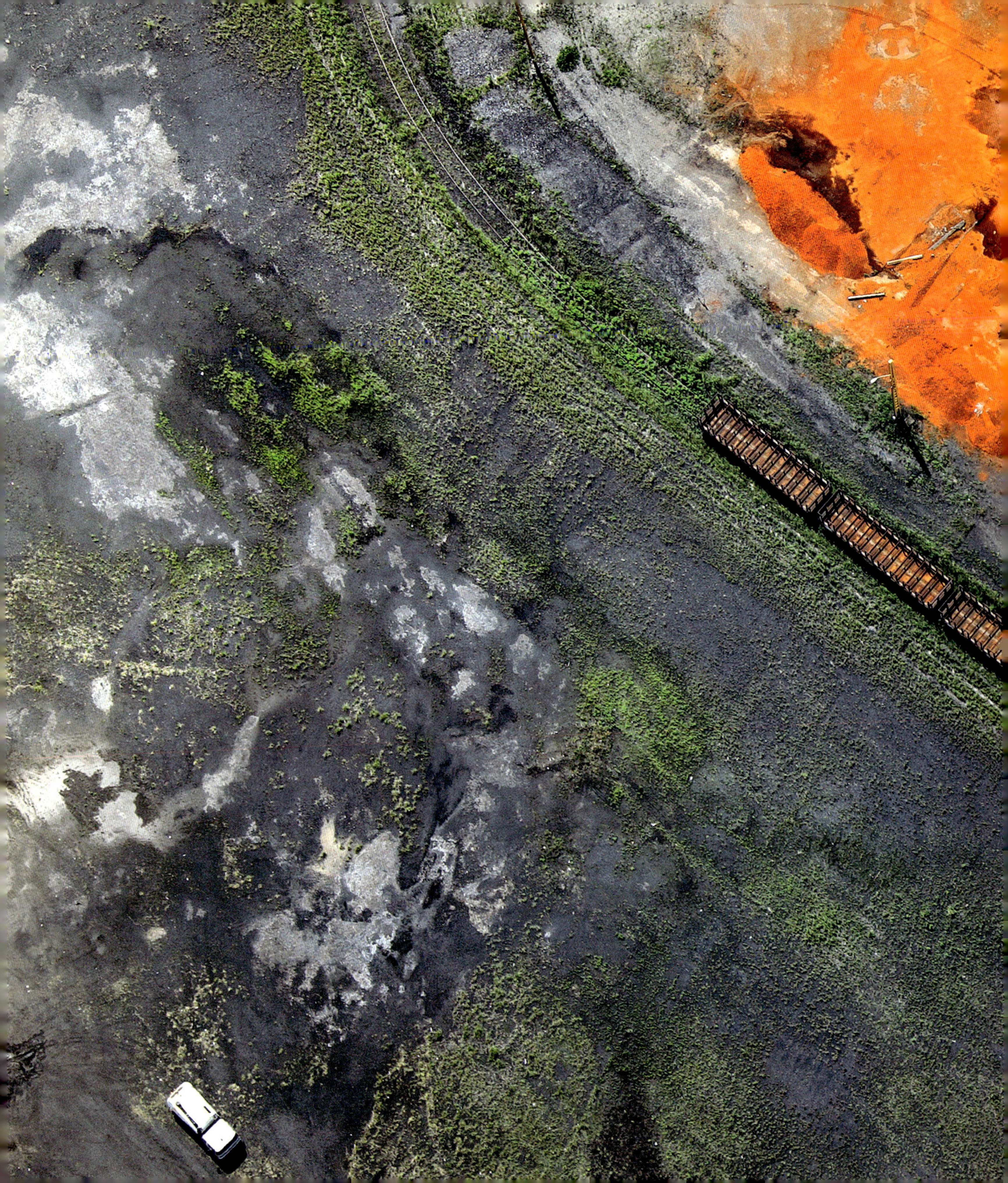

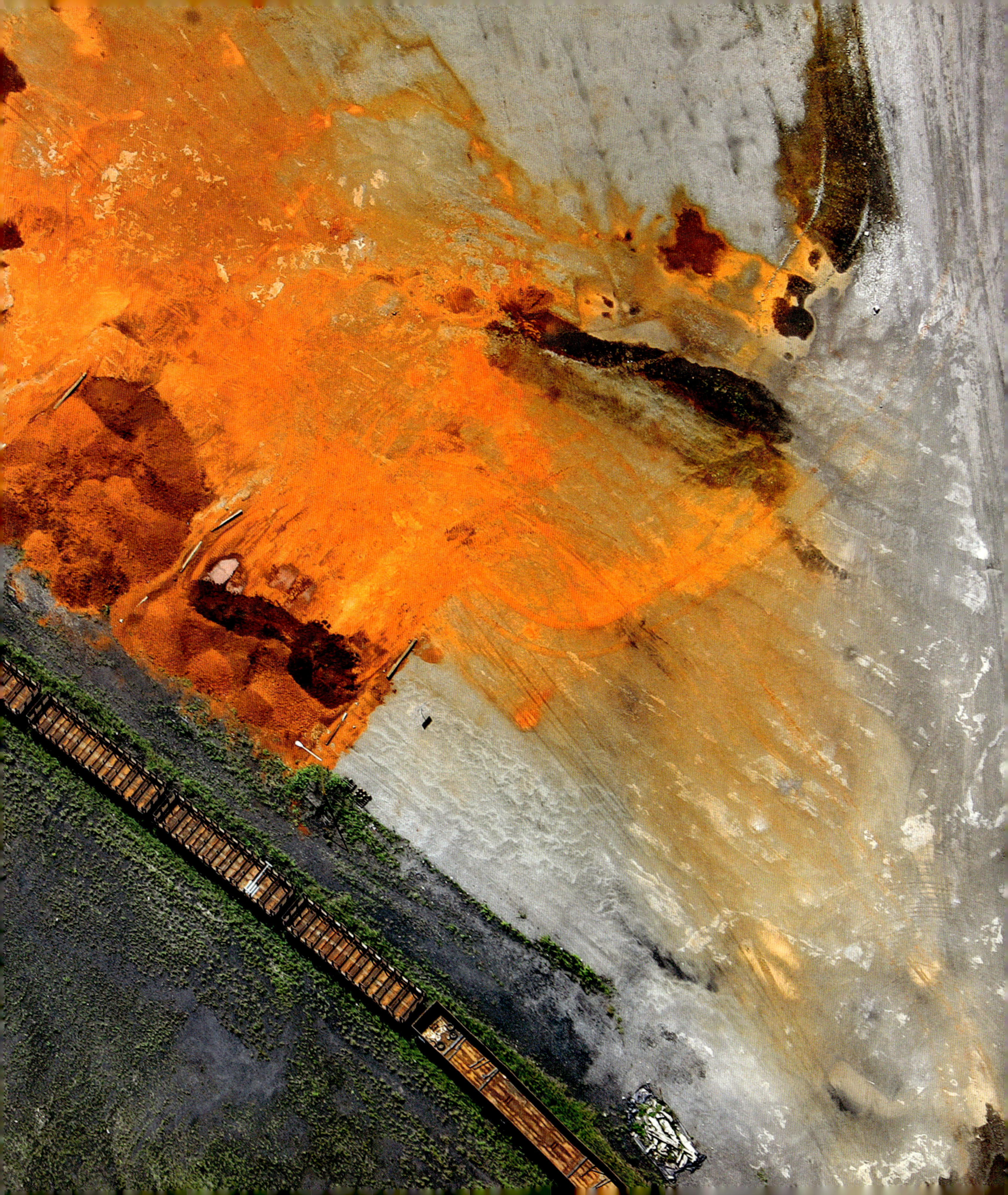

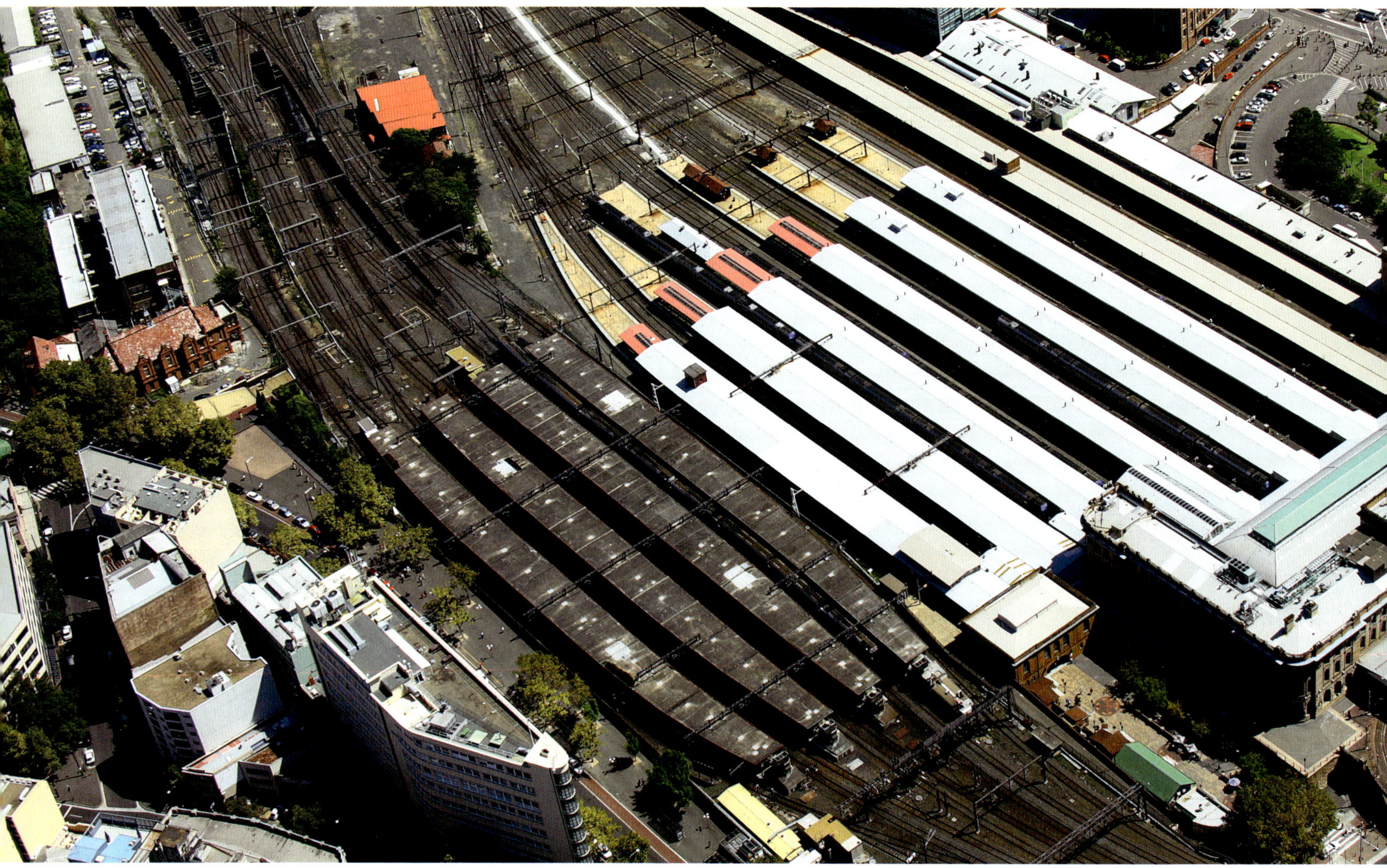

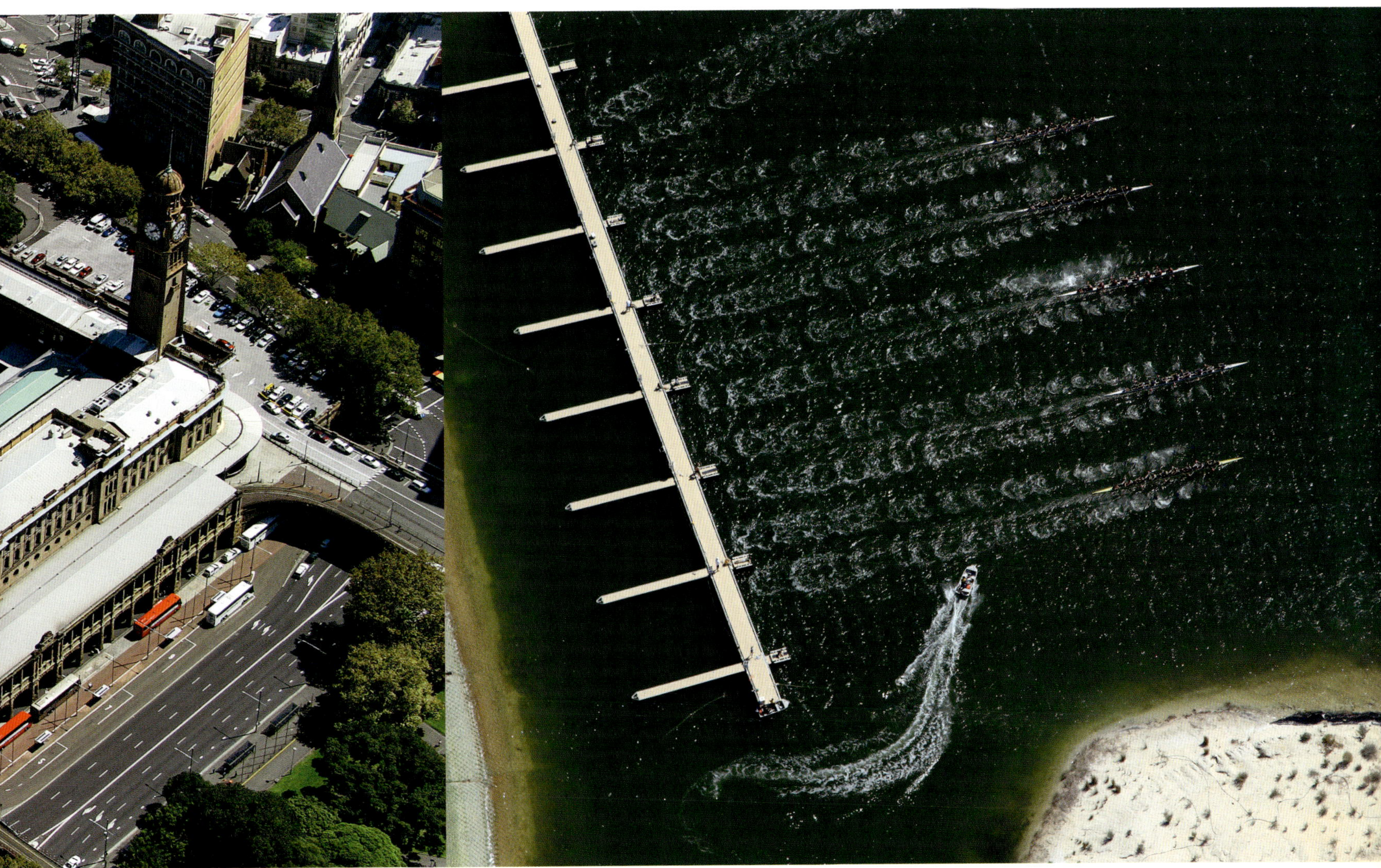

LEFT: Central Station in Sydney keeps 300,000 commuters on the move each weekday. **RIGHT:** Rowers depart from their own platforms at a regatta at man-made Champion Lakes Regatta Centre in Perth. **FOLLOWING PAGE LEFT:** Roma Street train station is at the centre of Brisbane's commuter movement. Five million people use the station each year. **FOLLOWING PAGE RIGHT:** A green keeper applies the finishing touches before a day of golf in Canberra.

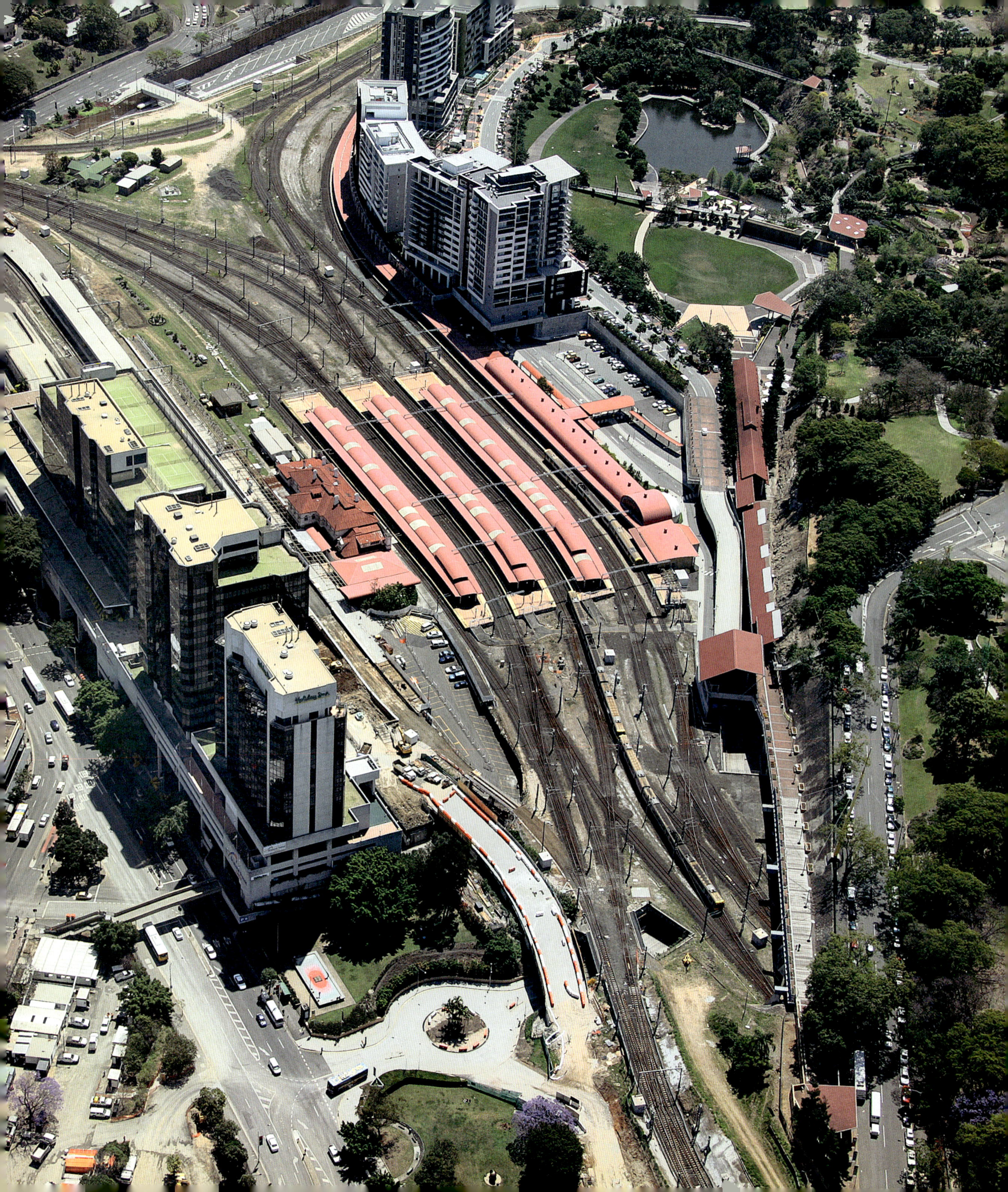

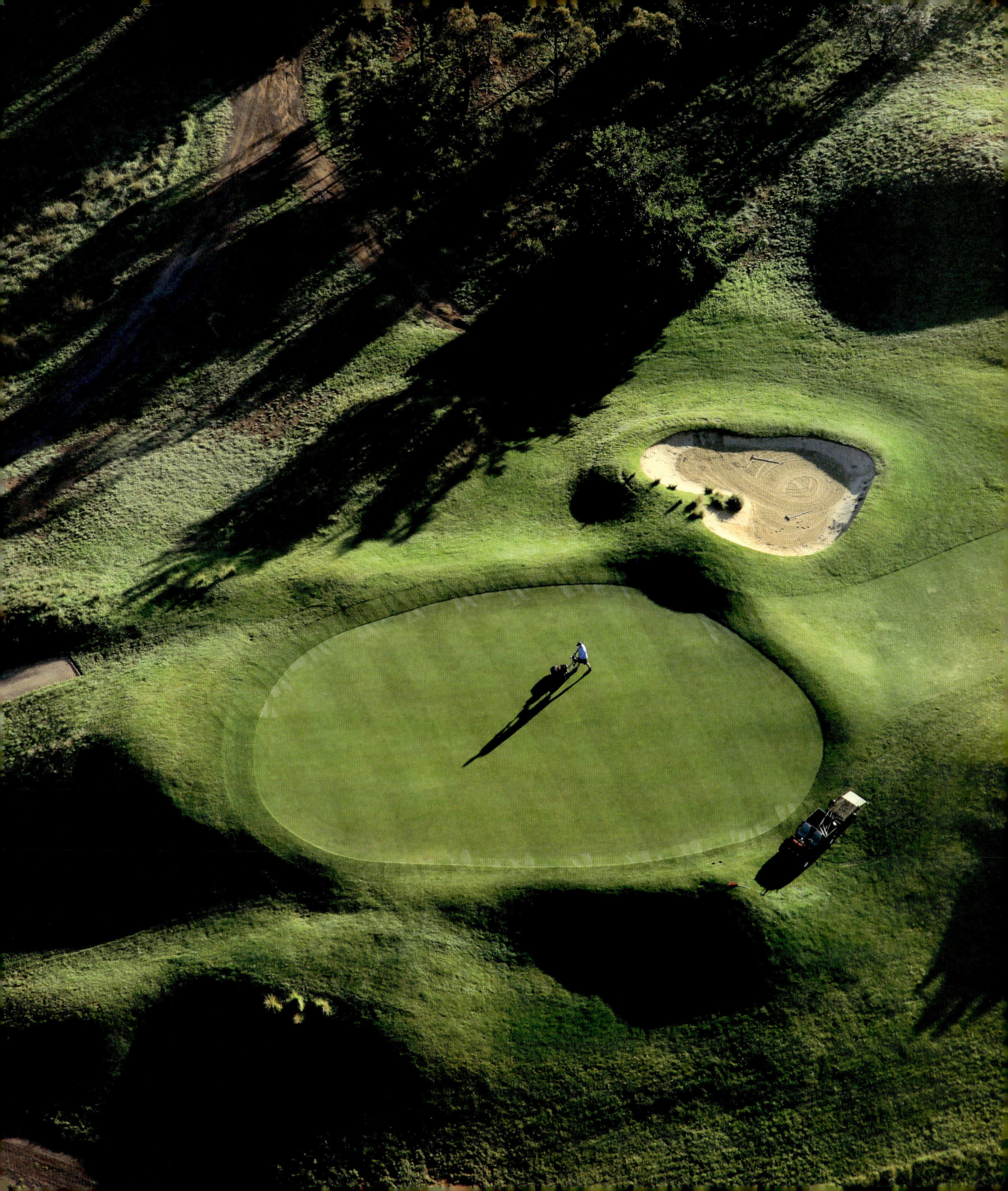

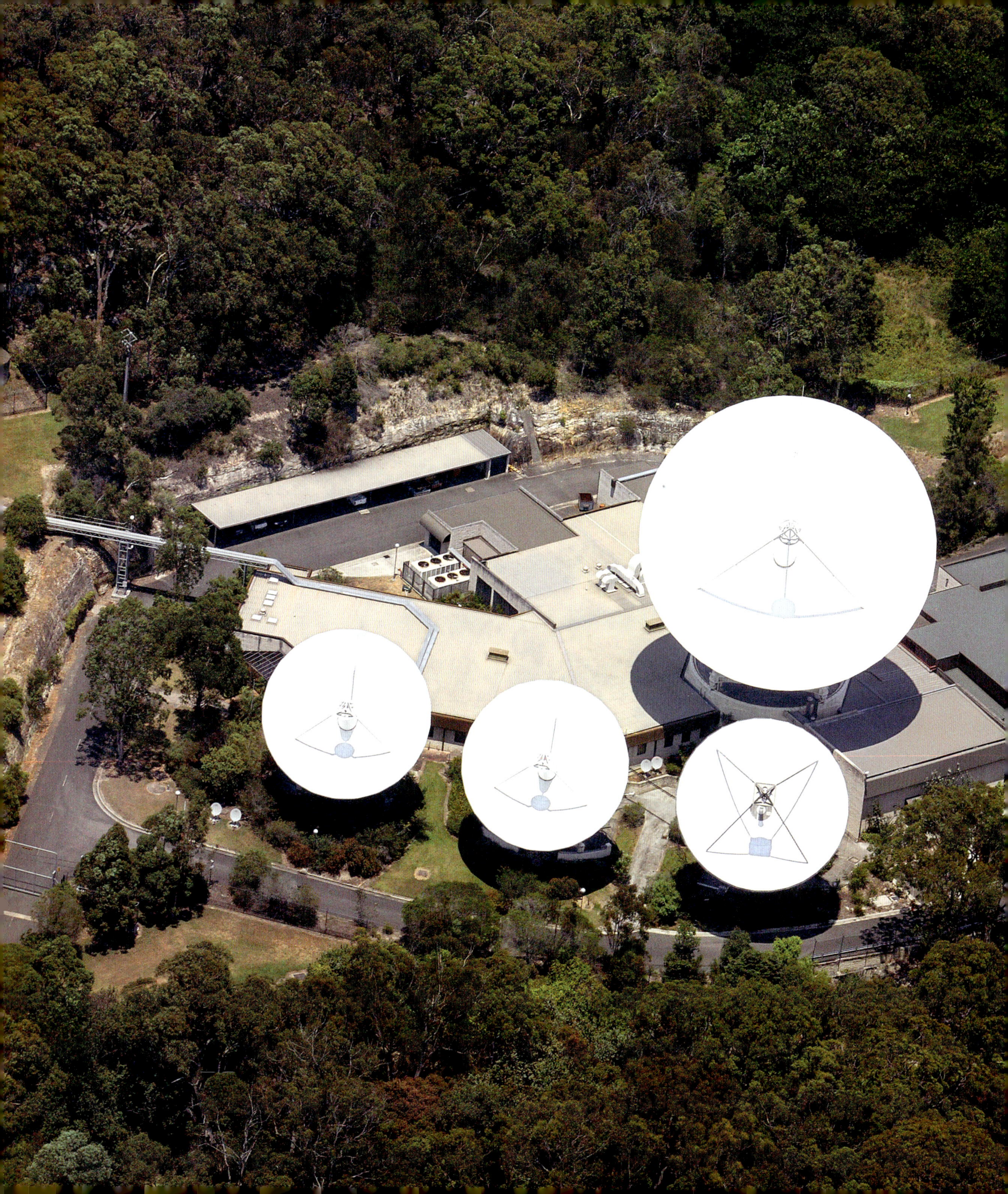

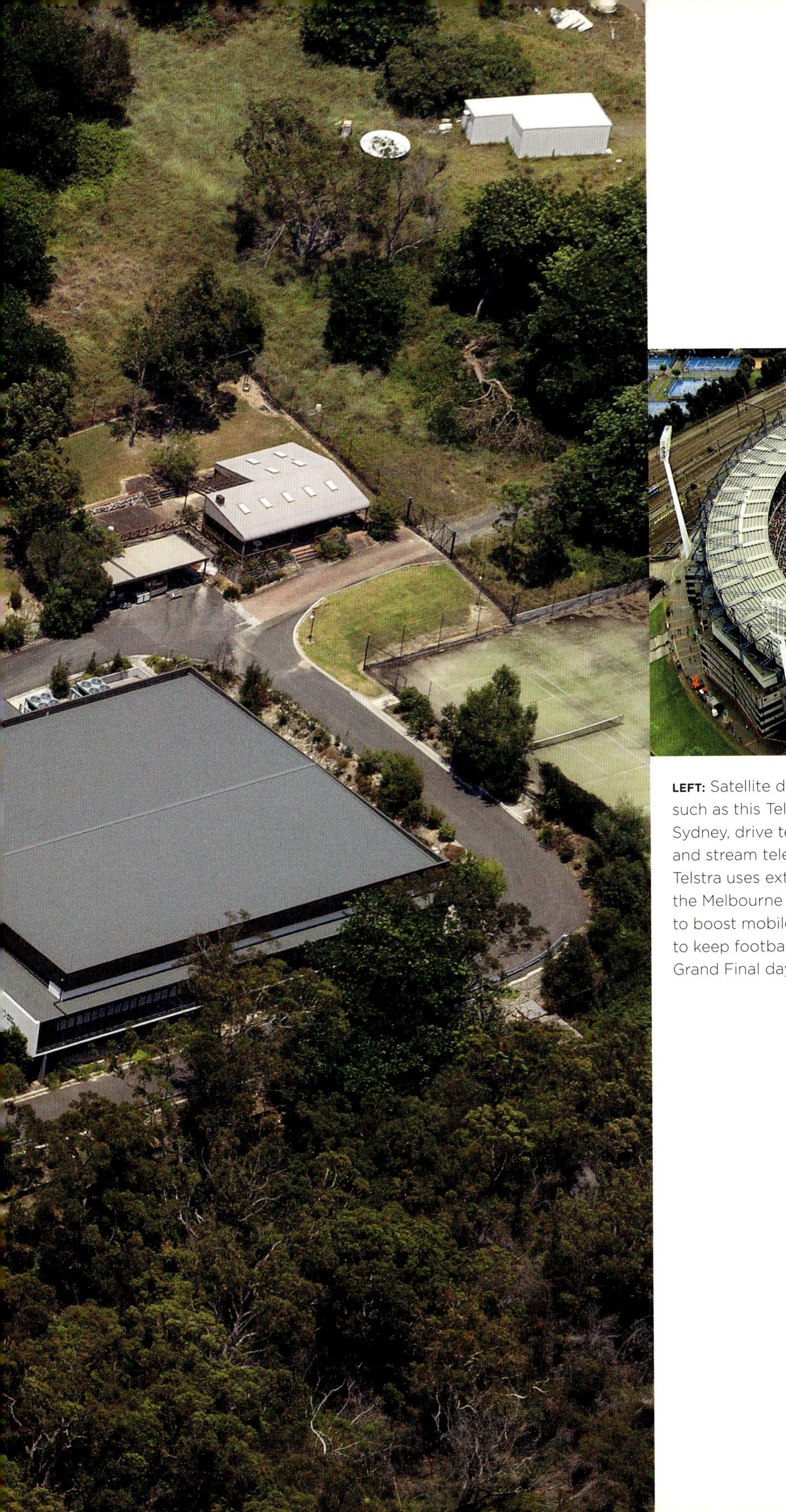

LEFT: Satellite dishes at earth stations such as this Telstra facility in northern Sydney, drive telecommunications and stream television programs. Telstra uses extra base stations at the Melbourne Cricket Ground **(RIGHT)** to boost mobile telephone signals to keep football fans connected on Grand Final day.

LEFT: Flemington Racecourse hosts more than 110,000 punters each November for the Melbourne Cup. Australians wagered more than $150 million on the Cup in 2012. **RIGHT:** Music fans come from all over Australia for the New Year's Eve Pyramid Rock festival on Phillip Island in Victoria.

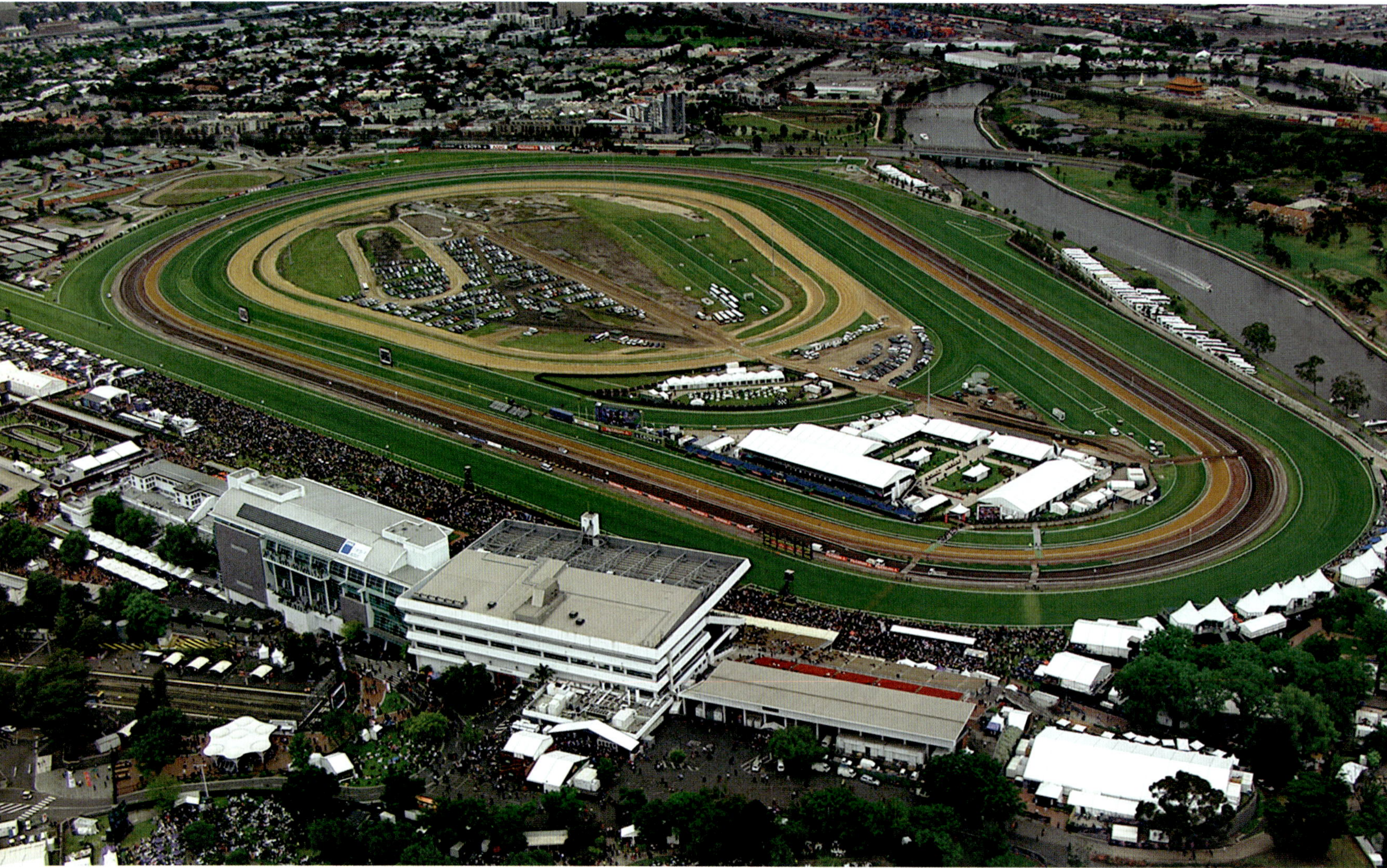

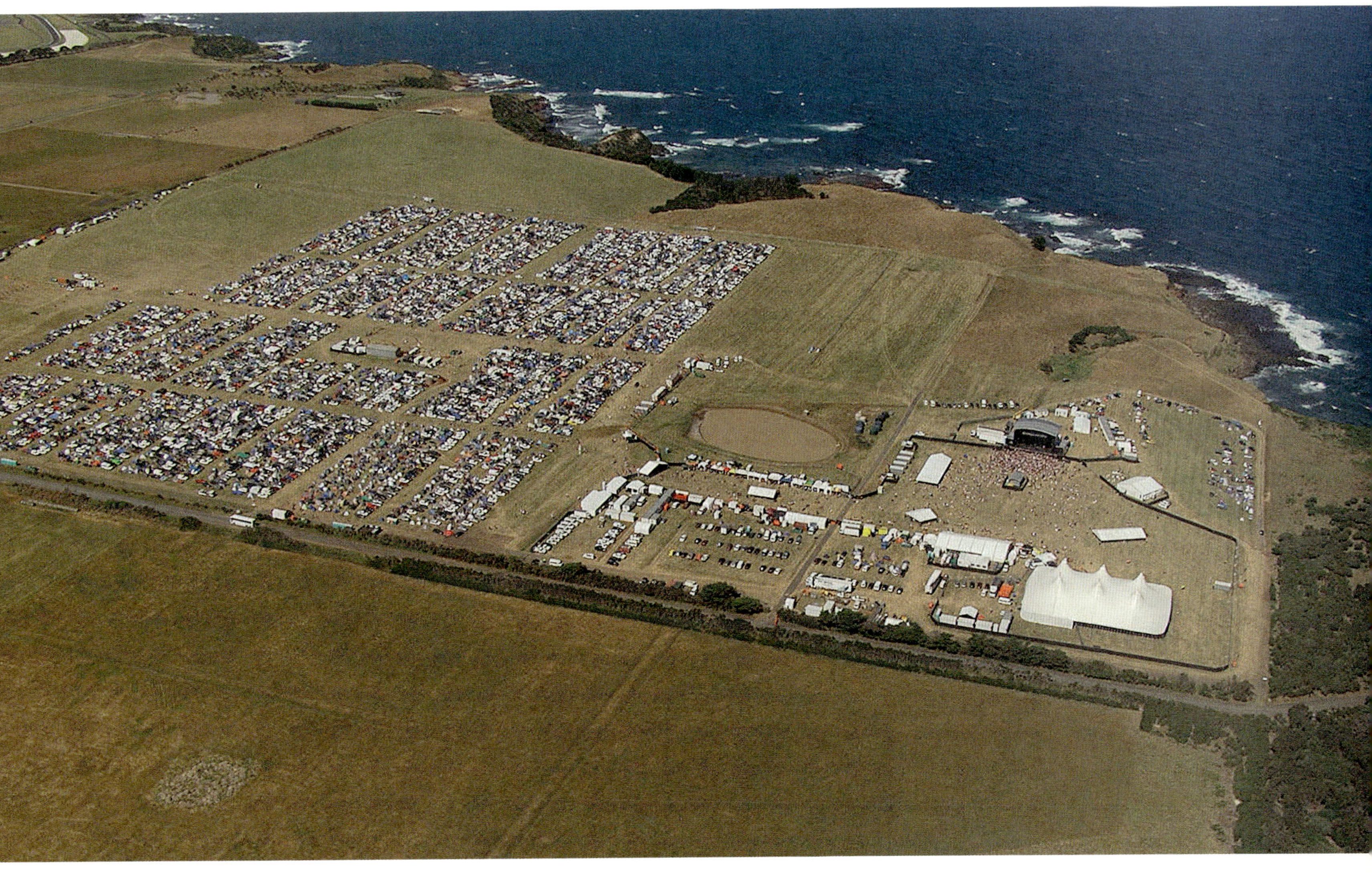

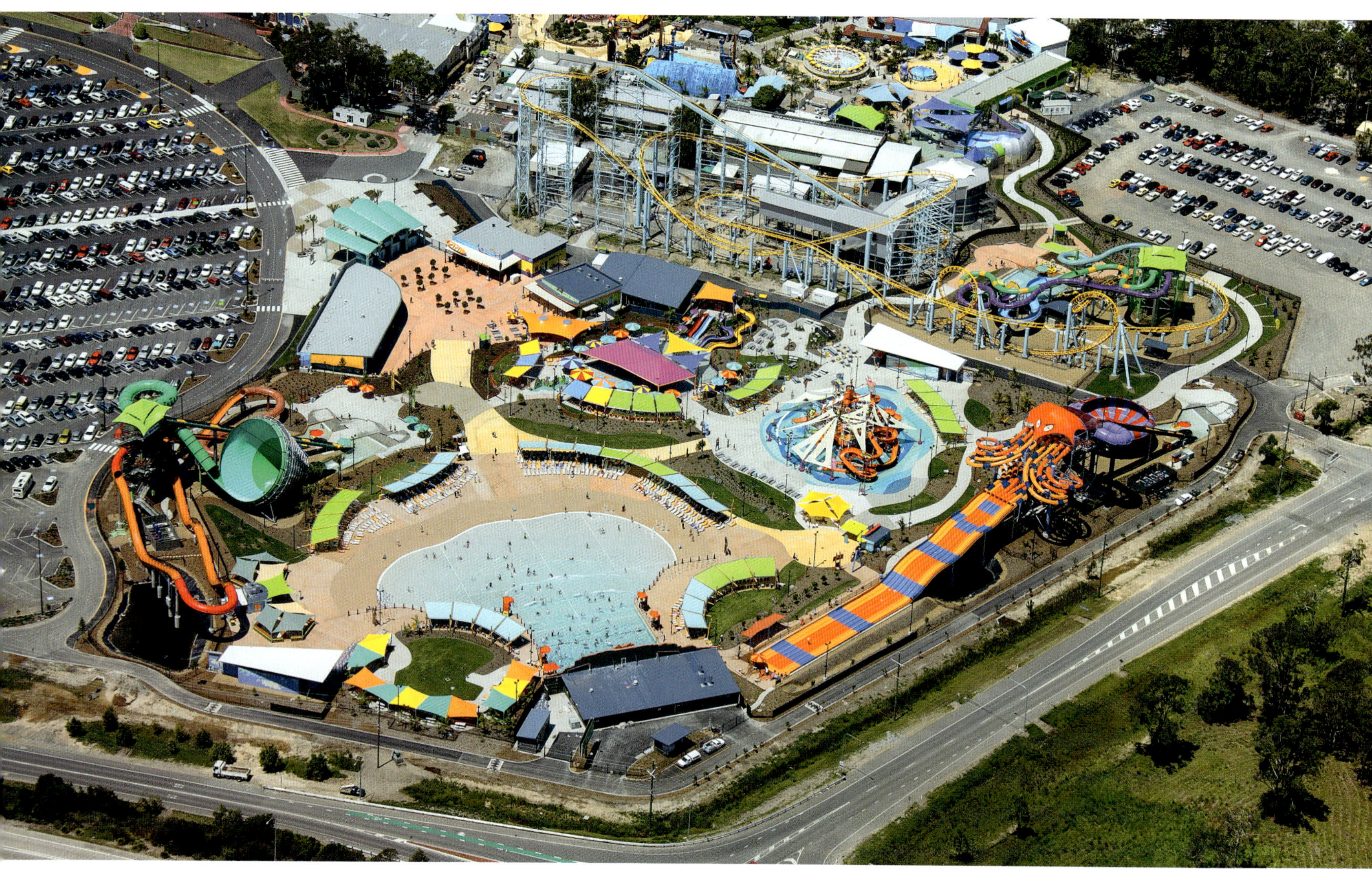

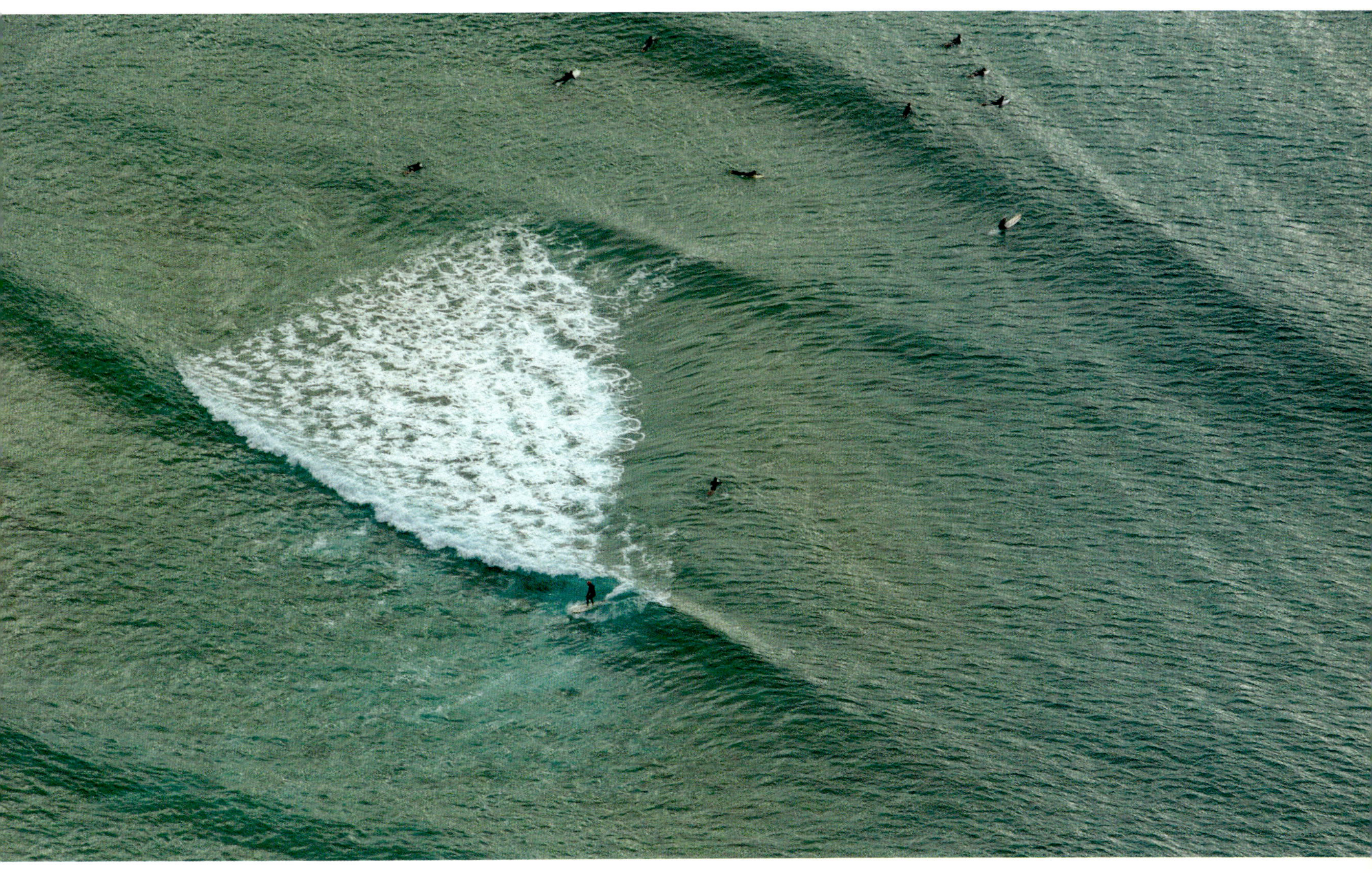

LEFT: Man-made rides at a fun park on the Gold Coast, Queensland. The Gold Coast's 70 kilometres of coastline and varied tourist attractions draw more than 10 million visitors each year. **RIGHT:** Surfers ride the real thing at the mouth of the Moruya River in southern New South Wales.

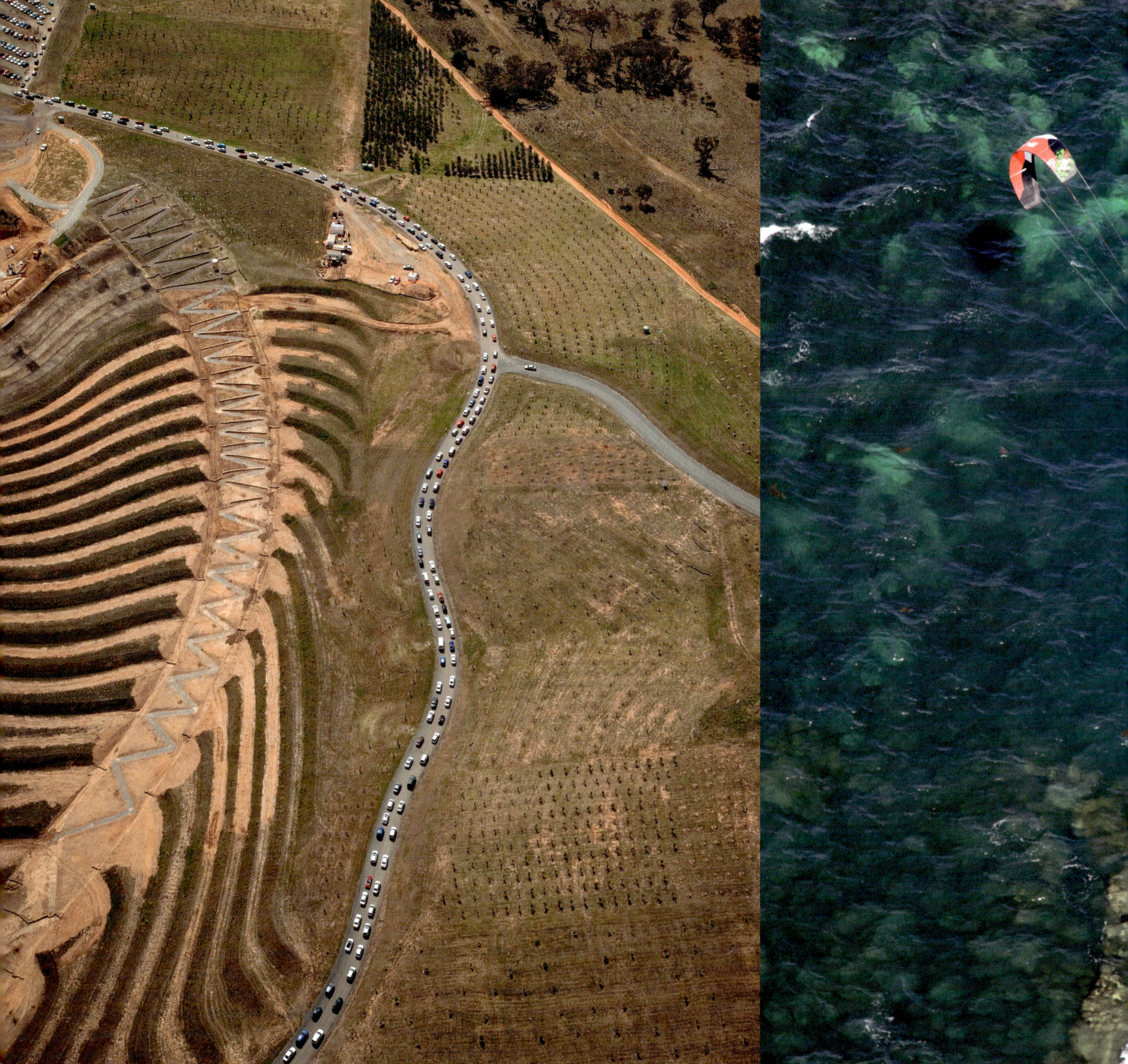

LEFT: A line of traffic snakes its way past the National Arboretum in Canberra, created after the bushfires of 2003. **MIDDLE:** A kitesurfer is on the move near Margaret River, Western Australia. **RIGHT:** The Pacific Motorway — alive at night — connects Brisbane and Tweed Heads.

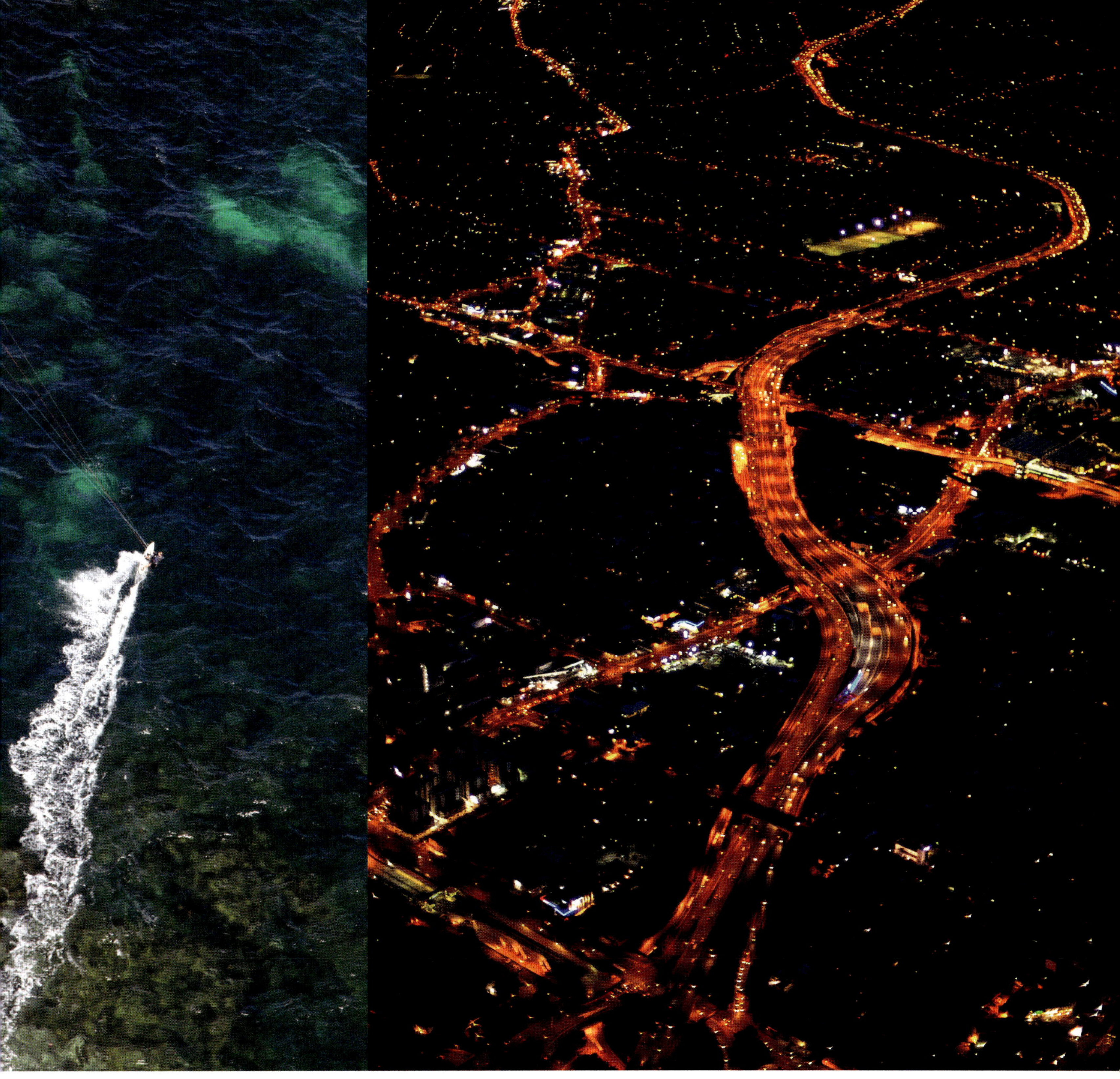

FOLLOWING PAGES: The Captain Cook Bridge in Brisbane is used by 127,800 vehicles every day while tens of thousands of pedestrians and cyclists share the smaller Goodwill Bridge each week.

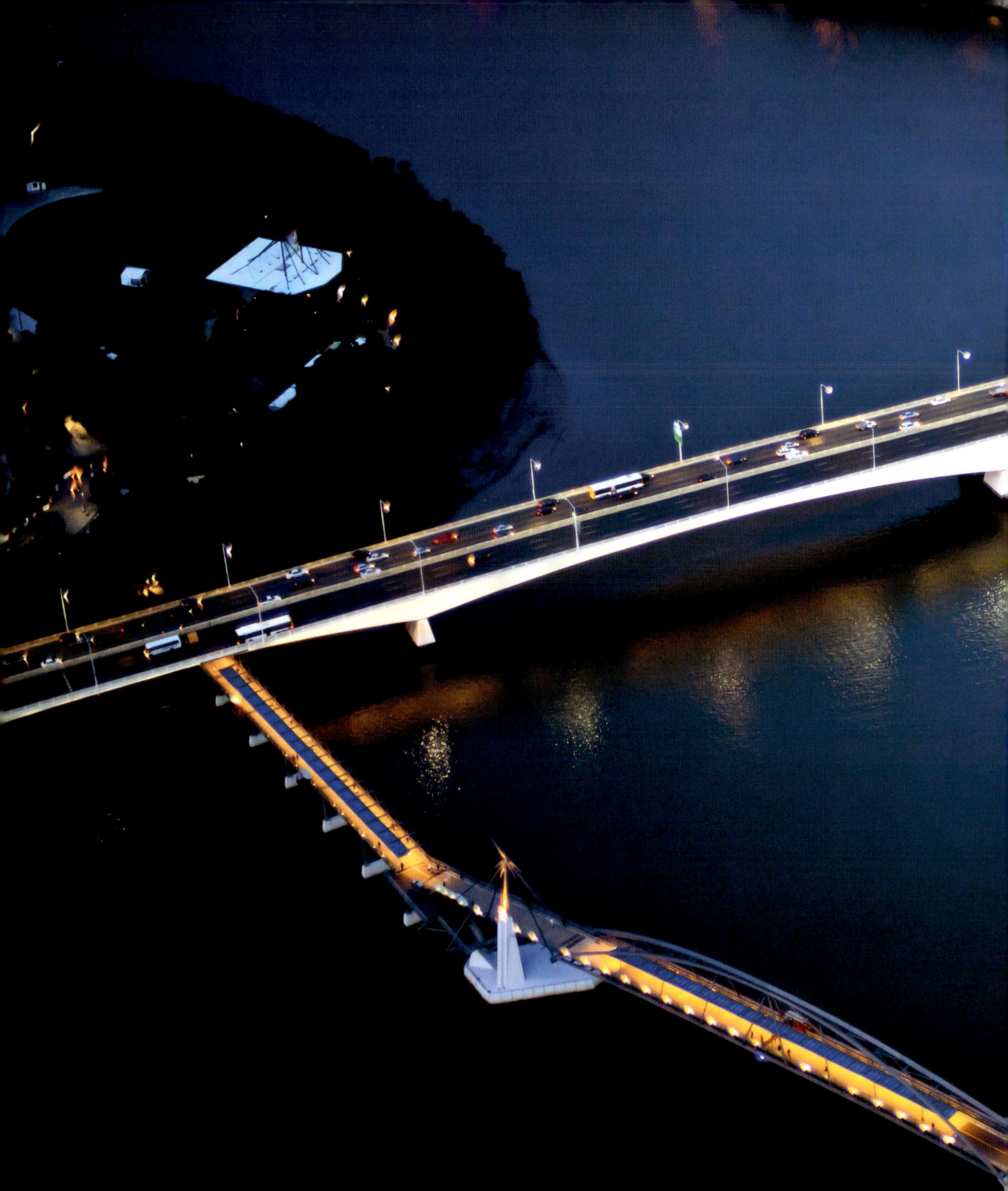

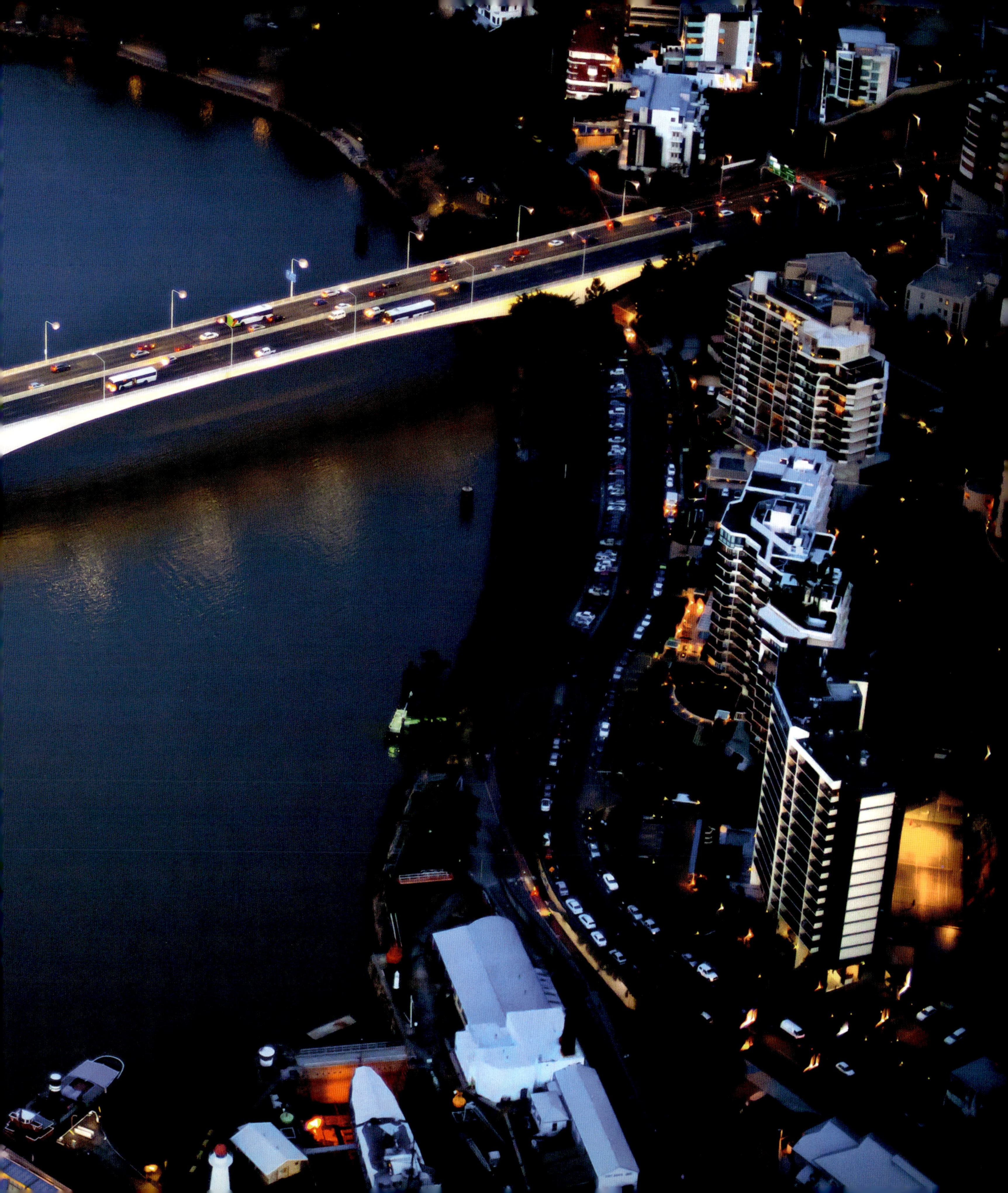

LEFT: Vehicles fresh off the ship sit at the terminal in Fremantle, Western Australia.
RIGHT: Australia Post is staging a comeback thanks to goods ordered online. Here, a truck crosses an overpass on the South Western Freeway near Douglas Park, southwest of Sydney.

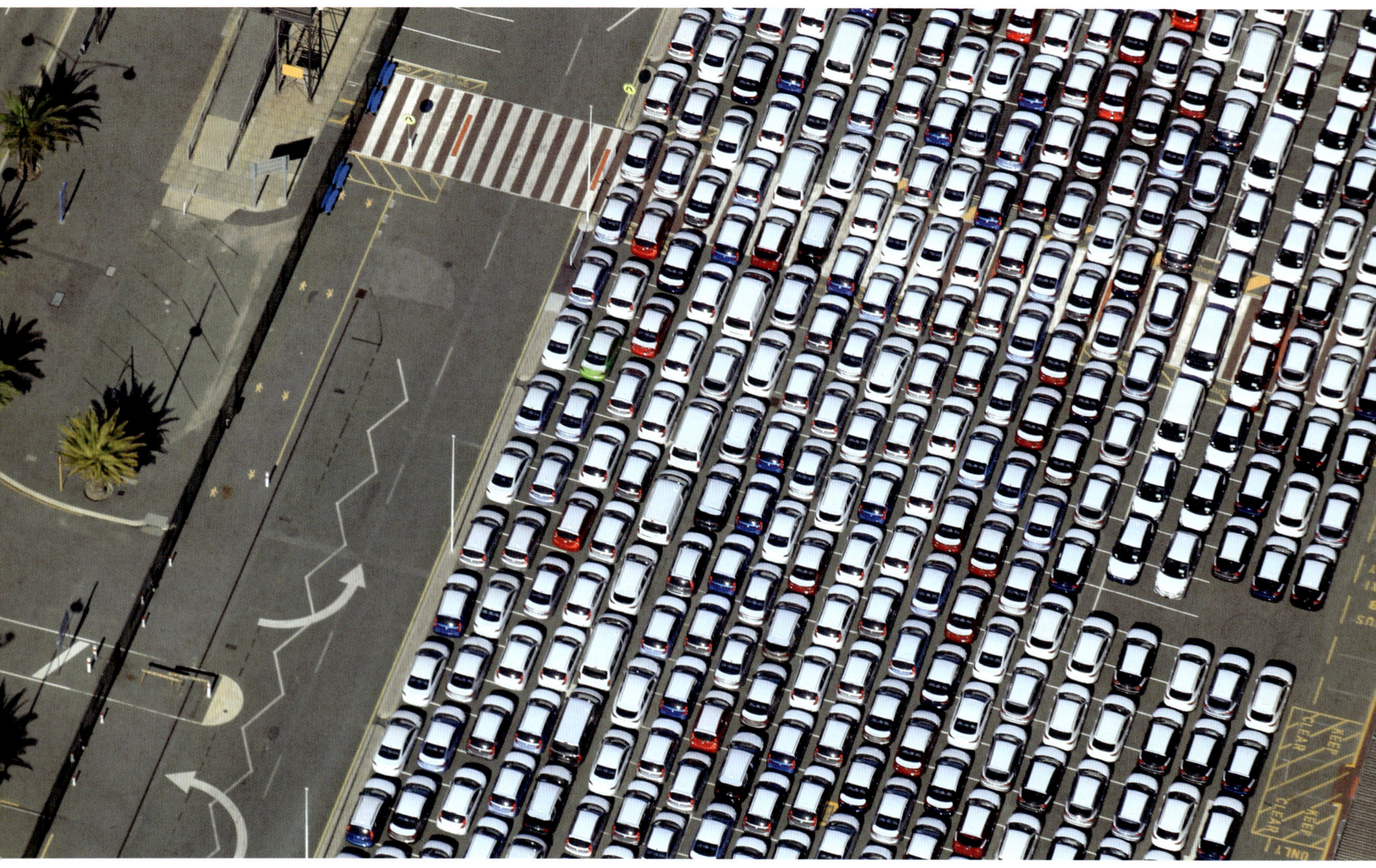

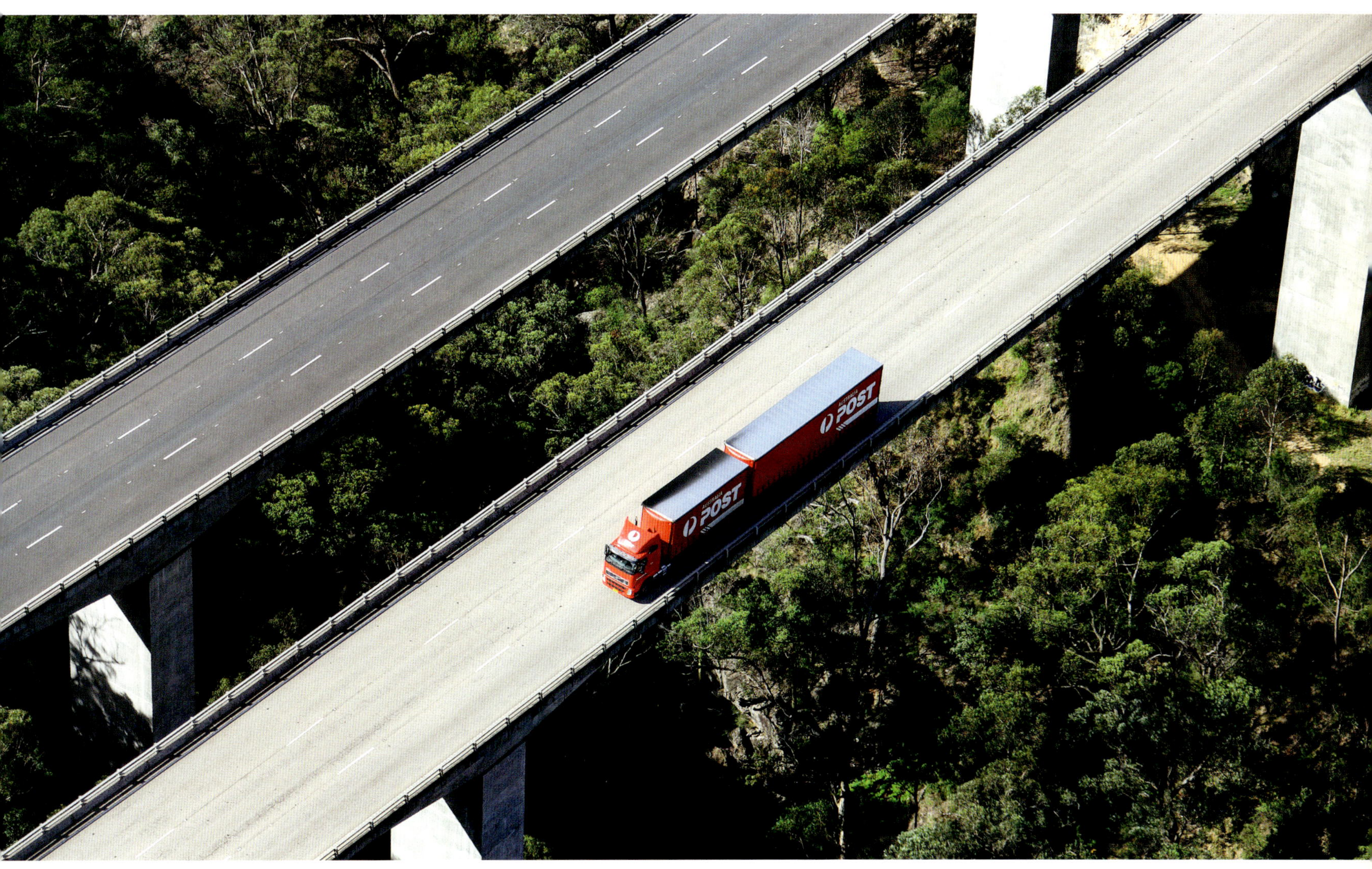
POST
POST

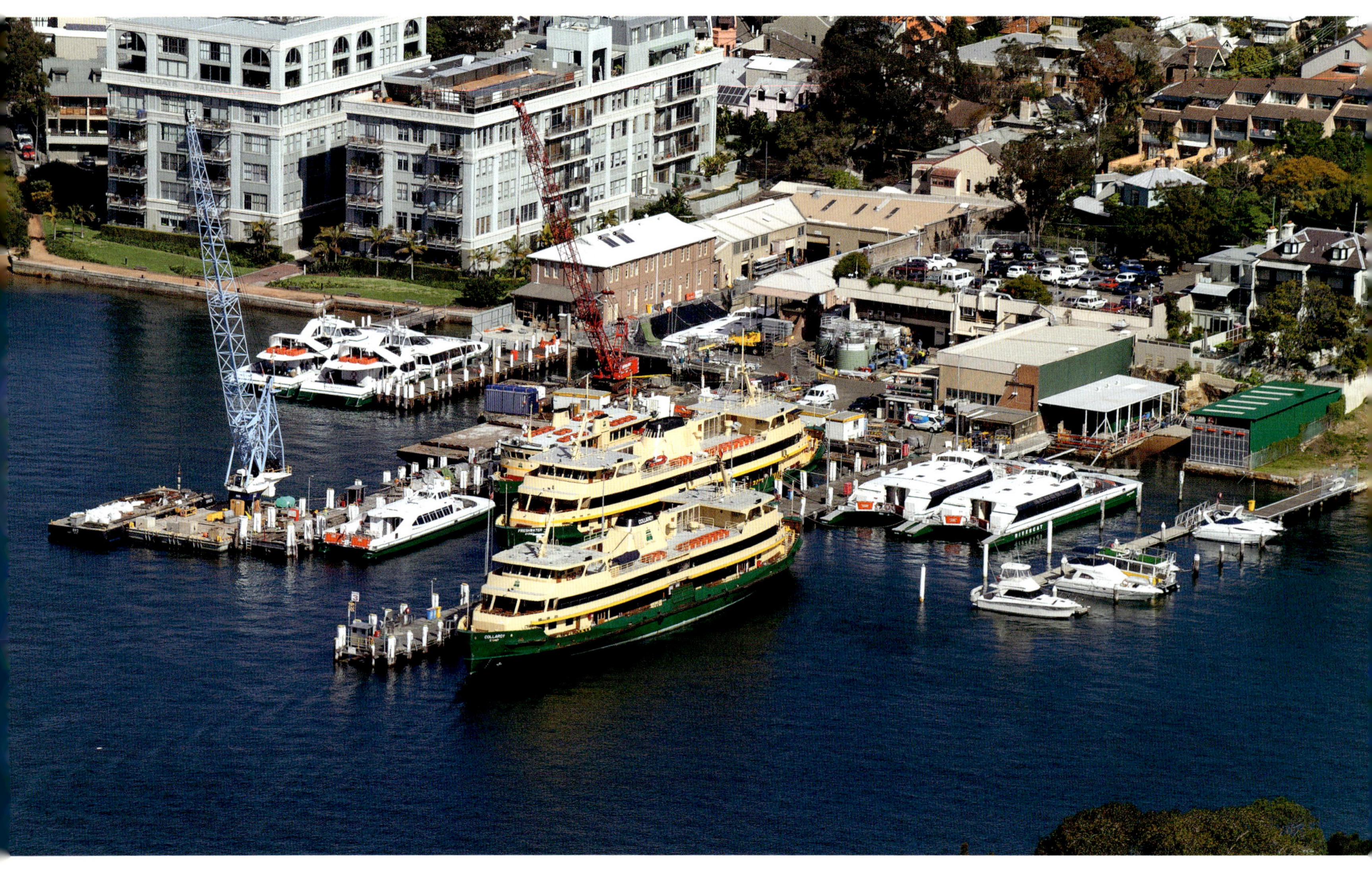

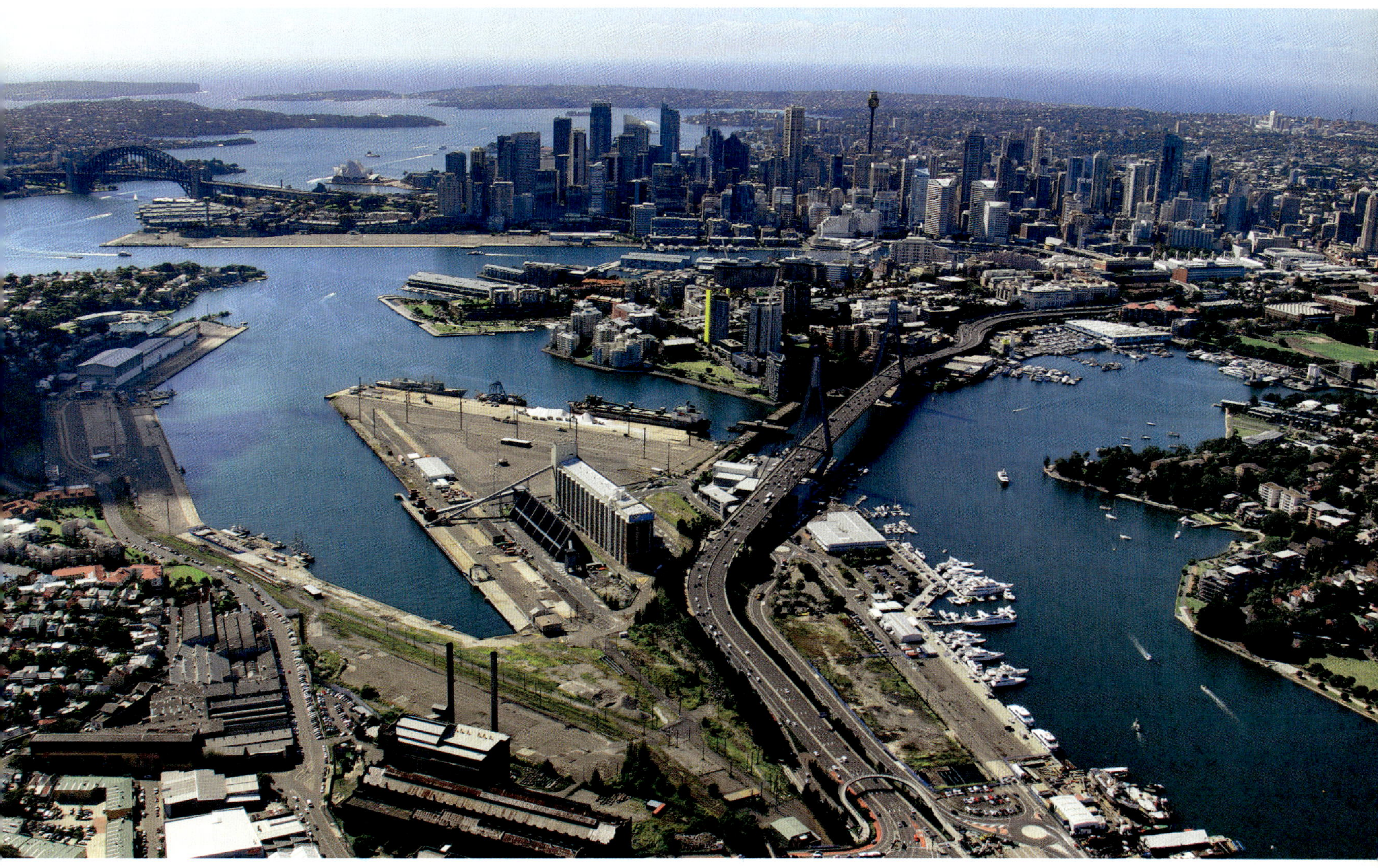

LEFT: Sydney ferries travel 1.3 million kilometres each year traversing the harbour. Maintenance work is conducted at the Balmain Shipyard in Mort Bay. **RIGHT:** White Bay (left of image) is an important facility for cargo and, eventually, cruise ships in Sydney. The Anzac Bridge is a key link between the inner west and the central business district in Sydney. It is the longest span cable-stayed bridge in Australia. **FOLLOWING PAGE:** Adelaide is one of a few Australian airports with a curfew on aircraft movements from 11pm to 6am. More than seven million passengers pass through the airport every year making it Australia's fourth largest.

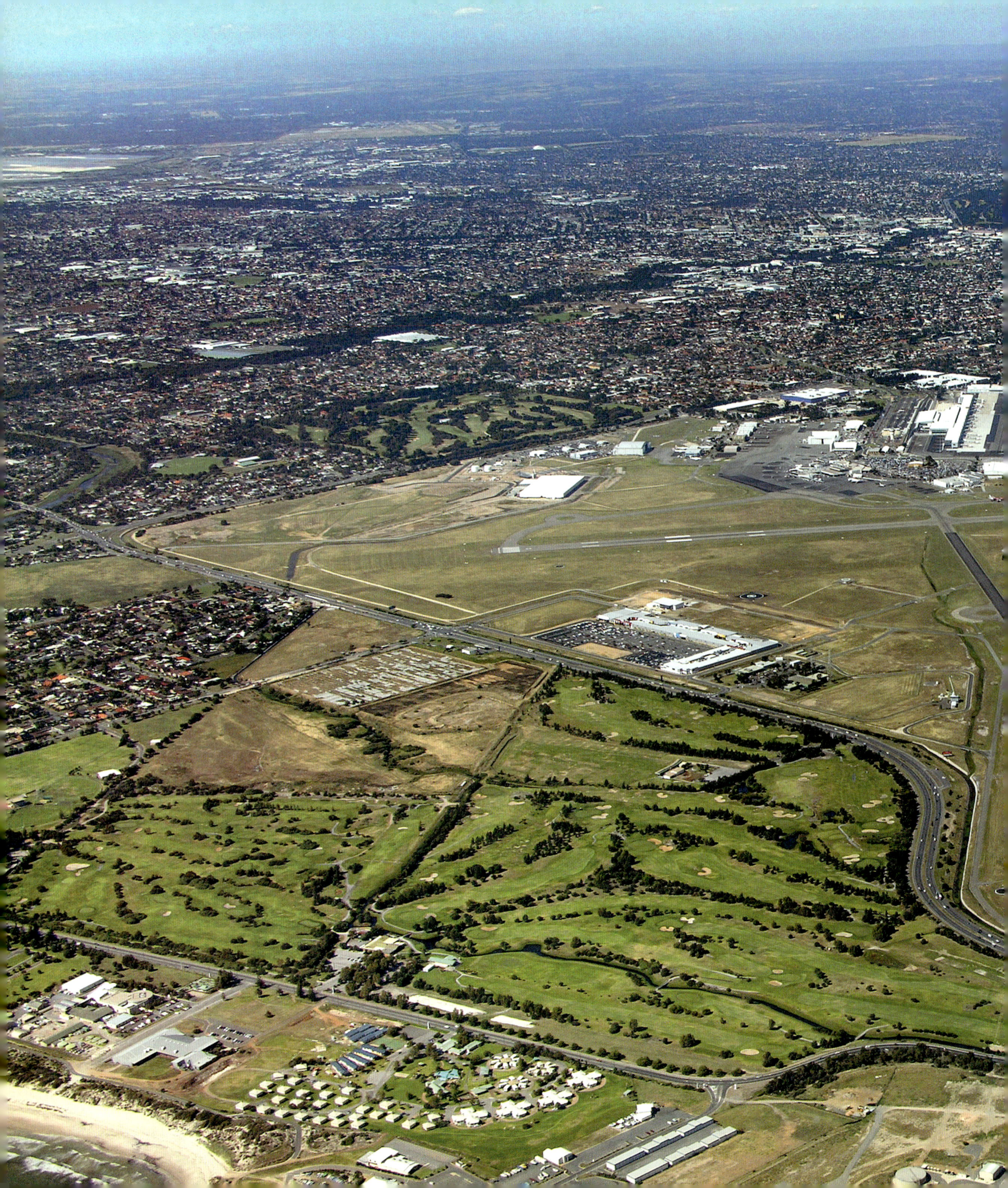

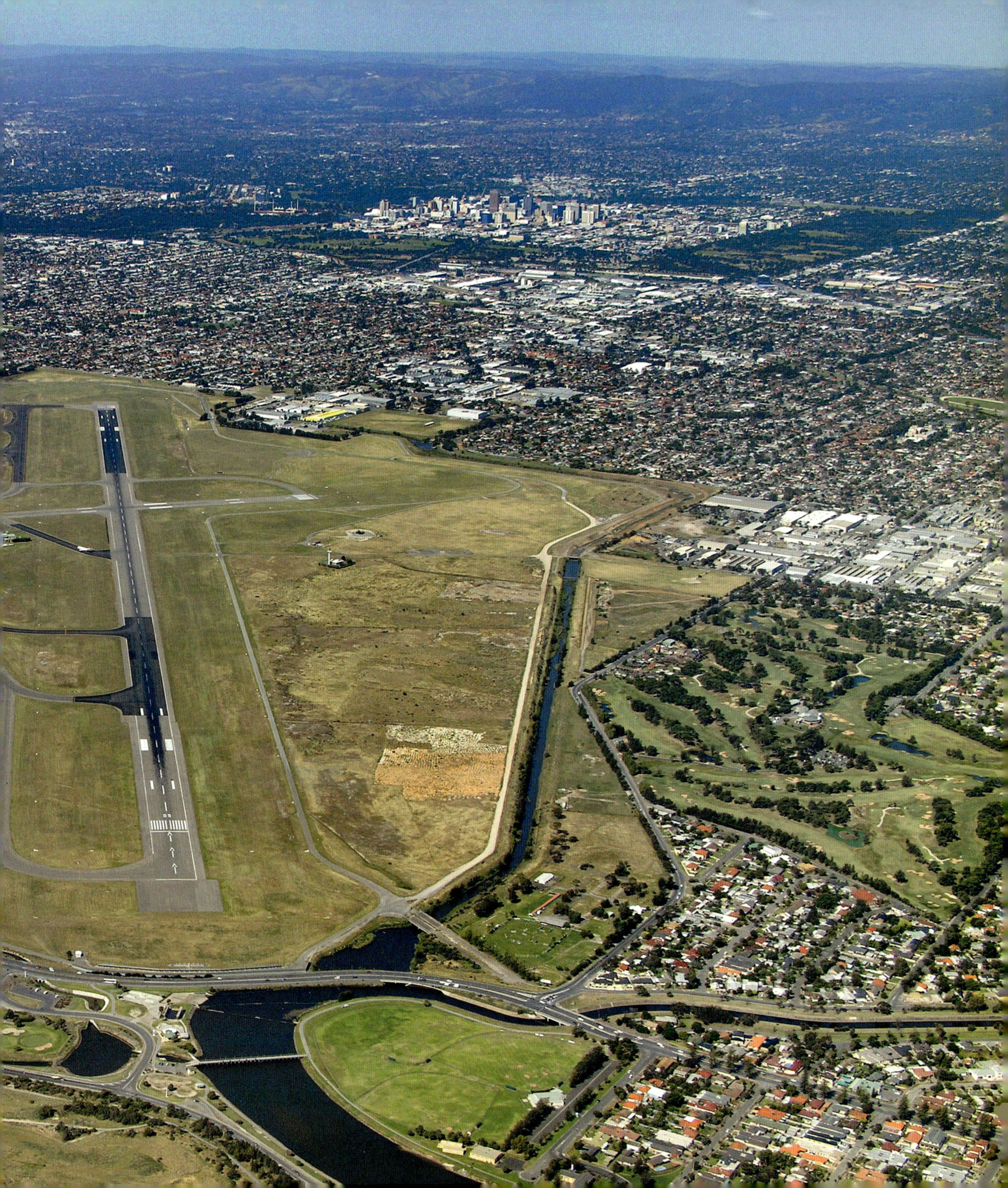

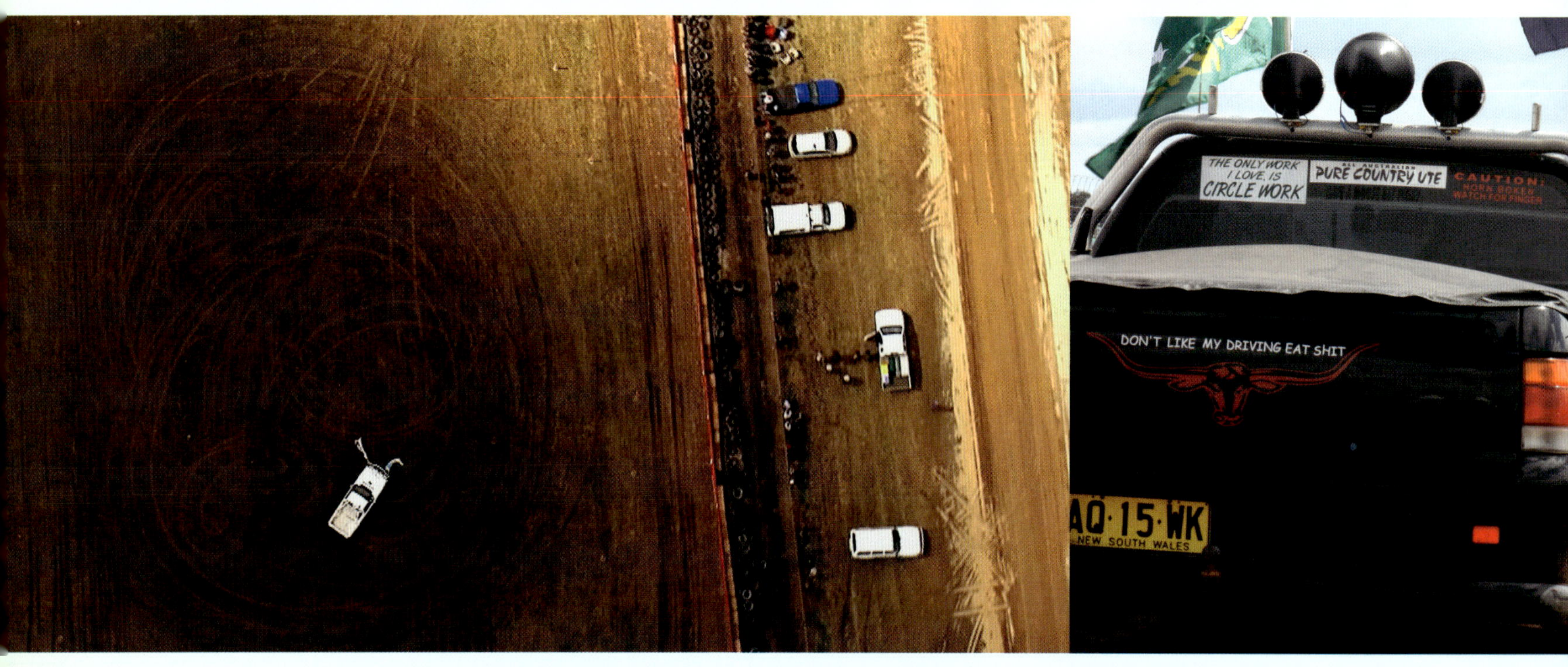
THE ONLY WORK I LOVE IS CIRCLE WORK
PURE COUNTRY UTE
CAUTION: HORN BOXER WATCH FOR FINGER
DON'T LIKE MY DRIVING EAT SHIT
AQ·15·WK
NEW SOUTH WALES

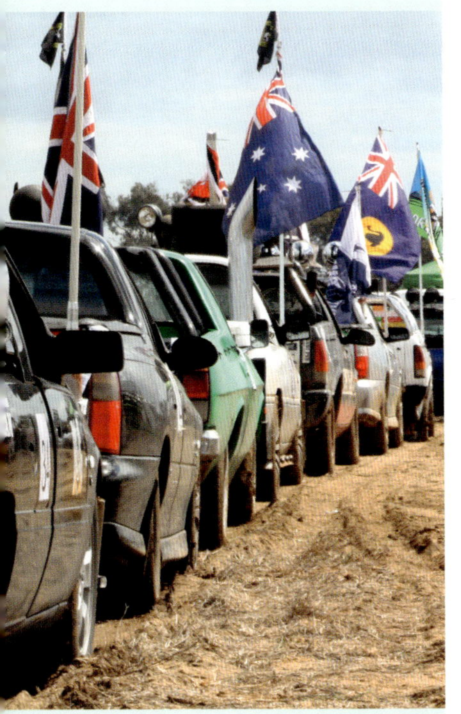

BUSH BASH COMES FULL CIRCLE

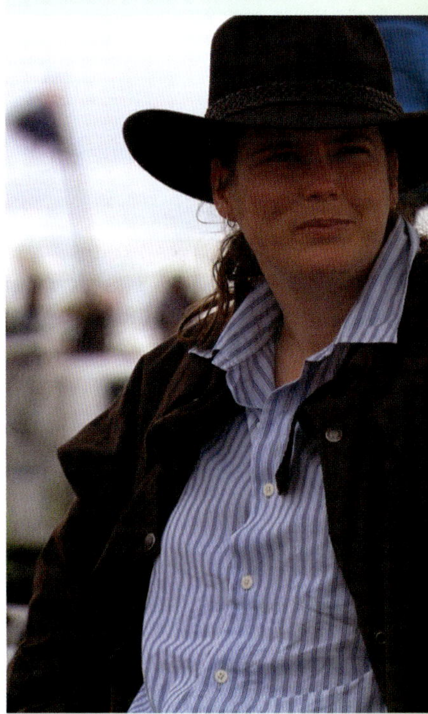

IN THE BUSH, road congestion is rare. There is really only one traffic jam that happens regularly — to be more precise, once a year — but it is a rather long one. In Deniliquin, in southern New South Wales, 5,000 utes are lined up to enter the grounds for the annual Ute Muster, a gathering of country folk from all over Australia. In the bush, these are the distances you must sometimes travel to have fun en masse. Among the drivers is Kelly-Ann Donnelly. She has driven for three days from Brisbane. 'I've been wanting to come to the Deni Ute Muster for a very long time,' she says, 'so to finally be here — it's amazing.'

For Donnelly, it isn't just pleasure that brings her to this side of the border. She is also a contestant in the event at the heart of the Ute Muster — the National Circle Work Championships. In a large paddock, Donnelly and her competitors will have a minute each to impress the judges with their ability to spin their utes around in sharp circles. There will be mud.

The siren sounds, Donnelly revs the engine and away she goes. The emcee's voice thunders through the loudspeakers: 'What do you reckon, ladies? Can we give Kelly-Ann a bit of support out there?' The crowd roars. It's an impressive effort and the emcee agrees: 'It's a great run! We love seeing the girls beat the guys, don't we?'

To say Donnelly has a love affair with her car is perhaps an understatement. 'I wouldn't know where to start about why I like the ute,' she says. 'But I think it's because it's tough, it's ballsy, and it's practical. You can go fishing; have the dog out the back ... and it looks hot. It's something unusual for a girl to have. My father wanted me to have a Ford Festiva.'

Even if Donnelly and her ute don't win the championship the trip to Deniliquin will have been a welcome return to her rural roots. 'I'm very honoured and privileged to be here. It's nothing like the city. You can't beat the country. You just can't!' Next year, Donnelly will be back, happy to sit in a traffic jam to do it all again.

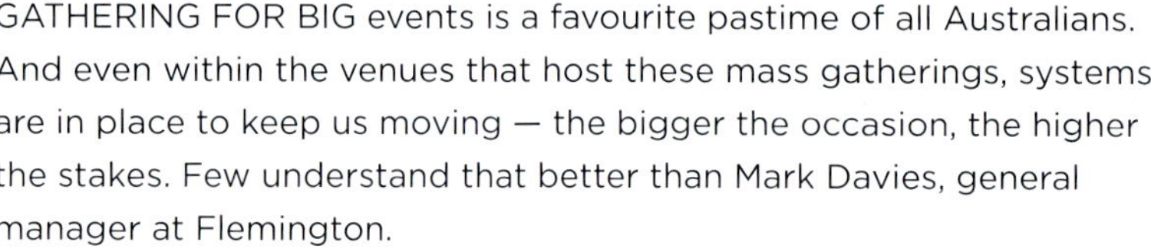

CROWDS LINE UP FOR THE CUP

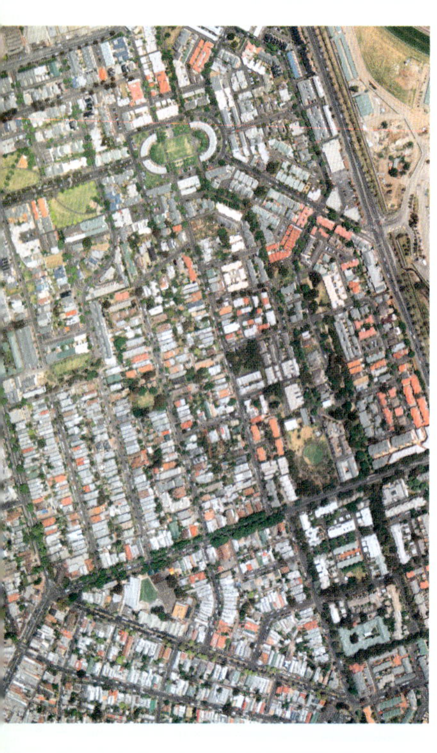

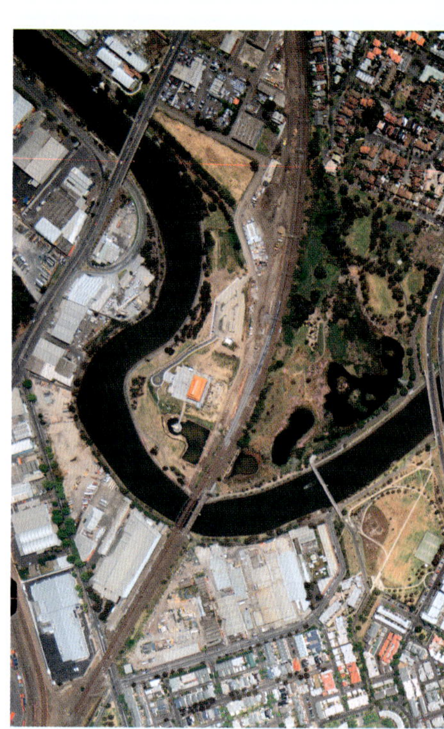

GATHERING FOR BIG events is a favourite pastime of all Australians. And even within the venues that host these mass gatherings, systems are in place to keep us moving — the bigger the occasion, the higher the stakes. Few understand that better than Mark Davies, general manager at Flemington.

They say the Melbourne Cup is the race that stops the nation, but each year at Flemington thousands are on the move. More than 100,000 people will be rubbing elegantly suited and frocked shoulders inside the racecourse. With that number of people crammed together, there is a risk of chaos and pandemonium. Thankfully, though, away from view, there are forces at work while people are at play.

From a helicopter, Davies takes in the sea of humanity swelling beneath him. The Melbourne Cup is the second largest gathering of race fans in the world, only beaten by a nose by the Kentucky Derby. Looking down, it is striking how orderly everything appears. On the concourse everyone seems stationary, waiting patiently for the race with a glass of bubbly in hand. The only people shuffling do so in defined alleyways, but without apparent boundaries.

Davies explains it is all down to two simple white lines drawn on the turf. 'It's an idea one of the guys in the office came up with,' he says. 'It seemed crazy at the time but it is amazing how many people follow the two white lines ... without anyone really knowing what is going on.' There are, of course, other forces here as well: police and ambulance are on call. But they only act in emergencies and most of the time everything runs smoothly. 'One of the things about managing crowds,' says Davies, 'is actually showing people that things are in control.'

But the big test for Davies comes after the race is run. And indeed, as soon as the winner crosses the line, a mass migration of people heading back to the city and its suburbs unfolds. Some 60,000 will leave by train from only two platforms just outside the racecourse's exit. 'It's fantastically accessible but it is also an Achilles' heel,' says Davies. 'Flemington has been here since the 1860s. At the time they thought we needed a rail track to get Melbournians out here and so they put it in the middle of the venue. If something goes wrong, it will be the first part that will show stress.'

To help manage an orderly exit, Davies and his team have created stages. Only 100 people are allowed on the platforms at any one time. Others move through a system of holding or queuing bays. It all works a treat. The Cup is yet another example of how so often we are blissfully unaware of the systems and networks keeping us on the move.

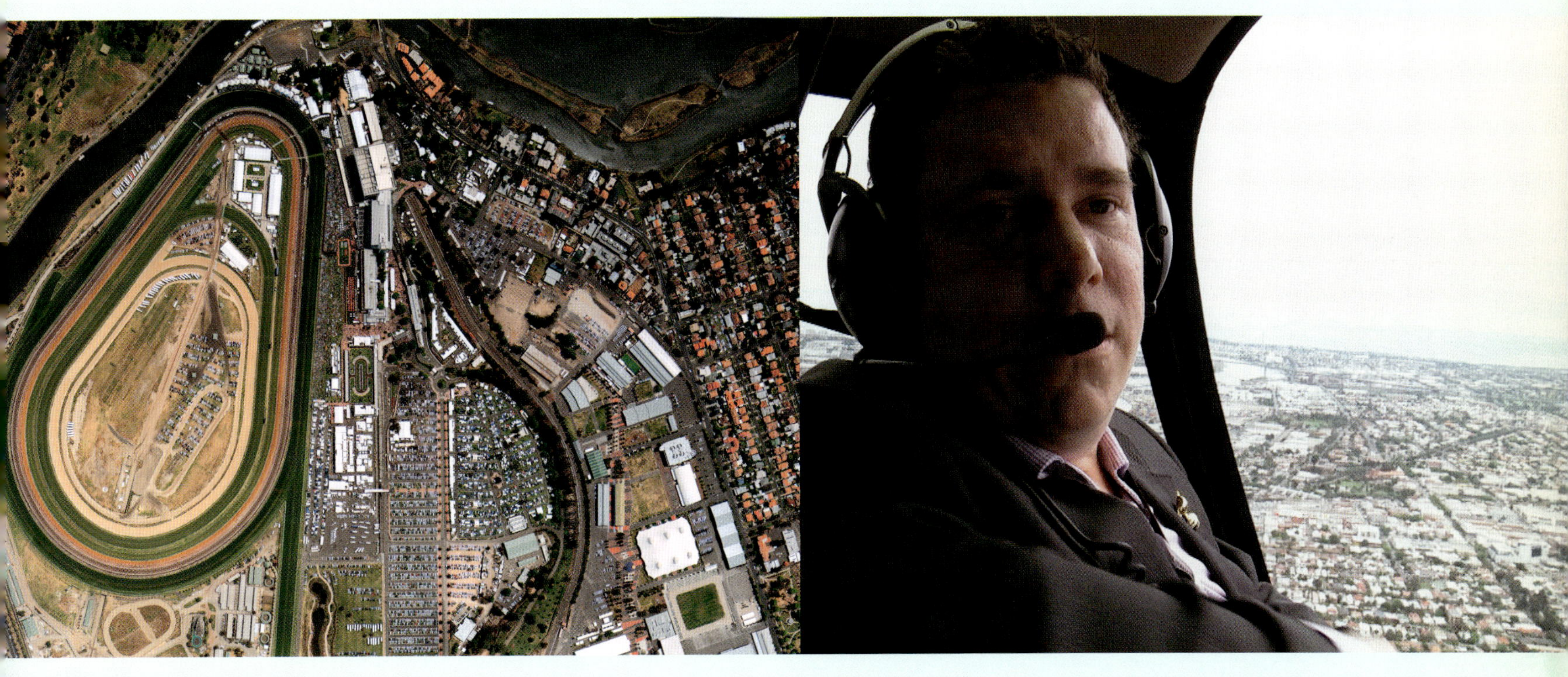

LIVING

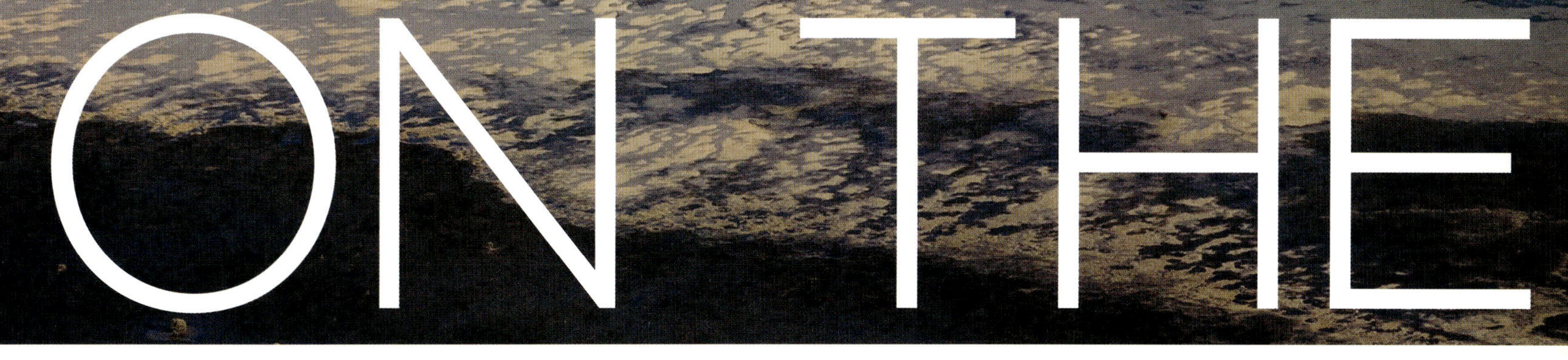

EDGE

Australia is the world's largest island nation. The coastline of states and territories stretches a staggering 60,000 kilometres – greater than the Earth's circumference. And it is on the continent's fringes that we've built our homes and major cities. Most of us – 85 per cent – have settled within 50 kilometres of the sea. But near the ocean, we do lead puzzlingly paradoxical lives. Two-thirds of all Australians live in just six major cities.

Highly urbanised yes, yet Melbourne, Adelaide, Perth, Sydney, Brisbane and Hobart are among the least densely populated cities on the planet. And that's because we like to sprawl. It's true we find safety and opportunity in numbers, but at the same time we value personal space like no other. For one, we live in the world's biggest houses – room to roam, we reckon, is not a privilege but a fundamental human right.

Our young nation, after all, sought escape from the close confines of Europe, and the allure of vast open spaces had from the onset of colonisation been irresistible. But as our population grows – expected to reach 40 million in 2050 – our big cities will get even bigger and sprawl even further. The question is, at what cost? How we sustainably manage the projected increase in numbers might be our biggest challenge yet.

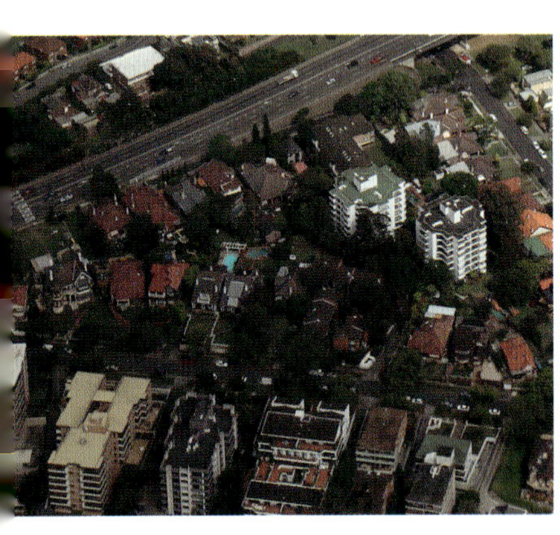

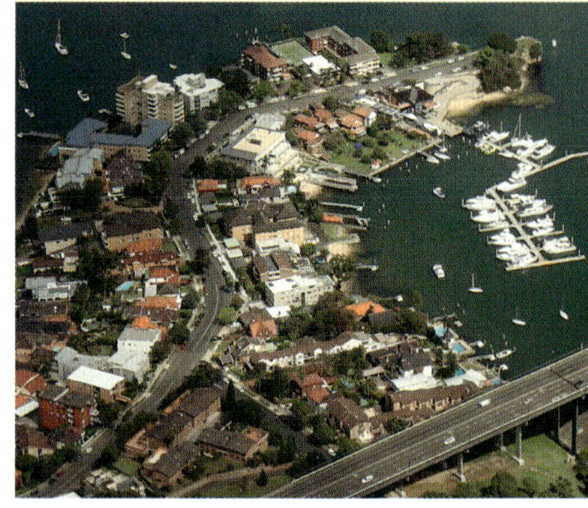

If there's one person with a bird's-eye view on sprawl, it's Aquila Gagnon. He is a window cleaner in Melbourne, our fastest growing metropolis. For more than a decade, Melbourne's relentless march has outstripped that of any other Australian city. More than four million people already call the garden city home, and every week they're joined by 1,500 new arrivals from interstate and abroad – all drawn to what's been called the world's most liveable city.

As Gagnon gently steers his 'building maintenance unit' over the 300-metre high edge of Eureka Tower in Southbank, the Melbourne Cricket Ground looms in the distance. 'I love that side of the city,' he says, 'the sporting precinct and the parkland. I hope that never changes.' His worries are not without reason. During his 15 years on the job, Gagnon has seen dramatic changes aplenty. 'When I first started you could see a bit of an end to it,' he says. 'Now, it's suburbia as far as the eye can see. It can't continue, it can't be good.'

The problem is that with inner-city houses in such short supply and prices soaring, most newcomers to Melbourne are pushed to its suburban fringes. In fact, half the population already lives more than 20 kilometres from the city centre. Melbourne's tentacles now reach an impressive 2,000 square kilometres, leaving international cities such as

London and Berlin, with 1,580 and 890 square kilometres respectively, in the shade. From his unique vantage point, Gagnon sees more than most. 'You can see the pollution – all the way from the city to the bay to the mountains. It's not a pleasant sight.'

For better or worse, sprawl is a story repeated throughout the country. In Perth, land grabs for housing developments are common, driven by the mining boom. In Adelaide, natural boundaries channel growth to the north and the south, while in Sydney's west, market gardens and farms make way for homes. Ultimately, endless outward growth *will* become untenable. If current population trends indeed prevail, the only way to curb sprawl is to reach for the sky. Arguably, we need more high-rises for people to live in, not just to work in. If only our love affair was with the balcony, not the back yard.

Oran Park, in Sydney's west, is a good example. There, 7,500 new back yards are being built. Still in an embryonic state, this former farmland will become home to 21,000 residents. And that's just the beginning. In the next three decades, 180,000 new homes will be built in Sydney's southwest. That's equal to 24 Oran Parks. More and more homes, built in the sweltering inland heat, further and further away from the city centre.

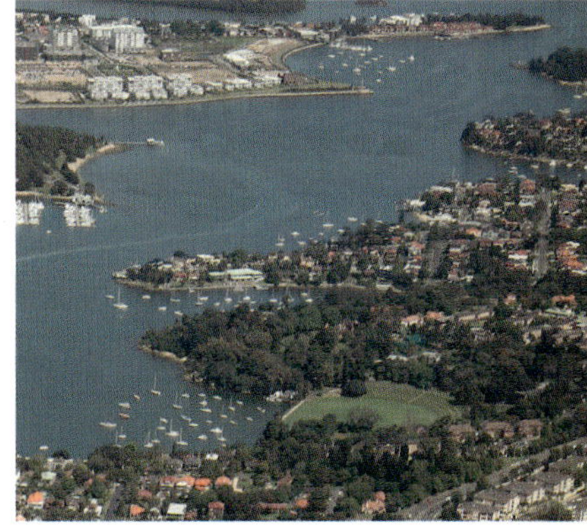

Where to build our future abodes requires thought and careful planning, not an unmitigated rush for the bush or, for that matter, the coast. For as Richard Adams will tell you, being close to the water can be a curse as much as a blessing. He's the economic development manager of the Tweed Shire Council who lives in Kingscliff, northern New South Wales. 'We have one of the nicest beaches in Australia,' says Adams. 'But in the last six weeks we have lost in the order of about 30 to 40 metres.'

In Kingscliff, the ocean is devouring the land. And Adams is now supervising the building of a great sandbag wall to fend off the might of Mother Nature. Bulldozers dig sand from further north and then dump it into huge bags to construct the wall on Kingscliff's beach's southern tip. It's a race against time – the town's adjoining holiday park has already lost its ocean-front cabins. Without tourism, Adams worries the town would struggle to survive. 'Kingscliff is essentially Kingscliff beach. To see it literally fall into the ocean is soul destroying,' he says.

Adams' contractors endeavour to stack as many sandbags as they can during low tide. 'We do what we can,' he says. 'But if Mother Nature really wants to take a big bite out of the holiday park there is really nothing we can do to stop her.' It's an all too familiar tale for erosion expert Professor Andrew Short. 'There is a real problem here,' he says as he views Kingscliff beach from a seaplane. 'A small community with limited funds dealing with a significant erosion problem.'

Short knows erosion when he sees it. He's spent 17 years studying each and every beach in the country, giving him an in-depth understanding of the dynamics between shoreline and ocean. 'We have 11,000 beaches in Australia,' he says, 'and 10,500 of them behave beautifully, no problem. But there is a minority of them where due to our lack of foresight, we have created problems.'

The main problem, he says, is that sometimes we have simply built too close to the water, disregarding the fact that shorefronts can move by hundreds of metres in just a matter of months. That movement is a natural phenomenon. Many of these problems exist, says Short, because early planning laws, some a century old, didn't take those natural dynamics into account. In other words, we didn't know any better. Kingscliff, says Short, is a prime example and its community has been paying the price for decades.

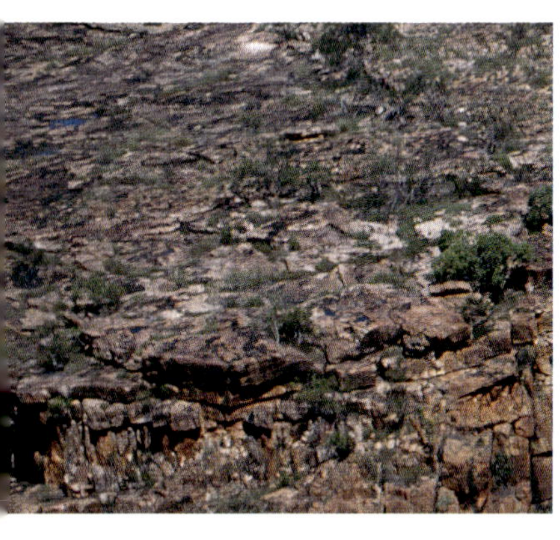

'You can see they have had a fairly mixed response along here. You've got two types of rock walls, some concrete in front of the surf club, you've got sandbagging and then there are areas where there is nothing.' The situation is typical, says Short, of other hotspots along the coast of New South Wales and elsewhere in Australia. 'The council does the best it can but with limited funding it is a real hotchpotch of solutions.'

In New South Wales, there are 15 such hotspots, but Short is concerned global climate change and rising sea levels could considerably worsen the situation. 'Instead of having your 15 hotspots, you'll have two or three hundred,' he says. 'Many areas that are sort of safe or not threatened today are going to be threatened in the future. It's just going to exacerbate the problem.'

If small towns such as Kingscliff struggle with 'makeshift' solutions, the neighbouring Gold Coast and its 'glitter strip' shows how spending big money can make a difference in getting it right. It's almost impossible to see, but a sea wall spans the length of the Gold Coast. 'They did a very good job,' says Short. 'They built it right at the end of the beach, covered it with sand, planted grasses and now it's a sand dune.'

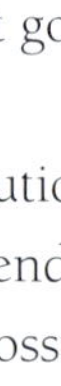

Hidden from view and unbeknown to most, it's the city's last line of defence. 'If all the sand was washed away,' says Short, 'it would still protect the houses, the roads and the hotels. It's quite expensive but

Sometimes we have simply built too close to the water, disregarding the fact that shorefronts can move by hundreds of metres in just a matter of months ... early planning laws, some a century old, didn't take those natural dynamics into account. In other words, we didn't know any better.

they can afford to do it.' In the Gold Coast we've successfully managed to reshape the natural world, just so we can safely live on the edge.

Our delicate relationship with the natural world is only one, albeit important, storyline in the greater narrative of urban growth. The other major story is how we provide our suburbs with the services we need and the creature comforts we crave. Our island nation largely depends on the 28,000 ships that visit our ports every year and do so in a fairly straightforward pattern: taking raw materials from our shores and bringing back containers filled with the goods we need, or think we need.

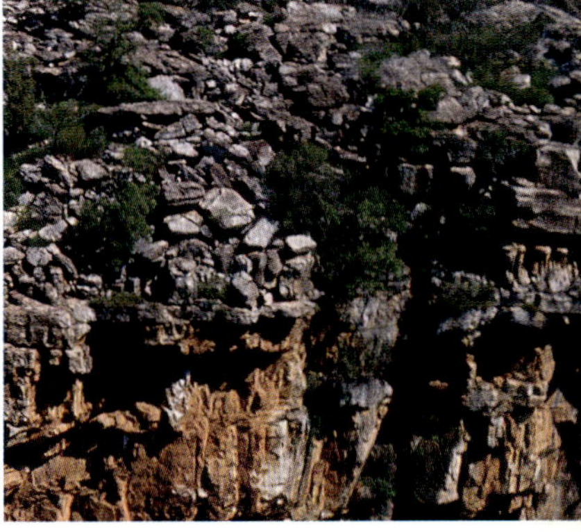

Modern-day wharfie Sharon Bowker is a link in a long and crucial supply chain. A crane driver at the Port of Melbourne, Bowker spends her day looking down on the world from 40 metres. 'It's everything you can possibly imagine,' she says while lifting a container, or 'box' as she calls it, out of a Japanese vessel. 'Clothing, food, white goods, furnishings – everything.'

Every week, Bowker and her colleagues load and unload 65 giant container ships – that's more than two and half million boxes a year. Two-thirds of everything they unload comes from Asia. At the touch of a lever, Bowker moves yet another box. 'There's a lot going on,' she says. 'There's the noise, the sirens going off, the amount of movement, there is just so much action under those cranes. Standing back you'd think nobody knows what they're doing, but we do.'

Together our ports handle almost seven million containers per year. 'It's really important,' says Bowker. 'Just imagine if we halved our productivity today. Just halved it. Where would you be? It's our job to keep everything flowing.' From Melbourne and other such ports in Fremantle, Adelaide, Brisbane and Sydney, trucks set off on journeys that can last from 30 minutes to three days. Many will head for distribution centres where anything from fridges to flatscreens and baked beans to bicycles get unpacked, repacked and redirected.

Ultimately, many of those products will end up in our modern suburban cathedrals – the shopping malls. In the Marion mall, in

Adelaide, we spend $770 million every year. Western Australia's biggest, Carousel, has a total floor space of more than 80,000 square metres. The mall in Carindale, Queensland, has 13 million visitors a year. In Parramatta, in Sydney's west, just one centre houses 550 shops. The biggest mall of them all, Chadstone in Melbourne, has 9,500 car parking spots. These statistics speak volumes. Shopping centres truly are our new places of worship. Our prayers, of course, are only heard if we have enough money.

It might be surprising in this day and age – the age of electronic payments and credit cards – to learn 70 per cent of all consumer spending in Australia is still in cash. Every day, we use $1 billion worth of notes and coins. Around the country, 30,000 ATMs are meant to make access to money easy and stress-free. And for most of us that's the case. It's a different story, though, if you happen to be the person responsible for filling these machines. If you are *that* person, life is anything but stress-free.

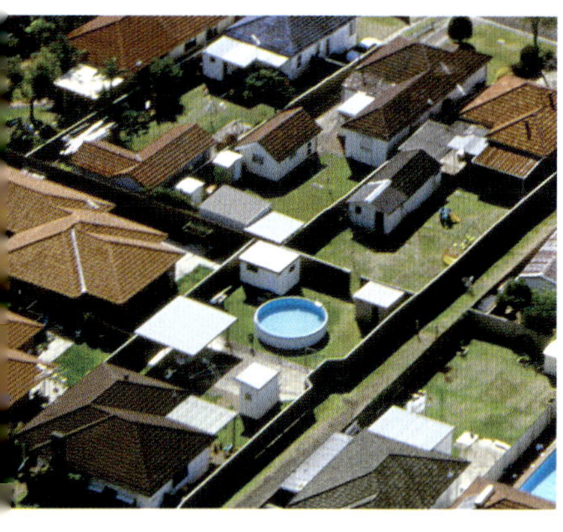

Before the start of Sydney's rush hour, armoured vans laden with cash try to beat the morning traffic. As the city wakes, the rush is on to fill the banks, ATMs, ticket-vending machines and shops before we, the public, get to them. Simon is at the wheel of one such van in the Sydney suburb of Chatswood. Riding shotgun is fellow guard Rob. The job's so dangerous their last names must remain a secret.

'The risks we have to manage,' says Simon, 'to get that money into where it's got to be … most people wouldn't understand.' For Simon the risk is very real – during the past five years there have been 47 attacks on cash van drivers. Curiously, and for unknown reasons, they have all happened in Sydney. On a typical run, Simon will pull up the van near a bank, jump out and keep his eye on the street while Rob takes an armoured suitcase containing cash.

'I think you have to be a little bit paranoid to do this job,' says Simon. 'It is pretty much your partner and yourself against the rest of the world for the whole day. It does drive you nuts, but it's just part of the job.' Throughout Australia, 400 other vans will be doing their rounds as well. All of them are tracked by satellites, so base command always knows where each vehicle is. There are other security measures, too: the guards are armed. But Simon says that instinct is still their most important weapon. 'If you've got a bad feeling, you should always go with that feeling. If it doesn't look good, it probably isn't good. There have been times the suspicion was so high and the tension so high, we just aborted jobs.'

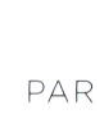

Rob emerges from the bank. He and Simon board the van and roll to the next job. A quick call to the office lets their security team know they are okay, safe and on schedule. In the industry it's called the welfare check. 'My mates think we are crazy,' says Simon. 'They couldn't handle thinking everyone was after what they had, the money and the guns. But it's an essential service.'

As our cities sprawl, unfortunately so too do emergencies and crime. Around the country, law enforcement officers are coming to grips with an ever-growing patch. Mission commander Grant Waddups is one of them. Most nights he'll take to the sky in Polair 2 – the call name for one of five police helicopters patrolling New South Wales, a state three times the size of Great Britain.

Following a call from the central control centre, Waddups instructs his pilot to head for Sydney's northwestern edge. In this sprawling metropolis, the chopper is no luxury. A city of four million people, Sydney has only half the population of New York but is twice its area. In Pennant Hills, a large number of outlaw motorcycle gang members have been spotted. Waddups' job is to monitor the gang from above and relay vital information about them – intelligence that ground police may not be aware of or unable to get quickly enough.

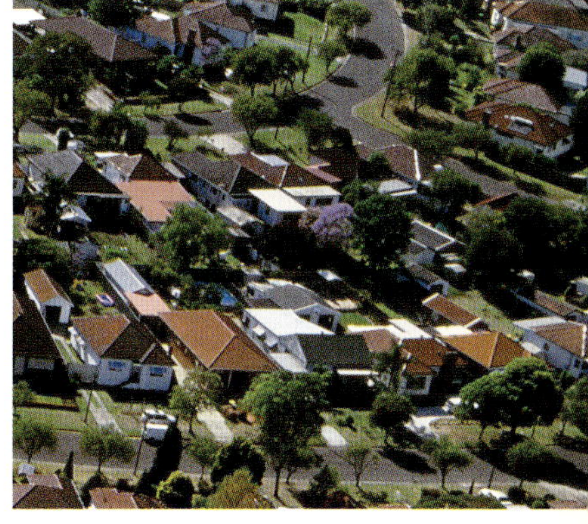

'Our role is like a command centre,' he says. 'We can obviously see a lot more than police on the ground' Often the helicopter arrives first on the scene. In this case, below the helicopter, about 20 bikies are congregating at a petrol station. Then the radio crackles. An incoming report suggests that a rival motorcycle gang is out and about in nearby Parramatta. Police are concerned a fight could break out. In bikie circles, such clashes can have deadly consequences.

Waddups and his team monitor the group below them, which has just pulled out of the station. 'Looks like they are all on the move towards Parramatta,' says Waddups. A team of ten patrol cars is dispatched to intercept them. The coordination between helicopter and ground police works well. The fleet of police cars quickly catches up with the bikies. Officers pull them over, managing to avoid an otherwise sure altercation. 'Let's get the night sun on them,' says the junior observer in the back of the chopper. A spotlight is turned on to assist the effort on the ground.

It's a short but successful intervention – the ability to take to the skies proving a useful tool in the law enforcement arsenal. Polair's helicopters already spend almost one-third of the year airborne. Between them, they travel half a million kilometres a year. And in time, as our cities continue to grow, they may become a permanent presence in our skies.

Our cities depend on a dazzling array of services to keep them ticking along. While police patrol the skies, another small nocturnal army roams our streets, making sure we're not just safe but clean.

Garbage collectors, on the road while most of us roll over in our beds one last time, pick up a whopping 43 million tonnes of rubbish a year. That's almost a two-tonne truckload for each and every one of us. Half of that is recycled but half of it still ends up in one of the country's 650 landfill sites. New technology, though, can now help turn even these wastelands to good use. For instance, in Woodlawn, near Canberra, a disused open-cut mine serves a valuable purpose. It's leading a second life of sorts. This hole alone takes 20 per cent of Sydney's garbage. It will take 70 years to fill, but already there's a clever twist to the operation.

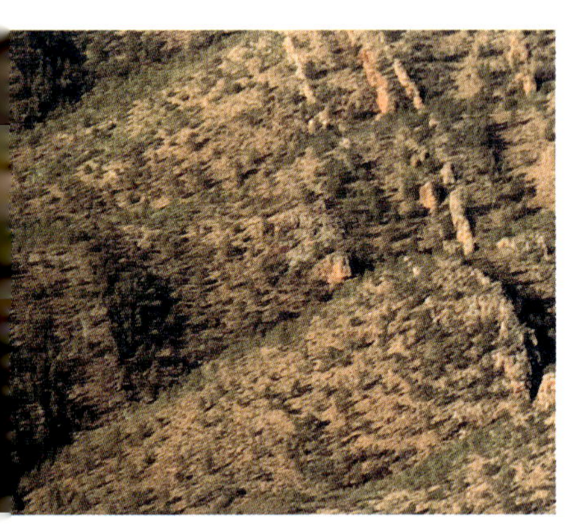

The site has effectively been turned into a bioreactor, turning waste into watts. Gas is captured from decomposing garbage, converted into electricity and fed into the grid. With the right technology, energy can be found in the most curious of places. With our rubbish projected to double in the next 10 years, it is crucial we find ever-smarter ways to process what we discard. That said, we could start by throwing away a little less.

Luckily, though, not *all* our waste scars the landscape. Just outside Werribee, in Victoria, ecologist Richard Loyn takes off in an ultralite to look at a most unusual phenomenon – 11,000 hectares of protected wetlands, courtesy of our sewage. 'About 40 species of shorebird visit this area from Arctic Siberia and Alaska,' says Loyn. 'Look at the concentration of birds on that pond. That is a big flock of white birds, mainly whiskered terns.' This is the first time Loyn has seen the wetlands from above – the unique vantage point allowing him to appreciate an ornithological oasis formed by human waste.

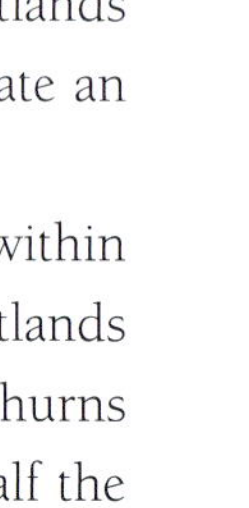

Each year, hundreds of thousands of birds migrate from within Australia and from abroad to this oasis. Incredibly, these wetlands are part of Melbourne's Western Treatment Plant. The facility churns through hundreds of millions of litres of our waste each year, half the Victorian capital's effluent. The nutrient-rich treatment lagoons create a bountiful habitat for birds.

It's hard to imagine but our Victorian forebears designed it that way, with exceptional foresight, more than a century ago. 'The main value of this place,' says Loyn, 'is a drought refuge.' During the past decade of drought the wetlands have regularly supported well over 100,000

Garbage collectors, on the road while most of us roll over in our beds one last time, pick up a whopping 43 million tonnes of rubbish a year. That's almost a two-tonne truckload for each and every one of us.

water birds, when there were very few other wetlands available to them elsewhere in Australia. 'It's very good to be able to see the products of the city being put to use to actually help a conservation purpose. There is no doubt these artificial habitats have greatly enhanced the value of the whole system,' says Loyn. Typically, as our cities grow we degrade and detract from our natural environment, but this is an example of us giving something back, about 2,500 tonnes of it every day.

How to manage the spiralling growth of our cities is a constant challenge and a source of argument. By 2050 there will likely be 17 million more of us … 40 million Australians huddled on the edge. With that type of growth, it is vital we maintain and extend our protected spaces. Our national parks and reserves temper our urban lives with a little bit of wilderness, which despite our obsession with city life, is still so important to the Australian psyche.

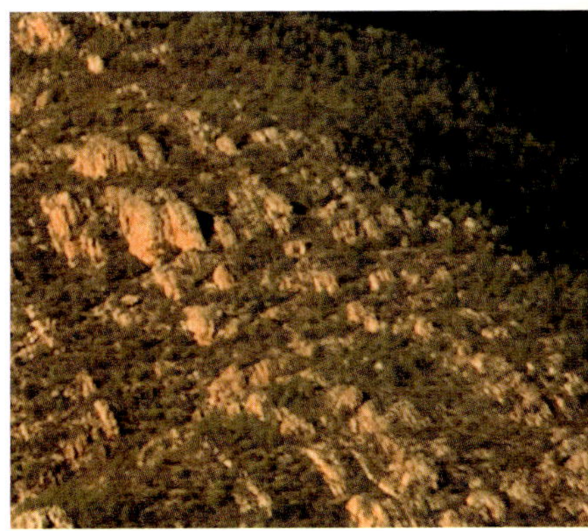

It is a little known fact that Australia is home to the world's second oldest national park, the Royal National Park, just 30 kilometres from Sydney's CBD. Gazetted as a national park in 1879, it's only outdone in age by Yellowstone in the United States of America. 'Nasho' as locals call it, is a 16,000-hectare tract of dense bushland and sandstone outcrops – a big, green lung, breathing in and purifying Sydney's pollution. It's also a buffer between Sydney and the northern reaches of the Wollongong region. Across Australia there are almost 9,500 such protected areas, equalling about 13 per cent of our land.

In the years to come, getting the balance right between keeping our growing cities liveable and protecting the natural environment will be an ever more challenging proposition. Our cities provide the opportunities, goods and services we crave, but they're bursting at the seams. Whether we'll go up instead of outwards is a matter for city planners, politicians and developers alike, but it is a question that needs urgent attention. It might have to mean curbing our enthusiasm to own open space in order to improve the sustainability of our major centres. The balcony might have to triumph over the back yard. And with that, quite possibly, a re-imagining of what life in Australia is about.

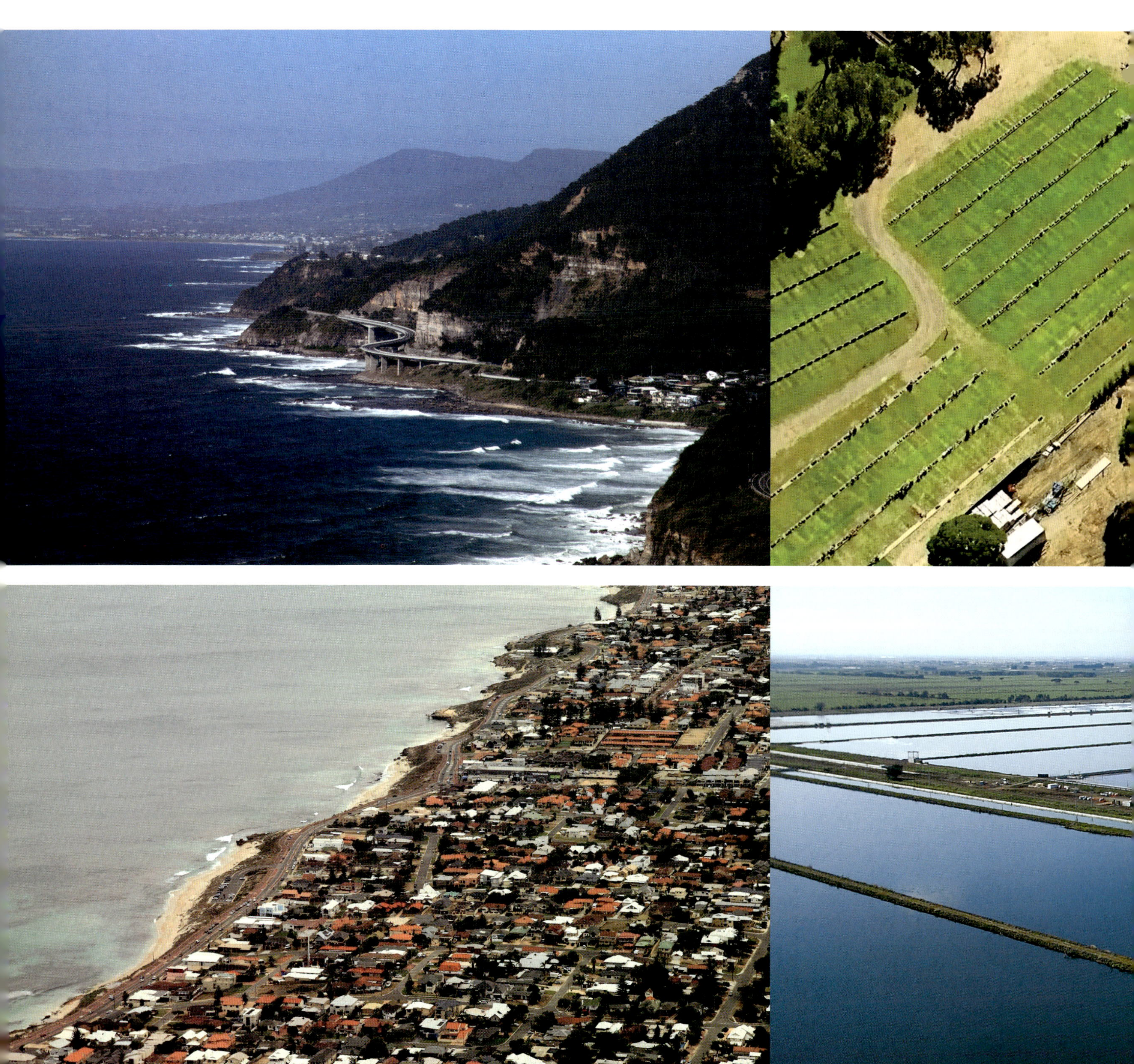

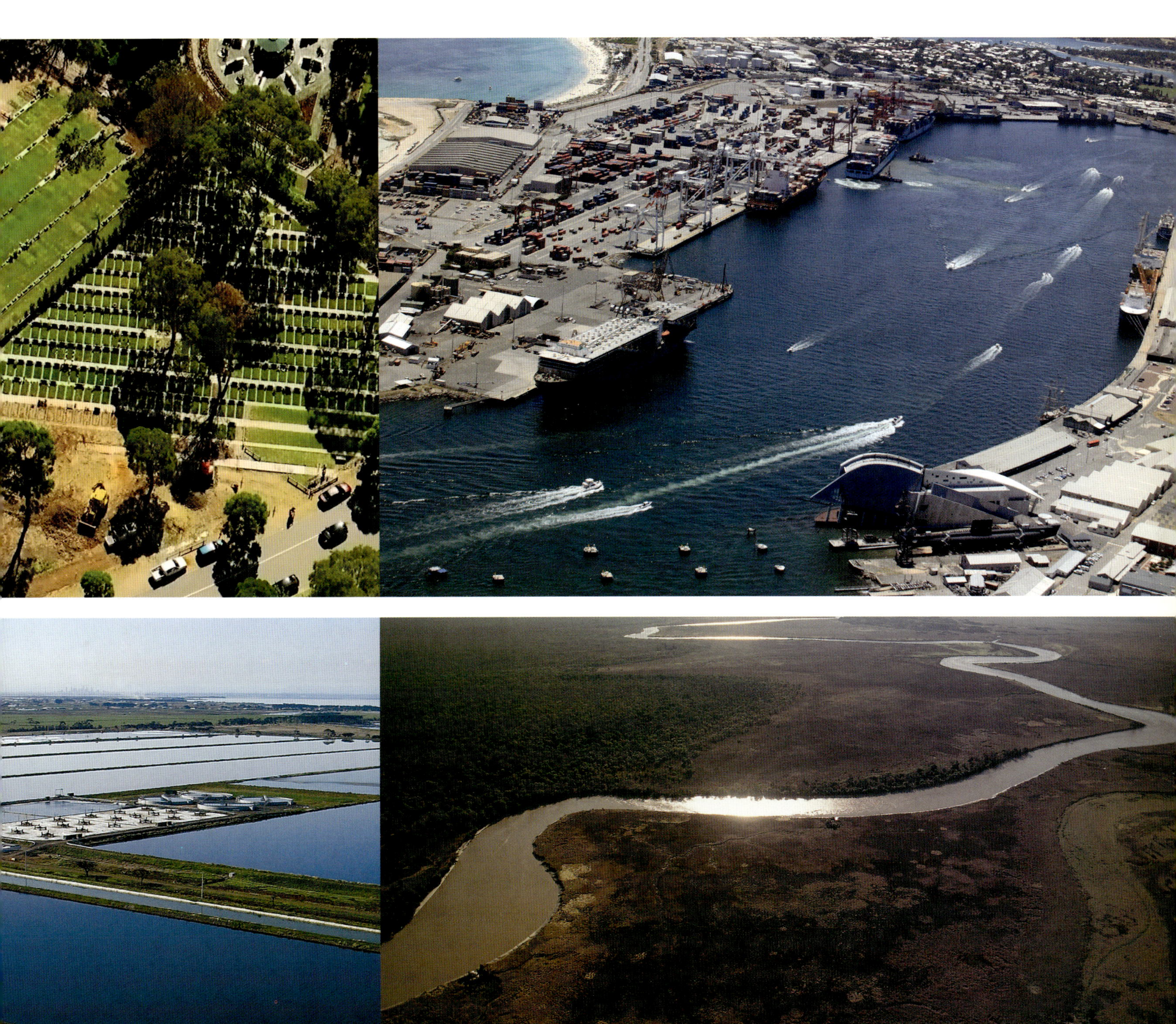

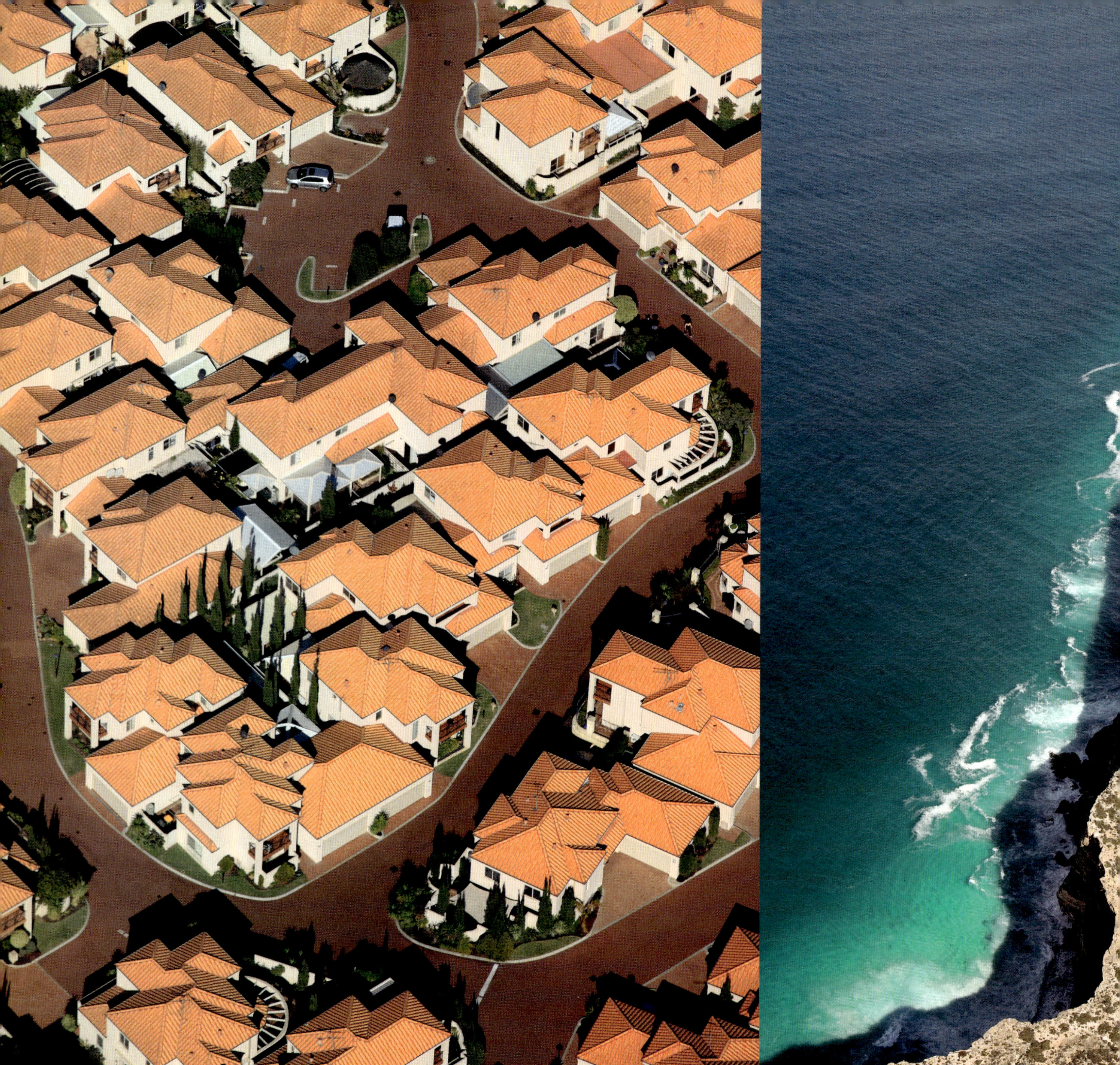

LEFT: The mining boom brought rapid growth to Perth's outer suburbs as bush and farmland gave way to new housing estates. **MIDDLE:** Cliffs on the remote edge of the Nullarbor Plain meet the Great Australian Bight. **RIGHT:** The Bungle Bungle Range in the World Heritage-listed Purnululu National Park in the Kimberley region of Western Australia. The Range rises to 578 metres above sea level.

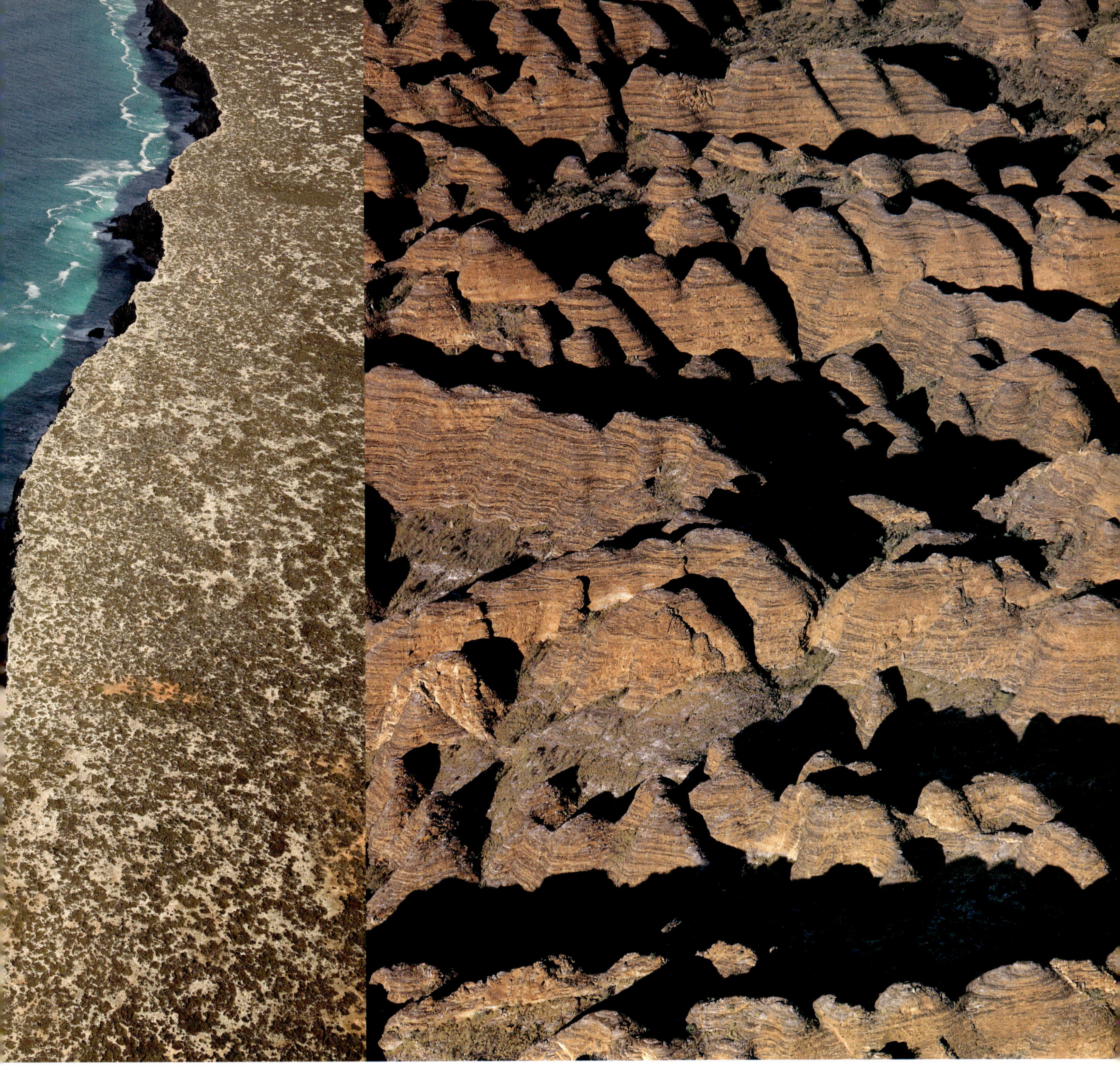

FOLLOWING PAGES: Apart from the capital cities, the Gold Coast in Queensland continues to be one of the fastest-growing areas in Australia. The region is home to more than half a million people, making it the sixth largest city in Australia.

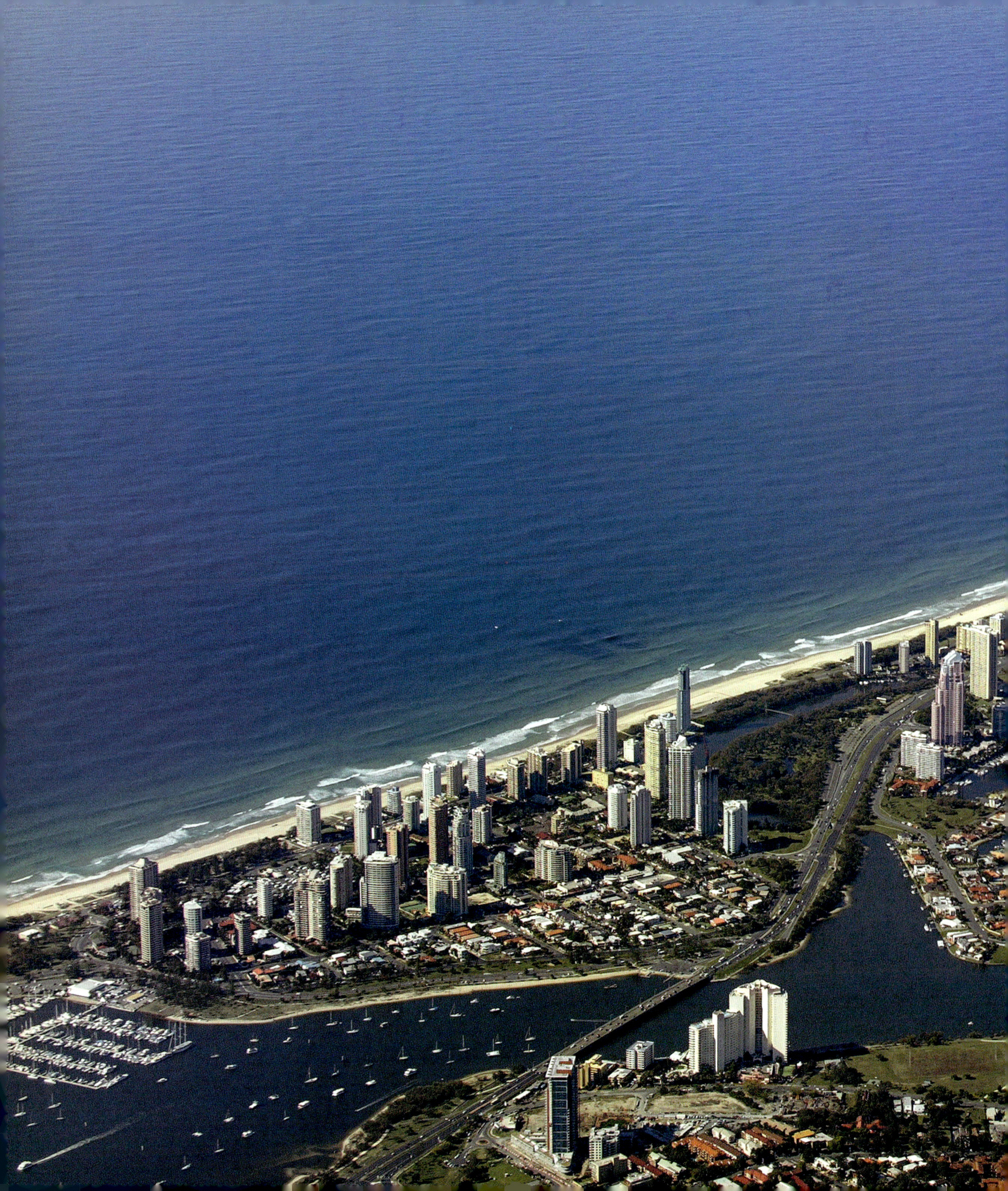

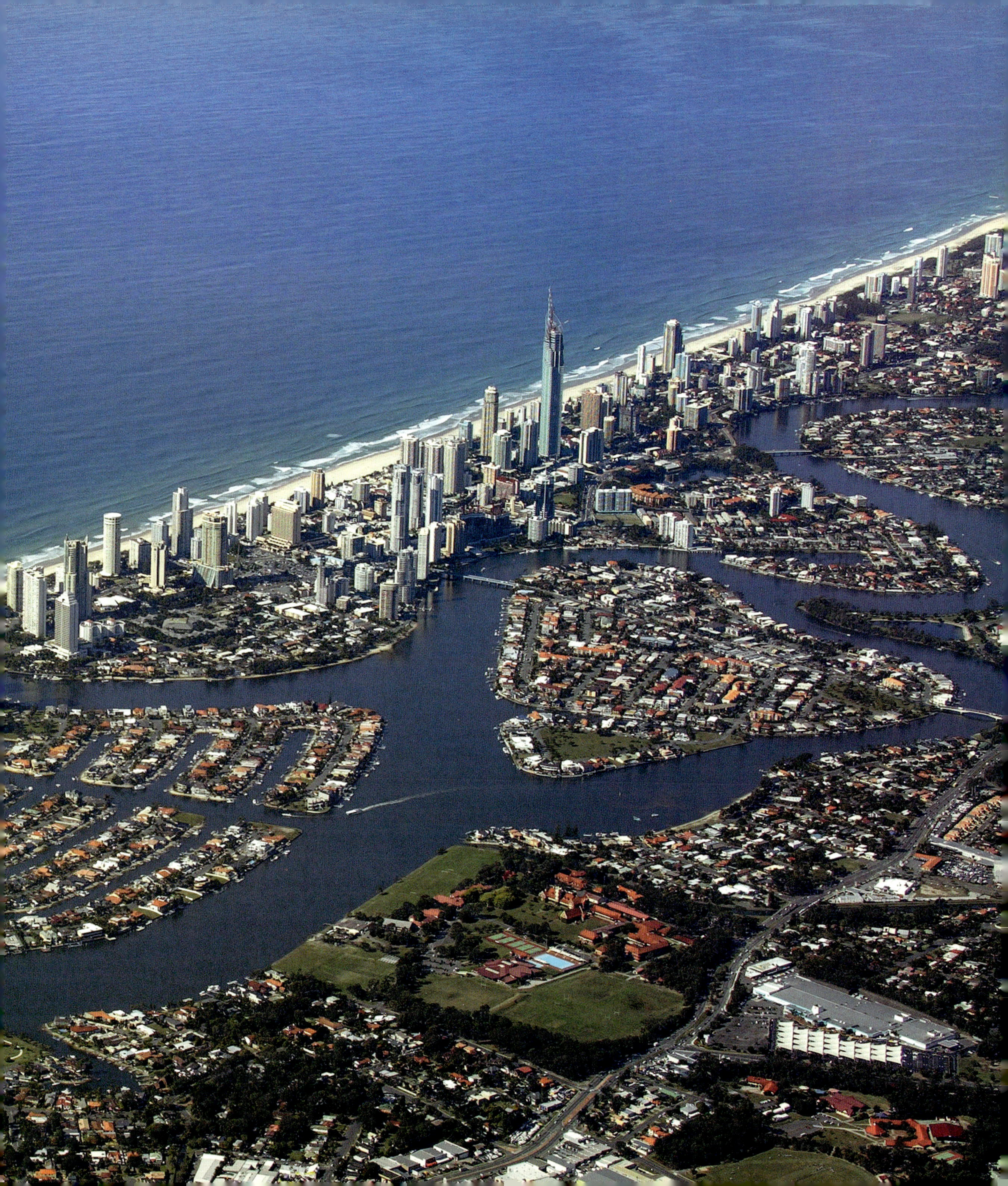

Eighty-five per cent of Australians live within 50 kilometres of the coast — sometimes too close for comfort. **LEFT:** Suburbia comes to Tuross Head in southern New South Wales. **RIGHT:** The concrete, sandbag and rock seawalls trying to stop erosion at Kingscliff near the New South Wales border with Queensland.

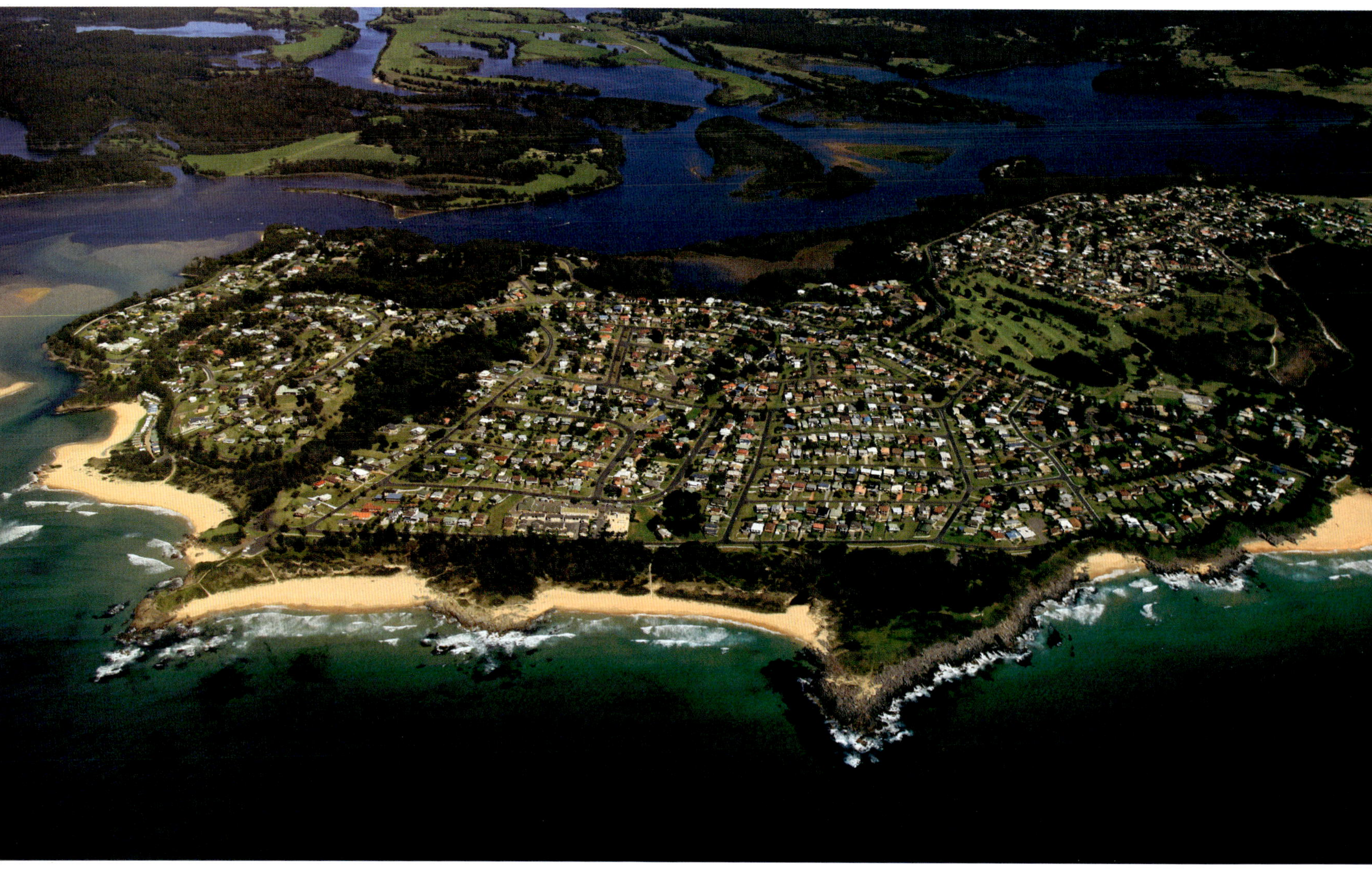

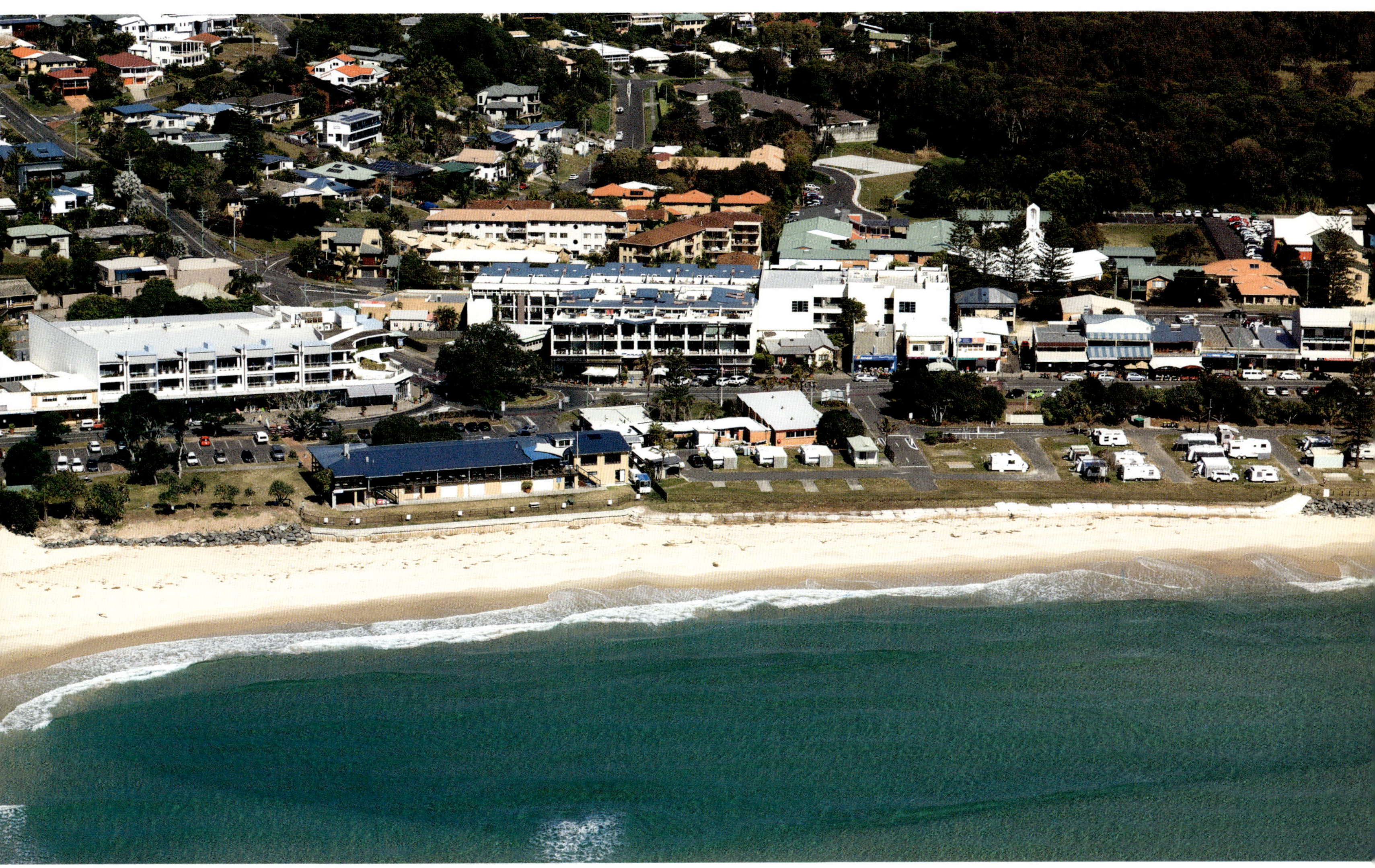

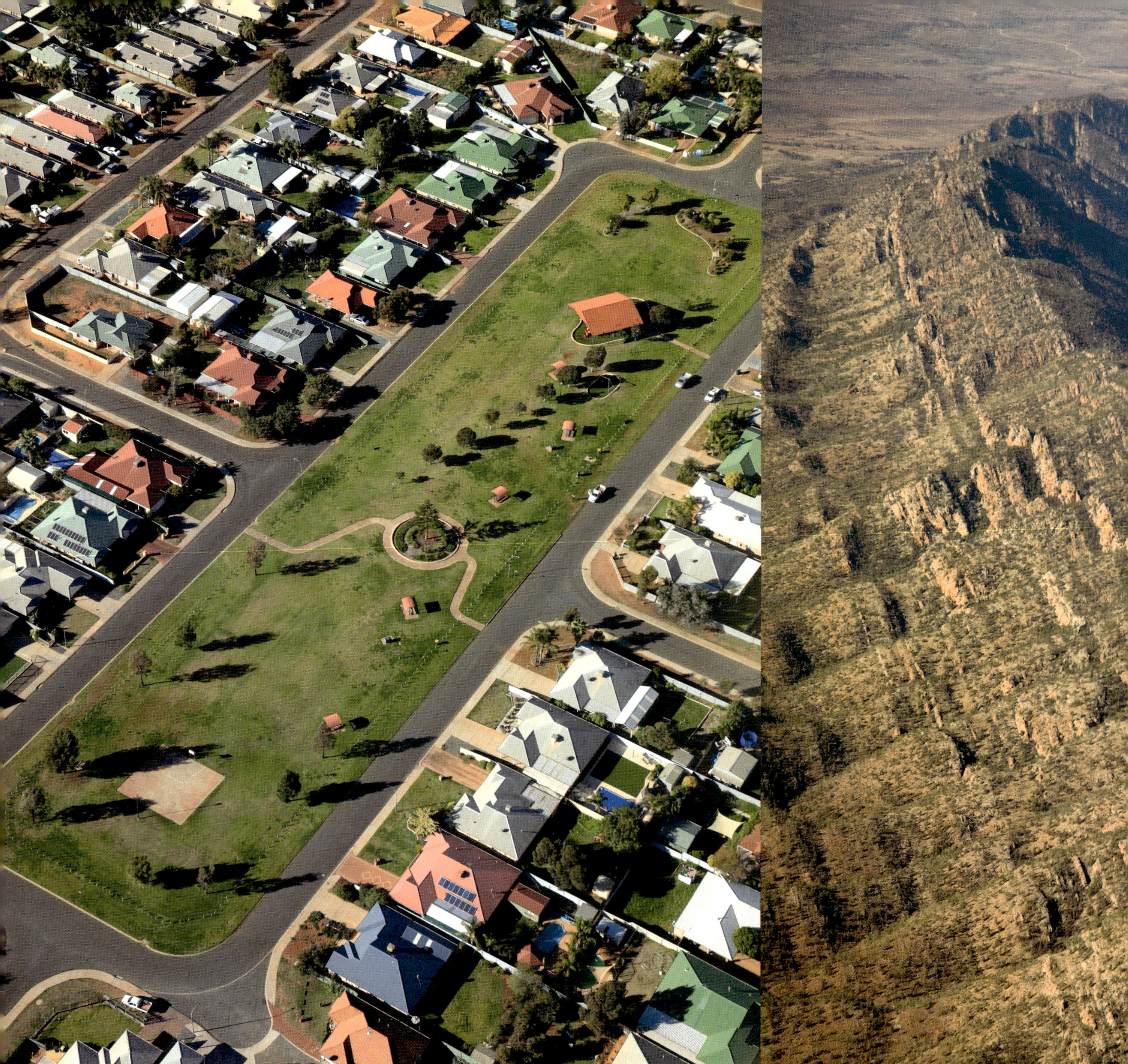

LEFT: Kalgoorlie's population in Western Australia has thrived on the back of mining and the Goldfields Pipeline, which brings fresh water to the region. **MIDDLE:** The remote Flinders Ranges is the largest mountain range in South Australia. **RIGHT:** Big blocks waiting for new homes to be built as Perth's suburban dream sprawls north.

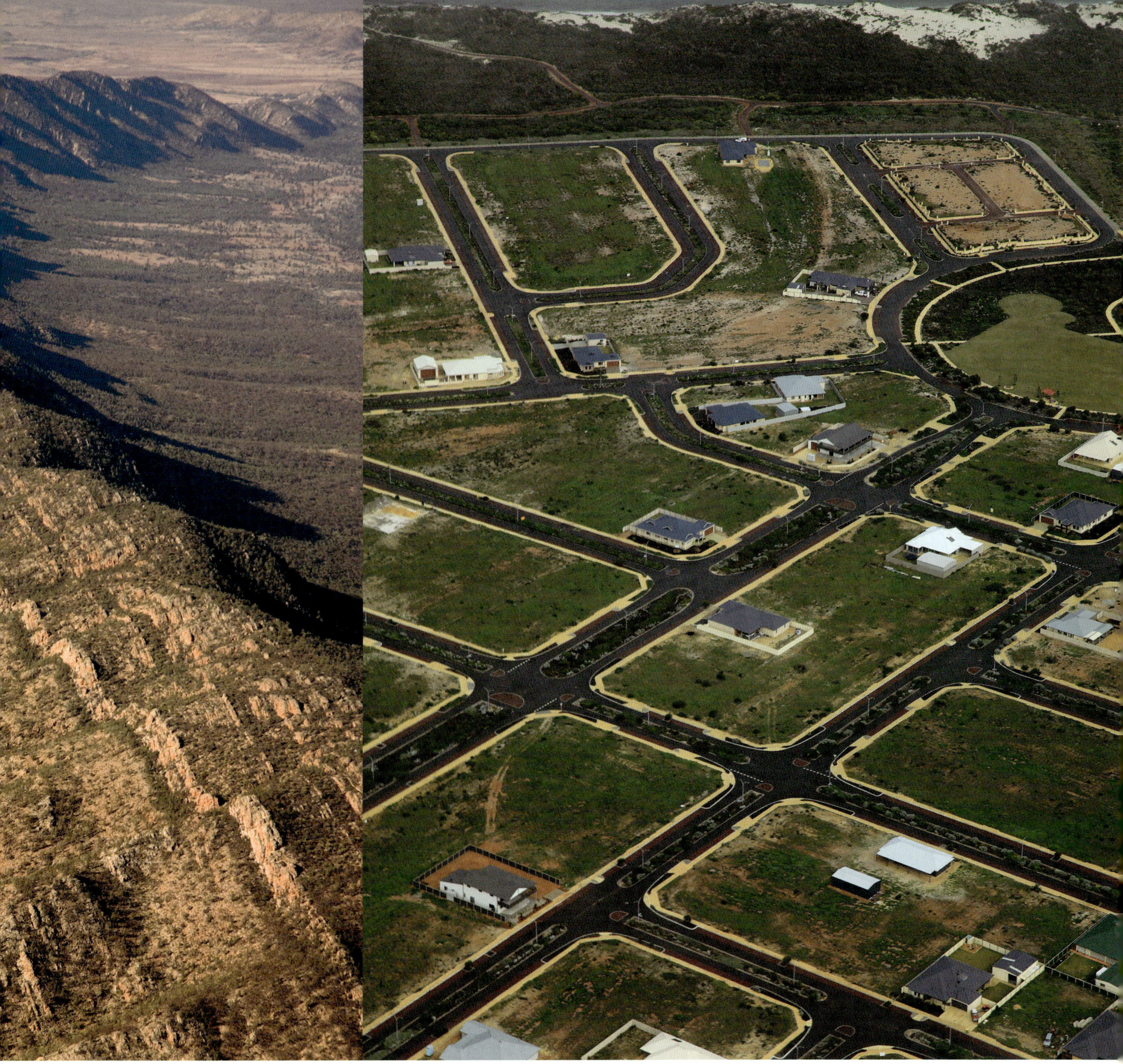

FOLLOWING PAGES: Greater Melbourne had the largest growth of all the capital cities in the decade to 2011 — increasing by 647,200 people. Most of the growth is in the city's outer western and southwestern suburbs.

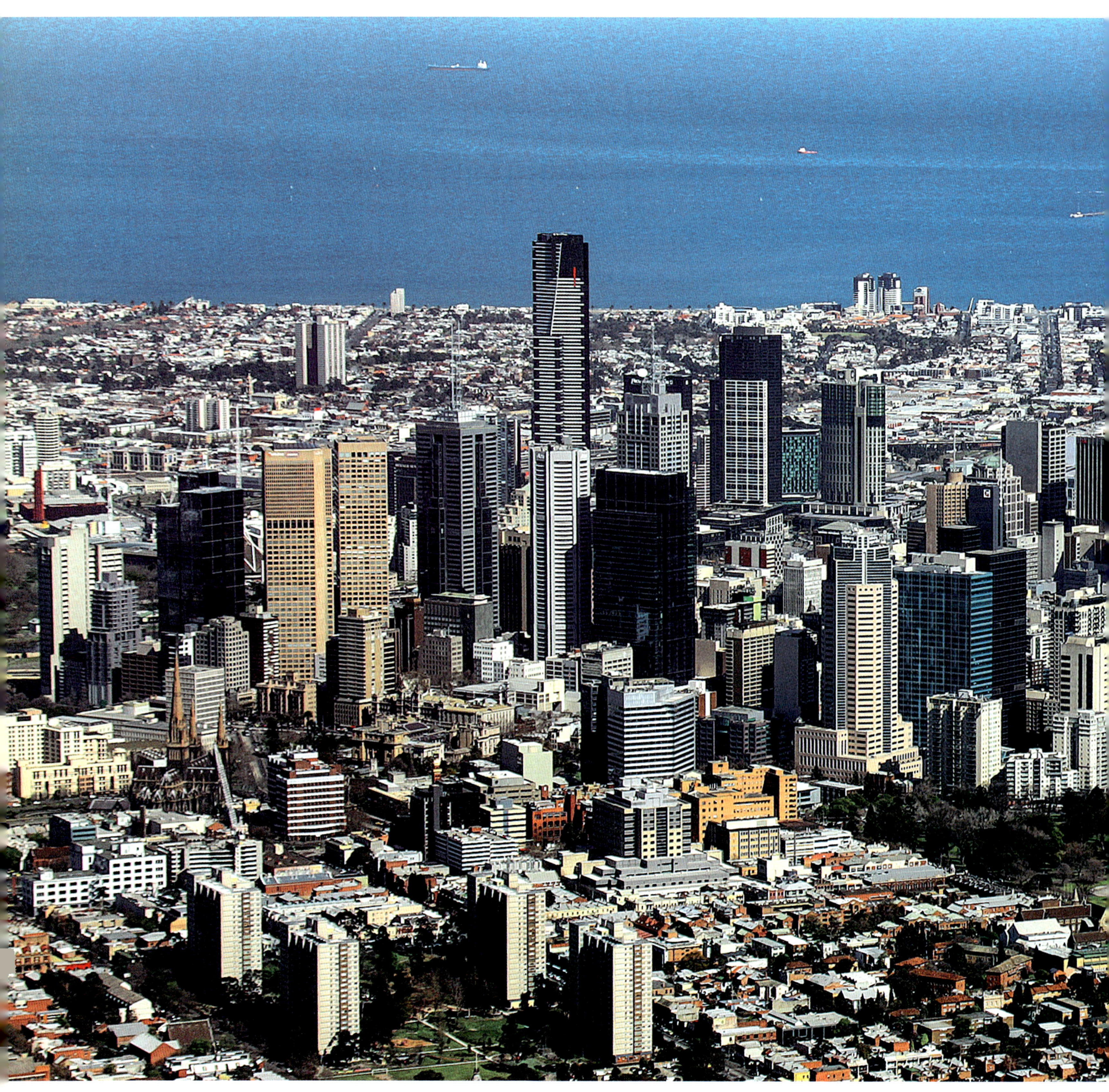

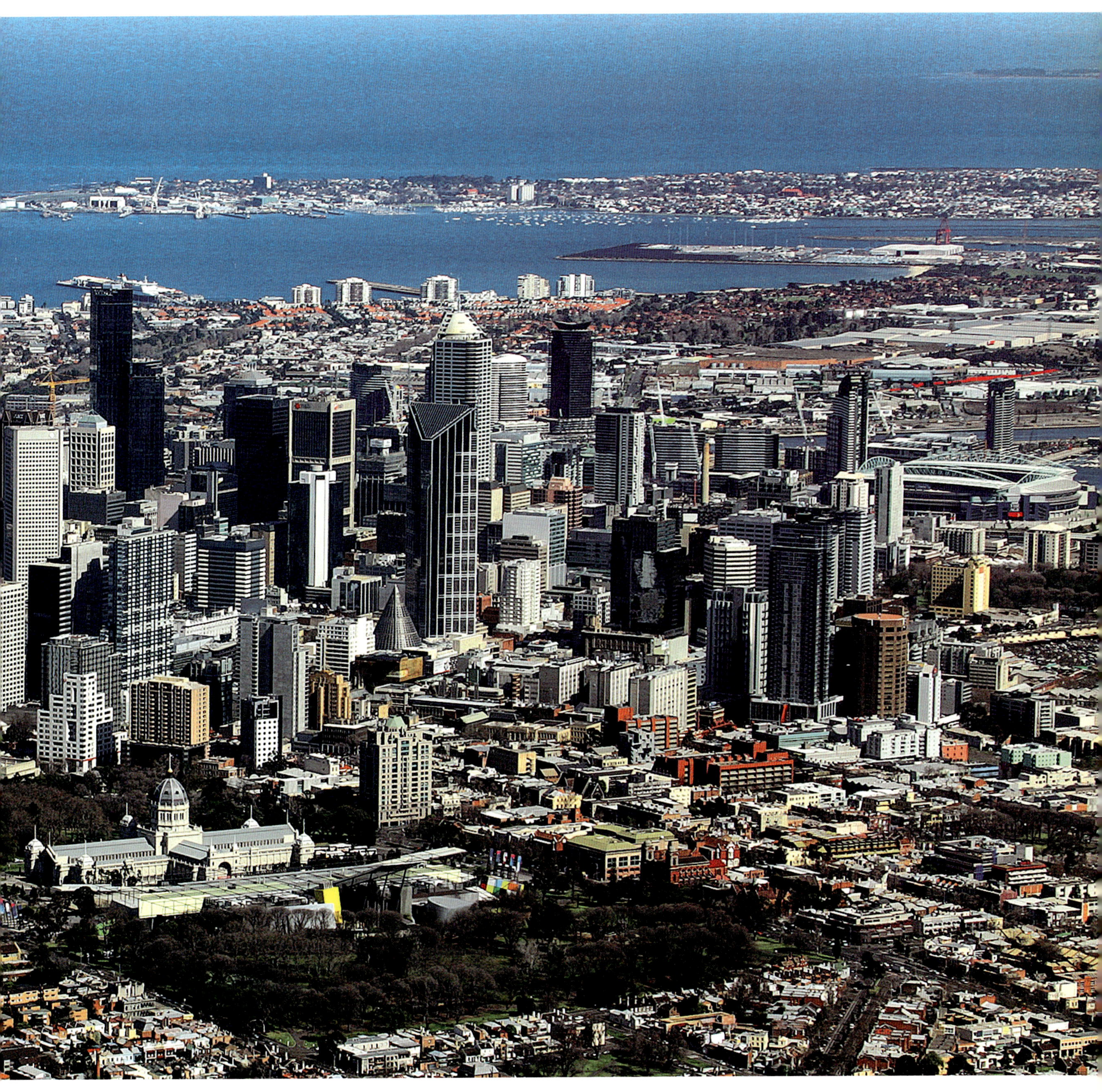

LEFT AND RIGHT: Two views of Brisbane's CBD. The population of Greater Brisbane has grown by 25 per cent in the past decade — the second fastest in Australia behind Perth in percentage terms. The southeast corner of Queensland is home to almost 3.2 million people.

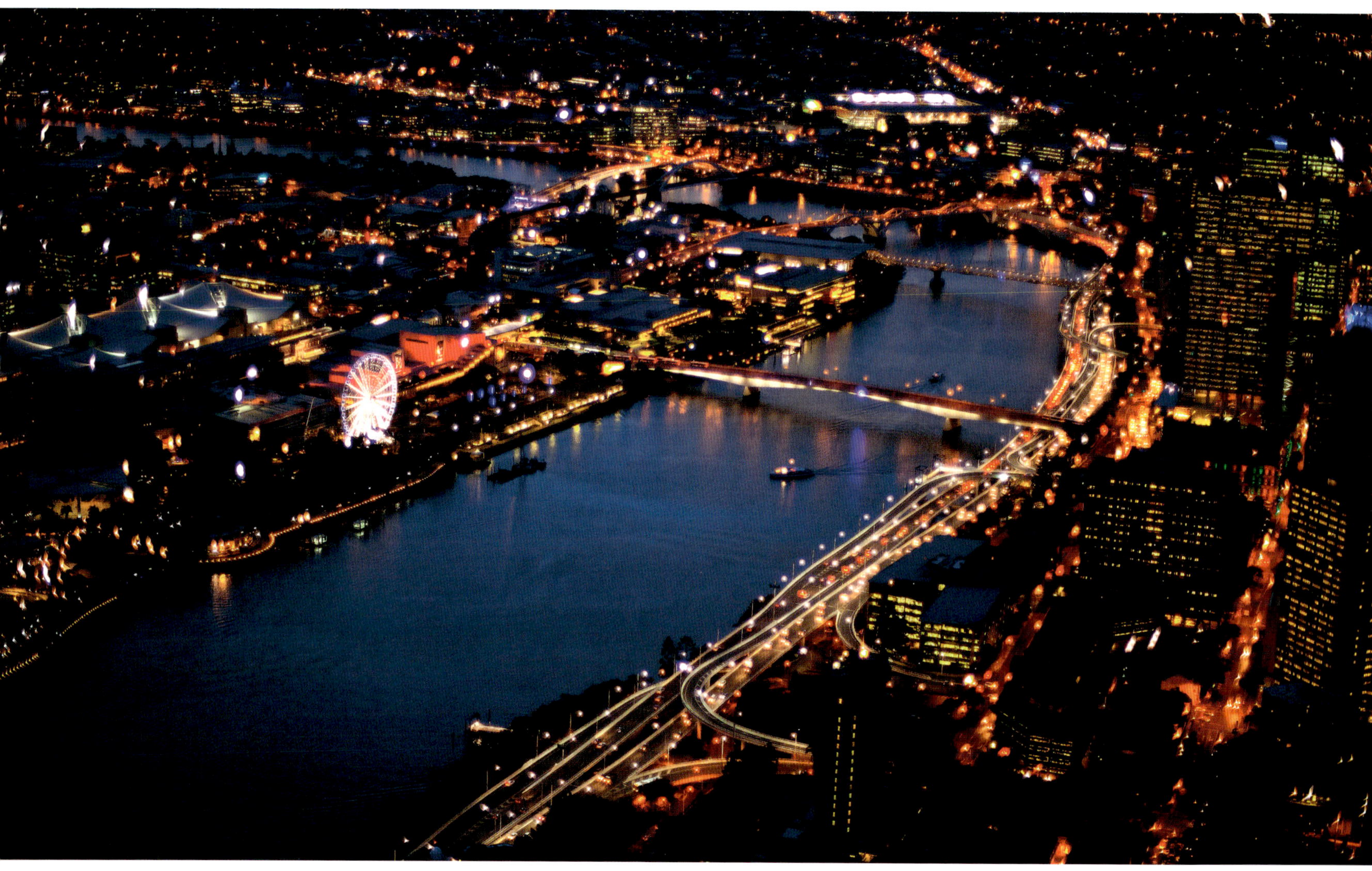

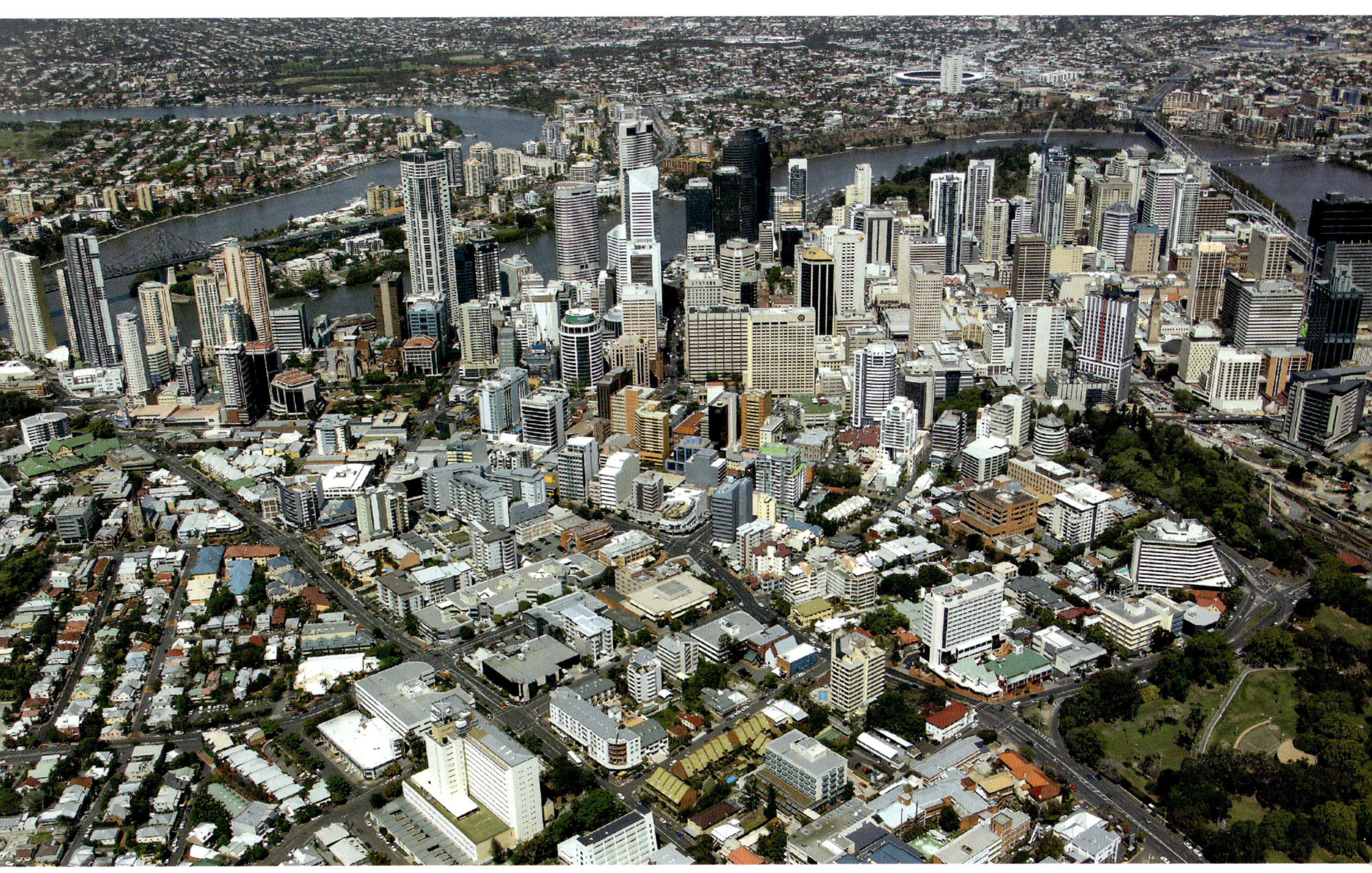

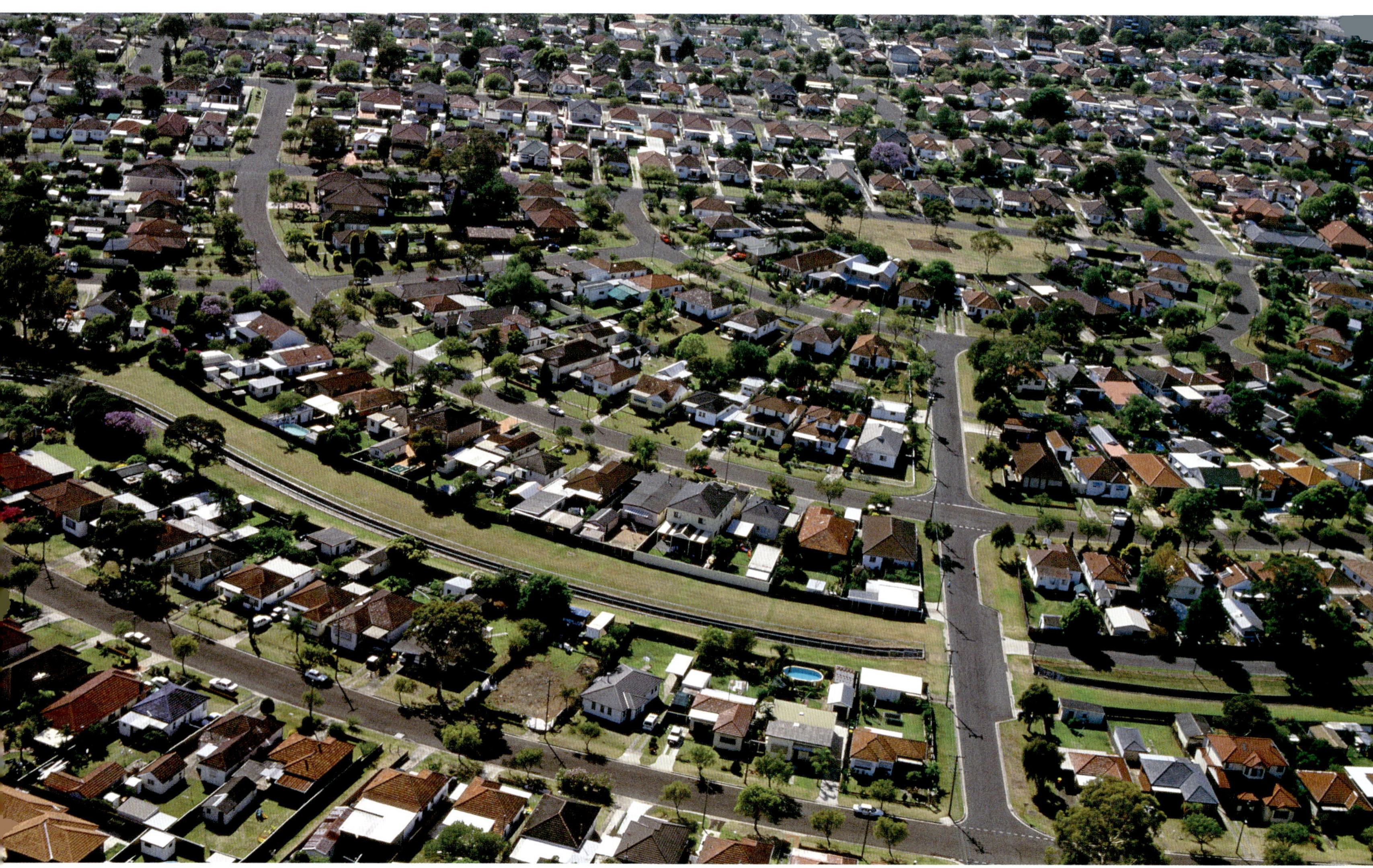

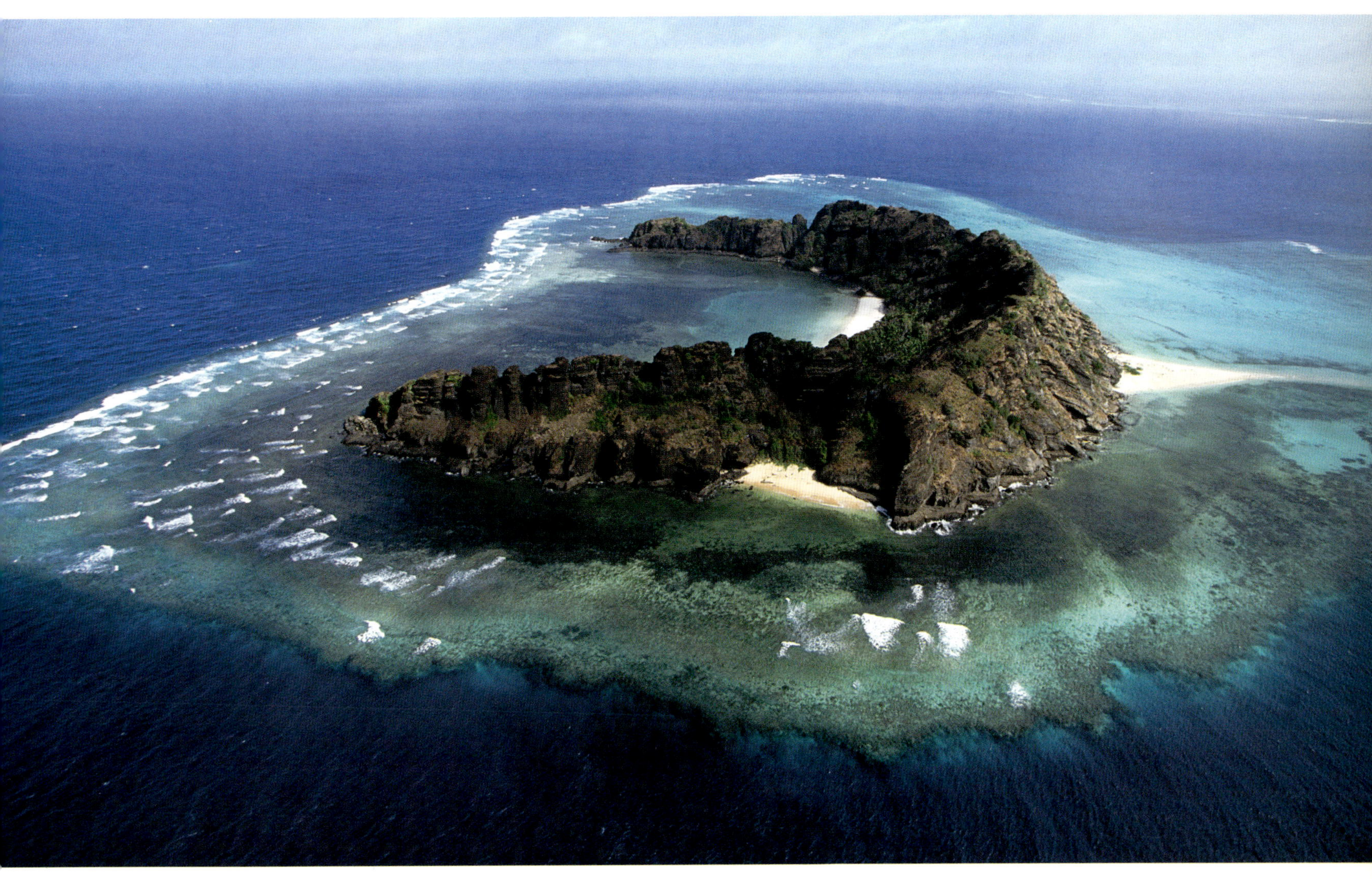

LEFT: A crowded crescent in Sydney's southwest is the epitome of urban sprawl.
RIGHT: In contrast, the pristine beauty of the crescent-shaped Waier Island in the remote eastern Torres Strait.

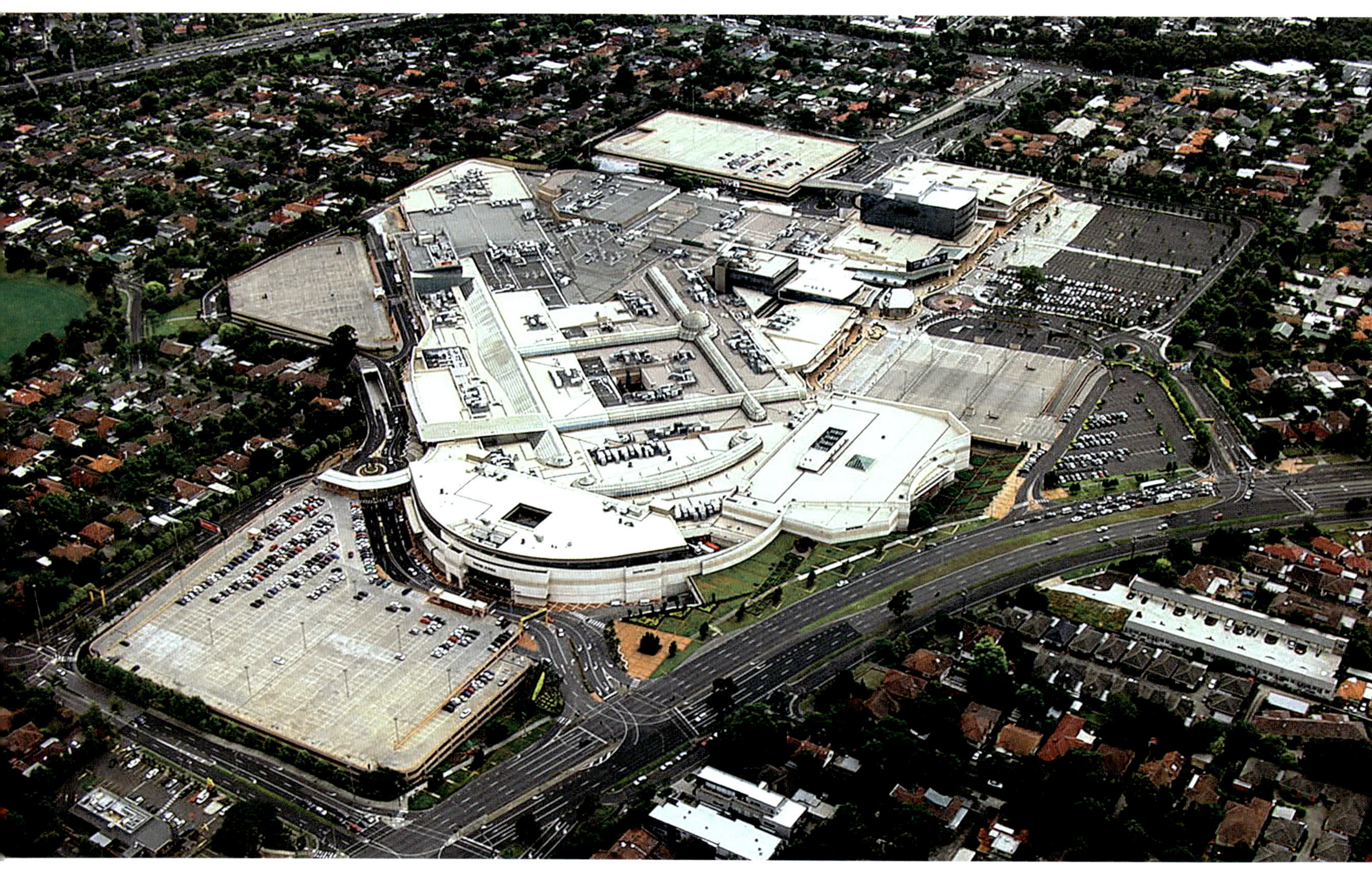

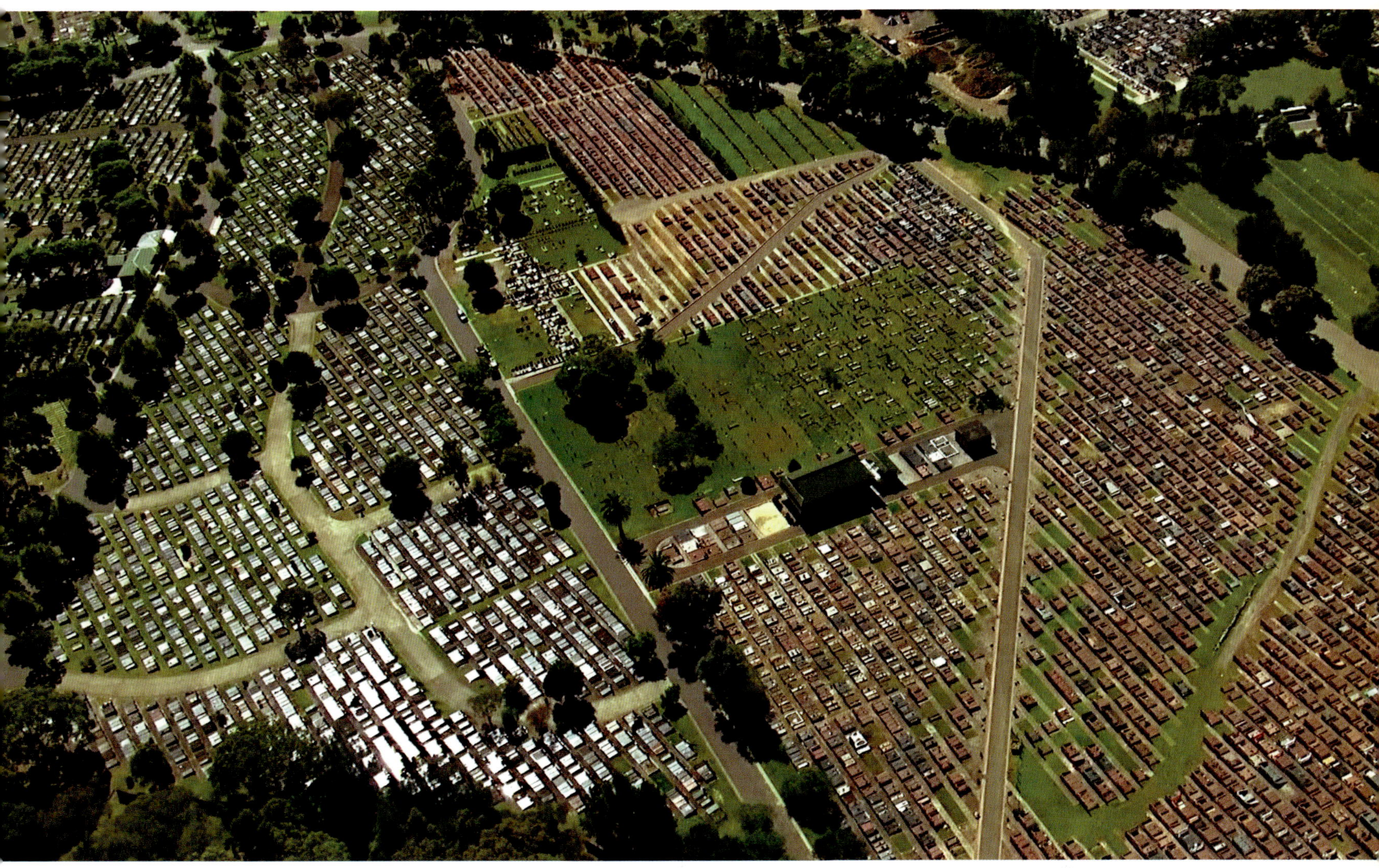

Competition for space is intense in the suburbs. **LEFT:** Australia's largest shopping centre is Chadstone in Melbourne. Total land area for Chadstone is 264,500 square metres, which includes parking space for 9,500 cars. **RIGHT:** Australia's largest cemetery is Rookwood in Sydney. Despite sprawling over 283 hectares, the cemetery is filling fast.

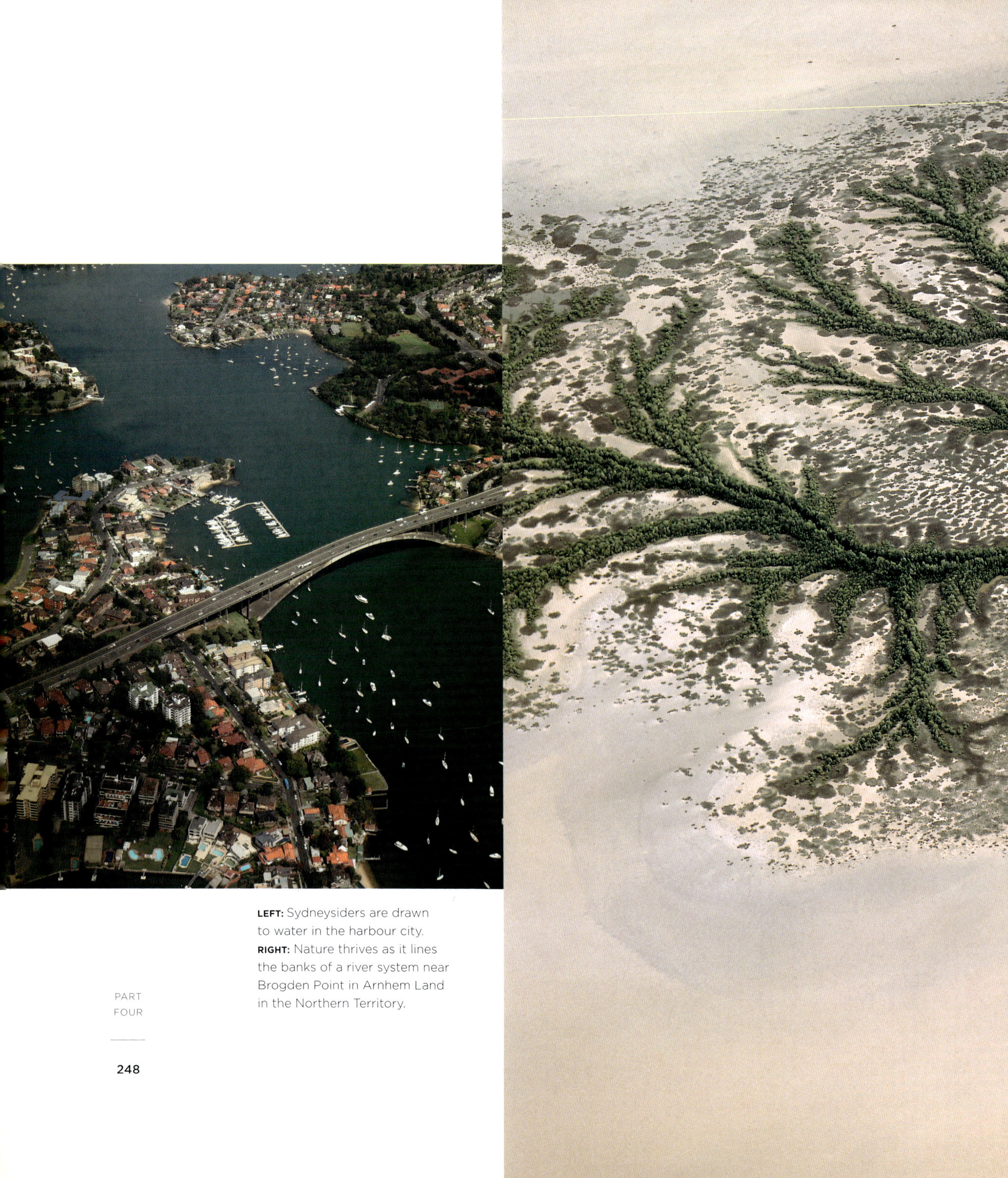

LEFT: Sydneysiders are drawn to water in the harbour city.
RIGHT: Nature thrives as it lines the banks of a river system near Brogden Point in Arnhem Land in the Northern Territory.

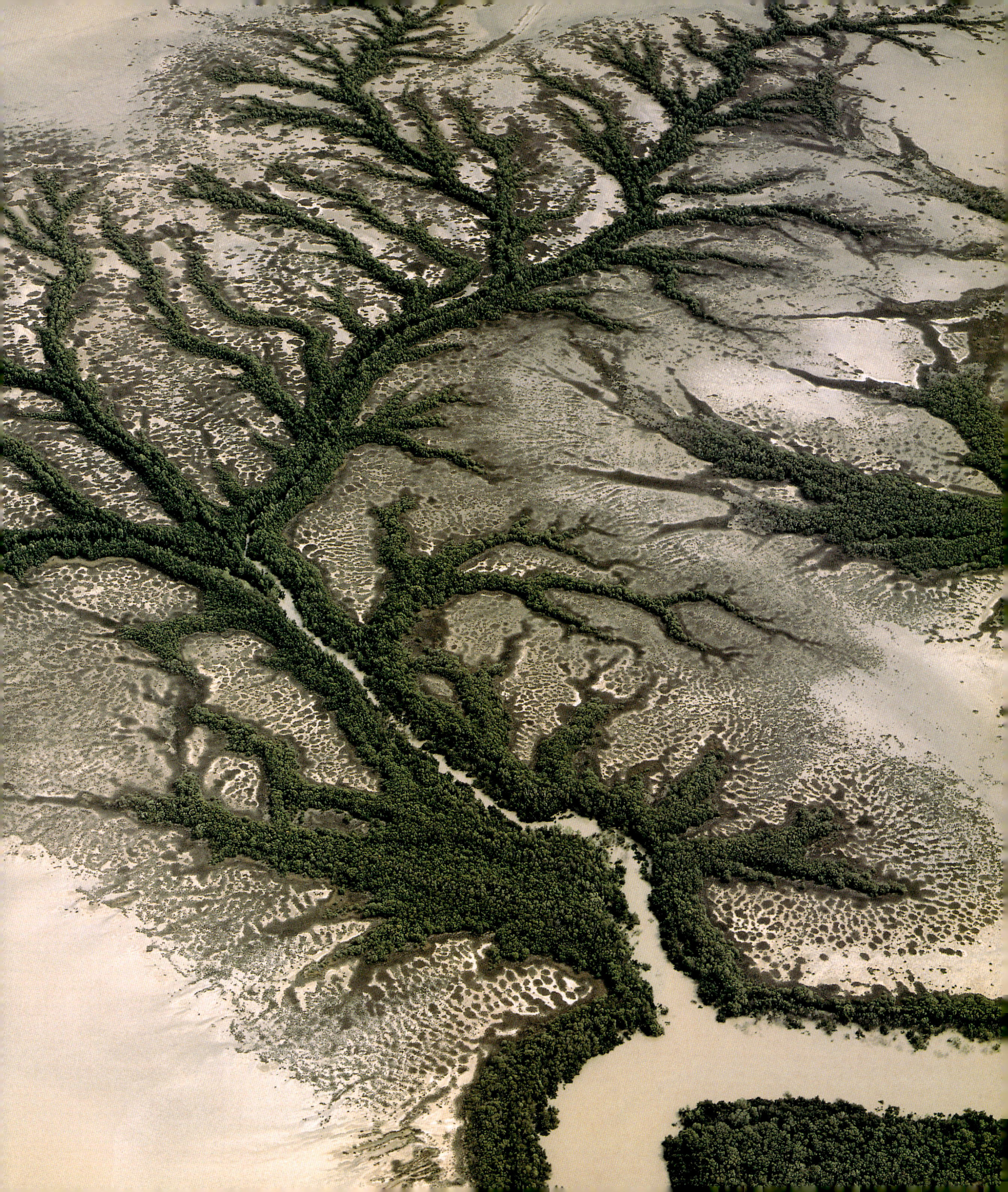

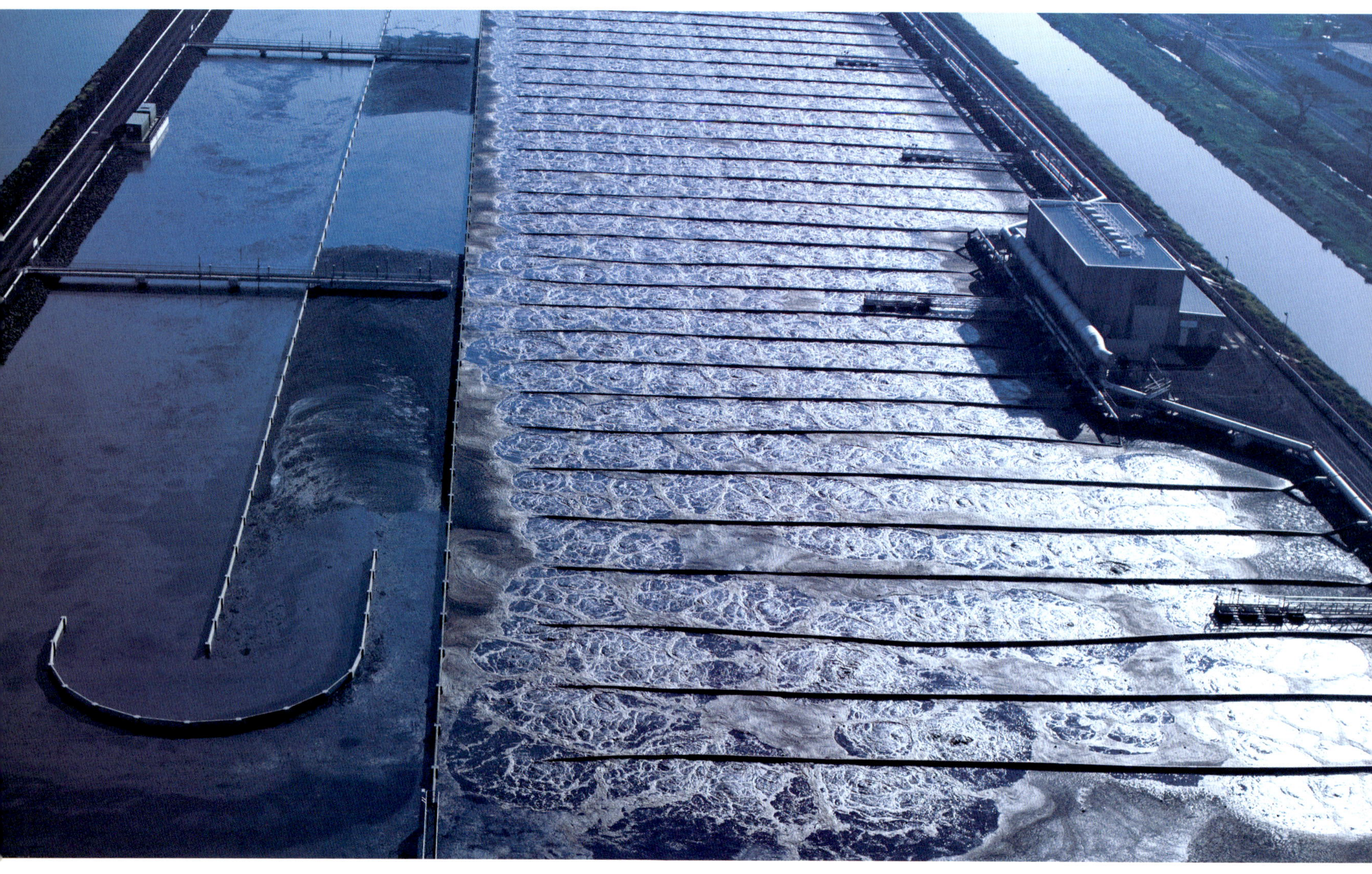

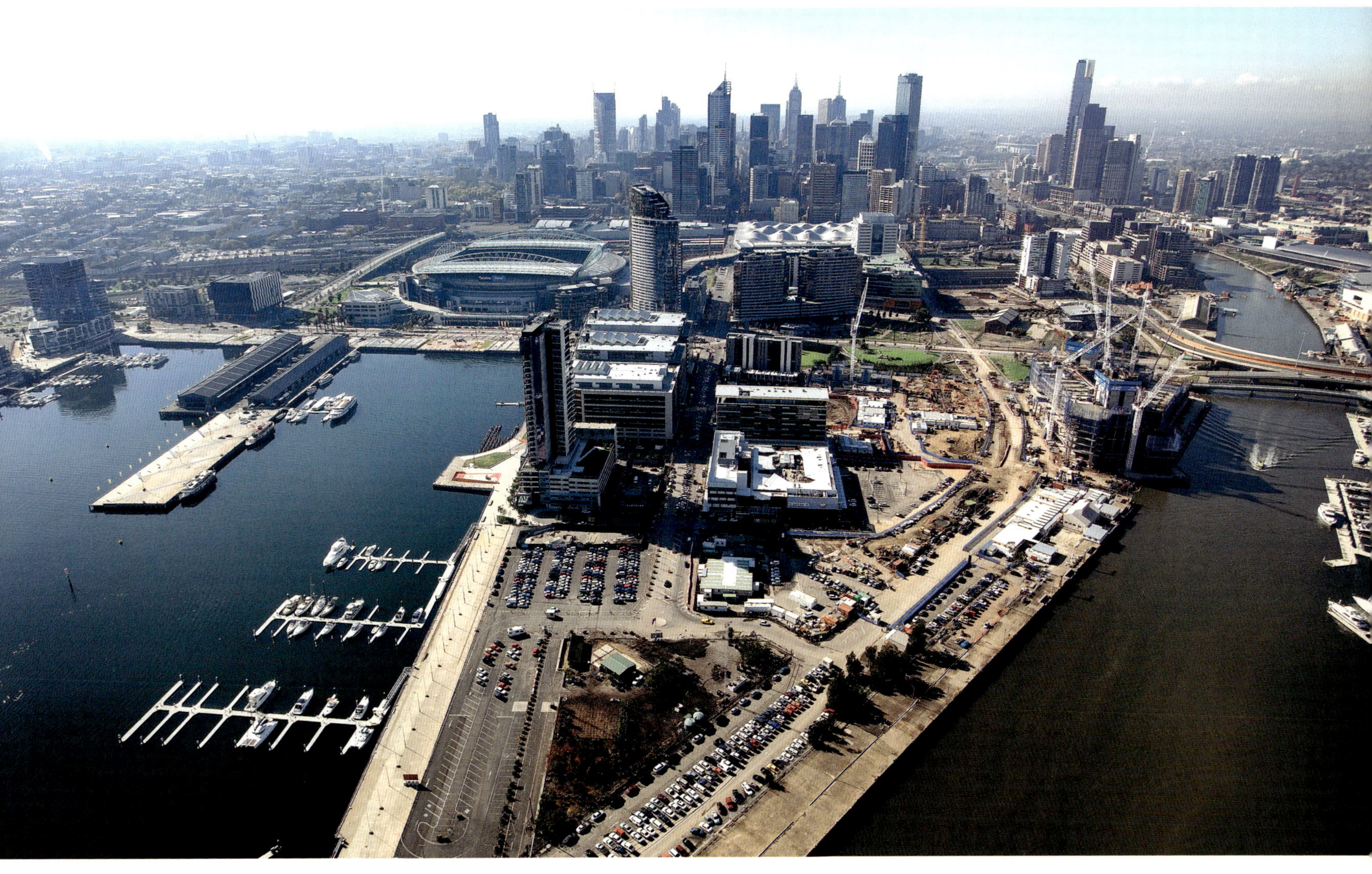

LEFT: The lagoon system at the Western Treatment Plant in Werribee generates almost 40 billion litres of recycled water a year. **RIGHT:** The plant processes about 50 per cent of sewage from nearby Melbourne.

LEFT: Greater Darwin has the lowest population density of any capital city in Australia with 41 people for every square kilometre. **RIGHT:** The shallow mouth of Entrance Point near the town of Onslow in Western Australia. In the state's remote coastal regions there is an average of one person for every square kilometre.

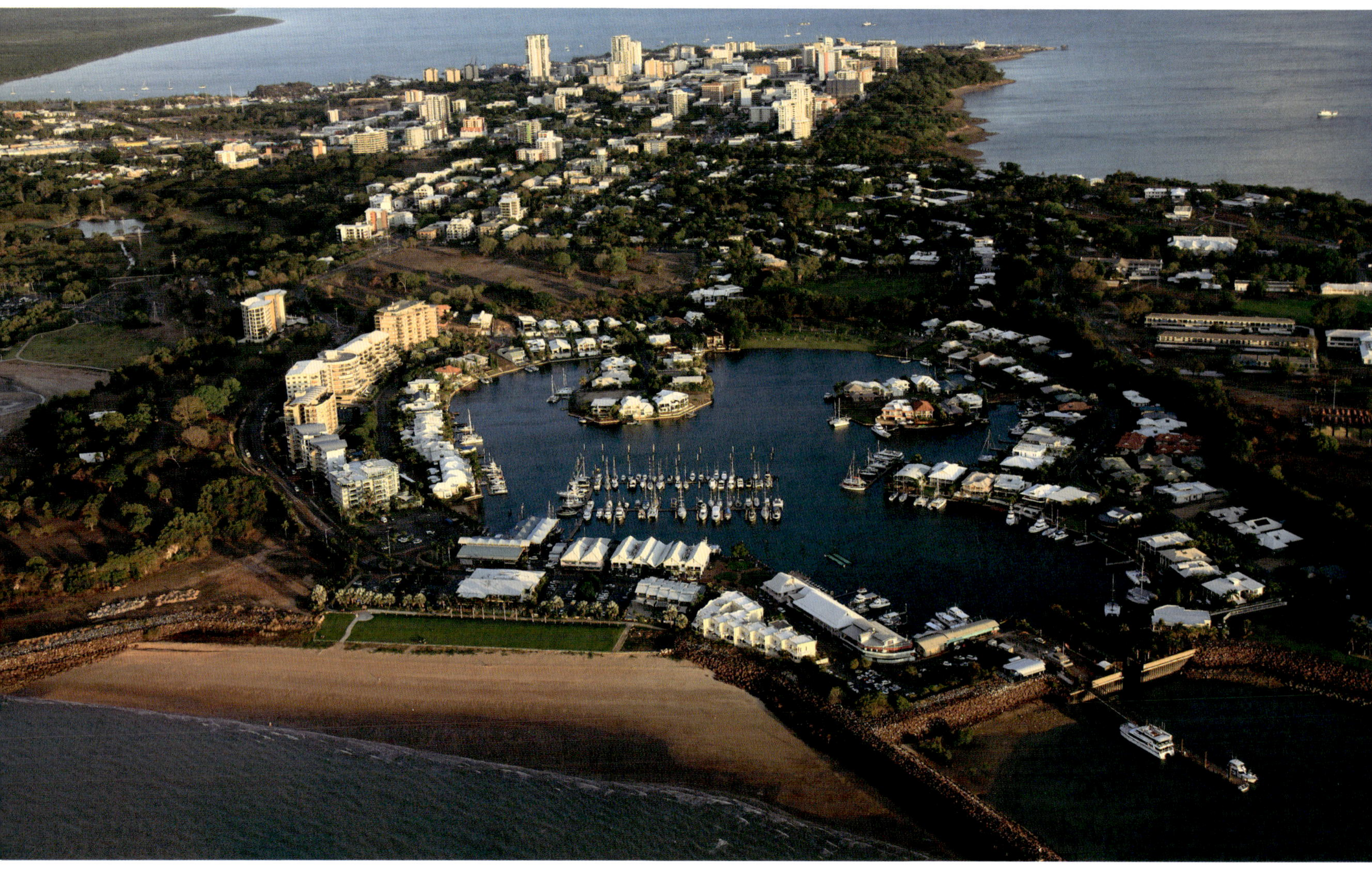

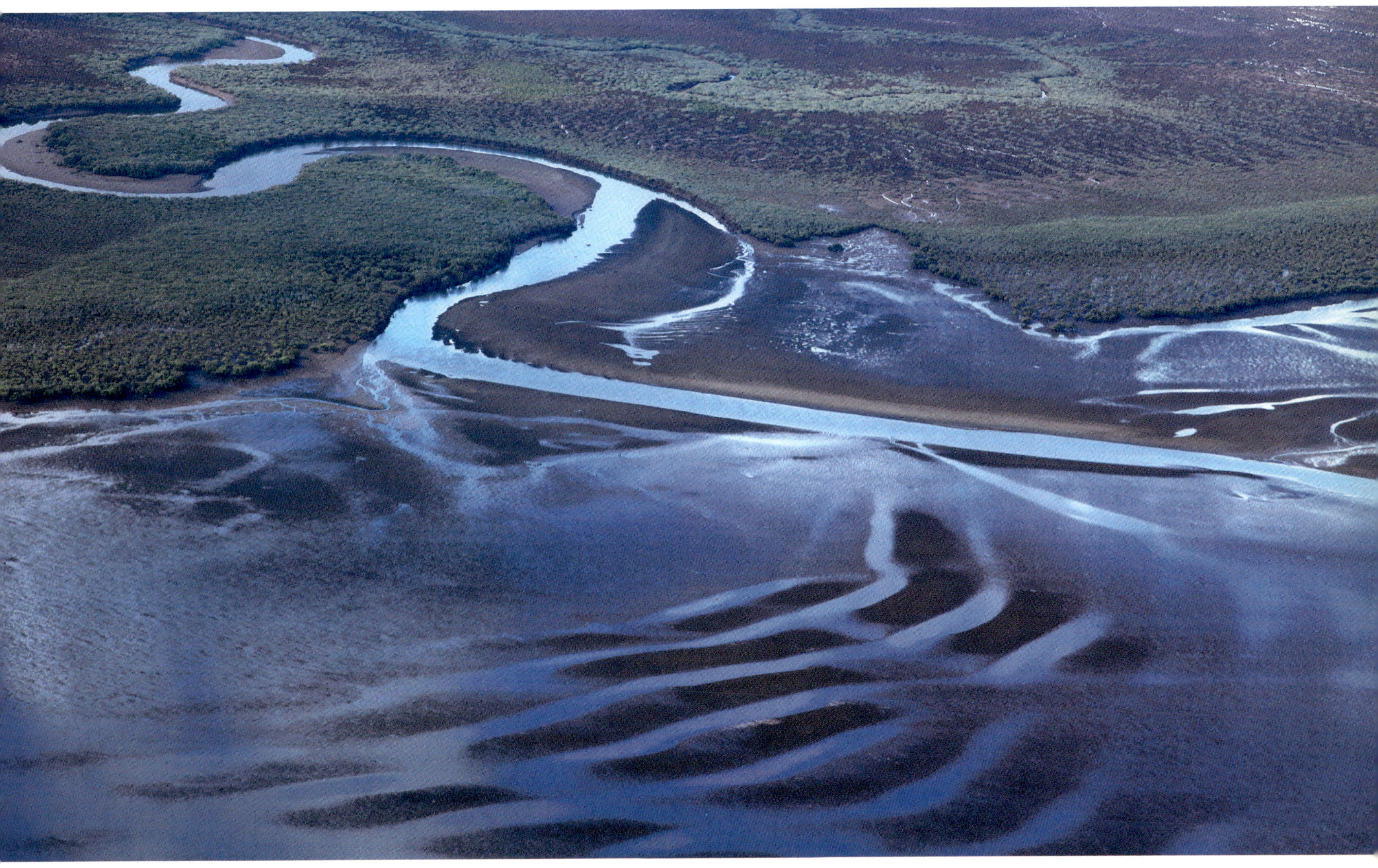

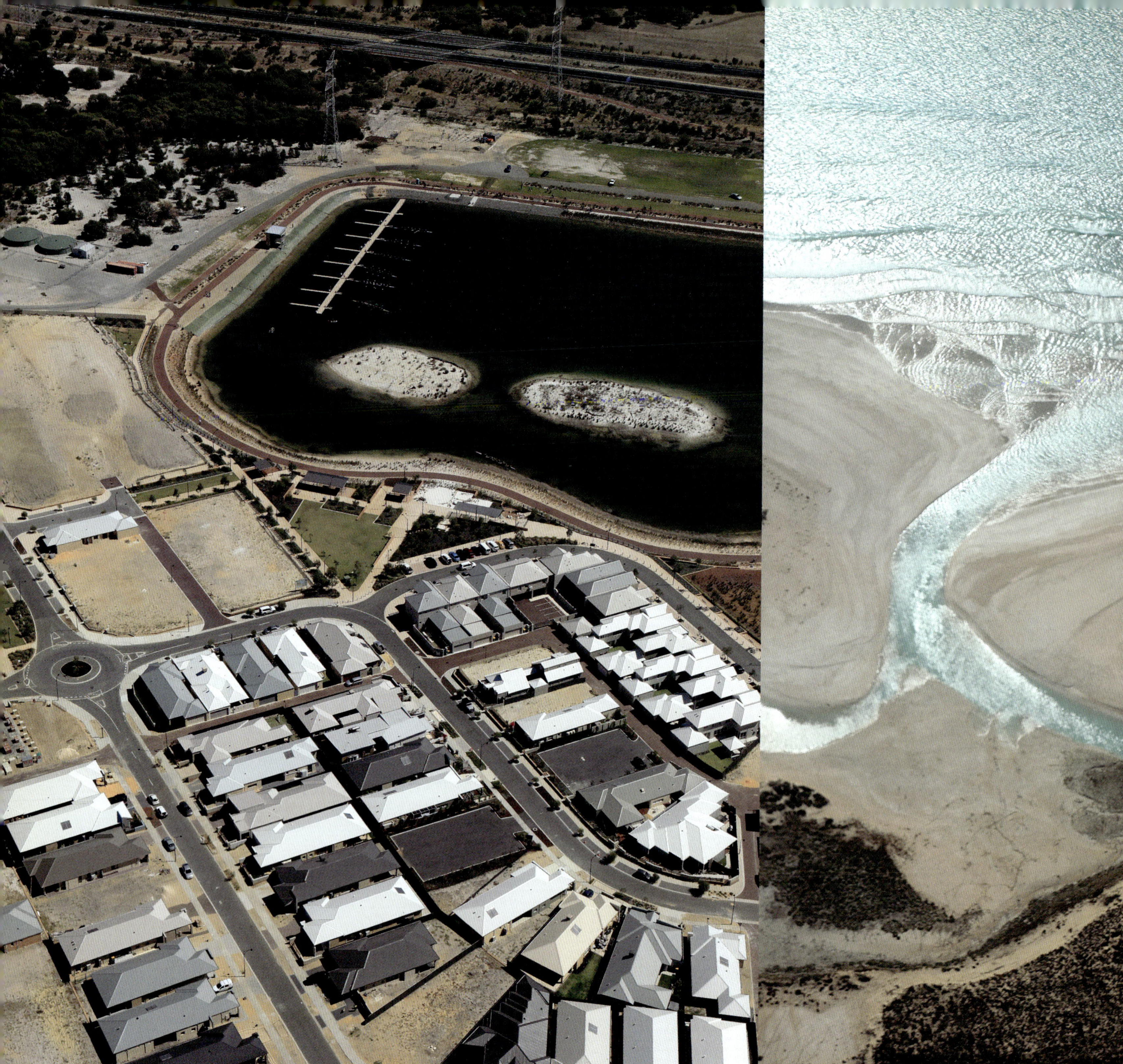

LEFT: New houses and vacant blocks sit next to man-made Champion Lakes in Perth. **MIDDLE:** The beautiful beaches of Cape Keraudren near Port Hedland in Western Australia. **RIGHT:** The cemetery in suburban Karrakatta is the largest in Perth at 98 hectares. It opened for burials in 1899. Like many city cemeteries, it is running out of space for burials.

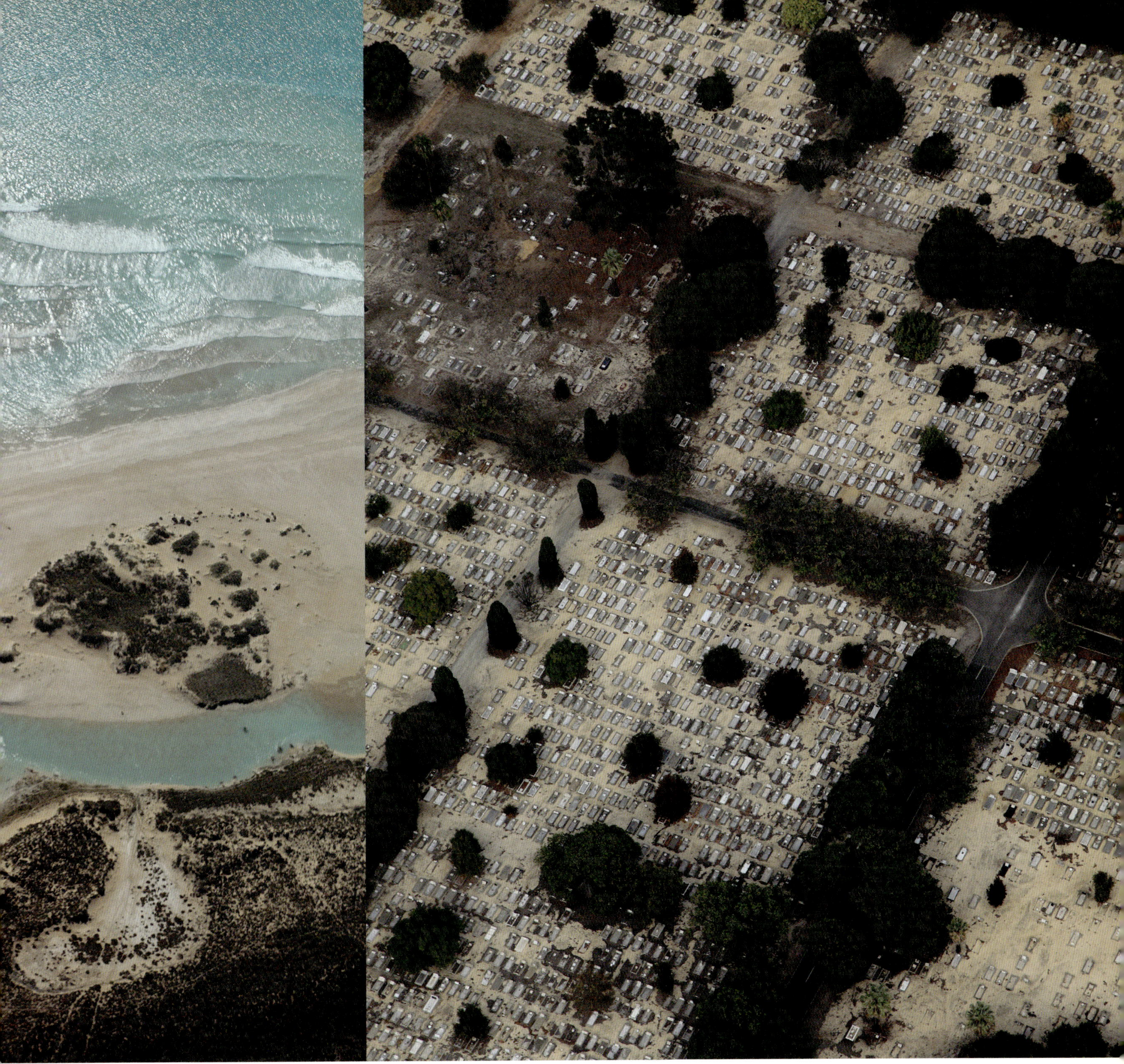

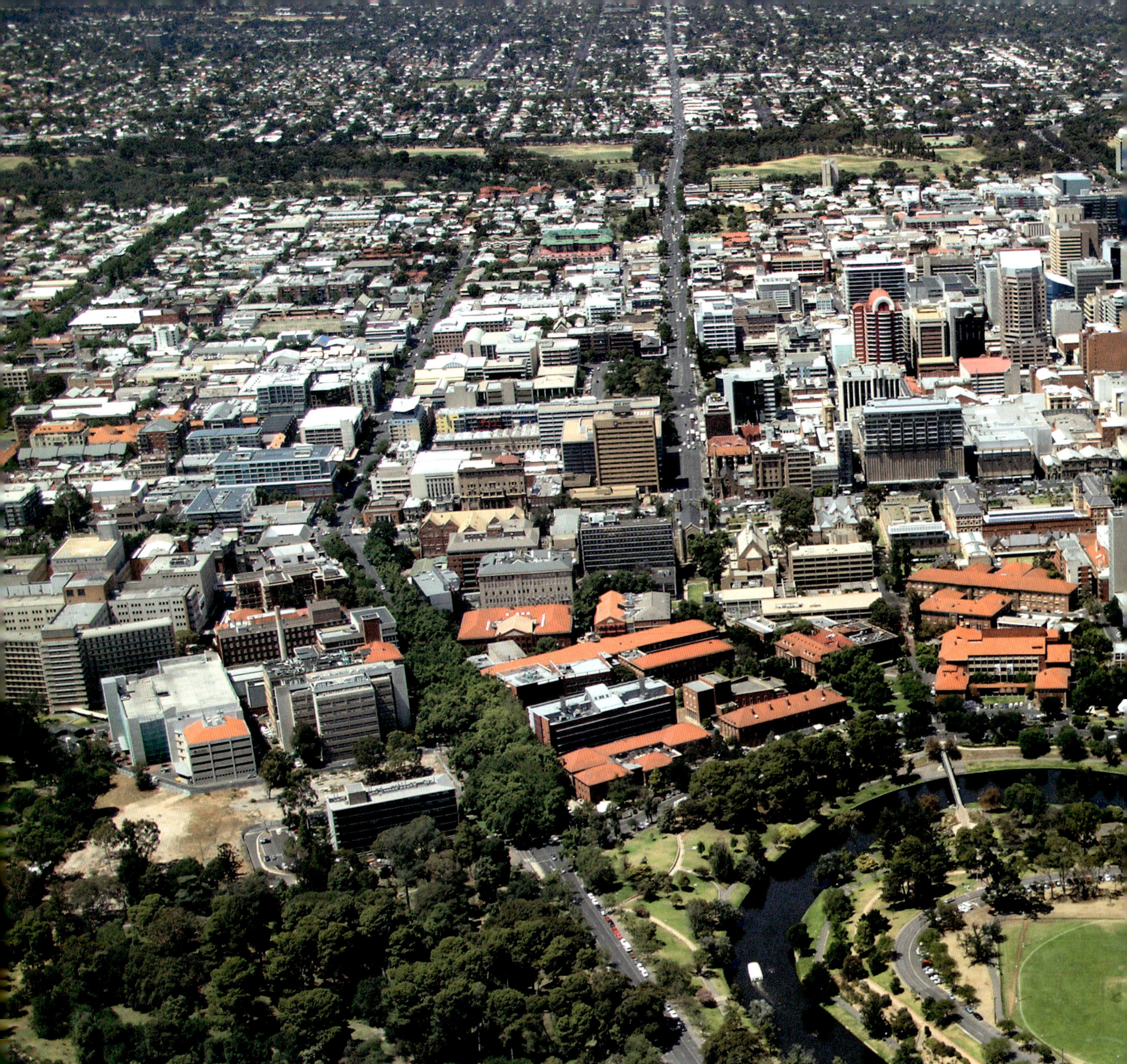

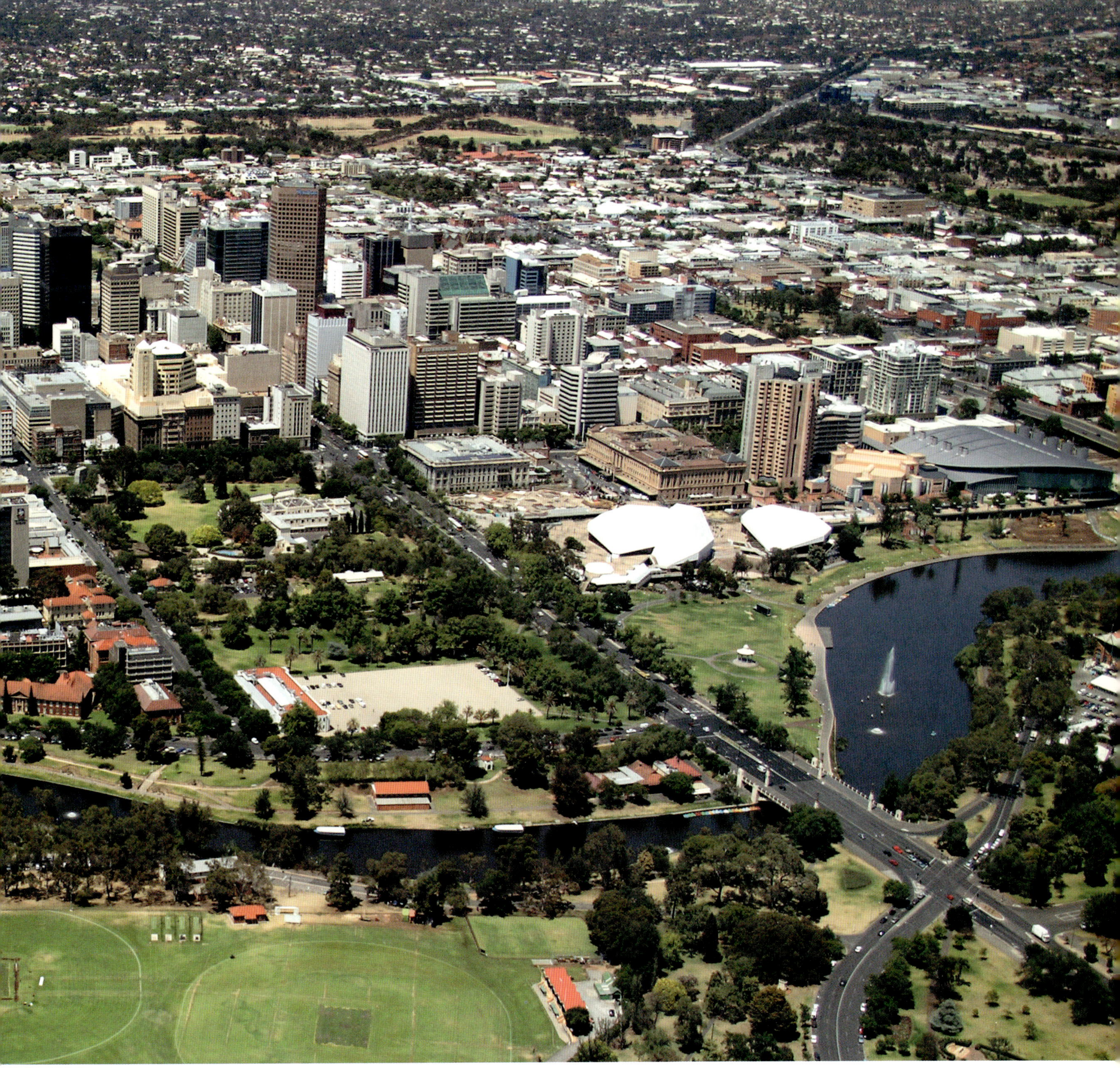

Three quarters of the people of South Australia — more than 1.2 million residents — live in the tree-lined capital, Adelaide.

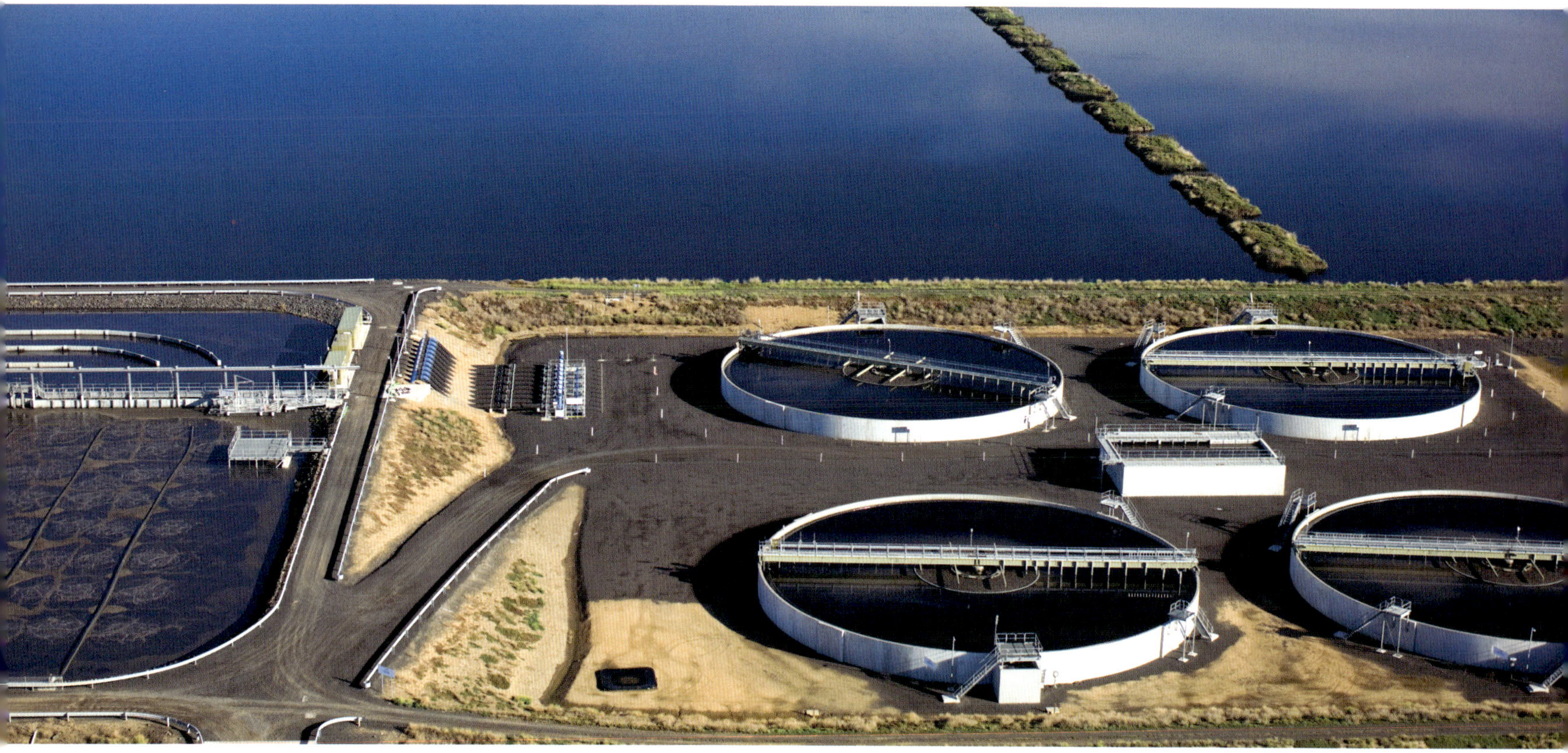

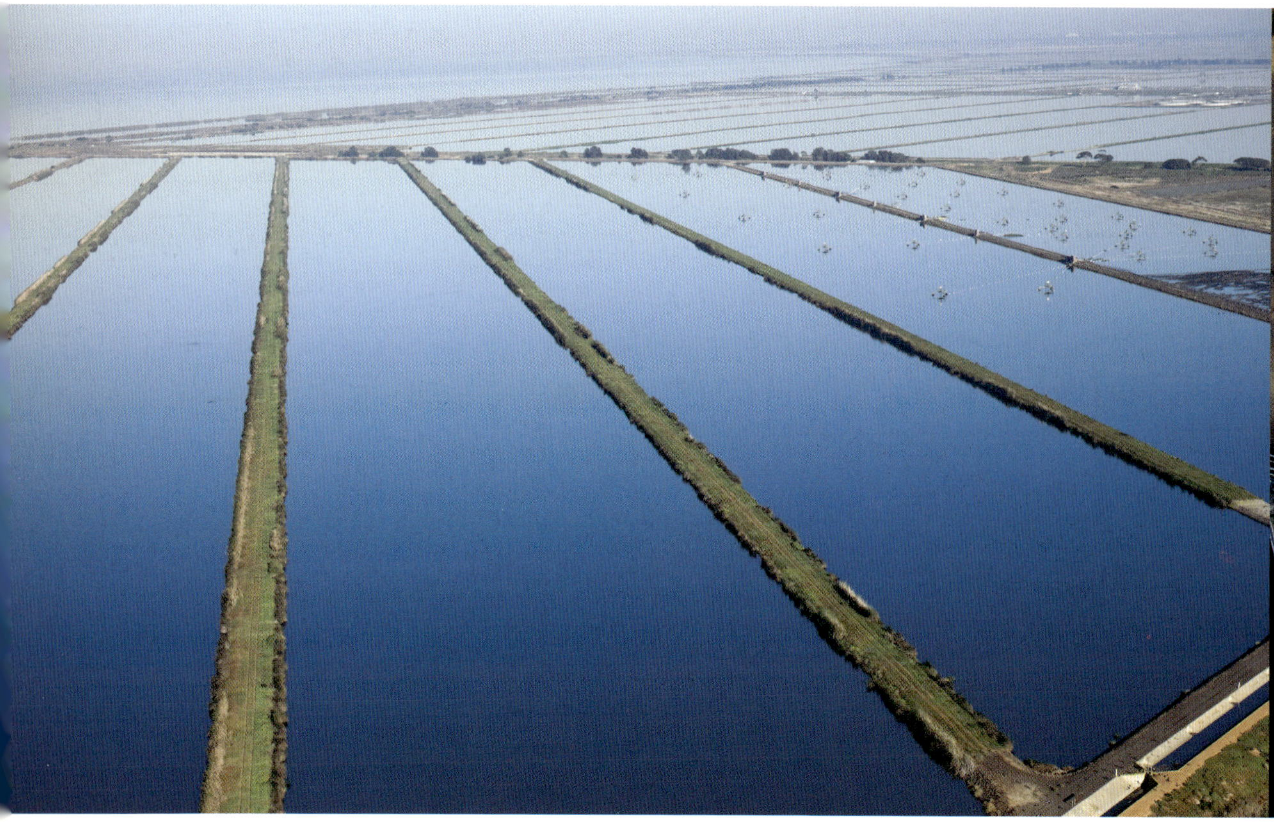

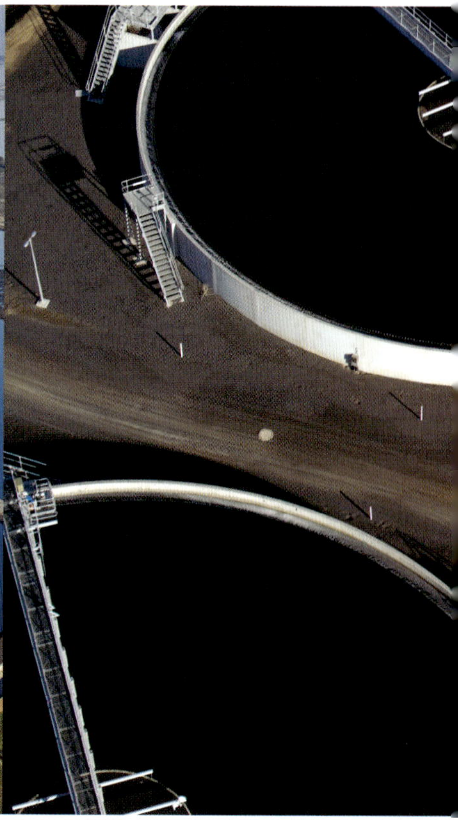

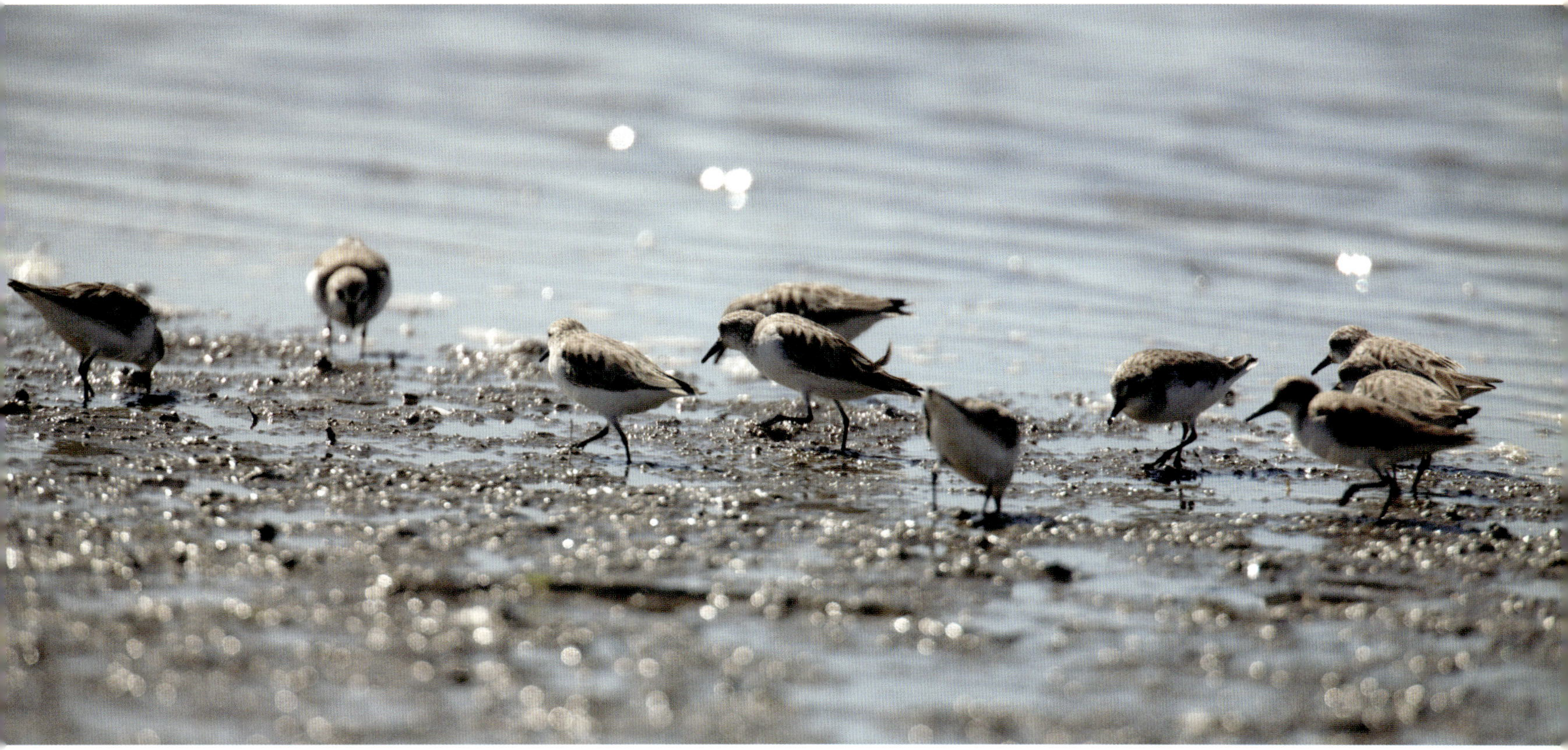

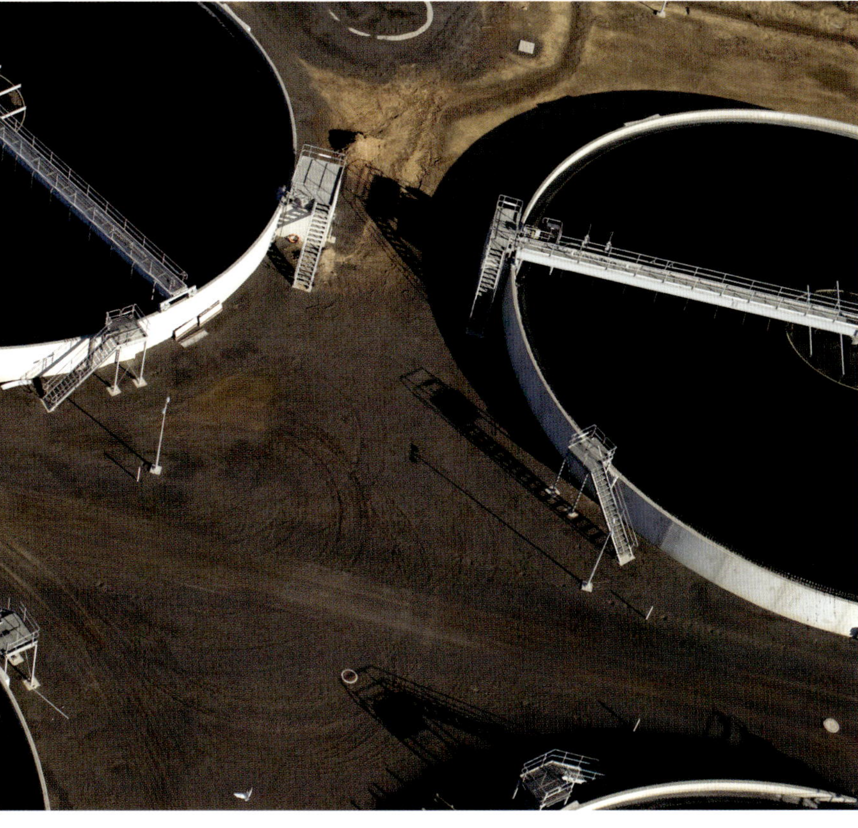

The Western Treatment Plant at Werribee, near Melbourne, is also one of Australia's most significant wetlands for water birds. A permanent water supply as well as insects and plant life attracts more than 280 species of birds from all over the world. The wetlands and birds are protected by legislation and the site is recognised as a wetland of international importance. **FOLLOWING PAGES:** Port Botany is the major import and export hub for Sydney. Stevedores handle more than two million containers a year. The port facilities are to be expanded.

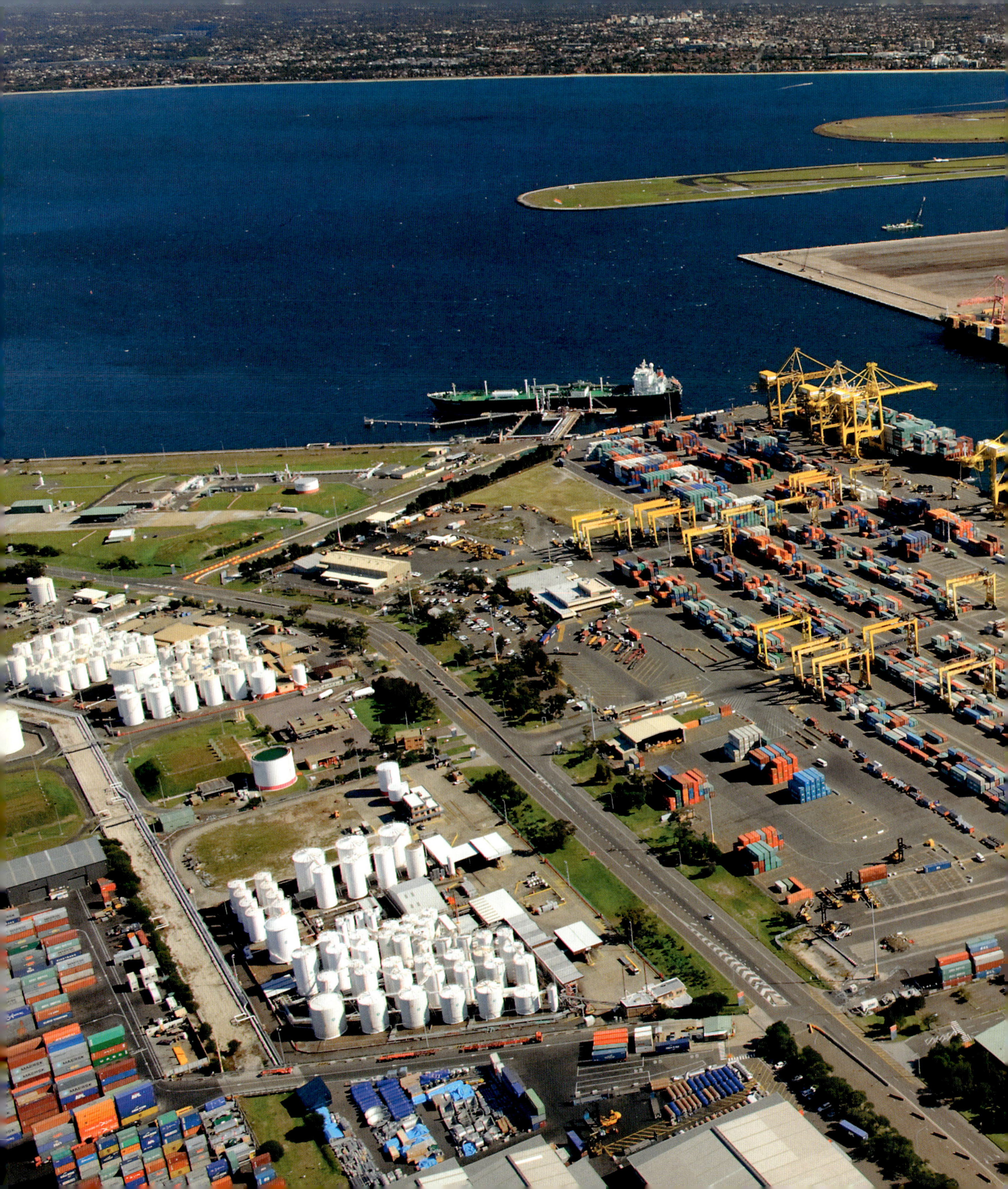

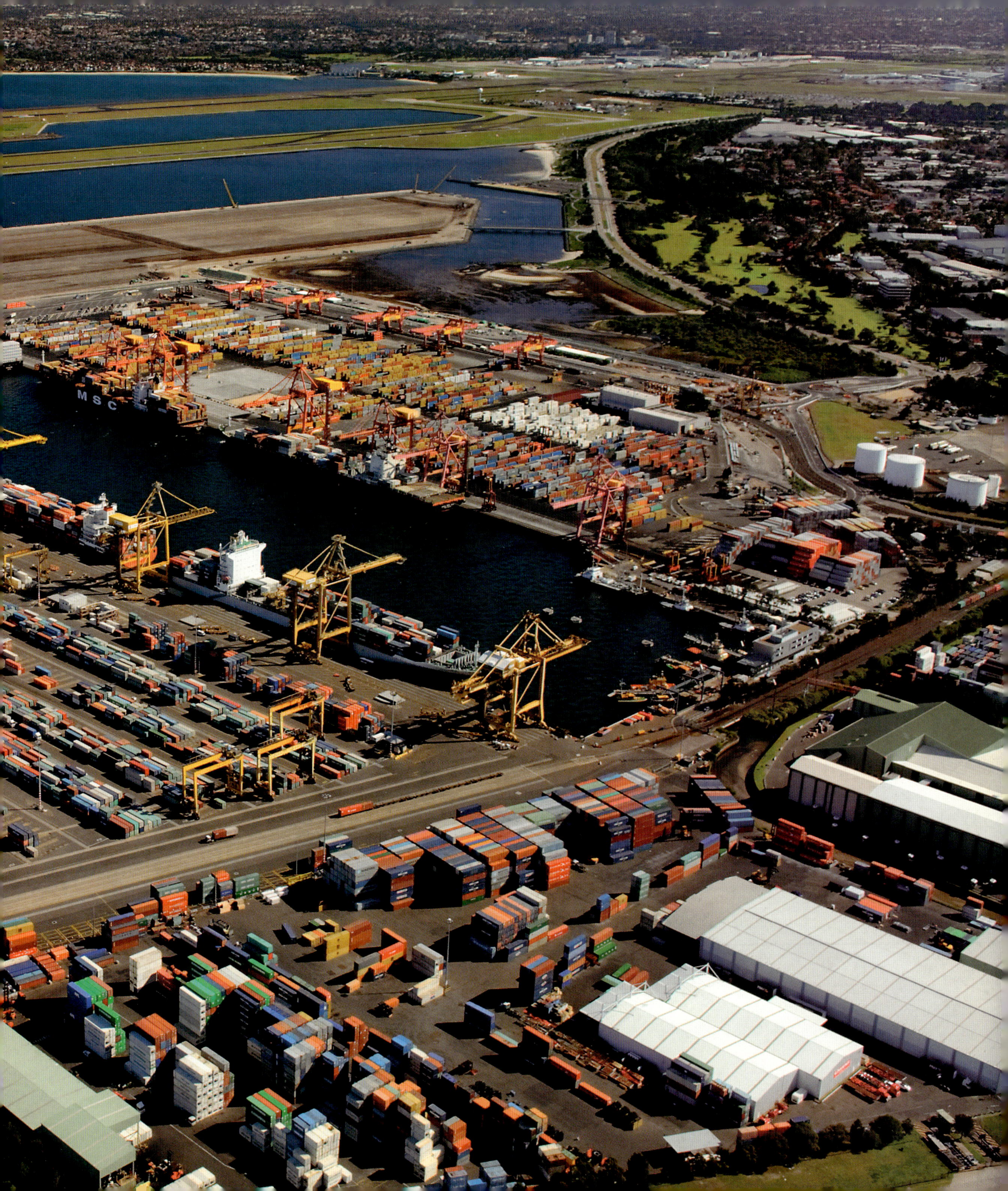

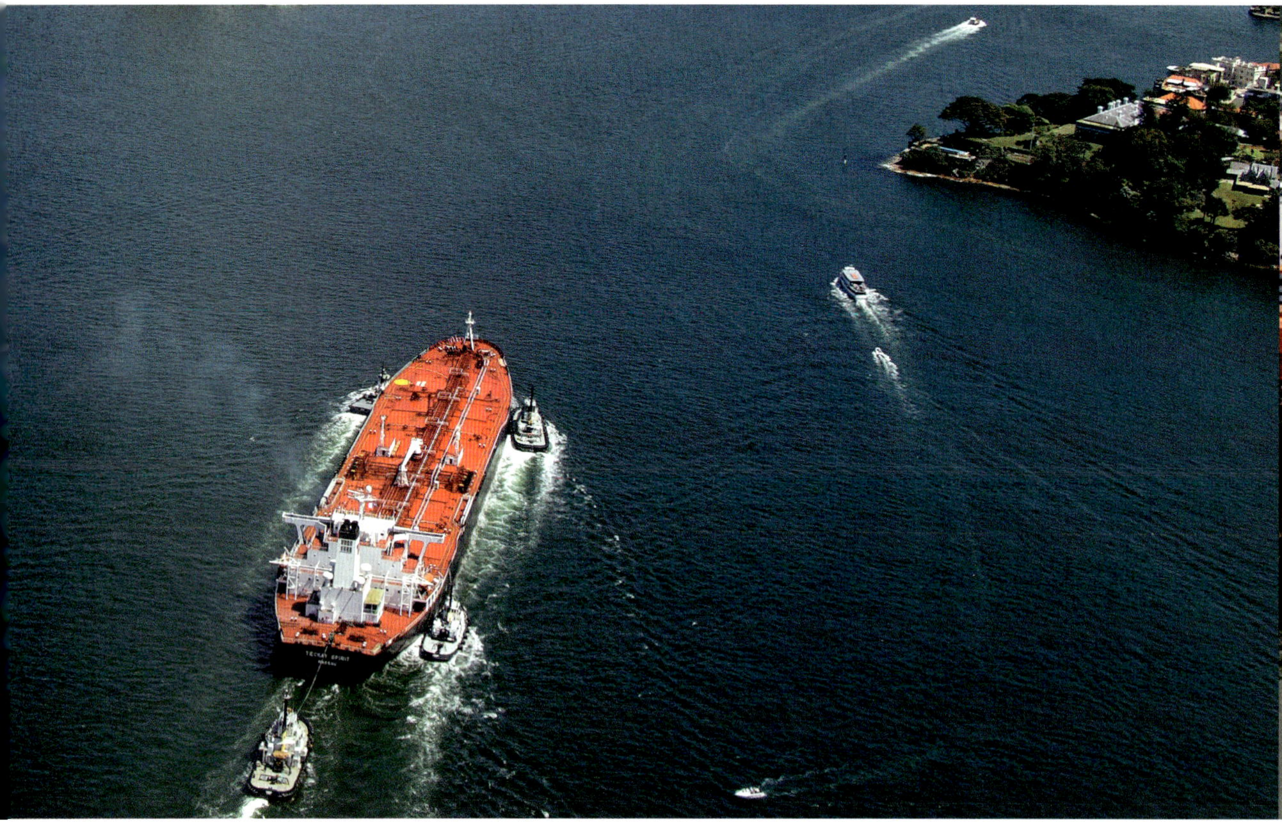

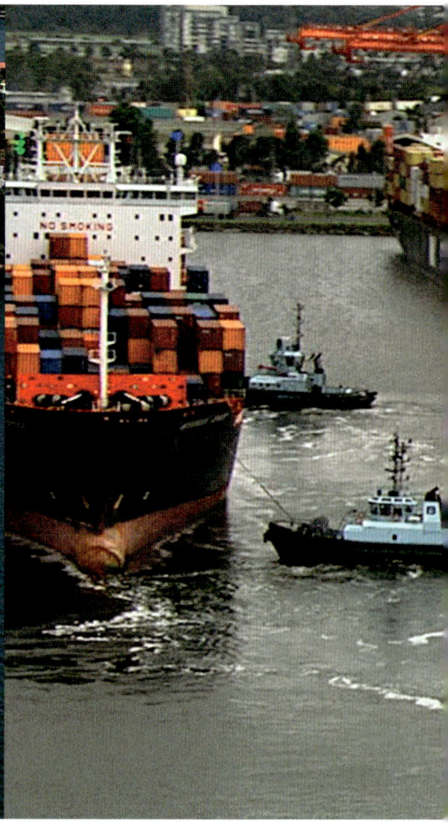

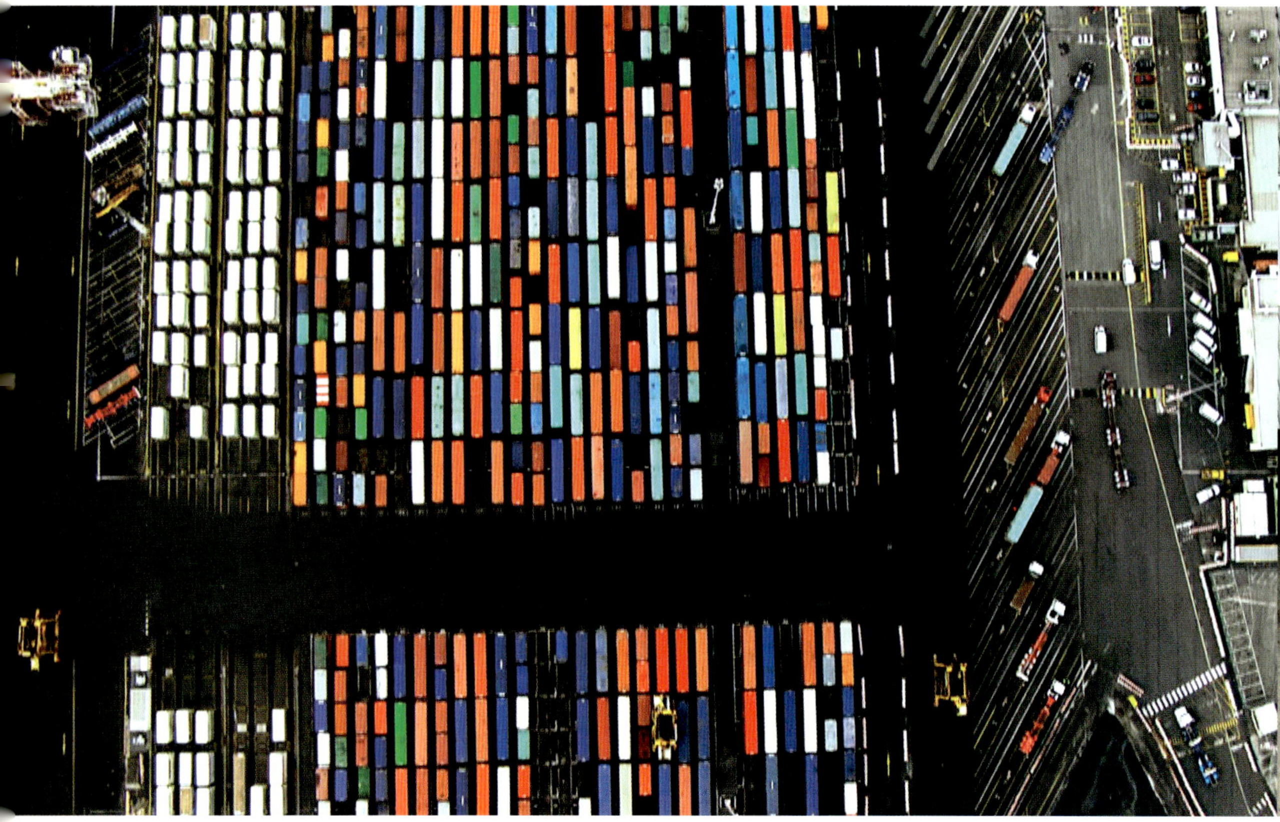

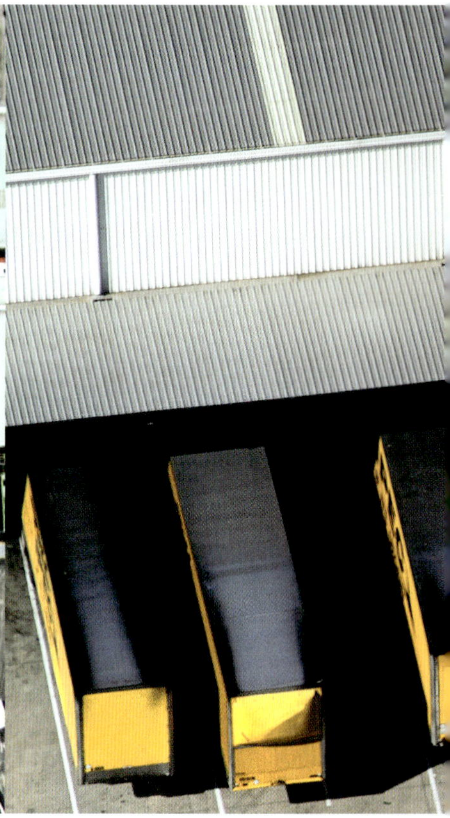

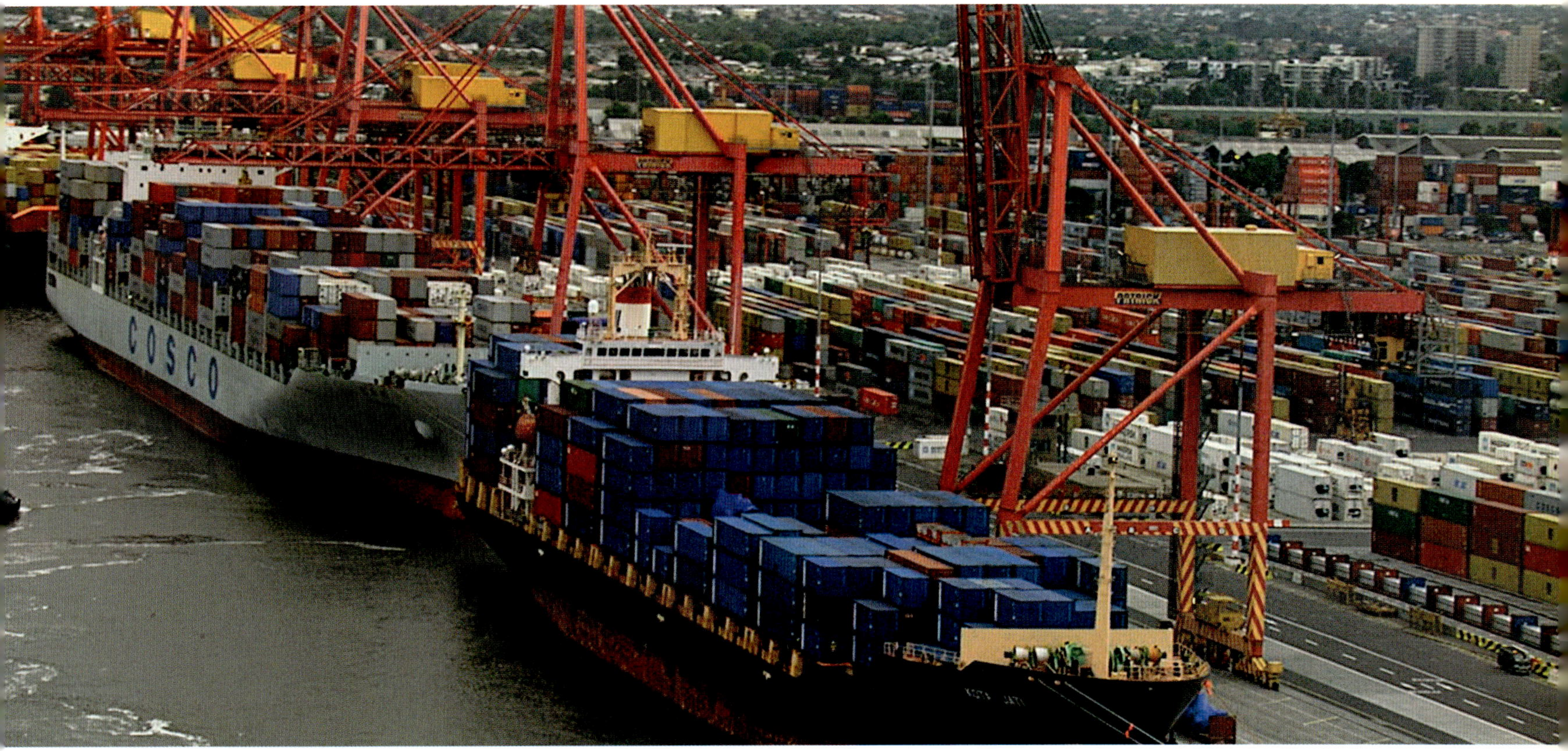

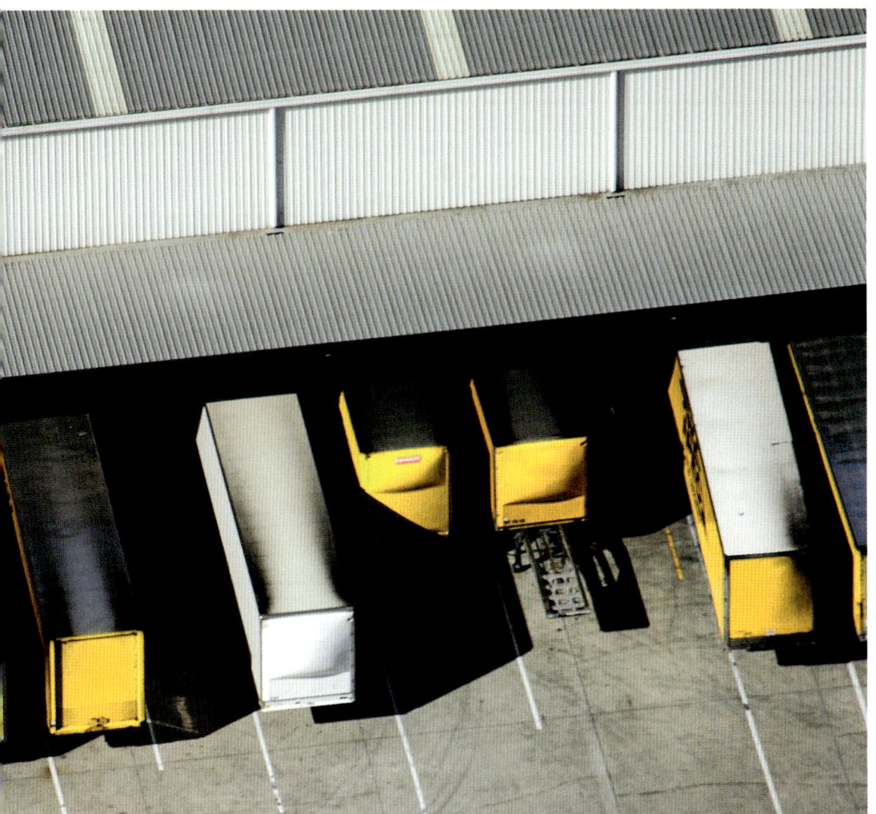

TOP LEFT: Four tugboats guide a crude oil tanker through Sydney Harbour. **TOP RIGHT AND BOTTOM LEFT:** The Port of Melbourne is Australia's largest and busiest container facility handling 87 million tonnes of cargo a year. **BOTTOM RIGHT:** Trucks in western Sydney play a vital part of the freight supply chain to help sustain urban sprawl.

LEFT: Perth's population has grown 26 per cent in the past ten years — the fastest of all capital cities. Greater Perth is home to more than 1.8 million people, which is almost 80 per cent of the state's population. **RIGHT:** A marina development at Port Coogee, south of Perth, is one of many infrastructure projects to support the growing population.

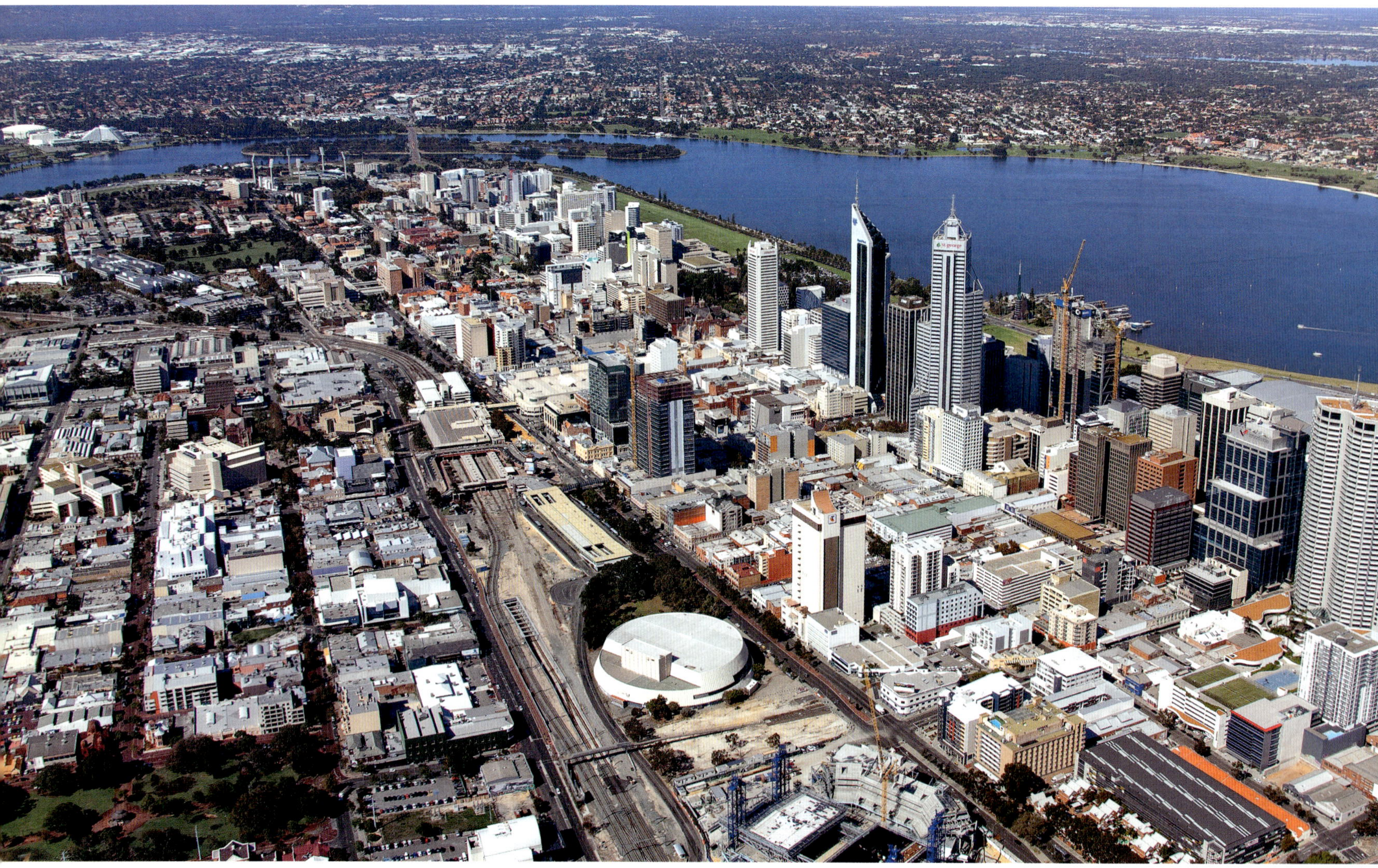

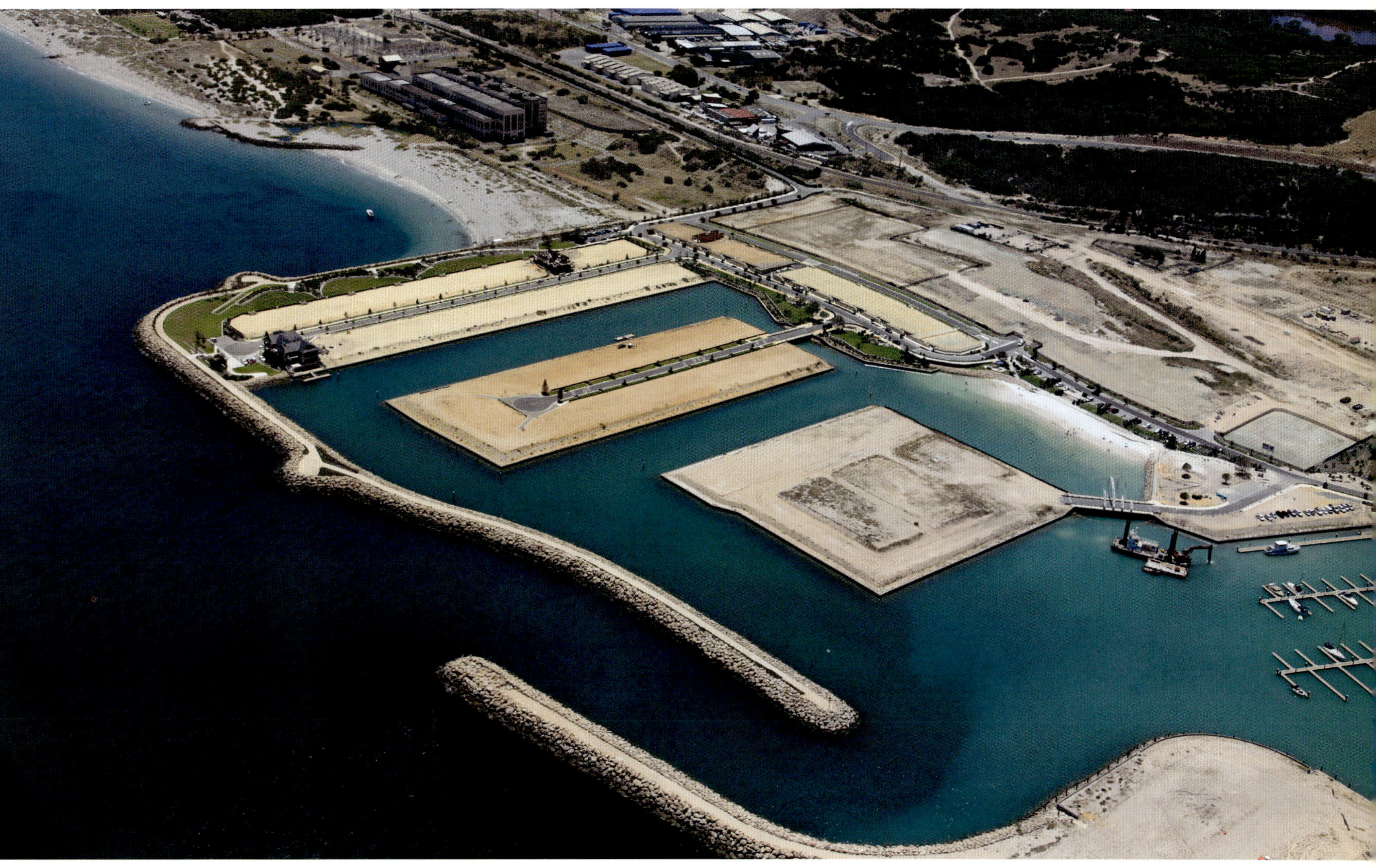

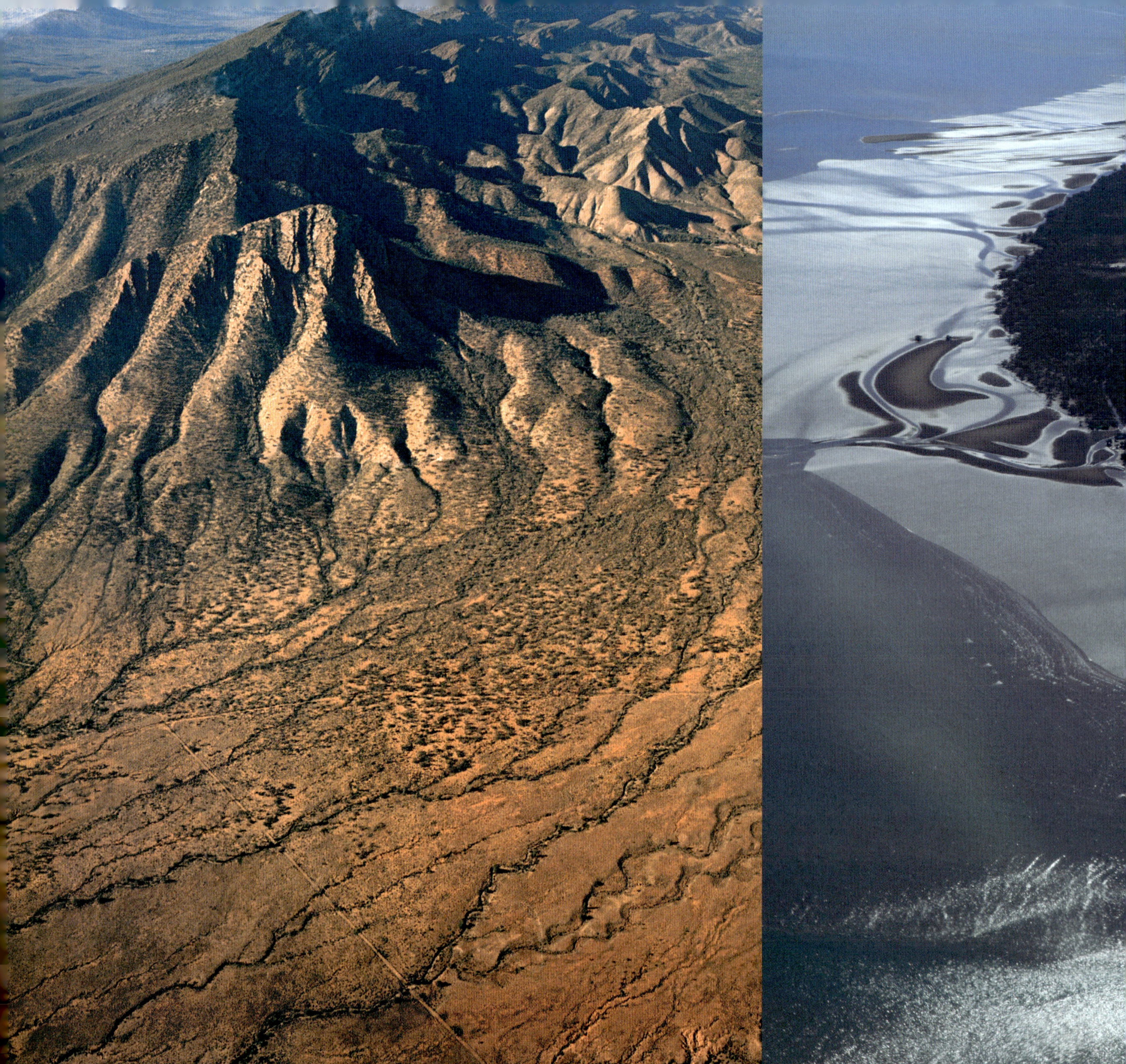

Australia's beautiful and remote wilderness, far from the madding crowd. **LEFT:** The Flinders Ranges in South Australia **MIDDLE:** The coastline near Dampier in the north of Western Australia. **RIGHT:** Ravines of the Oxley Wild Rivers National Park in New South Wales.

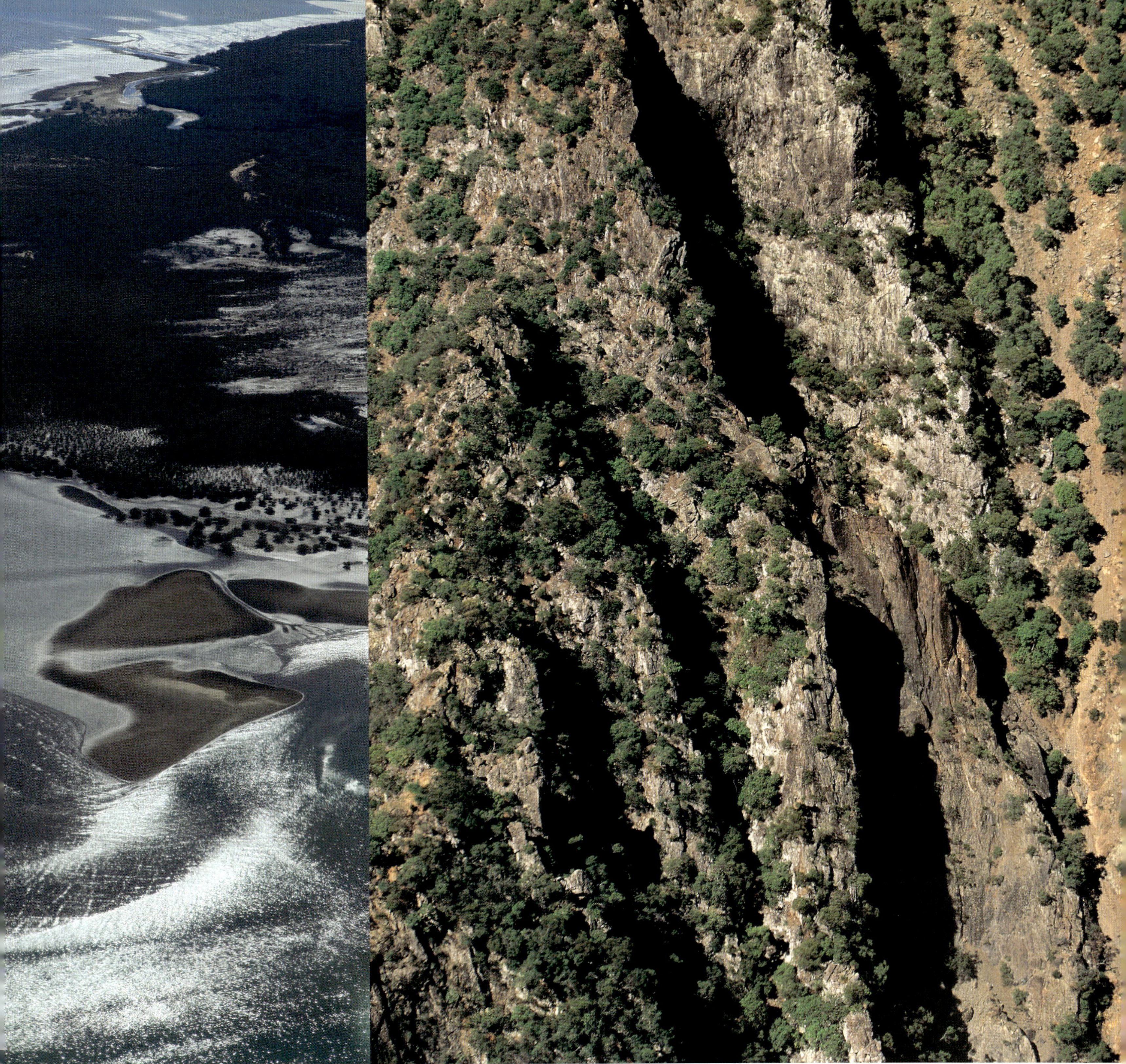

LEFT: Sydney's eastern suburbs have the highest population density in Australia with 8,900 people for every square kilometre. The population density for New South Wales, by contrast, is an average of nine people for every square kilometre. **RIGHT:** Lord Howe Island — a remnant of an extinct volcano — sits in the Tasman Sea and is home to about 350 people.

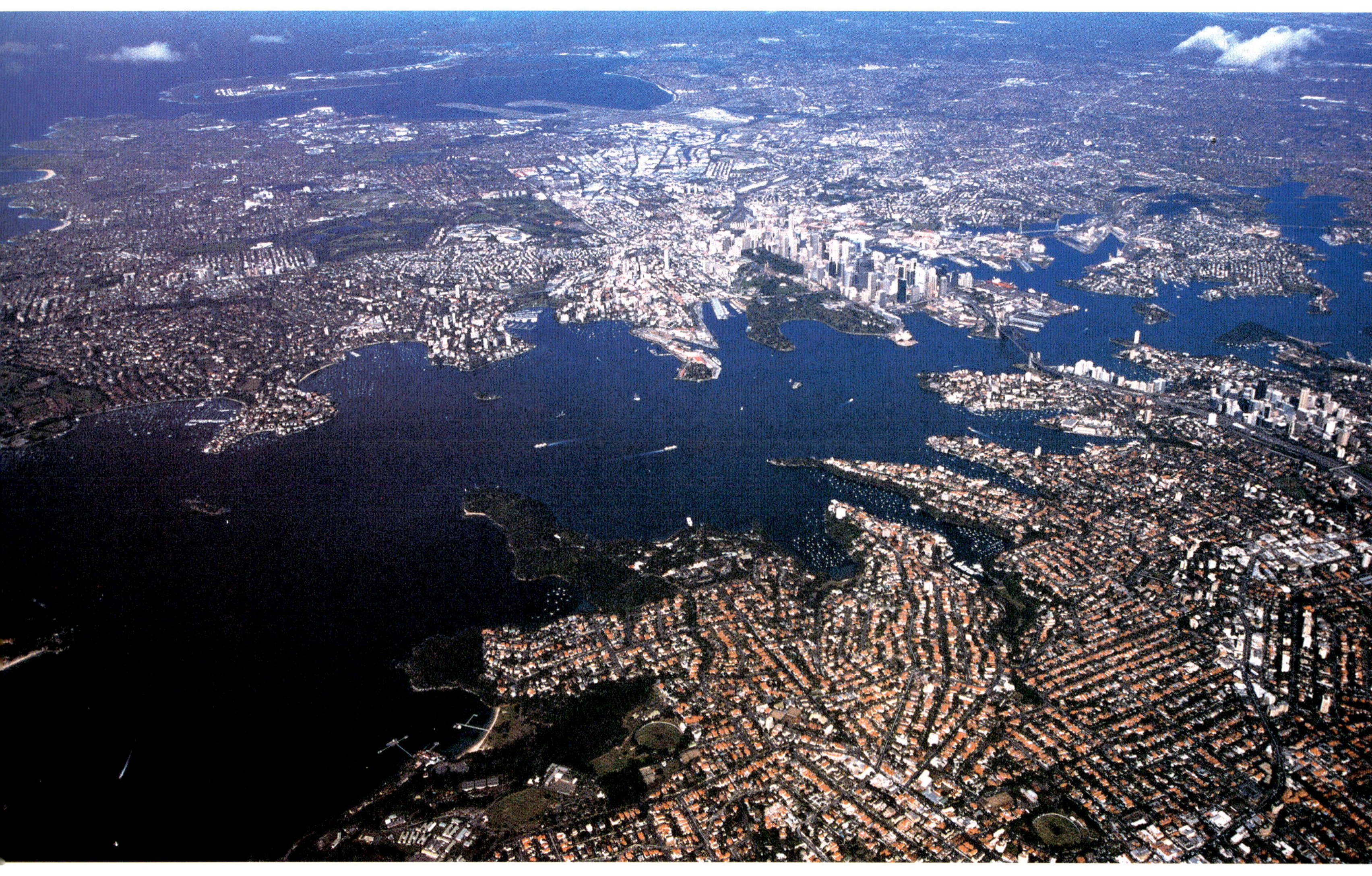

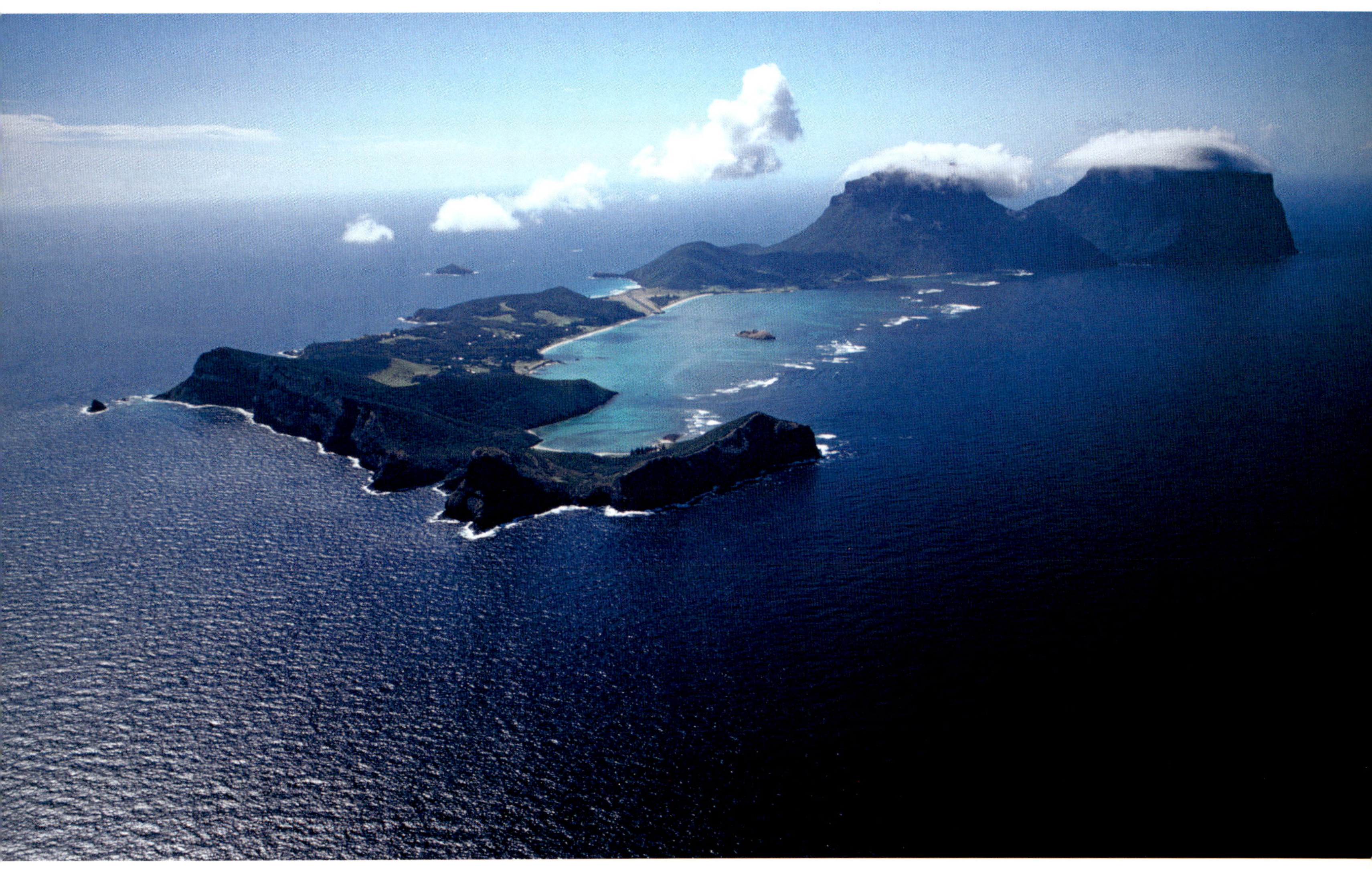

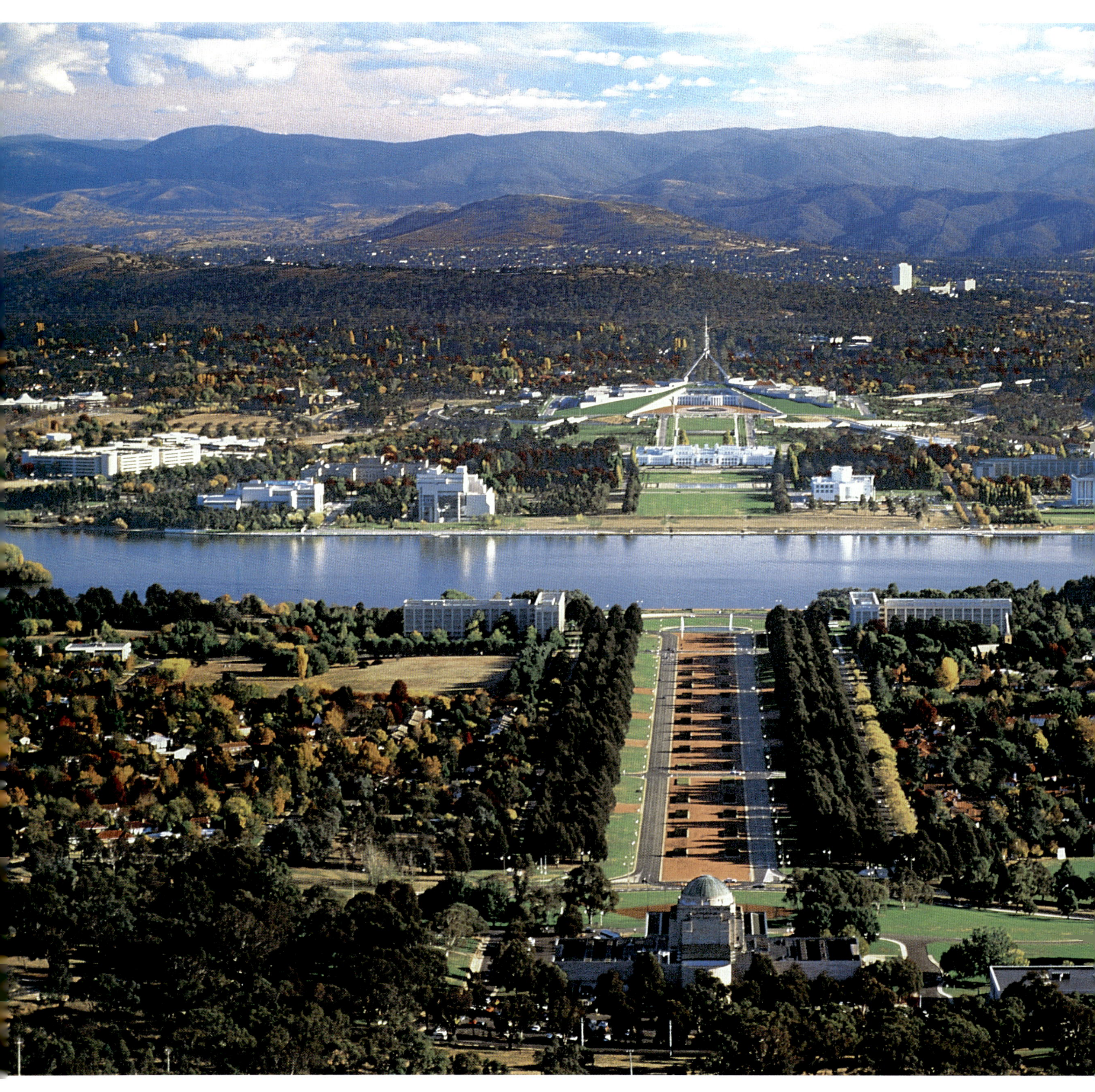

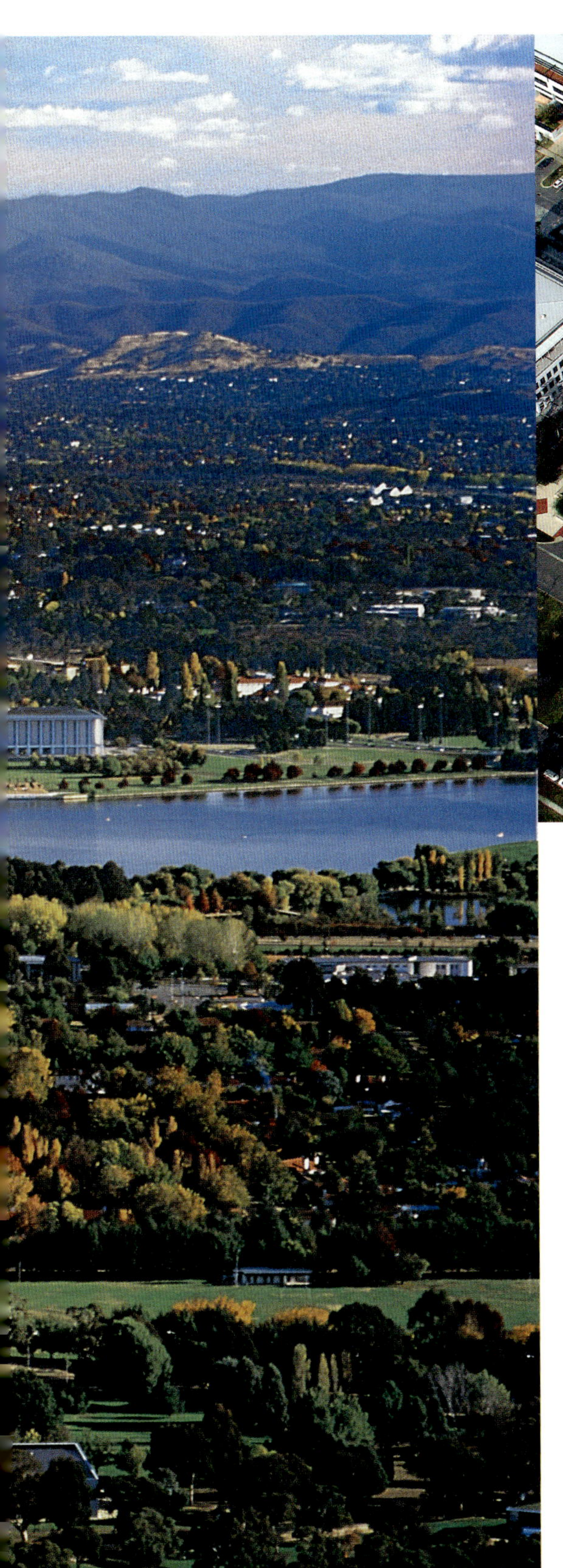

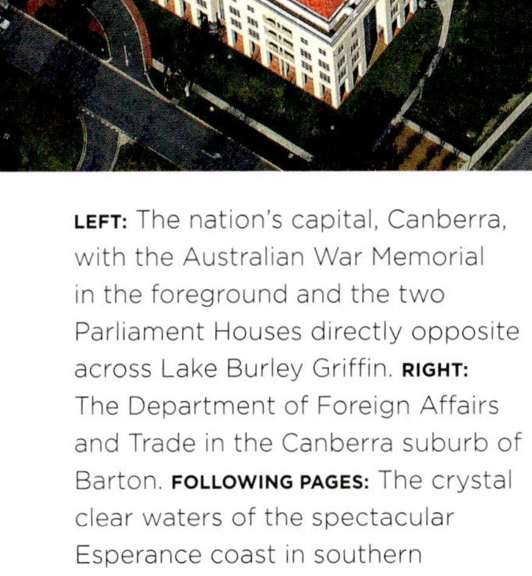

LEFT: The nation's capital, Canberra, with the Australian War Memorial in the foreground and the two Parliament Houses directly opposite across Lake Burley Griffin. **RIGHT:** The Department of Foreign Affairs and Trade in the Canberra suburb of Barton. **FOLLOWING PAGES:** The crystal clear waters of the spectacular Esperance coast in southern Western Australia.

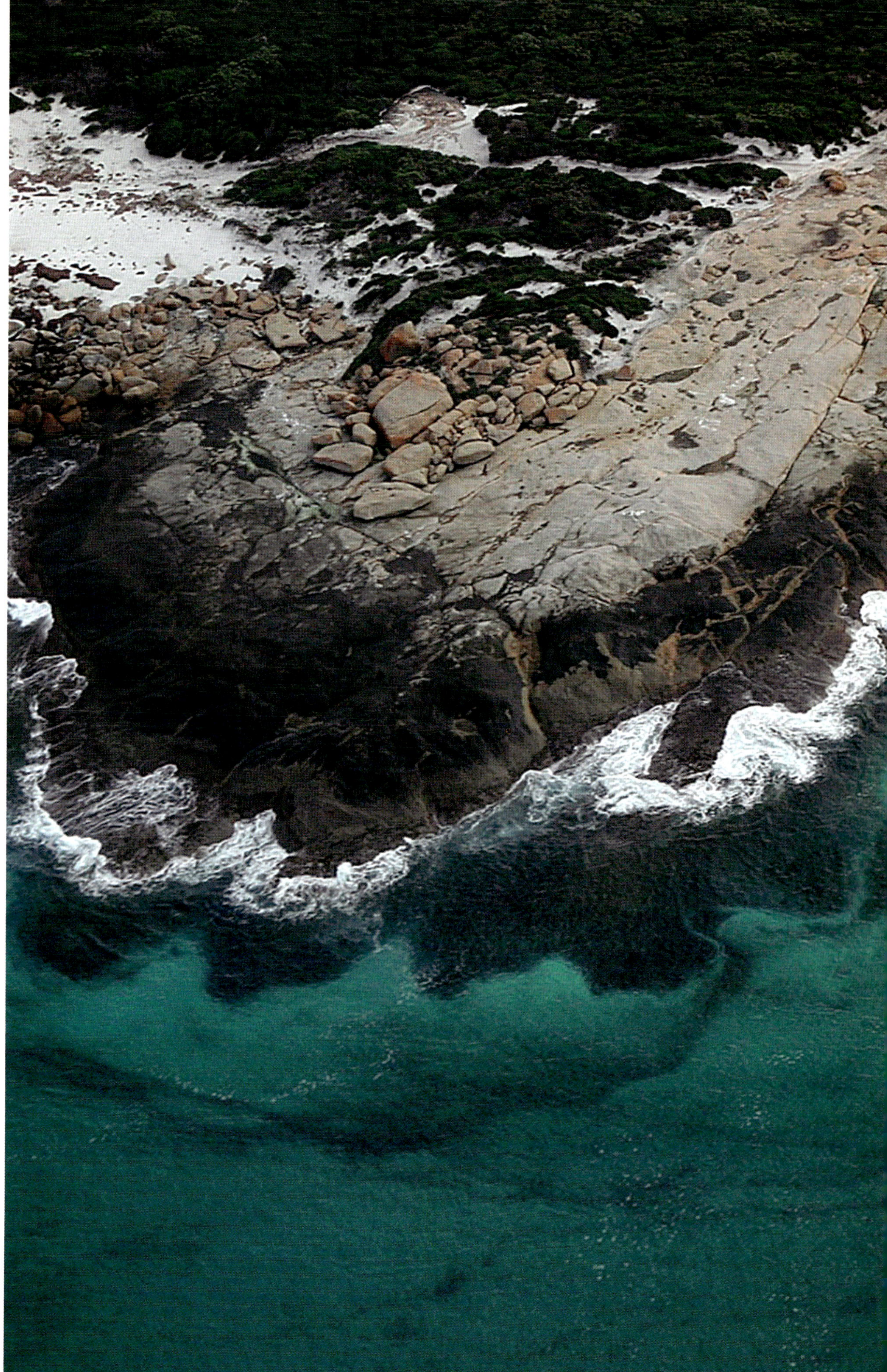

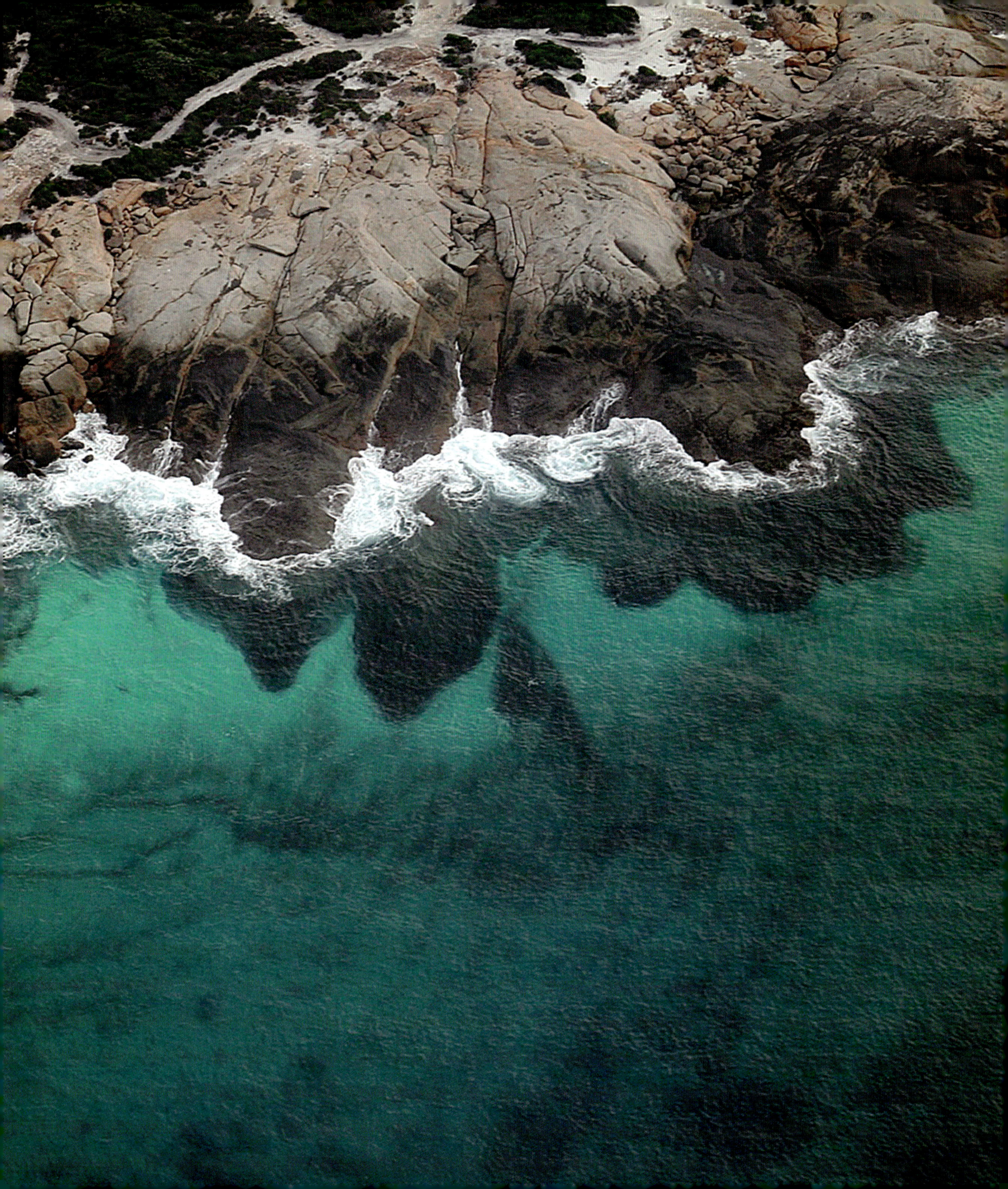

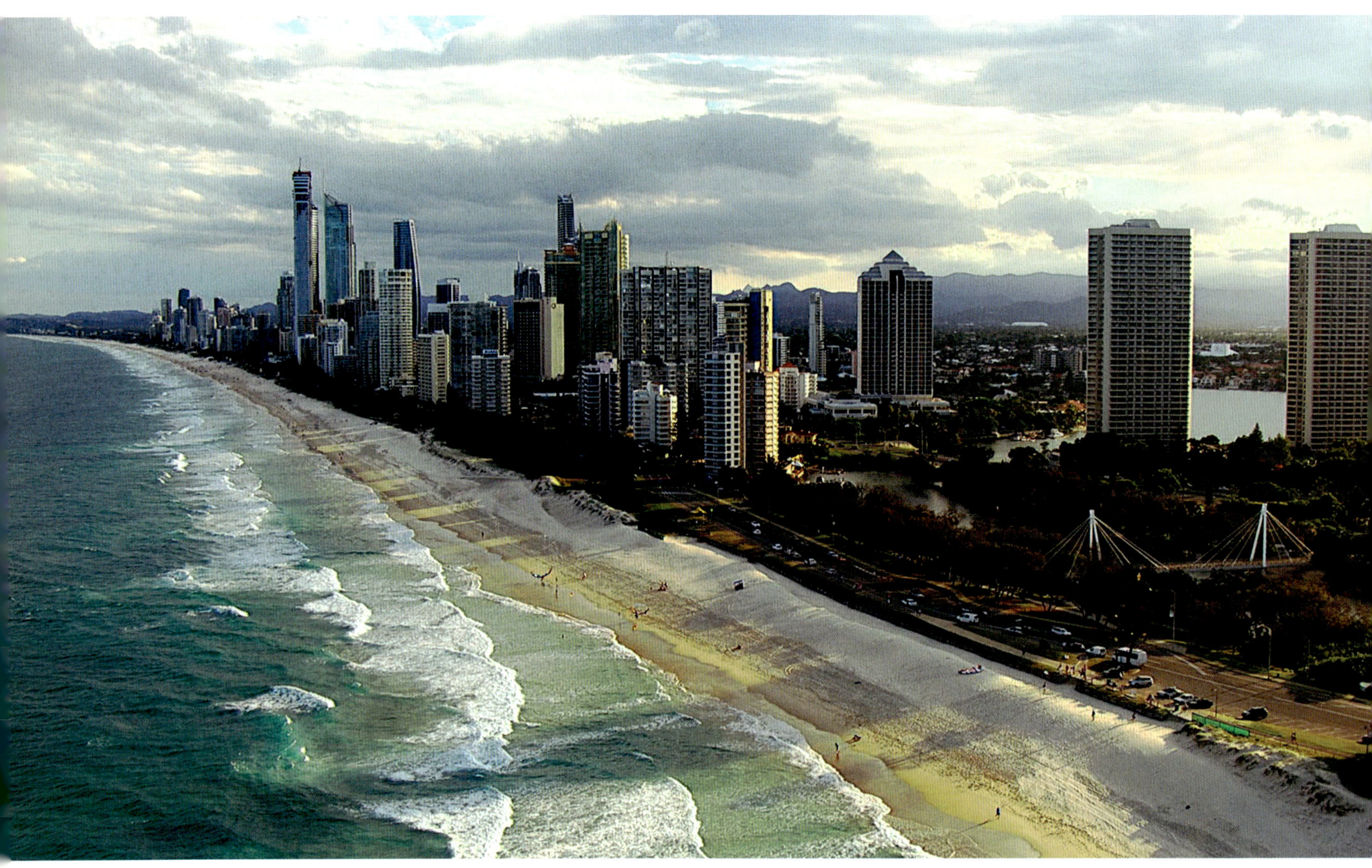

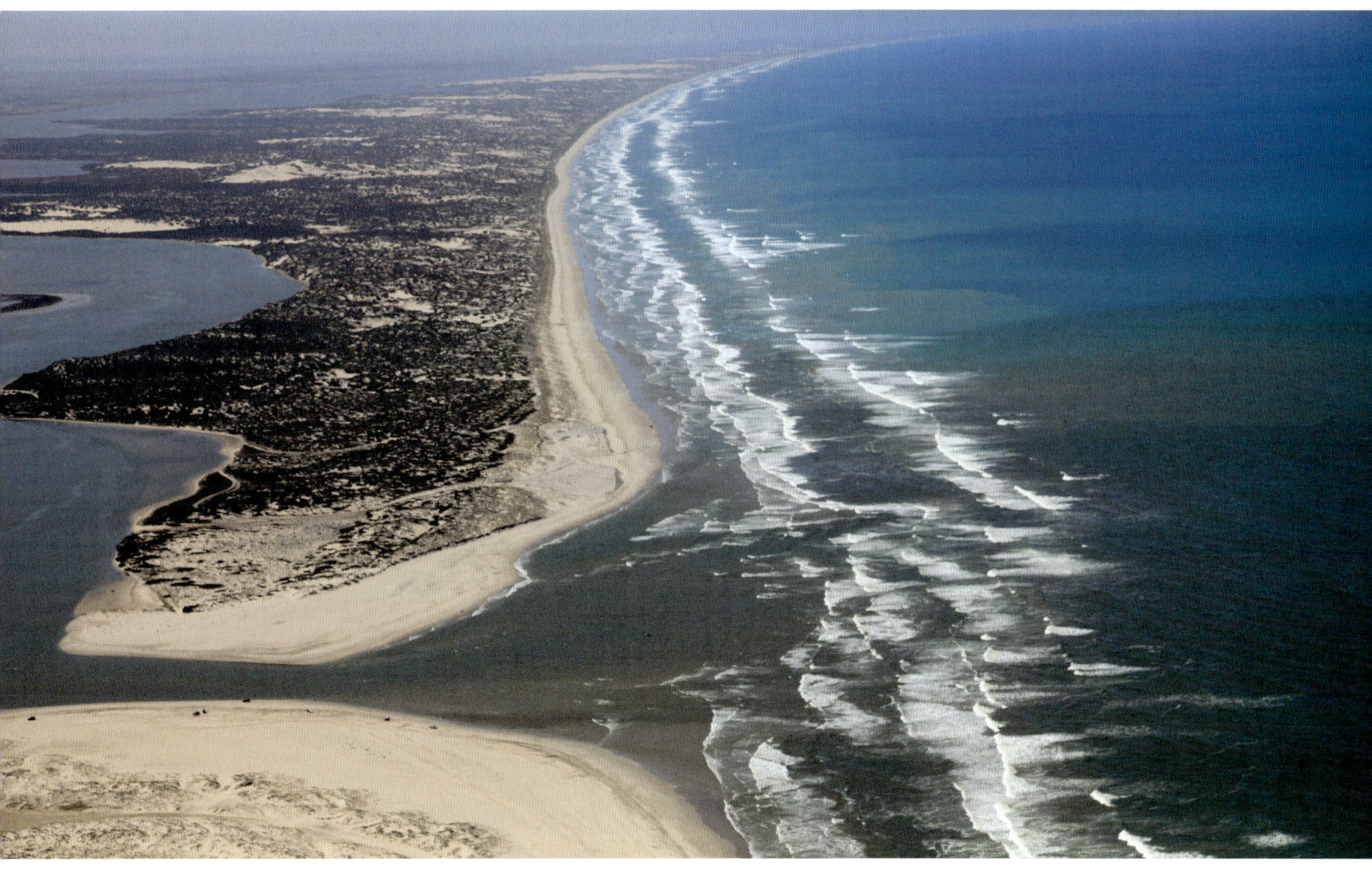

Australia is blessed with 11,000 beaches. **LEFT:** The Gold Coast today hides a protective seawall which is built the length of the beach and covered with sand and dunes. **RIGHT:** The mouth of the Murray — Australia's longest river at 2,375 kilometres — empties into the Great Australian Bight in South Australia.

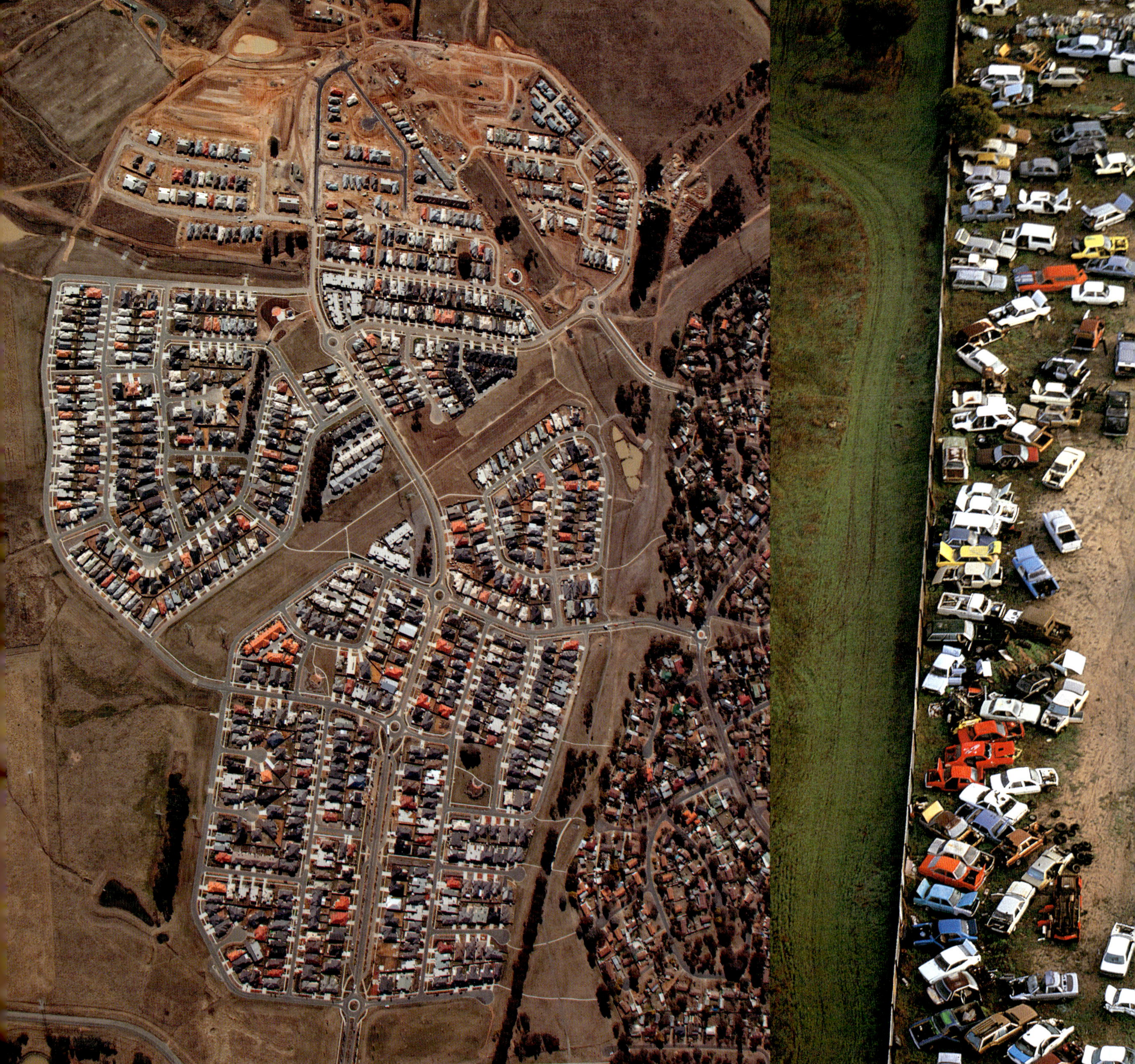

LEFT: A new development in the outer suburb of Macgregor in Canberra. **MIDDLE:** A wrecking yard is the final resting place for Australia's obsession with the motor vehicle. **RIGHT:** The cemetery in the town of Northam, Western Australia.

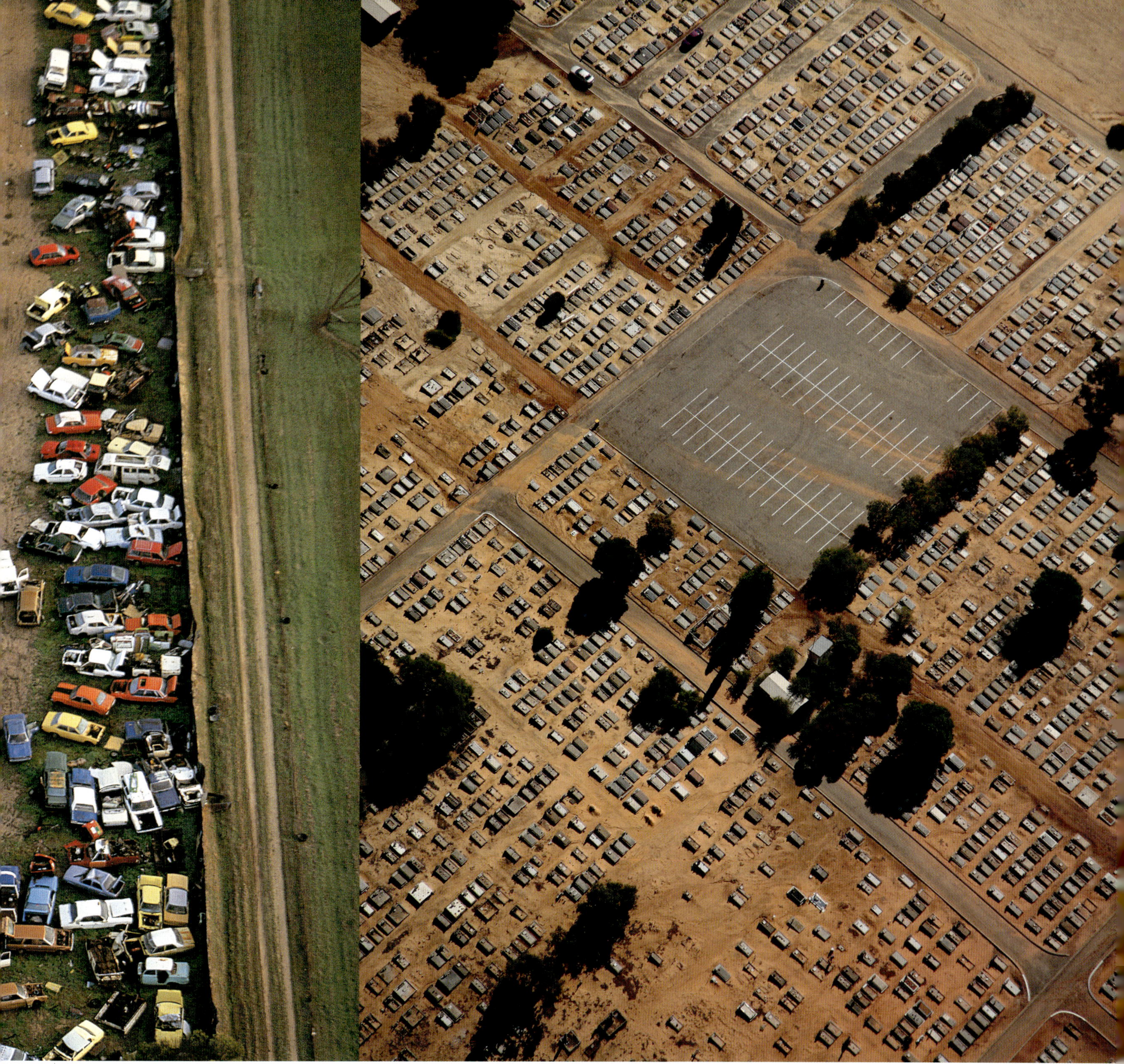

FOLLOWING PAGE LEFT: The shops and sprawl of suburban Arundel on the crowded Gold Coast hinterland. **FOLLOWING PAGE RIGHT:** The East Alligator River and the wide-open flood plains of Arnhem Land.

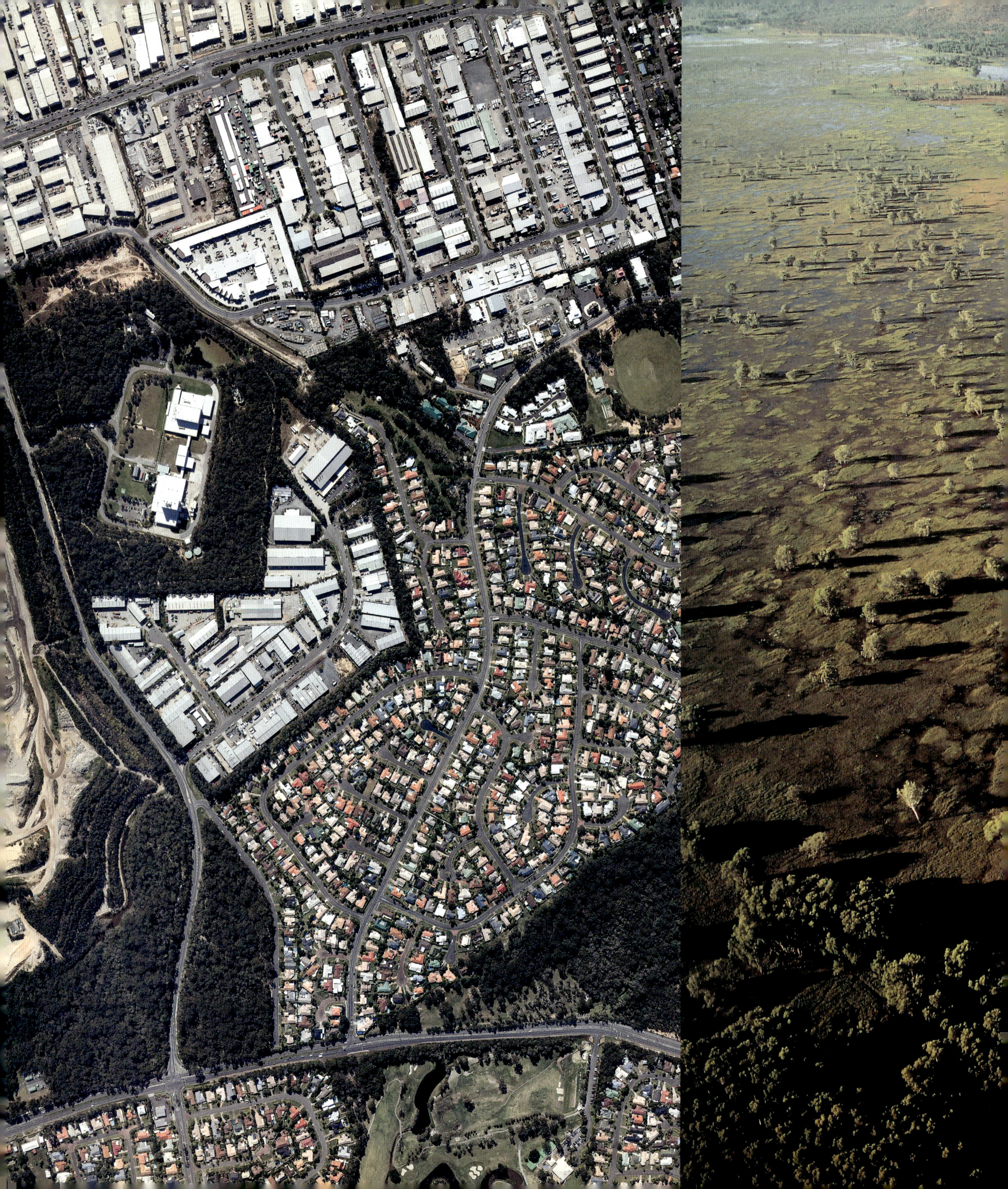

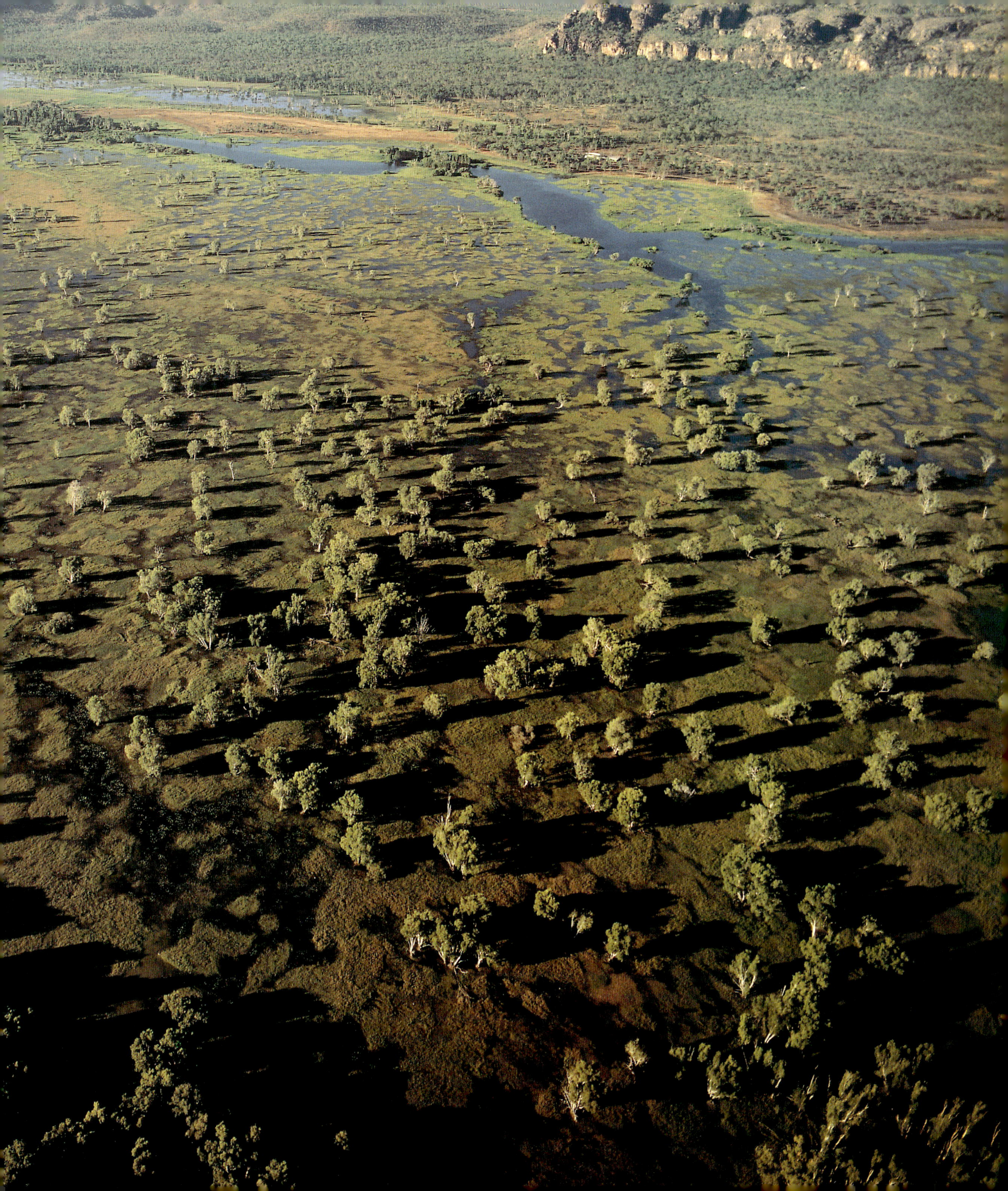

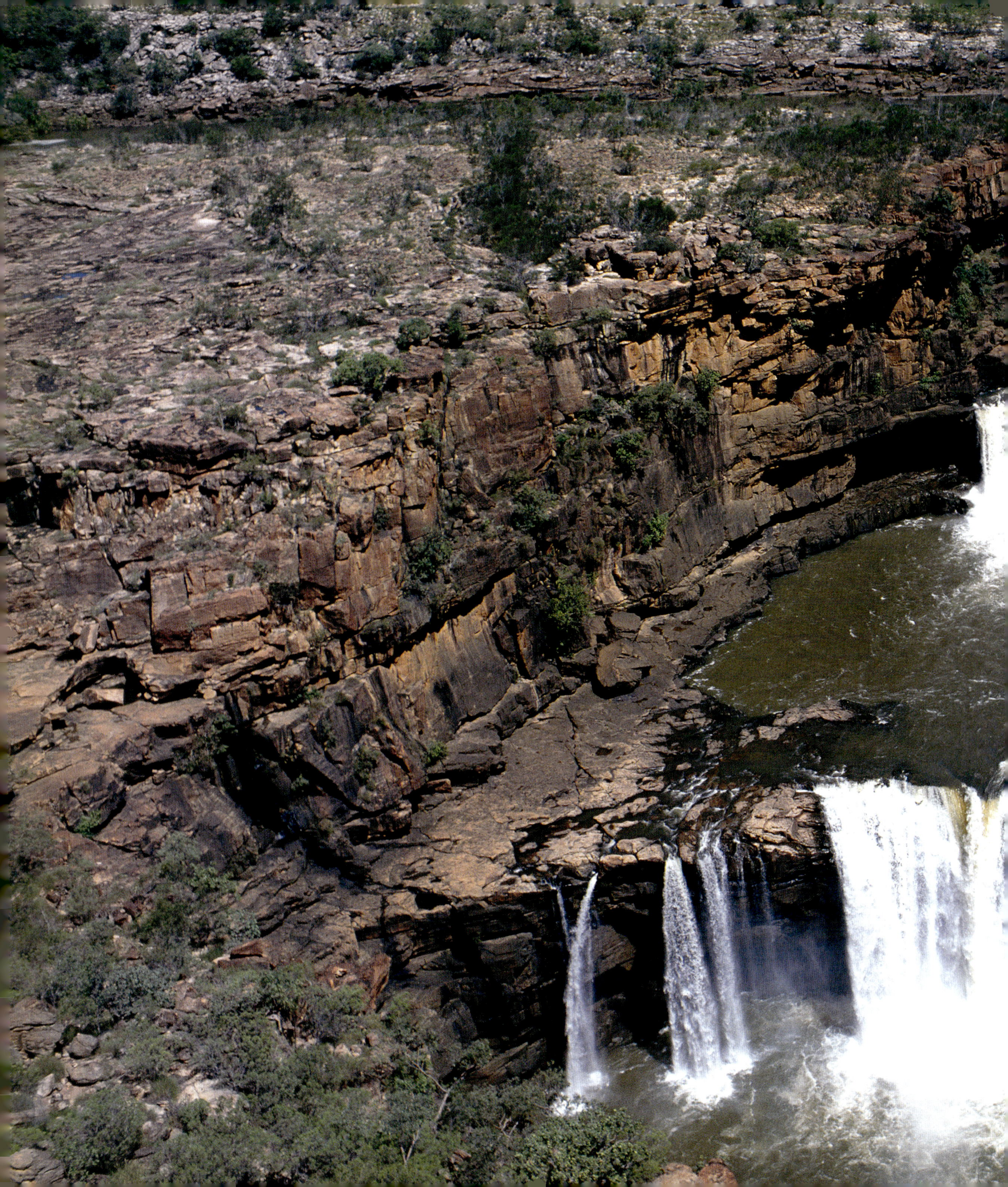

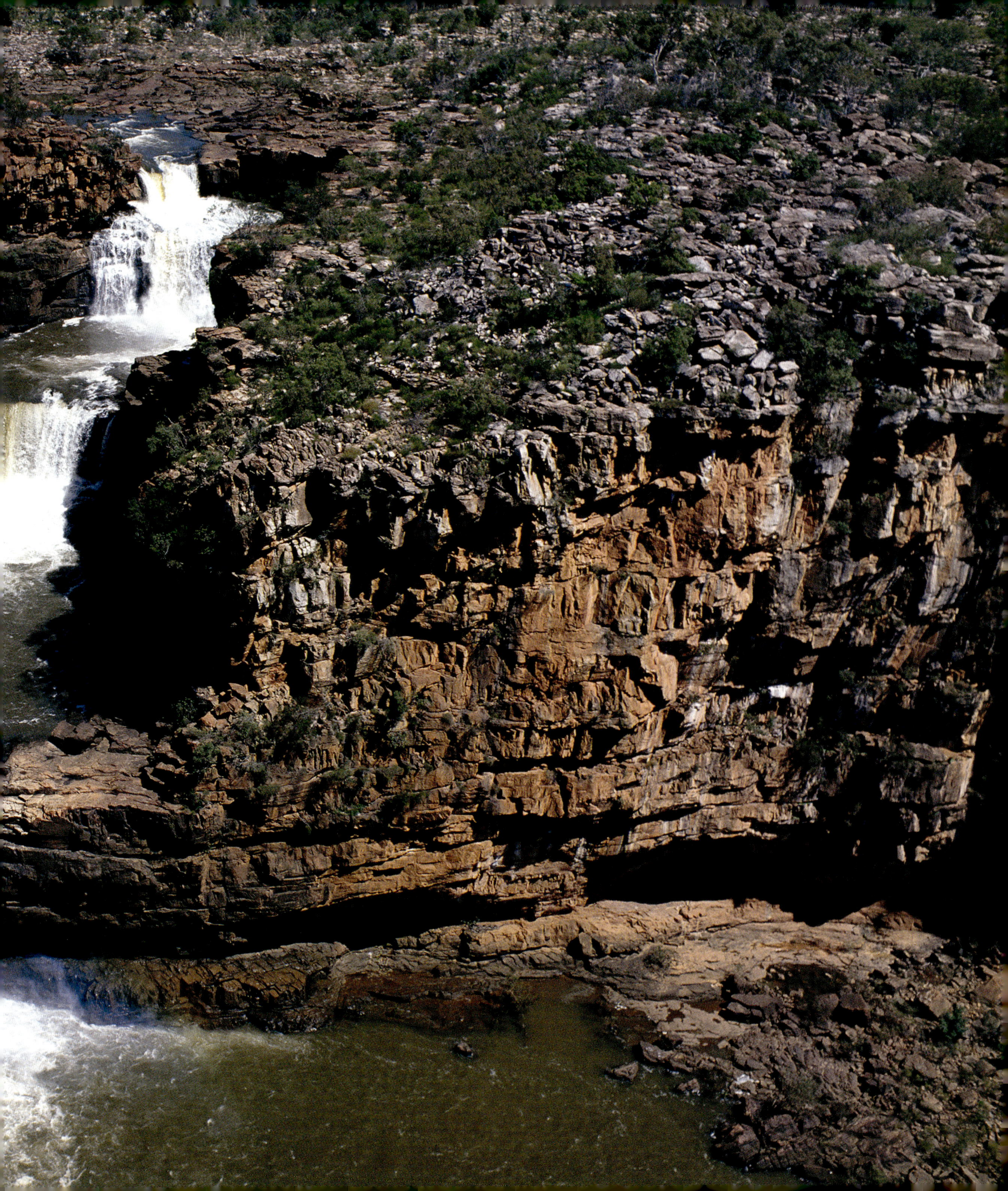

PREVIOUS PAGES: The spectacular Mitchell Falls in the Mitchell River National Park in the remote Kimberley region of Western Australia is a four-tier waterfall. The national park covers 115,300 hectares.

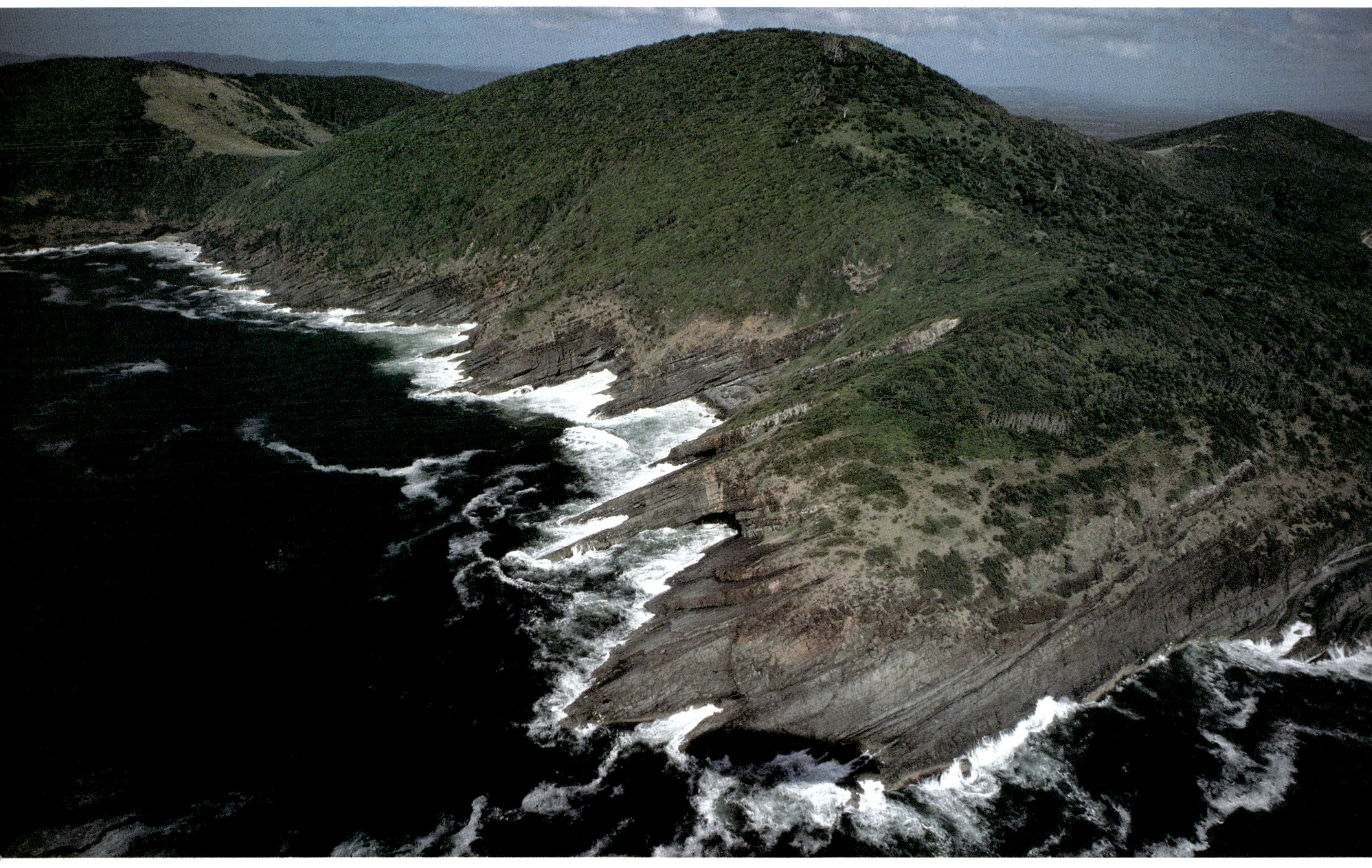

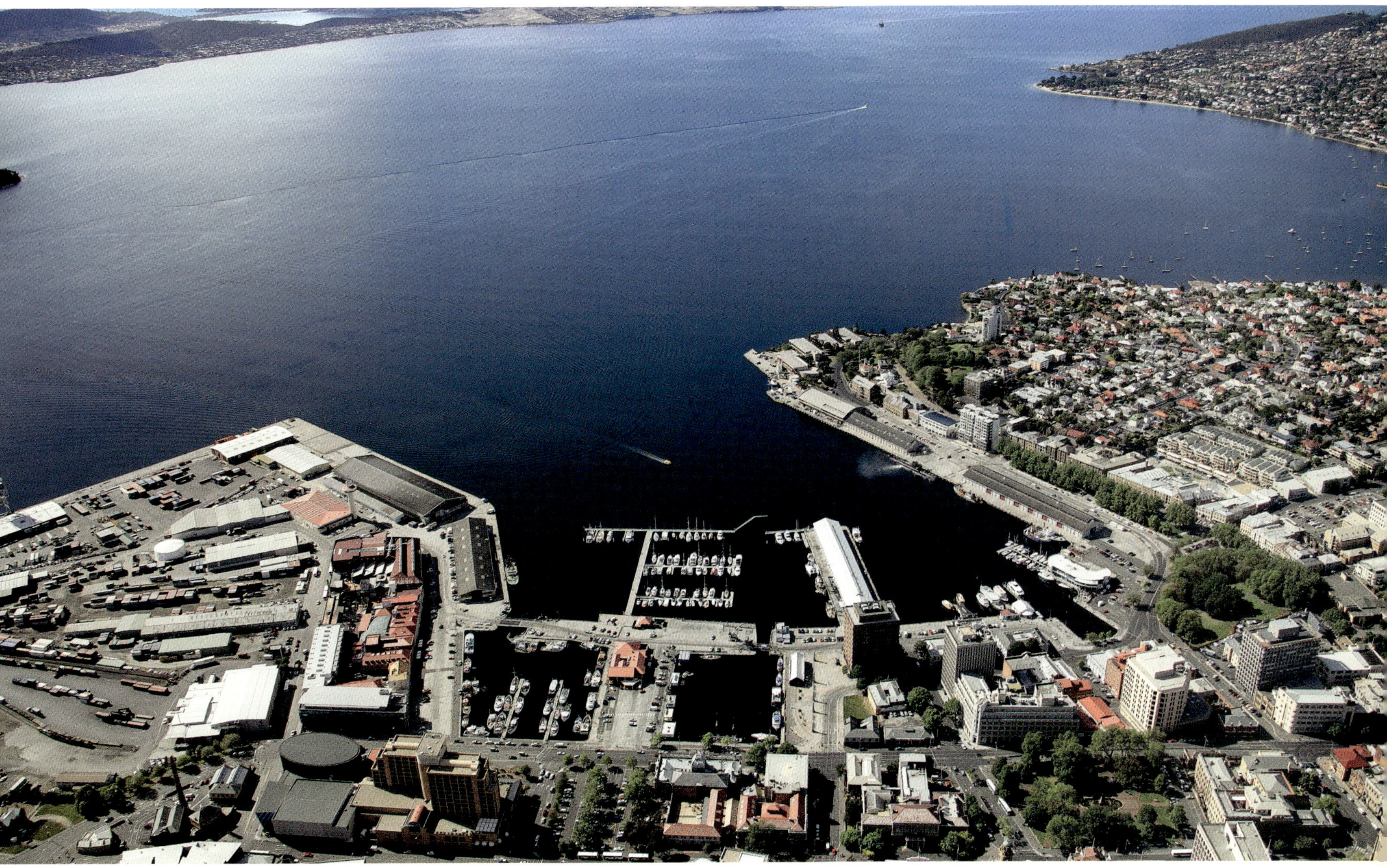

LEFT: A headland forms part of the Myall Lakes National Park near Newcastle on the east coast of New South Wales — a popular playground. **RIGHT:** The Derwent River, Sullivans Cove and the city of Hobart. The Tasmanian capital is home to 212,000 people with 160 people for every square kilometre — the lowest of any state capital city. **FOLLOWING PAGES:** Federation Peak in the Southwest National Park in Tasmania reaches a height of 1,224 metres. The park covers more than 600,000 square metres and is the state's largest national park.

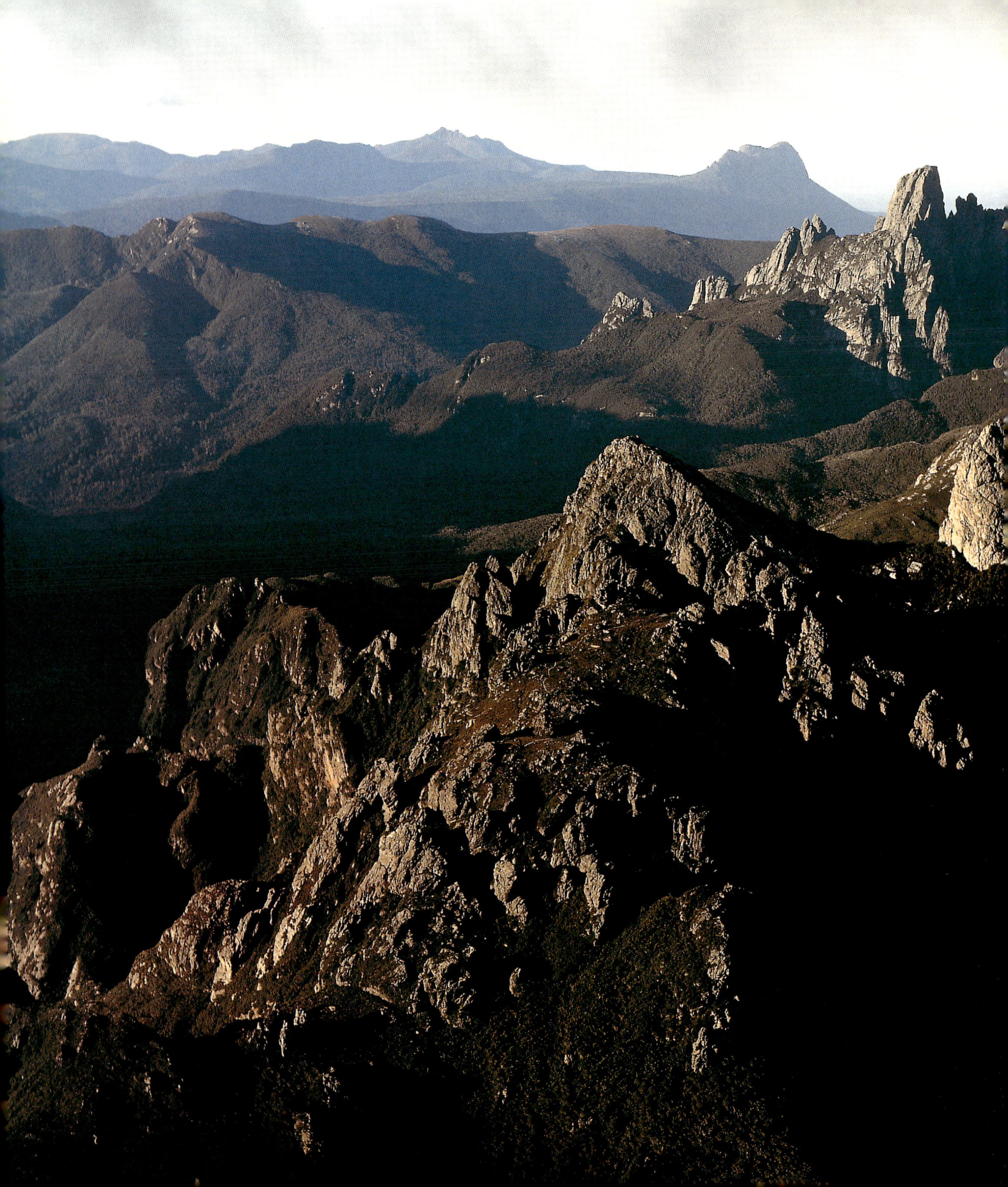

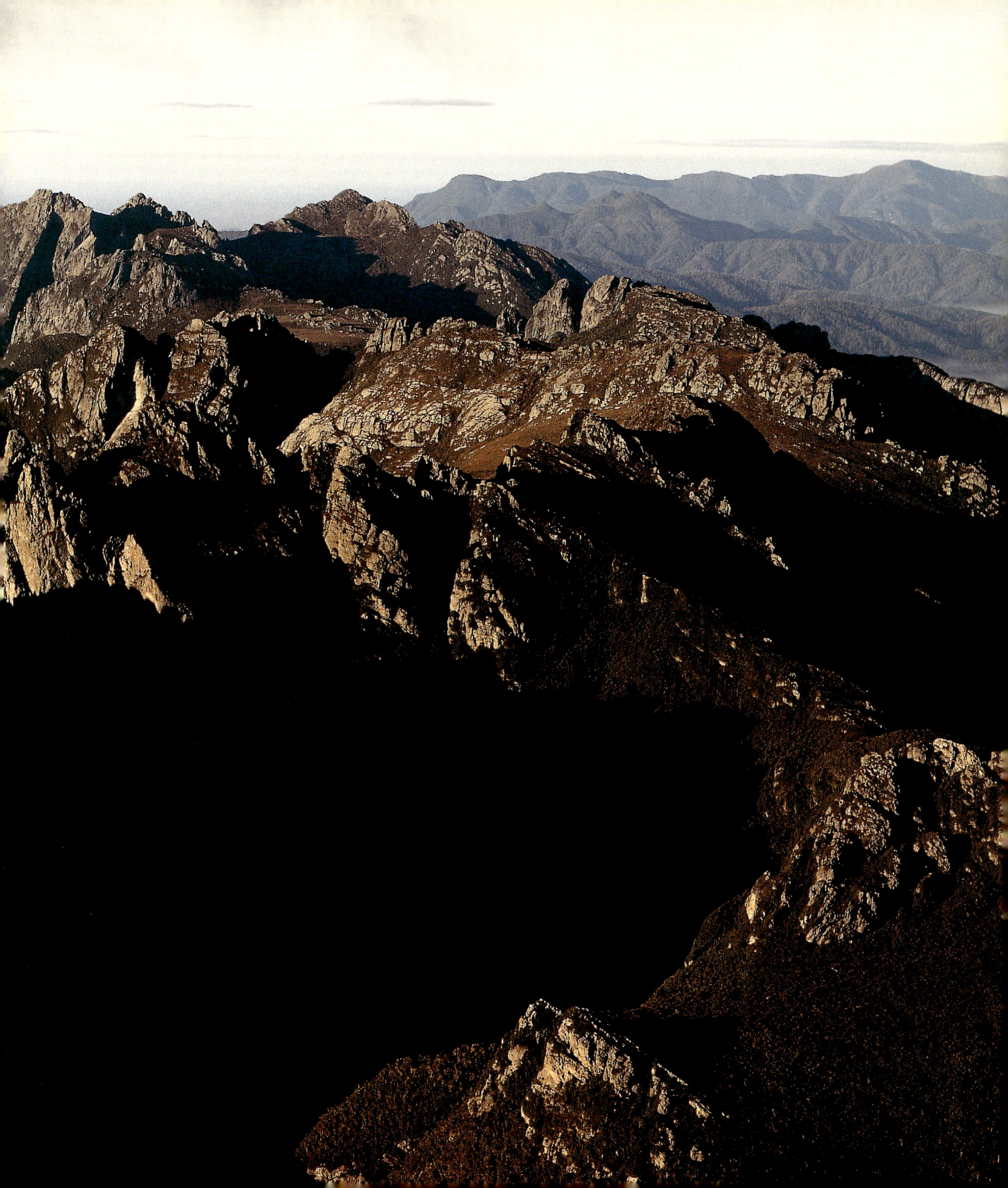

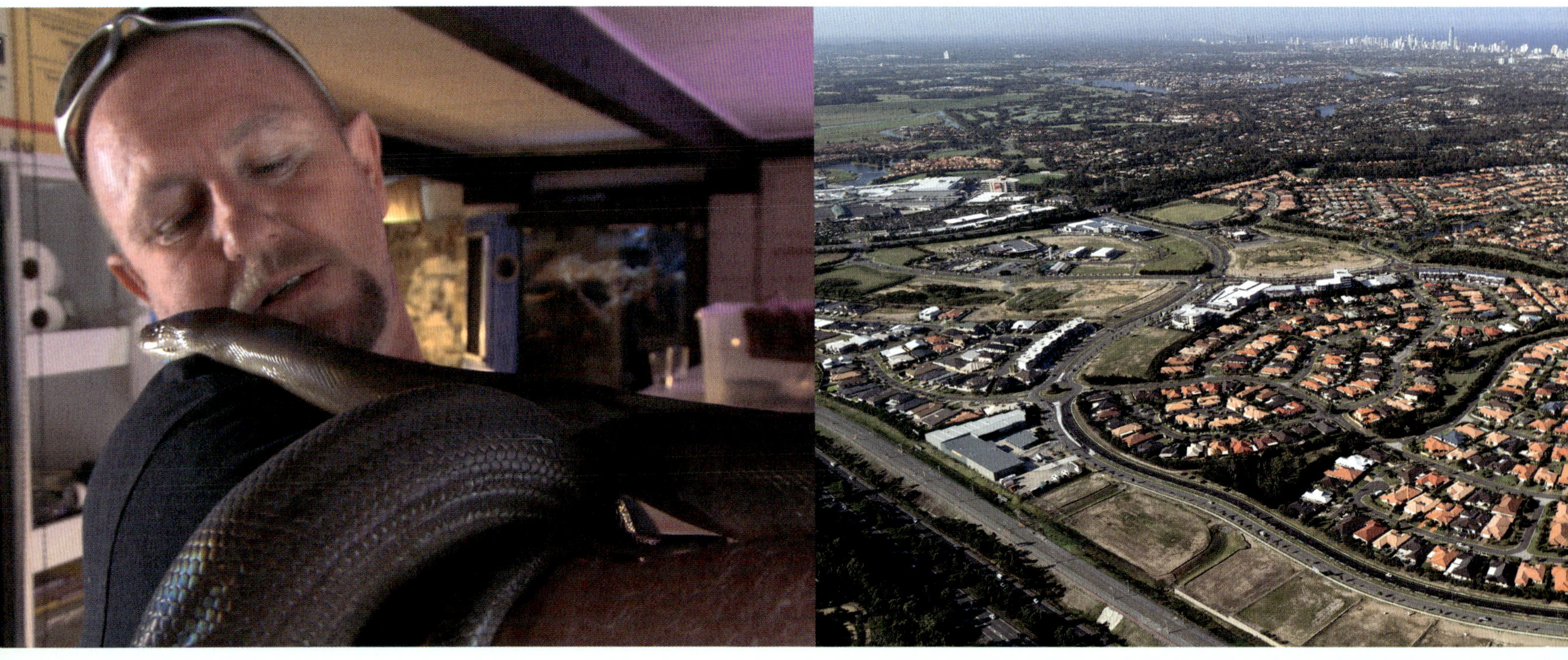

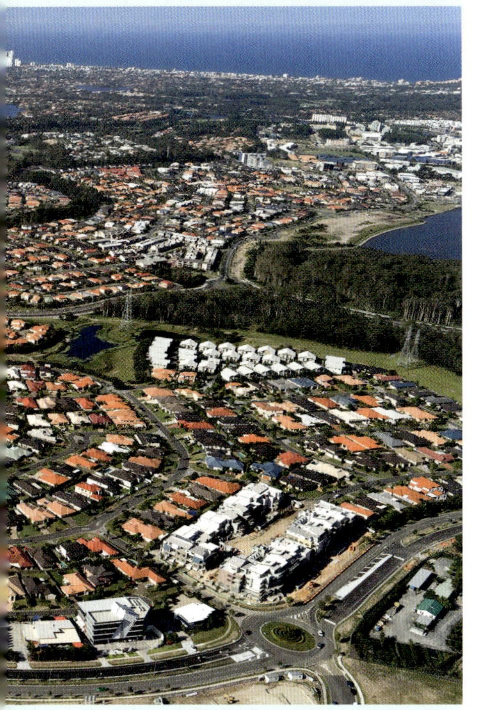

WHEN URBAN SPRAWL BITES BACK

TONY HARRISON IS a man who deals with trouble in paradise. As an urban snake catcher on the Gold Coast, Harrison helps protect more than half a million people against the sometimes unintended consequences of unbridled sprawl. In summer, Harrison receives up to 15 calls a day to remove snakes from buildings. 'The numbers would astound people,' says Harrison. 'It's a giant snake pit and everyone is building houses in it.'

Today Harrison pulls up his four-wheel drive at a residence where the owner greets him at the door. 'Every street has snakes,' Harrison says. There are 21 species of snakes on the Gold Coast. And indeed, there's one in the bathroom. 'Okay, yep, that is an eastern brown,' says Harrison. More Australians have been killed by eastern browns than by any other snake. 'It's the second most venomous snake on the planet,' he says. 'One drop can kill sixteen healthy adults.'

Venomous snakes have already landed Harrison in hospital four times. 'One bit me through the bag,' he recalls. 'It only took me ten minutes to get to hospital. An hour and a half later I started to feel the symptoms, three minutes after that I was unconscious. Four hours after that I woke up with doctors shaking their heads going "that was very close".'

At the house, Harrison must move quietly around the snake and then quickly lift it by the tail before gently manoeuvering and lowering it into a sack. He will then drive to the fringe of the city to release the reptile in the bush. It is a drive that gets longer all the time. 'We bulldoze the bush,' says Harrison as he heads out of town. 'Humans come along with their DC-9s. Habitat destruction, human encroachment — reptiles are pushed out of their normal land into our back yard.'

In recent years, Harrison has seen an alarming increase in requests for his services. And we only have ourselves to blame. Our suburban march seems unstoppable. 'Snakes don't sit down and have a few bourbons with their mates and say, "Let's go terrorising humans",' Harrison says while releasing the eastern brown. 'They never have those thoughts ... to wreak havoc on us. It's the other way around.'

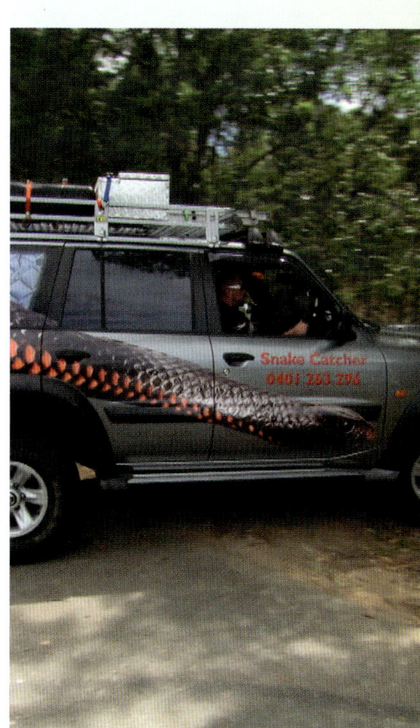

CEMETERIES FEEL THE SQUEEZE

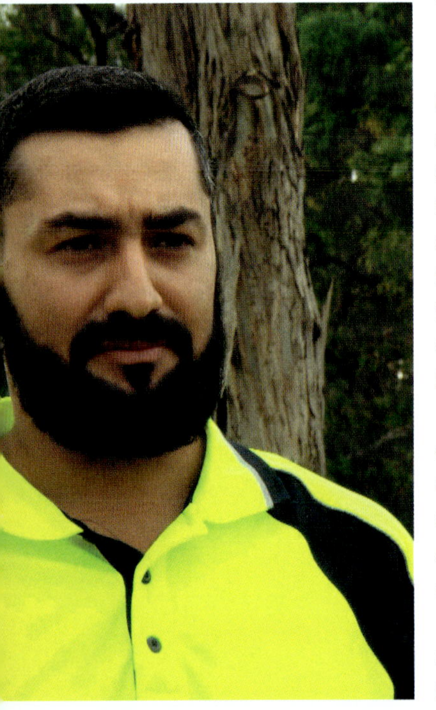

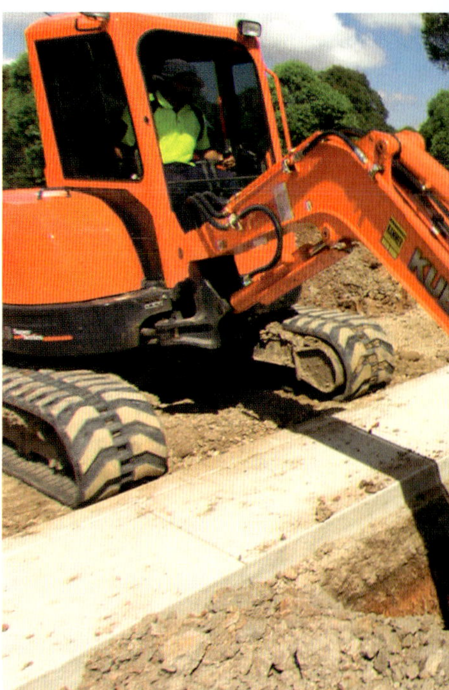

URBAN GROWTH DOES not just affect the living. The nation's cemeteries, too, are on the edge, filling up as fast as their surrounding suburbs. Take Rookwood necropolis, a 300-hectare Sydney suburb for the dead. It is the final resting place for a million souls - people from more than 90 different religions and backgrounds. Rookwood was built in the nineteenth century. Originally, the cemetery was positioned well away from the city centre to protect public health, but now this suburb of the dead has been enveloped by the sprawling suburbs of the living. And just like any other suburb, Rookwood has its own growing pains.

'It's a very big place,' says gravedigger Ammar Dakour. 'If I got a dollar for people asking me every day, how do I get out of the place, I wouldn't have to work.' Dakour and his colleague Jamal, both Muslims, are preparing a grave for burial at the Islamic section of the cemetery. Australia's Muslim population has more than doubled in the past 20 years and their section at Rookwood is rapidly running out of space.

'I think we've maybe got a year,' says Dakour. 'But you never know. It could be less.' Already the gravediggers at the Muslim plot are resorting to space-saving measures, digging holes deep enough to stack family members. 'It's two point two metres deep. The first person gets buried and then later a family member gets buried on top. It's new in the Muslim tradition because there is no land,' says Dakour.

After he finishes preparing the grave, a family arrives to farewell one of their own. The body, in a white shroud, is lowered into a bottomless casket already placed in the grave. 'In the Muslim tradition we bury the body as quickly as we can, within 24 hours,' says Dakour. 'There is no bottom in the casket because we return back to the soil, so the body has to be on the soil.'

Once the casket is closed, a layer of soil is scooped over it. With the family still present, Dakour climbs in his digger and lifts a second casket into the grave. It's only then that the burial comes to an end - the traditions of Dakour's faith adapting to the realities of an ever-growing population.

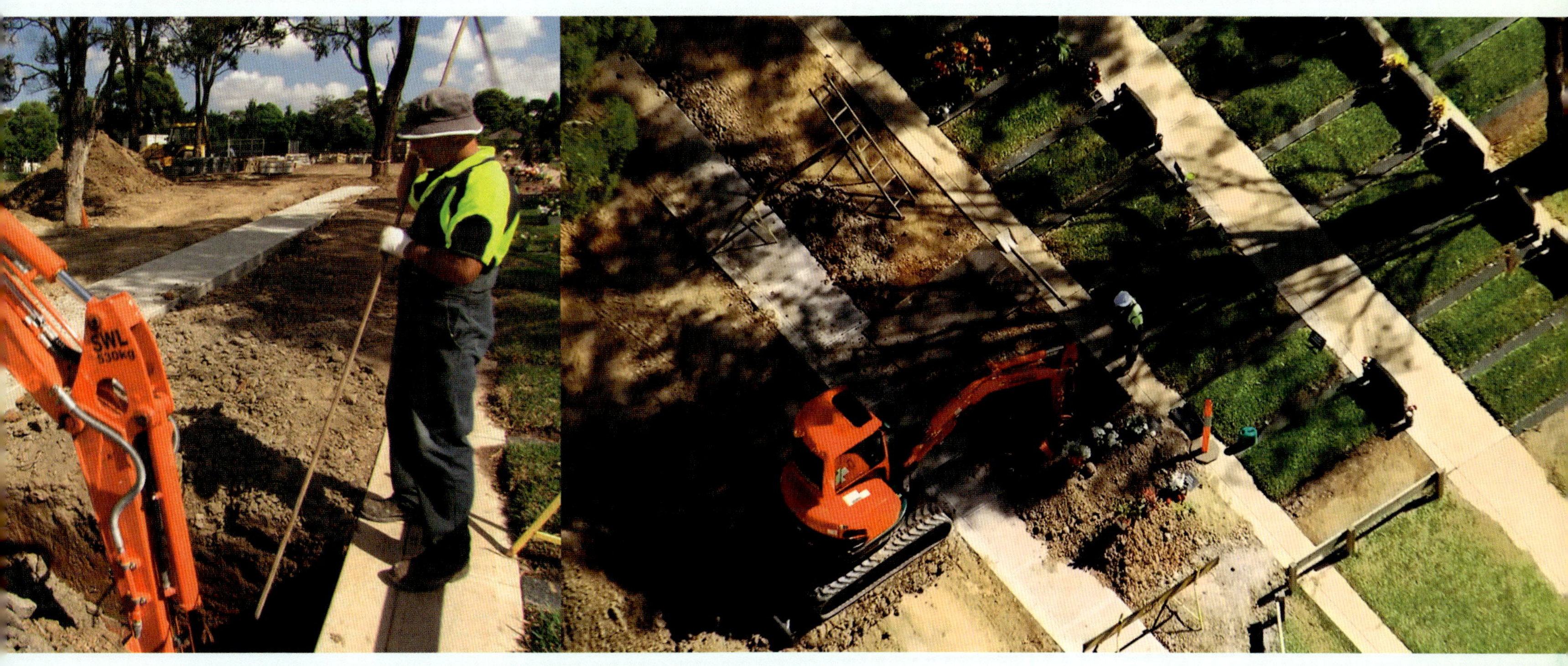
SWL
530kg

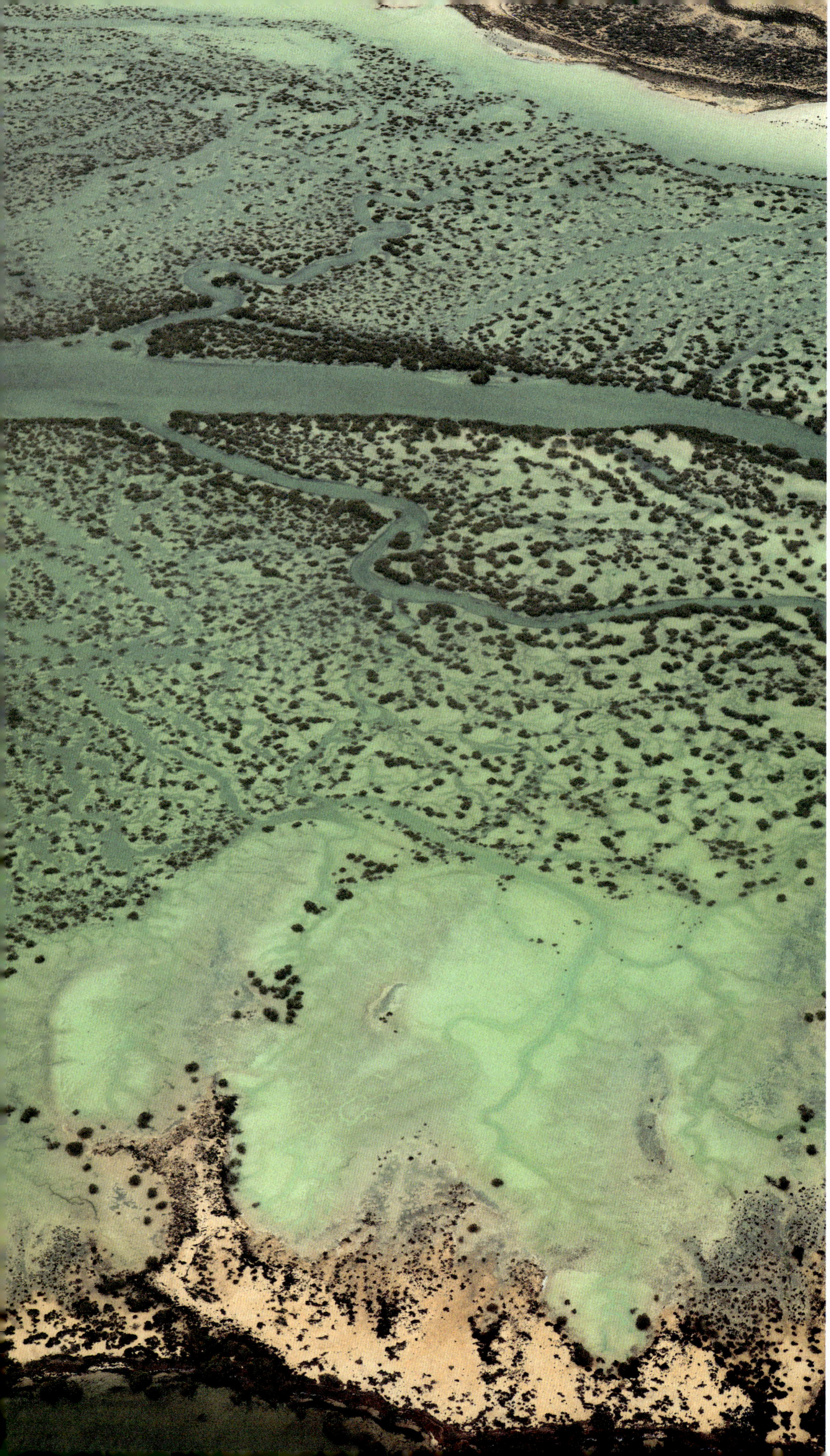

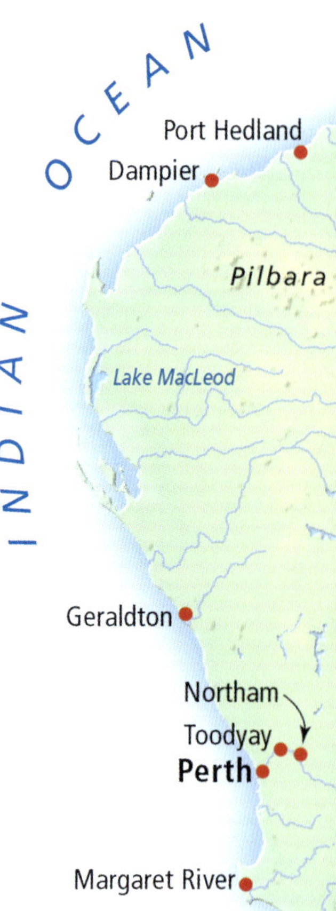
INDIAN OCEAN
Port Hedland
Dampier
Pilbara
Lake MacLeod
Geraldton
Northam
Toodyay
Perth
Margaret River

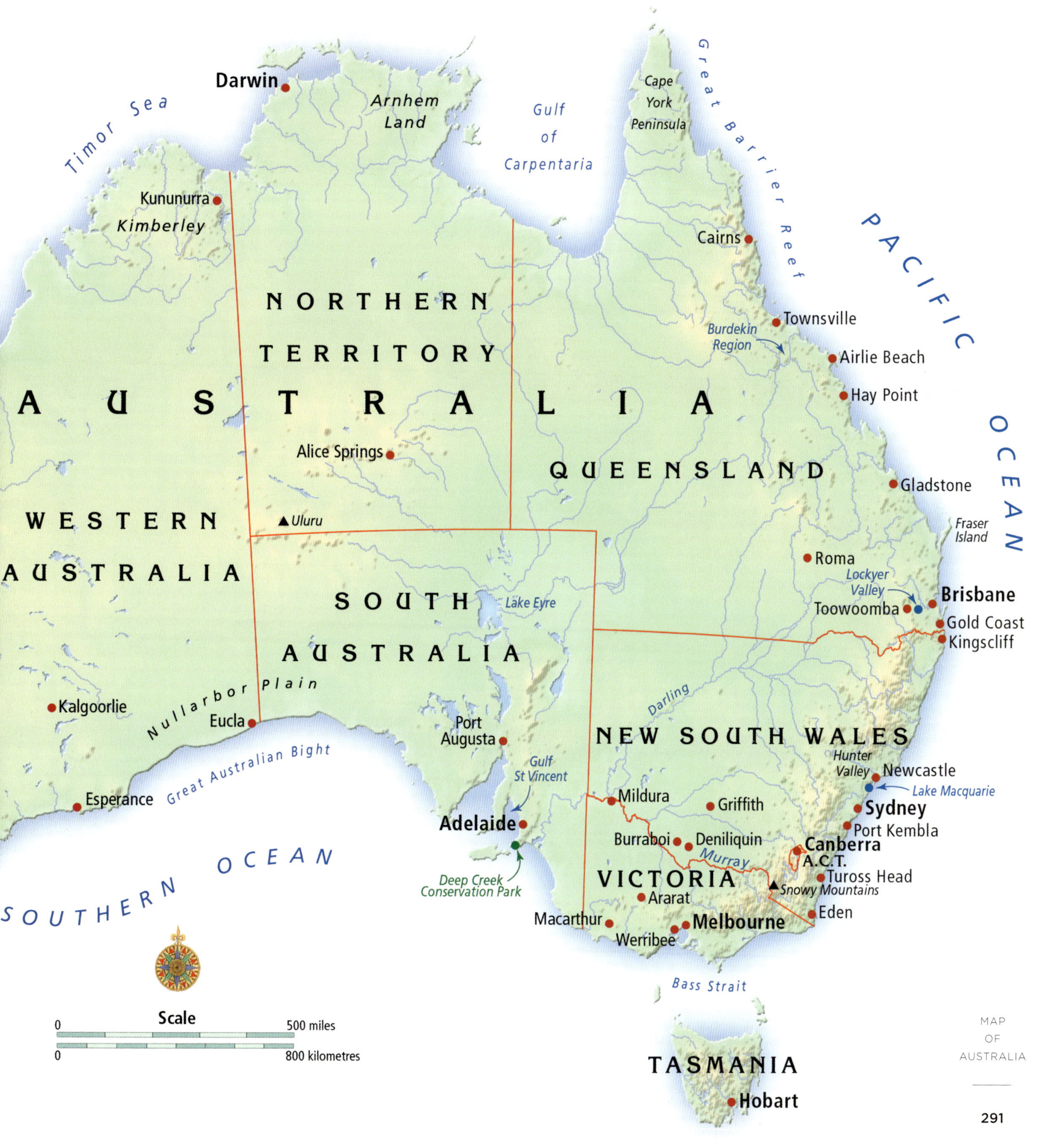
Darwin
Timor Sea
Arnhem Land
Gulf of Carpentaria
Cape York Peninsula
Great Barrier Reef
PACIFIC OCEAN
Kununurra
Kimberley
Cairns
NORTHERN TERRITORY
Townsville
Burdekin Region
Airlie Beach
Hay Point
AUSTRALIA
Alice Springs
QUEENSLAND
Gladstone
WESTERN AUSTRALIA
Uluru
Fraser Island
Roma
Lockyer Valley
Brisbane
Toowoomba
Gold Coast
Kingscliff
SOUTH AUSTRALIA
Lake Eyre
Nullarbor Plain
Kalgoorlie
Eucla
Darling
Port Augusta
NEW SOUTH WALES
Hunter Valley
Newcastle
Lake Macquarie
Great Australian Bight
Gulf St Vincent
Esperance
Mildura
Griffith
Sydney
Adelaide
Port Kembla
Burraboi
Deniliquin
Canberra
A.C.T.
Murray
SOUTHERN OCEAN
Deep Creek Conservation Park
VICTORIA
Tuross Head
Snowy Mountains
Ararat
Eden
Macarthur
Melbourne
Werribee
Bass Strait
Scale
0
500 miles
0
800 kilometres
TASMANIA
Hobart

ACKNOWLEDGEMENTS

This book is the result of extensive research by many people over a long period of time. The authors would like to express their thanks to the researchers from the television series, the many federal and state government agencies and departments, as well as the private companies who supported the research. The authors would like to acknowledge the support for this book, and the TV series on which it is based, from Michael Cordell, Nick Murray and Toni Malone at Cordell Jigsaw Zapruder; Brendan Dahill, Chris Thorburn and Stuart Menzies at the Australian Broadcasting Corporation; Mary-Ellen Mullane at Screen Australia; Nick Catliff and Richard Bradley at Lion Television; Kirsty Hunter; Sam Haynes for introducing Richard Woldendorp; Brigitta Doyle, Madeleine James and Natalie Winter at ABC Books and, last but not least, *Great Southern Land*'s presenter Professor Steve Simpson, academic director of the Charles Perkins Centre at Sydney University.

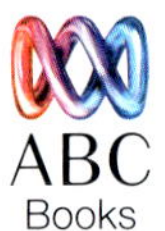

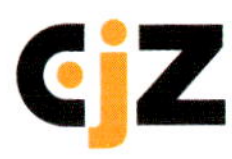

First published in Australia in 2013
by HarperCollins*Publishers* Australia Pty Limited
ABN 36 009 913 517
harpercollins.com.au

HarperCollins*Publishers*

Level 13, 201 Elizabeth Street, Sydney NSW 2000, Australia
31 View Road, Glenfield, Auckland 0627, New Zealand
A 53, Sector 57, Noida, UP, India
77-85 Fulham Palace Road, London W6 8JB, United Kingdom
2 Bloor Street East, 20th floor, Toronto, Ontario M4W 1A8, Canada
10 East 53rd Street, New York NY 10022, USA

National Library of Australia Cataloguing-in-Publication data:
Author: O'Mahoney, Ivan.
Title: Great southern land / Ivan O'Mahoney & Steve Bibb.
ISBN: 9780733332111 (hbk.)
Subjects: Australia.
Australia--Pictorial works.
Australia--Description and travel.
Other Authors/Contributors: Bibb, Steve.
Dewey Number: 994

Cover and internal design by Natalie Winter
Cover images by Richard Woldendorp
Map by Laurie Whiddon, Map Illustrations
Typeset in Berkeley Book 10.5/15
Colour reproduction by Graphic Print Group, South Australia
Printed and bound in China by RR Donnelley on 157gsm matt art
The papers used by HarperCollins in the manufacture of this book are a natural, recyclable product made from wood grown in sustainable plantation forests. The fibre source and manufacturing processes meet recognised international environmental standards, and carry certification.

5 4 3 2 1 13 14 15 16

PICTURE CREDITS

AIRVIEW ONLINE: 22-23 (centre), 34, 66, 118, 154-155, 164 (bottom left), 164-165 (bottom centre), 166-167, 169, 173, 172, 174-175, 176, 180, 181, 182, 183, 191, 192, 194-195, 196, 198, 200, 204, 207, 208-209, 211, 212, 213, 214-215, 234-235, 237, 240-241, 242, 243, 251, 256-257, 262 (top), 263 (bottom), 264, 271, 278, 283, 286-287 (centre)

BLUESFEST PTY LTD: 188

GEOFF COMFORT: 35, 115, 123, 205, 206, 276

MATT LEIPER: 151 (right), 288, 288-289 (centre)

MELBOURNE WATER: 230-231 (bottom centre), 250, 258 (top), 258 (bottom), 259 (top), 259 (bottom)

NATHAN TOMLINSON: 15 (top), 26, 29, 32-33, 37, 39, 42 (bottom), 42-43 (bottom centre), 44, 45, 46, 48, 49, 60 (left), 60 (right), 61, 62 (bottom), 63 (top right), 62 (top), 62-63 (top centre), 67, 70, 76, 77, 78-79 (centre), 80-81 (centre) 82-83, 97 (bottom right), 96 (top left), 101, 109, 127, 134, 136-137, 138, 142, 143, 144, 150-151 (centre), 164-165 (top centre), 168, 170, 171, 187, 193, 201, 202, 203, 217, 230-231 (top centre), 246, 247, 262 (bottom), 263 (top), 274, 277, 289

NICK OSBORNE: 150 (left), 151 (right)

NICOLA DALEY: 78, 80, 81, 219

PHIL BULL: 286, 287

KRISTIAN GERATHY: 40-41, 42 (top left), 43 (top right), 230 (top left)

RICHARD WOLDENDORP: i, ii-iii, iv, vi-vii, viii-ix, x-xi, xii-xiii, 2-3, 3-4, 6-7, 8-9, 10-11, 12-13, 14 (top left), 14-15 (top centre), 14 (bottom left), 14-15 (bottom centre), 15 (bottom right), 16, 17, 20, 20-21 (centre), 21, 22, 23, 24, 24-25 (centre), 25, 27, 28, 30, 31, 36, 38, 47, 50-51, 52, 53, 54, 55, 56, 56-57, 57, 58-59, 63 (bottom), 64 (top), 64-65 (centre), 67 (right), 68 (left), 68-69 (centre), 69 (right), 71, 72, 73, 74, 79, 84-85, 86-87, 88-89, 90-91, 92-93, 94-95, 96 (bottom left), 96-97 (top centre), 97 (top right), 98, 98-99 (centre), 99, 100, 102, 103 (left and right), 104, 105, 108, 110-111, 114, 116, 119, 120, 121, 122, 124-125, 126, 128, 129, 130, 131, 132, 133, 135, 140, 141, 145, 146, 147, 148-149, 156-157, 158-159, 160-161, 164 (top left), 165 (top right), 165 (bottom right), 177, 178-179, 184, 185, 186, 197, 199, 206-207 (centre), 210, 220-221, 222-223, 228-229, 230 (bottom left), 231 (top right), 231 (bottom right), 232, 232-233 (centre), 233, 236, 238, 238-239 (centre), 239, 248, 249, 252, 253, 254, 254-255 (centre), 255, 265, 266-267 (centre), 267, 272-273, 275, 276-277 (centre), 279, 282, 284-285, 290

RONAN SHARKEY: 216-217 (centre)

SNOWY HYDRO LIMITED: 18-19

SYDNEY PORTS CORPORATION: 260-261

TOBY OLIVER: 118, 216

TOURISM AUSTRALIA: 106-107, 139, 162-163, 189, 190, 224-225, 226-227, 244, 245, 266, 268, 269, 270, 280-281

TOURISM QUEENSLAND: 113, 117

VIC RACING CLUB: 218, 218-219 (centre)

WARWICK FIELD: 112, 152, 153 (left)

WAYNE RIGGS: 103 (left), 104